MAR 3 '70
RESERVE
BUS RESERVE

P9-APJ-175

THE

WILLARD J. GRAHAM SERIES

IN ACCOUNTING

BOOKS IN

THE WILLARD J. GRAHAM SERIES

IN ACCOUNTING

Holmes, Maynard, Edwards, and Meier ELEMENTARY ACCOUNTING
Neuner and Frumer COST ACCOUNTING: *Principles and Practice*
Holmes AUDITING: *Principles and Procedure*
Holmes BASIC AUDITING PRINCIPLES
Kennedy and McMullen FINANCIAL STATEMENTS
Anderson and Schmidt PRACTICAL CONTROLLERSHIP
Gordon and Shillinglaw ACCOUNTING: *A Management Approach*
Mikesell and Hay GOVERNMENTAL ACCOUNTING
Meigs PRINCIPLES OF AUDITING
Grinaker and Seiler AUDIT PRACTICE CASE
Pyle and White FUNDAMENTAL ACCOUNTING PRINCIPLES
Anthony MANAGEMENT ACCOUNTING: *Text and Cases*
Shillinglaw COST ACCOUNTING: *Analysis and Control*
Moore and Stettler ACCOUNTING SYSTEMS FOR MANAGEMENT CONTROL
Barr and Grinaker SHORT AUDIT CASE
Murphy AUDITING AND THEORY: *A CPA Review*
Ladd CONTEMPORARY CORPORATE ACCOUNTING AND THE PUBLIC
Welsch, Zlatkovich, and White INTERMEDIATE ACCOUNTING
Mattessich ACCOUNTING AND ANALYTICAL METHODS
Grinaker and Barr AUDITING: *The Examination of Financial Statements*
Paton CORPORATE PROFITS
Anthony MANAGEMENT ACCOUNTING PRINCIPLES
Nielsen CASES IN AUDITING
Hendriksen ACCOUNTING THEORY
O'Neil, Farwell, and Boyd QUANTITATIVE CONTROLS FOR BUSINESS: *An Introduction*
Murphy ADVANCED PUBLIC ACCOUNTING PRACTICE
Fremgen MANAGERIAL COST ANALYSIS
Griffin, Williams, and Welsch ADVANCED ACCOUNTING
Spiller FINANCIAL ACCOUNTING: *Basic Concepts*
Williams and Griffin MANAGEMENT INFORMATION: *A Quantitative Accent*

MANAGEMENT

INFORMATION

A Quantitative Accent

MANAGEMENT INFORMATION

A Quantitative Accent

THOMAS H. WILLIAMS
Professor of Accounting

CHARLES H. GRIFFIN
Professor of Accounting

The University of Texas

1967
RICHARD D. IRWIN, INC.
Homewood, Illinois

First printing, June, 1967

Printed in the United States of America

Library of Congress Catalog Card No. 67-17046

INTRODUCTION

THE PROCESSES of measurement in accounting have long appealed to the imagination, and have often provoked the criticism, of inventive accountants. It is disquieting, however, to note the slow reaction of accountants generally in adjusting to the rapidly evolving quantitative techniques that are designed to refine the bases for establishing management policies and strategies in business. It is evident that a gap—sometimes of cavernous proportions—exists between the conceptual framework of the quantitatively oriented approaches to the management decision function and the concepts of conventional managerial accounting. One may conjecture that the more deliberate pace of the accountant's reaction can be attributed, at least in part, to an acknowledged educational deficiency in quantitative methodology. It is therefore encouraging to note that revisions in college curricula in accounting and business administration within the past decade point to a strengthening of the mathematical sophistication of the accountant of the future.

Notwithstanding these evidences of progress, however, the editors are persuaded that there still exists no adequate educational framework (or none in suitable form) to facilitate the transfer of skills in the underlying mathematical techniques into operationally useful forms to meet the information needs of management. It would appear that this problem may be answered in the short run by increasing the accountant's awareness of those particular business variables which can be succinctly expressed in mathematical terms and which can be resolved more easily and rapidly by mathematical algorithms. Ultimately, however, the answer must be found in an enlargement of the accountant's understanding of the more fundamental structural elements of mathematics, as well as the development of a facility in the use of its notation in formulating and solving business problems.

In this collection of articles attention is focused on the first, and presently most important, facet of the problem, with the candid acknowledgment that this solution is necessarily transitional in nature. The compelling motivation in the compilation of the following articles was to accent the importance of the accounting-mathematics alloy in modern business information systems. Hopefully, the more imaginative student may be excited to venture beyond the pale of this admittedly incomplete enumeration of selected applications.

The primary article classification system chosen was based upon an observation of general problem areas of current topical interest. They are:

I. The Process of Measurement
II. Valuation of Business Resources
III. Analysis of the Distribution Function
IV. Production Planning and Control
V. Inventory Control
VI. Operations Budgeting
VII. Capital Budgeting
VIII. Integrated Planning Models
IX. Performance Review

It is patent that this classification correlates highly with important functional activities in business. The essential nucleus which delimits the scope of the illustrations is the relevance of the particular form of quantitative analysis for improving the quality of management information—both in respect to better and more efficient measurement processes and in optimizing models for operating decisions. This emphasis appears to be pedagogically superior to a procedurally oriented (mathematical techniques) classificational schema, as it provides a familiar and practical frame of reference for the business administration student. The use of this system also eliminates the constraint, often found in other works on quantitative analysis, of a preordered, and frequently rigid, sequencing between unit subdivisions. Only the emphasis desired in a particular course should condition the choice of illustrative applications; structural interdependency, either within or between divisions, is not intended.

Additionally, a secondary classification system defined in terms of the general types of methodological analyses employed in the various articles has been integrated into the overall structure of the book. The nature of this system is manifested in the accompanying Summary Tableau relative to the nine principal organizational units. This classification is then further extended to each of the separate units in tableaux which are structured relative to the individual articles included in each section. Selection of the classes was necessarily based upon the editors' appraisal of their potential relevance to an essentially technique-oriented classroom program or research project. Careful examination of the articles will, however, reveal the inherent multidimensional problem of such a classification effort—the presence of more than one methodology in a single article. In these instances, the tableau classification was determined from the dominant methodology implicit in the objective of the exposition.

The introductory commentary at the start of each unit is intended to provide an overview of the specific business problems included therein. These prefatory remarks may then be referred to the aforementioned unit tableaux to obtain an initial general impression of certain natural problem-technique associations. As an additional aid to selection and/or analysis of articles, a brief synopsis has been included immediately preceding each article.

In appraising the potential usefulness of such a collection of articles, the

SUMMARY TABLEAU

Methodological Analysis

Unit / *Methodology*	*I*	*II*	*III*	*IV*	*V*	*VI*	*VII*	*VIII*	*IX*	*Total*
General analysis of basic concepts	3				2			1		6
Descriptive models for analysis:										
Algebraic or symbolic:										
Deterministic	1	2	2	2		2		1		10
Probabilistic			1	1			2			4
Matrix methods		2		1				2		5
Markov processes		2								2
Simulation			1		2			1		4
Optimizing models:										
Linear programming			1	1				1		3
Game theory							2			2
Calculus			1	1	1		1			4
Other			1	1						2
Statistical theory:										
Sampling		2							3	5
Regression and correlation analysis						4				4
Total	4	8	7	7	5	6	5	6	3	51

NOTE: The individual elements of the matrix reflect the number of articles in a given unit (column) using a given methodology (row).

editors would iterate that the underlying objective in the compilation process has been to provide the reader with an introduction to the various types of quantitative analyses in their application to relevant business problems; manifestly, the articles are not designed to be didactic in nature. Accordingly, one may conclude that this book is intended to be a complementary reference work in graduate or advanced undergraduate courses in business administration which call for an understanding of the application of quantitative methods to the solution of business problems. It should have particular appeal in those instances where the basic text is principally oriented toward underlying mathematical properties, in which case both the primary and the secondary classification systems are relevant. Additionally, the collection should be useful for those graduate courses which include a survey consideration of developments in managerial accounting or management information systems.

The editors gratefully acknowledge the cooperation of the many authors and publishers who consented to the reprinting of the included articles. Additionally, special appreciation must be accorded John Stanley Fuhrmann whose perceptive and critical appraisal of the articles contributed significantly to the final compilation. Nonetheless, the editors do accept sole responsibility for errors of judgment regarding the final selection of the articles.

THOMAS H. WILLIAMS
CHARLES H. GRIFFIN

LIST OF CONTRIBUTORS

Charles B. Allen, *American Brass Company*
Hector R. Anton, *The University of California at Berkeley*
Herbert Arkin, *City University of New York*
Roland Artle, *Stockholm School of Economics*
William J. Baumol, *Princeton University*
Edward G. Bennion, *Standard Oil Company of New Jersey*
Sture Berglund, *Stockholm School of Economics*
Subodh Bhattacharjee, *The Johns Hopkins University*
Kenneth E. Boulding, *The University of Michigan*
Ronald Brenneck, *Ryan Aeronautics Company*
Pao L. Cheng, *The University of Massachusetts*
Neil Churchill, *Harvard University*
R. M. Cyert, *Carnegie Institute of Technology*
H. J. Davidson, *Touche, Ross, Bailey and Smart*
Don T. DeCoster, *The University of Washington*
George J. Feeney, *The General Electric Corporation*
Charles H. Griffin, *The University of Texas*
R. S. Gynther, *The University of Queensland*
David B. Hertz, *McKinsey and Company, Inc.*
Yuji Ijiri, *Stanford University*
Robert K. Jaedicke, *Stanford University*
F. K. Levy, *Rice University*
Irving J. Lieberman, *Herrnfeld Engineering Corporation*
R. C. Lyon, *Touche, Ross, Bailey and Smart*
John F. Magee, *Arthur D. Little, Inc.*
Richard Mattessich, *The University of California at Berkeley*
Hartsel G. McClain, *The Bendix Corporation*
Paul R. McClenon, *The Rand Corporation*
Edwin S. Mills, *The Johns Hopkins University*
Eliezer Naddor, *The Johns Hopkins University*
Robert D. Niemeyer, *Haskins and Sells*
Edgar S. Pessemier, *Purdue University*
Donald L. Raun, *San Fernando Valley State College*
Allen B. Richards, *The University of California (Davis)*
Alexander A. Robichek, *Stanford University*
Barry M. Rowles, *The National Supply Company*
Robert H. Roy, *The Johns Hopkins University*
K. F. Schumann, *Deere and Company*
Charles H. Sevin, *Lybrand, Ross Bros. and Montgomery*
John P. Shelton, *The University of California at Los Angeles*
Julian L. Simon, *The University of Illinois*
Spencer B. Smith, *Illinois Institute of Technology*
Wayland P. Smith, *State University of New York at Buffalo*
S. S. Stevens, *Harvard University*
Kenneth W. Stringer, *Haskins and Sells*

Marvin L. Taylor, *Ryan Aeronautics Company*
Arthur L. Thomas, *The University of Oregon*
G. L. Thompson, *Carnegie Institute of Technology*
R. M. Trueblood, *Touche, Ross, Bailey and Smart*
Donald S. Tull, *California State College*
Andrew Vazsonyi, *North American Aviation, Inc.*
M. L. Vidale, *Arthur D. Little, Inc.*
Spencer A. Weart, *Barrington Associates, Inc.*
T. M. Whitin, *Wesleyan University*
Thomas H. Williams, *The University of Texas*
H. B. Wolfe, *Arthur D. Little, Inc.*
Zenon S. Zannetos, *Massachusetts Institute of Technology*

TABLE OF CONTENTS

ARTICLE PAGE

I. THE PROCESS OF MEASUREMENT

1. Measurement and Man, *S. S. Stevens* 4
2. Axioms and Structures of Conventional Accounting Measurement, *Yuji Ijiri* 20
3. Some Aspects of Measurement and Accounting, *Hector R. Anton* . . 43
4. Reliability and Objectivity of Accounting Measurements, *Yuji Ijiri and Robert K. Jaedicke* 52

II. VALUATION OF BUSINESS RESOURCES

5. Discounted Services Again: The Homogeneity Problem, *Arthur L. Thomas* 70
6. Statistical Sampling Techniques in the Aging of Accounts Receivable in a Department Store, *R. M. Cyert and Robert M. Trueblood* . . . 84
7. Estimation of Allowance for Doubtful Accounts by Markov Chains, *R. M. Cyert, H. J. Davidson, and G. L. Thompson* 96
8. Application of Statistical Sampling Techniques to Lifo Inventory Valuation, *Barry M. Rowles* 114
9. Statistical Attributes of Group Depreciation, *Zenon S. Zannetos* . . 123
10. Matrix Theory and Cost Allocation, *Thomas H. Williams and Charles H. Griffin* 134
11. Linear Algebra and Cost Allocations: Some Examples, *Neil Churchill* 145
12. Mathematical Models for Public Utility Rate Regulation, *Robert H. Roy* 158

III. ANALYSIS OF THE DISTRIBUTION FUNCTION

13. Marketing Costs and Mathematical Programming, *William J. Baumol and Charles H. Sevin* 176
14. A Note on Manufacturers' Choice of Distribution Channels, *Roland Artle and Sture Berglund* 191
15. The Effect of Promotional Effort on Sales, *John F. Magee* 203
16. An Operations Research Study of Sales Response to Advertising, *M. L. Vidale and H. B. Wolfe* 214
17. A Simple Model for Determining Advertising Appropriations, *Julian L. Simon* 225
18. The Carry-Over Effect of Advertising, *Donald S. Tull* 241
19. Forecasting Brand Performance through Simulation Experiments, *Edgar A. Pessemier* 255

ARTICLE PAGE

IV. PRODUCTION PLANNING AND CONTROL

20. Economic Manufacturing Lot Size, *Subodh Bhattacharjee* 268
21. A Study of Optimum Assembly Runs, *Edwin S. Mills and Hartsel G. McClain* 285
22. An Investigation of Some Quantitative Relationships between Break-Even Point Analysis and Economic Lot-Size Theory, *Wayland P. Smith* 294
23. Planning Transistor Production by Linear Programming, *Spencer B. Smith* 308
24. The Use of Mathematics in Production and Inventory Control, *Andrew Vazsonyi* 316
25. Cost-Volume-Profit Analysis under Conditions of Uncertainty, *Robert K. Jaedicke and Alexander A. Robichek* 331
26. PERT/Cost: The Challenge, *Don T. DeCoster* 344

V. INVENTORY CONTROL

27. Inventory Control, *Robert D. Niemeyer* 358
28. Some Business Applications of Marginal Analysis—with Particular Reference to Inventory Control, *T. M. Whitin* 372
29. A Basis for Strategic Decisions on Inventory Control Operations, *George J. Feeney* 388
30. Markov Chains and Simulations in an Inventory System, *Eliezer Naddor* 404
31. The Application of Monte Carlo Analysis to an Inventory Problem, *Donald L. Raun* 419

VI. OPERATIONS BUDGETING

32. Operational Analysis—Statistical Approach, *Charles B. Allen* . . . 432
33. Statistical Techniques for Financial Planning and Forecasting, *Andrew Vazsonyi* 449
34. Improving Separation of Fixed and Variable Expenses, *R. S. Gynther* . 473
35. Cost Finding through Multiple Correlation Analysis, *Paul R. McClenon* 485
36. The Learning Curve—A Basic Cost Projection Tool, *Marvin L. Taylor* . 497
37. Learning Curve Techniques for More Profitable Contracts, *Ronald Brenneck* 502

VII. CAPITAL BUDGETING

38. A Contribution to the Theory of Capital Budgeting—The Multi-Investment Case, *Pao L. Cheng and John P. Shelton* 520
39. Risk Analysis in Capital Investment, *David B. Hertz* 534
40. How to Use Decision Trees in Capital Investment, *John F. Magee* . . 550
41. Capital Budgeting and Game Theory, *Edward G. Bennion* 571
42. Practical Application of the Theory of Games to Complex Managerial Decisions, *Spencer A. Weart* 586

ARTICLE PAGE

VIII. INTEGRATED PLANNING MODELS

43. General Systems Theory—The Skeleton of Science, *Kenneth E. Boulding* 602
44. Mathematical Models in Business Accounting, *Richard Mattessich* . . 614
45. Input-Output Accounting for Business, *Allen B. Richards* 626
46. Budgeting Models and System Simulation, *Richard Mattessich* . . . 636
47. A Linear Programming Model for Budgeting and Financial Planning, *Yuji Ijiri, F. K. Levy, and R. C. Lyon* 655
48. A Mathematical Model for Integrated Business Systems, *Irving J. Lieberman* 669

IX. PERFORMANCE REVIEW

49. Sampling and the Auditor, *Herbert Arkin* 684
50. Some Basic Concepts of Statistical Sampling in Auditing, *Kenneth W. Stringer* 692
51. Use of Sampling Procedures in Internal Auditing, *K. F. Schumann* . . 704

I

The Process of Measurement

TABLEAU I

Methodological Analysis

Article \ *Methodology*	*General Analysis of Basic Concepts*	*Descriptive Models for Analysis*				
		Algebraic or Symbolic (Deterministic)	*Algebraic or Symbolic (Probabilistic)*	*Matrix Methods*	*Markov Processes*	*Simulation*
1. Measurement and Man	X					
2. Axioms and Structures of Conventional Accounting Measurement		X				
3. Some Aspects of Measurement and Accounting	X					
4. Reliability and Objectivity of Accounting Measurements	X					

THE PROCESS OF MEASUREMENT

Accounting has been variously defined; yet most of these definitions accent the functions of recording, classifying, and summarizing transactions and events which either are financial in nature or have financial overtones. These defining expressions inevitably assume that some method (or methods) of measurement exist for giving quantitative expression to various business variables. But the process of measurement as a systematic, scientific theory has been inadequately examined by accountants; accordingly, a critical inquiry into the nature of accounting measurement may be useful.

Before one can proceed in this type of investigation, however, it is necessary that some understanding exist in respect to measurement itself, not merely that of which measurement consists in a specialized discipline. (The fact that a theory of measurement exists independently of any scientific discipline is in itself surprising to many individuals.) Some basic aspects of the theory of measurement are presented in article 1, including a description of the four basic scales of measurement.

Given some understanding of the term "measurement," it then appears appropriate to consider in a more definite manner what "accounting" measurement is or should be (articles 2, 3, and 4). Hopefully, from this distillate of accounting measurement attributes, better and more uniform accounting methods of measurement may be derived.

1

The author distinguishes measurement from mathematics, and identifies and describes the four basic scales of measurement. He also notes the role of measurement in psychophysics, illustrating some of the problems involved in measurement with an analysis of the measurement of two representative subjective quantities—brightness and sound intensity.

*MEASUREMENT AND MAN**

S. S. Stevens

IN SOME PARTS of science, we have reduced the business of measuring to simple routines, chores to be done by technicians—animate or inanimate. In these areas the basic and challenging problems of measurement have been solved, and the only task left is to implement, read, and record. In other parts of the discipline the problem of how and what to measure remains acute and real. The task is not simply to read a meter or gauge an effect; it is to devise a procedure by which to quantify some stubborn phenomenon—to reduce it to numerical order.

Much that pertains to man himself poses knotty problems of just this sort. How shall we measure his capacities, his attitudes, his sensations, or any of the many aspects of man that cannot be weighed in a balance or marked off on a stick? Is measurement possible here; and if so, to what degree? But first of all, what precisely do we mean by measurement, and what are the forms it may take?

MATHEMATICS VERSUS MEASUREMENT

"Probably more nonsense," said N. R. Campbell, "is talked about measurement than about any other part of physics."[1] Crotchety as this remark may sound, Campbell did not intend thereby to belittle the power and beauty of physical measurement or the superlative ingenuity of laboratory practice. But the art of measurement is one thing; the understanding of its fundamentals is another. And Campbell—the author of *Physics: The Elements*—was trying to teach us the same truth that Whitehead had in mind when he observed that "it is harder to discover the elements than to develop the science."[2]

* Reprinted from *Science*, Vol. 127, No. 3295 (February, 1958), pp. 383–89.

[1] N. R. Campbell, in Aristotelian Society, *Symposium: Measurement and Its Importance for Philosophy* (London: Harrison, 1938), Vol. XVII, Supplement.

[2] A. N. Whitehead, *Science and the Modern World* (New York: Macmillan Co., 1925; Pelican Mentor, 1948).

This is the way it has been with measurement. Here, as elsewhere, it has often taken our greatest minds to discover the simplest things.

One of these things is the relation between measurement and mathematics. It seems clear to us now that the process of measurement is the process of mapping empirical facts and relations into a formal model—a model borrowed from mathematics. But this conception took form only in very recent times. It is the product of long centuries of intellectual struggle, to which many of the foremost mathematicians contributed. It is a conception that was impossible, even unthinkable, until the nature of mathematics as a postulational system became clarified.

Once a basic and elementary notion dawns upon us in its full clarity, we often wonder how our fathers could have missed perceiving it. It is a curious fact that although the postulational method was applied to geometry some two millenniums ago, only in modern times were the fundamental assumptions of algebra exhumed from the hodgepodge of rules that govern algebraic practice. In this sense the modern postulates of algebra represent the distilled wisdom of more than 3,000 years of symbol juggling. They represent the outcome of our efforts to pare away the nonessentials in order to get a clear view of what constitutes the essence of a mathematical system.

And the essence is this: Mathematics is a game of signs and rules, man-made and arbitrary, like the game of chess. It begins with a set of undefined terms and a set of unproved assumptions regarding their interrelations. The mathematician invents symbols; and at the same time, he lays down rules to tell us how these symbols shall be allowed to combine and interact. Nowhere in this process, as we now conceive it, is there any reference to empirical objects—or any explicit concern for the world of sense and matter. Therein lies the revolutionary novelty, for not long ago, as human history goes, it was argued that negative numbers were "absurd" and "fictitious." For how could anything be less than nothing? You see, our ancestors thought it proper to test their mathematics by operations performed upon nature—upon actual objects—for they conceived arithmetic as a system of concrete numerical magnitudes whose relations should be verifiable in the empirical domain, and where in the real world were the negative objects?

The story of the slow and painful growth of the number system, the story of how the mathematicians, often against their own better judgment, began to write outlandish symbols, such as -3 and $\sqrt{-1}$, is a fascinating tale. It could occupy us at length, but we must forgo it. Its bearing on our present concern relates mainly to its outcome. With each new kind of number admitted to the number domain—the negatives, the irrationals, the imaginaries, and so on—it became more clearly impossible to prove arithmetic by appeal to experiment. So in the end the formal, syntactical system of mathematics achieved its full emancipation, its complete decoupling from empirical matters of fact. Thence it took off into the realm of pure abstraction, where it properly belonged in the first place.

Why did this decoupling take so long? Why so much travail to achieve something so simple and obvious? The difficulty, it seems, was measurement. In particular, it was the fact that the early mathematicians did not readily discern the difference between measurement and mathematics. Man was usually more interested in empirical measurement than in mathematics—as the scientist, no doubt, still is—and it was the problem of measurement that first gave rise to arithmetic. In the beginning, mathematics and measurement were so closely bound together that no one seemed to suspect that two quite different disciplines were involved. The earliest scales of measurement were scales of numerosity—scales for the counting of pebbles or cattle or warriors. In some dim era in the past, somebody invented the system of natural numbers precisely for the purpose of representing what he did with collections of objects. No doubt this forgotten genius was oblivious to the formal-empirical dichotomy, which we now consider so crucial. But that is beside the point. However he may have regarded it, the fact is that he built himself a formal model to stand for an aspect of the empirical world, much as an architect draws a plan for a house. Kronecker once said, "God created the whole numbers; all the others are the work of man." Passable theology, perhaps, but surely bad history.

Since arithmetic was invented for measurement, it is not surprising that the isomorphic correspondence between whole-number arithmetic and the empirical numerosity of piles of pebbles is tight and complete. It was, in fact, the very tightness of this isomorphism that blinded the ancients to the essential difference between mathematics and measurement. But modern mathematics is no longer constrained to serve only as a syntax for quantitative discourse. Far from limiting itself to serving as a model for numerosity, or even as a model for such continuous dimensions as length, it has become largely nonquantitative in some of its more abstract reaches. This outcome has suggested to Gödel a startling thought—namely, that it was purely a historical accident that mathematics developed along quantitative lines.[3] In one sense, Gödel is undoubtedly right, and his conjecture is a profound commentary on the nature of mathematics. But the story of measurement suggests that this "accident" had about it a certain inevitability. Striving somehow to count his possessions, ancient man seems destined in the nature of things to have hit upon the concept of number and to have made therein his first triumphant abstraction. Given the deeply human need to quantify, could mathematics really have begun elsewhere than in measurement?

It is not, however, only in history that we see the slow development of the formal-empirical dichotomy. An analogous development takes place in the lives of all of us. Just as ontogeny to some extent repeats phylogeny, so in the life of each maturing child the struggle of the ages is reenacted in the child's attempt to grasp the abstraction of mathematics. He learns his first arithmetic with the aid of fingers or buttons or beads, and only with great labor does he finally, if ever, achieve the reoriented view that mathematics is an abstract

[3] R. Oppenheimer, "Analogy in Science," *American Psychologist*, November, 1956, p. 127.

game having no necessary relation to solid objects. Each of us has suffered through this process of revision. Even though you may have shifted gears more smoothly than I, still you may well sympathize with my own dismay at my first encounter with imaginary numbers.

THE NATURE OF A SCALE

In its broadest sense, measurement is the business of pinning numbers on things. More specifically, it is the assignment of numbers to objects or events in accordance with a rule of some sort. This process turns out to be a fruitful enterprise only because some degree of isomorphism obtains between the empirical relations among the properties of objects or events, on the one hand, and some of the properties of the number system, on the other. Some of these properties and their uses in measurement are these:

1. *Identity:* Numbers may serve as labels to identify items or classes.
2. *Order:* Numbers may serve to reflect the rank order of items.
3. *Intervals:* Numbers may serve to reflect differences among items.
4. *Ratios:* Numbers may serve to reflect ratios among items.

These are ways in which we may deputize numbers to represent one or another aspect of a state of affairs in nature. Depending upon what kinds of empirical operations we are able to perform, one or more of these aspects of the number system may be used as a model to represent the outcome. The empirical operations are sometimes a matter of choice; more often, they are limited by our experimental ingenuity. In any case the nature of the operations determines that there may eventuate one or another of four kinds of scales.[4] These I have called "nominal," "ordinal," "interval," and "ratio." They are listed and described in Table 1.

The key to the nature of these different scales rests with the concept of invariance. How can we transform the numbers on the scale with no loss of empirical information? If all we can do about a set of objects is identify or classify them, we have only a nominal scale, and the numbers we assign can be permuted at will, for all that the numbers provide are labels. If operations exist for determining order, and if we have assigned numbers to reflect this fact, then the permissible scale transformation must be order-preserving. When intervals have empirical meaning—as on the ordinary temperature scale—we are limited to linear transformations. We can multiply by a constant and add a constant. And finally, if in addition to all this we can give empirical meaning to ratios, the only permissible transformation is multiplication by a constant, as when we convert from feet to inches. Any more liberal transformation entails a loss of information. In general, the richer

[4] S. S. Stevens, "On the Theory of Scales of Measurement," *Science*, 1946, p. 677; *idem*, "Mathematics, Measurement and Psychophysics," in S. S. Stevens (ed.), *Handbook of Experimental Psychology* (New York: John Wiley & Sons, Inc., 1951), pp. 1–49; *idem*, "Measurement, Psychophysics and Utility," in *Symposium on Measurement Held by the AAAS, December 1956* (New York: John Wiley & Sons, Inc., in press).

TABLE 1

A Classification of Scales of Measurement*

Scale	Basic Empirical Operations	Mathematical Group Structure	Permissible Statistics (Invariantive)	Typical Examples
Nominal	Determination of equality	Permutation group $x' = f(x)$ where $f(x)$ means any one-to-one substitution	Number of cases Mode "Information" measures Contingency correlation	"Numbering" of football players Assignment of type or model numbers to classes
Ordinal	Determination of greater or less	Isotonic group $x' = f(x)$ where $f(x)$ means any increasing monotonic function	Median Percentiles Order correlation (type 0: interpreted as a test of order)	Hardness of minerals Grades of leather, lumber, wool, and so forth Intelligence test raw scores
Interval	Determination of the equality of intervals or of differences	Linear or affine group $x' = ax + b$ $a > 0$	Mean Standard deviation Order correlation (type I: interpreted as r) Product moment (r)	Temperature (Fahrenheit and Celsius) Position on a line Calendar time Potential energy Intelligence test "standard scores" (?)
Ratio	Determination of the equality of ratios	Similarity group $x' = cx$ $c > 0$	Geometric mean Harmonic mean Percent variation	Length, numerosity, density, work, time intervals, and so forth Temperature (Kelvin) Loudness (sones) Brightness (brils)

*Measurement is the assignment of numbers to objects or events according to rule. The rules and the resulting kinds of scales are tabulated above. The basic operations needed to create a given scale are all those listed in the second column, down to and including the operation listed opposite the scale. The third column gives the mathematical transformations that leave the scale form invariant. Any number x on a scale can be replaced by another number x' where x' is the function of x listed in column 2. The fourth column lists, cumulatively downward, examples of statistics that show invariance under the transformations of column 3 (the mode, however, is invariant only for discrete variables).

the experimental operations, the greater is the isomorphism between them and the formal model of arithmetic, and the more restricted is the range of invariant transformations.[5]

Each of these scales has its uses, but it is the more powerful ratio scale that serves us best in the search for nature's regularities. On these ratio scales, we measure basic things like numerosity, length, and weight, and, depending on our artistry, we contrive more elusive measures, like the charge on the electron or the strength of a magnetic field.

Why, it may be asked, do we bother with the other types of scales? Mostly, we use the weaker forms of measurement only *faute de mieux*. When stronger forms are discovered, we are quick to seize them. But science is an art. There are no *ab initio* principles to tell us how to be clever in devising procedures of measurement. The way to empirical discovery lies not through mathematics, even, but through the exercise of uncommon experimental sense and ingenuity. We invent mathematical models, but we discover measures in the laboratory. As Norbert Wiener said, "Things do not, in general, run around with their measures stamped on them like the capacity of a freight car; it requires a certain amount of investigation to discover what their measures are."[6]

Perhaps those who stand apart from the practice of the scientific art and who philosophize about the "scientific method" think there really is such a thing, and that it can be captured in a book of rules. But the man on the laboratory stool is likely to agree with Hildebrand that "there is no such thing as *the* scientific method."[7] If you think science is a simple and unitary thing, try asking several scientists to define it. One of the entertaining things about science is that no one has succeeded in explaining precisely what it is.

However you define the scientific activity, measurement pervades most of the enterprise. Measurement is essential to the determination of functional relations, to the discovery of order and regularity. I need not extol it further, for we all know the reality of its power. In fact, we take it so much for granted that it becomes almost unthinkable that the pursuit of measurement did not always stand in high regard.

I vividly recall Professor Whitehead, peering over his lectern in Harvard's Emerson Hall and rasping out wisdom in his high-pitched voice: "If only the schoolmen of the Middle Ages had measured instead of classifying, how much they might have learned." Under the influence of Aristotelian logic, with its emphasis on classification, the schoolmen forsook the Pythagorean tradition, which taught the primacy of number and measurement. Classification, to be sure, is a first and essential step on the road up the hierarchy of scales. It gets

[5] For a possible fifth type of scale having a still different transformation group, see Stevens, "Measurement, Psychophysics and Utility"; *idem*, "On the Psychophysical Law," *Psychological Review*, 1957, p. 153.

[6] Norbert Wiener, "A New Theory of Measurement: A Study in the Logic of Mathematics," *Proceedings of the London Mathematical Society*, 1920, p. 181.

[7] J. H. Hildebrand, *Science in the Making* (New York: Columbia University Press, 1957).

us to the nominal level. But this is no more than a quarter-way house on the road to measurement in its more powerful forms. The revival of modern science in the 17th century—the century of genius—was a revival of the Pythagorean outlook, a revival of measurement. With Galileo, Newton, and the rest, science became primarily quantitative, and so it has remained.

In his diagnostic satire entitled *Science Is a Sacred Cow*, Standen perceived correctly the modern order of things when he put measurement at the top of the scientist's totem pole.[8]

MEASUREMENT IN PSYCHOPHYSICS

Measurement, as we have seen, is more than the pedantic pursuit of a decimal place. Its vital and absorbing aspect emerges most clearly, perhaps, when it becomes a question of measuring something that has never been measured—or better still, something that has been held to be unmeasurable. Quantification is a respectable enterprise in physics and chemistry, and even in much of biology. But what about man, and the measurement of his higher processes? Are we always objective and emotionally neutral about this prospect?

The economist Edgeworth once wrote, "There is an old prejudice still reviving, however often slain, against the reign of law in psychology, as incompatible with the higher feelings."[9] Some there are, I suppose, who still feel that quantification, by some brutal rigor, will shatter the human spirit if we probe with the aid of numbers. But man can hardly fall in stature by understanding man, or even by quantifying that understanding. The greater beauty of discovered order will surely more than compensate for the nostalgic pain of a romantic yearning to remain securely inscrutable.

However we regard this issue, the fact remains that man is undergoing measurement. We are all familiar with the highly developed business of testing human performance and ability, and with the pioneering work of Binet, who launched us on the road to the measurement of the IQ. This measure, with its approximate invariance over the child's growing years, stands as one of the first-rate contributions to human understanding. Interesting issues for the theory of measurement arise almost daily in these burgeoning fields of ability assessment. But since this is not my own area of interest, let me turn to another quest: the measurement of sensation.

Modern experimental psychology had its beginnings in this inquiry, which started just about a hundred years ago—in the 1850's.

Let me pose the problem in this way. Suppose you look at a photograph in the bright sunlight and then again in a dimly lighted room. The remarkable fact is that the picture looks much the same under the two conditions.

---

[8] See F. B. Silsbee, "Measure for Measure: Some Problems and Paradoxes of Precision," *Journal of the Washington Academy of Science*, Series 2, 1951, p. 213.

[9] F. Y. Edgeworth, *Mathematical Psychics* (London: Kegan Paul, 1881).

Despite a change of illumination of perhaps several thousandfold, the light parts of the picture look light and the dark parts dark. The perceived relation between light and shade within the picture remains highly stable, is subjectively constant. But just what it is that is subjectively constant, we may ask. There are at least two possibilities. One is that the subjective *difference* between the light and shade remains constant as we go from outdoors to indoors. The other is that the subjective *ratio* between the light and shade remains constant. If we could find out which of these relations holds, then we would know, for these conditions, the law that relates subjective brightness to the physical intensity of the stimulus.

Back in the 1850's, two major figures in science, Fechner and Plateau, both considered the problem and reached quite opposite conclusions (a fact that suggests that you cannot settle the matter merely by looking at pictures!). Fechner argued that the subjective *difference* between light and shade remains constant, and that therefore the subjective brightness is a logarithmic function of stimulus intensity. That is the well-known Fechner's law. Plateau argued that the *ratio* remains constant, and that therefore the subjective brightness is a power function of stimulus intensity.

Formulawise, we may state these two laws as the relation between psychological value Ψ and physical value ϕ in this way:

$$\text{Logarithmic law: } \Psi = k_1 \log \phi$$
$$\text{Power law: } \Psi = k_2 \phi^n$$

The exponent n is a constant whose value may vary with sense modality and with conditions of stimulation.

Of course, the champions of these laws cited other facts and evidence; and for a hundred years, this issue has stood as a kind of antinomy in psychophysics. If you have heard only of Fechner in this connection, it is because it was he who defended his view more fiercely, who more tirelessly outargued his critics. Plateau's interest was only casual; and as a matter of fact, he later changed his mind—and for a reason that was not really relevant.[10] So the field was left mainly to Fechner. But others revived the power law from time to time, and the contradiction persisted.

How can this conflict of opposing laws—the logarithmic and the power law—be resolved? By measurement, of course. All that is needed is a scale for the measurement of sensation. But that is easier said than done.

THE OPERATIONAL PRINCIPLE

At this point, let me try to clarify a sticky issue. This question of sensation and its measurement has often gotten itself bogged down in metaphysical debate. Ever since Descartes set mind apart from matter, we have been trying in one way or another to put them back together again, for if we accept the

[10] See Stevens, "On the Psychophysical Law."

dualistic view that mind is something apart, something inaccessible to science and measurement, the game is lost before the first move is made. To rescue science from this hopeless gambit, three modern developments have converged on a common solution. The three are behaviorism in psychology, operationism in physics, and logical positivism in philosophy.[11] Despite certain differences in language and emphasis, all three of these movements have sought to clarify our scientific discourse by ridding its concepts of metaphysical overtones and untestable meanings. Under the operational view, length is what we measure with rods; time is what we measure with clocks. However well grounded in common sense may seem the notions of absolute space and absolute time, the physicist, as physicist, can *know* nothing about them—for he can *do* nothing about them.

Equally inaccessible are the nonoperational aspects of sensation. What we can get at in the study of living things are the responses of organisms, not some hyperphysical mental stuff which, by definition, eludes objective test. Consequently, verifiable statements about sensation become statements about responses—about differential reactions of organisms. In psychology, perhaps even more than in physics, this operational stance is indispensable to scientific sense and meaning. In line with this necessity, let us agree that the term *sensation* denotes a construct that derives its meaning from the reactions, verbal or otherwise, made by an organism in response to stimuli. I know nothing about your sensations except what your behavior tells me. But what is equally true, we know nothing about the charge on the electron except for what its behavior discloses. We must be thoroughly operational in both instances.

Now, some will object that there is a difference here: that electrons do not study themselves, whereas men do. This is true enough. But if the science of man is to contain public, repeatable, verifiable generalizations, we must always in effect study the other fellow—we must pursue "the psychology of the other one." The psychologist as experimenter may look in upon himself if he cares to, and he may often thereby gain insight into fruitful hypotheses. But these hypotheses can lead to valid general laws only after they have been verified under experimental control on other people. If the experimenter serves as an observer in his own experiment, as I often do, he must proceed to treat his own responses as objective data, on a par with those of other observers. This manner of working, it seems to me, is the only sound, objective, operational approach. In what follows, therefore, I hope it will be taken for granted that I mean no more by sensation than what experiment tells us. Our goal is to make quantitative order of the reactions of sensory systems to the energetic configurations of the environment.

[11] S. S. Stevens, "Psychology and the Science of Science," *Psychological Bulletin*, 1939, p. 221; reprinted in M. H. Marx (ed.), *Psychological Theory: Contemporary Readings* (New York: Macmillan Co., 1951), pp. 21–54. See also P. P. Wiener (ed.), *Readings in the Philosophy of Science* (New York: Charles Scribner's Sons, 1953), pp. 158–84.

CONFLICTING LAWS

Let us return now to our problem. Fechner, as I have said, won the first round; and for almost a century, it looked as though the logarithmic law would prevail over the power law. Two rather convincing kinds of evidence seemed to favor it. First, there was the argument based on differential sensitivity, which we measure by noting how large an increment must be added to a stimulus for a person to detect the difference a certain percentage of the time. These just noticeable differences turn out to be roughly proportional to the magnitude of the original stimulus (Weber's law). There is a kind of relativity here. You can detect a candle added to a candle, but not a candle added to the light of the noonday sun. Fechner noted this principle and then proceeded to *postulate* that each just noticeable difference corresponds to a constant increment in sensation.

At this point, we are reminded of what Bertrand Russell said in another connection about postulation: "The method of 'postulating' what we want has many advantages; they are the same as the advantages of theft over honest toil."[12]

Be that as it may, if we grant Fechner's postulate, and if Weber's law is true, it follows that sensation grows as the logarithm of the stimulus.

The other line of evidence is exemplified in the astronomer's scale of stellar magnitude, which appears to date from Hipparchus (about 150 B.C.). Before the days of photometry, men looked at the stars and judged their apparent brightness on a scale from 1 to 6, where 1 stands for the brightest stars and 6 for the faintest. Successive numbers on the scale were assigned to successive equal-appearing intervals of stellar magnitude. Then an interesting thing happened. Men finally learned to measure the brightness of the stars by photometric methods; and much to Fechner's delight, it turned out that the magnitudes assigned by the simple process of looking and judging were spaced by approximately equal steps on a logarithmic scale of photometric value. In keeping with this fact, the step on the modern scale of stellar magnitude has now been standardized at 4 decibels (0.4 log unit).[13] (Actually, the early astronomers' scales differed among themselves, and most of them were slightly, but systematically, different from the logarithmic scale.[14])

So here we have two classes of sensory measures lending some degree of credence to the logarithmic law: the results of measuring differential sensitivity and the results of *partitioning* a sensory continuum into equal-appearing intervals.

---

[12] Bertrand Russell, *Introduction to Mathematical Philosophy* (2d ed.; New York: Macmillan Co., 1920), p. 17.

[13] P. Moon, "Photometrics in Astronomy," *Journal of the Franklin Institute*, 1954, p. 461; S. S. Stevens, "Decibels of Light and Sound," *Physics Today*, 1955, p. 12.

[14] J. Jastrow, "The Psycho-physic Law and Star Magnitudes," *American Journal of Psychology*, 1887, p. 112.

Then what about Plateau's view? Is there any experimental evidence that supports the power law? Actually, Plateau appears to have been the first experimenter to bring the partitioning method out of the heavens and into the laboratory—or more precisely, into the studio, for he asked eight artists to paint a gray that would appear halfway between extreme black and white. The eight grays, independently produced, turned out to be "*presque identiques.*" Furthermore, the goodness of the partition into equal intervals—black to gray to white—appeared to remain stable under different degrees of illumination. Starting from this latter fact, Plateau conjectured his power law.

Unfortunately, for reasons we will consider shortly, the method of partitioning is not capable of verifying the power law. It was because Plateau did not know this fact that he later felt obliged to change his mind about the law. Actually, however, he never should have changed it, for he was right in his basic conjecture. The correct law is the power law.

RATIO SCALE OF SENSORY MAGNITUDE

In our struggle to discover the measures of things, we do not always hit upon the simplest and easiest procedure first off. Fechner's method of constructing a scale by the tedious process of measuring just noticeable differences and counting them off was involved and indirect—and even included one of Russell's larcenous postulates in the bargain. Plateau's method was more direct, certainly; but it aimed, at best, only at the construction of an interval scale—one on which the zero point would be arbitrary and on which ratios could have no meaning.

Clearly, if a ratio scale was to be achieved, judgments of subjective ratios would have to be made. In the early 1930's the first serious efforts to get people to respond to ratios of sensory magnitude finally got under way, and over the past few years a swelling tide of ratio-scaling procedures has given this whole subject an exciting new look. It turns out that the ordinary thoughtful observer *can* make quantitative estimates of sensory events. He can adjust a light so that it appears half as bright as another, or a fifth as bright, or a tenth as bright. He can also set it to a given multiple of the apparent brightness of a standard light. Furthermore, given some standard brightness, to which is assigned an arbitrary value such as 10, the typical observer can assign numbers to other brightnesses proportional to their apparent level, as he sees them. These and several others are the procedures used.

On 17 different perceptual continua the application of these methods has resulted in power functions. To a fair approximation, estimated subjective magnitude is proportional to the stimulus magnitude raised to a power. The exponents, experimentally determined, have ranged from about 0.3 for loudness to 3.5 for the subjective intensity of electric shock applied to the fingers. The fundamental psychophysical law that emerges from these findings is simply this: Equal stimulus ratios produce equal subjective ratios. That is all there is to it. The proportionality between stimulus ratios and subjective ratios is a pervasive first-order relation, observed in empirical studies on numerous perceptual continua. Second-order departures from this law are sure to exist (we already know about some of them), but the wide invariance of the first-order relation is a matter of prime importance.

I was particularly interested to see what form the ratio scale of subjective magnitude would take for small luminous targets resembling a star, for the astronomers' estimates of stellar magnitudes gave us the first psychological

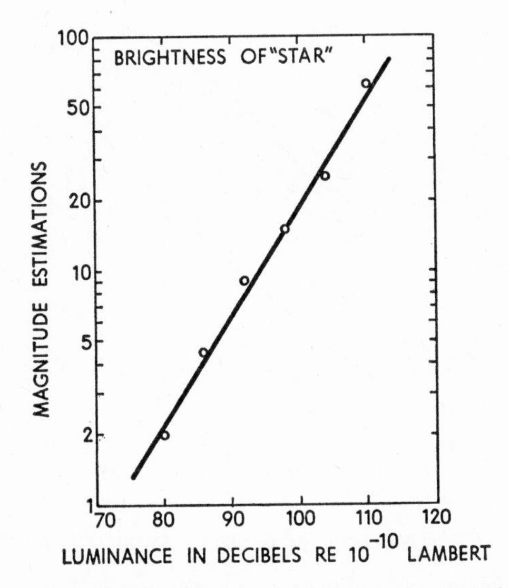

FIGURE 1. Direct magnitude estimations of the apparent brightness of a small target subtending an angle of about 1.5 minutes of arc. The observer was first shown a luminance of 92 decibels and told to call it "10." Relative to this modulus, he then estimated the other brightnesses, which were presented twice each in irregular order. Points are medians for 15 observers. The straight line in this log-log plot determines a power function with an exponent of 0.47.

scale, though it was not a ratio scale. Fifteen subjects were asked to assign numbers proportional to the apparent brightness of a small spot of light resembling a star, whose intensity was varied over a range of 30 decibels.[15] The median estimates gave a close approximation to a power function with an exponent of 0.47. Thus the apparent subjective magnitude of the "star" grows approximately as the square root of the photometric level (see Fig. 1). (The exponent here is greater than that for larger luminous targets, where the exponent is close to one third.)

Now the question arises, why did the early astronomers' scale approximate a logarithmic function, whereas direct estimations of apparent brightness give a power function? This stubborn question, which has long been a puzzle,

[15] S. S. Stevens and E. H. Galanter, "Ratio Scales and Category Scales for a Dozen Perceptual Continua," *Journal of Experimental Psychology*, 1957, p. 377. The experiments on the apparent brightness of the "star" were conducted by J. C. Stevens.

actually turns out to have a very simple answer. It hinges on the fact that a person's sensitivity to differences (measured in subjective units) is not uniform over the scale—a fact related to Weber's law. A given difference that is large and obvious in the lower part of the range is much less impressive in the upper part of the scale. This asymmetry in the observer's sensitivity to differences

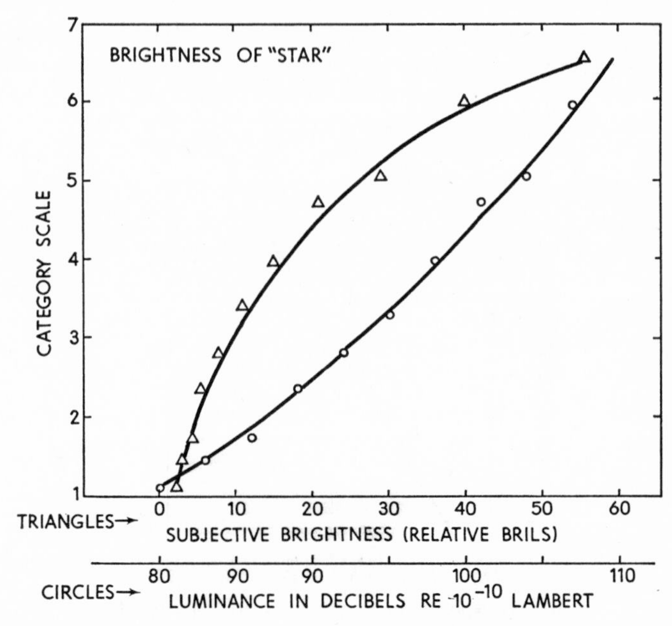

FIGURE 2. Judgments of brightness on a category scale from 1 to 7. A luminance of 80 decibels was presented and called "1," and one of 110 decibels was presented and called "7." The observer then judged the various levels twice each in irregular order. Points are averages for 15 observers. The results are plotted against two different abscissa scales. The triangles are plotted against the magnitude scale obtained from the line in Figure 1. The circles are plotted against the luminance scale in decibels. Note that the triangles determine a curve that is concave downward. The lower curve (circles) suggests that partitioning into a finite number of categories produces a function that is roughly logarithmic, but not precisely so.

produces a systematic bias whenever he tries to partition a continuum into equal-appearing intervals. On all continua of the class I have called "prothetic,"[16] of which brightness is one, we observe that the scale constructed by partitioning into categories is a convex function of the ratio scale obtained by direct estimation—that is, the category scale plotted against the ratio scale gives a curve that is concave downward (see the upper curve in Fig. 2).

The systematic bias that warps our judgments whenever we try to divide a segment of a prothetic continuum into equal-appearing intervals was presumably operating, of course, when the early astronomers arranged their scale of stellar magnitudes. The bias was apparently strong enough to make

[16] Stevens, "On the Psychophysical Law."

this scale approximate a logarithmic function of photometric intensity. But this roughly logarithmic outcome really helps Fechner's argument not at all, for when we look more carefully at the processes involved, we find that the form of the scale of stellar magnitudes is merely another example of the fact that man exhibits a built-in bias whenever he tries to partition a segment of a prothetic continuum. It is too bad that Plateau, when confronted with the results of another experiment on partitioning (conducted by Delboeuf), let himself be persuaded to renounce the power law.

Our confidence in the view that some kinds of partitioning are subject to bias gathers strength from the finding that not all partitioning is distorted in this manner. On another class of continua, called "metathetic," where sensitivity is not asymmetrical, the process of partitioning may produce an unbiased, linear scale.[17] Pitch is an example of a metathetic continuum, whereas loudness is prothetic. With loudness, the physiological process underlying our discriminations seems to involve the *addition* of excitation to excitation. With pitch, the process is believed to be the *substitution* of excitation for excitation, a change in the locus of the excitation. It is indeed interesting that the difference between these two basic classes of physiological mechanisms reflects itself in the behavior of the psychological scales which we construct from the sensory responses involved.

THE EAR AS A COMPRESSOR

Since scales of measurement bear little fruit if they do not serve to predict or explain anything, it is fair to ask what other insights into natural phenomena may stem from this boom in sensory measurement. I do not pretend to know where it all will lead, but I would like to cite one final example of its bearing on an interesting question.

One of the amazing properties of a sensory system like hearing is the almost incredible dynamic range of its operation. Energy ranges of billions to one are taken easily in stride.[18] In order to encompass such dynamic ranges, in order to detect sound vibrations whose amplitudes are less than the diameter of a hydrogen molecule and, at the same time, respond adequately to a thunderous roar, the sensory system must behave in some sense as a "compressor." The interesting question is, where does the compression take place—in the end organ or in the central nervous system?

First, it is to be noted that the degree of the compression we are concerned with is given by the exponent of the power function relating loudness to sound intensity.[19] This exponent of about 0.3 tells us that in order to double the apparent loudness, we must multiply the energy by a factor of about 10 (or the sound pressure by the square root of 10). Contrast this relation with the

[17] Stevens and Galanter, *op. cit.*

[18] S. S. Stevens, "The Measurement of Loudness," *Journal of the Acoustical Society of America*, 1955, p. 815.

[19] *Ibid.*

growth of the subjective intensity of electric shock, which shoots up as the 3.5 power of the current applied to the fingers.[20] Here, when we double the current, the typical observer judges the shock to be some 9 or 10 times as great as it was previously. There is no compression under this direct electrical stimulation. On the contrary, the system behaves as though it contained an "expander" of some sort. Through the direct measurement of sensory magnitudes, a striking difference is revealed between the behaviors of two sensory mechanisms.

Now the question is, what would happen if we were to stimulate the auditory nerve directly with an electric current? Some of us once explored this problem in a group of clinical patients whose middle ears had been opened for one reason or another, so that an electrode could be placed inside the open cavity.[21] Since other nerves, such as the facial and the vestibular, were readily stimulated under these circumstances, we have reason to believe that electrical stimulation also reached the auditory nerve, as indeed it must have done in those ears that heard only a noise whose character bore no systematic relation to the frequency of the stimulating current. A random, unpatterned excitation of the auditory nerve fibers would be expected to result from a current applied to the middle ear, and an unpatterned excitation of fibers should lead to the perception of noise rather than tone.

The interesting thing, from our present point of view, was the rapid growth of the loudness of the noise as the current was increased. The patient was asked to compare the noise with a sound produced by an acoustic stimulus led to his normal, unoperated ear. He adjusted the loudness in his normal ear to match the loudness of the noise in the operated ear. This simple procedure disclosed a startling fact. The growth of loudness was many times steeper under electrical than under acoustical stimulation. The exponent of the power function under electrical stimulation was, in fact, of about the same order of magnitude as that observed when a 60-cycle current was applied to the fingers.

Many interesting questions are raised by these measurements, but one implication is clear. The "compression" observed in the normal response of the auditory system to a sound stimulus is apparently not an affair of the central nervous system, for if we bypass the ear and stimulate the auditory nerve directly, we detect no compression. Rather, there results an "expansion" in the subjective response. Apparently, therefore, it is to the end organ itself that we must look for the mechanism of compression that governs the slow growth of loudness with acoustic intensity.

So it appears that with the aid of scales constructed for the measurement of sensation, we may have disclosed a fundamental difference between two transducer mechanisms. The transduction of sound energy into nervous

---

[20] S. S. Stevens, A. S. Carton, and G. M. Shickman, "A Scale of Apparent Intensity of Electric Shock," *Journal of Experimental Psychology*, in press.

[21] R. C. Jones, S. S. Stevens, and M. H. Lurie, "Three Mechanisms of Hearing by Electrical Stimulation," *Journal of the Acoustical Society of America*, 1940, p. 281.

energy is by way of an "operating characteristic" that somehow compresses the overall sensory response. The transduction of electrical energy into nervous energy seems to follow quite a different rule. To be sure, this outcome is but a trifle in the vast and relentless contest to unwind the tangle of nature; but it testifies, in simple example, to the profit that may accrue from measuring the "unmeasurable."[22]

---

[22] This research was aided by the Office of Naval Research and the National Science Foundation (report PNR–210).

2

The author suggests a set of accounting axioms which will approximate conventional accounting measurements, and enumerates basic measurement rules. Conventional accounting measurements are then represented mathematically, together with selected illustrative applications. Based upon his analysis, the author takes the position that future accounting measurements need not be restricted to expression in monetary units.

*AXIOMS AND STRUCTURES OF CONVENTIONAL ACCOUNTING MEASUREMENT**†

Yuji Ijiri

I. INTRODUCTION

1. This paper probes into the foundations of conventional accounting measurements in order to construct a relatively simple axiom system on which a purely mathematical measurement system can be erected and thus provide a consistent basis for examining pertinent aspects of conventional accounting practices.

2. The objective of this paper—as well as its mode of development—needs to be distinguished from other, prior attempts to axiomatize accounting.[1]

---

* Reprinted from *Accounting Review*, January, 1965, pp. 26–53.

† This work was supported in part by Office of Naval Research Contract Nonr–225(50) at Stanford University and in part by funds made available by the Ford Foundation to the Graduate School of Business, Stanford University. Reproduction in whole or in part is permitted for any purpose of the United States government.

An earlier draft of this paper was presented at the Eleventh International Meeting of the Institute of Management Science held in Pittsburgh, Pennsylvania, on March 12–14, 1964.

The author is indebted to Professor W. W. Cooper of Carnegie Institute of Technology and his colleague, Professor R. G. Brown of Stanford University, for their detailed review of an earlier draft of this paper, as well as for their helpful comments and suggestions.

[1] The first such attempt appears to be due to E. L. Kohler. See the definition of *axiom* and related terms in [12]. See also [1]–[9], [13]–[17], [19]–[21] for a more general approach to systematizing accounting principles and practices. In particular, [14] and [16] discuss specifically axiomatic approaches to accounting.

a) Unlike the attempt by Moonitz and Sprouse,[2] the object of our analysis is to develop and elucidate a uniform approach to *conventional* accounting measurement as such. That is, we take conventional accounting measurement as given rather than, *ab initio*, seeking to prescribe what we think accounting measurement should be.

b) Conventional accounting is analyzed in this paper from a purely mathematical viewpoint of measurement. Hence, we are not interested in factors which do not affect the measure. We consider any two accounting systems as being equal if the measures derived from the systems are equal for any set of inputs to the systems.[3] Therefore, unlike the approach by Mattessich adopted in [14], in which an emphasis is placed on a double classification scheme in accounting,[4] distinctions are not made in our analysis between an accounting system based upon double-entry bookkeeping and an accounting system based upon single-entry bookkeeping as long as methods of recording do not affect the measure which is of our primary interest.

c) The measurement system of conventional accounting is here viewed as though it consists of a set of axioms, on the one hand, and a set of measurement rules on the other hand. These are to be extracted from conventional accounting in such a way that the set of axioms and the set of measurement rules thus developed are not only *necessary* but also *sufficient* to explain the majority of the principles and practices in conventional accounting. Unfortunately, conventional accounting is a collection of many different accounting principles and practices. Moreover, in some cases, they are mutually inconsistent, and hence no systematic theories can describe all of them. Therefore, numerous axioms and measurement rules may be needed to cover *all* of the principles and practices in conventional accounting, whereas there may be no axioms and measurement rules that can be used commonly to explain *every* principle and procedure in conventional accounting. Thus, our attempt has been directed toward *approximating* conventional accounting by a relatively simple set of axioms and measurement rules, in the same manner that scientists in physics or chemistry have tried to develop a relatively simple set of concepts and theories in order to explain, in satisfactory degrees of approximation, complicated phenomena in this world.

d) The set of axioms and the set of measurement rules developed in this paper correspond to the set of axioms and the set of theorems (including lemmas and corollaries), respectively, in Euclidean geometry in the sense that if the set of axioms is granted, the measurement rules can be developed in a

[2] See Moonitz [16], and Sprouse and Moonitz [20].

[3] Two functions f and g are said to be equal if both are defined on the same domain X and

$$f(x) = g(x) \tag{1.1}$$

for every x in X. The same definition of equality applies to the equality of accounting systems in our discussions. In order to avoid any possibility of misunderstanding, we would like to postpone stating our view on what the things to be measured in conventional accounting are until we have presented all axioms and measurement rules.

[4] See, however, his recent work in [15] for a different approach.

purely mathematical way without requiring any empirical judgment. Furthermore, though the truth of the axioms cannot be proved (in the purely philosophical sense), they are empirically supported since the axioms are abstracted from what accountants have been doing in their daily practices. In addition, the number of axioms is minimized to avoid any redundant axioms coming into the set; i.e., the set of axioms developed here is necessary and sufficient to support the set of measurement rules, which is another half of the whole measurement system. Therefore, our set of axioms is *not a mere listing of concepts* that we think necessary for conventional accounting but is tied in logically and mathematically with the set of measurement rules and hence with the whole measurement system.

II. AXIOMS

Introduction

The set of axioms necessary for the system of accounting measurement that will approximate conventional accounting measurement consists of axiom of quantities, axiom of ownership, and axiom of exchanges. Since these three axioms are related to each other, one of the three axioms cannot be explained fully without having explained the rest of the axioms. Hence, we shall first explain each axiom separately in a less precise form and then state the three axioms in a more precise form.

Axiom of Quantities

1. Essentially, this axiom states that all objects which may be pertinent to accounting are quantifiable—i.e., measurable by some methods such as amount, volume, weight, length, time (service life), etc.

2. To state it more precisely:

a) Objects dealt with in accounting can be partitioned into a countable collection of classes (i.e., each object is classified into one and only one class).

b) For each class, there exists a function called a *physical measure* by which a unique number (quantity) is determined for the set of all objects in the class or for any subset of it.

c) For each class, if two sets of objects in the same class are of the same quantity derived by a physical measure for the class, they are mutually substitutable for the purpose of exchanges.[5]

The above statements will be made precise after the axioms of ownership and exchanges are introduced and similarly explained. For the moment, however, we may proceed to elucidate this axiom further, independently from the rest of the three axioms.

[5] Note that the axiom also implies that an object a is substitutable for itself (reflexive); if a is substitutable for a', then a' is substitutable for a (symmetrical); and if a is substitutable for a', and a' is substitutable for a'', then a is substitutable for a'' (transitive).

3. This axiom may be regarded as an axiom of classification based upon substitutability of objects. The physical measure defined for each class is used to define substitutability quantitatively.[6]

4. If an object is not substitutable for any other object (e.g., antiques), a class must be provided for the object with the physical measure whose value (quantity) is, say, one if the object is included in the class and otherwise zero.

5. In addition to the above requirements *a–c*, we require that a physical measure in each class satisfy all the requirements for a measure in mathematics, i.e.,

d) For each class the physical measure defined for the class must be always nonnegative, zero if the class is empty, and countably additive.[7]

This means that quantities derived by the physical measure are always positive or zero, and zero if the class contains no objects.[8] The requirement that the physical measure must be countably additive means that the quantity of distinct objects A and B combined together is the sum of the quantity of A and the quantity of B.[9] This is to assure that the quantity of 100 chairs is 100 no matter how we count them, or the quantity of 1,000 gallons of gasoline is 1,000 no matter how we measure it. On the other hand, so far as these requirements for a measure are satisfied, it does not matter whether gasoline is measured by gallons or pints or ounces.[10] Also, it should be noted that the value of a physical measure is allowed to take positive infinity, as in the example discussed in the next paragraph.

6. An object itself may be classified into a class different from one to which the *services* or *utilities* of the object belong. For example, land itself may be measured by its area (provided that two lots with the same area are substitutable—otherwise, they belong to different classes); whereas services obtained

---

[6] The substitutability must be recognized not only by the subject who owns the objects but also by other subjects who enter into the process of exchanges (economic and physical) of the objects. For example, brand A regular gasoline and brand B regular gasoline may be classified into the same class if they are to be used in a factory and if the differences in quality of the two brands are immaterial, since in such a case a given number of gallons of brand A gasoline is perfectly substitutable for the same gallon of brand B gasoline. On the other hand, if they are owned for resale purposes, and if for customers the two brands are not indifferent, though their quality difference may be insignificant, they should be classified into different classes.

[7] See, for example, Halmos [10] or Royden [18] for the properties of a measure.

[8] Mathematically, the physical measure can take zero on nonempty sets of objects in a class so far as other requirements for a measure are satisfied. However, since normally a nonempty set of objects and an empty set of objects are not substitutable, by the requirement *c* above such a trivial physical measure can be ruled out.

[9] More precisely, a physical measure q_i defined for the ith class must satisfy

$$q_i\left(\sum_{j=1}^{\infty} A_j\right) = \sum_{j=1}^{\infty} q_i(A_j) \qquad (i = 1, 2, \cdots) \tag{2.1}$$

for any sequence of disjoint subsets of A.

[10] Clearly, a function whose value is always equal to a multiple by a positive constant of the value of another measure is also a measure.

from the land may be measured by time. If the service life of land is considered to be infinite, the quantity of services of land is infinite. However, this does not disturb our measurement system at all, as becomes clear later.

7. One of the three amazing human abilities assumed in the three axioms is that a person is able to know that he is indifferent about two sets of objects when in fact the two are not identical. How can human beings acquire such an ability? Perhaps only by experiences. However, we shall not go into this psychological or rather philosophical question, but simply assume that such an ability has been granted by setting it in the axiom.

8. Though substitutability is essential in this axiom, what we need is not a simple substitutability but an *additive* substitutability. As mentioned in footnote 11, the substitutability must be reflexive, symmetrical, and transitive. However, in addition to this, we need the property that if a_1 is substitutable for b_1 and a_2 is substitutable for b_2, then a_1 and a_2 together are substitutable for b_1 and b_2 together. This is what is meant by an additive substitutability. Here is the need for introducing quantities or physical measures that generate quantities. Note that quantities discussed here presuppose substitutability. That is, *we are interested in quantities only insofar as they are supported by substitutability*. For example, paint and wine may be measured by the same unit of measure—e.g., by gallons. But "100 gallons of paint or wine" has no meaning at all in our accounting measurement system (even though the figure may be useful for some other purposes), since the figure is not based upon substitutability.

It seems to be extremely important to note this point. Quantities based upon substitutability are the essential factors in conventional accounting measurement.[11]

9. The set of objects that is dealt with in conventional accounting (we shall call it an *accounting set*) is not a simple collection of objects but a set with such properties as those described above. The axiom of quantities is to assure that there exists such an accounting set with which to start the construction of a measurement system.

Axiom of Ownership

1. The axiom of ownership—or more precisely, the axiom of ownership identifiability—involves four factors in its foundation: a subject, objects, a relation called ownership, and time.

2. *A subject:* A subject in this axiom is an identifiable thing that has a capacity for owning objects. A subject may be a person, a partnership, a corporation, or even an object or a collection of objects (estate). Conventional accounting exists only for one subject at a time. It is not defined for a simple

---

[11] We may say that two sets of objects, a and a', are *equal*, denoted by $a = a'$, if and only if both sets belong to the same class and the measure on a and the measure on a' are equal. This is another way of saying that two sets of objects are equal if and only if they are substitutable.

collection of subjects (e.g., a mob) unless such a collection is also considered as constituting a subject (a holding company). It is not defined for objects without a subject (minerals in the moon, unless the moon itself is considered as a subject). Therefore, except when there is a possibility of confusion, we shall always assume that we have a given subject.

3. *Objects:* Objects are any identifiable things that have a capacity for being owned by (or belonging to) a subject. Objects in conventional accounting include not only goods as such but also utilities that are generated from goods. It is an important accounting problem to decide what types of objects are to be included in the accounting set U. However, from the viewpoint of measurement, we shall assume that all issues concerning the objects in U have been settled (otherwise, no measurement systems can be developed) and the only property that we need to require is that objects in U be identifiable.

4. *Ownership relation:* The relation between a subject and objects is described as the latter "belonging" to the former. The belongingness need not be a legal ownership, though we use legal terms for convenience. Any mechanism can be used in defining ownership relation so far as at any point in time every element in the accounting set U is uniquely characterized either as belonging to the subject or as not belonging to the subject (but not both). Therefore, it may be a legal ownership, an economic ownership, organizational responsibility, or even a physical possession or a physical attachment to a subject. The essential point of the axiom is that the set of all objects that "belong" to a given subject at any given point in time must be uniquely identified. If there is any dispute about the belongingness of an object, whatever the definition of ownership may be, such a dispute must be settled before applying the measurement system.

5. *Time:* Since we are interested in changes over time in the set of objects that belong to a given subject, the set of all objects that belong to the subject at any given point in time must be identifiable at least at that time or later. (It need not be identifiable earlier than that time.) This also implies that any changes in the set of all objects that belong to the subject can also be recognized. We shall define the set of all objects that belong to the subject at time t to be the *property set* of the subject at time t, denoted by A_t, where A_t is a subset of U for any t.

6. The second amazing human ability assumed in the three axioms is the ability to identify an object as belonging to a given subject. Particularly in the case of a legal ownership, many objects do not have labels that identify the owner; nevertheless, the objects are recognized as belonging to a subject not only by the subject himself but also by the rest of the people in the society. Without the axiom of ownership, we are not able to identify A_t, on which we want to apply our measurement system.

7. By combining the axiom of ownership with the axiom of quantities, the set of all objects that belong to the subject at time t—i.e., A_t—can be uniquely identified, once we fix the order of the classes, by a vector

(2.2)
$$q^t = (q_1{}^t, q_2{}^t, \cdots): \quad q_i{}^t \geq 0 \quad (i = 1, 2, \cdots)$$

ıere q_i^t is the quantity of the objects that belong to the ith class and that are ʼned by the subject at time t. Then the problem for an accounting measure-ent system is, using the set of quantities q^t, to generate a unique real number r any given time t. Such a number, $m(A_t)$, is used as a measure on the set of objects that belong to the subject at time t.

8. A remarkable characteristic of the measurement system of conventional accounting is the fact that it is based on activities called exchanges. In other words, $m(A_t)$ is not determined arbitrarily, nor by the weight of the weighable objects in A_t, nor by the market value of the total objects in A_t, nor by anything else—but by the method called *measure imputation through exchanges.*

Axiom of Exchanges

1. By an exchange, we mean a phenomenon which decreases the property set of a given subject at a given point in time by a set of objects (called outgoing objects), denoted by d^-, and in return increases the property set by another set of objects (called incoming objects), denoted by d^+. Thus an exchange involves two sets of objects which are related with each other by a cause-and-effect relationship. An exchange may occur by an activity of the subject to whom the property set belongs, or it may occur by some other forces (by nature or by other subjects).

2. The third amazing human ability is that a person is able to know that a set of objects, d^+, is obtained in exchange for another set of objects, d^-. For example, a warehouse manager can see only goods coming in and going out, while a cashier can see only cash balance increased or decreased. But when we see the firm's operation as a whole, we are able to say that cash is increased in *exchange* for goods delivered. That is, we have a mechanism outside the measurement system, by which we are able to say that d^+ is obtained as a result of foregoing d^-, or in exchange for d^-. The axiom of exchanges is provided essentially to assure us that we can recognize such exchanges as they take place. We shall denote an exchange d by a pair of ordered sets

$$d = [d^+, d^-] \tag{2.3}$$

in which the first element shows the set of incoming objects and the second element the set of outgoing objects. When this concept of exchanges is applied to conventional accounting, it will be noted that this concept of exchanges is applicable for both *economic exchanges* (i.e., exchanges through market), and *physical exchanges* (i.e., exchanges through production processes). In our measurement system the two types of exchanges are not distinguished since there is no need for this from the viewpoint of accounting measurement.

3. For the reason that will become clear in the discussions of measurement rules, we shall require that the set d^+ of the incoming objects belongs to a single class only. If d^+ consists of objects in two or more classes, it is assumed that by some methods the exchange can be partitioned into a countable collection of (sub)exchanges each of which contains incoming objects that belong to a single class only.

4. The time dimension of an exchange has been deliberately postponed up to this point for a simpler explanation of the concept. We shall discuss this now in detail.

If, in every exchange d, an addition of d^+ to a property set A and a subtraction of d^- from the property set A are made *simultaneously*, the measurement system can be much simpler. If this is true, we can define an exchange at time t, denoted by d_t, to be a phenomenon that adds to A_t a set d_t^+ that is not in A_t, and subtracts from A_t a set d_t^- that is in A_t after d_t^+ has been added.[12]

However, in many cases, exchanges that are dealt with in conventional accounting contain objects that are to be added or subtracted in the future. For example, a sale on account is an exchange between goods to be subtracted now and cash to be added in the future. In order to take into account such exchanges, let us allow an addition of d^+ to occur at time t^+ and a subtraction of d^- to occur at time t^- with $t^+ \geq t$ and $t^- \geq t$ where t is the time at which the exchange has occurred. Because of such an extended notion of exchanges, objects to be added or subtracted in the future as the result of exchanges that have occurred in the past must be recorded and identified at any later time.

5. Let us, then, define an exchange in the following way: An exchange $d_t = [d^+, d^-]$ is a phenomenon at time t which results in adding the set d^+ of incoming objects (belonging to a single class) to the property set A_t^+ and subtracting the set d^- of outgoing objects from the property set A_t^- where $t^+ \geq t$ and $t^- \geq t$. With this definition of exchanges, we need an axiom by which it is guaranteed that any object that is to be added to or subtracted from the property set A can be associated with an exchange uniquely so that, for example, when cash is received a month later it can be recognized as a payment for the goods delivered earlier and not a simple increase in cash. Furthermore, we require that all exchanges that have occurred be countable and can be ordered completely and uniquely according to the time of their occurrence for the purpose of recording.

6. Considering all these factors, the axiom of exchanges is defined as follows: For any object that is added to or subtracted from the property set A_t, an exchange that has caused the addition or subtraction of the object can be uniquely identified; and all exchanges that have occurred are identifiable,

[12] More precisely, $d_t = [d_t^+, d_t^-]$ is an operation which changes A_t into A_t', where

$$A_t' = A_t \cup d_t^+ - d_t^- \tag{2.4}$$

subject to

$$d_t^+ \cap A_t = \phi \tag{2.5}$$

$$d_t^- \subset (A_t \cup d_t^+) \tag{2.6}$$

Here, A_t' is the set of objects that belong to the subject immediately after the exchange d_t, or more precisely,

$$A_t' = \underline{\lim}_{\Delta t \to 0} A_{t+\Delta t} = \overline{\lim}_{\Delta t \to 0} A_{t+\Delta t} \tag{2.7}$$

(I am indebted to Professor H. Uzawa of the University of Chicago for his remarks on this point.)

are countable, and can be ordered completely and uniquely according to the time of their occurrence.

Definitions and Three Axioms

1. The above discussions are now summarized in the following form of definitions and axioms:

Definitions

a) *A subject* is any identifiable thing that is capable of owning other things.

b) *Objects* are any identifiable things that are capable of being owned by a subject.

c) *Time* is a real variable; a smaller value of time means an earlier time and a larger value a later time.

d) *A physical measure* is a nonnegative set function that is defined on a class of objects and all of its subsets such that it is countably additive, that it takes zero on the empty set, and that two sets of objects in a same class are substitutable if they are of a same value of the physical measure. A class with such a function is called a measurable class.

e) *An accounting set* is a set of objects that may be partitioned into a countable collection of measurable classes.

f) *Ownership* is a well-defined relationship between a subject and objects at a given time by which for any object it is uniquely determined whether or not the object belongs to the subject at the given time.

g) *A property set* of a subject at time t is a subset of an accounting set and consists of all objects that belong to the subject at time t.

h) *An exchange* at time t is a phenomenon at time t which results in adding a set of incoming objects (all belonging to a single class) to the property set A_{t+} and subtracting a set of outgoing objects from the property set A_{t-}, where $t^{+} \geq t$ and $t^{-} \geq t$.

Axioms

Axiom of quantities: There exists an accounting set U—that is, a set of objects that may be partitioned into a countable collection of measurable classes.

Axiom of ownership: The property set A_t of a given subject at any time t can be uniquely determined at that time or later.

Axiom of exchanges: For any object that is added to or subtracted from the property set A_t, an exchange that has caused the addition or subtraction of the object can be uniquely identified; and all exchanges that have occurred are identifiable, are countable, and can be ordered completely and uniquely according to the time of their occurrence.

2. With this set of axioms, the set of measurement rules can be developed in a purely logical and mathematical way, as we shall see in the next section.

III. MEASUREMENT RULES

A Uniform Measure

1. By the axiom of quantities and the axiom of exchange, the property set can be described by a set of quantities, i.e., values of physical measures. Then

the problem for accounting measurement is to derive a measure of the property set by which a unique real number is assigned for any property set. The set of measurement rules to be discussed below is designed to generate such a measure, which will be called a uniform measure or simply a *u*-measure from a set of physical measures by means of exchanges.

2. For this purpose, we first select a class as a basic class and use the physical measure defined on the class to generate a *u*-measure. It is convenient to choose a class whose objects are often used in exchanges, but this is not essential from the viewpoint of mathematical measure. However, we shall require the class to be of finite measure; i.e., at any time t the set of objects in the property set A_t that belong to the class is always of a finite value of the physical measure defined on the class.[13]

3. Then

a) The *u*-measure of any set of (current and future) objects in the basic class is set equal to its quantity measured by the physical measure of the basic class.

b) The *u*-measure of the empty set is set equal to zero.

If cash is selected for a basic class, the *u*-measure of any set of cash, regardless of whether it is cash on hand (called current cash) or cash to be received or paid in future (called future cash), is given by its quantity measured by the physical measure of cash—e.g., dollars—and all receivables and payables as well as deposits and loans belong to the basic class. If gasoline is selected for a basic class, all receipts or deliveries of gasoline committed by exchanges are considered to belong to the basic class.

4. On the other hand, objects that belong to a nonbasic class, a class other than the basic class, are recognized in the measurement rules only at the time they are actually received or delivered. For example, if current cash is received in exchange for merchandise to be delivered 30 days from now, the exchange needs to be modified as if it were an exchange between current cash and future cash (advance receipt) and an exchange between current cash and current merchandise at the time when merchandise is actually delivered. Procedures for such modifications of exchanges will be discussed later in this section in more detail. Therefore, we shall proceed, assuming that no exchanges involve future nonbasic objects.

5. In order to start the measurement system, it is necessary to have the values of the *u*-measure given for each class of objects in the property set A at the beginning of a period for which we want to account. Therefore, we must require A to be empty or consist only of objects in the basic class, or values of the *u*-measure for each class be given as, for example, in a beginning balance sheet. If none of these cases apply, the *u*-measure of objects in a nonbasic class is arbitrarily set equal to zero in order to supply an artificial start. Initial proprietary investments of nonbasic objects belong to this category, which must be solved by means of evaluation by, say, market values. The set of

[13] This is necessary since we are going to have an operation called a subtraction of a set d^- from A, and if the *u*-measure of A and d^- are both infinite, $\infty - \infty$ is undefined.

three axioms is not capable of providing market values. This will be discussed later with other cases in which market values are used in conventional accounting.

Allocations, Imputations, and Comparisons of Measures

1. The basic part of measurement rules consists of the following three rules:

a) *Measure allocations:* Allocate the *u*-measure of a nonbasic class to the set of outgoing objects of the class and to the set of remaining objects in proportion to their physical measures.

b) *Measure imputations:* If incoming objects belong to a nonbasic class, assign as the *u*-measure of the incoming objects the sum of the *u*-measures of all outgoing objects in the exchange. Increase the *u*-measure of the class to which the incoming objects belong by the *u*-measure of the incoming objects.

c) *Measure comparison:* If the set of incoming objects is empty or belongs to the basic class, calculate a measure gain (or loss) by subtracting the sum of the *u*-measures of outgoing objects from the *u*-measure of the incoming objects.

2. The rule of measure allocations states the moving-average method, but rules for other methods of measure allocations used in conventional accounting can be well established. For example, rules for Fifo or Lifo may be determined by setting up a set of ordered subclasses in each class with each subclass having a pair of a physical measure and a uniform measure. Then, by specifying the order in which these subclasses are used for measure allocation together with the above rule for the moving-average method, we can derive rules for the Fifo or Lifo method.

3. The rule of measure imputations is a fundamental rule for the historical cost basis. The rule of measure comparisons, then, requires that a measure gain (or loss) is recognized if and only if incoming objects belong to the basic class (the revenue realization principle). Of course, all these operations for measure allocations, imputations, and comparisons are supported by the three axioms.

Modifications of Exchanges

1. When an exchange involves nonbasic future objects, i.e., objects in a nonbasic class that are to be received or delivered at some time later, the exchange must be modified before applying the above rules. This is done in the following way.

2. *Two sets of future objects:*

a) In an exchange $[d_1, d_2]$,[14] if both d_1 and d_2 are sets of future objects, do not recognize the exchange until one set is actually received or delivered, unless *both* d_1 and d_2 are sets of *basic* future objects, in which case recognize the exchange.

[14] In our notation the first element in the bracket always denotes the set of incoming objects; and the second element, the set of outgoing objects.

For example, even if a purchase order has been issued, it is the practice in conventional accounting not to make an entry until either goods have been received or cash has been paid. However, if a note is issued by a customer who owes the firm, an entry is immediately made by increasing notes receivable and by decreasing accounts receivable. To approximate these practices, the above rule was set up.

3. *Increase in nonbasic future objects:*

b) In an exchange $[d_1, d_2]$, if d_1 is a set of nonbasic future objects and d_2 is a set of current objects (basic or nonbasic), modify the exchange as if it were $[d_3, d_2]$ where d_3 is a set of basic future objects with $m(d_3) = m(d_2)$, where $m(d_i)$ is the u-measure of the set d_i, and recognize an exchange $[d_1, d_3]$ when d_1 is actually received.

Suppose that a purchase order has been issued and cash has already been paid but goods have not yet been delivered. Ordinarily, the cash paid is recorded as an advance payment until goods are received, even though it is possible, and actually done in some cases, to set up an account for future inventory. This is a rather trivial point in view of measurement of the property set since both methods yield exactly the same result. In any case, since the u-measure of current objects is uniquely determined by the rule of measure allocations, regardless of whether d_2 is basic or nonbasic, there is no problem in deriving d_3.

4. *Decrease in nonbasic future objects, I:*

c) In an exchange $[d_1, d_2]$, if d_2 is a set of nonbasic future objects and d_1 is a set of basic current objects, modify the exchange as if it were $[d_1, d_3]$, where d_3 is a set of basic future objects with $m(d_3) = m(d_1)$, and recognize an exchange $[d_3, d_2]$ when d_2 is actually delivered.

This is exactly the opposite case from the previous one. Suppose an order is sent from a customer with an advance payment; the cash received is treated as an advance receipt until goods are delivered. This is in line with the realization principle.

5. *Decrease in nonbasic future objects, II:*

d) In an exchange $[d_1, d_2]$, if d_2 is a set of nonbasic future objects and d_1 is a set of nonbasic current objects, modify the exchange as if it were an exchange $[d_1, d_3]$, where d_3 is a set of basic future objects with $m(d_3) = \bar{m}(d_2)$, where $\bar{m}(d_2)$ is the expected u-measure of d_2, and recognize an exchange $[d_3, d_2]$ when d_2 is actually delivered.

Here the expected u-measure of d_2 is given as the sum of the expected u-measures calculated for each class to which a subset of d_2 belongs, by multiplying the physical measure of the subset of d_2 by the average u-measure, i.e., the u-measure of the class divided by the (nonzero) physical measure of the class, and zero if the physical measure of the class is zero.

A problem arises when d_1, the set of incoming objects, is current objects belonging to a nonbasic class, since in such a case a u-measure cannot be determined for d_2 or d_1—for example, 500 barrels of crude oil received in exchange for 1,000 gallons of gasoline to be delivered in 30 days from now. (Note that this is different from the case in which crude oil was received on a consignment basis. In such a case, we need not consider that crude oil "belongs" to the subject.) The most likely treatment in conventional accounting is to use a so-called "replacement cost" of d_1, that is, the amount of cash to be paid if the exchange were made with cash. In our system, however, we do not have a mechanism to generate such a replacement cost or any other type of market values. Hence, as an approximation, we use the average costs, at the time of the exchange, of goods on hand in the classes that d_2 belongs to, provided that the average costs are defined for these classes. If they are not defined for a class that a subset of d_2 belongs to, we reluctantly set the u-measure of the corresponding subset of d_2 equal to zero. We will comment on this later again together with the discussions on market values.

A Uniform Measure on Property Sets

1. By means of these rules, we can uniquely determine the u-measure for any property set that a subject has owned, by adding the u-measures for each class in the property set. Future objects that are not included in the property set are all stated in terms of basic objects; hence the u-measure on these objects can be derived by the axioms of quantities and exchanges at any time. Let the u-measure at time t of all basic objects to be received (or added to a property set) in the future be represented by $m(B_t^+)$, and let the u-measure at time t of all basic objects to be delivered (or subtracted from a property set) in the future be represented by $m(B_t^-)$. Also, let us define an extended property set at time t, denoted by $\bar{A}_t$, as meaning the property set A_t together with the above two sets of basic future objects, i.e.,

$$\bar{A}_t = \{A_t, B_t^+, B_t^-\} \tag{3.1}$$

Then, since $m(A_t)$, $m(B_t^+)$, and $m(B_t^-)$ can all be determined uniquely by the above procedures, $m(\bar{A}_t)$ is well-defined by

$$m(\bar{A}_t) = m(A_t) + m(B_t^+) - m(B_t^-) \tag{3.2}$$[15]

2. By the rule of measure imputation, $m(\bar{A}_t)$ changes its value if and only if a nonzero measure gain g_t occurs, and $m(\bar{A}_{t'})$ after an exchange involving g_t has occurred is equal to the sum of $m(\bar{A}_t)$ before the exchange plus g_t generated by the exchange. Therefore, we always have an increase in the u-measure between two points in time, t_1 and t_2, i.e., $m(\bar{A}_{t_2}) - m(\bar{A}_{t_1})$, exactly equal to the sum of all measure gains during the period. We may compare

[15] The u-measure $m(\bar{A}_t)$ is no longer guaranteed to be nonnegative. However, it satisfies all the requirements for a *signed measure* in measure theory, since it is countably additive, is of finite values, and takes zero on the empty set. Refer to Halmos [10] or Royden [18].

this with a net profit figure derived from a balance sheet $[m(\bar{A}_{t_2}) - m(\bar{A}_{t_1})]$ and a net profit figure derived from an income statement

$$\left(\sum_{t_1 \leq t < t_2} g_t\right)$$

in conventional accounting.

3. It should be remembered that all of these rules are strictly based upon what is provided by the three axioms and nothing more. Of course, by increasing the number of axioms, these rules can be made more complicated for better approximations of principles and practices in conventional accounting. However, in order to focus on the fundamental factors, we have deliberately neglected minor points needed for further improvement in approximation.

IV. A MATHEMATICAL REPRESENTATION OF CONVENTIONAL ACCOUNTING MEASUREMENT[16]

1. The above discussions may be further clarified by the following mathematical representation of the axioms and the measurement rules.

2. By the axiom of ownership, we have for any given subject a unique set-valued function f of a real variable t:

$$A = f(t) \tag{4.1}$$

where A is a subset of a universal set U for all t.

3. By the axiom of quantities, A can be represented by a vector q for any t. Hence, we have a vector-valued function g of a real variable t:

$$q = g(t) \tag{4.2}$$

4. By the axiom of exchanges together with the rules of modifying exchanges discussed above, we can impose the following properties on the function $g(t)$:

The function $g(t)$ changes its values only at countable points of t. Hence the function is completely described by a sequence

$$(q^1, q^2, \cdots) \tag{4.3}$$

together with a sequence

$$(t^1, t^2, \cdots) \tag{4.4}$$

where

$$q^n = g(t) \quad \text{for all } t^{n-1} < t \leq t^n \qquad (n = 1, 2, \cdots)^{17} \tag{4.5}$$

and

$$t^n < t^{n+1} \qquad \text{for all } n = 1, 2, \cdots \tag{4.6}$$

[16] This section may be skipped without loss of continuity of the materials.

[17] Here the function g is assumed to be left continuous. However, the whole development may very well be done based on a right-continuous function.

with

(4.7) $$t^0 = -\infty \quad \text{and} \quad q^1 = 0$$

Also, if the first element in the vector q, denoted by q_1, represents the physical measure for the basic class, and all the subsequent elements q_i $(i = 2, 3, \cdots)$ the physical measures for nonbasic classes, we have

(4.8) $$q_i^n \geq 0 \qquad \text{for all } i = 2, 3, \cdots; n = 1, 2, \cdots$$

whereas q_1^n $(n = 1, 2, \cdots)$ is allowed to take a negative value due to negative future basic objects, and

(4.9) $$q_i^{n+1} - q_i^n > 0$$

for at most one i $(i = 1, 2, \cdots : n = 1, 2, \cdots)$, since the set of incoming objects always belongs to a single class.

5. Then the measurement rules are stated as follows:

For all $n = 1, 2, \cdots$

(4.10) $$p_1^n = q_1^n$$

and for all $n = 1, 2, \cdots$ and $i = 2, 3, \cdots$

(4.11) $$p_i^n = 0 \qquad \text{if } q_i^n = 0$$

(4.12) $$p_i^{n+1} = \frac{p_i^n}{q_i^n} \cdot q_i^{n+1} \qquad \text{if } q_i^{n+1} < q_i^n$$

(4.13) $$p_i^{n+1} = p_i^n \qquad \text{if } q_i^{n+1} = q_i^n$$

(4.14) $$p_i^{n+1} = p_i^n + \sum_{j \neq i} (p_j^n - p_j^{n+1}) \qquad \text{if } q_i^{n+1} > q_i^n$$

The u-measure $m(\bar{A}_t)$ of any extended property set $\bar{A}$ at time t is then given by

(4.15) $$m(\bar{A}_t) = \sum_i p_i^n$$

where n is the index which satisfies

(4.16) $$t^{n-1} < t \leq t^n \qquad (n = 1, 2, \cdots)$$

6. Therefore, with these axioms and measurement rules, we have a unique real-valued function h of a real variable t which generates the u-measure of an extended property set at time t; i.e.:

(4.17) $$m(\bar{A}_t) = h(t)$$

We may consider *a vector-valued function $g(t)$ as the input to the accounting measurement system and a real-valued function $h(t)$ as the output from the system.*[18] Also, as

[18] Let G be the set of all vector-valued functions g of a real variable t which satisfy the requirements in paragraph 4 above, and let H be the set of all real-valued functions h of a real variable t. Then the accounting measurement system m is a function which maps G into H, or

(4.18) $$G \xrightarrow{m} H$$

Note that the discrete nature of the functions in G is carried over to the functions that are in the range of the function m contained in H.

pointed out earlier, note that in conventional accounting the quantity

$$h(t_2) - h(t_1) \tag{4.19}$$

is used as an "evaluation" of the set of all activities that have taken place between time t_1 and t_2 (i.e., during the time period $t_1 \leq t < t_2$).

V. APPLICATIONS

Goods and Utilities

1. We shall now discuss some of the problems which may arise when we apply the above system in a practical situation. First of all, the distinction between goods and utilities that was mentioned earlier will be discussed in some detail.

2. Throughout our process of abstracting phenomena which are dealt with in conventional accounting, we have paid different consideration to *goods* themselves and *utilities* which may be generated by the goods. For example, suppose that a firm, K, rents a lot of its land to another firm, L. The ultimate right on the land still remains in the hands of K; hence, K may get a better title on the land than in a case in which K has only an obligatory right on L to deliver the land at a given future time. However, we need not distinguish the two cases from the standpoint of accounting measures. The land itself is in the hands of L anyway, and K has a right to receive the land in the future in both cases; hence, we may consider both of them as a case of a future object "belonging" to K.

3. Now, consider a rent on the land. This is actually a return for the utilities generated from the future object. In such a case, we do *not* consider that the current land is exchanged for the future land *plus* a given amount of money as a rent. If we considered so, the u-measure of the incoming objects, m(the future land plus cash), would be imputed from the u-measure of the outgoing object, m(the current land), by following the historical cost basis in conventional accounting that is reflected in our rule of measure imputation. However, this is not the method used in conventional accounting. Instead, the measure on the land is held constant, and the measure on incoming cash is recorded as income which corresponds to our concept of a measure gain. The only way that this procedure can be interpreted consistently with other procedures is to recognize the exchange

$$d = [\text{The future land, the current land}] \tag{5.1}$$

i.e., the future land was obtained in exchange for the current land (hence the measure of the future land is set equal to the measure of the current land), and then recognize another exchange, say:

$$d' = [\$1{,}000 \text{ cash, one-year service of the land}] \tag{5.2}$$[19]

[19] Though the service of the land is delivered continuously throughout the year, we can recognize it at discrete points in time by the axiom of exchanges.

That is, K obtained \$1,000 cash in exchange for "one-year *service* of the land." However, ordinarily the total service life of land is unlimited; namely, the physical measure of the services of the land is infinite. Since the u-measure for this class ought to be a finite number (by definition of the basic class measure), the u-measure that is to be allocated to the one-year services of the land is zero, according to the rule of measure allocation discussed above. On the other hand, the u-measure of \$1,000 cash is 1,000; hence, we recognize a measure gain of 1,000 in this exchange; i.e.:

$$m(\$1{,}000 \text{ cash}) - m(\text{the one-year services of the land}) = 1{,}000 \tag{5.3}$$

4. If, however, K rented a machine with 10 years of remaining life, and if the services of the machine in one year are comparable to the services of the machine in any other year (which is the basis for a straight line depreciation method), one tenth of the u-measure of the machine should be matched with the u-measure of the \$1,000 cash.[20] This, in effect, is what has been done in conventional accounting. (Although rent income and depreciation are calculated separately, the net effect of the u-measure of the property set is the same as the method described here.)

5. Now, let us extend this notion of future objects to the cases involving future cash. When \$1,000 of current cash is deposited in a bank now and \$1,050 of cash is returned a year from now, we should *not* consider this as an exchange:

$$d = [\$1{,}050 \text{ future cash}, \$1{,}000 \text{ current cash}] \tag{5.4}$$

Instead, we recognize the exchange:

$$d = [\$1{,}000 \text{ future cash}, \$1{,}000 \text{ current cash}] \tag{5.5}$$

and at the end of the one-year period, the exchanges:

$$d' = [\$50 \text{ current cash, one-year service of } \$1{,}000 \text{ cash}] \tag{5.6}$$

$$d'' = [\$1{,}000 \text{ current cash}, \$1{,}000 \text{ future cash}] \tag{5.7}$$

Since, as in the case of land, the "service life" of cash is unlimited, the u-measure of one-year service of \$1,000 cash is zero. Hence a measure gain of 50 is recognized in the exchange d' by the rule of measure comparison discussed above.[21]

A confusion arises in this case because of the fact that current cash is received in exchange for both cash delivered before and one-year service of cash; but if we compare this with the case of land, it will become clear that our way of interpreting interest is more consistent with the conventional accounting procedures than a way of looking at the exchange as the current cash forgone in exchange for an increased amount of cash in the future. We are not saying that this is the way that interest in general should be inter-

[20] If, say, one tenth of the services in the first year is comparable to the services in the tenth year, we should allocate the u-measure of the machine according to a physical measure that reflects the difference in services—e.g., by the sum of the years' digits method.

[21] A similar interpretation can also be made for interest on payables.

preted, but that by interpreting interest this way we can get a more *consistent* interpretation of conventional accounting principles and procedures with a simpler set of axioms and measurement rules.

6. But how about risks attached to future objects like accounts receivable? How can we interpret the practices of setting up reserves for bad debts? If, for example, in an exchange

$$d = [\$1{,}000 \text{ future cash, } 4{,}000 \text{ gallons of gasoline}] \tag{5.8}$$

where the u-measure of 4,000 gallons of gasoline is, say, 400, the firm expects, *at the time of the exchange*, that it can get only $800 cash, then the firm should recognize the exchange of

$$d' = [\$800 \text{ future cash, } 4{,}000 \text{ gallons of gasoline}] \tag{5.9}$$

yielding a measure gain of 400. (Note that we do not care whether this is done by setting up a reserve or by directly subtracting from the receivable so far as the net effect on the measure is the same.) This is exactly in line with the historical cost basis in conventional accounting. However, reserves for bad debts set up later, due to the changes in financial situations of customers or due to some other reason, must be considered as a departure from the historical cost basis that is similar to the application of market price in inventory when a market price becomes lower than the historical cost. (See discussions on market prices later.)

7. The rule of measure imputations developed above is directly in line with procedures in cost accounting. On the other hand, administrative expenses may be interpreted as exchanges which have no apparent incoming objects ($d^+ = \phi$); and since $m(\phi) = 0$, a measure loss is recognized at each exchange. A part of selling expenses may have direct incoming objects (reputation, goodwill, better salesmen), but we may consider that all such incoming objects are consumed when expenses occur. If so, there is no difference in the total measure gain. If they are not consumed at the time when expenses occur, we should, at least in principle, recognize the incoming objects and apply the rule of measure imputations.

8. It will also be noted that by utilizing the notion of "future cash," the principle of revenue realization and the accrual basis can be interpreted consistently with our measurement rules.

9. Finally, we would like to emphasize the fact that the concept of profit in conventional accounting cannot be derived independently from the concept of assets (or the property set in our system).

Profit in conventional accounting is derived as a measure (or evaluation) of the set of activities that have taken place during the given period of time. Unlike job evaluation or grading students' performance in a class, however, in conventional accounting we do not evaluate activities as such but evaluate them *through their effects on assets* (or a property set). The tendency of stressing the income determination side of accounting problems in current accounting theories should not be misinterpreted as if profit figures were derived as measures of activities independently from their effects on assets. In addition, just as the speed of an object is derived as the difference of the positions of the object at two different points in time relative to the length of the time period, profit is something that is derived as the difference of the u-measures of the property sets at two different points in time relative to the length of the time period; i.e., profit during the period between time t_1 and time t_2, denoted by $P(t_1, t_2)$, is given by

$$P(t_1, t_2) = m(\bar{A}_{t_2}) - m(\bar{A}_{t_1}) \tag{5.10}$$

Therefore, so far as the historical cost principle is adhered to, asset valuation and income determination are the two sides of the same coin, both concerned with *physical measures*, not with the uniform measure, when quantities of objects are hard to measure physically.

Some Problems in Applications

1. We shall now discuss principles and procedures that are used in conventional accounting but cannot be handled in the same way in our system.

2. *Market values:* The conventional accounting system that we have tried to approximate by our mathematical measure system is the one which is based upon such principles as the historical cost basis, the realization principle, the accrual basis, etc. Therefore, we have neglected such concepts as *market values, replacement costs, net realizable values,* etc. These concepts come into the conventional accounting systems and procedures in somewhat inconsistent ways. Some such examples may be listed as follows:

a) Cost-or-market-whichever-lower method applied to inventory and marketable securities
b) Donated assets or assets obtained at unusually low prices
c) Initial proprietary investment involving noncash assets
d) Allocation of joint costs based upon market values of joint products[22]
e) Reserves for bad debts

These are not incorporated into our system for an important reason that will be amplified more in the concluding section.

3. *Proprietary investments:* An exchange involving proprietary investment must be regarded as an exchange between current cash and future cash to be delivered at an indefinite time in the future, in order to operate the mathematical system developed here and generate a measure that approximates the one generated by the conventional accounting system, even though proprietary investment is different from loans and other payables from the standpoint of legal claims against the subject, the entity.

4. *Capital surplus:* An exchange involving capital surplus cannot be distinguished from an exchange involving earned surplus by our measure sys-

[22] Note that in the axiom of exchanges, we required that the set of incoming objects belong to a single class in any exchange to avoid this case. If an exchange involves incoming objects that belong to more than one class, the exchange must be decomposed before the measurement rules are applied on it.

tem. We consider, however, that the need to distinguish capital surplus and earned surplus comes from legal and managerial requirements concerning the distribution of income. This is a problem of allocation *policy* that arises after the total measure gain has been determined. We are, of course, not denying the importance of the contribution by conventional accounting in such an area, but we have set aside this area from our consideration of constructing a mathematical measure system.

5. *Reverse exchanges:* An exchange that is made in order to cancel another exchange that was made earlier (sales return, purchase return, etc.) is also unable to be handled in our system. Exchanges of this type presume the ability of human beings to identify an exchange as a reverse exchange of another one. While it is possible to set up an axiom to take care of this point, reverse exchanges themselves are rather unimportant, and hence we decided not to include such an axiom in our set of axioms in order to stress the most fundamental factors in conventional accounting.

VI. SUMMARY AND CONCLUSION

1. We have shown that if the set of three axioms—axiom of quantities, axiom of ownership, and axiom of exchanges—is granted, we can generate, by a set of measurement rules, a uniform measure from a set of physical measures by means of measure imputations through exchanges, in a purely mathematical wav without appealing to empirical judgment.

2. Furthermore, the empirical support for the measurement system imbedded in the set of three axioms is simple and very plausible; loosely speaking, all that is required in the axioms is that (*a*) objects can be quantified based on substitutability, (*b*) the set of all objects that belong to a subject can be identified, and (*c*) changes in such a set can be made through exchanges that are identifiable; or more simply, "I can identify things that are substitutable, things that I have, and things that are exchanged." As an example of simplicity, note that objects are defined to be simply identifiable things that can be "owned" by a subject, where ownership is attained through exchanges. It is therefore not necessary for objects to have any other properties such as usefulness for a subject in order to be dealt with in this measure system. We have used the term *utilities* to indicate things that may be generated from goods, but such utilities may very well be disutilities insofar as they are obtained through exchanges and can be quantified by a physical measure.

If, as we believe, the measurement system developed in this paper is a good abstraction of the measurement system of conventional accounting, then we may say that this simplicity of the empirical foundation of the measurement system is the reason for conventional accounting having been able to provide profit figures over the past several centuries.

3. In the last section, we discussed the fact that our system cannot handle the accounting practices of using *market values*. Here, we would like to point out an important difference between accounting measurement based upon

historical cost (or simply "historical cost measurement") and accounting measurement based upon market values, replacement cost, net realizable values, discounted future cash flows, etc. (or simply "market value measurement"). First of all, the basis for historical cost measurement is phenomena that *have occurred*, whereas the basis for market value measurement is phenomena that *could have occurred*, or *can occur*, or *will occur*.[23] Consider a tree as a representation of paths that a subject could have taken or can take in the future. At each branching point, regardless of the number of branches at that point, the branch that the subject has taken can be uniquely determined. Hence the whole path that the subject has taken up to the present time can also be uniquely determined. On the other hand, in most cases the paths that the subject could have taken or can take in the future are numerous, inexhaustible, and indeterminable (since we have to take into account possible reactions from the rest of the world which are mostly unknown).

This means that in historical cost measurement the path that is to be measured is uniquely given, and all issues are directed toward searching for the path, interpreting it, and measuring it; whereas in market value measurement, we must first agree on which path we are going to measure, and then resolve those same issues that are raised in historical cost measurement.[24,25] But how can we agree on a choice of a path among numerous alternatives, some of which are indeterminable, even if we decide to choose, say, an "optimum path" based upon agreed criteria? (Even in the game of chess that is far simpler than phenomena in the real world, we have not been able to find an "optimum path.")

Furthermore, information on market values, replacement cost, net realizable values, discounted future cash flows, etc., have two factors in common with other forecasted data; their usefulness depends very much upon the ability of the forecaster, and their usefulness is limited in time. [26,27] Considering these factors together with the point discussed in the above paragraph, it is clear that a system based upon market value measurement is not appropriate as an accounting measurement system that is to be applied continuously over a long period of time.

---

[23] For example, market values at which a firm could have replaced the machine or could have sold the securities at the date of the balance sheet.

[24] In terms of the mathematical representation of accounting measurement given in Section IV, this is equivalent to saying that in historical cost measurement, the value of the function $g(t)$ is uniquely determined, at time T, for all $t \leq T$, whereas in market value measurement this is not true.

[25] Of course, the uniqueness of the path does not necessarily imply that the path is recognized and interpreted uniquely by all accountants. We are, however, pointing out that the two measurement systems are in different dimensions of complexity.

[26] Nobody reads tomorrow's weather forecast the day after tomorrow, whereas historical records on weather are permanent.

[27] It is true that even in historical cost measurement, there exist needs for estimating the quantities of future objects or the quantities of objects that are consumed (e.g., depreciation). However, such needs exist only for objects involved in exchanges that a subject *has already committed*, unlike forecasting on alternatives that the subject *can* take.

4. We do not deny the usefulness of information based on market values, etc., as *ad hoc* information for particular decision making by a particular decision maker and perhaps as supplementary information to those provided by an accounting system based upon historical cost measurement. However, we should clearly recognize these fundamental differences between historical cost measurement and market value measurement and should not mix them together in one system at the same dimension.

5. It goes without saying that information generated from an accounting system must be *useful* for users. Therefore the usefulness of the uniform measure provided by an accounting system which was developed here as an abstraction of conventional accounting measurement must also be carefully looked at in view of users of the data provided by the system.[28]

Then, for example, we may very well change the basic class from cash to some other objects, say a class of inventories, if the user's needs are better satisfied by a measurement system based on inventories as a basic class, as in the case of inflation.[29] In our measure system, there is nothing to be changed in order to have a class of inventory for the basic class since the only requirement placed on a basic class is that the physical measure defined on the class is always of finite value.

Furthermore, we may very well change the set of measurement rules completely if this improves the usefulness of the information produced from the system. So far as we base our system upon the same set of axioms, the implementation of new measurement rules is relatively easy since they are purely mathematical (i.e., a part of the system which can be completely computerized), without requiring human ability or judgment. Such changes in measurement rules in order to generate more useful data ought to be explored in the future as a very prospective direction in which conventional accounting measurement can be fruitfully developed.

6. We believe that accounting in the future will be developed on a more general foundation without being restricted to monetary units in order to meet the ever-expanding needs for information by management as well as stockholders and other interested parties.[30] The idea of constructing a uniform measure from a set of physical measures by means of exchanges that have taken place will certainly supply very useful foundations for a development of accounting into such new areas.[31]

[28] An analysis of the mathematical relationship between a management goal and an accounting indicator for the goal by Ijiri [11] is an attempt to uncover this area.

[29] If a class of inventories is chosen as a basic class, cash is measured in terms of the physical measure defined on the basic class. We may apply Fifo, Lifo, or moving average method on cash.

[30] Professor W. W. Cooper of Carnegie Institute of Technology has been stressing the need for and possibility of designing an accounting system based upon nonmonetary units as well as axiomatic approaches to such an extended accounting system; it is this need which has stimulated the present work.

[31] A further extension of the axiomatic approach presented in this paper is given in Chapters 3 and 4 of Y. Ijiri, *The Foundations of Accounting Measurement: A Mathematical, Economic, and Behaviorial Inquiry*, Englewood Cliffs, N.J.: Prentice-Hall, Inc., 1967.

REFERENCES

1. American Accounting Association. "A Tentative Statement of Accounting Principles Affecting Corporate Reports," *Accounting Review*, June, 1936.
2. American Accounting Association. "Accounting Principles Underlying Corporate Financial Statements," *Accounting Review*, June, 1941.
3. American Accounting Association. "Accounting Principles Underlying Corporate Financial Statements—1948 Revision," *Accounting Review*, October, 1948.
4. American Accounting Association. "Accounting and Reporting Standards for Corporate Financial Statements," *Accounting Review*, October, 1951.
5. American Accounting Association. "Accounting and Reporting Standards for Corporate Financial Statements—1957 Revision," *Accounting Review*, October, 1957.
6. American Institute of Certified Public Accountants. *Changing Concepts of Business Income*. New York: Macmillan Co., 1952.
7. Canning, J. B. *The Economics of Accountancy*. New York: Ronald Press Co., 1929.
8. Chambers, R. J. "Blueprint for a Theory of Accounting," *Accounting Research*, January, 1955.
9. Gilman, Stephen. *Accounting Concepts of Profit*. New York: Ronald Press Co., 1939.
10. Halmos, P. R. *Measure Theory*. Princeton: D. Van Nostrand Co., Inc., 1950.
11. Ijiri, Yuji. "Goal Oriented Models for Accounting and Control." Unpublished Ph.D. dissertation, Carnegie Institute of Technology, 1963.
12. Kohler, E. L. *A Dictionary for Accountants*. Englewood Cliffs, N.J.: Prentice-Hall, Inc., 1952.
13. Littleton, A. C. *Structure of Accounting Theory*. New York: American Accounting Association, 1953.
14. Mattessich, Richard. "Towards a General and Axiomatic Foundation of Accountancy," *Accounting Research*, October, 1957.
15. Mattessich, Richard. *Accounting and Analytical Methods*. Homewood, Ill.: Richard D. Irwin, Inc., 1964.
16. Moonitz, Maurice. *The Basic Postulates of Accounting*. New York: American Institute of Certified Public Accountants, 1961.
17. Paton, W. A., and Littleton, A. C. *An Introduction to Corporate Accounting Standards*. New York: American Accounting Association, 1940.
18. Royden, H. L. *Real Analysis*. New York: Macmillan Co., 1963.
19. Sanders, T. H.; Hatfield, H. R.; and Moore, U. *A Statement of Accounting Principles*. New York: American Institute of Accountants, 1938.
20. Sprouse, Robert T., and Moonitz, Maurice. *A Tentative Set of Broad Accounting Principles for Business Enterprises*. New York: American Institute of Certified Public Accountants, 1962.
21. Vatter, W. J. *The Fund Theory of Accounting*. Chicago: University of Chicago Press, 1947.

3

The "effectiveness" of an accounting system is appraised in terms of its basic requirements, and comparisons are drawn with other system types. After considering the meaning of information, the author discusses the problem of structuring information, concluding that the process of measurement consists essentially of a decision to measure, the setting of the measurement scale(s), determination or preparation of the state, assignment of a numeric magnitude, and use of the measurement derived.

*SOME ASPECTS OF MEASUREMENT AND ACCOUNTING**

Hector R. Anton

RECENT STUDY in the behavior of organizations shows a close connection between the organization, its decision-making agents, and the information system of the organization. It is obvious that the accounting system is an important part of the firm's information system, and, almost as obvious but more arguable, that the accounting system is, or at least ought to be, the main structure for the entire information system. Without further belaboring the point here, at least we can assume that this is a reasonable hypothesis.

An information system approach to accounting gives some rather incisive insights to our theoretical problems. These are spelled out more fully elsewhere,[1] but a summary here is worthwhile for perspective. It may be useful first to point out that with regard to accounting systems, I will be using the term in a much more restrictive sense than most measurement theorists do. Torgerson, for example, defines a "particular system as roughly that which possesses such and so characteristics."[2] A system to him is a set or collection of properties. We are more concerned with unique characteristics of accounting systems which, though quite general, are not as abstractly general as in

* Reprinted from *Journal of Accounting Research*, Spring, 1964, pp. 1–9.

[1] Hector R. Anton, "Activity Analysis of the Firm: A Theoretical Approach to Accounting (Systems) Development," *Liiketaloudellinen Aikakauskirja* (*Journal of Business Economics*), Helsinki School of Economics, Helsinki, Finland, No. IV, 1961, pp. 291–305; *idem*, "Alcune Implicazioni della Teoria Dell'Informazione per le Organizzazioni Economiche" ("Some Implications of Information Theory for Business Organizations"), *Rivista Internazionale di Scienze Economiche e Commerciali*, Milan, Italy, Vol. IX, No. 9 (1962), pp. 825–37.

[2] Warren S. Torgerson, *Theory and Methods of Scaling* (New York: John Wiley & Sons, Inc. 1958), p. 9.

Torgerson. Briefly, the requirements of an effective accounting system are as follows:

1. An accounting system provides for continuous data gathering, processing, and dissemination.
   a) This requires analysis of information for the *selection* of data inputs into the system.
   b) A classificatory system is required; i.e., models are needed.
   c) Records must be kept, with relatively easy retrieval.
   d) Reports and other forms of communication are necessary.
2. An accounting system is to be integrated with the planning and control system.
   a) This requires integration of formal plans such as budgets and standards with controls, and the integration of the planning and control within the accounting system.
   b) Behavioral rules should be introduced to expedite decision making and/or to replace routine decisions. For example, control limits and standards may be set for automatic action as in automated production or inventory control, or items or programs out of limits may cause preparation of special warning reports which help only to expedite decisions.
3. The cost of the accounting system should be consistent with its output.

Compare this outline with the basic system properties of a military command-control system.

These basic system properties are inputs, processing, display, and feedback. . . . Data may enter the system through an intricate electronic device that leads directly into a computer or through as simple a process as a man carrying a piece of paper with some scribbled notes which are handed to a clerk for processing. But somehow the raw data *has* to be input into the system, and if the system is at all complicated, it will arrive for input in large quantities and be unusable in its raw form. Source data has to be combined and repatterned in a variety of ways to provide various kinds of information in answer to different kinds of management problems. The data may be transformed and processed by a computer or by a clerk working on a hand calculator, but some processing must be done before the system will function usefully. And once processing is completed, information must be output in a form that is meaningful to the action takers. Whether information is displayed directly from an electronic computer onto a complicated wall display, via line printer, or by manual methods is not of concern for the moment. The fact is the inputs have to be transformed into an output meaningful to people. In addition, if properly selected, display data stimulate ideas and requests for new types of information. This means that a feedback is required of the system so that the decision-makers, upon receiving one set of data, have an opportunity to loop back into the system and get new types of data, such as more detail or related information.

These simple properties are the basic elements of a command-and-control system. . . . And the basic properties of these systems, shorn of all frills, details, and complexities, are identical to those found in management systems.[3]

[3] Ramon J. Rhine, "Development of an Operational Management System," Systems Development Corporation (SP Series 1175), April 16, 1963, pp. 2–3. See also Robert W. Johnson, "Information System Design in a Complex Organization: Rand's LP–II Manned Simulation," RAND Corporation, May, 1962, p. 3.

A careful study of the two systems will indeed show that they are identical. Thus the accounting model provides for inputs (part 1*a*), processing (parts 1*b*, 1*c*, 2*a*, and 2*b*), display (parts 1*a*, 1*d*, and 2*a*), and feedback (parts 2*a* and 2*b*). Part 3, relating to cost, may be considered extraneous; but as will be demonstrated below, it is an integral part.

This parallel between the two systems is drawn for several reasons. First, it illustrates systems generality when a single basic system can serve two such dissimilar functions as expediting the delivery of an intercontinental ballistics missile and, say, the proper mix of ice cream or a myriad other more meaningful business decisions. Secondly, the generality shown means that accountants can benefit from, and should enlist the aid of, researchers in other information systems areas.[4] At least, they should make effective use of the results of such research. Conversely, and perhaps more important, researchers in other information areas, seeing the generality of accounting systems, may be enticed into the accounting area—the problems are tremendous and tremendously interesting, as I shall try to show below. Finally, and by no means least, perhaps accountants may be willing to undertake research based on command-and-control systems developments. What is important here is the fact that both systems fit my theoretic structure, and both systems have similar theoretical and practical measurement problems.

Let us now look more carefully into the implications of the accounting system outlined above and its import for the topic at hand. First, the systems outlined require *data* inputs into the system, but call for *information* as output. This surreptitious transformation is to be accomplished by something called "processing"—whose nature is slurred over. Now, data can be defined as collections of signs and characters generally arranged in some orderly way to represent facts—any facts that are a matter of direct observation. As I have indicated elsewhere,[5] this definition may be further generalized to treat as data the signs and characters themselves, whether or not they represent facts that are a matter of direct observation. This seems necessary in order to treat as data systems such things as simulations, or perhaps even more important, mixed systems where some data are subject to direct observation and other data are not. The latter, of course, will become more and more necessary as we develop systems that rely (make decisions based) on "hypothesized" data. This, of course, threads the thin line between objectivity and subjective interpretation. In any case, data comprise sets of signs and characters generally devoid of meaning in and of themselves.

Information, although it is variously defined, has the connotation of the *significance* derived from data. Information can be obtained from data, but it requires a further act from the receiver, namely, that something significantly

---

[4] See, for example, Abraham Charnes and W. W. Cooper, "Profile of the Profession: 1975—Consideration of the Quantitative Method," testimony presented to the Long Range Objectives Committee, American Institute of Certified Public Accountants, November 15, 1962 (mimeographed), pp. 2, 46.

[5] Anton, "Alcune Implicazioni," p. 827.

new be added to his memory. Significance here is to be tested not statistically but by some degree of added understanding of the source and/or usefulness in the receiver's context.

Information is usually considered at three different levels: the technical, the semantical, and the influence levels. At the technical level, at least in communication theory, no meaning is ascribed to information. The amount of information is a function of the degree of randomness of choice as to what can be said about the information source (the *H* field). Only in the technical sense of communication theory do data even approximate information. Even there, it is sharply distinguished since the degree of randomness of choice as to what could be said about an information source has implicit semantical relationships. For example, if the receiver *knows* the structure of the source, the *H* field, fewer bits are required to transmit the information. Extra bits (extra data) would be redundant and carry no information and can be eliminated. For example, if we are dealing with, say, a very simple double-entry system, in dollar values, with one debit and one credit account (and this is the structure of the information field), it is unnecessary to transmit all the "information" about the structure; all that is required is the sign, one bit, and the amount of the debit. The receiver of this information then gives it significance within the structure.

The semantical level of information, by definition, is concerned with attempts to furnish or convey meaning. This meaning clearly distinguishes between data and information—in information, there is a relationship between sign or symbol and the actual object or condition presented. It is obviously very important *whose* meaning is made effective, and whether that unique meaning is perceived. Cognition and perception on the part of the information receiver play major roles. There is no significance to be derived if the receiver does not recognize the signal (sign or symbol) or, except for the reinforcement of redundancy, if he already knows the "information" transmitted. Significance, of course, is proportional to the ability to use the information.

Another view of information that is consistent both with the above and with what is to follow is that information is *recorded experience*. Here the quantity of "information" is dependent on both the person receiving and the context in which he is acting. For our purposes, this poses problems about the accumulation of experiences recorded now which must be used in the future by unknown persons acting in unknown or vaguely known contexts.

> The potential of future reports has to be conceived in terms of conceptualizing a meaning of "amount of information" contained in the report which is independent of a particular decision-maker. This last means, in effect, that there should be a built-in utility for various potential decision-makers with differing purposes in varying contexts. The information systems designer thus has to make *predictions* with respect to potential decision-makers, the probability of use of the "stored experiences," and the usefulness of this information.[6]

[6] *Ibid.*, p. 289.

Structuring the information system will have to take into account the degree of certainty of use, projections of future value, and probabilistic estimates of the usefulness of the information in the future.

Processing, which forms such a central place in the systems under consideration, performs several theoretically different functions. As Rhine has pointed out, "if the system is at all complicated it [the data] will arrive for input in large quantities and be unusable in its raw form. Source data has to be combined and repatterned in a variety of ways to provide various kinds of information in answer to different kinds of management problems."[7]

The first function of processing necessarily is that of aggregation. This is also the simplest and least costly kind of structuring in an information system. As simple aggregation, it adds little information except the implicit assumption that the data are of the same class, and it (aggregation) is obviously done only to increase the perception of the user. However, it is a simple system indeed that will consist of data measurable in only one class. Beyond the simplest of systems, the processing function includes patterning and repatterning in a variety of ways. This is *structuring* in the sense used in communication theory; and here as there, it works on the *cognitive* as well as the perceptive faculties of the user. In brief, it structures the information field, and if the user knows the structure, it reduces the necessary data that have to be perceived in order to receive information.

Structuring (good or bad) costs money and time, and so does learning the structure (see point 3 above). Even more important, it affects the measurements. Inputs are conditioned (i.e., accepted, adapted, or rejected) by the structure; repatterning, in fact, means transformations with additional properties measured or eliminated. If we extend the process to summarizing, selective loss of information is incurred. How effective this is depends naturally on the "filter" that is used; that is, what kinds of information the system lets through the summarizing process. In many instances a summary is more meaningful than the total data; in others, vital information is lost. In other cases, redundancy may be eliminated and, quite often, noise.

Redundancy, which is useful only to prevent error, is insidious in that its growth goes largely unnoticed. Noise, unwanted signal that is introduced into the system in error or generated by the system itself, can be eliminated both by proper structure (this is one of the things double entry does well, for example) and by proper "filtering" action. This action can be illustrated, for example, by certain of the truncating averages, or by elimination of data outside preestablished norms. Accountants, in general, have not done enough work in these areas.

There is a striking parallel between the above ideas and leading theories of measurement in quantum mechanics. Compare, for example, the following statements by John L. McKnight:

> An important distinction was made by Margenau in 1937 between the preparation of a state and measurement. . . . Margenau states that the uncertainty arises in the preparation of the state and not in the measurement utilized to give a number.

[7] Rhine, *op. cit.*, p. 3.

At this stage the interaction of systems occurs, and here uncertainty enters, not in the measurement itself. The measurement occurs only if a number appears, but the quantum state is modified from the initial state, whether or not a measurement is made. Any other explanation runs the risk of reducing the statistical assertions of quantum mechanics to mere psychological measures of our lack of knowledge.[8]

In brief, structuring of an accounting system is analogous to the "preparation of a state," and it affects the properties whether a measurement takes place or not, and also whether the measurements are qualitatively good or bad. This, too, is at the root of Churchman's contention that "This amounts to saying that the assignment of costs to policies in an industry depends on the organization of the operations of the industry. . . ."[9]

Moreover, the systems call for data inputs; but except for the conditioning by the system structure, there are no input criteria. The criteria must be supplied from outside the system. If we assume an operationalist view—that is, that information ought to be for decision-making purposes—the criterion is based on an extension of significance, i.e., for what is the information significant. This approach soon leads to an emphasis on the influence level of information, and for data inputs that are consistent with the characteristics of the receiver of the information. While this gives us a purposive criterion, it also gives us the dilemma noted above as to who will be the decision maker and the uncertainty of his context.

The emphasis so far has been on data and information as they relate to accounting systems. This seems proper for perspective as well as for a statement of the conditions of measurement as they relate to accounting. Moreover, as Churchman has stated: "Everything that has been said here about measurement is applicable to a broader class called 'information' and 'data'."[10] As he sees it, measurement problems are subsidiary to the problems of data, just as I recognize data as subsidiary to information.

We need not drag out here the litany on measurement theories. That has been done amply by Firmin and others.[11] Nor, in fact, do we need to replicate the work done on the subject as it related to accounting. Rather, I would like to pursue the implications of Churchman's concept of measurement as it relates to the larger, more general, system that accounting must develop into if it is to keep pace with both modern technology and modern organization theory. Churchman postulates that we measure when we need fine distinction,

[8] John L. McKnight, "The Quantum Theoretical Concept of Measurement," in C. W. Churchman and P. Ratoosh (eds.), *Measurement: Definitions and Theories* (New York: John Wiley & Sons, Inc., 1959), pp. 193–96.

[9] Churchman, *Prediction and Optimal Decision: Philosophical Issues of a Science of Values* (Englewood Cliffs, N.J.: Prentice-Hall, Inc., 1961), p. 64.

[10] "Why Measure?" in Churchman and Ratoosh, *op. cit.*, p. 94.

[11] Peter Firmin, "Measurement Theory and Accounting Measurements," paper given at the 1963 American International Meeting of the Institute of Management Sciences, September 12–13, 1963, New York (mimeographed), pp. 1–32. See also Carl Devine, "Accounting—A System of Measurement Rules," in *Essays in Accounting Theory*, Vol. I, (privately published, 1962).

i.e., precision, and when we want to employ results obtained in one connection (presumably under rigid controls) in other, and perhaps many totally different, circumstances at the time of action.[12]

"The results obtained" apply to the *end* of a process. To beg the question, we may call this process the measurement; for example, following Lenzen's definition, "Measurement is the general procedure of assigning numbers to the properties or objects."[13] Or we may even rely implicitly on McKnight's "The measurement occurs only if a number appears."[14] But if we beg the question in this particular manner, we may devote our main attention to the selection of the measurement unit—a more trivial matter, since this is conventional.[15] In other words, it isn't so much the number or symbol assigned that is important, but the importance of that number or symbol *in its employment*. Of course, we may well argue that this is also a function of the "rigid controls" under which the initial "measurement" was made, and that the rigid control has to be construed as tightly as possible to take care of many eventualities in use.

But there are at least two possibilities here: (1) We have rigid standards of control, whether they are needed or not, and let the slack be taken in the action (inefficient use of overprecise data), or (2) the *standard* measurement is made with the characteristics of its use in mind. The point is that accuracy is a relative matter, and a "good" or "bad" measurement is relative to the accuracy required in its *use*. Measures of the cost of error are desperately needed; but unfortunately, few studies have appeared.[16] To further complicate matters, the degree of error in the measurement is also measured in its use, that is, in the outcomes which themselves have been at least partially determined by the measurement.

These approaches need not be mutually exclusive, but emphasis on the latter may serve a useful purpose since the former is well recognized. That is, no one is against setting up rigid controls for precise measurements—not even accountants, though they sometimes sound like it—it's like love and motherhood. But in a great many situations in accounting, and in the social sciences in general, it may be much more productive to start from the other end. We need standards; even more, we need to know the allowable deviation from the standards (Churchman's "adjustment rules") which implicitly allow for the accuracy of the standard. But more than this, *we need to measure* and *record* and *use* the measures of a great many properties and events that are now bypassed as "not being measurable." The list is long, and the items are of vary-

[12] Churchman, *Prediction and Optimal Decision*, chap. v.

[13] V. F. Lenzen, "Procedures of Empirical Science," *International Encyclopedia of Unified Science* (Chicago: University of Chicago Press, 1955), p. 289.

[14] McKnight, *op. cit.*, p. 196.

[15] Cf. Devine, *op. cit.*, p. 145.

[16] Cf. Johnson, *op. cit.;* also J. Marschak and Roy Radner, "Economic Theory of Teams," Center for Research in Management Sciences, University of California, Berkeley, Workpaper 67, August, 1963. Work on sensitivity analysis may be of some help in this area in the future.

ing importance—from the measurement of a lost sale to a successful lobbyist, from the shape of the Coca-Cola bottle to the shape of the front-office receptionist.

It behooves us to enable these measurements—all predicated on the operational systems approach; the user is to have such information as he needs to increase the efficiency of his decision-making process. Responsibility accounting, for example, was a first halting step in this direction. The system would go for beyond present financial-managerial accounting. Such a system would have the prime objective of facilitating decision making as a whole rather than in its parts. As such, separate systems such as "accounting systems," production control systems, inventory systems, and the like would be but component parts. Further, direct access to the information memory may be achieved through on-line, real-time access; quite possibly, new criteria such as opportunity and motivational costs may be used as well as predetermined decision functions. In short, decision making is to be facilitated by a decision-oriented system.[17]

This brings into focus a last remaining link in the process—the problem of communicating the measurement. Somehow a link must be forged between the information required, the "measured data," and the measurer. In terms of communication theory, these are the problems of the *encoding* and *decoding* process. The criteria have been established above; we now consider the more technical aspects of the communication problem. If there is "a wide variety of differing circumstances" of action, simple codes may not suffice.[18] Instead, a variety of codes may need to be used, which introduces redundancies into the system. Conversely, the codes may be made more general, like a language, with consequent loss of precision in unique uses. Each of these alternatives is costly—one requiring larger capacity from the system, the other facilitating inefficiencies in use. Indeed, the former is of vital importance in design, although if the criteria developed above are implemented, there will be capacity savings through better design of our present systems—especially in eliminating data that are *not* used.

The capacity problem also has a time dimension which creates a storage problem, and the storage problem, in the last analysis, is a *cost* problem. Cost, of course, is a relative between outlay and objective accomplishment. We see once again that we can trade structure for cost, precision for cost, capacity for cost, storage for cost, and, in the last analysis, *information* for cost. Accountants have done relatively little in testing efficiencies here.[19]

From the above discussion, the measurement process can now be said to consist of five parts:

[17] Cf. E. L. Weinthaler, Jr., "Developing Advanced Business Information Systems," *Data Processing for Management,* October, 1963, p. 10; Charnes and Cooper, *op. cit.*, pp. 40–41.

[18] Cf. Anton, "Alcune Implicazioni," p. 827.

[19] For an early attempt, see Robert Gregory and Richard Van Horn, *Automatic Data-Processing Systems* (San Francisco: Wadsworth Publishing Co., Inc., 1960), chap. x. This attempt was mostly abandoned in the 1963 edition.

1. A decision to measure
2. Setting of the measurement scale or scales
3. Determination or preparation of the state
4. Assignment—"a number appears"
5. Use of the measurement

All five are independent actions, but each is unimportant without the others. It is therefore one integrated process.

Lest we become overconfident due to recent advances, Churchman's warning is still applicable:

> The decision making problems of any of the aspects of measurement are enormously difficult, and even an approximation to their solution still escapes us. . . . A rather significant portion of our resources is devoted to generating and processing data. However, it is apparent that no one knows how the data should be expressed (the decision problem of data *language* is unsolved), what data are needed (the decision problem of data *specification* is unsolved), how the data are to be used in various contexts (the decision problem of *standardization* is unsolved), and how the data are to be evaluated (the decision problem of *accuracy* and *control* is unsolved).[20]

[20] "Why Measure?" p. 94.

4

The authors propose the general hypothesis that the fundamental criterion for selecting among alternative accounting measurements is relevance to the user. Based upon this proposition, the underlying problems of objectivity and reliability are discussed. The degree of objectivity implicit in the measurement of a single attribute is then defined as the standard deviation of a group of measurements of this attribute, and reliability is defined as the mean square error of these same measurements around an "alleged value." Finally, the relationship between these concepts is analyzed in statistical terms.

*RELIABILITY AND OBJECTIVITY OF ACCOUNTING MEASUREMENTS**

Yuji Ijiri and Robert K. Jaedicke

ACCOUNTING is a measurement system which is plagued by the existence of alternative measurement methods. For many years, accountants have been searching for criteria which can be used to choose the best measurement alternative. Generally, it is conceded by most accountants that the purpose for which the data are to be used (usefulness) is an important criterion to be considered in the choice of accounting method.[1] However, the use or purpose of the data still leaves much to be desired as a criterion since different accounting measurement methods are frequently suggested as being appropriate for a single user or group of users having the same purpose. For example, in a round-table discussion on "The Measurement of Property, Plant, and Equipment in Financial Statements" the participants agreed that usefulness would be one of the criteria for evaluating different accounting measurement methods. This general criterion ". . . was applied in the sense of *usefulness to investors who are willing and competent to read financial statements carefully and with discrimination for the purposes of assistance in arriving at rational investment deci-*

* Reprinted from *Accounting Review*, July, 1966, pp. 474–83.

[1] See, for example, Robert T. Sprouse, Reporter, *The Measurement of Property, Plant, and Equipment in Financial Statements* (Boston: Harvard University, Graduate School of Business Administration, 1964), p. 20.

sions."[2] In the above statement the user group and the purpose for which data will be used are both clearly identified. Yet, according to the moderator and reporter, three alternative measurement methods (for fixed asset accounting) represented by three different groups emerged from the discussion. One group would continue to use historical cost. "Some advocates of historical cost will continue to hold to this view unless they are given convincing evidence that an alternative will produce markedly *more useful results.*"[3]

A second group favored retention of historical cost, supplemented with statements where the data have been adjusted for general price level changes. Yet a third group believed that in certain situations, acquisition cost should be replaced with a market value or a specific price index measurement in order to reflect changes in specific prices and assets. Well-informed accountants and businessmen presumably disagree on what is the most useful measurement method even after the purpose for which the data are to be used and the user group are specified. When this happens, the use or purpose of the data is simply too broad and general a criterion to be of much help.

Usefulness is made up of many factors. Data must be timely, reliable, accurate, relevant, material, etc., to be useful. Our purpose here is not to deny the importance of usefulness as a criterion but rather to analyze one important aspect of usefulness. This aspect we shall refer to as *reliability*. Our two main purposes will be (1) to develop the concept of reliability as it relates to accounting and (2) to show how the criterion of reliability is related to the widely accepted criterion of objectivity. The concept of objectivity is first discussed.

THE CONCEPT OF OBJECTIVITY

Objectivity (like usefulness) of accounting measurements is usually regarded as an important criterion for choosing among measurement methods. For example, Paton and Littleton state, "Verifiable, objective evidence has therefore become an important element in accounting and a necessary adjunct to the proper execution of the accounting function of supplying dependable information."[4] Similarly, Moonitz writes that "changes in assets and liabilities, and the related effects (if any) on revenues, expenses, retained earnings, and the like, should not be given formal recognition in the accounts earlier than the point of time at which they can be measured in objective terms."[5] Still another example: Fertig concludes ". . . that a high degree of verifiable evidence is necessary as support for financial statement representa-

---

[2] *Ibid*, p. 21. Italics supplied.

[3] *Ibid.*, p. 63. Italics supplied.

[4] W. A. Paton and A. C. Littleton, *An Introduction to Corporate Accounting Standards* (New York: American Accounting Association, 1940), p. 18.

[5] Maurice Moonitz, "The Basic Postulates of Accounting" (New York: American Institute of CPA's, 1961), p. 41.

tions because accountants must always be in a position to assure their readers that financial statements are what they are represented to be."[6]

In spite of fairly common agreement that objectivity is important as a criterion for selecting accounting measurement methods, there is a surprising lack of agreement on just what the concept should mean and how it should be applied. On the one hand, Moonitz defines objective evidence as being subject to verification by a competent investigator. Thus the measurements have a meaning which is separate and apart from the measurer.[7] Paton and Littleton's definition of objectivity is similar to Moonitz's.[8] However, Arnett, in an article, "What Does Objectivity Mean to Accountants?" points out that the recognition that some useful measures are not objective has caused a loosening of the strict definition of objectivity as expressed by Moonitz and Littleton. He concludes that ". . . data still needs to be impersonal in order to be objective. However, 'impersonal' is now much more flexible in its application than under the strict construction."[9] Fertig joins those who want to broaden the definition of objectivity when he states, "First we will attempt to demonstrate that a more useful, less misleading definition of 'objectivity' is in terms of the measurements sought by accountants, rather than solely in terms of the verifiability of accounting evidence."[10] Of course, at the extreme, there are accountants who would contend that if the measurement is useful, further justification is unnecessary.[11] This latter viewpoint advocates dropping objectivity as a criterion for at least some accounting measurements.

Objectivity as a property of accounting measurements does have appeal. However, it is a difficult concept to define and in some cases leads to confusion and disagreement.

The *Winston Simplified Dictionary* (College Edition) defines the term *objective* as "existing outside of the mind; having a separate or independent existence." In other words, objectivity refers to the external reality that is independent of the persons who perceive it. However, the precise nature of the separate existence of the external reality is not clear, at least as it relates to accounting. For example, what is meant by the objective income figure of a given firm for a given period? If the above definition is used, it must be something that exists separately and independently from the accountants who measure it. While it may be convenient to assume the existence of such an objective income figure, it is impossible to ascertain what this value is without going through the thinking process of those accountants who made the measurement.

---

[6] Paul E. Fertig, "Current Values and Index Numbers: The Problem of Objectivity," *Research in Accounting Measurement* (New York: American Accounting Association, 1966).

[7] Moonitz, *op. cit.*, p. 41.

[8] Paton and Littleton, *op. cit.*, p. 18.

[9] Harold E. Arnett, "What Does Objectivity Mean to Accountants?" *Journal of Accountancy*, May, 1961, p. 68.

[10] Fertig, *op. cit.*

[11] W. B. McFarland, "Concept of Objectivity," *Journal of Accountancy*, September, 1961, p. 29.

Therefore, rather than basing the definition of objectivity on the existence of objective factors that are independent of persons who perceive them, it is far more realistic to define objectivity to mean simply the *consensus* among a given group of observers or measurers. For example, we can say that the amount of cash in a cashbox can be measured more objectively than the annual income of a firm. That is, if we asked a group of accountants to measure both the cash in the cashbox and the income of the firm, we would expect a higher degree of consensus on the former measure than the latter.[12] We will elaborate on the precise nature of consensus as applied to accounting by means of the following model of measurement.

There are three factors involved in measurement. They are (1) an object whose property is to be measured, (2) a measurement system which consists

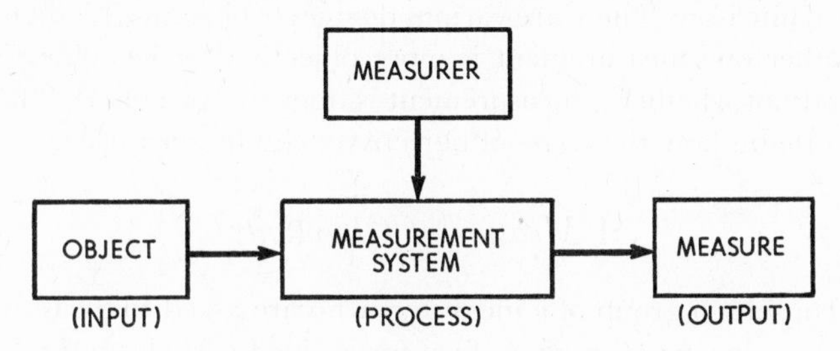

FIGURE 1. Measurement process.

of a set of rules and instruments, and (3) a measurer. These three factors collectively produce a quantity called a measure. (See Figure 1.) If the measurement rules in the system are specified in detail, we would expect the results to show little deviation from measurer to measurer. On the other hand, if the measurement rules are vague or poorly stated, then the implementation of the measurement system will require judgment on the part of the measurer; hence the output of the measurement system is more likely to show a wider deviation from measurer to measurer. In other words, the measurement system and the measurer's judgment are complementary with each other. Objectivity of a measurement system gives the degree of consensus in the results (output) or the degree to which the output of the system depends on the measurer.

The degree of consensus depends not only on the measurement system but also on the objects whose property is to be measured. For example, given two measurement systems for measuring income, the first may show a greater degree of consensus when the income of service firms is the object of measurement; however, the second may have a greater degree of consensus when the income of manufacturing firms is being measured. This could happen because the first measurement system contains vague measurement rules for

[12] This definition of objectivity agrees with that normally held by accountants (i.e., verifiability by an independent party) if we interpret the independent party to mean a representative of a given group of accountants. See, for example, the above quotations from Moonitz.

inventory treatment which shows up as a lack of objectivity (consensus) when inventory becomes important.

Further, the objectivity of a measurement system depends upon a particular group of measurers. For example, in measuring the income of a firm, a group of experts in accounting will produce a higher degree of consensus than a group of laymen. That is, accounting education tends to homogenize the way in which a group of measurers will measure income. In such a case an income figure which is highly objective from the viewpoint of the experts may be much less objective in the eyes of laymen. Therefore, in defining the objectivity of a measurement system, we must specify which group of measurers (i.e., which reference group) we are concerned with.

Finally, another important point to be noted here is that objectivity is not a black-or-white issue. There are various degrees of objectivity, and we should argue whether one measurement is more objective (or less objective) than another and not whether a measurement is objective or not. We shall therefore elaborate on how the *degree* of objectivity can be measured.

A Measure of Objectivity

Let us consider a group of n measurers who are asked to measure a given object, such as income of a given firm for a given period, under a specified measurement system. Let x_i be the quantity that the ith measurer ($i = 1, 2, \cdots, n$) reports by using the specified measurement system. We are now concerned with the degree of unanimity or the degree of variability of x_i's. One commonly used statistical measure of the variability of a set of observations is the variance. We may therefore use this as an indicator of the degree of objectivity of the given measurement system in measuring the given object. Namely, objectivity, V, may be defined to be

$$V = \frac{1}{n} \sum_{i=1}^{n} (x_i - \bar{x})^2 \tag{1}$$

where n is the number of measures in the reference group, x_i is the quantity that the ith measurer reports, and $\bar{x}$ is the average of x_i's over all measurers in the reference group.[13]

Next, we must note the fact that the above measure of variability depends upon a particular object. We must find a way to state the degree of objectivity of a measurement system independently from a particular object. This may be done by considering a set of all objects that are to be measured under the measurement system and taking an average (weighted, if necessary) of

[13] Obviously, there are many other ways of measuring the variability of observations. For example, we may use the average of $|x_i - \bar{x}|$ instead of $(x_i - x)^2$. Rel-variance, i.e., the variance divided by the square of the mean V/x^2, is another common measure of variability used in statistics. The latter measure has an advantage in that it does not depend upon the measurement unit of the x_i's, although difficulty arises as the mean (x) becomes closer to zero.

the above measure associated with the measurement of each object in the set.

One final remark before we move on to the discussion of reliability. If a measure is a highly objective one, it is irrelevant who in the measurement group has actually measured it, since most of the people in the group would have produced an identical (or a similar) result. This is the virtue of objectivity. That is, the measurement is relatively free from personal feelings or prejudice of the measurer if it is objective. Therefore the decision maker can use the measurement without being concerned about who the measurer is.

However, this does not mean that objectivity is the same as usefulness. For example, a highly objective measure, such as the cash balance, the number of shares of capital stock, etc., may not be as useful in predicting the future market price of a firm's stock as a highly subjective statement made by the president of the firm as to his expectation of the future stock price. Furthermore, a measure that is very useful for one purpose may not be useful at all for other purposes. Therefore *the usefulness of a measure cannot be determined until a specific use is given, whereas the objectivity of a measure can be determined independently of its use.*

THE CONCEPT OF RELIABILITY

Let us now move on to the discussion of the reliability of an accounting measurement. In general, a system is said to be reliable if it works in the way it is supposed to work.[14] For example, a barometer is said to be reliable if it reflects accurately the actual barometric pressure, since this is what a barometer is supposed to do. Similarly, a reliable man is one that will do what he is supposed to do; in other words, he can be "counted on."

However, there is another aspect of reliability which is especially important in dealing with reliability of an accounting information system. Consider the following question about the barometer example given above: "Is the barometer a reliable indicator of tomorrow's weather?" In this case the question is not whether the barometer indicates the actual barometric air pressure, but rather whether the barometer reading can be used for predicting tomorrow's weather. This type of question is more user-oriented. It is also the type of question which is of importance in evaluating the reliability of accounting measurements.

How can the degree of reliability be determined and measured when the barometer is used for forecasting the weather? Consider a case where the forecaster is simply interested in forecasting whether it is going to rain or not; i.e., the prediction contains two categories, "Fair" and "Rain." Similarly, suppose the barometer has only two readings, one for "Fair" and the other for "Rain," instead of a more detailed calibration. If the barometer points to Fair, the forecaster expects the weather tomorrow to be fair, and if the barometer points to Rain, he expects rain.

[14] Reliability is also not a black-or-white issue, as we shall soon see. But here, we are using the term loosely.

		Actual Weather Today	
		Fair	Rain
Barometer Reading Yesterday	Fair	Right	Wrong
	Rain	Wrong	Right

Figure 2. Barometer reading and actual weather.

On the other hand, the relationship can also be reversed. That is, if it is fair today, the expectation is that the barometer reading yesterday was Fair; if it rains today, the expectation is that the barometer reading yesterday was Rain. If, on the contrary, yesterday's reading was Rain when today is fair, or if the reading yesterday was Fair when today is rainy, the barometer gives a wrong indicator. If this occurs many times, the barometer would be considered unreliable for predicting the weather.

The degree of reliability of the barometer as used in predicting the weather may therefore be measured by the proportion of the total readings which are "right." Likewise, the degree of unreliability can be measured by the proportion of readings which are "wrong." This relationship is shown in diagram form in Figures 2 and 3.

If the above concept of reliability is to be used in accounting, the simple "right-or-wrong" classifications must be replaced with a detailed classification by introducing a finer calibration (or measurement). This can be done in the barometer example by using a method similar to the one discussed in dealing with objectivity. That is, reliability can be thought of as the degree of closeness to being right. However, there is one difference to be noted; the degree of closeness to being right depends primarily upon the way in which the user uses the indicator (barometer reading). This is something that was not observed in the discussion of objectivity. In fact, the point was made that the degree of objectivity could be measured independent of the manner in which the measurement is to be used.

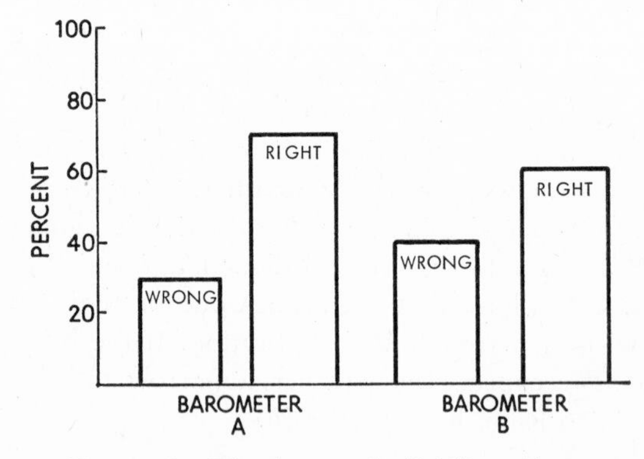

Figure 3. The degree of reliability of barometers: barometer A is more reliable than barometer B.

The relation between the reliability of the measurement and the manner in which the user uses the measurement can be seen by further examination of the barometer example. Assume, for example, that a user wants to use the barometer reading for predicting the amount of rain for the following day. In doing so, he creates in his own mind a relationship between today's barometer reading and the amount of rain tomorrow. However, this relationship that the user has determined (perhaps by past experiences) may not coincide exactly with the actual (real) relationship between today's barometer reading and tomorrow's rainfall. For example, assume that the actual and forecaster's relationships are as given in Figure 4. If the barometer reading is b, then the

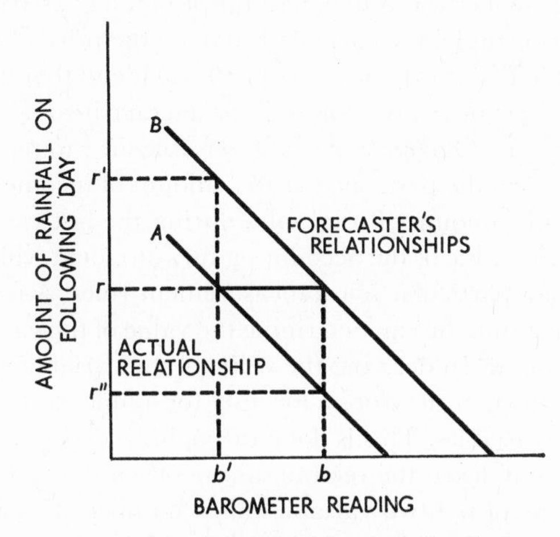

FIGURE 4. Actual and forecaster's relationships between today's barometer reading and tomorrow's rainfall.

forecaster would predict the amount of rainfall to be r. If the barometer reading is b', then r' amount of rain would be predicted. However, the actual relationship between the barometer reading and the rainfall is given by the line A. That is, if the reading is b, the actual amount of rainfall is r''; and if the reading is b', the actual amount of rainfall is r.

However, in spite of the actual relationship, if the actual amount of rainfall is r, a right barometer reading from the forecaster's viewpoint is b and not b'. That is, if the actual amount of today's rainfall is r, the forecaster alleges that yesterday's barometer reading should have been at b and not at b'. Let b (in this example) be called the alleged value. The alleged values will depend on the manner in which the forecaster uses the barometer readings for predicting rainfall. In the above example, the set of alleged values for various values of r (the rainfall) is represented by the line B.

The degree of "closeness to being right" is then represented by the difference between b and b'. As in the derivation of the objectivity measure, we may use this difference as a basis of the reliability measure, and by taking a suitable "representative" value of such differences at various levels of rainfall, we can define the reliability measure of the barometer.

Reliability of Accounting Measurements

Let us now consider the problem of reliability of accounting measurement. For a user of accounting data, the accounting measurement is only a means to an end. In other words, a user of accounting measurements is interested only insofar as the measurements give data which are helpful in his decision process. To make the argument more concrete, let the variable y be a factor which the decision maker wants to determine or predict based on the accounting measure. For example, the variable y may be the price of the firm's stock at a certain point in the future; or y may be the dividend that the firm will pay at the end of the year; or y may represent the average income of the firm during the next five years. Of course, it is also possible for y to represent an event which has occurred in the past, such as the amount of income tax paid in the previous period, the amount of total sales during the last two years, etc.

Now, let x be the value of the accounting measurement which results from the application of a particular set of measurement rules. A user of x uses the measure only if he thinks he can determine the value of the variable y from the value of the variable x. In deriving the value of the variable y from the value of the variable x, the user develops a formula (or a function) by which he can associate the two variables. This is done through his experience or by education. That is, he may learn the relationship between the variable x and y by observing the value of the two variables for a number of past periods, or he may be taught the relationship between the two. In any event, y and x are related by some function such as $y = f(x)$.

To illustrate, assume that a decision maker is interested in the amount of the future dividend per share of stock. He has discovered that the dividend in time period $t + 1$ is usually about one half of the per share income reported in time period t. Thus, he uses the relationship $y = 0.5x$, where y is the expected per share dividend in time $t + 1$ and x is the per share income reported in time period t, calculated by using a certain specified set of accounting measurement rules.

If income reported in time period t is \$10, then the decision maker, using his relationship $y = 0.5(x)$, would estimate the per share dividend in time period $t + 1$ to be \$5. Once a user of accounting data develops his own function f, he expects (and hopes) that the relationship between the variables x and y will be stable during future periods.

If, in the above example, the dividend in time period $t + 1$ actually turns out to be \$4 when reported income for time period t is \$10, this event decreases the degree of his reliance upon the reported per share income in estimating the future dividend. If the dividend on the stock turns out to be \$4, then the decision maker may say that the reported per share income should have been \$8. In other words, he *alleges* that the reported per share profit should have been \$8 now that the dividend on the stock is \$4. This is his *alleged value* given his decision function and given that the actual dividend was \$4. We may use this difference between the actual value (\$10) and the alleged value (\$8) as a basis for a reliability measure in the following manner.

The Measure of Reliability

First, we introduce the fact that the actual value (\$10) depends upon the measurers. Under a given set of measurement rules an accountant may derive \$12 as the income figure, whereas another accountant may give \$8. Therefore, we must average the differences between the actual value and alleged value over all measurers in the reference group in the same manner as in the case of the objectivity measure. Since we used the average of the square of the difference between the value derived by the measurer (x_i) and the mean of the values derived by all measurers ($\bar{x}$) in defining the objectivity measure, we shall use the same average of the square of the difference between the value derived by the measurer (x_i) and the alleged value (x^*) in defining the reliability measure R. Namely:

$$R = \frac{1}{n}\sum_{i=1}^{n}(x_i - x^*)^2 \tag{2}$$

This formula is exactly the same as that of the mean square error, another measure commonly used in statistics.[15]

Since the above reliability measure depends upon a particular object to be measured, we must apply the same averaging method as the one explained in connection with the objectivity measure in order to derive an expression for the reliability of a measurement system.[16]

Now, notice the similarity and difference between the measure of reliability (equation 2) and the measure of objectivity (equation 1). The degree of reliability of an accounting measurement system depends upon how close the actual measurements (x_i's) are to the alleged value (x^*), whereas the degree of objectivity depends upon how close the actual measurements (x_i's) are to the mean value ($\bar{x}$). A comparison of equations 1 and 2 shows this essential difference between objectivity and reliability. Note that the degree of reliability (R) as given in equation 2 can be rewritten as follows:

$$R = \frac{1}{n}\sum_{i=1}^{n}\{(x_i - \bar{x}) + (\bar{x} - x^*)\}^2 \tag{3}$$

---

[15] Both the objectivity measure V given by equation 1 and the reliability measure R given by equation 2 actually indicate the degree of "subjectivity" and the degree of "unreliability." That is, the degree of objectivity of the measurement system becomes greater as V gets smaller. Conversely, larger values for V (or R) are associated with lower degrees of objectivity (or reliability). The measurement system is *perfectly objective* if $V = 0$ and is *perfectly reliable* if $R = 0$.

[16] We may also consider a distribution of x^* based on various uses of the measure or various users of the measure and apply the same averaging method to derive a reliability measure for a given set of uses or users.

By squaring out the expression inside the brackets, we have

$$(4) \qquad R = \frac{1}{n}\sum_{i=1}^{n} \{(x_i - \bar{x})^2 + 2(x_i - \bar{x}) \cdot (\bar{x} - x^*) + (\bar{x} - x^*)^2\}$$

$$= \frac{1}{n}\sum_{i=1}^{n} (x_i - \bar{x})^2 + \frac{2}{n}(\bar{x} - x^*) \cdot \sum_{i=1}^{n} (x_i - \bar{x}) + \frac{1}{n}\sum_{i=1}^{n} (\bar{x} - x^*)^2$$

Since the (unsquared) sum of the deviations of any variable from its mean is zero,

$$\sum_{i=1}^{n} (x_i - \bar{x})$$

in the second term of the above expression is zero, and this entire term drops out. Hence:

$$(5) \qquad R = \frac{1}{n}\sum_{i=1}^{n} (x_i - \bar{x})^2 + \frac{1}{n}\sum_{i=1}^{n} (x - x^*)^2$$

Since the second term in equation 5 does not depend on i, it reduces to $(\bar{x} - x^*)^2$, and we have

$$(6) \qquad R = \frac{1}{n}\sum_{i=1}^{n} (x_i - \bar{x})^2 + (\bar{x} - x^*)^2$$

By using equation 1 and lettering $B = (\bar{x} - x^*)^2$, we have

$$(7) \qquad R = V + B$$

From equation 7, it is clear that the degree of reliability is the degree of objectivity plus a term, B, which may be called a "reliance bias" or simply a "bias." This means that R is always greater than or equal to V. R is equal to V if and only if the alleged value is equal to the mean of all measured values. Although several parts of the method would have to be more precisely specified to make it practically operational (such as how to choose the set of accounting measurers), equation 7 is an interesting and highly useful way to conceptualize the essential relationship between objectivity and reliability. These relationships are discussed below in detail.[17]

Reliability and Objectivity

Equation 7 shows that the concept of reliability is not independent of objectivity. If the bias factor B can be held constant, the degree of reliability can be improved by improving the degree of objectivity. This is shown in the diagram in Figure 5. Measurement system 1 is more reliable than system 2,

[17] In the above discussion, it is assumed that the alleged value is unique for each object that is measured. If it is not unique, we may define the bias factor B to be the smallest value of $(x - x^*)^2$ among all alleged values (x^*'s) in the measurement of a given object.

since $(\bar{x} - x^*)^2$ is the same for both methods, but $V_2 > V_1$.

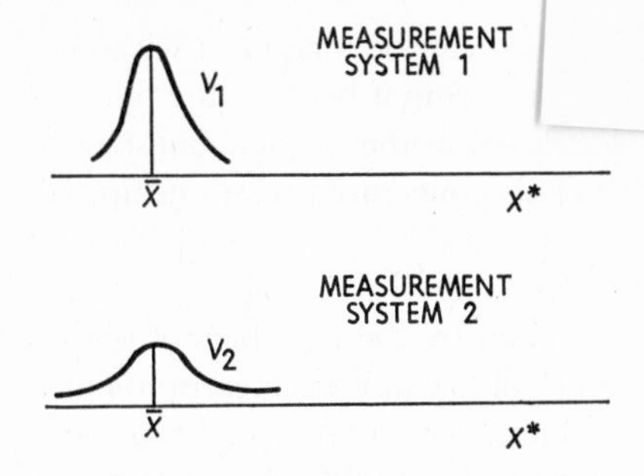

FIGURE 5. Reliability and objectivity, I.

On the other hand, equation 7 shows that the most objective measure is not necessarily the most reliable measure. This is so because the measurement system with the higher degree of objectivity (smaller V) may have a mean $(\bar{x})$ which is quite far from the alleged value, such that $V + B$ will be greater for a system with a small V than for a system where V is large but $(\bar{x} - x^*)^2$ is very small. This is shown in the diagram in Figure 6. System 4 is more reliable than system 3, despite the fact that $V_4 > V_3$; i.e., system 4 is less objective than system 3.[18]

If there is any misunderstanding on the part of the accountant as to what the user of the accounting data needs and wants, the mean of the reported values $(\bar{x})$ may be quite far from the alleged value (x^*). Even though the degree of objectivity of a measurement method can be determined independently of the use of the measurement, it does not make sense to think of the degree of reliability of an accounting measurement without studying how the measure will be used, how well the user understands the accounting process by which the measurement is made, and (above all) how, *in reality*, the variable x (the reported value) is related to the variable y which is of primary interest to the user of the data.

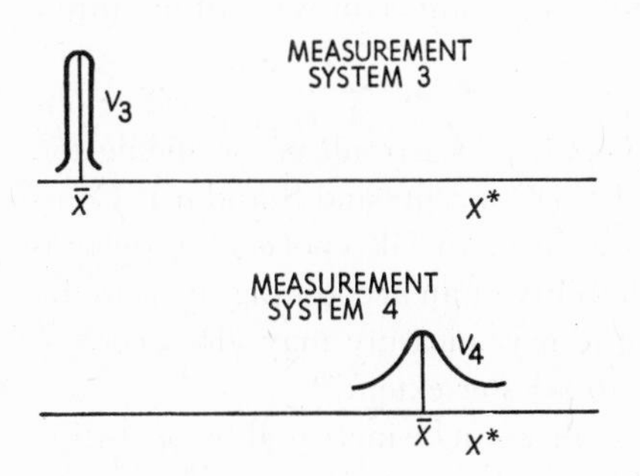

FIGURE 6. Reliability and objectivity, II.

SUMMARY AND CONCLUSIONS

The reliability of accounting measurements was defined as the degree of objectivity plus a bias factor. This relationship shows that the degree of ob-

[18] For years the advocates of, for example, market values have been urging a trade-off between usefulness and objectivity in favor of usefulness. In fact, it is usually agreed that the key problem in the selection of accounting methods is to achieve the proper balance between objectivity and usefulness. (See, for example, Sprouse, *op. cit.*, p. 65.) To the extent that reliability constitutes an important part of usefulness (materiality and timeliness of the data are also important), equation 7 is an effective way to characterize this trade-off using the statistical concept of variance and mean square error.

jectivity can be measured without regard for the use of the measure; but reliability cannot because the bias depends on the alleged value, which in turn is related to the particular use of the measure.

This conceptual relationship, which depends on the variance of measurement observations from their mean and the distance of this mean from the alleged value, gives valuable insights into some of the possible steps which can be taken by the members of the accounting profession to improve the reliability of accounting measurements.

First, accountants ought to cooperate to the fullest possible extent with the users of accounting data to search for and define those factors or quantities which will be useful in decision processes. These factors were designated as y's. Accountants must then undertake to develop measurements which will produce accounting measurements (x's) that will give good predictions of these decision variables (y's). Both of these research efforts should help to reduce the bias, B. Accountants should also attempt to educate the users of the accounting data as well as be educated in the manner described above. If users of accounting data can be more effectively educated, they might change their function for relating x and y, and this change can also result in decreasing the bias and improving reliability. Hence, reliability is definitely a two-way street. It may be that the reliability of a measurement can be improved by changing the measurement system; on the other hand, the reliability of the system may also be improved by changing the manner in which the output from the system is used.

Another way to improve the degree of reliability may be to sacrifice objectivity, if the bias can be made much smaller as a result of sacrificing the objectivity. The recent attempts by the 1964 Concepts and Standards Committees to include holding gains and losses in financial reports may be considered as an attempt to improve the reliability of an accounting measure by decreasing the bias factor even though the new measure may also decrease the degree of objectivity but, hopefully, to a lesser extent.[19]

Also of importance—the degree of reliability can be increased by operating on the degree of objectivity as well as by operating on the bias. Hence, accountants should constantly try to improve the degree of objectivity if the bias does not increase at a faster rate than the improvement in the degree of objectivity. Once the accounting profession finds what alleged values are to be measured, the degree of objectivity might be improved by establishing and more fully specifying a set of accounting measurement principles and procedures. These principles and procedures will, hopefully, produce measurements which are less dependent on the measurer than the situation we now have.

---

[19] American Accounting Association, Committee on Concepts and Standards—Long-Lived Assets, "Accounting for Land, Building, and Equipment," Supplementary Statement No. 1, *Accounting Review*, July, 1964, pp. 693–99; and 1964 Concepts and Standards Research Study Committee, "The Realization Concept," *Accounting Review*, April, 1965, pp. 312–22.

We must note that objectivity per se should not be the sole criterion for selecting accounting measurement systems. On the other hand, it is near-sighted to say that objectivity should be discarded altogether in favor of a vague and poorly defined notion of "usefulness." The degree of reliability (which encompasses objectivity) is the important criterion, and it will ultimately determine the extent to which the decision-making public will accept and use accounting measurements.

II

Valuation of Business Resources

TABLEAU II

Methodological Analysis

Article \ Methodology	*Descriptive Models for Analysis*					*Statistical Theory*	
	Algebraic or Symbolic (Deterministic)	*Algebraic or Symbolic (Probabilistic)*	*Matrix Methods*	*Markov Processes*	*Simulation*	*Sampling*	*Regression and Correlation Analysis*
5. Discounted Services Again: The Homogeneity Problem	X						
6. Statistical Sampling Techniques in the Aging of Accounts Receivable in a Department Store						X	
7. Estimation of the Allowance for Doubtful Accounts by Markov Chains				X			
8. Application of Statistical Sampling Techniques to Lifo Inventory Valuation						X	
9. Statistical Attributes of Group Depreciation				X			
10. Matrix Theory and Cost Allocation			X				
11. Linear Algebra and Cost Allocations: Some Examples			X				
12. Mathematical Models for Public Utility Rate Regulation	X						

VALUATION OF BUSINESS RESOURCES

Valuation is a specific instance or consequence of the process of measurement. Although some accountants reject as invalid the argument that accounting is directly concerned with valuation, an implied valuation is made whenever costs are allocated, depreciation is recorded, doubtful accounts are written off, etc. Given a general theory of accounting measurement, the accountant must nonetheless improvise or create tools to support and implement a theoretical basis of valuation. Such tools may be abstracted from mathematical and statistical analyses. These tools, or techniques, not only provide a logical, objective, and consistent basis for valuation but are frequently comparatively easy to apply in many cases.

Present value measurement has long been advocated as the proper theoretical basis for valuation of assets in the accounting records. However, this position is examined critically in article 5, and severe constraints are suggested. Following this conceptual analysis, several specific examples of practical valuation problems are discussed. These include the following:

1. *Aging of accounts receivable*
2. *Allowance for doubtful accounts*
3. *Inventory valuation*
4. *Depreciation*
5. *Cost allocation*
6. *Fixed asset (rate base) valuation*

The reader should remain alert in recognizing that these are but a sample, albeit a reasonably representative one, of several instances in which mathematical and statistical techniques may be useful in the valuation of resources; it should be further understood that the specific techniques described are not the only appropriate ones which may be used.

5

Given two inputs and a linearly homogeneous production function, the author demonstrates that the sum of the marginal net receipts equals total receipts, thus enabling one to use present value measurements in respect to valuing assets. However, the mathematical property of homogeneity is then analyzed, and several examples are provided for which the aforementioned equality does not obtain, including one in which the production function is not linearly homogeneous. The author thus concludes that discounted present values are not, in general, appropriate measurements to be reported in financial statements.

*DISCOUNTED SERVICES AGAIN: THE HOMOGENEITY PROBLEM**

Arthur L. Thomas

INTRODUCTION[1]

THIS IS an attempt to dig deeper into an important and surprisingly complicated issue: the valuation of assets in terms of the net discounted cash flows that they are expected to generate over their productive lives. In an earlier article,[2] some concern was expressed over certain accounting theorists tending to hold forth this discounted services approach as the only theoretically valid way to value assets, to present the approach as a standard against which conventional accounting practice should be compared, and to conclude from such a comparison that conventional accounting should be modified so as to make it a better approximation to this ideal.[3]

* Reprinted from *Accounting Review*, January, 1964, pp. 1–11.

[1] During its preparation, this paper received valuable criticism from Professor William J. Schlatter and Professor W. Allen Spivey, both of the University of Michigan, and neither of whom, of course, should be held responsible for any of its defects. Professor Schlatter made many helpful comments on its accounting aspects and presentation. Professor Spivey's role went even further: He offered some vague suspicions that the discounted services approach ran into a mathematical snarl; he first identified the specific issue involved, then patiently undertook to have this issue both understood and expressed properly.

[2] Arthur L. Thomas, "Precision and Discounted Services," *Accounting Review*, January, 1962, pp. 67–72.

[3] This earlier article lists a few examples of such normative uses of the approach. For more recent and good ones, see Donald A. Corbin, "The Revolution in Accounting," *Accounting Review*, October, 1962, especially pp. 629–31; and in the same issue, Stephen A. Zeff, "Replacement Cost: Member of the Family, Welcome Guest, or Intruder?" p. 620.

While there may be much to be said for modifying some features of conventional accounting, this article attempted to show that the discounted services approach was a snare in the way toward improvement; that, far from serving as an example of what accounting should be, the approach suffered from crippling internal weaknesses. Among other things, the article argued that whenever a stream of cash flows is jointly generated by more than one asset, the discounted services method cannot be used to value those assets individually without becoming very arbitrary.

MARGINAL NET RECEIPTS

As Zeff points out in his excellent article on replacement costs, it is a blunder to say just this and go no further. He notes that "The relevant future net receipts would be the *marginal* net receipts associable with the asset in question—not the total net receipts attributable to the single asset as though it were bereaved of the firm."[4]

This is quite true. Oddly enough, though, instead of changing our original conclusion, Zeff's comment turns out to give it powerful indirect support. For it is possible to demonstrate that the discounted services approach will usually be embarrassingly arbitrary just *because* the relevant net receipts are the marginal ones.

A SUMMARY OF WHAT WILL FOLLOW

Unfortunately, *showing* that this is so is a complicated job. It might be best to begin with a simple illustration wherein assets *can* plausibly be valued in terms of their discounted marginal net receipts. We will then try to see *why* the discounted services approach works so well in this illustration. Strangely enough, it will turn out that this success hinges on our assuming a particular mathematical property for the underlying relationship between the assets and their net receipts. It will become clear that if this property is not present, the discounted services approach will give capricious asset valuations. Finally, we will suggest that cases possessing the necessary mathematical properties are, in practice, fairly rare. We will, though, discuss this latter point only briefly, as the reader should by then be in a position to verify it for himself.

We will have to make use of a mathematical point which, while simple enough, is not the sort of thing that most accountants have any reason to be familiar with. Wherever possible, strictly mathematical matters will be kept below the surface. Where they must emerge, the casual reader is urged to skim them. While the mathematical issue is crucial to the whole discounted services approach, the general *drift* of the argument can be followed without a detailed understanding of the mathematics.

[4] Zeff, *op. cit.*, p. 624, n. 45. Zeff's further comment about probabilistic estimates of the future cash flows is also excellent. However, considering the degree of uncertainty inherent in any estimates of the future, mere *point* estimates of future cash flows could be very misleading. A system of asset valuation making use of confidence intervals rather than single dollar figures would seem to be called for here.

ASSUMPTIONS MADE IN THE ILLUSTRATIONS

In all of our illustrations, we will assume that the assets involved are machines, that there are only two kinds of them, that they jointly produce a single product, and that this product cannot be made without using both kinds of machine. We will assume that outputs are divisible but that inputs are not, that is, that it makes sense to speak of fractional units of product but that we are dealing with circumstances where no meaning can be attached to fractional machines. We will assume that the contributions of different types of machine to output are symmetrical, that is, for example, that the same output results from any combination of four machines of one type and six of the other, regardless of which is which.

These assumptions are made for simplicity only; all conclusions reached will be equally true in more complicated cases.

Finally, we will make two other assumptions, removing them only at the very end: that perfect markets exist for all inputs and that idle machines cost nothing. Removing *these* assumptions, it will be suggested, will actually reinforce our conclusions.

AN ILLUSTRATION WHEREIN THE DISCOUNTED SERVICES APPROACH WORKS SATISFACTORILY

Let us begin with an illustration in which the discounted services approach works satisfactorily, so as to see what such success involves. Let us call the two types of machines A's and B's, and designate the quantity of output by Z. There are a number of possible relationships between assets and their net receipts that are compatible with the discounted services approach. A fairly simple and fairly realistic possible relationship is based on the following production function:

$$Z = \frac{22AB - A^2 - B^2}{A + B}$$

As we might expect, this production function describes the quantity of output that will result from any possible combination of the two types of input. If we assume that the company is limited to 10 machines of each type, we can display these possible outputs as appears in Exhibit 1.

Several things should be observed here. If either input is fixed at any given level, additions to the other input quickly lead to diminishing returns—yet, for a while, still increase total output. (That total outputs also eventually diminish is a possible, but not necessary, feature of diminishing returns, and one that does not affect our discussion.) Suppose, for example, that we have only five A's available. The first B used will add 14 units to output, but the second B only 13.29, the third only 9.71, and so on.

The reason for building diminishing returns of this sort into our illustration is simply that they are a characteristic feature of actual situations in which net receipts are jointly generated by more than one asset. In actual business practice, it is usually possible to increase output by increasing some types of inputs while keeping others fixed. Indeed, this is often easier than increasing all inputs in proportion, at least in the short run.

However, after some level has been reached, the additional inputs will usually tend to add progressively less and less to output. For example, given a fixed plant, a point will eventually be reached where it is uneconomical to hire more labor, even if that additional labor is well trained and competent,

EXHIBIT 1

A										
10	10.82	28.00	42.38	54.57	65.00	74.00	81.82	88.67	94.68	100.00
9	11.60	28.27	42.00	53.46	63.14	71.40	78.50	84.65	90.00	94.68
8	12.33	28.40	41.36	52.00	60.85	68.29	74.60	80.00	84.65	88.67
7	13.00	28.33	40.40	50.09	58.00	64.54	70.00	74.60	78.50	81.82
6	13.57	28.00	39.00	47.60	54.45	60.00	64.54	68.29	71.40	74.00
5	14.00	27.29	37.00	44.33	50.00	54.45	58.00	60.85	63.14	65.00
4	14.20	26.00	34.14	40.00	44.33	47.60	50.09	52.00	53.46	54.57
3	14.00	23.80	30.00	34.14	37.00	39.00	40.40	41.36	42.00	42.38
2	13.00	20.00	23.80	26.00	27.29	28.00	28.33	28.40	28.27	28.00
1	10.00	13.00	14.00	14.20	14.00	13.57	13.00	12.33	11.60	10.82
	1	2	3	4	5	6	7	8	9	10 *B*

if only because labor cannot be indefinitely substituted for machines. The same is true of most other inputs.

PROPORTIONAL RETURNS TO SCALE

On the other hand, it can happen that if *all* inputs are increased in proportion, output will also increase proportionally. This characteristic is often called "proportional returns to scale" and is entirely consistent with there being diminishing returns when one or more input is kept *fixed.* While we will suggest later that proportional returns to scale are not a necessary property of all production functions, our illustration was chosen to show them. Six *A*'s and six *B*'s yield twice the output of three *A*'s and three *B*'s. Eight *A*'s and four *B*'s yield four times the output of two *A*'s and one *B*.

Thus, in summary, our illustration involves diminishing returns when one input is held fixed, accompanied by proportional returns to scale.

VALUATION OF THE MACHINES IN TERMS OF THEIR MARGINAL NET RECEIPTS

Our production function gives us a relationship between assets and *output*, but we do not yet have a relationship between assets and *net receipts*. To obtain this, we need to know what the output sells for and what it costs to run the machines. Assume that we can sell as much product as we wish at a price of \$1, and that a period's services for one A and one B cost \$4 and \$3, respectively. Then, if we let R stand for net receipts, we get the following relationship between assets and net receipts:

$$R = \frac{22AB - A^2 - B^2}{A + B} - 4A - 3B$$

$$= \frac{15AB - 5A^2 - 4B^2}{A + B}$$

It is easy to verify that if the company is limited to 10 machines of each type, it will maximize its net receipts at \$30 by using all 20 of them to produce 100 units of output. We can calculate the individual *marginal* net receipts of each type of machine at this output,[5] add them up, and compare the results with total net receipts, obtaining the figures given in Exhibit 2.

EXHIBIT 2

Type of Machine	*Individual Marginal Net Receipts*	*Number of Machines Used*	*Total Marginal Net Receipts*
A	\$1	10	\$10
B	\$2	10	20
Total net receipts			\$30

It is easy to see that the marginal net receipts from each machine "add up" to the total net receipts. Because of this, the total net receiptsc an be divided up among the machines, and the discounted services approach applied to value them, without any apparent arbitrariness.

EXHAUSTION OF PRODUCT

This property, whereby the marginal net receipts add up to the total net receipts, is sometimes called "exhaustion of product." It would be awkward

[5] The individual marginal net receipts for either type of asset can be calculated by taking the partial derivative of the function expressing the relationship between both assets and the net receipts, solving the result in terms of the actual numbers of each type of machine employed to generate the assumed output.

were the product *not* exhausted. Suppose that in the previous illustration our individual marginal net receipts had turned out to be, say, \$1.50 and \$1.30. Then, total marginal net receipts (\$28) would have been \$2 less than total net receipts (\$30). The extra \$2 would either have had to be allocated to the machines, or ignored, or else treated as goodwill of some sort. If we allocated the \$2, we could do so by giving a uniform bonus to each machine, or according to the original marginal net receipts, or marginal productivity, or *average* net receipts, or average productivity, or in several other ways. Any such treatment would necessarily be arbitrary. It is therefore important to ask whether we can always be sure that our relationships will be such that product is exhausted.

Unfortunately, there is no assurance that they will be. Indeed, exhaustion of product turns out to be an unusual case.

HOMOGENEITY[6]

To explain *why* this is true, it is essential to introduce a bit of mathematics. For there is a mathematical issue that underlies the whole discounted services approach and which must inevitably be faced sooner or later. This issue is related to a possible property of functions called "homogeneity." Fortunately, the mathematical points involved are not very complicated.

FUNCTIONS

First of all, we should be clear as to what a function is. A function can be regarded as a particularly clear, unambiguous rule for associating members of one set of things with members of another set of things. For example, consider the function $f(x) = x^2$. We can imagine the set of all possible values that x might have. The function gives us a rule whereby each x value is associated with another number, the *value of the function* for that particular x value. For instance, the x value of 2 is associated with the function value 4, the x value of 6 with the function value 36. In each case the function lets us associate an x value with a function value.

Of course, it is possible to have more complicated kinds of functions. Our production function in Exhibit 1 is a function of *two* variables instead of one. It associates function values with *pairs* of A and B values. For instance, it associates the function value 27.29 with the pair $5A$, $2B$; it associates the function value 41.36 with the pair $3A$, $8B$; and so on. The principle involved is the same, though.

[6] Homogeneous functions are defined and their properties discussed in a number of mathematical works. Two that might be of particular interest to accountants are Taro Yamane, *Mathematics for Economists* (Englewood Cliffs, N.J.: Prentice-Hall, Inc., 1962), pp. 90–100, 127–29; and R. G. D. Allen, *Mathematical Analysis for Economists* (New York: Macmillan Co., 1939), pp. 315–22.

The basic production function used as an illustration in this paper is based on one mentioned by Allen on page 322.

DEFINITION OF HOMOGENEITY

While the concept is unfamiliar to most accountants, homogeneity is just a possible property of functions, involving a very convenient and rigid sort of predictability. Consider again the function $f(x) = x^2$. There are a number of questions that we might want to ask about this function. One of them turns out to be quite important, even though at first it seems a rather surprising thing to ask.

Suppose that we picked some constant (call it k) and multiplied any x value by k. Obviously, this will give us a new x value. Since the function is a rule associating all x values with function values, we will also end up with a new *function value*. We might ask, "What will be the relationship between the old function value and the new function value?" Our function is simple enough here that we can answer this by using a little algebra. If we let $f(kx)$ represent $f(x)$ after we have multiplied the x value by the constant k, then:

$$\begin{aligned} f(kx) &= (kx)^2 \\ &= k^2x^2 \\ &= k^2f(x) \end{aligned}$$

Regardless of what x values we consider, our new function value will just be k^2 times the old function value. Note that the relationship between the new and old function values is thus entirely independent of the particular values that we might choose for x. It depends only on the value that we choose for k (and, strictly speaking, on the function involved, a point that we will discuss shortly). The relationship between the old and new function values is therefore highly predictable. Call this property "homogeneity," and call functions that have this property "homogeneous."

This homogeneity property can be generalized to functions of more than one variable. For example, our previous relationship between assets and their net receipts is also homogeneous:

$$R = f(A, B) = \frac{15AB - 5A^2 - 4B^2}{A + B}$$

Therefore:

$$\begin{aligned} f(kA, kB) &= \frac{15kAkB - 5k^2A^2 - 4k^2B^2}{kA + kB} \\ &= \frac{k^2}{k}\,\frac{(15AB - 5A^2 - 4B^2)}{A + B} \\ &= kf(A, B) \end{aligned}$$

Once again, to predict what the relationship is between the old and new function values associated with any pair of A and B values, all that we need to know is the form of the function and the value chosen for k.

NONHOMOGENEOUS FUNCTIONS

There are many functions that do not have this property, where the relationship between the old and new function values is not so conveniently predictable. As an example, consider the function $f(x) = x^2 + x$. If we multiply an x value by k, we get

$$f(kx) = (kx)^2 + kx$$

Here, the relationship between the old and new function values cannot be predicted without knowing the particular x value that was involved, for

$$\begin{aligned} f(kx) &= (kx)^2 + kx \\ &= k^2x^2 + kx \\ &= k(kx^2 + x) \\ &= k(x^2 + x) + (k^2 - k)x^2 \\ &= kf(x) + (k^2 - k)x^2 \end{aligned}$$

Were someone to ask us what the relationship was between the old and new function values, we would have to reply, "That depends; what original x value did you have in mind?"

Call functions of this sort "nonhomogeneous." The notion of a nonhomogeneous function can also be generalized to functions of any number of variables. Note finally that, as in our example, a function can be nonhomogeneous and yet be perfectly regular, well-behaved, and reasonable. A lack of homogeneity does not imply any lack of respectability, just the lack of a particular mathematical property.

HOMOGENEITY OF VARIOUS DEGREES

The predictability of homogeneous functions lets us describe them more fully than we have so far. When our function was $f(x) = x^2$, it turned out that the new function value was k^2 times our old function value. But when our function was

$$f(A, B) = \frac{15AB - 5A^2 - 4B^2}{A + B}$$

it turned out that our new function value was only k times our old function value. It is simple and natural to classify homogeneous functions in terms of the power to which k has to be raised in order to express the relationship between old and new function values. Thus, $f(x) = x^2$ would be homogeneous to the second power of k, and $f(A, B)$ to the first power of k. Instead of using quite this language, though, mathematicians prefer to speak of functions being "homogeneous of degree two," or "homogeneous of degree one." This means the same thing, and we will use their standard phraseology.

It is possible to find functions that are homogeneous of any degree that you wish. The function $f(x) = x^{37}$ is homogeneous of degree 37;

$$f(x, y) = \frac{x + y}{2x - y}$$

is homogeneous of degree zero; $f(x) - x^{1/2}$ is homogeneous of degree one half;

$$f(x, y) = \frac{x + y}{3x^2 - 5xy - 2y^2}$$

is homogeneous of degree -1; and so forth.

We are now equipped with the materials that we need to complete our discussion of the discounted services approach.

A REQUIREMENT FOR EXHAUSTION OF PRODUCT

We asked earlier whether we could always be sure that the individual marginal net receipts of assets jointly producing a single product would always add up to that product's total net receipts, whether we could always be sure that product would be exhausted. We are now in a position to answer this. For it can be proven mathematically that *product will be exhausted only if the relationship between assets and net receipts is homogeneous of degree one.*[7]

In other words, for the relationship between assets and net receipts to be compatible with the discounted services approach, it must have a special mathematical property. It turns out that "homogeneity of degree one" can be interpreted as being the same thing as our previous notion of "proportional returns to scale." Thus, in economic language, we can conclude that for the discounted services approach to avoid arbitrariness, returns to scale must be proportional. We should keep in mind, too, that these proportional returns to scale must be a property of the relationship between assets and net receipts, not just of the production function.

A CASE WHICH IS NOT HOMOGENEOUS OF DEGREE ONE

Our previous relationship between assets and net receipts was homogeneous of degree one. Let us turn it into a function that is homogeneous of degree *two* and see what happens. The result is not intended to be realistic, only illustrative.

Keep the $1 selling price the same; assume, though, that it costs nothing to operate either type of machine, and alter the production function so as to get the following relationship between assets and net receipts:

$$R = \frac{66AB - 3A^2 - 3B^2}{200}$$

[7] For proofs of this, see Allen, *op. cit.*, pp. 317–20; and Yamane, *op. cit.*, pp. 97–98, 127–29.

Assuming again that we are limited to 10 of each type of machine, we find that once more we can maximize our total net receipts at $30 by using all 20 machines. But when we calculate individual marginal net receipts at this output, we get the disturbing result shown in Exhibit 3.

Total individual marginal net receipts are *twice* the total net receipts! In general, it can be shown that if the relationship between assets and net receipts is homogeneous of degree d, then total marginal net receipts will be d times total net receipts.[8] As we suggested before, this leaves us with a missing $30 that in this case must either be ignored, shown as a sort of negative goodwill, or else prorated somehow among the machines.

At least, any arbitrariness here is predictable. But matters could be worse than this. Though we are forced to be a bit arbitrary here, at least we can decide in advance what arbitrary rule we are going to follow. So long as the relationship is homogeneous, we can *predict* how much bigger (or smaller) total individual marginal net receipts will be than total net receipts. Our rule will not depend upon the particular output that we end up producing, with its particular mix of inputs.

EXHIBIT 3

Type of Machine	*Individual Marginal Net Receipts*	*Number of Machines Used*	*Total Marginal Net Receipts*
A	$3	10	$30
B	$3	10	30
Total marginal net receipts			$60
Total net receipts			$30

It would be really serious if we could not even predict, if in each case we had to wait, see how things worked out, then eventually make a capricious adjustment of the individual marginal net receipts in terms of a hindsight knowledge of the extent to which we had used our assets. This latter would resemble balancing one's checkbook by writing oneself a check.

Yet, as we shall soon see, this is exactly what we would often have to do under the discounted services approach.

THE PROBLEM OF NEGATIVE ASSETS

Before showing this, though, it is worth while pointing out that even when we are dealing with relationships that are homogeneous of degree one, a serious problem can develop. Let us return to the example used in Exhibit 2, where the product sells for $1 and the production function is

$$Z = \frac{22AB - A^2 - B^2}{A + B}$$

[8] See Allen, *op. cit.*, pp. 319–20; and Yamane, *op. cit.*, pp. 97–98.

Let us suppose instead, though, that *A*'s cost \$6 and that *B*'s cost \$4. This gives us a relationship between assets and net receipts that is still homogenous of degree one:

$$R = \frac{12AB - 7A^2 - 5B^2}{A + B}$$

If we are still limited to 10 machines of each type, we have the possible input mixes and related net receipts that appear in Exhibit 4 (only positive net receipts are shown).

EXHIBIT 4

A \ *B*	1	2	3	4	5	6	7	8	8	10
10										
9										0.68
8									0.65	0.67
7								0.60	0.50	
6							0.54	0.29		
5						0.45				
4					0.33					
3				0.14						
2										
1										

We see that total net receipts can be maximized at 68 cents by using 9 *A*'s and 10 *B*'s. If we compute individual marginal net receipts at this output, we find, as expected, that the relationship "adds up." But, as can be seen in Exhibit 5, something very strange has happened: The individual marginal net receipts of the *A*'s are negative! Both types of asset are necessary to produce the output and have symmetrical effects on the production of output. Short-run total net receipts have been maximized. Yet the discounted services

EXHIBIT 5

Type of Machine	*Individual Marginal Net Receipts*	*Number of Machines Used*	*Total Marginal Net Receipts*
A..........................	\$0.352*	9	\$3.17*
B..........................	\$0.385	10	3.85
Total net receipts..............			\$0.68

* Negative

approach would lead to showing one type of assets as asset contrast (or, perhaps, as liabilities)!

This is not the sort of result that we would expect from something purporting to serve as a standard for financial accounting.

NONHOMOGENEOUS RELATIONSHIPS

The final and most serious flaw in the discounted services approach is simple to describe: As we saw earlier, many regular and reasonable functions are nonhomogeneous. Let us see what happens when the relationship between assets and net receipts is nonhomogeneous.

Suppose that, once again, our production function is the one shown in Exhibit 1, and that *A*'s cost \$4 and *B*'s cost \$3. Up to now, we have been assuming that the demand for the company's product is completely elastic. Assume instead that the company's demand function shows some inelasticity. One of the simplest such demand functions is

$$P = \$2 - \frac{Z}{100}$$

where P represents the unit price that the company can get for the product and Z, as before, stands for quantity of output. We can interpret such a relationship as arising either from the need to charge less to sell progressively more product or from the need to spend more on marketing.

The resulting relationship between assets and net receipts is a bit complicated but leads to the possible total net receipts at different levels of output shown in Exhibit 6, assuming again that we are limited to 10 machines of each type.

EXHIBIT 6

	1	2	3	4	5	6	7	8	9	10
10		2.16	17.80	27.36	32.75	35.24	35.69	34.72	32.72	30.00
9		6.55	21.36	30.34	35.41	37.82	38.38	37.64	36.00	33.72
8		10.73	24.61	32.96	37.67	39.94	40.55	40.00	38.64	36.72
7		14.63	27.48	35.09	39.36	41.43	42.00	41.55	40.38	38.69
6		18.16	29.79	36.54	40.25	42.00	42.43	41.94	40.82	39.24
5	3.04	21.13	31.31	37.01	40.00	41.25	41.36	40.67	39.41	37.75
4	7.38	23.24	31.62	36.00	38.01	38.54	38.09	36.96	35.34	33.36
3	11.04	23.94	30.00	32.62	33.31	32.79	31.48	29.61	27.36	24.80
2	13.31	22.00	24.94	25.24	24.13	22.16	19.63	16.73	13.55	10.16
1	12.00	14.31	13.04	10.38	7.04	3.30				

B

Inspection shows us that we can maximize total net receipts at $42.43 by using six *A*'s and seven *B*'s. After making our calculations, we have the information given in Exhibit 7.

Here the discounted services approach would not only treat essential machines as negative assets but would pick as negative the ones that cost the least to operate.[9] Even worse, there is no predictable relationship between total marginal net receipts and total net receipts. As we have suggested, this last will be true of any nonhomogeneous relationship. Any allocation of total net receipts among the 13 machines would have to be done in an essentially capricious fashion. The facts *could* be ground to fit the theory, but only in a frivolous and peremptory way.

EXHIBIT 7

Type of Machine	*Individual Marginal Net Receipts*	*Number of Machines Used*	*Total Marginal Net Receipts*
A	$0.226	6	$ 1.36
B	$0.083*	7	0.58*
Total marginal net receipts			$ 0.78
Total net receipts			$42.43

* Negative

HOW SERIOUS WOULD THESE PROBLEMS BE?

Our final task should be to ask how often the discounted services approach would be apt to display these flaws. A little experimentation with possible production and demand functions should persuade the reader of several things:

1. To be homogeneous of degree one, the relationship between assets and net receipts must involve proportional returns to scale.
2. Most *plausible* production functions involving diminishing returns are nonhomogeneous.
3. It is rare that coupling a demand function with a production function leads to a homogeneous relationship between assets and net receipts if either or both are nonhomogeneous.
4. Similarly, regardless of the properties of the production function, it is very hard to get a homogeneous relationship between assets and net receipts except by using a linear demand function, and preferably an infinitely elastic one. In short, it is very hard to couple functions and get a homogeneous result.

In ordinary business life, most net receipts are generated jointly by more than one input. While proportional returns to scale are theoretically possible,

[9] This is not a necessary consequence of nonhomogeneity, but it is not an uncommon one.

it is difficult to be sure how common they are. Certainly the outputs and net receipts of large plants and large enterprises often seem disproportionate to those of small plants and small enterprises. Some of what might look like increasing or decreasing returns to scale is, of course, just due to difficulties in varying all inputs (including managerial talent) in exact proportion, and gives a spurious appearance of disproportionality. Even so, it is hard to believe that this is always the entire explanation.

Even if it turns out that a *production* function involves proportional returns to scale, it is rare for the relationship between assets and net receipts to do so. Few companies have perfectly elastic demand functions or even *linear* ones. Moreover, our discussion has not even touched upon certain other common features of business life which, if present, seem even harder to build into a homogeneous relationship between assets and net receipts. These include imperfect *input* markets, market segmentation, idle capacity costs, and the like.

It seems, therefore, that most actual relationships between assets and net receipts would be nonhomogeneous, and that few if any companies would be able to escape the severe flaws of the discounted services approach. To recommend this approach as a standard for financial accounting seems, therefore, in most cases, to unintentionally recommend arbitrary asset valuation.

CONCLUSIONS

What room, then, is left for the discounted services approach? Very little, it seems, as far as financial accounting goes: It can be used to value receivables and other cash claims, retired plant, and other scrap. These assets may fit the approach's specialized mathematical requirements; few others do.

Outside of financial accounting, the discounted services approach is largely unaffected by our arguments. Nothing that we have said bars a company from using this approach in capital-budgeting or bond-refunding decisions, for here no attempt is made to value all assets at the same point in time. Nothing bars its use in economic theory or investment analysis, for here the intention is to come to a single net asset value for the entire company. The approach breaks down only when we try to use it to value individual assets for balance sheet purposes.

But this is just another way of saying that it breaks down when we try to make it serve as a standard for financial accounting or as an approach to emulate in the continuing development of financial accounting theory.

6

This article deals with both accounting and statistical considerations in respect to the aging of accounts receivable in a department store. Statistical sampling techniques in respect to a specific case are described and evaluated.

*STATISTICAL SAMPLING TECHNIQUES IN THE AGING OF ACCOUNTS RECEIVABLE IN A DEPARTMENT STORE**

R. M. Cyert and Robert M. Trueblood

STATEMENT OF THE PROBLEM

IN THE ECONOMIC SYSTEMS of most industrial countries the bulk of the sales made by business concerns of any significant size is in the form of credit sales. In large retail outlets such as department stores, credit sales become even more important, and the number of accounts receivable becomes exceedingly large. Under such conditions the proper credit policy to be followed becomes a management problem of the first magnitude. In addition to the proper credit policy, it is necessary for management to determine the proper reserve for uncollectibles. One of the traditional methods of generating information on these questions has been the aging of the accounts receivable. It is precisely on management problems of this kind, where good information about large masses of data must be derived, that modern statistical sampling techniques can play an important role. When the data for decision-making purposes are the result of a statistical sample, management has an objective measure of the quality of the data on which the decision may be made. The specific objective of this paper is to demonstrate the usefulness of statistical

* Reprinted from *Management Science*, January, 1957, pp. 185–95.

The research underlying this article is part of a broader study of the application of statistical techniques to accounting and auditing problems carried on at the Graduate School of Industrial Administration of Carnegie Institute of Technology. The authors wish to acknowledge the aid of W. W. Cooper, R. W. Johnson, E. Mansfield, and R. J. Monteverde in the preparation of this paper.

sampling in the aging of receivables for the purpose of setting the allowance for uncollectibles.

Stated in terms of statistics, receivables aging is the process of determining the frequency distribution of the dollars in the total accounts receivable according to the length of time the dollars have been owed to the company. If the enterprise has a large number of accounts, the aging is usually performed on a sample drawn from the universe, the total accounts receivable. The frequency distribution of dollars grouped according to age is estimated for the universe from the sample. Loss expectancy rates, rough estimates of the proportion of dollars in each age category liable to become uncollectible, are then applied to each age group of the frequency distribution to estimate an allowance for uncollectible accounts.[1] The estimated allowance based on the aging results is one of the factors typically used by management in establishing the allowance for uncollectibles for financial statement purposes.

The particular store studied is a large metropolitan department store doing a heavy volume of credit sales. It carries about 100,000 receivables from customers. The practice of the store has been to select for detailed aging about 15,000 of the regular accounts. The customers' accounts are filed alphabetically in more than 500 trays with approximately 200 accounts in each tray.[2]

Historically, in drawing the sample of 15,000 accounts, the store selected on a judgmental basis 75 individual trays. These were completely aged. In addition, all of the regular retail accounts in the universe with balances in excess of $2,500 were aged in detail.

Each dollar in the balance of all accounts under $2,500 included in the sample is classified on the basis of its age into one or more of five categories: 0 to 2 months, 2 to 4 months, 4 to 6 months, 6 to 10 months, and over 10 months old. On the basis of the proportion of the total dollars of the sampled accounts falling into each age category, the dollars of total accounts receivable (excluding those over $2,500) which would fall into each age category are estimated.

In relation to the accounts with balances in excess of $2,500, the aging is performed in detail, and the precise accumulation of the dollars involved in each age classification is obtained.

Loss expectancy rates for each age category, based in part on experience, are then applied to the estimated dollars of receivables in each age category as a guide to the determination of the amount of the allowance for uncollectibles.

For example, assume that the 15,000 accounts aged carry an aggregate

---

[1] The loss expectancy rates are "policy parameters." The rates will vary as a function of such things as the firm's expectations of economic conditions, the firm's desires as to the degree of caution to be followed in financial policy, past experience, etc. For the study described in the paper, the loss expectancy rates had to be taken as given.

[2] The trays are, for accounting control purposes, grouped into about 100 subcontrols. The entire portfolio of regular accounts is carried in a single general ledger account.

balance of \$450,000 and that the total accounts aggregate \$3 million. Further, assume that of the \$450,000 of account balances aged in detail, it is established that \$30,000 of balances fall into the 4 to 6 months category, and that this category carries a loss expectancy rate of 15 percent. It could be estimated, therefore, that

$$\$200{,}000 = [(\$30{,}000/\$450{,}000) \times (\$3{,}000{,}000)]$$

of the total accounts are 4 to 6 months old and that \$30,000 (15 percent of \$200,000) should be included in the approximation of the total allowance for uncollectibles for this age class.

In establishing the accuracy of the client's detailed aging work in this particular case, the public accountant has customarily checked the detailed aging of 10 percent, or roughly 1,500, of the individual accounts. The auditor has typically used judgment criteria in selecting his sample and has followed no explicit pattern. For example, he has checked relatively more of the accounts aged during the early phases of the operation, and he has attempted to check the work of as many different clerks as practicable. Where the quality of work fell below acceptable standards, he has returned entire blocks of work for rechecking by the client and, wherever possible, has had corrections made in the client's detailed aging.

A number of preliminary studies were made on past data to determine the feasibility of utilizing statistical techniques in this case. At the same time, as part of a larger study, discussions were held on the proper relationships among statistics, accounting, and management. After the preliminary studies and the discussions the following objectives were decided upon in this case:

1. The sample design being used for selecting accounts to be aged should be analyzed with a view toward improving the method of selection and determining the optimum sample size.
2. The plan for selecting accounts already aged to be test-checked by the auditor was to be examined with a view toward installing an appropriate acceptance sampling scheme.

It was felt that these objectives would throw light on the general relationship existing among the three fields in that the requirements placed on the two sampling plans would have to take into account the purposes for which the information would be utilized by both the public accountant and the management. At the same time, the flexibility of the statistics would be tested in the process of serving two masters.

CONCLUSIONS

The general conclusion evolving from the study is that it is possible to apply statistical sampling methods to the accounting data involved in the study. The problem handled is, of course, only a peripheral one in relation to the total audit area. Nevertheless, the problem exhibits the characteristics of problems concerning accounting data such as the determination of a sampling method with certain administrative constraints and the selection of precision and reliability criteria by the auditor, with management desires taken into account. It was in fact because of this reason that the problem was selected as one of the first to be analyzed in the broader study under way.

In the particular case, both objectives of the study were satisfied. A sampling method was devised on the basis of which it is possible to measure the precision of the estimate of the allowance for uncollectibles with a given reliability coefficient. The method resulted in a substantial reduction in sampling over what had been the practice. However, it should be noted that this reduction was the result of relaxing the precision required of the estimate. It was not the result of merely using a statistical sample rather than a judgmental sample. It could well be that other cases would result in a larger sample. The important benefit is that the precision of the estimate is measured and that the risk of being wrong is known.[3] A basis for further extension is provided since much needs to be done in the way of getting a start on explicit measures of this kind.

The second objective of revising the test-check sample was met by devising a sequential sampling plan. In following a sequential sampling procedure, the auditor successively selects, at random, individual aged accounts and establishes whether they have been properly or improperly aged. After each selection, he reaches one of three decisions: (1) accept the entire aging work, (2) continue to pick other accounts for test checking, or (3) reject the complete aging work—depending on the number of accounts test-checked and the number of defective accounts found to that time. At any particular point in the process the auditor decides to accept, to reject, or to accumulate more evidence.

In this particular instance the entire aging work could not be accepted before at least 55 individual agings had been test-checked, and then only if no errors had been found. The lot could be rejected by the examination of a minimum of three items, if each of the first three items examined was defective. The sequential sampling plan was so devised that the maximum number of accounts that would be test-checked by the auditor would be 376; but on the average, only 126 would have to be test-checked before a decision could be reached.

In selecting the sequential sampling procedures for test-checking purposes, the public accountants stipulated that on the basis of past practice the acceptance and rejection levels should be as follows:

1. If 3 percent or less of the individual agings performed by the store were in error, the entire aging work of the store should be accepted by the public accountant at least 90 percent of the time.
2. If 8 percent or more of the individual agings performed by the store were in

[3] M. H. Hansen, W. N. Hurwitz, and W. G. Madow, *Sample Survey Methods and Theory* (New York: John Wiley & Sons, Inc., 1953), Vol. I, pp. 17–34.

error, the entire aging work of the store should be rejected by the public accountant at least 95 percent of the time.

These criteria of acceptability were based upon the level of error which analysis had shown to be implied by past practice, together with the auditor's conception of a reasonable level of error.

In designing the test-check sample, the combined work of all the employees involved was regarded as a single batch. This arbitrary assumption was made solely for purposes of experimentation. In most cases, it would probably be preferable to view the agings performed by each employee as a group of distinct and separate batches of work. If this view were adopted, the procedures for selecting the auditor's test-check sample would be the same as those described above—the only change being in the number of accounts which would have to be test-checked by the auditor before he could make a decision. Generally, the number of accounts having to be test-checked by the auditor would increase with the number of employees actually involved in the detailed aging work. For example, if four of the client's employees each aged 425 accounts, then on the average 504 (4 × 126) accounts would have to be test-checked by the auditor.

FURTHER WORK

Since the work on aging has been completed, a number of other applications have been made. The same basic method has proved successful, although the results in terms of sample-size reduction have not always been as spectacular as in the present case.

One of the interesting developments of the additional applications has been the interest of the various business firms to the estimates of the total dollars in each age category. In at least one instance the major interest was in the estimates of dollars per age category. The reason for the interest is the desire to have accurate information for the evaluation and modification of credit policies.

However, as a result of the manner in which the sample is selected, the precision of the estimate of the various age categories is generally not equal. The smaller the age category in terms of the number of accounts, the poorer will be the precision of the estimate of the dollars in that age category. From the stand-point of management, it is necessary to improve the precision of the smaller age categories because the smaller categories are usually the older categories which may need management attention. For management to know whether current credit policies need corrective action or not, the older age categories need close examination. This is another example of the relationships among accounting, management, and statistical sampling.

Many stores, however, use a system of flasher cards to designate in the files those accounts which are delinquent. The system of flasher cards, through variation in color, shape, position, etc., is generally detailed enough cate all of the age categories. The primary purpose of the flasher ca highlight those accounts which need special attention for collection purposes. The most recent work on aging has been an attempt to utilize the data from the flasher system to supplement the regular aging sample in those age categories which are smaller and also older. The regular aging sample is used to estimate the allowance for uncollectibles. The dollars in each age category are supplemented to the extent necessary to attain the required precision by sampling from those accounts that the flasher cards designate as belonging to the appropriate age category. It is quite clear that a good deal depends upon the flasher system being accurate, and a number of tests have been developed which measure the quality of the flasher system.

ACCOUNTING CONSIDERATIONS

Management and the public accountant have a mutual interest in the aging of accounts receivable. Accounts receivable aging assists management in its appraisal of the results of credit policy, provides a measure of the performance of credit personnel, and gives a partial story with respect to the worth of the firm's accounts receivable as of any given date. From an internal control standpoint, the public accountant is necessarily concerned with the operations of the credit department. He must also particularly concern himself with the worth of the firm's accounts receivable both from the balance sheet point of view and in relation to income determination.

Accounts receivable aging is typically used by management as one of several factors in the establishment of an allowance for uncollectible accounts. Although management has primary responsibility in determining the amount of such an allowance, the public accountant must appraise management's action in establishing the allowance. As an aid in judging the adequacy of the allowance for uncollectibles, the public accountant customarily reviews management's aging analysis. This is an accepted control procedure in modern corporate practice.

Typically, a business enterprise ages its accounts receivables monthly, or at other fairly frequent intervals. However, in the case of certain enterprises such as retail department stores, where the receivables are high in volume and where the individual balances are low in amount, monthly aging is not practical. In such cases, accounts receivable aging may be performed only once a year. Further, present accounting and auditing practice, in enterprises such as department stores, permits the determination of aging for the entire receivables portfolio on something less than a 100 percent basis. In such a situation, there is merit in pursuing the possibility of using statistical sampling methods. In short, the accounts receivable aging process in a typical metropolitan department store of some size is a type of problem where aid may fairly be sought from statistics to improve business practice.

STATISTICAL CONSIDERATIONS

In this section an attempt will be made to demonstrate the manner in which the sample design and the type of estimator were developed in this case. In some instances, as will be seen, the data were not available and had to be improvised. This situation is probably characteristic of industrial applications.

The initial objective of the statistical analysis was to evaluate the aging procedure with a view to determining the optimum sample design. In order to achieve such an objective, it was obvious that a good deal of analysis of the data would be necessary. The past data available were from a judgmental sample. Some preliminary rank correlation studies indicated that the data could probably be treated as random with respect to the age distribution. However, it was decided that a preferable approach would be to have the store proceed to draw 75 trays, as in the past, but insure the randomness of the sample of the trays by the use of a random number table for selecting the trays. Arrangements were also made to have all the data on each account recorded so that analyses to find the optimum sampling unit could be made.

One important step in the study was to determine the form of the estimator to be used. There were two alternative possibilities. One method that could be used would be to estimate the average dollars required in the reserve for each account (or whatever other sampling unit was used) and estimate the total reserve by multiplying by the number of accounts:

$$\bar{y} = \frac{\sum_{k=1}^{n} \sum_{j=1}^{m} \sum_{i=1}^{5} f_{ijk} l_i}{nm}$$

$$\hat{Y} = NM\bar{y} = \frac{NM}{nm} \sum_{k=1}^{n} \sum_{j=1}^{m} \sum_{i=1}^{5} f_{ijk} l_i$$

where

f_{ijk} = Dollars classified in the ith age category of the jth account of the kth tray
l_i = Loss expectancy rate of the ith age category
n = Total number of trays selected in the sample
N = Total number of trays in the universe
m = Number of accounts sampled in each tray
M = Number of accounts in each tray
$\bar{y}$ = Estimated average reserve per account
$\hat{Y}$ = Estimated total reserve for the universe

A second method which could be used is a ratio estimate. The ratio would be the sum of the dollars required for the reserve for each account (or whatever sampling unit was used) divided by the sum of the total dollars in the accounts. Symbolically:

$$y = nm\bar{y} = \sum_{k=1}^{n} \sum_{j=1}^{m} \sum_{i=1}^{5} f_{ijk} l_i$$

$$x = \sum_{k=1}^{n} \sum_{j=1}^{m} x_{jk}$$

$$r = \frac{y}{x}$$

$$\hat{Y}_R = \frac{y}{x} X$$

where

x_{jk} = Total dollars in the *j*th account of the *k*th tray
X = Total dollars of accounts receivable in the universe
r = Estimated reserve ratio

In both examples, it is of course possible to estimate the reserve directly rather than in two steps as illustrated above for purposes of expositional clarity.

A second important choice that had to be made was that of the sampling unit. There is no single best method of making such a choice. As Cochran puts it, "Information about optimum type of unit is more usually procured as an ingenious by-product of a survey whose main purpose is to make estimates."[4] In this case the smallest practicable unit was the individual account. It was not feasible to try to sample individual dollars. The accounts were not numbered; but for two stage designs, with the tray as the first stage, the individual account could be used as the sampling unit. However, an unrestricted random sample of accounts was ruled out because of the cost of identifying and selecting the accounts.

A third problem of concern that had to be faced was that of the procedure by which the sample was to be selected. A stratified design was considered and discarded. The basis for stratification would have been the size of the account. However, it would have been extremely costly, if not impossible, to stratify. The particular accounts in the universe would have to be selected from the trial balance tapes and the actual accounts in each tray determined by counting accounts from the beginning of the trial balance tape and then by counting individual accounts from the first account in the first tray. It was decided that stratified sampling would not be practicable.

A second procedure that had more merit was a two-stage design in which the tray would be the first stage and the sampling unit the second stage. It was decided, therefore, to proceed to analyze the sample of 75 trays as a two-stage sample. The procedure was to try both the mean per unit estimate and the ratio estimate. By means of a cost function, it would be possible to find the optimum subsampling ratios. The more efficient estimator, that is, the one with the smaller sampling error, could then be selected.

[4] W. G. Cochran, *Sampling Techniques* (New York: John Wiley& Sons, Inc., 1953), p. 195.

The first step in the analysis, then, was to draw a random subsample from each of the 75 trays for purposes of estimating the within and between-tray variances. The two estimators being compared were as follows:

(1)[5]
$$\hat{Y} = NM\bar{y} = \frac{\sum_{k=1}^{n}\sum_{j=1}^{m} y_{jk}}{nm} NM$$

$\hat{Y}$ = Estimated reserve for the universe
y_{jk} = The amount of the jth account in the kth tray going into the reserve = $\sum_{i=1}^{5} f_{ijk} l_i$
N = The total number of trays
M = The total number of accounts per tray

(2)[6]
$$\hat{Y}_R = \frac{\sum_{k=1}^{n}\sum_{j=1}^{m} y_{jk}}{\sum_{k=1}^{n}\sum_{j=1}^{m} x_{jk}} X$$

where

$\hat{Y}_R$ = The estimated allowance for uncollectibles based on the ratio estimate
x_{jk} = The balance of the jth account in the kth tray
X = The total value of accounts receivable

The variances for the two estimates can be calculated from the following expressions:

$$V(\hat{Y}) = \frac{N^2M^2}{mn}\left\{\frac{N-n}{N}\,\frac{m\sum_{k=1}^{n}(\bar{y}_k - \bar{y})^2}{n-1} + \frac{M-m}{M}\,\frac{n}{N}\,\frac{\sum_{k=1}^{n}\sum_{j=1}^{m}(y_{jk} - y_k)^2}{n(m-1)}\right\}$$

where

$$\bar{y}_k = \frac{\sum_{j=1}^{m} y_{jk}}{m}$$ = The average amount per account in the kth tray going into the reserve

$$\bar{y} = \frac{\sum_{k=1}^{n} \bar{y}_k}{n}$$

$$V(\hat{Y}_R) = \frac{N(N-n)}{n(n-1)}\sum_{k=1}^{n}(\bar{y}_k - r\bar{x}_k)^2 + \frac{N(M-m)}{nMm}\sum_{k=1}^{n}(s^2_{ky} + rs^2_{kx} - 2rs_{kyx})$$

---

[5] *Ibid.*, p. 225.
[6] P. V. Sukhatme, *Sampling Theory of Surveys with Applications* (Ames: Iowa State College Press, 1954), pp. 315–35.

where

$$\bar{x}_k = \frac{\sum_{j=1}^{m} x_{jk}}{m} = \text{The average balance per account in the } k\text{th tray}$$

$$r = \frac{\sum_{k=1}^{n}\sum_{j=1}^{m} y_{jk}}{\sum_{k=1}^{n}\sum_{j=1}^{m} x_{jk}} = \text{The reserve ratio as estimated from the sample of } mn \text{ accounts}$$

s^2_{ky} = The variance of the y values in the kth tray
s^2_{kx} = The variance of the x values in the kth tray
s_{kyx} = The covariance of the y's and the x's in the kth tray

On the basis of the estimates of the variances derived from the first sample, it was possible to determine the optimum size for the second-stage sample for a given cost function. There were no specific cost figures in existence. However, by means of some experimental timing and evaluation of the factors involved in tray selection versus account selection, it was concluded that a rough approximation to the cost curve would be as follows:

$$C = c_t n + \frac{c_t}{12} nm$$

In this function, c_t is the cost of selecting a tray, and $c_t/12$ is the cost of selecting an account. With this information and the estimated variances, it was possible to determine the optimum value for m by use of the Lagrange multiplier technique.[7] Let

$$S_t^2 = \frac{\sum_{k=1}^{n} (\bar{y}_k - r\bar{x}_k)^2}{n - 1}$$

$$S_a^2 = \sum^{n} (s_{ky}^2 + r s_{kx}^2 - 2r s_{kyx})$$

$$K = nm$$

Then:

$$V(\hat{Y}_R) = \frac{N^2 S_t^2}{n} - NS_t^2 + \frac{NS_a^2}{K} - \frac{NS_a^2}{Mn} + \lambda\left(C - c_t n - \frac{c_t K}{12}\right)$$

Differentiating with respect to n and K, and setting the derivatives equal to zero, we have

[7] Cochran, *op. cit.*, pp. 225–29.

$$-\frac{N^2S_t^2}{n^2}+\frac{NS_a^2}{Mn^2}=\lambda C_t$$

$$-\frac{NS_a^2}{K^2}=\lambda\frac{C_t}{12}$$

Therefore:

$$m=S_a\sqrt{\frac{12M}{MNS_t^2-S_a^2}}$$

In this particular case the value for m came out to be somewhat greater than 200, which was the total number of accounts per individual tray. The result indicates, then, that the whole tray should be taken as the sampling unit and that the minimum sampling error for a given sample size is obtained when the sampling unit is a whole tray. In a similar fashion the optimum subsample size for the mean per unit can be determined. In this case the optimum value for m again came out to be approximately equal to M, that is, 200. The effect of this outcome was to make the sample the equivalent of a random sample of the trays.

The next step was then to compare the resulting precision from each of the two estimates when the 75 trays were completely subsampled. The resulting precision of the total estimated allowance for uncollectibles was considerably better for the ratio estimate than for the mean per unit method. The standard error was $560 for the estimate based on the ratio estimate as against approximately $1,600 for the estimate based on the mean per unit. On the basis of these results, it was decided to use the ratio estimate for estimating the allowance for uncollectibles and to make the sample an unrestricted random sample of trays.

The precision of the estimated allowance of $140,000 resulting from the sample of 75 trays was about $1,100 at the 95 percent reliability level and $1,680 at the 99.73 percent level. The auditors, in reviewing these results, attempted to reconcile the statements of precision and reliability with their intuitive feelings about the problem. There was complete agreement among them that the estimated precision given by the past sample was unnecessarily tight at either level of reliability. The consensus was that a precision of $3,000 with a coefficient of reliability of 95 percent would equal or exceed the audit conception of reasonableness with respect to the estimate. It should be noted that one of the reasons the degree of precision could be relaxed is that the estimated allowance is only one of several factors which determine the final decision on the size of the allowance to be carried in the financial statements.

With the precision requirement given, it was then possible to compute the sample size necessary for the aging. The necessary sample size was determined to be nine trays. However, because of the difficulties of getting an accurate estimate of the variance with a sample size that small, it was decided to use a sample of 30 trays.[8]

[8] The question is immediately raised, of course, as to the validity of the formula for the variance of a ratio estimate with a sample of nine trays. The working rule is that the large-

In summary, approximately 6,000 accounts rather than 15,000 accounts would be selected for aging. The sample would be selected by choosing, with the aid of a table of random numbers, 30 trays. From this sample the allowance for uncollectibles can be estimated, and the estimate should have a precision of approximately $3,000 at the 95 percent confidence level.

This particular case is, of course, only one example of the role statistical techniques can play in management and audit problems. A number of extensions can easily be suggested. The confirmation of accounts receivable is an obvious area where sampling techniques can be applied. Estimation of such measures as product or departmental gross profit ratios and labor performance ratios are examples of other types of potential application. In the audit area the use of sampling in making the tests of transactions is both a challenging and an important extension.

In general, the auditor faces a mixture of problems in contrast to a straightforward business-optimizing decision. In assessing the internal control system of a firm, the auditor is performing an important role for management. At the same time the auditor is testing the internal control system for his own purposes, namely, to determine whether such a system could lead to accurate financial statements. For both objectives the use of statistical techniques can contribute significantly to both auditing and management through economical data collection and analysis. In addition, the use of statistical methods enables the auditor to make a precise statement as to what was actually achieved, in the sense of specifying confidence limits with a given probability level. The use of statistical techniques in this way makes the audit process itself more objective; and by using more objective methods, the auditor himself becomes more independent.

---

sample results may be used if the sample exceeds 30 and the coefficients of variation of x and y are both ≤ 0.10. Cf. Cochran, *op. cit.*, p. 114.

The necessity of jumping to a sample of 30 with the ratio estimate raises the question as to whether the alternative estimator might not be better despite the analysis for larger samples. Actually, the answer is twofold. First, when the sample size for the alternative method was determined to meet the required precision and reliability, the sample size was greater than 30. Second, it was desired to install a method of estimation which could be made uniform for a number of stores. Since the ratio estimate had proved more efficient in this case, it was desirable to use it on the assumption that it would also be preferable in the other cases.

7

The objective of this analysis is the determination of loss expectancy rates for various classes of receivables. A model is presented using a square matrix to describe the changes in classification of an account over a specified time period. Given this formulation, transition probabilities are derived for use in a Markov chain process. The Appendix provides five numerical examples which illustrate the principal results of the symbolic model.

ESTIMATION OF THE ALLOWANCE FOR DOUBTFUL ACCOUNTS BY MARKOV CHAINS*†

R. M. Cyert, H. J. Davidson, and G. L. Thompson

IN RETAIL ESTABLISHMENTS and in other businesses that commonly use the reserve method of accounting for bad debts, the estimation at fiscal year-end of the allowance for doubtful accounts[1] has a direct and often significant effect on income. The allowance, which represents the estimated amount of receivable balances which will ultimately prove uncollectible, is estimated. The difference between the estimated allowance and the allowance on the books is taken into income via a charge or credit to bad debt expense. Where a significant portion of a firm's assets are tied up in accounts receivable, the accurate estimation of the allowance for doubtful accounts assumes a special importance.

In most retail establishments the method of determining the allowance for doubtful accounts has historically been a two-step process. First, the accounts have been classified into age categories which reflect the stage of account delinquency—e.g., current accounts, accounts one month past due, accounts two months past due, and so forth. If the enterprise has a large number of accounts, the aging has been customarily performed on a sample basis and the

* Reprinted from *Management Science*, April, 1962, pp. 287–303.

† This research has been sponsored in part by Touche, Ross, Bailey and Smart. This paper was written as part of the contract "Planning and Control of the Industrial Operations" with the Office of Naval Research and the Bureau of Ships, at the Graduate School of Industrial Administration, Carnegie Institute of Technology.

[1] The reader may be more familiar with the allowance for doubtful accounts as the reserve for bad debts. The former terminology is preferred by the accounting profession.

frequency distribution of dollars, grouped according to age category, estimated from the sample for the total universe of accounts.

The second step in the process of estimating the allowance for doubtful accounts involves the application of "loss expectancy" rates to the dollars in each age group of the frequency distribution obtained by the sampling process. The loss expectancy rates are judgment estimates of the proportion of dollars in each age category liable to become uncollectible. In a sense, these loss expectancy rates are "policy parameters," for they are not only based on past experience but are also functions of such things as the firm's expectations of economic conditions, the firm's conservatism in financial policy, and other similar factors.

Investigation of more accurate and efficient methods of estimating the allowance for doubtful accounts was begun in the early 1950's by R. M. Cyert and Robert M. Trueblood.[2] At this time, studies were confined primarily to investigation of more efficient methods of performing the first step in the estimation procedure: determining the age distribution of accounts. In particular, the applicability of statistical sampling techniques was evaluated. A number of retail establishments now use scientific sampling methods to perform the first step in the estimation of the allowance for doubtful accounts.

As a continuation of research, the second phase of the allowance estimation problem was a logical area for investigation. While it did not seem likely that all of the judgment factors involved in the setting of loss expectancy rates could be eliminated, it did appear feasible to develop a scientific approach to determining these rates. Accordingly, research into this problem was initiated. This paper discusses a method which has been developed. In addition, some of the managerial implications of the method are discussed.

MODEL DEVELOPMENT

Before describing the methods which have been developed for estimating loss expectancy rates, it will be helpful to define the allowance for doubtful accounts. *The allowance for doubtful accounts at any point in time is the dollar amount (estimated) of accounts receivable at that point in time which will, in the future, prove to be uncollectible.* For example, on December 31, 1960, the XYZ Department Store might have $4 million of accounts receivable. If each of these $4 million were followed subsequently, one would find that a fraction of the dollars would eventually be repaid; a small number of dollars, say $40,000, would never be repaid. In this situation a perfect estimate of the reserve for doubtful accounts as of December 31, 1960, would be $40,000.

From this description of the allowance for doubtful accounts, it may be noted that a loss process is involved. Our approach to developing a method of estimating loss expectancy rates and the allowance has been through development of a model describing this loss process.

---

[2] R. M. Cyert and Robert M. Trueblood, "Statistical Sampling Techniques in the Aging of Accounts Receivable in a Department Store," *Management Science*, January, 1957, pp. 185–95.

Consider a balance of accounts receivable at time i. The dollars of this balance can be classified then, or at any subsequent time, into each of n age categories.[3] For a balance of receivables at time i, let

B_0 = Dollars of receivables which are zero periods or payments past due (current)
B_1 = Dollars of receivables which are one period or payment past due
.
.
.
B_j = Dollars of receivables which are j periods or payments past due
.
.
.
B_{n-1} = Dollars of receivables which are $n - 1$ periods or payments past due
B_n = Dollars of receivables which are *n or more* periods or payments past due

These classifications correspond to the customary classifications used in aging. B_0 is the dollar amount in the current age category, B_1 the dollar amount in the one-month past-due category, and so forth. B_n corresponds to the aging classification commonly called the "bad debt" category. A delinquent account may be repaid eventually; however, it is customary accounting procedure to lump all accounts more than some fixed number of periods or payments past due into a bad debt category.

Consider now a balance of receivables as of time i, at the next later time period $i + 1$. At time $i + 1$ the balance at time i can be classified in two ways, according to the age category from which it came and according to the age category where it now is. In general, we will let B_{jk} equal the balance in category k at time $i + 1$ which came from category j at time i.

Using this two-way classification, we must make one modification to account, at time $i + 1$, for all the receivables at time i. Another "age" category must be added to those categories previously described. This category, which we will denote by the subscript $\bar{0}$, corresponds to a "paid" classification. Dollars in any age category at time i may move to category $\bar{0}$ as well as to categories 0 to n at time $i + 1$.

Using this system of classification, a balance of receivables at time i can, in general, be described by an $n + 2$ square matrix, B. The individual entries, B_{jk}, equal the amount of the balance in category j at time i which moves to category k at time $i + 1$:

$$B = \begin{bmatrix} B_{\bar{0}\bar{0}} & \cdots & B_{\bar{0}k} & \cdots & B_{\bar{0}n} \\ \cdot & & \cdot & & \cdot \\ B_{j\bar{0}} & \cdots & B_{jk} & \cdots & B_{jn} \\ \cdot & & \cdot & & \cdot \\ B_{n\bar{0}} & \cdots & B_{nk} & \cdots & B_{nn} \end{bmatrix}$$

[3] The number of age categories will vary in practice. The last category will depend upon the rules for "writing off" accounts. The data in Exhibit 1 (p. 100) and Exhibit 2 (p. 101) are taken from a store which classifies the accounts as bad debts when the dollars pass out of age category 6.

From this $n + 2$ matrix of balances, B, it is possible to develop an $n + 2$ matrix of transition probabilities, P. The transition probability entries in this matrix, P, measure the likelihood that dollars in a particular category will move to another category during the applicable period of time. An implicit assumption is that this transition probability is measured over the same period of time that is used for the classification of accounts receivable.

In general, the transition probability, P_{jk}, will be defined as the probability of a dollar in classification j at time i transiting to classification k at time $i + 1$. In terms of the balance matrix entries, B_{jk}, the transition probabilities, P_{jk}, are defined:

$$P_{jk} = \frac{B_{jk}}{\sum_{\bar{0}}^{n} B_{js}} \qquad (k = \bar{0}, 0, 1, \cdots, n)$$

As applied to the movement of receivables balances, several special characteristics of the matrix of transition probabilities may be noted. First, any dollar amount entering the $\bar{0}$ (paid) category cannot transit to another category but must remain in the paid category. It follows that $P_{\bar{0}\bar{0}} = 1$, $P_{\bar{0}0} = 0$, $P_{\bar{0}1} = 0, \cdots, P_{\bar{0}k} = 0, \cdots, P_{\bar{0}n} = 0$. A second special characteristic involves the bad debt classification. It is assumed in our model that any amount reaching the bad debt classification remains in this classification.[4] Thus:

$$P_{n\bar{0}} = 0,\ P_{n0} = 0,\ P_{n1} = 0, \cdots, P_{nn} = 1$$

Note that many of the probabilities in the P matrix are zero or small. The number of zero entries that occur will depend upon the aging method employed. There are two general approaches that are used in aging. In one—the total balance method—all dollars in the account balance are put in the age category corresponding to the oldest dollar. Hence a current purchase charge by a customer with a five-month past-due balance would be classified in the five-month age category. The "partial balance" method, which is the second approach, allocates the dollar balance of an account among the age categories on the basis of the age of each of the dollars. Under either method an amount in age classification j at time i cannot move beyond age classification $j + 1$ at time $i + 1$. Thus, all entries in the diagonals above the one beginning with P_{12} will be zero.

The calculation of transition probabilities and the resulting matrix of transition probabilities as prepared from a random sample of approximately 1,000 department store accounts is illustrated in Exhibit 1 and Exhibit 2.

---

[4] In practice, some accounts are repaid after reaching the bad debt category. This does not materially affect the realistic nature of the model. First, the bad debt category may be selected so that the prospect of subsequent recovery is small. Second, the model treatment corresponds to common accounting treatment; i.e., accounts are written off on reaching a specified age category, and recoveries are treated as separate transactions.

EXHIBIT 1

DOLLAR MOVEMENT AND TRANSITION PROBABILITIES

Age Movement		*October–November, 1959*		*November–December, 1959*		*Combined*	
From	*To*	*Dollars*	*Probability*	*Dollars*	*Probability*	*Dollars*	*Probability*
0	0̄	$ 9,608	0.194	$11,623	0.228	$ 21,232	0.211
0	0	33,769	0.682	33,112	0.648	66,881	0.665
0	1	6,173	0.124	6,358	0.124	12,530	0.124
Total........		$49,550	1.000	$51,093	1.000	$100,643	1.000
1	0̄	$ 2,107	0.141	$ 2,002	0.125	$ 4,108	0.133
1	0	2,827	0.189	2,965	0.186	5,792	0.187
1	1	6,576	0.440	7,070	0.443	13,646	0.442
1	2	3,434	0.230	3,923	0.246	7,356	0.238
1	3						
1	4						
Total........		$14,944	1.000	$15,960	1.000	$ 30,902	1.000
2	0̄	$ 1,583	0.117	$ 1,701	0.138	$ 3,284	0.127
2	0	1,121	0.083	958	0.078	2,079	0.081
2	1	2,054	0.152	3,116	0.254	5,170	0.200
2	2	5,315	0.394	4,026	0.328	9,341	0.362
2	3	3,422	0.254	2,492	0.202	5,913	0.230
Total........		$13,495	1.000	$12,293	1.000	$ 25,787	1.000
3	0̄	$ 788	0.101	$ 732	0.094	$ 1,520	0.098
3	0	82	0.011	123	0.016	210	0.014
3	1	210	0.027	493	0.064	704	0.045
3	2	1,731	0.222	867	0.112	2,598	0.167
3	3	1,879	0.241	2,617	0.334	4,497	0.288
3	4	3,109	0.398	2,928	0.380	6,037	0.388
Total........		$ 7,799	1.000	$ 7,760	1.000	$ 15,566	1.000
4	0̄	$ 590	0.189	$ 416	0.101	$ 1,005	0.138
4	0	2	0.001	169	0.041	170	0.024
4	1	....	.....	....	.....	....	.....
4	2	376	0.120	297	0.072	674	0.093
4	3	600	0.192	800	0.195	1,400	0.194
4	4	1,068	0.342	1,905	0.464	2,972	0.411
4	5	488	0.156	517	0.126	1,005	0.140
4	6						
Total........		$ 3,124	1.000	$ 4,103	1.000	$ 7,226	1.000
5	0̄	$ 355	0.110	$ 268	0.069	$ 623	0.087
5	0	55	0.017			55	0.008
5	1	43	0.013	88	0.023	131	0.018
5	2			91	0.023	91	0.013
5	3	624	0.193	91	0.023	715	0.100
5	4	261	0.081	592	0.153	853	0.120
5	5	1,739	0.538	1,601	0.413	3,340	0.470
5	6	158	0.049	1,148	0.296	1,306	0.184
Total........		$ 3,234	1.000	$ 3,879	1.000	$ 7,114	1.000

To complete the description of the model, two assumptions that are made must be noted. First, it is assumed that the matrix of transition probabilities is constant over time and independent of the initial age distribution of account balances. The empirical validity of this assumption is discussed in more detail in a later section. Second, it is assumed that all accounts are the same size when the "total balance" method of aging is used. This assumption is necessary because it is not the individual dollars which move but rather all of the dollars in the account. Thus a skewed distribution of account balances could distort the limiting probabilities. Empirically, this assumption is troublesome. However, the difficulty can be handled by stratifying balances on the basis of size and making the estimate of the limiting probabilities on

EXHIBIT 2

MATRIX OF TRANSITION PROBABILITIES (P)

To / *From*	*Paid* ($\bar{0}$)	*Current* (*0*)	*Months Past Due* *1* (*1*)	*2* (*2*)	*3* (*3*)	*4* (*4*)	*5* (*5*)	*6: Bad Debt* (*6*)
($\bar{0}$)........	1.00	0.00	0.00	0.00	0.00	0.00	0.00	0.00
(0)........	0.21	0.67	0.12	0.00	0.00	0.00	0.00	0.00
(1)........	0.13	0.19	0.44	0.24	0.00	0.00	0.00	0.00
(2)........	0.13	0.08	0.20	0.36	0.23	0.00	0.00	0.00
(3)........	0.10	0.01	0.04	0.17	0.29	0.39	0.00	0.00
(4)........	0.14	0.02	0.00	0.09	0.20	0.41	0.14	0.00
(5)........	0.09	0.01	0.02	0.01	0.10	0.12	0.47	0.18
(6)........	0.00	0.00	0.00	0.00	0.00	0.00	0.00	1.00

this basis. Still another, and perhaps simpler, way of avoiding this assumption would be to follow the transitions of accounts rather than account balances. The assumption does not need to be made when the "partial balance" method of aging is used.

THE MODEL AS A MARKOV CHAIN PROCESS

The model as previously described can be recognized as a Markov chain process with $n + 2$ states and transition matrix given by P. Moreover, since there are two absorbing states (the collection state $\bar{0}$ and the bad debt state n), and since, from every nonabsorbing state, it is possible to reach one of these two absorbing states, we see that the process is a Markov chain with two absorbing states.[5] We shall make use of certain known results from Markov chain theory, and also derive some additional results. These will be interpreted in terms of the accounts receivable problem.

[5] John G. Kemeny and J. Laurie Snell, *Finite Markov Chains* (New York: D. Van Nostrand Co., Inc., 1959), p. 35.

There are three questions that can be answered by the use of Markov chain theory:

1. Suppose that at a given time, i, there are certain amounts in each of the various age classifications. We know that if the process is permitted to continue indefinitely, all of these dollars will end up in either the paid state, 0, or the bad debts state, n. What fraction of the total dollars involved will end up in each of these states?

2. Suppose a retail establishment receives c new dollars (charge sales) in its accounts each period. These c dollars enter distributed in the various age categories. If c new dollars are received in this manner each period, what will be the steady-state distribution of receivables by age category?

3. Suppose a retail establishment receives c_i new dollars (charge sales) in its accounts each period. The amount of new dollars, c_i, and the distribution of the dollars among the age categories varies cyclically. The amounts, c_i, may also be affected by a growth trend. If c_i new dollars are received in this manner each period, what will be the distribution of receivables by age category at the end of any period?

RESULTS AND INTERPRETATION

In the following discussion, we shall adopt the notation of Kemeny and Snell.[6] The transition matrix, P, is square with $n + 2$ rows and columns. Reorder the states so that the first state is the absorbing (paid) state, 0; the second state is the absorbing (bad debt) state, n; and the remaining transient states are the age categories $0, 1, \cdots, n - 1$. The matrix P can be partitioned:

$$P = \left[\begin{array}{c|c} I & O \\ \hline R & Q \end{array}\right]$$

I is the 2×2 identity matrix; O is a $2 \times n$ zero matrix; R is a $n \times 2$ matrix; and Q is an $n \times n$ matrix

$$N = (1 - Q)^{-1} = I + Q + Q^2 + Q^3 + \cdots + Q^k + \cdots$$

exists and is called the *fundamental matrix* of the absorbing Markov chain.

The entries of the $n \times 2$ matrix, NR, give the probabilities of absorption in each of the absorbing states, 0 and n.[7] The entries in the first column give the probabilities of dollars in each of the age categories being paid; the second column gives the probabilities of becoming bad debts. These entries in the second column correspond to the loss expectancy rates now developed on a judgment basis by most retail establishments.

As noted above, Markov chain theory provides an estimate of loss expectancy rates; however, its results are more general. A direct estimate of the allowance for doubtful accounts and the variance of this estimate can also be

[6] *Ibid.* See especially chap. iii.

[7] *Ibid.*, pp. 52–53.

obtained. First, we must define some matrix operations. If A is any matrix, let A_{sq} be the matrix obtained by squaring each entry in A; let A_{rt} be the matrix obtained by taking the square root of each entry in A.

Suppose that at time i the n-component vector

$$B_i = (B_{i0}, B_{i1}, \cdots, B_{i,n-1})$$

gives the dollars in each age category. Let b be the sum of all these amounts, the total value of accounts receivable. The vector, $\pi = (1/b)B$, is a probability vector with nonnegative components whose sum is one. The components of the vector represent the fraction of total accounts receivable in each age category. If we assume that the movement of small blocks of the dollars in each of these age categories is independent, then we can regard the vector π as being the initial vector for the Markov chain.

The following theorem can be proved. (NOTE: In an Appendix (p. 110), we work out numerical examples of the formulas to be derived. The reader may wish to read the Appendix in parallel with the text.)

Theorem 1

The entries of the two-component vector, BNR, give the expected payments and bad debts resulting from the accounts receivable vector, B. The components of

$$A = b[\pi NR - (\pi NR)_{sq}] \tag{1}$$

give the variances of payments and bad debts. The components of A_{rt} give the standard deviations of these same amounts.

Proof. As previously noted, the components of the first column of the matrix, NR, give the probabilities of a dollar moving from each of the transient states to the absorbing (paid) state. The components of the vector, $\pi = (1/b)B$, give the initial probabilities of a dollar moving to each of the transient states each time the process is started. Hence the probability of a dollar ending in the paid state is given by the first component of the vector, πNR. If the process is started b times, the mean number of dollars ending in the paid state is the first component of $b\pi NR = BNR$. The first component of the vector, πNR, is the mean value of a function, f, that takes a value of one when a dollar ends in the paid state and otherwise takes on value zero. The variance of this function is given by the first component of

$$V(f) = M(f^2) - [M(f)]^2$$

Since $f^2 = f$, then $M(f^2) = M(f)$, and hence the variance of f is given by the first component of $\pi NR - (\pi NR)_{sq}$. If the process is started b times, the variance of the total amount in the paid state is given by the first component of formula 1. The analysis for the bad debt state is similar.

The reader may note the similarity of the mean and variance of the above function with the corresponding formulas for a binomial distribution. Theorem 1 thus gives the answer to the first question posed.[8] Note also that the variances of the two components of BNR are equal.

At this point, we turn to the second question, the prediction of the steady-state age distribution of receivable balances. Suppose that c dollars of new receivables are received each period and that these dollars are distributed among the different categories as indicated by the components of the vector:

$$C = (C_0, C_1, \cdots, C_{n-1})$$

Define the vector, $\eta = (1/c)C$. The vector η is a probability vector and can be regarded as the initial vector for the Markov chain. Suppose the Markov process is started c times each period with the initial vector η. What is the steady-state distribution of receivable balances, and what are the variances of these balances? We may also inquire as to the amount each period of expected payments and bad debts, and their respective variances.

Theorem 2

If the Markov chain process is started c times each period with the initial vector η, the components of the vector, CN, give the steady-state receivable balances in each age category. The number $CN\xi$ (where ξ is an n-component column vector with all entries one) gives the steady-state value for the total accounts receivable balance. The two-component vector, CNR, gives steady-state values for payments and bad debts each time period.

Proof. If the process described has run for many periods, the amount in the various states will consist of η from new receivables, ηQ from new receivables of the previous month, ηQ^2 from new receivables of two months past, and so forth. The sum of all these is

$$\begin{aligned} \eta + \eta Q + \eta Q^2 + \eta Q^3 + \cdots &= \eta(1 + Q + Q^2 + Q^3 + \cdots) \\ &= \eta N \end{aligned}$$

---

[8] Mr. Yuji Ijiri has kindly pointed out to us that the present value of the accounts receivable can be computed in a similar manner as follows. If b is the interest rate, let $\beta = 1/(1 + b)$ be the discount factor. Then, if B is the accounts receivables vector and R_1 is the first column of the matrix R, we can expect collections of BR_1 during the present time period; BQR_1 from the next time period, when it will be worth only βBQR_1, etc.; and in the $(k + 1)$ time period, we expect BQ^kR_1, when it will be worth $\beta^kBQ^kR_1$, etc. Adding these discounted values together, we get as the present value of the accounts receivables

$$\begin{aligned} BR_1 + \beta BQR_1 + \cdots + \beta^kBQ\mathrm{R}_1 + \cdots &= B[I + \beta Q + \cdots + \beta^kQ^k + \cdots]R_1 \\ &= BN_\beta R_1 \end{aligned}$$

where we have set $N_\beta = I + \beta Q + \cdots + \beta^kQ^k + \cdots$.

Most department stores follow the *a* practice of charging interest on certain kinds of accounts. Exactly the same kind of reasoning can be used to compute the present value of these accounts with the interest charge added. Thus, if b is the interest charged the customer and we set $\beta = 1 + b$, then the formula just given will compute the present value of these accounts. Of course, if we both discount and charge interest on future payments, then there will be either a net discount factor or a net interest factor; and again the same formula —namely, $BN_\beta R_1$—will give the present value, where β is the net discount or interest factor.

If this process is started c times each period, accounts receivable balances in each of the states are given by the vector $c\eta N = CN$.

If ξ is a column vector with unitary components, $CN\xi$ is the sum of the components of the vector, CN, and represents the total balance of accounts receivable.

If the process has run for many periods, there will be ηR dollars absorbed from the new receivables of the first period, ηQR absorbed from the new receivables of last month, ηQ^2R from the new receivables of two months past, and so forth. The sum of these is

$$\eta R + \eta QR + \eta Q^2R + \cdots = \eta(1 + Q + Q^2 + \cdots)R$$
$$= \eta NR$$

If the process is started c times, steady-state payments and bad debts each period are given by $c\eta NR = CNR$. This completes the proof of the theorem.

Combining theorems 1 and 2, we get the following corollary.

Corollary

Let $t = CN\xi$ and $\pi = (1/t)CN$; then, CN^2R and $t[\pi NR - (\pi NR)_{sq}]$ are the predicted mean and variance of collections and bad debts.

Note that this prediction is made by using the new charges to estimate the accounts receivable.[9]

Let us call a *repetitive Markov chain* the process in which we start off a Markov chain a number of times each period and follow all of these until absorption. Then, theorem 2 shows that the mean number of dollars in each transient state is the same as the expected number of times a nonrepetitive Markov chain will be in each transient state. However, as we will see in theorem 3, the variances of two quantities will not be the same.

Theorem 3

The variances for the quantities in theorem 2 are given by the formulas

$$V = c[\eta N - \sum_{k=0}^{\infty} (\eta Q^k)_{sq}] \tag{2}$$

$$v = c[\eta N\xi - \sum_{k=0}^{\infty} (\eta Q^k\xi)_{sq}] \tag{3}$$

$$W = c[\eta NR - \sum_{k=0}^{\infty} (\eta Q^kR)_{sq}] \tag{4}$$

where formula 2 gives the variances of the components of CN, formula 3 gives the variances of the components of $CN\xi$, and formula 4 gives the variances of

[9] Combining theorem 2 with the result of n. 8, we find $CNN_\beta R_1$ to be the estimated value of the steady-state accounts receivables.

the components of CNR. The standard deviations are of course given by the square roots of these quantities, V_{rt}, v_{rt}, and W_{rt}, respectively.

Proof. The proofs of these assertions involve the rearrangement of absolutely convergent series and are all very similar. We give the details of formula 2 only. If η is the starting vector of new charges made in the current month and c new dollars are charged, then the variance vector of amounts of new charges in each age category is given by $c[\eta - \eta_{sq}]$, by reasoning similar to the proof of formula 1. Similarly, the variance vector of charges carried over from last month is given by $c[\eta Q - (\eta Q)_{sq}]$, and those carried from the month before are given by $c[\eta Q^2 - (\eta Q^2)_{sq}]$, etc. Adding up these quantities, we get

$$\begin{aligned} V &= c[\eta - \eta_{sq} + \eta Q - (\eta Q)_{sq} + \eta Q^2 - (\eta Q^2)_{sq} + \cdots] \\ &= c[(\eta + \eta Q + \eta Q^2 + \cdots) - (\eta_{sq} + (\eta Q)_{sq} + (\eta Q^2)_{sq} + \cdots)] \\ &= c[\eta N - (\eta Q)_{sq} + (\eta Q^2)_{sq} + \cdots)] \end{aligned}$$

which is formula 2.

Note that the variances of the two components of CNR are equal.

Formulas 2–4 involve unsummed series. Lower-bound estimates for them can be made by taking a few terms of each series. It is also possible to find upper-bound formulas for these quantities that may be useful for computation. These are given in the next theorem.

Theorem 4

Let $N^* = (I - Q_{sq})^{-1}$; then the variances given in theorem 3 may be estimated by the following upper bounds:

$$V \leq c[\eta N - \eta_{sq} N^*] \tag{5}$$

$$v \leq V\xi \leq c[\eta N - \eta_{sq} N^*]\xi \tag{6}$$

$$W \leq c[\eta NR - \eta_{sq} N^* R_{sq}] \tag{7}$$

Proof. Let A, B, and C be nonnegative matrices with C a square matrix and such that the product ACB is defined. Then

$$(AC^kB)_{sq} \geq A_{sq}(C^k)_{sq}B_{sq} \geq A_{sq}(C_{sq})^k B_{sq} \tag{8}$$

These inequalities are established by noting that a given expression is obtained from the one on its immediate left by ignoring certain nonnegative cross-product terms. To prove formula 5, we note that, using formula 8:

$$\begin{aligned} -(\eta_{sq} + (\eta Q)_{sq} + (\eta Q^2)_{sq} + \cdots) &\leq -\eta_{sq}(I + Q_{sq} + (Q^2)_{sq} + \cdots) \\ &\leq -\eta_{sq}(I + Q_{sq} + (Q_{sq})^2 + \cdots) \\ &= -\eta_{sq} N^* \end{aligned}$$

The proofs of formulas 6 and 7 are similar.

CYCLICAL MONTHLY INPUTS

The results of theorems 2, 3, and 4 were based on the assumption that the monthly input of dollars, c, was constant. In most retail establishments, however, the monthly input—charge sales—follows a cyclical pattern, with peaks at Christmas, Easter, and the opening of schools in autumn. In addition, yearly sales of a company may expand or contract due to growth, inflation, and so forth. Here, we consider the effect on the model of introducing these considerations.

To be specific, let C_i be the vector of new charges at a given month i; let c_i be the total amount of new charges; let $\eta_i = (1/c_i)C_i$ be the ith probability starting vector; we assume that

$$\eta_{i-T} = \eta_i \tag{9}$$

$$C_{i-T} = \alpha C_i \tag{10}$$

where α is the reciprocal of the growth factor. [For example, if the business expands at the rate of 2 percent a year, then $\alpha = 1/(1 + 0.02) = 1/1.02$.] The length of the cycle period is T, where in the department store case $T = 12$, typically. Note that formulas 9 and 10 imply $c_{i-T} = \alpha c_i$. Let us answer question 2 again under these assumptions.

Recall that a repetitive Markov chain is an ordinary Markov chain that is started off the same number of times each period, always with the same initial vector. By a *cyclic repetitive Markov chain*, we shall mean a repetitive Markov chain in which the number of times the process is started and the initial vectors used vary in a cyclic pattern. Thus, formulas 9 and 10 define a cyclic repetitive Markov chain in which the pattern repeats every T periods. We shall generalize the results for repetitive Markov chains to those for cyclic repetitive Markov chains.

Theorem 5

Let $N_\alpha = (I - \alpha Q^T)^{-1}$; then the entries of

$$A_i = \left[\sum_{k=0}^{T-1} C_{i-k}Q^k\right]N_\alpha \tag{11}$$

$$a_i = \left[\sum_{k=0}^{T-1} C_{i-k}Q^k\right]N_\alpha\xi \tag{12}$$

$$D_i = \left[\sum_{k=0}^{T-1} C_{i-k}Q^k\right]N_\alpha R \tag{13}$$

give for month i the expected amounts in the various age categories (formula 11), the expected total accounts receivable (formula 12), and the expected collections and bad debts (formula 13).

Proof. Let $C_i, C_{i-1}, \cdots, C_{i-T+1}$ be the actual new charges in the ith month and in the preceding $T - 1$ months. By means of formula 10, we can deduce, knowing the expansion rate, all charges for earlier months as well. From the ith month, we can expect C_i to be the charges to the various age categories; from the $(i - 1)$ month, we can expect $C_{i-1}Q$; from C_{i-2}, we can expect $C_{i-2}Q^2$, etc.; from C_{i-T+1}, we can expect $C_{i-T+1}Q^{T-1}$; from $C_{i-T} = \alpha C_i$, we expect $\alpha C_i Q^T$, etc. Adding together these vectors, we obtain

$$\begin{aligned} A_i &= C_i + C_{i-1}Q + C_{i-2}Q^2 + \cdots + C_{i-T+1}Q^{T-1} \\ &\quad + \alpha C_i Q^T + \alpha C_{i-1}Q^{T+1} + \cdots + \alpha C_{i-T+1}Q^{2T-1} \\ &\quad + \alpha^2 C_i Q^{2T} + \alpha^2 C_{i-1}Q^{2T+1} + \cdots + \alpha^2 C_{i-T+1}Q^{3T-1} + \cdots \\ &= C_i(I + \alpha Q^T + \alpha^2 Q^{2T} + \cdots) + C_{i-1}Q(I + \alpha Q^T + \alpha^2 Q^{2T} + \cdots) \\ &\quad + \cdots + C_{i-T+1}Q^{T+1}(I + \alpha Q^T + \alpha^2 Q^{2T} + \cdots) \\ &= [C_i + C_{i-1}Q + C_{i-2}Q^2 + \cdots + C_{i-T+1}Q^{T-1}]N_\alpha \end{aligned}$$

which is formula 11. Formulas 12 and 13 are established similarly.

Note that these estimates for the ith month depend on the new charges in the ith and preceding $T - 1$ months. It is not surprising that this should give a more accurate prediction than the one given by theorem 2. Also, note that if Q^n goes to zero rapidly, it may be possible to use only the new charges in the last few months to obtain a reasonably accurate estimate.

Corollary

Combining theorems 1 and 5, we find $A_i NR$ and $a_i[\tau_i NR - (\tau_i NR)_{sq}]$, where $a_i = A_i\xi$ and $\tau_i = (1/a_i)A_i$, as the mean and variance estimates of the collections and bad debts[10] that will result from the accounts receivable existing at time i.

Theorem 6

Let $N_\alpha{}^* = (I - \alpha Q^T_{sq})^{-1}$; then the entries of

$$\begin{aligned} V[A_i] &= A_i - \sum_{k=0}^{T-1} c_{i-k}\left[\sum_{h=0}^{\infty} \alpha^h(\eta_{i-k}Q^{Th+k})_{sq}\right] \\ &\le A_i - \left[\sum_{k=0}^{T-1} c_{i-k}(\eta_{i-k})_{sq}(Q_{sq})^k\right]N_\alpha{}^* \end{aligned} \tag{14}$$

$$\begin{aligned} V[a_i] &= a_i - \sum_{k=0}^{T-1} c_{i-k}\left[\sum_{h=0}^{\infty} \alpha^h(\eta_{i-k}Q^{Th+k}\xi)_{sq}\right] \\ &\le a_i - \left[\sum_{k=0}^{T-1} c_{i-k}(\eta_{i-k})_{sq}(Q_{sq})^k\right]N_\alpha{}^*\xi \end{aligned} \tag{15}$$

$$\begin{aligned} V[D_i] &= D_i - \sum_{k=0}^{T-1} c_{i-k}\left[\sum_{h=0}^{\infty} \alpha^h(\eta_{i-k}Q^{Th+k}R)_{sq}\right] \\ &\le D_i - \left[\sum_{k=0}^{T-1} c_{i-k}(\eta_{i-k})_{sq}(Q_{sq})^k\right]N_\alpha{}^*R_{sq} \end{aligned} \tag{16}$$

give the variance and variance estimates for the corresponding quantities in theorem 5.

[10] Continuing the results of nn. 8 and 9, we find $A_iN_\beta R_1$ as the estimated present value of the accounts receivable at time i.

We shall not give proofs for these formulas since no new ideas beyond those used in the proofs of theorems 3 and 4 are involved. Note that formulas 14–16 generalize formulas 2–4 and 5–7.

The amount of work needed to use the formulas for cyclic repetitive Markov chains is more than that for repetitive chains, largely due to the fact that more data are being utilized. How much more accurate the new formulas are than the old we do not know at present. However, we plan to make tests on real data in the near future.

SUMMARY

Direct Results

In the preceding sections, we have developed a model describing the behavior of accounts receivable balances. Given a matrix of transition probabilities, P, and given a vector of new sales (either constant or variable by period), the following results may be obtained:

1. Estimated loss expectancy rates by age category
2. The estimated allowance for doubtful accounts
3. The steady-state age distribution of accounts receivable
4. Variances for the estimates described in 2 and 3 above
5. Generalization of the above results to the cyclic case

All of these results are useful in managing and in accounting for accounts receivable.

The Constant P Matrix Assumption

The results enumerated above are subject to the assumption, stated earlier, that the matrix of transition probabilities is constant over time. We do not of course expect this assumption to be perfectly true. There may well be cyclical changes in transition probabilities, just as there are cyclical changes in sales of most retail assumptions. The validity of the constant transition probability assumption will depend on the magnitude of these changes. Empirical investigation of the actual changes in transition probabilities and their effect on model results is currently under way.

The primary problems associated with changing transition probabilities would seem to be one of estimation. If these probabilities change, however, it seems likely that they change as a function of changes in business activity. It may be possible to predict the changes in transition probabilities, if any, by correlation with indices of local economic conditions.

Indirect Results

As noted earlier, research leading to development of the model described was initiated with the aim of estimating loss expectancy rates. Gratifyingly, the formal results obtained go beyond this initially limited aim. More importantly, perhaps, the informal results of the approach developed are believed to be of value. These informal results stem from the fact that the transition probability–Markov chain description of accounts receivable behavior provides a valuable insight into better methods of managing accounts receivable.

Accounts receivable management in most retail establishments is a major problem. Typically, accounts receivable are the most important single asset in the balance sheet of many retail firms. The overall control of this asset by means of credit policy continually poses questions. Should credit terms be tightened and a more active collection policy be pursued? Should credit restrictions be relaxed in order to stimulate sales?

To aid in arriving at a decision on these matters, a variety of statistics are used by retail establishments to reflect current economic conditions and the overall status of accounts receivable. Many stores rely heavily upon collection data in various forms: ratios to sales, accounts receivable balances, previous months' collections, and so forth. Some stores rely on the comparison of annual aging results and, in many instances, supplement annual aging data with agings on a monthly basis. Bad debt write-offs and any subsequent recoveries are followed closely. Periodic service charge income, which is related to accounts receivable outstanding, is also used as an overall measure of credit conditions.

All of these measures have some value as indices of the current behavior of accounts receivable. None, however, seem to provide the comprehensive picture of accounts receivable behavior that is provided by the matrix of transition probabilities and allied model results. This indirect use of model results—the use of transition probabilities for management information for accounts receivable control—promises to be as fruitful as the use of results directly obtainable from the model.

The techniques of this paper are obviously applicable to many other kinds of problems. Such problems can be characterized as "inventory" problems in which we consider items produced and stored in inventory. Eventually, the items leave the inventory either by being "sold" or by "spoiling." Any class of items that is perishable or otherwise subject to obsolescence can be so studied. Examples of such goods are metal coins, automobiles, produce, photographic film, employees, style goods (dresses, etc.), canned goods, etc. The reader will doubtless think of other possibilities.

APPENDIX

To illustrate the computation of the formulas derived in the paper, we shall work out several variants of a simple problem. Suppose $n = 2$—i.e., accounts two periods old—are declared bad debts. Suppose the transition matrix is

$$P = \begin{array}{c} \\ \bar{0} \\ 2 \\ 0 \\ 1 \end{array} \begin{array}{c} \begin{array}{cccc} \bar{0} & 2 & 0 & 1 \end{array} \\ \begin{pmatrix} 1 & 0 & 0 & 0 \\ 0 & 1 & 0 & 0 \\ 0.3 & 0 & 0.5 & 0.2 \\ 0.5 & 0.1 & 0.3 & 0.1 \end{pmatrix} \end{array}$$

where we have already arranged the states so that the absorbing states appear first. From the matrix, we see that

$$R = \begin{pmatrix} 0.3 & 0 \\ 0.5 & 0.1 \end{pmatrix}$$

and

$$Q = \begin{pmatrix} 0.5 & 0.2 \\ 0.3 & 0.1 \end{pmatrix}$$

From Q, we can obtain

$$N = (I - Q)^{-1} = \begin{pmatrix} 0.5 & -0.2 \\ -0.3 & 0.9 \end{pmatrix}^{-1} = \begin{pmatrix} 2.31 & 0.51 \\ 0.77 & 1.28 \end{pmatrix}$$

$$NR = \begin{pmatrix} 0.95 & 0.05 \\ 0.87 & 0.13 \end{pmatrix}$$

A. To illustrate theorem 1, we assume $B = (70, 30)$ to be the accounts receivable vector; then

$$BNR = (70, 30) \begin{pmatrix} 0.95 & 0.05 \\ 0.87 & 0.13 \end{pmatrix} = (92.6, 7.4)$$

The variances of each component are equal to

$$100\,[0.926 - (0.926)^2] = 6.2$$

which makes the standard deviation equal to 2.5. Hence, of the \$100 accounts receivable, we expect to collect 92.6 and to lose 7.4 to bad debts. If, for safety, we wanted to reserve one standard deviation more than the expected bad debts, we would set aside $7.4 + 2.5 = 9.9$ as the reserve for bad debts.

B. To illustrate present value calculations, suppose that the period in question is a six-month interval and that we discount accounts 3 percent per period. Then, $BN_\beta R_1$ can be calculated as follows:

$$B = 1/1.03 = 0.97$$

$$N_\beta = (I - \beta Q)^{-1} = \begin{pmatrix} 0.515 & -0.194 \\ -0.281 & 0.903 \end{pmatrix}^{-1} = \begin{pmatrix} 2.19 & 0.47 \\ 0.68 & 1.25 \end{pmatrix}$$

so that

$$BN_\beta R_1 = (70, 30) \begin{pmatrix} 2.19 & 0.47 \\ 0.68 & 1.25 \end{pmatrix} \begin{pmatrix} 0.3 \\ 0.5 \end{pmatrix} = 87.3$$

and we see that the expected collections of 93.2 have a present value of 87.3.

Suppose the retail establishment charges a 9 percent service charge per half year on its accounts and discounts them at 3 percent per half year, leaving a net interest charge of 6 percent per half year. Then, $\beta = 1.06$ and

$$N_\beta = (I - \beta Q)^{-1} = \begin{pmatrix} 0.470 & -0.212 \\ -0.318 & 0.894 \end{pmatrix}^{-1} = \begin{pmatrix} 2.53 & 0.60 \\ 0.90 & 1.34 \end{pmatrix}$$

so that

$$BN_\beta R_1 = (70, 30) \begin{pmatrix} 0.253 & 0.60 \\ 0.90 & 1.34 \end{pmatrix} \begin{pmatrix} 0.3 \\ 0.5 \end{pmatrix} = 102.4$$

is the present discounted value of the accounts receivable.

C. To illustrate theorem 2 and its corollary, suppose $C = (40, 10)$ is the steady-state vector of new charges; then

$$CN = (40, 10) \begin{pmatrix} 2.31 & 0.51 \\ 0.77 & 1.28 \end{pmatrix} = (100.1, 33.2)$$

gives the steady-state amounts in each of the receivable age categories. Also

$$CNR = (100.1, 33.2) \begin{pmatrix} 0.3 & 0 \\ 0.5 & 0.1 \end{pmatrix} = (46.7, 3.3)$$

are the steady-state average collections and bad debts per period.

To estimate the eventual collections and bad debts from a given period's accounts receivable (which total 133.3), we compute

$$CN^2R = (CN)(NR) = (100.1, 33.2) \begin{pmatrix} 0.95 & 0.05 \\ 0.87 & 0.13 \end{pmatrix} = (124.0, 9.4)$$

The variances of each of these quantities are 9.32, which gives standard deviations of 3.05. We leave present value calculations to the reader.

D. To illustrate theorems 3 and 4, we compute

$$N^* = (I - Q_{sq})^{-1} = \begin{pmatrix} 0.75 & -0.04 \\ -0.09 & 0.99 \end{pmatrix}^{-1} = \begin{pmatrix} 1.36 & 0.055 \\ 0.124 & 1.03 \end{pmatrix}$$

$$\eta = (0.8, 0.2)$$

$$\eta N = (0.8, 0.2) \begin{pmatrix} 2.31 & 0.51 \\ 0.77 & 1.28 \end{pmatrix} = (2.00, 0.664)$$

$$\eta NR = (2.00, 0.664) \begin{pmatrix} 0.3 & 0 \\ 0.5 & 0.1 \end{pmatrix} = (0.932, 0.07)$$

$$\eta_{sq} N^* = (0.64, 0.04) \begin{pmatrix} 1.36 & 0.055 \\ 0.124 & 1.03 \end{pmatrix} = (0.875, 0.076)$$

$$\eta_{sq} N^* R_{sq} = (0.875, 0.076) \begin{pmatrix} 0.09 & 0 \\ 0.25 & 0.01 \end{pmatrix} = (0.098, 0.001)$$

so that

$$\begin{aligned} V &\leq 50[(2.00, 0.664) - (0.88, 0.076)] = (55.6, 29.3) \\ v &\leq 84.9 \\ W &\leq 50[(0.932, 0.07) - (0.098, 0.001)] = (41.7, 3.5) \end{aligned}$$

By computing a few terms of the exact formulas for these variances, it was found that the above variance estimates were about 5 percent larger than the true value.

E. To illustrate the cyclical case, assume that $T = 2$ and $\alpha = 1/1.02$ (i.e., the growth rate is 2 percent per year). Then

$$\alpha Q^2 = \begin{pmatrix} 0.316 & 0.122 \\ 0.184 & 0.071 \end{pmatrix}$$

$$N_\alpha = (I - \alpha Q^2)^{-1} = \begin{pmatrix} 0.684 & -0.122 \\ -0.184 & 0.929 \end{pmatrix}^{-1} = \begin{pmatrix} 1.51 & 0.199 \\ 0.30 & 1.11 \end{pmatrix}$$

Suppose $C_0 = (35, 15)$ and $C_1 = (40, 10)$. Then

$$\begin{aligned} C_0 + C_1 Q &= (35, 15) + (40, 10) \begin{pmatrix} 0.5 & 0.2 \\ 0.3 & 0.1 \end{pmatrix} \\ &= (58, 24) \end{aligned}$$

and

$$\begin{aligned} A_i &= (58, 24) \begin{pmatrix} 1.51 & 0.199 \\ 0.30 & 1.11 \end{pmatrix} = (94.8, 38.2) \\ a_i &= 133 \\ D_i &= (94.8, 38.2) \begin{pmatrix} 0.3 & 0 \\ 0.5 & 0.1 \end{pmatrix} = (47.5, 3.82) \end{aligned}$$

We omit variance and present value calculations for this example.

8

The author cites several sources of error in traditional indices used for Lifo inventory calculations; he concludes that modern sampling techniques provide a reliable, economical alternative means of measurement and control of the Lifo inventory. An illustrative case is provided in which accounting and statistical considerations are outlined. Operations specifically discussed include the sampling approach, sample experimentation, and the selection of a sample. Results of the sampling application are then presented and evaluated.

*APPLICATION OF STATISTICAL SAMPLING TECHNIQUES TO LIFO INVENTORY VALUATION**†

Barry M. Rowles

THE PRIMARY OBJECTIVE of the program described in this paper is to produce, through statistical sampling methods, accurate estimates of current physical inventories valued in terms of base year costs. These estimates may be used either directly in Lifo inventory computations, or they may be used to substantiate or to control base year cost inventory valuations. Other objectives, mentioned at the end of this paper, will not be discussed unless they relate directly to the inventory valuation program.

In spite of the many controversies which have flared around Lifo inventory valuation during the past decade, one important phase has received comparatively little attention from users or their public accountants. The underlying principle of Lifo, valuing inventory on a base cost system for book and tax purposes, has been largely dependent upon indexes relating current to base year costs. In many cases, these index methods of valuing inventory at base

* Reprinted from *Accounting Review*, April, 1954, pp. 244–50.

† The author is indebted to D. Rosenblatt of American University and to W. W. Cooper of Carnegie Institute of Technology for their instruction and guidance while consultants to this program. R. M. Trueblood and R. W. Johnson of the firm of Touche, Niven, Bailey and Smart actively participated in the program's inception and development.

This paper was presented informally at the Conference on Modern Statistical Methods in Business and Industry, Carnegie Institute of Technology, on May 1, 1953. It has been incorporated as one of the case studies in a paper, "The Use of Statistics in Accounting Control," given by R. M. Trueblood at the 1953 NACA annual meeting in Los Angeles.

year costs (including total-count techniques) are unnecessarily expensive. What is more important, they are frequently used, whatever their source, without explicit consideration of their accuracy or the consequences of inaccuracy. They are extremely critical in the Lifo computations, since if they contain even small amounts of error or bias, the Lifo elector's income and tax figures can be significantly distorted.

The Internal Revenue Service's stated policy concerning Lifo price indexes in relation to retail accounting is this:

> Any price indices must be based upon sound statistical principles of construction and upon adequate records to be kept available for examination by the Bureau . . . indices may be prepared by an individual taxpayer based upon his own data on prices and inventory quantities, if adequate, and if proof is submitted that sound statistical methods have been employed that assure reliable indices, not only for the particular year in question, but for subsequent years.[1]

In actual practice, these indexes are usually obtained either from a Lifo user's own inventory data, using total-count pricing procedures, or from a published price index series such as those compiled by the U.S. Bureau of Labor Statistics. These sources may or may not conform to the foregoing statement of policy, depending upon the IRS's definition of "sound statistical methods" and "adequate" data on prices and inventory quantities. Under certain conditions, which very frequently exist, however, these sources will produce indexes containing various types and degrees of error. Furthermore, these errors can be of sufficient magnitude to disqualify the indexes under professional statistical and accounting standards vigorously applied.

The possible errors contained in indexes computed on the basis of data from the total economy stem from two factors. One, an index computed from total industry data, may not properly reflect either the price level or the inventory mix of any given member of the industry. Even if the national index were extremely accurate, it should not be used without some assurance that it is within a defined range of what the user's actual Lifo price index would be if it were computed. This point is equally valid in the cases where national indexes have been computed specifically for Lifo computation purposes.[2]

The second possible source of error in national indexes lies in the statistical methods generally used to obtain them. It is difficult, if not impossible, to objectively evaluate the degree of control of bias and error in these indexes because of the lack of published evidence and accompanying measurements.

Internally computed Lifo price indexes present problems of their own, particularly when the inventory on Lifo is large and heterogeneous and when its mix fluctuates over time. If total-count pricing procedures are used, the indexes are theoretically free from error and completely satisfactory. In

---

[1] Mimeograph 6244 (IR Cum. Bull. 1948–1), referring to the use of Lifo by taxpayers using the retail inventory method.

[2] For an excellent example of how a particular Lifo user's indexes can deviate from indexes computed on a national scale, see *Hutzler Bros. Co.*, 8 Tax Court 14 (1947).

actuality, pricing or computing errors may exist in the indexes because of the sheer size of the inventory, the appearance of new items, lack of base year cost data, lack of capable personnel, or the usual year-end time restrictions. The pricing error effect could be magnified over time and could be cumulative.

If internally computed Lifo price indexes are built up on a cumulative chain basis, the possibility of product mix bias exists. This bias occurs because of shifts in the mix of an inventory containing elements with different current-to-base cost ratios. The bias can be in either direction and can reverse itself, so that the chain indexes can be either higher or lower than the true Lifo price index would be at any given time. However, because the mix shifts which cause the bias are frequently consistent in nature and direction over a period of several years, the bias effect may become increasingly pronounced.

For the foregoing reasons, it is as unwise as it is illogical to assume that either national indexes or internally computed indexes are completely accurate. Therefore an effort should be made to measure and control the amount of error involved. This point becomes reinforced when it is realized that the use of modern statistical methods may yield improved quality and increased control at reduced cost when compared to other methods. Traditionalism does not provide adequate justification for the continued use of these other methods when a more satisfactory alternative is available.

These considerations underlie the statistical installation discussed in this paper. The company concerned is a large manufacturer and supplier of various types of machinery and equipment. A section of its inventory valued at over $17 million in current costs, and including about 250,000 items in over 100 different locations, was covered by the program. This inventory has been valued on a Lifo basis for book and tax purposes for several years.

CONCLUSIONS

In summary, it can be said that it has been substantiated, on the basis of this first attempt, that the objections to present methods of valuing inventory in base costs can be effectively overcome through sampling techniques. In addition, several inventory control methods are made possible that would otherwise be difficult to obtain.

Carried out at the company level, the sampling is performed on the actual inventory for which a base cost valuation estimate is desired. Thus the problems encountered in national indexes are eliminated from consideration.

The problems of internally computed indexes are difficult but also surmountable. Base-pricing difficulties, including errors, can be attacked once the amount of the base pricing is reduced by sampling methods. In this program, for example, a subsampling system was set up to check the quality of the base prices being used on the sample elements and the extent of clerical error in the calculation. In this fashion, error control and correction factors were obtained for application as desired. Initially, the base pricing involved in the sampling program covered about 25 percent of the items included in the usual total-count amount. By refinement of the procedures, this figure has been reduced to about 4 percent for future inventory-sampling purposes.

Calculation and control of sampling and other errors is undertaken, and it follows that estimates can be made as precise and reliable as desired. A method of balancing costs and benefits is thus provided as a basis for rational decisions by both the firm and the tax authorities. This will provide indexes which can be audited in two senses: The clerical computations can be repeated and the same results obtained, and the procedures can be followed to the point of drawing a new and independent sample and computing another index, which will fall, with a stated probability, within a given range of the true Lifo index.

Where chain indexes are used, the constant possibility of bias due to product mix variations can be watched and existing bias determined and controlled.

By a slight extension, such a sampling program offers the user important collateral advantages. He can accurately and economically compute Lifo inventory valuation at interim points—e.g. quarterly—during each year. For a large, complex inventory, such calculations may not be feasible or economical under total-count base pricing or chain index methods. Such valuations are important for resolving questions of voluntary and involuntary liquidations prior to the year-end, as well as for many other accounting and management purposes.

ACCOUNTING CONSIDERATIONS

Company terminology which will be used in describing the program is defined as follows:

A *product class* is a homogeneous group of items, the basic classification in the inventory accounting system. The inventory covered in this study contained over 30 product classes. Each product class may contain up to 3,500 items; and theoretically, each item can appear in each of over 100 branches.

A *branch* is a sales outlet holding inventory composed of various items. No single branch in the company would stock all of the items in any one product class at any one time.

The Lifo price index which was taken as the standard of comparison in this program is defined as

1. An index which relates the user's current physical inventory valued in terms of current costs to the same inventory valued in terms of base year costs, that is, a pure price index with the same current quantity weights used in the denominator and in the numerator.
2. An index free from pricing, clerical, or other errors.

This index would be the most desirable for use in the index method of Lifo valuation because of its accuracy and its strict conformation with Lifo inventory accounting principles, but it is frequently difficult to obtain in practice. National indexes and internally computed chain indexes are often regarded as administratively convenient approximations of it. Although the IRS is becoming more liberal in its attitude toward Lifo as time passes, this same passing of time from "base year" increases the probability of significant error in the above approximation methods. This error may have serious tax implications and should be measured and controlled. Once a case of inadequate base valuation computing techniques has set in, with or without the complication of increasingly inaccurate base prices, retroactive correction can be difficult even if legally possible.

The general question of the acceptability of such a sampling program to the IRS will undoubtedly and properly be raised. As yet, this question cannot be positively answered, but the statement of IRS policy for department store Lifo indexes given previously is concise.

It seems reasonable to assume that Lifo indexes used by firms not on the retail inventory method should also qualify under that policy statement. In any event, a sound statistical approach to the Lifo inventory problem could not logically be rejected. Such an approach provides consistent index accuracy over time, without danger of cumulative bias, through the measuring and control of clerical, costing, and sampling errors.

STATISTICAL CONSIDERATIONS

This section of the paper is concerned with details of the program's installation, with particular attention directed to the statistical techniques used. Data from the program will be used for examples wherever possible, consistent with space limitations and the degree of generality intended. In all cases, details of formula derivations have been omitted, but it is hoped that no loss of significance will result since most of the statistical techniques are contained in generally available literature.

Considerations Prior to Beginning Sampling Experimentation

Before beginning to consider sample designs, it was essential to establish a solid foundation upon which the program could be built. Initial attention was devoted to the precision[3] required in the estimates that would be derived from the sampling program, considering the effect of error in these estimates upon the resulting Lifo inventory valuation. Actually, this precision determination evolved, subject to change, as cost and error considerations were more thoroughly explored with program progress. Because of possible transmission of errors to other accounts, it is unwise to freeze such a decision on a once-and-for-all basis in any accounting program.

[3] For a simple definition, see Trueblood, *op. cit.* For a more explicit definition, see E. L. Kohler, *A Dictionary for Accountants* (Englewood Cliffs, N.J.: Prentice-Hall, Inc., 1952).

The initial phase of this program was concerned with a single section of the inventory, comprising about $11 million at Lifo valuation. After consideration of the various factors involved, the desired precision of the overall estimate of the inventory valued in base-year costs was set at about 1 percent with a reliability[4] of 95 percent. The underlying structure of the inventory was such that to achieve this precision in the overall estimate, it was apparently necessary to design for a precision of 4 percent at the product class level (product classes were considered to be strata[5] within the inventory universe).

The next step was the layout of the universe "frame"[6] from records and reports as they existed at the most recent physical inventory date. Wherever possible, the frame was laid out in terms of the basic inventory units: the items within product classes. This frame was set up primarily for sampling experimentation; as a general principle, such an experimental frame should allow access to the smallest units obtainable, since combination of units into larger aggregates may reduce the number of alternate statistical methods that might be explored. Such a reduction of alternatives may force the temporary use of needlessly inefficient methods until further detail can be acquired by sampling methods or otherwise.

The distribution of inventory dollar value at the item level, across different product classes and across different stores, was examined at this point preparatory to beginning experimentation. The frame provided the data to which a standard statistical technique known as the analysis of variance was applied. Marked skewness was found in the distribution of dollar value at the first three levels of aggregation: (1) the distribution among items from the inventory in one product class held in one branch; (2) the distribution among branch inventory totals in each product class; (3) the distribution among entire branch totals or among entire product class totals. The coefficient of variation[7]—the ratio of the standard deviation to the mean—was consistently high at each of the above levels, ranging from about 1 to 1.7.

Since much of the information obtained during this phase of the program was to be used in sample design and size computations later on, universe variances and means were obtained wherever feasible, rather than sample estimates of them. It became increasingly obvious during these investigations that the program would require adaptation and development of existing statistical methods.

As a final step in this initial investigation, a group of several product classes (strata) was selected which had distribution and variance characteristics that were representative of the total inventory. Various sample designs were tested on these product classes, which represented about 25 percent of the total inventory for which a base cost valuation estimate was desired.

---

[4] *Ibid.*

[5] *Ibid.*

[6] *Ibid.*

[7] *Ibid.*

General Sampling Approach

Various methods of sample estimation could have been used in connection with the sample designs considered. These ranged from regression estimates (least squares) to ratio estimates, where the ratios were composed of current and base year cost valuations. Each method had advantages and disadvantages. Regression estimates, for example, are at least as efficient as ratio estimates[8] but are more cumbersome. The ratio estimate was selected as the preferred approach for three reasons:

1. The form of the ratio estimate is identical to that of the Lifo price indexes historically used, which has definite psychological advantages.
2. The superior efficiency of the regression estimate effectively disappears when the regression line nearly passes through the origin, which it does in this case.
3. The ratio estimate is easier to compute.

Sampling Experimentation

After the selection of an area of the inventory for sample design experimentation, a variety of sample designs were applied, samples drawn, estimates formed, and errors of these estimates ascertained. Current cost inventory data were used for this experimentation, rather than base year cost data. This provided an additional margin of safety, since it was verified that the inventory generally exhibited higher variance in current cost terms. This resulted from the fact that the characteristic price movements since the base year have been upward at varying rates for different items. Therefore, any sample size determinations made on the basis of current cost valuation variances would be more than adequate for use on base cost data.

The following comparisons were made between the various designs:

1. Efficiency, defined as sample size necessary to obtain an estimate of the current cost valuation of each product class with a precision of 4 percent at 95 percent reliability.
2. Stability over time, measured by the precision of estimates when the same sampling plans were applied to inventory data over a period of years.
3. Administrative difficulty of computing errors of estimates, considering time and type of personnel required if the computations were to be done on a monthly basis.
4. Flexibility of the designs, as indicated by the ease with which the resulting samples could be supplemented or the extent to which the designs could be efficiently applied to related areas of analysis such as sales data. Because of time limitations, this flexibility had to be determined primarily through judgment rather than through computations, except for a few applications of designs to sales data.

---

[8] See W. G. Cochran, *Sampling Techniques* (New York: John Wiley& Sons, Inc., 1953), pp. 148–49.

As a result of this experimentation, it was determined that unrestricted random sampling[9] and systematic sampling[10] were inefficient. Various methods of stratified random sampling were definitely better, but these still resulted in up to 50 percent samples to obtain the precision and reliability desired.

The sample design ultimately selected was developed specifically for the program[11] and was essentially a nonindependent stratified sample. Previous inventory data, branch inventory totals within each product class, were ranked and stratified; the strata were then placed side by side, forming clusters of branch-by-product class totals. An unrestricted random sample of these clusters was drawn from each product class. This design is characterized by relatively high efficiency, stability, ease of computations for sample-size determination and later estimates, and the possibility of simple supplementations.

Sample Selection

The determination of total sample size in a survey to be run in coordination with a regular accounting function such as inventory taking involves careful consideration of the timing of related operations, in addition to the purely statistical aspects such as variances and cost factors. A total sample size of 25 percent of the items in the inventory was determined to be necessary on the basis of the above considerations and computations. This was larger than desired, primarily because aggregative inventory units had to be selected initially. After the initial sampling was completed, it was possible to reduce the total sample size to 4 percent of the items in the inventory. This sample size is expected to be sufficient for future surveys.

The 25 percent sample was drawn and priced in terms of both current and base year costs via the regular inventory-pricing procedure but with special priorities to speed the return of the information.

Other Features of the Program

In this program, certain special sample designs were set up to run concurrently with the regular survey, covering inventory areas of particular interest; this included areas exhibiting historic instability, or those for which certain hypotheses were to be tested—e.g., similarity of price movement in comparison with the total inventory.

To determine the extent of base costing error in the total sample, a subsample was drawn systematically (for administrative convenience), and for this subsample the base costs were independently checked. By this device,

[9] See Kohler, *op. cit.*

[10] *Ibid.*

[11] This design was conceived and developed by D. Rosenblatt.

correction factors were obtained which, if significant, could have been applied to the final estimate of the base cost valuation. Alternatively, the check could have been used as a quality control method, since portions of the inventory sample with a high probability of possessing base costing errors in excess of some predetermined level could have been rejected and base-costed again.

As a test, and to meet time limitations, one section of the sample was base-costed by using regression formulas[12] computed from base and current cost information already received for similar material. Provision was made to verify these estimated base costs by actually performing the costing on a subsampling basis at a later date.

Results of the Sample Survey

The final computations of sample estimates for the total inventory covered by this program were:

1. Estimate of current cost valuation derived from sample data = $17,567,000.
   Precision of above estimate at 95 percent reliability = 0.96 of 1 percent.
2. Estimate of base year cost valuation derived from sample data = $11,072,000.
   Precision of above estimate at 95 percent reliability = 0.98 of 1 percent.
3. Ratio, or index of current-to-base valuations = $\frac{\$17,567,000}{\$11,072,000} = 158.66\%$.
   Precision of above index at 95 percent reliability = 0.253 of 1 percent.
4. Although the estimate of base year cost valuation in item 2 could be used directly in the Lifo calculations, it is possible to improve upon this estimate. If the index in item 3 is divided into the actual total current cost valuation, obtained from the year-end physical inventory, the resulting figure is a better estimate of the base year cost valuation. This estimate will have the same precision and reliability as the index, or:
   Ratio or index estimate of base year cost valuation = $17,672,000 ÷ 158.66% = $11,138,000.
   Precision of above estimate at 95 percent reliability = 0.253 of 1 percent, which is an increase in precision of 0.727 percent with the same reliability.

With the initial survey completed and the total sample size for future surveys reduced by subsampling, the usual "mopping-up" operations are completed at this writing. Permanent reporting, recording, and computation systems have been established to keep the program on a continuing basis, which includes monthly indexes of inventory cost.

Provision has been made for redesign and supplementation of the program's sampling plans as necessary, to keep them consistently reliable. This will assure the future integrity of the program, which is to be used as a springboard to other fruitful areas for statistical sampling. Inventory control as well as inventory valuation, sales and cost analyses, and predictions offer inviting prospects which are now being explored.

---

[12] See A. Wald, "The Fitting of Straight Lines if Both Variables Are Subject to Error," *Annals of Mathematical Statistics*, September, 1940.

9

In brief outline the chief accounting considerations and advantages of group depreciation are presented in this article; the importance of bias in estimation errors is accented. A Markov process model is then presented which provides for the calculation of accumulated depreciation at any given point in time, and which also yields reliable information relative to the economic life of assets for use in studies in capital budgeting, maintenance, etc.

*STATISTICAL ATTRIBUTES OF GROUP DEPRECIATION**

Zenon S. Zannetos

THE DISTINCTION between unit versus group depreciation is based on the definition of the depreciable entity. If each unit is kept in a separate account and depreciated by itself, then the process is called the unit depreciation method. If, on the other hand, a lot of similar assets are included in one account and depreciation is taken on the total cost of the group, then we have group depreciation. In effect, the mechanics of group depreciation are based on the notion of the statistical average of the lives of the various items included in the account and ignore each and every particular item's life.

Some people further classify depreciation methods on the basis of the definition of the term *similar assets*. If the grouped assets are similar with respect to purpose (use) but not necessarily with respect to expected life and nature, then they define this type of depreciation as composite depreciation. These people reserve the term *group depreciation* for assets that are not only similar with respect to purpose (or use) but are also homogeneous with respect to generic classification—for example, trucks, electrical motors, steam turbines, and utility poles.

This discussion will be concerned with the last-mentioned category (assets that are similar with respect to life, use, and nature) and those groups of assets that have similar lives and similar end uses even though they may not belong to the same generic classification.

One of the acknowledged advantages of group depreciation is that it saves clerical work. While under the unit depreciation method one has to calculate separate charges for each individual asset, under group depreciation one

* Reprinted from *Accounting Review*, October, 1962, pp. 713–20. The author wishes to thank his colleagues Myron J. Gordon, Otto H. Poensgen, and Andrew C. Stedry for their comments. He is also grateful to the School of Industrial Management at Massachusetts Institute of Technology for the use of its 1620 computer for several empirical tests and to Harvey Wilson for writing the program that he used.

lation is made on the basis of the sum total of all the assets included in the p. Furthermore, the retirement of assets depreciated as a group is simpler, no loss or gain on retirement is recognized. In the past, because most of the calculations were either manual or mechanical, savings of this nature were significant. Today, however, with modern electronic data processing systems, this advantage has been reduced extensively, computational cost included. So one has to look for other justifications of group depreciation.

In my estimation, the major advantages of group depreciation have not been in the area of clerical savings. Much more important is the predictive value that a statistical average of a group of units provides. To the extent that the accountant must project himself into the future in order to decide on the appropriate economic life, the actual life of any particular unit may be different from the estimated because of

1. Errors in estimates
2. Quality differences among otherwise identical units of assets
3. Technological obsolescence
4. Any combination of the above

While no one can claim that group depreciation will eliminate errors in the estimated life of any particular unit, it is well known that the statistical variance of the average life of all units in a group (squared deviations from the expected life of all similar units in the universe) decreases proportionately with the size of the group. Consequently, the probability of a given size of error in the life of a group of assets is much smaller than it is in the case of an individual unit. For the same reasons the probability that the actual life will deviate by a given amount from the expected life because of stochastic quality differences, is greater in the case of any particular asset unit than it is for a group of units with similar expected lives. In the case of technological obsolescence, again the grouping of assets into one depreciable classification offers advantages in terms of deviations from the expected life, as long as there exists stability (predictability) in the impact of technological obsolescence on the life of the assets in the particular statistical universe. The assumption that the impact of technological obsolescence on the economic life of assets can be predicted does not seem to be overly restrictive because, either by nature or through pressure, innovation seems to be perpetuated within certain firms or industries. If, as is occasionally the case, obsolescence is a function (parabolic or hyperbolic) of the degree of maturity of the firm or industry, still the changes in life-spans caused by obsolescence may be predicted; and furthermore, they would be small between the life-spans of successive assets.

At this point, one may wonder as to whether "control" may not be lost if one concentrates on a group of assets rather than on the individual units. Of course, this is not so! Because controllability implies that there exists stability in the universe, which stability is manifested in terms of expected values and not in terms of particular observations. Consequently, it does not make any sense to take each and every observation in isolation, measure its deviation from the estimated mean and then erase the "memory" by closing this difference to the profit and loss statement. No one is justified in concluding that something is wrong (out of control) and taking action on the outcome of one comparison, because no matter how large the deviation, there is a probability, however small, that the observation and the mean come from the same universe. In other words, a deviation from an estimate does not necessarily imply that the estimate is wrong. Deviations are to be expected under probabilistic conditions because this is the meaning of an estimate or expected value under uncertainty.

In contrast to what we have just expounded, we know that the mean of a sample is an unbiased estimator[1] of the mean of the universe; therefore, group depreciation offers opportunities for storing the information—deviations of particular observations from the estimated mean—that is necessary for testing whether the actual and estimated means are the same. We must also note in this context that if stability does not exist in the particular universe, then we have no rational way of predicting what the future holds in store for us, and consequently cannot even classify anything on an *ex ante* basis.

The use of the group depreciation method, however, offers not only advantages but also vexing problems. The latter are manifested if the actual life of the group proves to be different than the estimate on which depreciation is being calculated. While under- or overestimation of economic lives of assets is not a unique characteristic of group depreciation, the mechanics of group depreciation, as we will shortly show, tend to compound the errors if these errors are biased in any one direction. Consequently, unless surveys are made periodically for determining the remaining economic life of the equipment in the group, there is a danger of either having insufficient balance in the allowance for depreciation for absorbing the retirement of assets or else depreciating a new acquisition over a small fraction of its estimated life if the total group is very close to being fully depreciated. For example, let us suppose that at the end of a particular year, say 19X0, a group asset account depreciated on a straight line basis at 10 percent per year appears as follows:

Equipment	1,000,000	
Less: Depreciation to date	900,000	100,000

Let us further assume that a new asset or group of assets is acquired for \$50,000 at the beginning of the following year. At the end of 19X1 the asset account will be:

Equipment	1,050,000	
Less: Depreciation to date	1,005,000	45,000

As the above example indicates, if the old assets are not retired in 19X2, then the company will succeed in depreciating in less than two years a new asset with a life of 10 years. The opposite results, of course, will be manifested if the group is depreciated on the basis of an exaggerated estimated life.

[1] We say that X is an unbiased estimator of Y if the expected value of X is Y.

The impact of the aforementioned shortcomings of group depreciation on balance sheets and income statements is all too obvious to merit any extensive elaboration. No doubt, it can be shown that the value of group depreciation for managerial decisions is by far greater than any disadvantages that emanate from "honest" balance sheet misrepresentations. This is not meant to diminish the importance of balance sheet data, however imperfect the latter may be. Conscious misrepresentations of balance sheets are deplorable, and unconscious ones undesirable if they can be avoided without excessive costs. Luckily, however, we do not have to make a choice between the statistical advantages of group depreciation and erroneous balance sheet data. Troubles such as the one illustrated here will arise only in cases where the information generated by the group depreciation method is not used properly.

The purpose of this note is to suggest a way for reaping the advantage offered by the group depreciation method while at the same time avoiding its pitfalls. In the process, it will become obvious that group depreciation not only could provide meaningful data for determining the life and allowance for depreciation of assets in a particular group, but it could also aid in capital budgets and forecasts and raise some very poignant questions. If the latter are investigated, management is likely to get an invaluable experience in estimation and statistical inference and knowledge of the impact of obsolescence on assets.

By using a finite Markov chain[2] with an empirically derived transition probability matrix, one can calculate at any moment of time the amount of depreciation allowance that reflects the statistical value of cost expirations. Furthermore, in the process of deriving the transition probability matrix, a lot of information can be obtained on the peculiarities of the various factors that affect the economic life of assets, information that is of great value to managerial planning and control.

MARKOV PROCESS MODEL

The assets of a firm can be grouped in different ways, depending on the purpose and viewpoint. In the following, we choose a classification based upon the remaining economic life of the assets.

Let A_j represent the total dollars of assets that have j years of life remaining at the end of a time period. The values of j go from zero to n. By utilizing double subscripts, we can identify the dollar amounts of assets that move from one classification to another. In notation $A_{i,j}$, we denote the assets (in dollars) that made the transition from group i to group j during one time time period (from the last time of aging of the assets to now).

Proceeding in the above-mentioned way, we will eventually complete the entries in an $n + 1$ square matrix A as follows:

[2] For a treatise on this subject, see John G. Kemeny and J. Laurie Snell, *Finite Markov Chains* (Princeton: D. Van Nostrand Co., Inc., 1960).

From/To:

$$A = \begin{array}{c} \\ S_0 \\ S_1 \\ \vdots \\ S_n \end{array} \begin{array}{c} \begin{array}{cccc} S_0 & S_1 & \cdots & S_n \end{array} \\ \begin{pmatrix} A_{0,0} & A_{0,1} & \cdots & A_{0,n} \\ A_{1,0} & A_{1,1} & \cdots & A_{1,n} \\ \vdots & & & \\ A_{n,0} & A_{n,1} & \cdots & A_{n,n} \end{pmatrix} \end{array}$$

To repeat, an entry in the above matrix A represents the assets that made the transition from the classification indicated by the first subscript to the classification shown by the second. For example, entry $A_{n,n-1}$ gives the dollar total of assets that were new at the beginning of the period and became a year old or, alternatively, had $n - 1$ years of life remaining a period later. Age here is determined by *economic* and not physical life. The entry $A_{k,0}$ represents the asset dollars that had k years of life remaining at the beginning of the year but by the end of the year became uneconomical and had to be retired. The various S_i's represent the "states" or classifications into which the assets fall, the subscripts indicating the years of economic life remaining in the assets.

If we now assume that the above entries are representative[3] of the factors (obsolescence, mechanical defects, errors) that exercise influence on the economic lives of the assets in a group, we can develop the matrix P of the "transition probabilities" that describe the process. A transition probability gives the likelihood of assets (in dollars) moving from one classification to another. In our notation, $P_{i,j}$ denotes the probability that one dollar of assets will move from classification i, where it is at the beginning of the period, to classification j at the end. These probabilities are:

$$P_{i,j} = \frac{A_{i,j}}{\sum_{k=0}^{n} A_{i,k}} \qquad i, j = 0, 1, \cdots, n$$

$$0 \leq P_{i,j} \leq 1 \quad \text{and} \quad \sum_{j=0}^{n} P_{i,j} = 1$$

Translated in everyday language, the transition probability $P_{i,j}$ represents the assets that had i years of life remaining at the beginning of the period *and* j *at the end*, as a fraction of all assets that had i years of economic life at the beginning of the period.

[3] One way of achieving better representation is by taking observations over a number of years (m). In that case the matrix A will be equal to

$$A = \sum_{t=1}^{m} A_t$$

and the entries

$$A_{i,j} = \sum_{t=1}^{m} (A_{i,j})_t$$

We will later have a little more to say about the general problem of estimation, however.

In case the assets in the group are not many and/or not distributed more or less uniformly with respect to age so as to allow a close estimation of $P_{i,j}$, one may accumulate data over time. Then, $P_{i,j}$ will become

$$P_{i,j} = \frac{\sum_{t=1}^{m} (A_{i,j})_t}{\sum_{t=1}^{m} \sum_{k=0}^{n} (A_{i,k})_t}$$

Under conditions of absolute certainty the transition probability matrix will have all ones in the diagonal immediately to the left of the main diagonal; $P_{0,0}$ will be equal to one; and all the other entries will be zero. In other words, under complete certainty, each asset will lose exactly one year of economic life at the end of each period, nothing more and nothing less. Under uncertainty, however, which is a fact of everyday life, most of the entries in the matrix P will be greater than or equal to zero and less than one. The entry $P_{0,0}$ will be equal to one, indicating that once an asset enters into this state (zero life remaining) the probability of getting out of this classification is zero. That is to say, upon reaching state S_0, the asset must be retired. This also implies that all the other entries $P_{0,j}$ for $j \neq 0$ in the remaining columns 1 to n of the transition probability matrix must be equal to zero, because

$$\sum_{j=0}^{n} P_{0,j} = 1$$

Any state S_i whose $P_{i,i} = 1$ is called an absorbing state. States that belong to a set whose members cannot be contacted by members of any other set are called transient states.[4] The transition probability matrix P will thus be

$$P = \begin{array}{c} \\ S_0 \\ S_1 \\ \cdot \\ \cdot \\ \cdot \\ S_n \end{array} \begin{array}{c} \begin{array}{cccc} S_0 & S_1 & \cdots & S_n \end{array} \\ \begin{pmatrix} 1 & 0 & \cdots & 0 \\ P_{1,0} & P_{1,1} & \cdots & P_{1,n} \\ \cdot & \cdot & \cdots & \\ \cdot & \cdot & \cdots & \\ \cdot & \cdot & \cdots & \\ P_{n,0} & P_{n,1} & \cdots & P_{n,n} \end{pmatrix} \end{array}$$

and its canonical form,[5]

$$P = \left(\begin{array}{c|c} I & 0 \\ \hline R & Q \end{array}\right)$$

[4] Since all states but S_0 are transient, the assets in every other state will eventually gravitate toward S_0 and thus be absorbed (retired).

[5] The notation used here is consistent with Kemeny and Snell, *op. cit.*

where I is the identity submatrix of dimension one, 0 is the zero submatrix, R is an n *by* 1 submatrix and includes the transition probabilities from the transient states to the absorbing state, and Q concerns the transition from transient states to other transient states and is of dimension $n \times n$.

Given that the firm's assets can be classified in terms of their remaining life, one can derive the initial input vector π_0. This is

$$\pi_0 = \frac{A_j}{\sum_{j=0}^{n} A_j}$$

where again A_j represents the total dollars of assets that have j years of life remaining. One can readily see that the input vector is nothing more than the distribution of the lives of assets at that moment of time.

The product $\pi_0 P$ gives us the input vector π_1 a period later, which represents the probability mass function[6] of the lives of the *initial assets* at the end of the first period, and the product

$$\sum_{j=0}^{n} A_j \pi_0 P$$

yields the dollar amounts of assets in the various age categories. If the matrix P is stable,[7] π_2 will be equal to $\pi_1 P$ or $\pi_0 P^2$. Consequently, the multiplication of π_0 by the various powers of P will yield the input matrices for later periods. For example:

$$\pi_k = \pi_0 P^k$$

will give us the probability mass function applicable to the *initial* group of assets at the end of the kth period, and

$$\sum_{j=0}^{n} A_j \pi_0 P^k$$

the respective dollar amounts of the original assets that will belong to the various age classifications at the end of the kth period. These results show that if for any asset group of i age we wish at any moment of time to determine the

---

[6] The probabilistic weights assigned to the lives of the assets. The term *probability mass function* is used rather than *probability distribution* because the function is discrete (not continuous).

[7] A matrix is stable if its entries can be predicted (probabilistically). In other words, the sample which the matrix represents is part of a universe whose matrix is invariant with respect to time. The long-run stability of matrix P is guaranteed by the stability of the universe of lives of assets from which our group is drawn. In the absence of such a stability in the universe the data will be useless for predictive purposes. In fact, if it were not for this stability, one would not be able to even classify newly acquired assets by age groups for depreciation purposes. So the assumption of stability is not in any sense overly restrictive. Adjustments in the empirical matrix P should be expected, however, in order to achieve better and better approximations to the universal transition probability matrix.

probabilistic mass function that describes the economic life of its members k years later, we can obtain it in the ith row of the kth power of the transition matrix P.

It can be easily shown that for an *initial* group of assets (before any additions or retirements take place) the allowance for depreciation that properly represents the accumulated expirations of economic lines at the end of year k is equal to:[8]

$$\left[\sum_{j=0}^{n} A_j(\pi_0 - \pi_k)N^T\right]\frac{1}{n} \quad \text{for} \quad k < n$$

where N^T is the transpose (or column form) of the vector of years $(0, 1, \ldots, n)$. The depreciation expense D_k for the kth year is

$$D_k = \left[\sum_{j=0}^{n} A_j(\pi_{k-1} - \pi_k)N^T\right]\frac{1}{n}$$
$$= \left[\sum_{j=0}^{n} A_j\pi_{k-1}(I - P)N^T\right]\frac{1}{n}$$

The above calculations are based on straight line depreciation, that is to say, on the assumption that years of life expiration are of equal value no matter where they occur in the course of the asset's use. By making the proper adjustments in the vector N^T, other methods can be generated.

Our previous discussion laid the foundation for the extension of the model to the most important case where the input vectors π_k change not only because of the changes in the age distribution within the initial group but also because of the acquisition and retirement of new and old assets. Even though we will no longer be able in this case to arrive at the various π_k's recursively (by multiplying π_0 with the various powers of P), as we did when dealing with an initial group of assets, the general formulation is still valid. Each new input vector will simply be obtained from the previous one, multiplied by P, and then adjusted for new acquisitions and retirements.

One can readily see that the depreciation expense as determined by the method suggested here (Markov chain method) may vary from year to year, depending on the components of the input vectors and the magnitude of the entries in the transition probability matrix. This is true whether the calculations are based on initial assets or assets as affected by subsequent acquisitions and retirements. The calculations, however, can be easily performed mechanically or electronically, so this is not a limitation in any sense. Furthermore, even under the traditional depreciation methods, the impact of acquisitions and retirements necessitates a recalculation at the end of each year.[9] If, however, new assets are acquired every year, and provided these are of the same

[8] The subtraction $(\pi_i - \pi_j)$ is an operation defined on vector components.

[9] Of course, with some of the so-called "accelerated depreciation" methods the mechanics may get very involved. Since the group depreciation method suppresses information on the lives of the particular units within the group, it is incompatible with the mechanics of the sum of the years' digits method.

dollar magnitude, then the age distribution of the total assets will after an initial number of years c approach a steady state, and the yearly depreciation charges will approach stability. This is so because the input vectors π_k, before any adjustments are made for retirements and new acquisitions, will all be equal to $\pi_c P$, and after the adjustments all equal to π_c. Consequently, the depreciation charges,[10] D_k, for any year $k > c$ (c being the number of years required for reaching asymptotic convergence) will be

$$D_k = \left[\sum_{j=0}^{n} A_j(\pi_k - \pi_{k+1})N^T \right] \frac{1}{n}$$

$$= \left[\sum_{j=0}^{n} A_j(\pi_c - \pi_c P)N^T \right] \frac{1}{n} \quad \text{for all} \quad k > c$$

$$= \left[\sum_{j=0}^{n} A_j \pi_c (I - P)N^T \right] \frac{1}{n}$$

which is invariant with respect to k for $k > c$. The rate of convergence which determines c is a function of the initial age distribution of the assets and the state distribution of the rows of the transition probability matrix.

Finally, a few words on estimation. While no one can claim that the process of estimation is an easy task, the difficulties are not insurmountable either. Let us take, for example, the expected number of years of economic life for a group of assets. Whether the initial estimate (on which the number n of states S_i is determined) is slightly high or low is not critical, because if the transition probabilities are established correctly and are representative, then the depreciation as determined by the method previously suggested will still be correct. Any over- or underestimation of the initial economic life will be washed out in the transition probabilities almost entirely.

In view of what we have just expressed in the previous paragraph concerning the relationship between the number of states S_i and the "actual" economic life, one may wonder how we can establish the expected life of assets. Such information is necessary for both *ex ante* and *ex post* capital-budgeting evaluations, and it is not difficult to obtain. One only has to establish the expected number of times the process is in each transient state having started from state S_n (new assets) and then add the resulting figures.

It can be shown[11] that the mean number of "years" the assets spend in any given transient state j, having originated in state i, is given by the respective entry in a matrix N, where

$$N = (I - Q)^{-1}$$

In the above relation, I is an identity matrix of dimension $n \times n$ in our case, and Q is the $n \times n$ submatrix of the transition probability matrix P (in canonical form). As the reader will recall, Q concerns the transition from the

[10] We assume here that the yearly acquisitions are all bought or start depreciating at the beginning of the period.

[11] For proof of the relationships that are presented here, see Kemeny and Snell, *op. cit.*, chap. iii.

transient states to other transient states. Having obtained the matrix N, if we then add the entries in the first row, we will have the expected life of assets in the group. In general, if we let $M_i(t)$ represent the mean number of steps (time t) that an asset has to take in order to reach from a transient state i to the absorbing state, then

$$M_i(t) = N\xi = (I - Q)^{-1}\xi$$

where ξ represents the summing operation of row entries. The variance of t is equal to

$$\text{Var}_i(t) = (2n - I)N\xi - N\xi_{sq}$$

The term $N\xi_{sq}$ stands for the entries of $N\xi$ squared.

The process of testing whether the entries of the transition probability matrix and subsequent observations come from the same universe—in other words, testing to determine whether the entries of matrix P are valid—can be carried out in one of two ways: either by means of the classical method of testing hypotheses, which method among other things involves the difficult task of establishing meaningful α and β errors, or by the so-called "Bayesian" approach.[12] Using the latter approach, one establishes prior probabilistic distributions for values around the empirical mean and then on the basis of subsequent observations adjusts this mean (generates posterior probabilities).[13] Utility functions may also be introduced in the Bayesian formulation

[12] Modern statistical decision theory relies very heavily on Bayesian statistics. See Herman Chernoff and Lincoln E. Moses, *Elementary Decision Theory* (New York: John Wiley& Sons, Inc., 1959); Howard Raiffa and Robert Schlaifer, *Applied Statistical Decision Theory* (Boston: Division of Research, Harvard Business School, 1961); also Jack Hirshleifer, "The Bayesian Approach to Statistical Decision—An Exposition," *Journal of Business*, October, 1961, pp. 471–89.

[13] Let us assume, for example, that x_1 is a value which was established as the most probable (either empirically on insufficient data or by means of pure judgment) with prior probability (subjective) of $P(x_1)$. Furthermore, assume that the only other possible values are x_2 with $P(x_2)$ and x_3 with $P(x_3)$. We obtain an event e and wish to find the probability (posterior) that e and x_1 came from the same universe before we take action. In effect, we wish to find the conditional probability $P(x_1 \mid e)$. From Bayes's rule, we know that

$$P(x_1 \mid e) = \frac{P(e \cap x_1)}{P(e)} = \frac{P(e \mid x_1)P(x_1)}{P(e)}$$

Since we have assumed that e can occur only in conjunction with any one of the *mutually exclusive* x_i's, then

$$P(e) = P(e \cap x_1) + P(e \cap x_2) + P(e \cap x_3)$$
$$= \sum_{i=1}^{3} P(e \cap x_i)$$

Consequently,

$$P(x_1 \mid e) = \frac{P(e \mid x_1)P(x_1)}{\sum_{i=1}^{3} P(e \mid x_i)P(x_i)}$$

in order to assign the proper gain or penalty if equal deviations are associated with unequal consequences.

SUMMARY

It has been argued in this paper that the benefits of group depreciation go far beyond the bookkeeping simplification and its concomitant cost savings. Far more important are the statistical attributes of group depreciation that yield reliable information on the economic life of the assets included in the group. By means of finite Markov chains, one can derive empirical probabilistic distributions of the age of the various assets, which should provide management with better data, not only for asset depreciation but also for maintenance, utilization, and replacement of capital equipment. Once the transition probability matrix is established and the initial aging of assets accomplished, data can be generated automatically for forecasts of retirements of assets, balances in the asset accounts, and allowance for depreciation, as well as depreciation charges for each year over the forecasting horizon. The information generated can then be introduced and aid in the development of capital and cash budgets and forecasts.

Often the advantages of the so-called "operations research" techniques do not so much emanate from any miracles inherent in analytical solutions as from the discipline of logical investigation in the existing relationships between the various factors affecting decisions and operations, and the deductive as well as inductive reasoning that is enforced upon the investigators. This can be said also of many of the aspects of the process suggested here, especially those related to the development of the transition probability matrix. The dynamics of adjustment at the least will subject those involved in a demanding and informative exercise in statistical estimation. More than that, however, analysis of the reasons for such adjustments will yield information on the process of obsolescence itself, its cycles, if any, and the paths that it takes.

10

The authors point out the accommodation of matrix theory to problems involving reciprocal relationships. An illustration of the cost allocation problem for which there exists manufacturing and service department interdependency is then presented in matrix notation and solved. Other applications of matrix theory to accounting relationships are briefly alluded to.

*MATRIX THEORY AND COST ALLOCATION**

Thomas H. Williams and Charles H. Griffin

MUCH OF THE ACCOUNTING DATA used in management control and administrative decision making is a product of antecedent processes of cost allocation and expense distribution. Both of these operations assume the validity of cost divisibility and recombination. Existing practices of accountants in allocating costs and expenses to relevant production orders, products, processes, and/or departments would appear to confirm the general acceptability of such an assumption. Effective cost control depends upon an identification of costs with responsibility centers, and the calculation of unit costs is especially important in measuring product or process profitability. In these and other types of analyses the property of cost and expense analysis and synthesis is a uniquely useful accounting attribute.

In the analysis of costs an important first problem which confronts the accountant is the measurement of benefits to be derived from the cost or expense elements which are not clearly identifiable with specific departments or cost centers. The reliability of successive allocations necessarily rests upon this first, basic determination. Once the interdepartmental relationships or associations are established quantitatively, there remains a second problem of arithmetically distributing costs in the previously established allocation ratios. The complexity of the latter problem increases geometrically with the increase in number of mutually related departments. In respect to reciprocally related accounting elements, matrix theory may be usefully applied both in aiding calculational simplicity and in promoting a clearer understanding of the basic structure of the interrelated elements.

---

* Reprinted from *Accounting Review*, July, 1964, pp. 671–78.

RECIPROCAL RELATIONSHIPS

The problem of cost distribution is but a particular instance of the more general problem of reciprocal relationships. Consequently, by first examining the nature of the more general problem and the several solution techniques which are available, it may be possible to establish a broader basis for the solution of a variety of similarly structured accounting problems.

The nature of reciprocal relationships may be illustrated by examining the details of calculating an employee profit-sharing bonus. Assuming that an allowable bonus is computed as a percentage of net profit after income taxes and is also deductible in determining the tax liability, an interdependency relationship clearly exists. Determination of the income tax obligation is dependent upon the amount awarded as a bonus; concurrently, the bonus is also evaluated in terms of the income tax liability. These variables may be expressed symbolically in the following equations:

$$B = \alpha(P - T)$$
$$T = \gamma(P - B)$$
$$P = \text{Parameter}$$

where B = bonus, P = net profit before bonus *and* income tax, T = income tax, and α and γ the bonus percentage and the income tax rate, respectively. Although the mutual dependence of bonus and tax variables may be expressed in numerous ways, an algebraic formulation as given above is perhaps the most precise expression of such a reciprocal association.

A similar dependency structure is evident in many other accounting problems. For example, in the preparation of consolidated financial statements involving bilateral stockholdings, the investment elimination requires an analysis similar to that indicated above. Reciprocal distributions are also required where there are several mutually related service departments. In such mutual dependencies, there exists the same type of algebraic structure as illustrated previously. While accountants have traditionally dealt with such problems on an isolated individual basis—and with the use of familiar mathematical techniques—significantly they have often failed to recognize that each is essentially a specific instance of a more *general* problem to which a *general* mathematical system may often apply. The previous tax-bonus formulation is used again following to illustrate a general mathematical theory appropriately descriptive of reciprocal relationships. Thereafter, this theory will be applied to a more complex, yet frequently recurring practical problem of cost allocation.

SOLUTION TECHNIQUES

Two basic mathematical methods are frequently employed to solve problems involving interdependency elements. One is a variate on a trial-and-error procedure, viz., the successive iteration method; the other is the traditional solution form for systems of simultaneous linear equations.

In applying the successive iteration method, a correct problem solution proceeds from a progression of successive estimates. Each value estimate makes use of a previous estimate until solution values stabilize. For example, assuming that α (the bonus percentage) equals 10 percent, γ (the tax rate) equals 50 percent, and P (the profit before bonus and tax) equals \$100,000, the order of solution is given following:

Step	*Bonus*	*Tax*
1	\$10,000.00	\$45,000.00
2	5,500.00	47,250.00
3	5,275.00	47,362.50
4	5,263.75	47,368.13
5	5,263.19	47,368.41
6	5,263.16	47,368.42
7	5,263.16	47,368.42

The first approximation of bonus is based upon a zero tax amount; thereafter, tax and bonus values are calculated sequentially, appropriate recognition being given to the previous calculation. Reference to the previous schedule discloses that the values stabilize with a bonus of \$5,263.16 and a tax obligation of \$47,368.42.

Using the same data, the problem may be more formally expressed as a system of algebraic equations, simplified as follows:

$$\begin{aligned} B &= 0.10(P - T) \\ T &= 0.50(P - B) \\ P &= \$100,000 \\ B &= 0.10[100,000 - (50,000 - 0.50B)] = \$5,263.16 \\ T &= 0.50(100,000 - 5,263.16) = \$47,368.42 \end{aligned} \tag{1}$$

Significantly, these values confirm the amounts previously established by the successive iteration method. Where an equation system is relatively simple, i.e., the system consists of a small number of variables and equations, the algebraic solution is perhaps the most efficient solution form. However, where there exist many variables, the successive iteration method is usually a more convenient algorithm. Most accountants are familiar with both of these solution techniques.

There exists, however, a more fundamental mathematical schema-matrix algebra—which will accommodate larger and more complex systems of equations involving many variables. In point of fact, the solution of simultaneous equations is based upon principles implicit in the theory of matrices.

THE MATRIX STRUCTURE

A matrix is a rectangular array of elements—numbers, functions, etc.—which can be used to examine problems involving *relations* between these elements. Although operations such as addition and multiplication can be performed on matrices, the matrix is not evaluated quantitatively. A matrix A may be represented

$$A = \begin{bmatrix} a_{11} & a_{12} & \cdots & a_{1n} \\ a_{21} & a_{22} & \cdots & a_{2n} \\ \cdots & \cdots & \cdots & \cdots \\ a_{m1} & a_{m2} & \cdots & a_{mn} \end{bmatrix} \tag{2}$$

In the above expression the first subscript for a given element indicates the *row* in which it appears, and the second subscript denotes the *column*. Such a matrix with m rows and n columns is normally referred to as a $m \times n$ *matrix*, or a matrix of *order* (m, n).

One of the most important applications of matrix algebra relates to the study of systems of simultaneous linear equations. Consider the system of three linear equations in P, T and B given earlier, viz.:

$$\begin{aligned} B - 0.10P + 0.10T &= 0 \\ 0.50B - 0.50P + \quad T &= 0 \\ P \qquad\qquad &= 100{,}000 \end{aligned} \tag{3}$$

The 3×3 *matrix of coefficients* assumes the form

$$\begin{bmatrix} 1 & -0.10 & 0.10 \\ 0.50 & -0.50 & 1 \\ 0 & 1 & 0 \end{bmatrix} \tag{4}$$

An ordering of coefficients of the equation system is a first condition to an application of the general solution technique for linear equations.

Once the elements are ordered, it is then appropriate to refer to *operations* on the matrix. For example, a matrix *sum* may be formed by adding corresponding elements of matrices of the same order; also, it is appropriate to multiply a given matrix by a scalar or by another matrix. In scalar multiplication, each element of the matrix is multiplied by a real number. Where one matrix is to be multiplied by a second matrix, however, multiplication is possible only where the matrices are conformable for multiplication, i.e., where the number of columns in the first matrix is equal to the number of rows in the second. Given a 2×3 matrix A and the 3×2 matrix B, the matrix product AB, a 2×2 matrix, is given following:[1]

$$AB = \begin{bmatrix} a_{11} & a_{12} & a_{13} \\ a_{21} & a_{22} & a_{23} \end{bmatrix} \begin{bmatrix} b_{11} & b_{12} \\ b_{21} & b_{22} \\ b_{31} & b_{32} \end{bmatrix}$$

$$= \begin{bmatrix} a_{11} \quad b_{11} + a_{12} \quad b_{21} + a_{13} \quad b_{31} & a_{11} \quad b_{12} + a_{12} \quad b_{22} + a_{13} \quad b_{32} \\ a_{21} \quad b_{11} + a_{22} \quad b_{21} + a_{23} \quad b_{31} & a_{21} \quad b_{12} + a_{22} \quad b_{22} + a_{23} \quad b_{32} \end{bmatrix}$$

[1] Substituting integers for the symbols for each element of the two matrices, a matrix product is given below:

$$AB = \begin{bmatrix} 0 & 2 & 3 \\ 1 & -2 & 0 \end{bmatrix} \begin{bmatrix} -1 & 0 \\ 4 & -3 \\ 1 & 2 \end{bmatrix} = \begin{bmatrix} 11 & 0 \\ -9 & 6 \end{bmatrix}$$

A facile use of this multiplicative process is especially important in the solution of systems of linear equations.

A knowledge of other matrix operations is also important in order to more completely describe the general technique for the solution of a system of linear equations; however, these few elementary matrix operations enable one to preview the ultimate objective, viz., to develop an economical and efficient method of handling cost allocation problems. Consider the following general system of linear equations:

$$\left\{\begin{array}{l} a_{11}x_1 + \cdots + a_{1n}x_n = b_1 \\ \cdots\cdots\cdots\cdots\cdots \\ a_{m1}x_1 + \cdots + a_{mn}x_n = b_m \end{array}\right. \tag{6}$$

where m may not be equal to n; i.e., the number of equations is unequal to the number of unknowns. Using matrix notation, such a system may be written:

$$\begin{bmatrix} a_{11} & \cdots & a_{1n} \\ \cdots & \cdots & \cdots \\ a_{m1} & \cdots & a_{mn} \end{bmatrix} \begin{bmatrix} x_1 \\ \cdots \\ x_n \end{bmatrix} = \begin{bmatrix} b_1 \\ \cdots \\ b_m \end{bmatrix} \tag{7}$$

This formulation parallels the system presented in equation 6, and may be verified by performing the indicated multiplication. If the coefficient matrix is denoted A, the vector of unknowns X, and the vector of constants B, the equation may be further abbreviated

$$AX = B \tag{8}$$

If values are determined for $x_1, x_2, \ldots, x_n$ which satisfy equation 7, these values also satisfy the linear equations 6, and conversely. A determination of these values thus is equivalent to a solution of the set of equations.

DETERMINATION OF AN INVERSE—THE ESSENCE OF THE PROBLEM

The solution of equation 8 may be compared to the solution of an equation with one unknown variable. The solution of

$$ax = b \tag{9}$$

can be expressed as

$$x = b/a \tag{10}$$

Equation 9 was solved by multiplying both sides of the equation by $1/a$, frequently written a^{-1}. Using the matrix inverse notation, equation 8 may be rewritten

$$X = A^{-1}B \tag{11}$$

In the event that the coefficient matrix remains constant, the solutions for $x_1, \ldots, x_n$ can be easily evaluated merely by a simple matrix multiplication operation, once the initial calculation of A^{-1} has been made.[2] It is this property of the matrix solution technique that makes it especially useful to accountants in simplifying problems involving reciprocal relations.

The matrix notation easily accommodates both simple and complex systems of equations. For the relatively simple tax-bonus illustration used earlier, the equation system 3 may be easily cast in the following matrix form:

$$\begin{bmatrix} 1 & -0.10 & 0.10 \\ 0.50 & -0.50 & 1 \\ 0 & 1 & 0 \end{bmatrix} \begin{bmatrix} B \\ P \\ T \end{bmatrix} = \begin{bmatrix} 0 \\ 0 \\ 100{,}000 \end{bmatrix} \tag{12}$$

The equivalence of this formulation and that given by equation system 3 can be verified by performing the indicated matrix multiplication.

Equation 12 may be expressed in matrix inverse form as follows:

$$\begin{bmatrix} B \\ P \\ T \end{bmatrix} = \begin{bmatrix} 1 & -0.10 & 0.10 \\ 0.50 & -0.50 & 1 \\ 0 & 1 & 0 \end{bmatrix}^{-1} \begin{bmatrix} 0 \\ 0 \\ 100{,}000 \end{bmatrix} \tag{13}$$

Determination of values for B, P, and T reduces to a problem of computing the inverse of the coefficient matrix and subsequently performing a simple matrix multiplication. In this instance the following solution is derived:[3]

$$\begin{bmatrix} B \\ P \\ T \end{bmatrix} = \begin{bmatrix} 1.052631578 & -0.105263157 & 0.052631579 \\ 0 & 0 & 1 \\ -0.52631578 & 1.05263157 & 0.47368421 \end{bmatrix} \begin{bmatrix} 0 \\ 0 \\ 100{,}000 \end{bmatrix} \tag{14}$$

$$= \begin{bmatrix} 5{,}263.16 \\ 100{,}000.00 \\ 47{,}368.42 \end{bmatrix}$$

THE COST ALLOCATION MODEL

The previous example illustrates, for a simple equation system, the use of the matrix notation in solving an elementary problem involving reciprocal relationships. The application to more complex systems is identical, although the arithmetic involvements are necessarily somewhat more tedious. The following problem in cost allocation for a manufacturer with five service departments and three producing departments is a case in point.

Assume that after primary distributions have been made—and before reciprocal distributions are begun—the following account balances obtain:

---

[2] Various procedures exist for the systematic calculation of the inverse, depending upon the complexity of the problem. For problems involving relatively few variables, several manual computation techniques can be found in Franz E. Hohn, *Elementary Matrix Algebra* (New York: Macmillan Co., 1950); for more complex problems, standard computer programs for the determination of a matrix inverse are available.

[3] The technique of synthetic elimination was used to calculate the inverse. See Hohn, *op. cit.*, pp. 73–74.

Manufacturing department A	\$120,000
Manufacturing department B	200,000
Manufacturing department C	80,000
Service department X_1	8,000
Service department X_2	12,000
Service department X_3	6,000
Service department X_4	11,000
Service department X_5	13,000

The measure of interdependency of the various departments in respect to distributing service department expenses is given following:

Service department X_1:	
To manufacturing department A	.25%
To manufacturing department B	.25
To manufacturing department C	.25
To service department X_3	.10
To service department X_4	5
To service department X_5	.10
Service department X_2:	
To manufacturing department A	.80
To service department X_3	.10
To service department X_5	.10
Service department X_3:	
To manufacturing department A	.20
To manufacturing department B	.30
To manufacturing department C	.20
To service department X_1	5
To service department X_2	.10
To service department X_4	.10
To service department X_5	5
Service department X_4:	
To manufacturing department B	.40
To manufacturing department C	.40
To service department X_1	.10
To service department X_2	5
To service department X_3	5
Service department X_5:	
To manufacturing department A	.10
To manufacturing department B	5
To manufacturing department C	5
To service department X_1	.20
To service department X_2	.20
To service department X_3	.20
To service department X_4	.20

Accountants have traditionally solved this type of problem by the *successive iteration* method. Once the service department expenses have been successively distributed, the balance increments added by the reciprocal relationships are then distributed. The process is repeated until account balances stabilize. However, as noted earlier, these relationships can be expressed more precisely as a system of simultaneous equations and solved by methods of matrix algebra. If the *total* service department costs *after* reciprocal distribution are denoted $X_1, \ldots, X_5$, the relationship between service departments can be represented

(15)
$$\begin{aligned}
X_1 &= 8{,}000 + 0.05X_3 + 0.10X_4 + 0.20X_5 \\
X_2 &= 12{,}000 + 0.10X_3 + 0.05X_4 + 0.20X_5 \\
X_3 &= 6{,}000 + 0.10X_1 + 0.10X_2 + 0.05X_4 + 0.20X_5 \\
X_4 &= 11{,}000 + 0.05X_1 + 0.10X_3 + 0.20X_5 \\
X_5 &= 13{,}000 + 0.10X_1 + 0.10X_2 + 0.05X_3
\end{aligned}$$

Rearranging the equations to preserve vertical symmetry among the variables, the equation system is

(16)
$$\begin{aligned}
X_1 \qquad\qquad - 0.05X_3 - 0.10X_4 - 0.20X_5 &= 8{,}000 \\
X_2 - 0.10X_3 - 0.05X_4 - 0.20X_5 &= 12{,}000 \\
-0.10X_1 - 0.10X_2 + X_3 - 0.05X_4 - 0.20X_5 &= 6{,}000 \\
-0.05X_1 \qquad - 0.10X_3 + X_4 - 0.20X_5 &= 11{,}000 \\
-0.10X_1 - 0.10X_2 - 0.05X_3 \qquad + X_5 &= 13{,}000
\end{aligned}$$

From the above, the matrix of coefficients is easily determined to be:

(17)
$$\begin{pmatrix} 1 & 0 & -0.05 & -0.10 & -0.20 \\ 0 & 1 & -0.10 & -0.05 & -0.20 \\ -0.10 & -0.10 & 1 & -0.05 & -0.20 \\ -0.05 & 0 & -0.10 & 1 & -0.20 \\ -0.10 & -0.10 & -0.05 & 0 & 1 \end{pmatrix} \begin{pmatrix} X_1 \\ X_2 \\ X_3 \\ X_4 \\ X_5 \end{pmatrix} = \begin{pmatrix} 8{,}000 \\ 12{,}000 \\ 6{,}000 \\ 11{,}000 \\ 13{,}000 \end{pmatrix}$$

The desired objective is, as before, a determination of appropriate values for $x_1, \ldots, x_5$; and it is now clear that the problem reduces to a calculation of the inverse of the coefficient matrix; i.e., if the coefficient matrix is denoted A, the vector of unknowns X, and the vector of constants B, the solution is of the form

(18)
$$X = A^{-1}B$$

The inverse of A is determined to be:[4]

(19)
$$V^{-1} = \begin{pmatrix} 1.0385469 & 0.0330747 & 0.0787780 & 0.1094473 & 0.2519694 \\ 0.0408924 & 1.0377815 & 0.1247000 & 0.0622133 & 0.2531175 \\ 0.1353058 & 0.1316976 & 1.0409525 & 0.0721631 & 0.2760238 \\ 0.0883998 & 0.0375576 & 0.1225132 & 1.0168434 & 0.2530628 \\ 0.1147092 & 0.1136705 & 0.0723954 & 0.0207742 & 1.0643098 \end{pmatrix}$$

Once the inverse is determined, the problem is essentially an exercise in matrix multiplication:

(20)
$$\begin{pmatrix} X_1 \\ X_2 \\ X_3 \\ X_4 \\ X_5 \end{pmatrix} = \begin{pmatrix} 1.0385469 & 0.0330747 & 0.0787780 & 0.1094473 & 0.2519694 \\ 0.0408924 & 1.0377815 & 0.1247000 & 0.0622133 & 0.2531175 \\ 0.1353058 & 0.1316976 & 1.0409525 & 0.0721631 & 0.2760238 \\ 0.0883998 & 0.0375576 & 0.1225132 & 1.0168434 & 0.2530628 \\ 0.1147092 & 0.1136705 & 0.0723954 & 0.0207742 & 1.0643098 \end{pmatrix} \begin{pmatrix} 8{,}000 \\ 12{,}000 \\ 6{,}000 \\ 11{,}000 \\ 13{,}000 \end{pmatrix}$$

$$= \begin{pmatrix} 13{,}657.46 \\ 17{,}503.59 \\ 13{,}290.64 \\ 16{,}368.06 \\ 16{,}780.64 \end{pmatrix}$$

[4] The technique of synthetic elimination can again be used to determine the inverse.

A summary of the allocated costs is shown in Table 1. Since $X_1, \ldots, X_5$ are defined as total costs *after* distributions, the upper half of the table can be prepared merely by multiplying the values of these variables by the predetermined distribution percentages. Values for the lower half of the table (cost transfers out) can be easily derived from the accumulations in the upper half. The completed summary of cost allocations indicates the flow of costs both in and out of relevant departments. The accounting function is especially sensitive to these data both in respect to traditional record keeping and in appraising the effectiveness of cost management.

TABLE 1

SUMMARY OF COST ALLOCATIONS

	Dept. A	*Dept. B*	*Dept. C*	*Dept.* X_1	*Dept.* X_2	*Dept.* X_3	*Dept.* X_4	*Dept.* X_5	*Total*
Total cost before distribution	$120,000	$200,000	$80,000	$ 8,000	$12,000	$ 6,000	$11,000	$13,000	$450,000
Cost transfers from:									
Department X_1	3,415	3,414	3,414			1,366	683	1,366	13,658
Department X_2	14,003					1,750		1,750	17,503
Department X_3	2,658	3,986	2,658	665	1,329		1,329	665	13,290
Department X_4		6,548	6,547	1,637	818	818			16,368
Department X_5	1,679	839	839	3,356	3,356	3,356	3,356		16,781
	$141,755	$214,787	$93,458	$13,658	$17,503	$13,290	$16,368	$16,781	$527,600
Cost transfers to:									
Department A				$ 3,415	$14,003	$ 2,658		$ 1,679	$ 21,755
Department B				3,414		3,986	$ 6,548	839	14,787
Department C				3,414		2,658	6,547	839	13,458
Department X_1						665	1,637	3,356	5,658
Department X_2						1,329	818	3,356	5,503
Department X_3				1,366	1,750		818	3,356	7,290
Department X_4				683		1,329		3,356	5,368
Department X_5				1,366	1,750	665			3,781
				$13,658	$17,503	$13,290	$16,368	$16,781	$ 77,600
Total cost after distribution	$141,755	$214,787	$93,458	0	0	0	0	0	$450,000

The "permanency" of the inverse is a particularly useful property. Once it is determined, the cost allocation problem remains essentially one of matrix multiplication so long as the distribution percentages remain invariate. Often, these ratios continue unchanged for relatively long periods of time; and in consequence, the method assures important accounting simplification. Although the previous illustration was limited to multivariate cost distribution, parallel accounting treatment would be accorded the traditional preparation of consolidated financial statements where intercorporate reciprocal stockholdings exist. In the latter case, present solution methods are unusually cumbersome where the number of mutually related companies is large or the involvement of stockholdings complex.

COMPUTER APPLICATIONS

The previous illustrations have emphasized the nonmechanical solution of complex problems involving reciprocal relationships by the use of matrix algebra. As the number of departments or variables increases, this method of manual calculation becomes increasingly difficult. In such instances, resort may be had to electronic computers in calculating the matrix inverse. For most computer installations, standard library routines (programs) are available for calculating the inverse and/or solving simultaneously systems of linear equations. In problems of cost allocation involving large numbers of departments, only one computer-based determination of the matrix inverse is required so long as the distribution ratios remain invariate. In each allocation the solution derives from a multiplication of the inverse matrix by the new matrix (vector) of initial cost values. The IBM 1620—using a standard library program—determines the inverse of a given 5×5 matrix in approximately one minute (including input-output time). Where the matrix to be inverted is 30×30, calculation time approximates five minutes.[5] Accountants have been especially sensitive to the advantages of this compression in calculation time.

> The National City Bank of New York announced recently that it had developed, in conjunction with the International Business Machines Corporation, an approach to [the distribution of overhead costs] which reduced actual computation time from 1000 man-hours to 9½ minutes.
>
> In one steel company . . . , 51 overhead departments, or cost centers, make about 600 interdepartmental charges, and the monthly distribution [of these charges] required formerly about 300 man-hours. This was reduced to 35 minutes on an electronic calculator—in this case a smaller machine than the one on which the [above] bank problem was calculated.[6]

Other impressive evidences of economies in accounting calculation time might be cited; these are but a small sample of the time consequence of computerized accounting. The cost allocation problem is but a single illustration of a catalog of similar problems to which the accountant may usefully apply matrix notation.

NEW APPLICATIONS

Apart from its value in simplifying the difficulty and shortening the time span of many accounting operations, the matrix concept has also been appropriately applied in developing a number of *theoretical* formulations. The Leontief input-output model used in economic theory relies upon the matrix formulation to explain the interrelationships between relevant variables. This model has also been used in accounting analysis and was recently appraised in the following terms:

> The input-output system provides a method whereby management can predict changes in the level of the balance sheet accounts which arise from some level of

---

As is evident in the previous illustration, the size of the matrix to be inverted is unaffected by departments (generally manufacturing) which have no reciprocal distributions. These departments are incorporated into the final solution when the summary of cost allocations is prepared.

[6] Grandjean G. Jewett, "The Distribution of Overhead with Electronic Computers," *Journal of Accountancy*, June, 1954, p. 698.

operations, analyze the impact on the accounting system and level of accounts brought about by changes in operating levels and conditions. The framework, common to all firms, also provides a uniform procedure for aggregating firm data and thus is a method of consistently establishing an inter-firm analysis for an industry or an inter-industry analysis for the economy.[7]

Professor Richard Mattessich also foresees special usefulness of the matrix notation in the creation of an abstract generalized model for accounting theory:

> There are strong indications that the matrix formulation of accountancy facilitates not only the classifying analysis of flows, but also the explanation *why* such flows occur. The combination of accounting equations with production functions by means of matrix concepts has been successfully initiated in input-output accounting and might find further application and extension (to liquidity preference and investment functions, and so on) in other kinds of accounting systems.[8]

To the extent that matrix formulations of accounting analysis contribute to more rigorous and logical models of accounting theory, additional support is adduced for such methods. Surely this use provides an appropriate complement to the more practical benefits immediately available to the accounting practitioner.

---

[7] Allen B. Richards, "Input-Output Accounting for Business," *Accounting Review*, July, 1960, p. 436.

[8] Richard Mattessich, "Towards a General and Axiomatic Foundation of Accountancy," *Accounting Research*, October, 1957, p. 348.

11

The article discusses the application of linear algebra to four types of cost allocation problems. These illustrations focus on the following situations: (1) reciprocal cost allocations, (2) cost allocations between arbitrary cost collection centers in process cost operations, (3) determination of the internal composition of asset and expense balances under varying inputs, and (4) analysis of product costs (job or process cost system) under varying levels of expenditures.

LINEAR ALGEBRA AND COST ALLOCATIONS: SOME EXAMPLES[*][†]

Neil Churchill

INTRODUCTION

THE USE OF systems of linear equations in financial analysis and accounting is a relatively recent and promising development. One of the first papers in this area appeared in *Accounting Research* in 1957.[1] Since then, much additional work has been done. For example, a recent study sets forth the accounting system in terms of the linear programming model and thus brings to bear on the problems of accounting the entire body of network analysis and linear programming theory.[2]

---

* Reprinted from *Accounting Review*, October, 1964, pp. 894–904.

† The basic work on this paper was done in the Summer of 1960 when the author participated in the Westinghouse Summer Professors' Program as a member of the Business Systems Research and Development group of the Westinghouse Electric Corporation. The author is indebted to Professor Andrew C. Stedry of Massachusetts Institute of Technology for directing his attention to the interrelationship of linear algebra with accounting and to Professors Charles T. Horngren of the University of Chicago and Otto A. Davis and Stanley Zionts of Carnegie Institute of Technology for their comments on this paper.

1 Richard Mattessich, "Towards a General and Axiomatic Foundation of Accountancy," *Accounting Research*, October, 1957, pp. 328–55. See also the early works of O. Pichler and K. Wenke. The most readily available reference is probably Klaus Wenke, "On the Analysis of Structural Properties of Large Scale Microeconomic Input-Output Models," Preprint No. 4, *Papers Presented at the 6th Annual International Meeting of the Institute of Management Sciences, September, 1959, Paris* (London: Pergamon Press, 1959).

2 Yuji Ijiri, "Goal Oriented Models for Accounting and Control" (unpublished Ph.D. dissertation, Carnegie Institute of Technology, 1963). See also A. Charnes, W. W. Cooper, and Yuji Ijiri, "Breakeven Budgeting and Programming to Goals," *Journal of Accounting*

In cost accounting, linear algebra can be useful in representing and solving allocation and analysis problems. The purpose of this paper is to illustrate the application of linear algebra to the problem of reciprocal cost allocation and three additional allocation problems:

1. The analysis of costs charged to various departments and inventory accounts in a simple process cost system
2. The analysis of residual cost balances in cost collection centers under changing cost incurrence conditions
3. The analysis of product costs under varying levels of expenditures

The potential usefulness of these illustrations is commented upon in each case. In addition, these formulations have three overall benefits in the teaching of accounting. One is the insight such a system of notation gives toward further developments in cost analysis and cost accounting. *A second is the ease with which problems so formulated can be programmed on digital computers.* Finally, such a formulation reinforces the student's competency in mathematics and increases his understanding of both the mathematics and the accounting system.

RECIPROCAL COST ALLOCATIONS

The allocation of costs from a service department or a service division to one or more operating units is normally done individually, department by department, by algebra or by successive approximations. When the number of units or the extent of the reciprocal interactions becomes very large, either simplifying assumptions are made, or the problem becomes very hard to handle by ordinary methods. Expressing the problem as a series of linear equations leads naturally to the application of matrix algebra. Consider the following such problem (see Fig. 1), where four operating departments, A, B, C, D, are supported by three service departments, S_i, with some interactions. Let the total costs for the operating departments, including alloca-

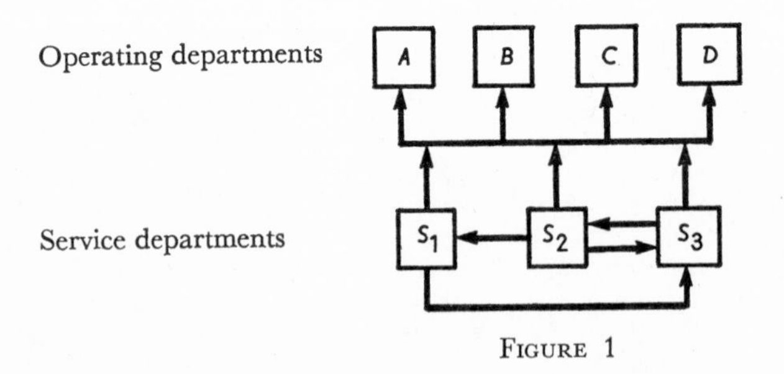

FIGURE 1

Research, Spring, 1963, pp. 16–43; and Yuji Ijiri, F. K. Levy, and R. C. Lyon, "A Linear Programming Model for Budgeting and Financial Planning," *Journal of Accounting Research*, Autumn, 1963, pp. 198–212.

tions from the service departments, be as follows, with the E's representing departmental expenses:

$$
\begin{aligned}
A &= 0.2S_1 + 0.1S_2 + 0.1S_3 + E_A \\
B &= 0.4S_1 + 0.2S_2 + 0.1S_3 + E_B \\
C &= 0.1S_1 + \quad 0 \quad + 0.3S_3 + E_C \\
D &= 0.1S_1 + 0.2S_2 + 0.4S_3 + E_D
\end{aligned}
$$

Let the costs for the service departments, including allocations to each other, be as follows:

$$
\begin{aligned}
S_1 &= 0.2S_2 + E_{S_1} \\
S_2 &= 0.1S_3 + E_{S_2} \\
S_3 &= 0.2S_1 + 0.3S_2 + E_{S_3}
\end{aligned}
$$

We can express the above in tabular form as follows:

SOURCES OF ALLOCATION

	S_1 S_2 S_3	E_A	E_B	E_C	E_D	E_{S_1}	E_{S_2}	E_{S_3}
A =	0.2 + 0.1 + 0.1	+1						
B =	0.4 + 0.2 + 0.1		+1					
C =	0.1 + 0 + 0.3			+1				
D =	0.1 + 0.2 + 0.4				+1			
S_1 =	0 + 0.2 + 0					+1		
S_2 =	0 + 0 + 0.1						+1	
S_3 =	0.2 + 0.3 + 0							+1

Note that the sum of each column equals one since all the service department costs are completely allocated. This tabulation can be represented in matrix form as follows.[3]

	s	e
u	M_{11}	M_{12}
s	M_{21}	M_{22}

Hence:

$$
\begin{aligned}
[u] &= [M_{11}][s] + [M_{12}][e] \\
[s] &= [M_{21}][s] + [M_{22}][e]
\end{aligned}
$$

[3] There are several excellent books on linear algebra and other topics in modern mathematics which require little or no mathematical prerequisites. Among those written with business and the social sciences in mind are John G. Kemeny and others, *Finite Mathematics with Business Applications* (Englewood Cliffs, N.J.: Prentice-Hall, Inc., 1962); F. Parker Fowler, Jr., and E. W. Sandburg, *Basic Mathematics for Administration* (New York: John Wiley & Sons, Inc., 1962); and George Hadley, *Linear Algebra* (Reading, Mass.: Addison-Wesley Publishing Co., Inc., 1961).

or

$$[I - M_{21}][s] = [M_{22}][e]$$
$$[s] = [I - M_{21}]^{-1}[M_{22}][e]^4$$

Thus:

$$[u] = [M_{11}][I - M_{21}]^{-1}[M_{22}][e] + [M_{12}][e]$$

where

$$[u] = \begin{pmatrix} A \\ B \\ C \\ D \end{pmatrix}$$

$$[s] = \begin{pmatrix} S_1 \\ S_2 \\ S_3 \end{pmatrix}$$

$$[I] = \begin{pmatrix} 1 & 0 & 0 \\ 0 & 1 & 0 \\ 0 & 0 & 1 \end{pmatrix}$$

and

$$[e] = [E_A, E_B, E_C, E_D, E_{S_1}, E_{S_3}, E_{S_2}]^T$$
$$(T = \text{Transpose})$$

with the M's given as above.

This example can be further partitioned for convenience in later manipulations. Let $[e_1]$ and $[e_2]$ be the direct expenses incurred by the operating and the service departments, respectively. Then

	s	e_1	e_2
u	M_{11}	I	0
s	M_{21}	0	I

since each direct cost (the E) is incurred only in its respective department. Where this is the case, the equations above can be expressed as follows:

$$[u] = [M_{11}][I - M_{21}]^{-1}[I][e_2] + [I][e_1]$$

After the inversion of the matrix $[I - M_{21}]$, $[u]$ appears as the following function of the direct expenses, $[e_1]$ and $[e_2]$:

[4] This formulation requires $[I - M_{21}]$ to have an inverse. While it is mathematically possible for $[I - M_{21}]$ to be singular (not to have an inverse), this condition would be unrealistic from a managerial point of view, for it can be shown that where $[I - M_{21}]$ is singular, either (*a*) one or more departments are assigned all of their own costs or (*b*) at least two departments allocate their entire costs to each other and hence none to any other department. Neither of these cases are important, but if they exist, they can be dealt with by combining all such interacting departments into one which will behave as an operating department. It can also be shown that the $[I - M_{21}]$ matrix for the remaining departments, if any, will be nonsingular, and hence this formulation will hold.

$$[u] = \begin{pmatrix} 0.2 & 0.1 & 0.1 \\ 0.4 & 0.2 & 0.1 \\ 0.1 & 0 & 0.3 \\ 0.1 & 0.2 & 0.4 \end{pmatrix} \begin{pmatrix} 1.00414 & 0.20704 & 0.02070 \\ 0.02070 & 1.03520 & 0.10352 \\ 0.20704 & 0.35199 & 1.03520 \end{pmatrix} [e_2] + [I][e_1]$$

or

$$(1) \qquad [u] = \begin{pmatrix} 0.22360 & 0.18013 & 0.11801 \\ 0.42650 & 0.32506 & 0.13250 \\ 0.16253 & 0.12630 & 0.31263 \\ 0.18737 & 0.36854 & 0.43685 \end{pmatrix} \begin{pmatrix} E_{S_1} \\ E_{S_2} \\ E_{S_3} \end{pmatrix} + \begin{pmatrix} 1 & 0 & 0 & 0 \\ 0 & 1 & 0 & 0 \\ 0 & 0 & 1 & 0 \\ 0 & 0 & 0 & 1 \end{pmatrix} \begin{pmatrix} E_A \\ E_B \\ E_C \\ E_D \end{pmatrix}$$

Substituting direct charges in the above example:

$$[e_1] = [10{,}000,\ 12{,}000,\ 14{,}000,\ 8{,}000]^T$$
$$[e_2] = [2{,}000,\ 2{,}000,\ 5{,}000]^T$$

Then

$$\begin{pmatrix} A \\ B \\ C \\ D \end{pmatrix} = \begin{pmatrix} 1{,}398 \\ 2{,}166 \\ 2{,}141 \\ 3{,}296 \end{pmatrix} + \begin{pmatrix} 10{,}000 \\ 12{,}000 \\ 14{,}000 \\ 8{,}000 \end{pmatrix} = \begin{pmatrix} 11{,}398 \\ 14{,}166 \\ 16{,}141 \\ 11{,}296 \end{pmatrix}$$

Given any set of direct charges, if the proportions to be allocated to each of the operating departments and between each of the service departments remain the same, the coefficient matrix 1 above can be used. The calculations are simple, fast, and straightforward no matter what the direct operating or service department charges might be. Thus, where many allocations of varying costs are made in essentially the same proportions, or where costs must be allocated with interactions between several departments, the above could prove advantageous.

COST ALLOCATIONS WITH INVENTORIES

The preceding formulation can be extended beyond the allocation of service department costs to include any allocation of cost from one set of cost collection centers to another. These cost collection centers can of course represent actual, operating, or service departments. They also can represent inventory accounts since these too are collection points for certain costs. As an example, consider the illustration (Fig. 2) of a simple process cost operation with two inventory accounts.

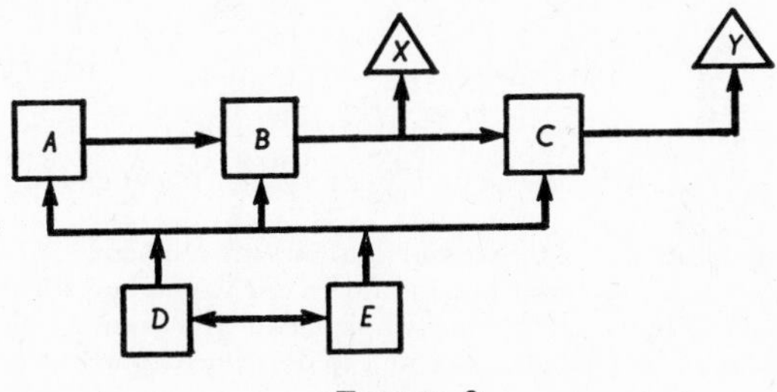

FIGURE 2

Department A performs operations on material which then goes into department B for further processing. Department B performs a different set of operations, and its output is either ready for sale as product X or is processed further by department C and then sold as product Y. In addition, two service departments, D and E, provide assistance to all three operating departments and, if desired, to each other. Finally, let each of the five departments incur direct departmental costs of three types: employees' salaries, L_i; purchased goods and services from outside the company, M_i; and directly incurred and/or allocated and reapportioned overhead costs such as depreciation, rent, etc., O_i. These relations can be expressed as a series of equations as follows:

$$
\begin{aligned}
C_A &= L_A + M_A + O_A + k_{AD}C_D + k_{AE}C_E \\
C_B &= L_B + M_B + O_B + k_{BD}C_D + k_{BE}C_E + C_A \\
C_C &= L_C + M_C + O_C + k_{CD}C_D + k_{CE}C_E + k_{CB}C_B \\
C_D &= L_D + M_D + O_D + k_{DE}C_E \\
C_E &= L_E + M_E + O_E + k_{ED}C_D \\
C_X &= (1 - k_{CB})C_B \\
C_Y &= C_C
\end{aligned}
$$

where C_i equals total costs that are charged *to* department i, ($i = A, B, C, D, E$) or to either inventory account ($i = X, Y$) and k_{ij} equals the proportion of the total cost of the jth department that flows *into* the ith department.

Representing the above as in the previous section:[5]

	C_A	C_B	C_C	C_D	C_E	C_X	C_Y	M	L	O
C_A				k_{AD}	k_{AE}			M_A	L_A	O_A
C_B	1			k_{BD}	k_{BE}			M_B	L_B	O_B
C_C		k_{CB}		k_{CD}	k_{CE}			M_C	L_C	O_C
C_D					k_{DE}			M_D	L_D	O_D
C_E				k_{ED}				M_E	L_E	O_E
C_X		$(1 - k_{CB})$								
C_Y			1							

or

	u	v
u	M_{11}	M_{12}

where $[M_{12}]$ represents each cost center's share of the total of each primary expense.

Then

$$
\begin{aligned}
[u] &= [M_{11}][u] + [M_{12}][v] \\
[u] &= [I - M_{11}]^{-1}[M_{12}][v]
\end{aligned}
$$

[5] The material, labor, and overhead costs in each department can be represented either as a proportion of the total appropriate costs, as shown in the table, or in dollar amounts. In the latter case the table would be expanded to include a material, labor, and overhead variable for each department. In this presentation a one would be inserted in place of each of the M_i's, L_i's, and O_i's in the table, and each departmental expense would be treated as a primary expense which is completely allocated to only one department.

where v_i represents the amount of each direct or primary expense charged directly to the ith cost center. Each u_i represents the total costs that flow *into* each cost center or inventory account.

This is done in three parts:

1. Since the matrix $[M_{11}]$ expresses the flows of costs directly between cost collection centers, the individual cells, the a_{ij}, of the $[I - M_{11}]^{-1}$ matrix represent the portion of the costs originating in the jth cost center that ultimately flow into the ith cost collection center.
2. The matrix $[M_{12}]$ expresses the portion of each of the total primary costs that originates in each cost center.
3. The vector $[v]$ expresses the total amount of each of the primary costs that enter the system.

The product $[M_{12}][v]$ can be expressed alternatively as a vector, $[e]$, of the total primary costs incurred in each cost collection center. This would be desirable where the relative amounts, $[M_{12}]$, of the primary costs change substantially or are not readily available. Where $[M_{12}]$ can be calculated, it is quite useful. In fact, the real practicality of this formulation lies in the ease with which changes in the primary cost comprising $[v]$ can be traced to all the cost centers. Such changes might be an increase in the price of purchased materials, the signing of a new labor contract, or the introduction of replacement cost depreciation. Changes in the allocation of these primary costs to various cost centers, the elements of the $[M_{12}]$ matrix, and the flow of costs between cost centers, the elements of the $[M_{11}]$ matrix, can also be readily made to complete the usefulness of this technique for estimating the cost effects of various alternatives.

As an example, take the following simplified representation of the situation illustrated in Figure 2 (reciprocal costs are neglected to restrict the solution to whole numbers). Let

$$
\begin{aligned}
C_X &= 0.4C_B \\
C_Y &= C_C \\
C_A &= 0.2C_D + 0.3C_E + 0.8M + 0.2L + 0.3O \\
C_B &= 0.3C_D + 0.2C_E + C_A + 0.2L + 0.1O \\
C_C &= 0.3C_D + 0.5C_E + 0.6C_B + 0.1M + 0.2L + 0.1O \\
C_D &= 0.1M + 0.2L + 0.3O \\
C_E &= 0.2C_D + 0.2L + 0.2O
\end{aligned}
$$

Then:

$$
[u] = \begin{pmatrix} 0 & 0 & 0 & 0.4 & 0 & 0 & 0 \\ 0 & 0 & 0 & 0 & 1 & 0 & 0 \\ 0 & 0 & 0 & 0 & 0 & 0.2 & 0.3 \\ 0 & 0 & 1 & 0 & 0 & 0.3 & 0.2 \\ 0 & 0 & 0 & 0.6 & 0 & 0.3 & 0.5 \\ 0 & 0 & 0 & 0 & 0 & 0 & 0 \\ 0 & 0 & 0 & 0 & 0 & 0.2 & 0 \end{pmatrix} \begin{pmatrix} C_X \\ C_Y \\ C_A \\ C_B \\ C_C \\ C_D \\ C_E \end{pmatrix} + \begin{pmatrix} 0 & 0 & 0 \\ 0 & 0 & 0 \\ 0.8 & 0.2 & 0.3 \\ 0 & 0.2 & 0.1 \\ 0.1 & 0.2 & 0.1 \\ 0.1 & 0.2 & 0.3 \\ 0 & 0.2 & 0.2 \end{pmatrix} \begin{pmatrix} 2{,}000 \\ 4{,}000 \\ 3{,}000 \end{pmatrix}
$$

or

$$[u] = \begin{pmatrix} 1 & 0 & 0.4 & 0.4 & 0 & 0.24 & 0.2 \\ 0 & 1 & 0.6 & 0.6 & 1 & 0.76 & 0.8 \\ 0 & 0 & 1 & 0 & 0 & 0.26 & 0.3 \\ 0 & 0 & 1 & 1 & 0 & 0.60 & 0.5 \\ 0 & 0 & 0.6 & 0.6 & 1 & 0.76 & 0.8 \\ 0 & 0 & 0 & 0 & 0 & 1 & 0 \\ 0 & 0 & 0 & 0 & 0 & 0.20 & 1 \end{pmatrix} \begin{pmatrix} 0 & 0 & 0 \\ 0 & 0 & 0 \\ 0.8 & 0.2 & 0.3 \\ 0 & 0.2 & 0.1 \\ 0.1 & 0.2 & 0.1 \\ 0.1 & 0.2 & 0.3 \\ 0 & 0.2 & 0.2 \end{pmatrix} \begin{pmatrix} 2{,}000 \\ 4{,}000 \\ 3{,}000 \end{pmatrix}$$

and

$$[u] = \begin{pmatrix} 0.344 & 0.248 & 0.272 \\ 0.656 & 0.752 & 0.728 \\ 0.826 & 0.312 & 0.438 \\ 0.860 & 0.620 & 0.680 \\ 0.656 & 0.752 & 0.728 \\ 0.100 & 0.200 & 0.300 \\ 0.020 & 0.240 & 0.260 \end{pmatrix} \begin{pmatrix} 2{,}000 \\ 4{,}000 \\ 3{,}000 \end{pmatrix} = \begin{pmatrix} 2{,}496 \\ 6{,}504 \\ 4{,}214 \\ 6{,}240 \\ 6{,}504 \\ 1{,}900 \\ 1{,}780 \end{pmatrix}$$

To analyze the effect of an increase in the purchased material prices of 5 percent, an increase in labor costs of 10 percent, and a decrease in overhead of $300, only the $[v]$ vector need be changed, and the result is readily calculated as follows:

$$[u] = \begin{pmatrix} 0.344 & 0.248 & 0.272 \\ 0.656 & 0.752 & 0.728 \\ 0.826 & 0.312 & 0.438 \\ 0.860 & 0.620 & 0.680 \\ 0.656 & 0.752 & 0.728 \\ 0.100 & 0.200 & 0.300 \\ 0.020 & 0.240 & 0.260 \end{pmatrix} \begin{pmatrix} 2{,}100 \\ 4{,}400 \\ 2{,}700 \end{pmatrix} = \begin{pmatrix} 2{,}548 \\ 6{,}652 \\ 4{,}290 \\ 6{,}370 \\ 6{,}652 \\ 1{,}900 \\ 1{,}800 \end{pmatrix}$$

In this manner the effects of varying budgetary plans can be traced throughout the cost system. Similarly, variable costs flowing through the system can readily be determined by eliminating the fixed costs from $[v]$ and the effects traced through the system as above.[6]

FINANCIAL STATEMENTS AND RESIDUAL BALANCES

The matrix formulation is advantageous when the cost composition of asset or expense account balance is desired. That is, what are the purchased goods and services, the employee labor costs, or the allocated costs *left* in any asset or expense account? These are not the charges into the account as before but the residue or the *balance* that remains. Mixtures of costs almost inevitably arise in organizations which collect costs by cost centers and

[6] Similarly, for any decision-making purpose, the relevant costs can be applied to the coefficient matrix and the effects on all the cost centers in the system determined.

allocate them from one cost center to another by some predetermined rate. In these cases the composition of the allocated costs is lost in the allocation and reallocation process. For budgetary purposes, or when making up pro forma statements, the composition of costs of various types in the balance of financial accounts may be desired. Alternatively, the effect of various allocation rates may be traced to financial statements.

The charges into each cost center are the sum of the primary expenses originating in the cost center and the charges from other cost centers. As before, this can be expressed as follows:

$$[u] = [A][u] + [k][v] = [I - A]^{-1}[k][v]$$

where

u_i = The charges *into* the ith department, account, or cost center
a_{ij} = The portion of the total charges in the jth cost center distributed to the ith account or cost center
k_{ij} = The portion of the jth primary expense charged directly to the ith cost center
v_j = The direct primary expenses

The u_i are the total charges into the account. What is needed, however, are the undistributed charges that remain in the account. Since the undistributed charges remaining in the account are one minus the charges distributed to other accounts, the undistributed charges for the jth cost center are

$$1 - \sum_i a_{ij}$$

Thus, if we let u_j' equal the undistributed charges,

$$u_i' = (1 - a_{.j})u_j$$

where

$$u_j = u_i$$

and

$$a_{.j} = \sum_i a_{ij}$$

Then

$$[u'] = [W][I - A]^{-1}[k][v]$$

where

$$[W] = \begin{pmatrix} 1 - a_{.1} & 0 & 0 & \cdot & \cdot & \cdot & 0 \\ 0 & 1 - a_{.2} & 0 & \cdot & \cdot & \cdot & 0 \\ 0 & 0 & 1 - a_{.3} & \cdot & \cdot & \cdot & 0 \\ 0 & 0 & 0 & \cdot & \cdot & \cdot & 0 \\ \cdot & \cdot & \cdot & \cdot & \cdot & \cdot & \cdot \\ \cdot & \cdot & \cdot & \cdot & \cdot & \cdot & \cdot \\ \cdot & \cdot & \cdot & \cdot & \cdot & \cdot & \cdot \\ 0 & 0 & 0 & \cdot & \cdot & \cdot & 1 - a_{.n} \end{pmatrix}$$

To illustrate, assume the following cost classifications and direct charges:

	M	L	O	Σ
A	0	8	3	11
B	3	4	5	12
C	9	4	2	15
Σ	12	16	10	38

and assume that A receives 0.40 of B's and 0.20 of C's costs, and B receives 0.30 of C's costs.

Then

$$[u] = \begin{pmatrix} A \\ B \\ C \end{pmatrix}; \quad [A] = \begin{pmatrix} 0 & 0.4 & 0.2 \\ 0 & 0 & 0.3 \\ 0 & 0 & 0 \end{pmatrix}; \quad [k] = \begin{pmatrix} 0 & 0.50 & 0.30 \\ 0.25 & 0.25 & 0.50 \\ 0.75 & 0.25 & 0.20 \end{pmatrix}; \quad [v] = \begin{pmatrix} 12 \\ 16 \\ 10 \end{pmatrix}$$

$$[u] = \begin{pmatrix} 0 & 0.4 & 0.2 \\ 0 & 0 & 0.3 \\ 0 & 0 & 0 \end{pmatrix} \begin{pmatrix} A \\ B \\ C \end{pmatrix} + \begin{pmatrix} 0 & 0.50 & 0.30 \\ 0.25 & 0.25 & 0.50 \\ 0.75 & 0.25 & 0.20 \end{pmatrix} \begin{pmatrix} 12 \\ 16 \\ 10 \end{pmatrix}$$

$$[u] = \begin{pmatrix} 1 & 0.4 & 0.32 \\ 0 & 1 & 0.30 \\ 0 & 0 & 1 \end{pmatrix} \begin{pmatrix} 0 & 0.50 & 0.30 \\ 0.25 & 0.25 & 0.50 \\ 0.75 & 0.25 & 0.20 \end{pmatrix} \begin{pmatrix} 12 \\ 16 \\ 10 \end{pmatrix}$$

$$[u] = \begin{pmatrix} 0.340 & 0.680 & 0.564 \\ 0.475 & 0.325 & 0.560 \\ 0.750 & 0.250 & 0.200 \end{pmatrix} \begin{pmatrix} 12 \\ 16 \\ 10 \end{pmatrix} = \begin{pmatrix} 20.60 \\ 16.50 \\ 15.00 \end{pmatrix}$$

$$[u'] = [W][u] \quad \text{where} \quad [W] = \begin{pmatrix} 1 & 0 & 0 \\ 0 & 0.6 & 0 \\ 0 & 0 & 0.5 \end{pmatrix}$$

$$[u'] = \begin{pmatrix} 1 & 0 & 0 \\ 0 & 0.6 & 0 \\ 0 & 0 & 0.5 \end{pmatrix} \begin{pmatrix} 20.60 \\ 16.50 \\ 15.00 \end{pmatrix} = \begin{pmatrix} 20.60 \\ 9.90 \\ 7.50 \end{pmatrix}$$

and of course

$$\sum_i u_i' = \sum_i v_i = 38$$

In the above example, if the material costs decrease by $2, the labor costs increase by 25 percent, and the overhead costs remain the same, then the expense classifications would change as follows:

$$\begin{pmatrix} A \\ B \\ C \end{pmatrix} = \begin{pmatrix} 0.340 & 0.680 & 0.564 \\ 0.475 & 0.325 & 0.560 \\ 0.750 & 0.250 & 0.200 \end{pmatrix} \begin{pmatrix} 10 \\ 20 \\ 10 \end{pmatrix} = \begin{pmatrix} 22.64 \\ 16.85 \\ 14.50 \end{pmatrix}$$

$$\begin{pmatrix} A' \\ B' \\ C' \end{pmatrix} = \begin{pmatrix} 1 & 0 & 0 \\ 0 & 0.6 & 0 \\ 0 & 0 & 0.5 \end{pmatrix} \begin{pmatrix} 22.64 \\ 16.85 \\ 14.50 \end{pmatrix} = \begin{pmatrix} 22.64 \\ 10.11 \\ 7.25 \end{pmatrix}$$

Here a decrease in material costs of 16.67 percent and an increase in labor costs of 25 percent caused the balance in the A account to increase 9.9 percent, in B to increase 2.1 percent, and in C to decrease 3.33 percent. The vector $[u']$ can of course be expressed directly in terms of $[v]$ as follows:

$$[u'] = [W][I - A]^{-1}[k][v]$$

or

$$[u'] = \begin{pmatrix} 1 & 0 & 0 \\ 0 & 0.6 & 0 \\ 0 & 0 & 0.5 \end{pmatrix} \begin{pmatrix} 0.340 & 0.680 & 0.564 \\ 0.475 & 0.325 & 0.560 \\ 0.750 & 0.250 & 0.200 \end{pmatrix} \begin{pmatrix} M \\ L \\ O \end{pmatrix}$$

$$[u'] = \begin{pmatrix} 0.340 & 0.680 & 0.564 \\ 0.285 & 0.195 & 0.336 \\ 0.375 & 0.125 & 0.100 \end{pmatrix} \begin{pmatrix} 10 \\ 20 \\ 10 \end{pmatrix} = \begin{pmatrix} 22.64 \\ 10.11 \\ 7.25 \end{pmatrix}$$

The same process can be used to trace the effects of any set of relevant costs, including the use of variable costs alone, on the cost flows and on the account balances. If, in the original example, none of the materials, one fourth of the labor, and all of the overhead represented fixed costs, recording only the variable costs in the system involves only a change in $[v]$. This would allocate the costs through the system as follows:

$$[u] = \begin{pmatrix} 0.340 & 0.680 & 0.564 \\ 0.475 & 0.325 & 0.560 \\ 0.750 & 0.250 & 0.200 \end{pmatrix} \begin{pmatrix} 12 \\ 12 \\ 0 \end{pmatrix} = \begin{pmatrix} 12.24 \\ 9.60 \\ 12.00 \end{pmatrix}$$

$$[u'] = \begin{pmatrix} 1 & 0 & 0 \\ 0 & 0.6 & 0 \\ 0 & 0 & 0.5 \end{pmatrix} \begin{pmatrix} 0.340 & 0.680 & 0.564 \\ 0.475 & 0.325 & 0.560 \\ 0.750 & 0.250 & 0.200 \end{pmatrix} \begin{pmatrix} 12 \\ 12 \\ 0 \end{pmatrix}$$

$$[u'] = \begin{pmatrix} 0.340 & 0.680 & 0.564 \\ 0.285 & 0.195 & 0.336 \\ 0.375 & 0.125 & 0.100 \end{pmatrix} \begin{pmatrix} 12 \\ 12 \\ 0 \end{pmatrix} = \begin{pmatrix} 12.24 \\ 5.76 \\ 6.00 \end{pmatrix}$$

Whether one is interested in the level of expenditure, $[u]$, or the residual balance, $[u']$, the result is readily provided. Where the cost collection point is a departmental budget, the level of expenditure $[u]$ is of interest. If, however, the cost collection point is an account for a financial statement, then the residual balance $[u']$ is of prime concern. In either case the above formulation provides a flexible mechanism for analysis and modification.

PRODUCT COSTS

A final example of the use of an algebraic formulation in cost allocation problems is in the determination of costs of products in either a job or a process cost system. The products can be represented as a set of cost collection accounts, $P_1, P_2, \cdots, P_n$. Costs flow into these accounts from operating cost centers, $C_1, C_2, \cdots, C_m$. These operating cost centers, in turn, receive charges from other cost centers as well as incurring their own labor, material, and overhead costs—expressed in dollar amounts or as a portion of aggregate expense categories, $E_1, E_2, \cdots, E_h$. If, as before, we let k_{ij} represent the costs flowing into the ith cost collection center or collection account from the jth cost center or expense category, then

$$P_i = \sum_{j+1}^{m+h} k_{ij}C_j \qquad i = 1, 2, \cdots, n$$

$$C_i = \sum_{j=1}^{m+h} k_{ij}C_j \qquad i = 1, 2, \cdots, m$$

In matrix form

$$\begin{bmatrix} p \\ c \end{bmatrix} = [M]\begin{bmatrix} c \\ v \end{bmatrix}$$

where

$$\begin{bmatrix} p \\ c \end{bmatrix} = [P_1, P_2, \cdots, P_n, C_1, C_2, \cdots, C_m]^T$$

$$[M] = [k_{ij}] \qquad i = 1, 2, \cdots, m + n$$
$$j = 1, 2, \cdots, m + h$$

$$\begin{bmatrix} c \\ v \end{bmatrix} = C_1, C_2, \cdots, C_m, E_1, E_2, \cdots, E_h]^T$$

We can partition $[M]$ as before so that

$$[M] = \begin{bmatrix} M_{11} & M_{12} \\ M_{21} & M_{22} \end{bmatrix}$$

Then

$$[p] = [M_{11}][c] + [M_{12}][v]$$
$$[c] = [M_{21}][c] + [M_{22}][v]$$

and

$$[p] = [M_{11}][I - M_{21}]^{-1}[M_{22}][v] + [M_{12}][v]$$

If the product accounts distribute their charges in turn, the balance left after such distributions can be obtained as in the preceding section and $[p'] = [W][p]$ where $[W]$ is defined on page 153.

Thus the cost of products can be determined for varying sets of manufacturing conditions merely by changing the k_{ij}'s. More important, however, is the ability to readily determine the cost of each product at varying levels of activity, $[v]$, since $[p]$ can be expressed as a function of $[v]$ in all but the exceptional case where $[I - M_{21}]$ has no inverse. The converse, however, is more difficult. Determining a "bill of materials," $[v]$, given only the desired level and distribution of production outputs, $[p]$, requires that $[v]$ be a function of $[p]$. For the problem to have a unique solution, the number of products and the number of primary expense classifications must be equal, and the matrix

$$[M_{11}][I - M_{21}]^{-1}[M_{22}] + [M_{12}]$$

must possess an inverse.[7]

CONCLUSION

With the exception of the procedures for service cost allocation, the first example, the usefulness of the foregoing applications depends upon the stability of the underlying relationships, the k_{ij}'s, when one of the variables or the level of one of the variables is changed. As in the case of Richards' "input-output analysis,"[8] measurement of the relationships presents a formidable problem.

Immediate applicability was not, however, the intent of this paper, nor was an exhaustive coverage of all the areas in accounting which could benefit from the application of mathematical techniques (such as multireciprocal consolidations in financial accounting). Rather, the purpose here was to explore some possible areas for mathematical analysis in the research and the teaching of accounting.

---

[7] $\underset{h \times 1}{[v]} = \Big[\underset{\text{"}n \times m\text{"}}{[M_{11}]}\ \underset{m \times m}{[I - M_{21}]^{-1}}\ \underset{\text{"}m \times h\text{"}}{[M_{22}]} + \underset{n \times h}{[M_{12}]}\Big]^{-1}\ \underset{n \times 1}{[p]}$

Work currently going on in the theory of a generalized inverse promises some relief from this restriction.

[8] Allen B. Richards, "Input-Output Accounting for Business," *Accounting Review*, July, 1960, pp. 429–36.

12

The author develops a mathematical model which describes the relationships between income, the tax rate, depreciation, stocks, bonds, and other variables. An illustrative example is then presented, including an analysis of the effect of inflation and deflation. Although emphasis is placed upon the valuation problems associated with the determination of an equitable rate base, the model would also appear to have important implications for commercial enterprises where inflation or deflation patently affects pricing decisions.

*MATHEMATICAL MODELS FOR PUBLIC UTILITY RATE REGULATION**†

Robert H. Roy

THE EARNINGS of public utilities, as is widely known, are regulated by government commissions of various kinds, which exist for the dual purpose of preventing uneconomic duplication of utility facilities and services and, at the same time, exploitation of the public through monopoly position. Public service commissions thus serve as a substitute for competition by control and regulation of the prices at which each utility sells its services to the public. In general, such regulation is exercised by seeking to determine the value of a utility's property and deciding upon an equitable rate of return to apply to that value. The product of these (value times rate of return) then becomes the projected income of the utility, and price schedules are established with the objective of yielding that amount.

In countless rate cases, there have of course been many disputes about these two factors, value and rate of return; and since World War II, many of these have concentrated upon the determination of value during a long period of inflation. Utilities have argued that public service commissions must determine *present* value when setting a rate base, taking due account of the decline in the purchasing power of the dollar in evaluating plant con-

* Reprinted from *Journal of Industrial Engineering*, January–February, 1962, pp. 8–14. The *Journal* is the official publication of the American Institute of Industrial Engineers, Inc., 345 East 47th Street, New York, New York 10017.

† The author is indebted to Dr. Eliezer Naddor, associate professor of industrial engineering, Johns Hopkins University, for reviewing the manuscript and for making suggestions concerning notation. Special thanks are due to Dr. Sidney Davidson, professor of accounting, University of Chicago, for his penetrating comments and criticism.

structed at an earlier time for a relatively smaller number of more valuable dollars. Contrariwise, opponents of "current fair value," to use the customary term, have held to the position that value can properly be determined only by assessing the aggregate original cost of plant in current use and subtracting from it accumulated depreciation to yield net book cost as an expression of value to be used as rate base.

Because accounting for utility investments in plant and depreciation is subject to regulatory governance and control, proponents of original cost have claimed—often with telling effect—that any other method of determining value, by appraisal, by "reproduction cost new" studies, by the application of price indexes, is speculative and therefore incapable of verification and devoid of meaning. Proponents of current fair value have countered these arguments by showing that adherence to net original cost during years of inflation seriously impairs the purchasing power of utility income and, in effect, results in partial confiscation of the assets of the corporation.

By the development of mathematical models, this article will endeavor to shed some light upon the effect of inflation or deflation on utility income. It will further propose a verifiable and reproducible method for calculating rate base, which takes account of inflation or deflation no matter how such changes in the value of the dollar may occur.

NOTATION

Let

G = Income before payment of income taxes
I = Income after payment of income taxes but before bond interest, that is, the income to all who have furnished long-term capital
B = Investment in plant financed by debt capital
S = Revenue from sales in any fiscal year
E = Operating expenses in any fiscal year
D_e = Depreciation expense in any fiscal year
D_p = Accumulated depreciation reserve of plant still in service
T = Income taxes in any fiscal year
C = Total original book cost of plant still in service
R_I = Rate of return based on income after taxes
b = Interest rate on debt capital
x = Tax rate on income
t = Subscript denoting any designated base year
$t - 1, t - 2$, etc. = The preceding year, year before that, etc.
$t + 1, t + 2$, etc. = The following year, year after that, etc.
$t - m$ = Year of oldest plant not yet retired
$t + n$ = Any future year
$u_1, u_2 \cdots u_i$ = Units of service
$p_1, p_2 \cdots p_i$ = Corresponding unit prices charged for service, such that

$$\left(\sum_i u_i p_i\right)_t = S_t$$

(NOTE: The final step in regulation is the assignment of values for p to yield the rate of return, R_I, established by a public service commission.)

$e_1, e_2 \cdots e_i$ = Individual items of operating expense, such that

$$\left(\sum_i e_i\right)_t = E_t$$

$c_1, c_2 \cdots c_i$ = Original cost of individual items of plant not yet retired, regardless of year of purchase, such that $\left(\sum_i c_i\right)_t = C_t$

(NOTE: $c = 0$ for any item of plant which has been retired.)

$d_1, d_2 \cdots d_i$ = Depreciation rates corresponding to each individual item of plant not yet retired such that[1] $\left(\sum_i c_i d_i\right)_t = (D_e)_t$ and $\left(\sum_{t-m}^{t} \sum_i c_i d_i\right)_t = (D_p)_t$

(NOTE: Not all depreciation rates are expressible as constant percentages, and it should be understood that any given cd represents depreciation expense for that particular item, however calculated. Similarly, any given cd summed over time represents depreciation reserve for that particular item, however calculated.)

GENERAL RELATIONSHIPS

$$I_t = [R_I(C - D_p)]_t \quad (1)$$

Equation 1 represents essentially the first step in regulatory procedure followed by public service commissions in original cost jurisdictions. The rate of return, R_I, and the rate base, $C - D_p$, are determined by the regulatory body, after evidence and argument have been presented on behalf of the utility and the public. The product of the two terms then yields the anticipated permissible income of the utility from which charges to customers are determined. All of the other relationships set forth below are derived from this first step.

Income also may be related to sales, operating expenses, depreciation, and income taxes, as shown in equation 2.

$$I_t = (S - E - D_e - T)_t = [R_I(C - D_p)]_t \quad (2)$$

In this equation

$$(S - E - D_e)_t = G_t \quad (3)$$

and[2]

$$T_t = x(G - bB)_t = x(S - E - D_e - bB)_t \quad (4)$$

[1] Whenever the subscripts t, $t + 1$, etc., are used outside parentheses or brackets, it is to be understood that they apply to all of the terms enclosed within.

[2] Note that bond interest, bB, is deductible in the usual way in the calculation of income taxes, as shown in equation 4, but is included in utility income, I, as previously defined.

Substituting equation 3 and equation 4 in equation 2 gives:

$$
\begin{aligned}
I_t &= [S - E - D_e - x(S - E - D_e - bB)]_t \\
&= [G - x(G - bB)]_t \\
&= [(1 - x)(S - E - D_e) + x(bB)]_t \qquad (5)\\
&= [(1 - x)(G) + x(bB)]_t \\
&= [R_I(C - D_p)]_t
\end{aligned}
$$

From this

$$
\begin{aligned}
(R_I)_t &= \frac{[(1 - x)(S - E - D_e) + x(bB)]_t}{(C - D_p)_t} \qquad (6)\\
&= \frac{[(1 - x)(G) + x(bB)]_t}{(C - D_p)_t}
\end{aligned}
$$

DETAILED RELATIONSHIPS[3]

For the year t, equation 6 may be expressed in greater detail as follows:

$$
(7) \qquad (R_I)_t = \frac{\left[(1 - x)\left(\sum_i u_i p_i - \sum_i e_i - \sum_i c_i d_i\right) + x(bB)\right]_t}{\left(\sum_i c_i - \sum_{t-m}^{t} \sum_i c_i d_i\right)_t}
$$

For the year $t + 1$, assume an additional investment in plant of $(c)_{t+1}$. Then

$$
(8) \qquad (R_I)_{t+1} = \frac{(1 - x)\left\{\left(\sum_i u_i p_i - \sum_i e_i\right)_{t+1} - \left[\left(\sum_i c_i d_i\right)_t + (cd)_{t+1}\right]\right\} + x(bB)_{t+1}}{\left(\sum_i c_i - \sum_{t-m}^{t+1} \sum_i c_i d_i\right)_t + (c - cd)_{t+1}}
$$

Similarly, if plant investments $(c)_{t+2}$, $(c)_{t+3}$, $\cdots$, $(c)_{t+n}$ are made in succeeding years, we have

$$
(9) \qquad (R_I)_{t+2} = \frac{(1 - x)\left\{\left(\sum_i u_i p_i - \sum_i e_i\right)_{t+2} - \left[\left(\sum_i c_i d_i\right)_t + (cd)_{t+1} + (cd)_{t+2}\right]\right\} + x(bB)_{t+2}}{\left(\sum_i c_i - \sum_{t-m}^{t+2} \sum_i c_i d_i\right)_t + (c - 2cd)_{t+1} + (c - cd)_{t+2}}
$$

[3] Utilization of a much simpler system of notation would have been possible in the sections which follow, but the more complex form has been adhered to as better representing the accounting process actually employed. Depreciation reserve, for example, is calculated by summing depreciation for all items of plant not yet retired for all years of service, and the double summations used do convey this procedure better than would the substitution of single-letter symbols.

and

$$(10)\quad (R_I)_{t+n} = \frac{(1-x)\left\{\left(\sum_i u_i p_i - \sum_i e_i\right)_{t+n} - \left[\left(\sum_i c_i d_i\right)_t + (cd)_{t+1} + (cd)_{t+2} + \cdots (cd)_{t+n}\right]\right\} + x(bB)_{t+n}}{\left(\sum_i c_i - \sum_{t-m}^{t+n}\sum_i c_i d_i\right)_t + (c - ncd)_{t+1} + [c - (n-1)cd]_{t+2} + \cdots (c - cd)_{t+n}}$$

Equation 10 may be arranged to give

$$(11)\quad (I)_{t+n} = (R_I)_{t+n}\left\{\left(\sum_i c_i - \sum_{t-m}^{t+n}\sum_i c_i d_i\right)_t + (c - ncd)_{t+1} + [c - (n-1)cd]_{t+2} + \cdots (c - cd)_{t+n}\right\}$$

$$= (1-x)\left\{\left(\sum_i u_i p_i - \sum_i e_i\right)_{t+n} - \left[\left(\sum_i c_i d_i\right)_t + (cd)_{t+1} + (cd)_{t+2} + \cdots (cd)_{t+n}\right]\right\} + x(bB)_{t+n}$$

The first line of equation 11 simply shows that income is derived from annual increments, each of which is the product of a rate of return determined by a regulatory commission and the net book value (original cost minus depreciation reserve) of the plant purchased in each year, either back to the base year t, as shown, or back to any other year—$t - m$, for example. As stated before, once the value of $(I)_{t+n}$ is determined in this way, quantities of u are estimated for the future period, and price schedules for p are set to yield the income specified. This relationship is shown in the second line of equation 11.

NUMERICAL EXAMPLE

This method of calculating income may be illustrated by a few simple assumptions, as follows.

Let

$$R_I = 10 \text{ percent}$$

$$\left(\sum_i c_i\right)_t = \$10{,}000$$

$$\left(\sum_{t-m}^{t}\sum_{i} c_i d_i\right)_t = \$5{,}000$$

$$\left(\sum_{i} c_i d_i\right)_{t+1}, \left(\sum_{i} c_i d_i\right)_{t+2}, \left(\sum_{i} c_i d_i\right)_{t+3} = \$500 \text{ per year}$$

$$(c)_{t+1},\ (c)_{t+2},\ (c)_{t+3} = \$1{,}000 \text{ each year}$$

$$(cd)_{t+1},\ (cd)_{t+2},\ (cd)_{t+3} = \$100 \text{ per year for each}$$

Then

$$(I)_t = 0.10[10{,}000 - 5{,}000] = 500 = \$500$$

$$(I)_{t+1} = 0.10[(10{,}000 - 5{,}500) + (1{,}000 - 100)] = 450 + 90 = \$540$$

$$(I)_{t+2} = 0.10[(10{,}000 - 6{,}000) + (1{,}000 - 200) + (1{,}000 - 100)]$$
$$= 400 + 80 + 90 = \$570$$

$$(I)_{t+3} = 0.10[(10{,}000 - 6{,}500) + (1{,}000 - 300) + (1{,}000 - 200) + (1{,}000 - 100)]$$
$$= 350 + 70 + 80 + 90 = \$590$$

From these figures the process may be stated: Income is derived from the product of rate of return and net book value for each vintage year; each year, vintage increments of income are reduced by the product of rate times increase in depreciation reserve (which is the same as annual depreciation expense for each vintage); and each year, income rises because the net book value of the plant as a whole rises, that is, the utility is expanding, from a net original cost of $5,000 in the year t to $5,900 in the year $t + 3$. Other examples could be devised, of course, to show either stable or declining income by selecting figures from which income derived from investment in new plant is equal to or less than the annual increments added to depreciation reserve.

THE EFFECT OF INFLATION OR DEFLATION

Returning now to equation 11, it is clear that this model takes no account of changes in the value of the dollar. Dollar income derived from investment in the year t will decline in each succeeding year because of depreciation, but the purchasing power of such income may change in either direction. Progressive inflation will reduce the purchasing power, while progressive deflation will increase the purchasing power of vintage dollar income.

To sustain the purchasing power of utility income during periods of inflation and deflation, assuming a fixed rate of return, we must rewrite equation 11.

Let

I' = Income of constant purchasing power

$(v)_t, (v)_{t+1}, \cdots (v)_{t+n}$ = Index numbers representing the relative purchasing power of the dollar for each year

During inflation

$$(v)_t > (v)_{t+1} > \cdots (v)_{t+n}$$

During deflation

$$(v)_t < (v)_{t+1} < \cdots (v)_{t+n}$$

Then

$$(I')_{t+n} = (R_I)_{t+n}\left\{\left(\sum_i c_i - \sum_{t-m}^{t+n}\sum_i c_i d_i\right)_t\left(\frac{v_t}{v_{t+n}}\right) + (c - ncd)_{t+1}\left(\frac{v_{t+1}}{v_{t+n}}\right) + [c - (n-1)cd]_{t+2}\left(\frac{v_{t+2}}{v_{t+n}}\right) + \cdots (c - cd)_{t+n}\right\}$$

$$(12) \qquad = (1 - x)\left\{\left(\sum_i u_i p_i - \sum_i e_i\right)_{t+n} - \left[\left(\sum_i c_i d_i\right)_t\left(\frac{v_t}{v_{t+n}}\right) + (cd)_{t+1}\left(\frac{v_{t+1}}{v_{t+n}}\right) + (cd)_{t+2}\left(\frac{v_{t+2}}{v_{t+n}}\right) + \cdots (cd)_{t+n}\right]\right\} + x(bB)_{t+n}$$

Two observations about equation 12 are necessary:

Since I' has been defined as income of constant purchasing power, *all* of the vintage items on *both* sides of the equation have been multiplied by ratios of v. But there are two quite separate issues involved: (1) multiplication of vintage rate base values by ratios of v requires only regulatory commission approval of the fair value concept, whereas (2) multiplication of vintage depreciation expense items by ratios of v would not only require commission approval but approval of the Internal Revenue Service as well, since it is from the operating side of the equation that income tax is calculated. Most utilities have been content to fight the rate base issue of fair value before regulatory commissions and to waive questions related to vintage depreciation expense. Although logical consistency demands the modification of all vintage values by ratios of v, the question will be waived here also, since we are not concerned with determination of values for p.

The operating sides of equations 11 and 12 to the right of each second equal sign call for multiplication of sales, expenses, and depreciation expense by $1 - x$ and for addition of $x(bB)$. These terms relate to the calculation of income tax and bond interest and are interdependent, as indicated in equation 4. By definition, B is that portion of the rate base represented by debt capital, for which a fixed interest rate is specified. By contract, then, bB is impervious to either inflation or deflation. This, in turn, means that the equity shareholder will receive income of *higher* purchasing power in a period of inflation and *lower* purchasing power in a time of deflation, if all values in the rate base are multiplied by ratios of v and no other adjustment is made. This will be made clear by returning to the numerical example used previously.

NUMERICAL EXAMPLE, ASSUMING INFLATION

Let $(v)_t = 1.0$, $(v)_{t+1} = 0.8$, $(v)_{t+2} = 0.6$, and $(v)_{t+3} = 0.4$. Then

$$(I')_t = 0.10(10{,}000 - 5{,}000)\frac{1.0}{1.0} = 500 = \$500$$

$$(I')_{t+1} = 0.10\left[(10{,}000 - 5{,}500)\frac{1.0}{0.8} + (1{,}000 - 100)\frac{0.8}{0.8}\right] = 563 + 90 = \$653$$

$$(I')_{t+2} = 0.10\left[(10{,}000 - 6{,}000)\frac{1.0}{0.6} + (1{,}000 - 200)\frac{0.8}{0.6} + (1{,}000 - 100)\frac{0.6}{0.6}\right]$$
$$= 667 + 106 + 90 = \$863$$

$$(I')_{t+3} = 0.10\left[(10{,}000 - 6{,}500)\frac{1.0}{0.4} + (1{,}000 - 300)\frac{0.8}{0.4} + (1{,}000 - 200)\frac{0.6}{0.4} + (1{,}000 - 100)\frac{0.4}{0.4}\right]$$
$$= 875 + 140 + 120 + 90 = \$1{,}225$$

These figures compare with those given previously, as shown in Table 1.

TABLE 1

	I	I'	I'/I
t	\$500	\$ 500	1.00
$t+1$	540	653	1.21
$t+2$	570	863	1.51
$t+3$	590	1,225	2.08

The ratio of $(I'/I)_{t+3}$ indicates that income has had to rise by a factor of about 2.08 in order to preserve purchasing power over four years of progressive inflation. But the payment of bond interest out of income and the amounts remaining for the owners of the enterprise, the equity shareholders, reveal a different story.

To illustrate, let

Q = Portion of income available for equity shareholders, after payment of bond interest, without adjustment for inflation

Q' = Portion of income available for equity shareholders, after payment of bond interest, with adjustment for inflation

If we then assume that $bB = \$100$ in each of the previous examples, we get the figures for equity income shown in Table 2, which reveals that adjustment in income by a factor of about 2.08 has yielded adjustment in equity's share by a factor of about 2.30, thereby proving a "windfall" to the equity stockholder. If the portion of plant financed by debt were higher and $bB =$ \$150, these factors respectively would have been 2.08 and 1,075/440 = 2.44,

TABLE 2

	Q	Q'	Q'/Q
t	\$400	\$ 400	1.00
$t+1$	440	553	1.26
$t+2$	470	763	1.62
$t+3$	490	1,125	2.30

and the equity shareholder would have profited still more. Some proponents of fair value argue that there is nothing wrong with such a windfall, because the risks of ownership rise with increase in the debt ratio. Nevertheless, the windfall to common stockholders, the *additional* purchasing power of equity income during inflation, is one of the most frequent arguments used against the concept of fair value.

Without taking sides, it may be pointed out that readjustment of equity income to a basis of *stable* purchasing power may be made by multiplying $(Q')_{t+3}$ by the ratio of the factors $2.08/2.30 = 0.904$, or by taking the product of $(Q)_{t+3}$ and the ratio $(I'/I)_{t+3}$, processes which are of course identical. Thus if we let

$$Q'' = \text{Readjusted equity income}$$
$$I'' = \text{Readjusted net income}$$

the figures for $t + 3$ become

$$(Q'')_{t+3} = \left(Q' \times \frac{I'/I}{Q'/Q}\right)_{t+3} = 1{,}125 \times \frac{2.08}{2.30} = \$1{,}019$$
$$= (Q \times I'/I)_{t+3} = 490 \times 2.08 = \$1{,}019$$

and

$$(I'')_{t+3} = (Q'' + bB)_{t+3} = 1{,}019 + 100 = \$1{,}119$$

For the assumption $(bB)_{t+3} = \$150$, $(Q'')_{t+3} = 440 \times 2.08 = \$915$, and $(I'')_{t+3} = 915 + 150 = \$1{,}065$.

A readjustment of this kind will be shown in the case study which follows. It may be noted in passing that such a readjustment procedure would result in an *increase* in equity's share of income during a period of deflation.

CASE STUDY

Although the data which follow are taken from an actual case and are part of a public record, certain simplifications and assumptions have been made for purposes of convenience. Original cost and depreciation reserve items in Table 3 have been rounded to the nearest \$100,000; debt capital has been assumed to be \$100 million at an average interest rate of 3½ percent; the tax rate x used is 52 percent; and the rate of return, specified by the Public Service Commission, is 6¼ percent, based upon net original cost.

TABLE 3*

Year (t = 1929) ($t - m$ = 1899)	Original Cost $\sum_i c_i$	Depreciation Reserve $\sum_t \sum_i c_i d_i$	Net Original Cost (Col. 2 − Col. 3)	CPI Translator $\frac{v}{v_{t+n}}$	Net Fair Value (Col. 4 × Col. 6)
1	2	3	4	5	6
1929	$ 16.9	$10.2	$ 6.7	1.685	$ 11.29
1930	2.1	1.1	1.0	1.730	1.73
1931	1.1	0.6	0.5	1.900	0.95
1932	1.0	0.5	0.5	2.115	1.06
1933	0.2	0.1	0.1	2.233	0.22
1934	0.4	0.2	0.2	2.159	0.43
1935	0.8	0.4	0.4	2.104	0.84
1936	0.9	0.5	0.4	2.083	0.83
1937	1.8	0.9	0.9	2.011	1.81
1938	3.8	1.9	1.9	2.048	3.89
1939	3.1	1.6	1.5	2.079	3.12
1940	4.4	1.9	2.5	2.062	5.16
1941	6.4	2.6	3.8	1.963	7.46
1942	7.3	2.8	4.5	1.772	7.97
1943	1.3	0.5	0.8	1.669	1.34
1944	1.2	0.4	0.8	1.642	1.31
1945	1.9	0.8	1.1	1.606	1.77
1946	4.9	1.8	3.1	1.481	4.59
1947	9.8	2.9	6.9	1.293	8.92
1948	28.6	8.4	20.2	1.201	24.26
1949	20.6	5.2	15.4	1.213	18.68
1950	10.3	2.8	7.5	1.201	9.01
1951	13.4	3.1	10.3	1.113	11.46
1952	18.8	3.6	15.2	1.088	16.54
1953	20.2	3.8	16.4	1.080	17.71
1954	30.1	4.0	26.1	1.076	28.08
1955	22.8	3.0	19.8	1.079	21.36
1956	41.4	3.8	37.6	1.063	39.97
1957	46.2	2.6	43.6	1.027	44.78
1958	53.8	1.0	52.8	1.000	52.80
TOTAL	$375.5	$73.0	$302.5		$349.34

* Figures in columns 2, 3, 4, and 6 are in millions of dollars.

Use of actual figures would add detail and verisimilitude but in no way alter the results.

Since the purpose here is to reveal the effect of inflation on the purchasing power of utility income, the Consumers' Price Index has been used for values of v. Use of other indexes, such as the Wholesale Commodity Price Index or the Gross Private Product Price Deflator, would yield essentially similar results. Detailed figures are given in Table 3. Column 1 shows

$t = 1929$ as the base year and $t + n = 1958$ as the current year, with elements of surviving plant dating from $t - m = 1899$. Columns 2, 3, and 4 portray detailed elements of the rate base as used in equation 11. Column 5 shows ratios of v from $t = 1929$ to $t + n = 1958$, and column 6 shows elements of the rate base adjusted for ratios of v as applied in equation 12.

From these data, we can now calculate I, I', Q, Q', and Q'' and I'' for the year 1958:

$I = 0.0625 \times 302{,}500{,}000$
$= \$18{,}906{,}250$ Income based upon net book cost, taking no account of inflation

$I' = 0.0625 \times 349{,}340{,}000$
$= \$21{,}833{,}750$ Income based upon "current fair value," taking account of inflation

$I' = I = 21{,}833{,}750 - 18{,}906{,}250$
$= \$2{,}927{,}500$ Gain in income permitted through recognition of current fair value

$Q = I - bB = 18{,}906{,}250 - 0.035 \times 100{,}000{,}000$
$= 18{,}906{,}250 - 3{,}500{,}000$
$= \$15{,}406{,}250$ Portion of income available to equity shareholders, without adjustment for inflation

$Q' = I' - bB = 21{,}833{,}750 - 3{,}500{,}000$
$= \$18{,}333{,}750$ Portion of income available for equity shareholders, adjusted for inflation

$I'/I = 21{,}833{,}750/18{,}906{,}250 = 1.155$

$Q'/Q = 18{,}333{,}750/15{,}406{,}250 = 1.190$

$Q'' = Q \times I'/I = 15{,}406{,}250 \times 1.155$
$= \$17{,}794{,}219$ Portion of income available for equity shareholders, adjusted for inflation and readjusted to prevent "windfall"

$I'' = Q'' + bB = 17{,}794{,}219 + 3{,}500{,}000$
$= \$21{,}294{,}219$ Income adjusted for inflation and readjusted to prevent windfall to equity shareholders

$I'' - I = 21{,}294{,}219 - 18{,}906{,}250$
$= \$2{,}387{,}969$ Gain in income through recognition of current fair value, adjusted to prevent windfall to equity shareholders

The adjustment of Q' to Q'' to maintain the purchasing power of the equity shareholders' portion of income reduces the effective rate of return to

$$R_I'' = \frac{I''}{349.34} = \frac{21{,}294{,}219}{349{,}340{,}000}$$
$$= 0.06096 \text{ or } 6.1\%$$

OBSERVATIONS AND CONCLUSIONS

While the possibility of increasing income by substantially more than \$2 million through recognition of the principle of current fair value is worth a great deal of effort, the development of equations 11 and 12 may have seemed unnecessarily tedious and complex for the achievement of fairly simple results. However, the models represented by these equations are not presented simply for the purpose of making a calculation in any single utility for any single year. That has been done and will be done again by utilities, as they continue to seek recognition for fair value. They will present their arguments for a fair value rate base by reproduction cost studies, by appraisal studies, by application of various price indexes; and commission counsel will rebut by stating that these techniques are subjective, that they pile speculation upon speculation, that fair values so derived should be disallowed because they have been calculated by biased utility accountants, supported perchance by biased company-retained experts. Such rebuttal has been effective in the past and will no doubt be effective in the future.

But whether one accepts fair value in principle or not, the models escape the charge of subjectivity and bias. The models and the data which go into them are describable, specifiable, regulatable, and, in the language of science, reproducible and verifiable. Give the data to any sufficiently capable person, and the same answer will be found.

This does not mean to say, of course, that *all* judgment will be removed from the regulatory process; not at all. But once a suitable index has been decided upon, the degree of judgment necessary for application of the models will be no more than that required by the net original cost method. Adherents of this much more familiar approach are rather inclined to feel that the subtraction of depreciation reserve from book cost yields a sacred and immutable result, because the data come from company records which are both regulated and audited. But judgment is still necessary in full measure: Depreciation expense and depreciation reserve, which affect both the operating and the rate base sides of the equation, are hardly precise determinations; decisions are made every day, often by subordinate personnel, as to whether work shall be charged to a capital account or to maintenance expense; the forecast of service units to be sold and the determination of price schedules are necessarily speculative; the prudence of a debt ratio, like beauty, lies in the eye of the beholder; and the rate of return, so vital to the calculation of income, is subject to an array of traditional, economic, and political constraints too subtle to be described. The models, it is claimed, do not diminish the importance of judgment, but neither do they increase its need.

A second claim for the models is that they may be applied to any set of data, over any span of years, for any rate and amount of inflation or deflation. Aside from the important fact that rate base computations could be made as routine as they are when based on book cost, there are philosophical considerations as well. If one postulates either runaway inflation, as in the case of Germany in the early 1920's, or sudden deflation, as when French currency was recently devalued by a factor of 100, it is impossible to believe that public service commissions could continue to regulate on a net original cost basis. To do so would result in almost total expropriation in the first instance and a hundredfold enrichment in the second. It is this extension of argument to its logical conclusion which gives strongest support to sustaining the buying power of utility income. If it is necessary to adjust for a lot of inflation or deflation, then it is logical to adjust for a little. Routine use of the models would meet any such situation as it occurred.

These are extreme and, one hopes, unlikely cases. But more reasonably, assume that the investment of $257 million made during the years 1950–58 had been made in reverse order by years, with $53.8 million applied to 1950, $46.2 million to 1951, etc. If we further assume no changes in depreciation reserve, then the total net book cost would remain at $302.5 million. The assumption of constant depreciation reserve is of course somewhat unrealistic but is made simply in order to leave net book cost unchanged. In any event, this kind of situation, a different investment pattern leading to the same net book cost, easily could occur in an actual case. In this case, under these assumptions, the figures for net fair value shown in column 6 of Table 3, because of application of the CPI translators in reverse order, would rise by $12.54 million, to a new total for net fair value of $361.88 million.

Under these circumstances, values for I and Q would remain unchanged at $18,906,250 and $15,406,250, respectively, but new computations would be needed for I', Q', I'', and Q'', as follows:

$$
\begin{aligned}
I' &= 0.0625 \times 361{,}880{,}000 = \$22{,}617{,}500 \\
I' - I &= 22{,}617{,}500 - 18{,}906{,}250 = \$3{,}711{,}250 \\
Q' &= 22{,}617{,}500 - 3{,}500{,}000 = \$19{,}117{,}500 \\
I'/I &= 22{,}617{,}500/18{,}906{,}250 = 1.196 \\
Q'' &= 15{,}406{,}250 \times 1.196 = \$18{,}425{,}875 \\
I'' &= 18{,}425{,}875 + 3{,}500{,}000 = \$21{,}925{,}875 \\
I'' - I &= 21{,}925{,}875 - 18{,}906{,}250 = \$3{,}019{,}625
\end{aligned}
$$

Under these assumptions, recognition of current fair value would have added more than $3 million to income, an increment obviously of considerable significance to corporate health.

To further illustrate the flexibility of the models, assume that in the actual case the interest rate on bonds was 4 percent and debt capital comprised $150 million instead of the $100 million used in the original calculations. Under these conditions, I and I' would remain unchanged at $18,906,250 and $21,833,750, respectively, but new calculations would be needed for Q, Q', Q'', and I'', as follows:

$$
\begin{aligned}
Q &= 18{,}906{,}250 - 0.04 \times 150{,}000{,}000 = 18{,}906{,}250 - 6{,}000{,}000 = 12{,}906{,}250 \\
Q' &= 21{,}833{,}750 - 6{,}000{,}000 = 15{,}833{,}750 \\
I'/I &= 1.155 \text{ (as before)} \\
Q'' &= 12{,}906{,}250 \times 1.155 = \$14{,}906{,}719 \\
I'' &= 14{,}906{,}719 + 6{,}000{,}000 = \$20{,}906{,}719 \\
I'' - I &= 20{,}906{,}719 - 18{,}906{,}250 = \$2{,}000{,}469
\end{aligned}
$$

In this case the figure $I'' = \$20{,}906{,}719$ represents a little less than a 6 percent rate of return on the fair value rate base of $349.34 million, necessary to sustain the purchasing power of income available for equity shareholders.

RATE OF RETURN

While it is too much to expect the models to resolve the many controversial questions relating to rate of return, they can shed some light on the problem. Some proponents claim that adjustment in the rate base is quite unnecessary in order to meet inflation, that the simple and easy way is to adjust the rate of return. To leave the multiplicand alone and raise the multiplier can yield precisely the same answer but is not likely to have the same total effect. In the case history, for example, an adjusted net income of $21,294,219 can come from applying a 6¼ percent rate of return to the $349.34 million fair value rate base and then adjusting for equity's share, or from applying a 7.04 percent rate of return to the net original cost of $302.5 million. In the case where investment patterns were reversed, adjusted net income of about $21.9 million could come from a 6¼ percent return through the model, or from 7¼ percent of net original cost.

The answers in each case are the same, but the effects are not. The models rest upon the hypothesis that the purchasing power of utility income should be preserved during changes in the value of the dollar. They adopt as a point of departure a rate of return stabilized by custom and practice and acceptable to the public, to investors, and to government. Procedure thereafter is prescribable, verifiable, and flexible. Accomplishment of the same result by alteration in the rate of return would require picking a rate of return from the air, on the one hand, and disturbing a tradition-bound number, on the other. The first is arithmetically awkward; the second is politically impracticable.

It would appear, therefore, that application of models such as these could diminish some part of the subjectivity of public utility rate making and perhaps provide a prescribable, regulatable, and acceptable method of procedure.

III

Analysis of the Distribution Function

TABLEAU III

Methodological Analysis

Article \ *Methodology*	*Descriptive Models for Analysis*					*Optimizing Models*			
	Algebraic or Symbolic (Deterministic)	*Algebraic or Symbolic (Probabilistic)*	*Matrix Methods*	*Markov Processes*	*Simulation*	*Linear Programming*	*Game Theory*	*Calculus*	*Other*
13. Marketing Costs and Mathematical Programming						X			
14. A Note on Manufacturers' Choice of Distribution Channels								X	
15. The Effect of Promotional Effort on Sales		X							
16. An Operations Research Study of Sales Response to Advertising	X								
17. A Simple Model for Determining Advertising Appropriations									X
18. The Carry-Over Effect of Advertising	X								
19. Forecasting Brand Performance through Simulation Experiments					X				

ANALYSIS OF THE DISTRIBUTION FUNCTION

The distribution function (marketing) is traditionally conceived to be that functional area encompassing decisions related to choosing salable products, determining appropriate prices, planning the advertising effort, and electing alternative distribution channels. While subjective criteria and traditional accounting data may be useful in respect to some of these decisions, mathematical and statistical techniques may also be used, at least in part, as other reliable decision bases. Some of the more prominent areas of application are enumerated following:

1. *Choice of distribution channel*
2. *Measurement of advertising effect or consequence*
3. *Determination of consumer reaction to a given product*

Quantitative approaches to the first problem are presented in articles 13 and 14. Articles 15, 16, 17, and 18 deal with quantitative methods that are concerned with measuring the effect of advertising. Article 19 offers an example of how quantitative methods may be combined with behavioral assumptions in predicting consumer response. Although an example of the direct application of quantitative methods to the pricing problem is not presented, it may be readily seen that the techniques outlined in the following articles can be applied to this problem; to regard price as a variable in the models presented would be a useful and valid extension of the arguments cited.

13

The comment is often made that the marketing effort is improperly allocated. The authors argue that the combined use of distribution cost analysis and mathematical programming may achieve an optimum allocation. Both analysis and programming problems are evaluated, and an Appendix is provided which includes a simple example and discussion of marginal and average cost data.

*MARKETING COSTS AND MATHEMATICAL PROGRAMMING**

William J. Baumol and Charles H. Sevin

IT IS DIFFICULT to exaggerate the opportunities for reduced marketing costs and increased marketing efficiency, and hence greater profits, which are offered to management by the combined techniques of distribution cost analysis and mathematical programming. In the offing may be a revolution in the planning and execution of distribution that is fully comparable to the triumph of time and motion studies and cost analysis in the factory.

In the pages to follow, we shall describe some of the more important techniques that management can profitably use, and we shall show that

1. The misallocation of marketing effort in industry is greater than most people realize.
2. The separation of (*a*) fixed costs incurred in common for different types of sales effort, (*b*) separable fixed costs, and (*c*) variable costs which are related to different segments of the business is one of the key steps in analyzing a company's distribution problem.
3. The techniques of mathematical and linear programming can be used to derive approximately, on the basis of these cost data, the most profitable allocation of a firm's marketing expenditures and resources.
4. Once the needed data on cost-volume relationships are obtained and the computations are completed, the businessman can proceed to redirect his marketing effort in a way that is virtually guaranteed to increase his profits.

In a short Appendix, we shall suggest a few inexpensive computations that will help to improve a distribution cost analysis.

* Reprinted by permission of the publishers from Edward C. Bursk & John F. Chapman (eds.), *New Decision-Making Tools for Managers* (Cambridge, Mass.: Harvard University Press). Copyright, 1963, by the President and Fellows of Harvard College.

TREMENDOUS OPPORTUNITIES

In most businesses a very large proportion of the customers, orders, products, and territories brings in only a very small proportion of the sales. But selling, advertising, and other marketing efforts all too frequently are expended in proportion to the area covered, the number of customers, the number of orders, and so forth; management does not give enough explicit consideration to their actual and potential contribution to sales volume and profit.

Even the better managed firms seldom realize how much of their marketing effort brings in only very small sales returns, since it is difficult to find out which sales can be ascribed to which selling and promotion work. They make little or no systematic attempt to evaluate the results of specific portions of marketing effort and usually measure their success solely by the firm's total dollar sales in each product line. Moreover, the manufacturers of branded consumer goods with a national market typically follow a policy of 100 percent coverage of the market in order to support their national advertising.

For these and other reasons, there is widespread misallocation of sales effort. A business as a whole may be making a good profit; but if you analyze its costs and sales carefully, you will usually find that a large number of sales are not very profitable at all—at least as compared with certain other sales.

Also, such sales are a heavy drain on potential profits. When time on an expensive television program is devoted to the promotion of a low-profit item, or a salesman spends time on an unpromising retailer, or limited warehouse space is tied up by large stocks of a low-turnover, low-markup item, the costs to the firm are high. Valuable television time, sales effort, and warehouse space are thereby withheld from more profitable uses. If a salesman divides his time between one product which earns the company $5 an hour and another which nets $12 an hour, then every hour spent promoting the former, in effect, costs the company $7. This is quite elementary, yet its lesson is ignored all about us every day. For instance:

1. One company made a distribution cost analysis and found that 68 percent of its customers, bringing in only 10 percent of the volume, were responsible for a net loss of as much as 44 percent of sales.
2. A distribution cost analysis in another firm revealed that 95 percent of all the customers in one territory were unprofitable—with losses ranging up to 86 percent of sales.

Profit Tools

The substantial losses on unprofitable sales resulting from disproportionate spreading of marketing effort can be minimized or even eliminated simply by making certain that the marketing dollar goes where it can do the most good. This can be done with the help of two related tools—distribution cost analysis and mathematical programming. These tools can indicate to management where and how to apportion marketing effort to make the most of potential net profit possibilities. In fact, companies which have used just distribution cost analysis as a management tool—without the use of mathematical programming—have achieved startling reductions in their distribution costs by correcting only the more obvious maldistributions of market effort. For example:

1. In one company, marketing expenses were cut nearly in half, from 22.8 percent to 11.5 percent of sales, and a net loss of 2.9 percent on the books was turned into a net profit of 15 percent, after shifting some effort from the 68 percent of accounts which had been unprofitable.
2. Another company shifted selling and advertising effort from less profitable to more profitable territories and achieved a 78 percent increase in average sales per salesman, a reduction of 33 percent in the ratio of selling and advertising expense to sales, and an increase of about 100 percent in the ratio of net profits to sales.[1]

Steps in Cost Analysis

How is management to find out what the different parts of the firm's marketing process contribute to its costs, its profits, and its sales? It is not so easy as it sounds. Prevalent accounting techniques for recording the results of marketing activities are insufficiently detailed; their information is distorted by arbitrary cost allocations, and their figures are only part of what is required.

The first step is a finer breakdown of the firm's average cost and profit data. The overall distribution costs for the entire business must be allocated to *the specific segments of the business for which they are incurred.* For example, through distribution cost analysis, we find that the sale of a thousand cases of product A through medium-size retailers located in the Chicago metropolitan area requires x dollars worth of salesman time, y dollars in transportation and warehousing costs, z dollars in advertising expenditure, and so on. We then get the production costs and figure the net profits or losses for each segment separately. This is not the place for an extended discussion of the principles and methods of distribution cost analysis, but two basic principles of the techniques used can readily be summarized:

1. The distribution expenditures of a particular business, which are usually recorded on a *natural* expense basis, are reclassified into *functional* cost groups, which bring together all of the indirect costs associated with each marketing activity or function performed by that company.
2. The functional cost groups are allocated to products, customers, and other segments of sales on the basis of measurable factors, or product and customer char-

[1] These two cases are taken from Charles H. Sevin, *How Manufacturers Reduce Their Distribution Costs* (Washington, D.C.: U.S. Government Printing Office, 1948).

acteristics which bear a cause-and-effect relationship to the total amounts of these functional costs.[2]

TREATMENT OF COSTS

Fixed (overhead) costs may be defined as those which, in the short run, do not change in total amount as sales increase (although, as we shall see later, costs which are fixed in one problem can be variable in another). This may be the result of contractual obligations assumed by the firm, or it may represent salaries, sunk or irrecoverable expenditures in buildings, equipment, and so forth.

Not all fixed costs should be treated alike, however. In fact, one of the crucial steps in distribution cost analysis is to distinguish between those costs which can be charged to specific types of sales and those which cannot. The management which is ready and able to do this well can confidently go on with the job of deciding where its unrealized potentials for profit lie.

Exclude if Common

Some fixed marketing costs are incurred in *common* for several different sales segments—for example, the advertising of a company's brand name, which must automatically influence the sale of all package sizes in one degree or another. Any breakdown of these advertising costs among the various package sizes must be arbitrary because the facts only entitle us to say that the advertising program is serving all of the package sizes at once.

Here we run into a serious problem. Two different methods of allocating such fixed costs can easily yield totally different results; and clearly, both cannot be right. There is, in fact, no really correct method of allocating fixed costs incurred in common by sales for different products or customers.

The solution to this problem is simple: Fixed costs which are common to several sales segments and whose magnitudes do not vary with the volume of sales in any one segment should be omitted from all cost and profit computations. Sales income should be viewed as a contribution to profit and fixed cost together. The situation is like a family debt; what each brother brings in helps both to support the family and to pay off the family's obligations, although it does not affect the size of the rent, food, and heating bills.

Include if Variable

None of this applies, of course, to *variable* costs, which increase with sales and therefore can be allocated. For instance, more sales in Wisconsin help to pay the company's transportation bill, but they also increase the magnitude

[2] For further details on classification of distribution costs by functional categories and bases for their allocation to specific segments of a business, see Sevin, *op. cit.*

of this bill. It is a variable cost. The addition to the freight bill cannot be ignored in seeing how much these Wisconsin sales are worth to the firm. But a fixed cost of the sort we are discussing does not vary with sales. The added income from Wisconsin contributes to the payment of fixed costs but adds nothing to their size.

It follows, therefore, that an allocation of marketing costs which omits fixed elements can show how much a particular type of sale contributes to the well-being of the firm and can indicate how a revision of the firm's distribution efforts can help sales and profits. Costs which include arbitrarily allocated fixed elements can be seriously misleading, and they do not add any useful knowledge to a management analysis of sales and profits. To illustrate: Suppose that a company correlates its sales and profits in a certain territory and finds a curve like the solid line in Exhibit 1. It learns that the sales dollar is most profitable when total sales volume is at point x. Now suppose that warehouse rental goes up and adds $5,000 to fixed cost. This lowers the profit

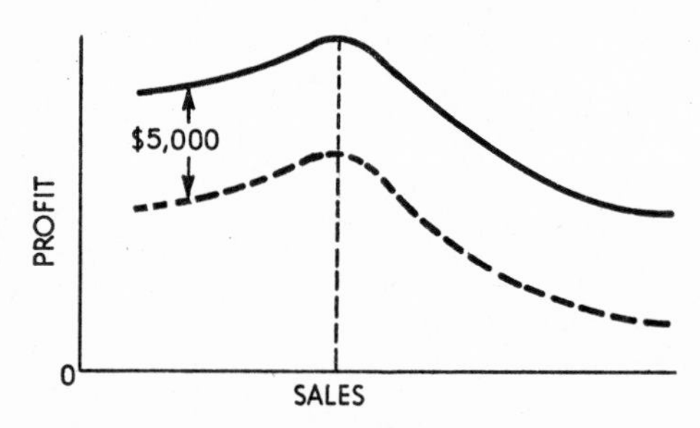

EXHIBIT 1. Relation of profits to sales unaffected by fixed costs.

curve at every point; the dotted line now represents profits. But the highest point of the new curve still occurs at x, simply because warehouse rental is a fixed cost at all sales volumes. A change in such a cost does not tell management anything it did not know before about the sales–maximum profits relationship. It would be important to know only in the exceptional case where the increased fixed costs make it impossible for the firm to break even.

Of course, the elimination of fixed expenses from the allocation of costs is not quite so simple in practice as it may sound. It is often difficult to distinguish between variable and fixed marketing costs. For instance:

1. Warehousing cost, which is fixed when the warehouse is not used to capacity, becomes variable *when*, with all the storage space filled up, management considers the construction of more space to eliminate a bottleneck.
2. A sales manager's salary may be a fixed cost *unless* the company considers firing him altogether rather than transferring his services from one product line to another.
3. Most, if not all, costs which are fixed in the short run become variable after enough time passes, or if a large enough change in sales volume occurs. The costs

of plant and equipment are usually fixed *until* the facilities wear out and have to be replaced.

In dealing with such questions, the nature of the problem is most often crucial in determining whether a cost is fixed or variable. If a firm is considering how many trucks it should use, the purchase cost of its truck fleet is clearly variable. But when the firm wishes to know how best to allocate the trucks which it already possesses, the assumption being that no new trucks are to be bought or old ones scrapped, then the nature of the problem dictates that the purchase cost of the truck fleet is fixed.

Again, if the problem is one of long-range planning, certain plant and equipment costs will be variable because the machines will wear out during the period under consideration, whereas these costs would be fixed for a problem in, say, short-run production programming or control. In any event, the segregation of fixed costs requires caution, skill, and experience; the job is an important one, but it is full of pitfalls for the unwary.

Include if Separable

The fixed costs just considered are not the only kind of distribution costs which are fixed expenses for a company. In fact, most fixed marketing costs are different in the sense that they *can* and *should* be allocated to sales. These are what we shall call the *separable* fixed costs. To illustrate: If the sales manager's job is not in question, his salary is, as we have seen, a fixed cost to the firm. No change in sales affects the magnitude of his salary (although it may affect his bonus). However, the time and effort which he spends on specific sales segments is variable. He can spend 5 percent of his time—or more, or less—working to promote sales in the New Orleans district. The more time he spends here, the less time he has left to spend on the promotion of other sales. Accordingly, we may be able to allocate his time with ease, even though his salary is a fixed cost.

Similarly, the floor space in a warehouse for finished goods inventory whose rental is fixed, or the capacity of a delivery truck fleet, is divided among the different products in terms of the space needed by each.

Such costs are not a direct deduction from the income which accrues to the firm as its sales increase and need not enter the profit calculation any more than do fixed costs which are common to several sales segments. But they are nonetheless crucial for distribution cost analysis, for its purpose is to show where the firm's marketing effort can be used most effectively. Clearly, the sales manager should devote his time to a sales sector which yields $50 per hour in preference to another sector which offers only $30 return for an hour of his effort.

As we shall see, it is this consideration which makes the methods of mathematical programming relevant to a distribution cost analysis. Separable fixed costs usually pertain to efforts or resources that are *limited* in total.

Accordingly, the marginal cost of separable fixed expenses—for instance, the cost of the manager's time which would be required to make *additional* sales in each segment of the business being costed—should be computed if possible. And these figures should be kept distinct from variable costs.

CHANGES IN SALES POLICY

Suppose now it is found that, on the average, the sale of a dollar's worth of product x through medium-size retailers in Kansas City contributes more to profits than a dollar sale of product y through small retailers in Richmond. It is tempting to jump to the conclusion that more sales effort should be allocated to the former and less to the latter. But does this follow? Suppose, for example, that sales of product x in Kansas City have saturated the market, while the Richmond market is ripe for development. Clearly, it would not be wise to shift effort to Kansas from Virginia.

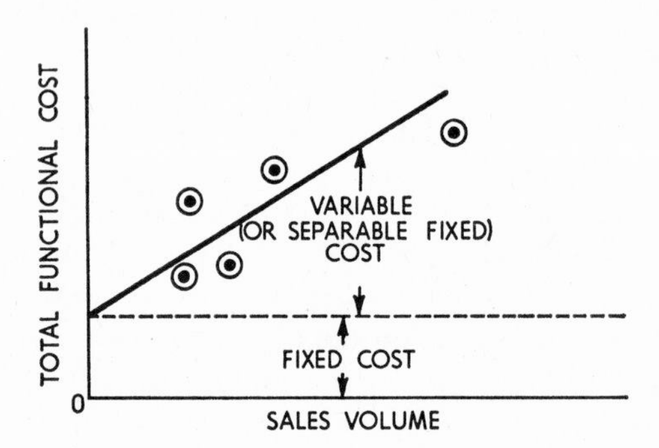

EXHIBIT 2. Example of sales cost data needed for statistical decision.

Thus the cost *currently* incurred by a specific segment of sales may be the right answer to the wrong question. It tells us how well the firm is doing now; but the firm wants to know whether it can do better in the future and, if so, how and where. Accordingly, we must know the answer to the following hypothetical questions: What would happen to marketing costs *if* more effort were pointed in one direction rather than in another? More specifically, how are changes in total costs in each sales category related to changes in volume in the same category?

In effect, for each sales segment and each functional cost group, we want the kind of information contained in Exhibit 2. We need these data for both variable costs and separable fixed costs. Once these figures are obtained, the businessman can proceed to apportion his distribution effort in a way virtually guaranteed to increase his profits.

This means that in the simplest case where there is only one type of marketing effort in question (the more complicated—and more common—cases will be discussed later), effort should be reallocated as much as possible to those segments of sales where an additional unit of marketing effort will yield the highest contribution to net profits and overhead, after deduction of variable costs; i.e., effort should be increased in that sales sector where there is the highest value of the fraction

$$\frac{\text{Additional sales—Additional variable costs}}{\text{Additional effort or resource devoted to this sector}}$$

Further discussion and a rigorous derivation of this criterion are included in the Appendix to this article. However, here is a simple illustration: Suppose the figures show that in Boston an additional $2 in the field sales force's fixed budget will yield an additional $10 in sales and that the additional variable cost of those sales is $4. Then the value of the fraction in question will be $(10 - 4) \div 2 = 3$. If the corresponding figure for Oklahoma City is 2.6, it is clear that selling effort should be reallocated from Oklahoma to Boston.

Often, as shown in an example in the Appendix dealing with use of a limited resource (warehouse space), the proper allocation of effort will actually be completely different from that indicated by the conventional approach via per unit net profit.

Cost-Volume Relation

How do we find out how the functional costs vary with sales? The obvious answer is to see what has happened to costs when sales changes occurred in the past. But past events are not controlled experiments; past sales changes are often the result of a variety of causes, many of which are no longer pertinent. Moreover, unlike most production costs, which are a function of volume, changes in distribution costs are often both a cause and an effect of changes in sales volume. Past experience may therefore be an unreliable test. There are, however, a number of techniques which will help us cope with this difficulty.

MATHEMATICAL PROGRAMMING

Usually, there are several types of distribution effort or cost which a company must allocate carefully. The funds available for advertising may be limited, the salesmen's time be fully occupied, and warehouse space may constitute a bottleneck. The objective is to promote those sales which make the best use of all three of these factors.

No one sales segment is likely to use all three effectively. One product may use advertising dollars very efficiently because its sales can be increased with the aid of relatively little additional advertising expenditure. But if this product is also bulky, its inventory will employ relatively large amounts of warehouse space. Similarly, another product may yield much greater profits for each additional hour of the sales force's time but small returns on each additional advertising dollar. The problem, therefore, is to select that *combination* of sales activities that will make optimal use of the company's facilities and know-how. This is what the mathematician calls a programming problem.

What does programming do that other techniques cannot do?[3] In many cases the standard optimization technique, i.e., differential calculus, can, given adequate data, indicate precisely what is the maximum (profit) or minimum (cost) achievable. But in some problems of optimization, there is a complication in that the outcome, to be acceptable, must meet certain specifications which the mathematician calls "side conditions."

For example, it may be most profitable for a firm to sell 10,000 pairs of shoes a week. This is, then, a sort of optimum. However, if the firm's warehouse can stock only 8,000 pairs of shoes, the optimum is an unattainable goal, and it becomes necessary to recompute a more modest and practicable target. The aim is to find the most profitable combination of outputs which do not violate the "inequality side condition" that production must be less than or equal to 8,000 pairs per week.

Programming is the mathematical method for analyzing and computing optimum output decisions which do not violate the limitations imposed by inequality side conditions. In other words, it attacks the same problem that distribution cost analysis seeks to solve. Its purpose is to find a pattern of sales which maximizes profits and yet does not exceed the available capacities of the firm.

Setting Up the Problem

The mathematical programming problem consists of two essential parts: (1) something which is maximized (e.g., profit) and (2) the inequality side conditions.

As for the first, it is generally assumed that the business is trying to maximize the sum of the gross (dollar) margins in the various segments of sales minus the sum of their variable costs. This is where our variable costs are used in the distribution cost analysis.

Next, we examine the relevant inequality side conditions. These describe the various limitations imposed on the firm by a fixed advertising budget or sales force, limited warehouse space, and so forth. There will be an inequality which corresponds to each of these limitations. For example, one inequality will state that the amount of warehouse space used by the various sales segments must not exceed the available capacity. More specifically, if, say, the warehouse space used for finished goods inventories is strictly proportional to the sales in each category, we will require that the warehouse space used up by the different categories of sales add up to an amount less than or equal to the available warehouse space. We can put all of this more comprehensively and concisely in mathematical terms:

[3] See Alexander Henderson and Robert Schlaifer, "Mathematical Programming: Better Information for Better Decision Making," *Harvard Business Review*, May–June, 1954, p. 73; and *idem*, "Solution of Management Problems through Mathematical Programming," *Cost and Profit Outlook*, May, 1956 (published by Alderson and Sessions, Philadelphia).

$$a_1(W) + a_2(X) + a_3(Y) + a_4(Z) \leq A$$
$$b_1(W) + b_2(X) + b_3(Y) + b_4(Z) \leq B$$
$$c_1(W) + c_2(X) + c_3(Y) + c_4(Z) \leq C$$

where A is the available warehouse space, B is the available sales force time, C is the budgeted advertising funds; and where $a_1(W)$ is the warehouse space used by W sales, $a_2(X)$ is the space used by X sales, $b_1(W)$ is the salesmen's time used by W sales, and so forth. (For illustration, it is assumed that there are exactly four sales segments.)

It is here our separable fixed cost figures are used. We see now why these were not added to the variable cost statistics. The two types of figures play totally different roles in the analysis and appear in completely separate parts of the mathematical program. The variable cost represents a deduction from the firm's income; the separable fixed cost represents a drain on its limited marketing effort; and they must each be treated accordingly.

There remain two stipulations that must be made before the mathematician takes over:

1. We must specify that sales in any segment can fall to zero but can never be negative, or

$$W \geq 0, X \geq 0, Y \geq 0, \text{ and } Z \geq 0$$

This may seen so obvious and unimportant that it is not worth mentioning; however, it turns out that this apparently trivial requirement is fundamental for the mathematical analysis. One reason is that the computations are usually done by electronic calculators, which are not really as bright as sometimes supposed. They may do computations quickly, but they do not realize (unless told so specifically) that negative sales are out of the question. If some particular sales segment is especially unprofitable, the machine will figure out that the less the firm sells in that segment, the better off it will be. But if so, why stop cutting down when we get to zero? Unless instructed otherwise, the machine is very likely to end up recommending negative sales in unprofitable segments!

2. The nature of the problem may change so that a cost once fixed becomes variable and the corresponding capacity limitation disappears. In a planning problem, for instance, if present warehouses would be inadequate for increasing sales, the construction of new warehouses might be considered by the planners, and then the amount of construction would vary with the amount of sales. The effect on the mathematical program is simple; the corresponding inequality is dropped, and the variable cost figures in the profit expression are increased to include the new variable costs.

LINEAR PROGRAMMING

The word *programming* most frequently occurs in the term *linear programming*. When the facts of the situation state that costs will always be proportionate to sales so that, for example, a threefold increase in the level of sales in any one segment will always exactly triple all the costs incurred by the segment, the relevant program is said to be linear. This is because the graph showing the relationship between sales in a sector and the magnitude of some cost will then be a straight line, as in Exhibit 2.

In a linear case, there are great economies in data collection and computation. As Exhibit 2 indicates, it takes fewer dots or statistics to locate a straight line than to plot a curved line. The few dots shown on the graph would obviously not be sufficient to permit the fitting of a curved line with any degree of confidence; yet even these few are expensive to collect.

Limited Advantages

Linear programming has practical uses in distribution cost analysis; but to appreciate them, it is necessary to look first at its limitations.

To begin with, it almost never fits the facts. If pursued to its logical conclusion, it is virtually certain to give the wrong answer. One reason is that in marketing, various costs involve quantity discounts. For example, if we ship one third of a carload of goods, the less-than-carload rates apply, and it will cost considerably more than one third the amount required to ship a full carload. It is easy to think of other costs which do not rise strictly in proportion with sales. Inventory levels, and hence the costs of storage, do not usually rise exactly in proportion to sales volume; neither does the cost of sales management. One could make quite a list.

Moreover, linear programming has an inherent bias which often leads to seriously incorrect answers in distribution cost analysis. It usually suggests the elimination of a large number of sales categories; for example, it may suggest that a firm end up selling to only a certain type of retailer and in only a few major cities. This happens because of the basic theorem of linear programming, which in effect states that if there are, say, just three inequality side conditions in a problem, then maximum profits can be obtained by confining sales to no more than three sales segments.

To illustrate, if we are trying to get the most out of our warehouse capacity, our salesmen's time, and our advertising expenditure, linear programming would lead us to concentrate on three sales segments—one which produces large profits per square foot of warehouse space, another which returns large profits per salesman-hour, and a third which yields high returns per advertising dollar. Any types of sales which are second best to these three would be eliminated.

Of course, this is all wrong. For one thing, there are diminishing returns to effort; markets become saturated. If one twentieth of the national advertising budget is used in Chicago, moving the entire advertising effort to Chicago will not increase sales there twentyfold. The transfer of effort would be a good thing only up to a point, and it would be most profitable to devote much of the advertising budget to other market areas.

Best Direction

All of this is not to say, however, that linear programming has no uses. Quite the contrary. While a linear program usually will not compute a correct optimum because the changes it suggests will go too far, there is yet a very strong presumption that it will correctly indicate the best *directions* of change. It will identify correctly the sales segments to which more effort should be allocated. Accordingly, where it is too expensive to undertake a full-scale non-linear programming analysis, or where the necessary data are simply not available, linear programming can still be exceedingly helpful.

CONCLUSION

In practice, the great bulk of the savings which distribution cost analysis has made possible can be ascribed to its ability to find those sales sectors to which marketing effort is most glaringly misallocated. Using this technique, many sales managements have been able to redirect their efforts and achieve very substantial additions to profits.

As most sales executives know, the data available are rarely so accurate that the analysts can trust a very refined calculation. But when their information points out a very costly case of misdirected effort, they can confidently proceed to take remedial action, for no small error in data and computation will normally account for the considerable losses which distribution cost analysis often reveals. In sum, even fairly inaccurate data and fairly crude computational techniques will usually turn up those inefficiencies which are most glaringly and which constitute the most important opportunities to increase profits.

Accordingly, even though they may not have the data, the time, or the budget for a mathematical programming analysis, managers usually can still obtain much of the benefit of a full-scale distribution cost analysis by using a linear programming approximation or just the general approach outlined in this article. They can increase the accuracy of their information with only inexpensive modifications in distribution cost analysis procedures, as we indicate in the Appendix to this article. Thus the principles alone of mathematical programming will serve, when used in conjunction with a distribution cost analysis, to help management achieve from its marketing operations a marked increase in efficiency and substantially higher profits.

APPENDIX: SOME SUGGESTIONS FOR COMPUTATIONS

Profit Computation for Allocation Decisions

When the firm is considering the allocation of the currently available amount of some type of marketing effort, it is posing a question which requires that the expenditure on that type of effort be treated as a fixed cost. In posing such a question, the analyst is told, in effect, that the firm has, let us say, so many salesmen at its disposal, and he is then asked how the members of the sales force can best divide their time among products, customers, territories, and so forth.

In distribution cost analysis the various separable fixed costs (e.g., the warehouse floor space) allocated to each sales segment are translated into money terms, and the sum of these and the allocated variable costs are subtracted from the dollar gross margins to obtain a net profit or loss figure for each segment of the business. The implication is that marketing effort ought to be decreased in the sectors which show a large net loss and increased in the sectors having the highest per unit net profit figures. In many cases, however, this implication may be incorrect and misleading.

For simplicity, we will illustrate this with the linear case where variable and separable fixed costs per unit for any sales sector do not change with the volume of sales in that sector. We will also assume that warehouse space is the only separable fixed cost. We will deal with the sales W and X in two sectors.

Now, it is usually suggested that effort should be transferred from X to W if and only if W's per unit net profit is greater than X's; that is, if and only if (formula 1):

Gross margin of W − Variable cost of W − Separable fixed cost of $W >$
Gross margin of X − Variable cost of X − Fixed separable cost of X

But formula 1 does not always correctly indicate the most profitable reallocation of marketing effort. The most profitable thing to do is to increase the effort devoted to the sector which yields the highest contribution to profit and overhead *per dollar of warehouse space*. That is because warehouse space is the separable fixed cost—the effort or resource factor which needs to be economized—and the best profit-making strategy is to use that space where it earns the most. This proposition is easily proved.

If A is total available warehouse space and is completely utilized, we have:

$$A = A_w W + A_x X$$

or

$$X = A/A_x - A_w W/A_x$$

where A_w and A_x are the respective number of square feet of warehouse space used up per unit of W and X. Now, let T_w and T_x represent the contribution to profit plus overhead per unit of W and X, respectively. Substituting the expression just obtained for X, the total contribution to profit plus overhead of both sectors then will be:

$$\begin{aligned} WT_w + XT_x &= WT_w + A/A_x T_x - A_w W/A_x T_x \\ &= A/A_x T_x + W(T_w - A_w/A_x T_x) \end{aligned}$$

Thus an increase in W will add to this figure if and only if $T_w - A_w A_x T_x > 0$; i.e., if $T_w/A_w > T_x/A_x$. To put it in another way, an increase in W will add to the profit figure only if T_w/A_w, the contribution per unit of warehouse space from stocking W, is greater than T_x/A_x, the contribution per unit of warehouse space from stocking X.

The significance of all this for our main question is that actually more effort should be allocated to W from X if and only if the figure for W's contribution to profit and overhead in ratio to W's use of warehouse space is greater than the corresponding figure for X; that is, if and only if (formula 2):

(Gross margin of W − Variable cost of W) ÷ Separable fixed cost of W >
(Gross margin of X − Variable cost of X) ÷ Separable fixed cost of X

Now the important thing to note is that formulas 1 and 2 will not always point in the same direction. For example, if both gross margins are equal to one, if the unit variable cost of W is 0.3 and the separable unit fixed cost of W is 0.2, and if the variable cost of X is 0.1 and the separable fixed cost of X is 0.3, then the net profit computation under formula 1 yields *less* unit net profit for W, because

$$1.0 - 0.3 - 0.2 = 0.5 < 1.0 - 0.1 - 0.3 = 0.6$$

Thus, distribution cost analysis, as often practiced, would infer that effort should not be shifted from X to W, or that the shift should be in the other direction. But the correct computation under formula 2 shows that W's contribution to profit and overhead per unit of warehouse space is really *greater* than X's, because

$$(1.0 - 0.3) \div 0.2 = 3.5 > (1.0 - 0.1) \div 0.3 = 3$$

In other words, the firm should shift effort from X to W, in precisely the opposite direction from that indicated by the usual net profit computation of formula 1.

It should be remembered, however, that the procedure which has just been shown to be correct is valid if there is only one category of fixed cost and one corresponding facility to be allocated optimally. Where the number of facility limitations is greater than this, it is necessary to utilize the standard mathematical programming computations discussed earlier in this article.

Marginal versus Average Data

As we have seen, average costs per unit cannot tell us how to reallocate effort. The information needed to decide whether a shift of effort will be profitable is the *addition* to costs and sales which will result from such a shift, i.e., the marginal costs and revenues. In practice, however, it is much easier and less expensive to obtain average gross profit and cost figures than to acquire the corresponding marginal figures. Most distribution cost analysis, therefore, employs average data in its calculations. We believe that this often yields satisfactory approximations, but good practice requires that the data be corrected for the most glaring divergences between the marginal and average cost figures. In many cases, it should be possible to recognize such differences fairly easily.

Here, economic analysis provides us with several simple rules:

1. All fixed costs must be eliminated from the average cost figures. In particular, if there are setup costs which must be incurred for the firm to operate at all, these must be omitted. A perusal of the accounting practices of the firm may indicate gross profit or cost figures in which such costs enter heavily, and appropriate corrections should be made.

2. If demand does not respond readily to effort, marginal revenues will be considerably lower than average revenues. In effect, this is because there will be diminishing returns to effort in such markets, so that *additional* effort will normally yield smaller revenues than does most of the present effort. This means that if experience suggests that market M is pretty much saturated and will not respond readily to further marketing effort, the average gross profit figure for this market must be *reduced* to obtain a number closer to the marginal gross profit.

In a few cases, marginal revenues will be greater than average revenues because additional selling activity can increase the effectiveness of effort already expended. In such cases an upward adjustment of the average gross profit is called for.

Of course, it will not be possible to identify all of the sales segments requiring this sort of adjustment or to determine the precise magnitude of the required changes. But with a little experience, one usually can recognize, on the basis of interviews with management and examination of the available records, the most extreme cases of divergence between marginal and average gross profit; the analyst can then eliminate the most serious sources of error.

3. On the cost side, we have a similar rule. Where there are seriously diminishing returns, increase the average costs; if demand does by any chance respond more readily to added sales effort, reduce the average costs. This rule applies in the same way to production and to distribution costs.

4. The magnitude of the required change in an average gross profit figure and in an average cost figure can be inferred with the help of the following standard formulas:

a) Marginal gross profit = Average gross profit + Sales × Rate of change in gross profit per sale

b) Marginal cost = Average cost + Sales × Rate of change in average cost per sale

The rate of change in average cost per sale would mean, for example: (Average cost in sector X when sales are $1,001,000 − Average cost when sales are $1,000,000) ÷ Increase in sales ($1,000).

14

A mathematical description is given for a hypothetical situation involving a choice among three distribution channels, after which a model is developed which accommodates the determination of a minimal manufacturing and distribution cost—given the assumption that sales are affected by the choice of the channel of distribution. This analysis is then modified in the form of a profit maximization model. In respect to each model, critical variables are discussed, and numeric examples are provided.

*A NOTE ON MANUFACTURERS' CHOICE OF DISTRIBUTION CHANNELS**

Roland Artle and Sture Berglund

GENERAL APPROACH

MANY MARKETING PROBLEMS are usually analyzed in verbal terms only. For instance, different alternatives as regards the marketing routes, or channels, through which goods and services or their titles flow, are mostly considered in terms of "advantages" and "disadvantages." Recently, however, techniques aiming at quantification—such as linear programming and search theory—have been gaining favor. This essay purports to clarify, in quantitative terms, some of the considerations that may underlie a manufacturer's choice of distribution channels. We shall limit ourselves to a comparison of two alternatives, namely, selling through wholesalers and selling directly to retailers.

There is a simple relationship that is sometimes used to explain why a manufacturer of products such as groceries, drugs, and dry goods very often sells his goods through wholesalers. This relationship can be illustrated as follows:

Given 4 manufacturers and 10 retailers buying goods from each manufacturer, the number of contact lines necessary will be found to vary with the number of wholesalers, as Figure 1 shows. When selling directly, each manufacturer contacts 10 retailers, in all adding up to 40 contact lines. If the manufacturers turn to selling through a wholesaler, the necessary number of con-

* Reprinted from *Management Science*, July, 1959, pp. 460–71.

tacts reduces to 14. If the manufacturers sell their products through 2 wholesalers, there will be 28 contact lines needed, and so on.

As is easily seen, however, this relationship rather simplifies too much. There are, in fact, differences in costs hidden in the diagram: Any two contact lines may differ from the point of view of costs. This is obvious when, for example, the line between a manufacturer and a wholesaler is compared with the line between a manufacturer and a retailer. One may be used more or less frequently or with smaller or greater inputs per time than the other.

However, it seems to us that the above-mentioned relationship may serve as a fruitful starting point for further analysis. By splitting up each contact

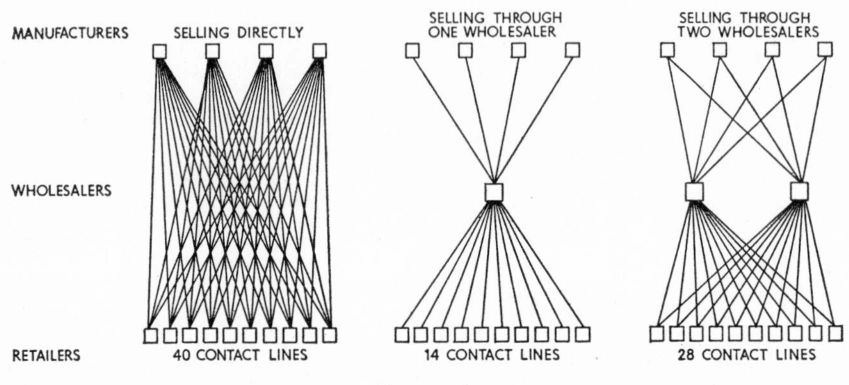

FIGURE 1

line into its components, functions, a much more realistic basis seems to be provided for computations of the inputs involved in different choices of distribution channels. The evaluation of each function may then be carried out in terms of standard costs, in order to facilitate comparisons between different alternatives. Further, the amounts of all the necessary inputs as well as the size and structure of the unit or standard costs applied to them may be adapted to those conditions that one may want to analyze.

For the sake of simplicity, we shall limit ourselves to a study of the pure selling function, and we shall start with a practical illustration of the method. Other distributive functions, such as transportation, order routine, and handling of the goods, could be treated similarly. Obviously, there is in reality a great variety of alternatives as regards channels of distribution. The examples described here are chosen because they are considered simple and sharply outlined.

PRACTICAL ILLUSTRATION[1]

Suppose there are 10 retailers selling some particular goods in a town. The distance between any 2 neighboring retailers is on the average one mile.

[1] In order to give the examples more clarity and generality, the computations have been given both algebraic and numerical form. The following symbols and assumed values of the parameters will be used in the examples:

Further, it is assumed that there are four manufacturers supplying the 10 retailers with their goods. Each manufacturer produces and sells one particular good. The factories are situated at different places, each place being some 15 miles away from the town where the retailers are located.

In the first case, we shall assume that the manufacturers sell their products directly to retailers. Each manufacturer sends his salesman to call at each retailer some 50 times per year, on the average. Thus, each retailer is assumed to receive 200 calls per year by salesmen. Every call gives rise to an order of 25 units. Each of the four goods has the same price, namely, $1.50 per unit, when sold to retailers. The total costs, per year, of the personal contacts will then be:

A. The manufacturers' costs:

1. Assume that it will take the salesmen 20 minutes to drive in to a central point in the town and that their salaries per hour amount to $4.50. The cost of the car is estimated at 12 cents per mile. To get to the central point some 50 times per year will then cost:

$$\begin{aligned} \text{Salaries: } cgk &= \$\ 75 \\ \text{Motoring costs: } cfh &= \underline{\ \ 90} \\ \text{Costs of each manufacturer: } c(gk + fh) &= \$165 \\ \text{Total costs: } ac(gk + fh) &= \$660 \end{aligned}$$

2. Assume that it takes some four minutes to get from one customer to the next, on the average. The distance between the central point and the first customer is also assumed to be covered in four minutes. Total costs of traveling between the customers will then be:

$$\begin{aligned} \text{Salaries: } bcgm &= \$150 \\ \text{Motoring costs: } bchi &= \underline{\ \ 60} \\ \text{Costs of each manufacturer: } bc(gm + hi) &= \$210 \\ \text{Total costs: } abc(gm + hi) &= \$840 \end{aligned}$$

	Symbol	Unit	Value
Number of manufacturers	a		4
Number of retailers	b		10
Number of calls per retailer and manufacturer	c		50
Number of units per order and manufacturer	d		25
Price per unit, to retailers	e		$1.50
Distance between each manufacturer and a central point in the town	f		15 miles
Salesmen's salary, per hour	g		$4.50
Traveling costs per mile	h		$0.12
Distance between any two neighboring retailers	i		1 mile
Time to drive from factory to town	k	hours	20 minutes
Time to drive from one retailer to the next	m	hours	4 minutes
Fixed time per call	n	hours	18 minutes
Time varying with number of order lines	o	hours/line	0.6 minutes/line
Time varying with order value	p	hours/$	0.8 minutes/$20
Salesman's waiting time per call	q		4 minutes
Number of contacts between wholesaler and each manufacturer	r		10
Wholesaler's or manufacturer's cost per contact between them	s		$1
Fixed costs of manufacturing	t		$20,000
Variable costs of manufacturing	j		$0.90/unit

3. On the basis of some empirical studies a regression analysis was carried out that showed visiting time to consist of the following parts: 18 minutes (fixed time) + 0.6 minutes per order line + 0.8 minutes per $20 of sales.

   These results need further validation. But if we do accept the equation as giving the approximate length of visiting time, the following computations will give total costs of calling at retailers:

Cost of fixed time: $bcgn$	=	$ 675.00
Cost of time varying with the number of order lines: $bcgo$	=	22.50
Cost of time varying with sales: $bcdegp$	=	56.25
Costs of each manufacturer: $bcg(n + o + dep)$	=	$ 753.75
Total costs: $abcg(n + o + dep)$	=	$ 3,015

4. The salesmen's costs of returning to their factories:

$$ac(gk + fh) = \$660$$

   (The salesmen's costs of returning to their factories from the last customer are assumed to equal those given in point 1 above.)

B. The retailer's costs: It is assumed that the salesman will have to wait some four minutes, on the average, until the retailer can spare the time to see him. The time the retailer spends will thus be given by the equation above, with the modification that the fixed time should be reduced by four minutes. Total costs of retailers will then be, assuming the retailer's time to be of the same value as the salesmen's:

Cost of fixed time: $abcg(n - q)$	=	$2,100
Variable costs: $abcg(o + dep)$	=	315
Total costs: $abcg(n - q + o + dep)$	=	$2,415

In the second case, it is assumed that the manufacturers sell their goods through a wholesaler, located at the center of the town. The wholesaler also calls at each retailer some 50 times per year, on the average. His sales of each of the four goods are assumed to equal the manufacturers' sales in case they sell directly. The wholesaler's salesman has the same salary as the manufacturer's, that is, $4.50 per hour. The wholesaler orders his goods some 10 times per year from each manufacturer. The contact between manufacturer and wholesaler is assumed to cost both $1 per order irrespective of order size (contact by telephone). Total costs per year can then be calculated as follows:

A. The manufacturers' costs:

The cost of receiving orders: ars = $40

B. Wholesaler's costs:

1. The cost of ordering from manufacturers, as above: ars = $40
2. The cost of driving to every customer (compare the first case, A[2]):

Salary: $bcgm$	=	$150
Motoring costs: $bchi$	=	60
Total costs: $bc(gm + hi)$	=	$210

3. The cost of calling at retailers (the same formula as in the first case is assumed to apply):

Fixed time cost: $bcgn = \$675$
Variable costs: $abcg(o + dep) = 315$
Total costs: $bcg(n + ao + adep) = \$990$

C. Retailers' costs: The calls of the wholesaler's salesman will cause the retailers to have the following costs:

$$bcg(n - q) + abcgo + abcdegp = \$840$$

Let us now, as *a third case*, assume that the manufacturers sell their products through *two* wholesalers. Suppose, for the sake of illustration, that only every second visit that the two wholesalers' salesmen make to retailers results in a sale, but that all other conditions remain as above. Each wholesaler will then receive 25 $150 orders per year, on the average. In this case, total costs will be computed thus:

A. The manufacturers' costs:

$$2ars = \$80$$

B. The wholesalers' costs:

1. The cost of ordering from manufacturers, as above:

$$2ars = \$80$$

2. The cost of driving to every customer (as in the second case, point B[2] but doubled, since there are now two wholesalers):

$$2bc(gm + hi) = \$420$$

3. The cost of calling at retailers (compare the second case, point B[3]):

$$2bcgn + 2ab\frac{c}{2}go + 2ab\frac{c}{2}degp = \$1,665$$

C. The retailers' costs:

$$2bcg(n - q) + 2ab\frac{c}{2}go + 2ab\frac{c}{2}degp = \$1,365$$

Comparison between the three cases gives the selling costs shown in Table 1. Thus, under the conditions given, total contact costs of manufacturers and

TABLE 1

Case 1	Case 2	Case 3
$2ac(gk + fh)$	....	....
....	$2ars$	$4ars$
$abc(gm + hi)$	$bc(gm + hi)$	$2bc(gm + hi)$
$abcg(n + o + dep)$	$bcg(n + ao + adep)$	$2bcg\left(n + \frac{ao}{2} + \frac{adep}{2}\right)$
$abcg(n - q + o + dep)$	$bcg(n - q + ao + adep)$	$2bcg\left(n - q + \frac{ao}{2} + \frac{adep}{2}\right)$
= \$7,590	= \$2,120	= \$3,610

retailers will amount to $7,590 if manufacturers sell directly to retailers. Do they turn to selling through a wholesaler, contact costs will decrease to $2,120. Costs rise sharply, however, when another wholesaler enters the stage: With two wholesalers, contact will amount to $3,610.

Which Choice Gives the Lowest Manufacturing and Distribution Costs?

A manufacturer may sometimes consider it possible to sell more if he sells directly to retailers than if he sells through wholesalers. The fixed part of the cost of manufacturing would then be spread over a larger number of units sold; that is, manufacturing costs per unit would be reduced. The results might be a reduction in the total costs of manufacturing and selling, namely, if the reduction in manufacturing costs would more than counterbalance the probable increase in selling costs. The question may then be raised: At what point will a rise in sales, when manufacturers sell directly to retailers, give the same total costs per unit as when manufacturers sell through wholesalers? Some answers to this question will be given in the following. To begin with, conditions earlier specified will be applied once again. It will further be assumed that manufacturing costs consist of a fixed part (that does not vary with moderate changes in the number of units produced) and another part that varies proportionately with the number of units. As before, the study will be limited to costs of personal contacts. Other selling costs will be neglected.

In principle, a rise in sales may be thought to come about through

1. An increase in the number of calls upon customers, with sales per call remaining unchanged
2. An increase in sales per call, with the number of calls remaining unchanged
3. Some combination of changes in the number of calls and in sales per call

We shall proceed by analyzing each of these alternatives. Variable manufacturing costs will be neglected, since they will not affect results. Throughout, it will be assumed that the fixed costs will amount to $20,000.

Example 1. Suppose a retailer buys the same amount of each product each time a salesman calls upon him irrespective of whether the salesman comes slightly more often or slightly more seldom than he used to. Let it further be assumed that he buys the same amount irrespective of whether the salesman represents a wholesaler or a manufacturer. The question is then posed: How much should the manufacturers' salesmen increase their number of calls upon retailers in order to make the manufacturers' total costs (of manufacturing and personal contacts) just about as low as when manufacturers sell through a wholesaler?

Let the average number of calls that a salesman makes upon each retailer equal x_1.

Let A stand for the expression

$$ac\{2(gk + fh) + b[(gm + hi) + g(n + o + dep)]\}$$

i.e., the costs of selling in case 1, the retailers' costs not included, and B stand for the expression

$$2ars + bc[(gm + hi) + g(n + ao + adep)]$$

i.e., the costs of selling in case 2, the retailers' costs not included.

The four manufacturers in our example will then incur the following costs of manufacturing (fixed costs) and selling (costs of personal contacts), when selling directly to retailers:

$$T + \frac{x_1 A}{c}$$

or $20{,}000 + 4x_1 \cdot 25.875$.

The unit cost will be calculated as

$$\frac{T + \dfrac{x_1 A}{c}}{abdx_1}$$

or

$$\frac{20{,}000 + 4x_1 \cdot 25.875}{1{,}000x_1}$$

This figure is to be compared to the unit cost when selling through a wholesaler:

$$\frac{T + B}{abcd}$$

or

$$\frac{20{,}000 + 1{,}280}{50{,}000} = \$0.4256$$

The two unit costs are then put equal in order to solve the problem:

$$\frac{T + \dfrac{x_1 A}{c}}{abdx_1} = \frac{T + B}{abcd}$$

or

$$\frac{20{,}000 + 103.5x_1}{1000x_1} = \$0.4256$$

$$x_1 = c\frac{T}{T - (A - B)}$$

or

$$x_1 = 62.1 \text{ calls}$$

Thus, we find that manufacturers must send their salesmen to visit retailers at least 63 times per year to get the same costs per unit sold as when selling through a wholesaler, provided that the wholesaler's salesman calls upon retailers some 50 times per year.

From an overall, macroeconomic point of view it might be argued that the retailers' costs of receiving salesmen should also be included. If they are, the break-even point will naturally be found to increase. In our example, it would amount to 68.8 calls.

Example 2. In this case, it will be assumed that manufacturers let their salesmen call upon retailers the same number of times as the wholesaler does. Instead, manufacturers are assumed to aim at increasing order sizes. Here the problem will be: Which order size is required to obtain the same cost per sold unit (when manufacturers sell directly) as that which would have arisen had manufacturers sold through a wholesaler?

Let the average number of units that a manufacturer sells each time his salesman calls upon a retailer equal u_1 (order size).

Manufacturers will then incur the following costs when selling directly to retailers:

$$T + A + abcegp(u_1 - d) \text{ or } 20{,}000 + 4{,}950 + 9u_1$$

The unit cost will be calculated as:

$$\frac{T + A + abcegp(u_1 - d)}{abcu_1}$$

or

$$\frac{24{,}950 + 9u_1}{2{,}000u_1}$$

The corresponding cost when selling through a wholesaler will be (as above):

$$\frac{T + B}{abcd}$$

or \$0.4256. When the two unit costs are put equal, we find:

$$\frac{T + A + abcegp(u_1 - d)}{abcu_1} = \frac{T + B}{abcd}$$

or

$$\frac{24{,}950 + 9u_1}{2{,}000u_1} = 0.4256$$

$$u_1 = d\left(\frac{T + A - abcdegp}{T + B - abcdegp}\right)$$

or 29.6 units.

It should be observed that *abcdegp* represents the cost of selling time, varying with order value. It is identical in cases 1, 2, and 3. If we call it V, we can write the expression

$$u_1 = d\left(\frac{T + A - V}{T + B - V}\right)$$

The manufacturers' salesman must thus try to get at least 30 units per order in order to compensate for the lower cost of personal contacts when manufacturers sell through a wholesaler. This is to be compared to the order size that the wholesaler is assumed to get, namely, 25 units (of each manufacturer's goods). In case retailers' costs of receiving salesmen are included, as above, the point of equilibrium will be found to lie at 31.3 units per order.

Example 3. In reality, a rise in sales is likely to come about through a combination of the two variables studied in isolated form above, namely, number of calls and size of order. We pose the question: Which combinations of the two will give the same costs per unit when selling directly as when selling through a wholesaler?

Let x_1 and u_1, as above, stand for number of calls and order size, respectively.

Total costs per unit when selling directly to retailers will then be

$$\frac{T + x_1\left[\frac{A}{c} + abegp(u_1 - d)\right]}{abx_1\, u_1}$$

or

$$\frac{20{,}000 + 4x_1(24.75 + 0.045u_1)}{40x_1\, u_1}$$

Corresponding costs per unit when selling through a wholesaler will be

$$\frac{T + B}{abcd}$$

or \$0.4256. And so we get the following equation:

$$\frac{T + x_1\left[\frac{A}{c} + abegp(u_1 - d)\right]}{abx_1\, u_1} = \frac{T + B}{abcd}$$

or

$$\frac{20{,}000 + 4x_1(24.75 + 0.045u_1)}{40\, x_1\, u_1} = 0.4256$$

$$x_1 = \frac{cdT}{u_1(T + B - V) - d(A - V)}$$

or

$$x_1 = \frac{1{,}187}{u_1 - 5.88}$$

This equation can be expressed graphically as shown by Figure 2. The curve *A* shows all those combinations between number of calls and size of order that give the same added costs of manufacturing and selling per unit.

The diagram shows, for example, that 50 calls, each resulting in an order of 29.6 units on the average (=1,480 units per manufacturer and year), give the same total costs per unit as 60 calls, each resulting in an order of 25.7 units on the average (=1,540 units per manufacturer and year), or as 40 calls, each

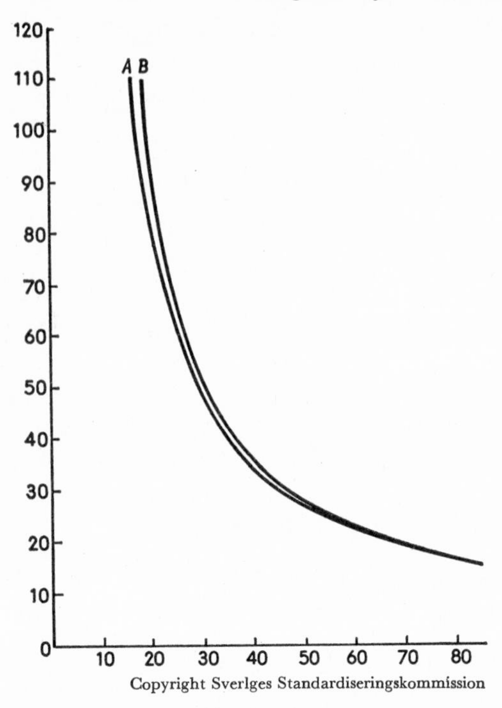

FIGURE 2

Figure 2 shows those relations between number of calls and size of order that give, respectively, the same costs per unit (curve *A*) and the same contribution to profits (curve *B*) when selling directly to retailers as when selling through a wholesaler.

resulting in an order of 35.6 units (=1,423 units per manufacturer and year). All these alternatives, relating to direct selling from the manufacturer, render the same total costs per unit as when selling through a wholesaler.

If, in this case, retailers' costs of receiving salesmen are included, the relation between number of calls and size of order in the points of equilibrium will have the form

$$x_1 = \frac{1{,}154}{u_1 - 8.24}$$

Which Choice Gives Maximum Profits?

Example 4. The preceding examples, numbers 1–3, have illustrated the computation of an equilibrium point (or rather a set of points) where selling directly results in the same total costs per unit sold as when selling through a wholesaler.

If, on the other hand, the manufacturers aim at maximal profits by maximizing the contribution to fixed costs, a somewhat different method of computation is called for. The problem is here to compute the equilibrium point, where the dollar amount of this contribution is the same, whether selling directly or through a wholesaler.

Let us assume, as before, that each manufacturer and the wholesaler have priced their goods identically, viz., \$1.50 per unit, when sold to retailers, and further that the variable manufacturing costs of each manufacturer amount to 90 cents per unit.

When selling directly, the total contributions will then be

$$abx_1\, u_1(e-j) - x_1\left[\frac{A}{c} + \frac{V}{cd}(u_1 - d)\right]$$

or

$$(4)(10x_1u_1)(1.50 - 0.90) - (4x_1)(24.75 + 0.045u_1) = 4x_1(5.955u_1 - 24.75)$$

When selling through a wholesaler, the contribution, computed correspondingly, will be

$$abcd(e-j) - B$$

or

$$30{,}000 - 1{,}280 = 28{,}720$$

The equilibrium point desired can then be expressed in the equation

$$abx_1\, u_1(e-j) - x_1\left[\frac{A}{c} + \frac{V}{cd}(u_1 - d)\right] = abcd(e-j) - B$$

or

$$4x_1(5.955u_1 - 24.75) = 28{,}720$$

$$x_1 = \frac{abcd(e-j) - B}{u_1\left[ab(e-j) - \frac{V}{cd}\right] - \frac{A-V}{c}}$$

$$= \frac{1{,}205.7}{u_1 - 4.16}\ \text{calls}$$

The curve B in Figure 2 shows all those combinations between number of calls and size of order that give the same contribution to fixed costs when selling directly as when selling through a wholesaler.

Figure 2 shows, for example, that in this case, *50* calls, each resulting in an order of *28.3* units on the average (=*1,414* units per manufacturer and year), give the same contribution as *60* calls, each resulting in an order of *24.3* units (=*1,456* units per manufacturer and year), or as *40* calls, each resulting in an order of *34.3* units (=*1,372* units per manufacturer and year). These figures should be compared to those of the preceding example (*1,480*, *1,540*, and *1,423* units, respectively).

Table 2 shows those relations between number of calls ($=x_1$) and size of order ($=u_1$) that give, respectively, the same costs per unit sold (example 3) and the same contribution to profits (example 4) when selling directly to retailers as when selling through a wholesaler.

TABLE 2

Example 3			Example 4		
x_1	u_1	M*	x_1	u_1	M*
15	85.04	1,276	15	84.54	1,268
16	80.09	1,281	16	79.52	1,272
17	75.73	1,287	17	75.08	1,276
18	71.85	1,293	18	71.14	1,281
19	68.37	1,299	19	67.62	1,285
20	65.25	1,305	20	64.45	1,289
22	59.85	1,317	22	58.96	1,297
24	55.36	1,329	24	54.40	1,306
26	51.55	1,340	26	50.53	1,314
28	48.29	1,352	28	47.22	1,322
30	45.46	1,364	30	44.35	1,331
35	39.81	1,393	35	38.61	1,351
40	35.57	1,423	40	34.30	1,372
50	29.63	1,483	50	28.27	1,414
60	25.67	1,540	60	24.26	1,456
70	22.84	1,599	70	21.38	1,497
80	20.72	1,658	80	19.23	1,538
90	19.07	1,716	90	17.56	1,580
100	17.75	1,775	100	16.22	1,622
110	16.67	1,834	110	15.12	1,663

* $M = x_1 u_1$.

CONCLUSION

Since the aim of this paper has only been to present a method, no comments will be made here on the significance of the results of the numerical examples. But it seems as if these and similar examples could be developed in various directions and thus increase our understanding of the relation between such factors as order size, number of calls, quantity sold, the contribution to fixed costs, total costs per unit, etc. It is probable, too, that by posing different assumptions about the number of calls and the order size of a wholesaler, and by taking into account the fixed costs on the wholesaling and retailing level, one could make the examples more instructive and interesting.

As was pointed out earlier, it will be necessary to include in the computation other functions beside the selling function—e.g., paper work, warehouse routines, transportation, etc. If the costs of different alternative ways of distribution are given a general algebraic form, it should be easy to study the changes in costs effected by specific changes in the methods of operation.

Also, we ought to get a more reliable picture of the effect of changes in methods of distribution by introducing into our calculations probability models, especially concerning the expected effects on sales volume.

In an economy where the supremacy of selling directly or through a wholesaler is often discussed, the existence of an adjustable method of computation, like the one described here, may help to introduce into the discussion more exact and unbiased arguments.

15

The general functions derived in a case study relating sales and promotional effort are outlined by the author. In seeking to determine an optimum allocation of advertising among dealers, the Poisson distribution is assumed in respect to orders of units of product by a given dealer. Given the relevance of this distribution and the determination of the probability density of the average number of units ordered by all dealers, one can calculate the percentage of dealers who will order a specified number of units. The effect of promotional effort is then formulated mathematically by comparing the functions for dealers with and without promotional aid, thus providing a quantitative basis for evaluation of alternative promotional plans.

*THE EFFECT OF PROMOTIONAL EFFORT ON SALES**

John F. Magee

INTRODUCTION

THE MANAGEMENT of an industrial enterprise is constantly faced with the problem of deciding how much advertising, selling, or promotional effort is economically justified. A reasonable response to this question implies at least an intuitive knowledge of the relation between sales volume and promotional effort. This paper presents a case study of the development of such a relationship.

This development yielded an objective measure of relative efficiency of the distribution of promotional effort. The relative efficiency of use of promotional effort was not hitherto measured, and the company had no real idea how efficient the distribution method was. This measure provided a guide in directing further research effort and evaluating alternative schemes for distributing promotional effort. A quantitative measure of the effectiveness of the promotion was obtained as a first step in a thorough analysis of the promotional material itself. Finally, the construction of a quantitative statement of the relation between promotion and sales was the first and most difficult step in the construction of a general theory of company operations.

Industrial security requires that this case be disguised. We believe this has

* Reprinted from *Journal of Operations Research*, March, 1953, pp. 64–74.

been accomplished without essential distortion of the methodology involved, but we hope the reader will be lenient if certain unrealities appear in the statement of the problem.

The company studied distributes coffee to a large number of retail grocery stores throughout the country. The main promotional effort is carried on by a group of promotional salesmen who travel from store to store, working with dealers. These salesmen distribute point-of-sale advertising and displays, try to obtain favorable display locations for stock from dealers, and educate the dealers in the merits of the merchandise.

The cost of promotional salesmen is such that the company has felt for many years that promotional calls on all dealers were not justified. It was felt that promotional salesmen could profitably call on about 40 percent of the dealers. Study of ways of selecting dealers for promotion had gone on for about two decades and led to the system in current use based on the sales records of the preceding two months. For example, the 40 percent of the dealers purchasing in the greatest volume during April and May would be subjected to the promotional program for June.

OBJECTIVES OF THE STUDY

The questions asked initially were:

1. How good is the existing procedure for selection of dealers for promotion? Can an "ideal" be set; and if so, how close to ideal is the present system?
2. How much further effort in refining this dealer selection method is warranted?
3. How much promotional effort is justified as long as the present method of directing this effort is unchanged?

To answer these questions, the first step was to study the effects of the existing promotional effort on the dealer accounts. At the time the study was begun, it was known only that promotional effort appeared, on the average, to have some effect on business from dealers promoted. The business from individual dealers was subject to large random fluctuations. Furthermore, the effect of the promotional effort was confounded with the fact that only those dealers from whom a larger volume of business was expected were promoted.

The salient features were found to lie in the purchasing habits of the dealers, and these were expressible by a relatively simple mathematical model. The model was a first approximation, neglecting interactions among dealers and effects of current promotion on future business.

DATA AVAILABLE

The purchase record of each of the many thousands of dealers for a one-year period was available. These records gave the name, location, sales route number, and promotional territory code of each dealer, the date of each purchase, the size of each order, and whether promotional effort was given to the account in any month.

Records of past experiments were also available. The variety and number of dealers, and the number of random influences affecting the purchases of each, raised complications in running such promotional experiments. The method used had been to select two large groups of dealers from the same region, equally distributed among the several classes and types of dealers, which in total had purchased close to equal amounts during several preceding time periods. The normal promotional program was given to eligible dealers in one group, the experimental program to eligible dealers in the other, and conclusions were based on a comparison of total business from each group. The time required and the random errors in the results of these experiments made them both costly and inflexible. Moreover, they had been designed to compare specific promotional programs rather than to gather information for study of the operation. The most useful were several such experiments in which *all* dealers in the test group had been subjected to the typical or conventional promotional program.

The company's products were sold to dealers by the case. The cost of one case was fixed. Whether a dealer purchased frequently in small quantities or less frequently in larger quantities was insignificant, nor was the particular product or products purchased important; the most important characteristic of a dealer was the expected number of cases he would order in a specified time.

When the average number of cases ordered per month by individual dealers was computed from several months' observations and compared with the number of cases ordered in later months, a substantial amount of persistence was observed. A fair amount of random variation between past and future performance, however, remained to be explained.

CHARACTERIZATION OF INDIVIDUALS AND GROUPS OF DEALERS

We denote by c the average number of cases ordered per month by a particular dealer. Then the best estimate of the number of cases this dealer will order in a future month is also c. Actually, however, a dealer is likely to order more or fewer cases in any particular month. The number he actually orders will depend somewhat on chance: on his customers' impulses to buy, on his needs, and on his inclination toward the company. That is, the actual number of cases ordered in any period will follow some sort of probability distribution related to his expected number.

The hypothesis was made that the distribution of actual number of cases ordered could be approximated by the Poisson distribution

$$E(n) = \frac{e^{-c}c^n}{n!} \tag{1}$$

where $E(n)$ is the probability that a dealer with an expected frequency of ordering or characteristic order, c, will actually order n cases in a month.

This hypothesis is not simple to check. The values of c for individual dealers were not known; they could only be estimated from past records. Moreover, the estimate of c depends not only on the average number of cases ordered by the individual dealer but also, where the number of time periods is small, on the distribution of c's for the dealer group as a whole.

One simple check was made. The average number of cases ordered per month and the observed variance were computed for each of several hundred dealers. Under the hypothesis of equation 1, these should be approximately equal. A fair check was obtained. Otherwise, validation of equation 1 depended on more general tests of consistency. That is, if we assume the Poisson distribution to be the proper one and go on to further analyses of dealer behavior, do we obtain results consistent with observed data in any manipulations of the model we may make? This checks whether errors introduced by the Poisson assumption are satisfactorily compensated in other parts of the model, rather than checking the assumption itself.

If an individual dealer can be characterized, at least in part, by his characteristic order, c, what can be said about a group of dealers—for example, the group of all dealers, or the dealers in a particular area? We know some will be what we would call "excellent" dealers who average many cases per month. Others who order little will, in the present form of our analysis, be considered "poor" dealers, while the rest will fall somewhere between these two extremes. Thus, if we array the dealers according to their characteristic order, c, we will get some sort of probability density of dealers as a function of their expected number of cases ordered, which we call $\Upsilon(c)$.

The probability density $\Upsilon(c)$ will presumably depend in some fashion on the promotional program followed. For convenience, $\Upsilon(c)$ will be defined as the probability density under the condition that all dealers are given the normal promotional aids.

The fraction of dealers who will order n cases will be given by the equation

$$f(n) = \int_0^\infty \frac{e^{-c}c^n}{n!}\,\Upsilon(c)\,dc \tag{2}$$

That is, the fraction of dealers ordering n cases in a given month is the sum of the fractions who will order n cases from the groups of dealers whose *average* number of orders, c, is between 0 and 1, between 1 and 2, between 2 and 3, and so on.

Results of past experiments where all dealers had been given promotional help gave information on the form of $\Upsilon(c)$. Figure 1 shows the observed values of $f(n)$ for one such experiment, and suggested that $\Upsilon(c)$ should be an exponential or sum of exponentials in form. The simple exponential form

$$\Upsilon(c) = \frac{1}{s}\,e^{-c/s} \tag{3}$$

was tried, where s is the average number of cases ordered by one dealer per month for the group of dealers as a whole. Substituting equation 3 in equation 2 yields

$$f(n) = \frac{s^n}{(s+1)^{n+1}} \tag{4}$$

The fit of equation 4 to observed values of $f(n)$ is shown in Figure 1. The value of s used was simply the total number of orders from the group, divided by the total number of dealers in the group.

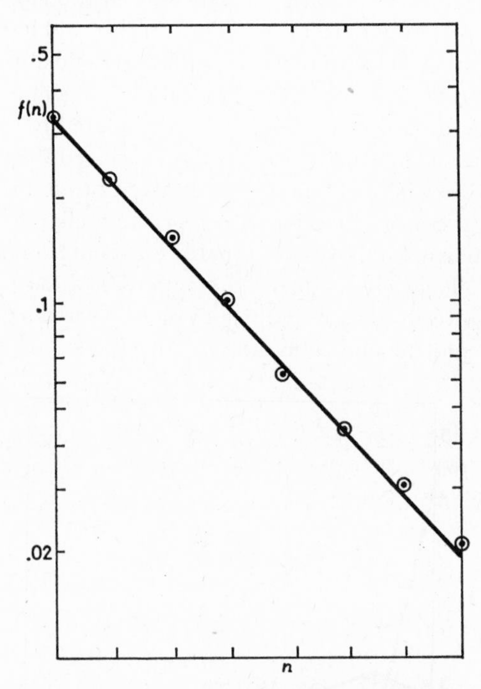

FIGURE 1. The observed fractions of dealers ordering n cases in a month; all dealers given special promotional help. The full line is a plot of equation 4 with $s = 2$.

The validity of the Poisson distribution to describe the behavior of individual dealers was tested, using equation 3. If an individual dealer orders n_k cases in k months, the expected value of his characteristic order, c, is

$$\begin{aligned} E(c|n_k, k) &= \int_0^\infty c' \frac{(ks+1)^{n_k+1}(c')^{n_k}}{s^{n+1}n_k!} e^{-c'\left(\frac{ks+1}{s}\right)} dc' \\ &= \frac{n_k+1}{k+\frac{1}{s}} \end{aligned} \tag{5}$$

Since the expected value of the number of cases ordered in a future month, n_f, is c, the number of orders n_f should be related to the number of orders in k past months by the equation

$$E(n_f) = \left(\frac{s}{sk+1}\right) n_k + \left(\frac{s}{sk+1}\right) \tag{6}$$

When tested on several hundred dealers in the experimental groups, the slope and intercept of equation 6 were found to agree with the observed values.

THE EFFECT OF PROMOTIONAL EFFORT

A routine procedure was used by the sales organization for ranking dealers. The top 40 percent of the dealers according to this ranking was then given promotional attention. The system was sufficiently flexible, however, that fractions from 30 percent to 100 percent of the total group had been given promotion in some instances. It was possible to isolate the records of the top 40 percent of dealers who would normally have received the promotion in the experimental groups where 100 percent was given promotional attention.

The probability density function $\Upsilon_p(c)$ for these eligible dealers (top 40 percent) was unknown, but it was presumably different from that of the group as a whole, $\Upsilon(c)$. Plots were made of the fractions of these groups ordering n cases, $f_p(n)$, as shown by the circles in Figure 2. Various approximations to $\Upsilon_p(c)$ were tried, and the one giving the best prediction of the $f_p(n)$ was

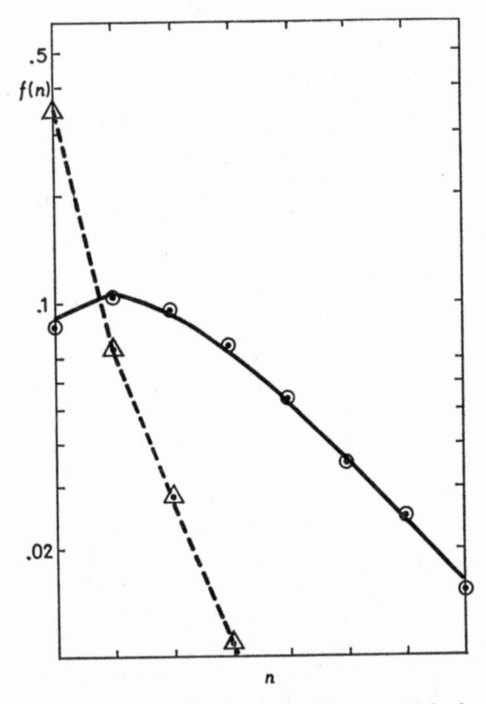

FIGURE 2. The observed fractions of dealers ordering n cases in a month. Those normally receiving promotional help are plotted as circles and those normally not receiving promotional help as triangles. The full line is a plot of equation 8, and the dashed line of equation 10*a*.

(7) $$\Upsilon_p(c) = \frac{(1 - e^{-g(c/s)})e^{-c/s}}{s}$$

where a is the fraction of the dealers promoted, and $g = (a/1 - a)$. The values of $f_p(n)$ would then be given by

(8) $$\begin{aligned} f_p(n) &= \int_0^\infty E(n)\Upsilon_p(c)\, dc \\ &= s^n\left\{\frac{1}{(s+1)^{n+1}} - \frac{1}{(s+g+1)^{n+1}}\right\} \end{aligned}$$

By comparing equations 3 and 7, we see that $\Upsilon_{np}(c)$, the distribution of characteristic orders of dealers normally not promoted (the lower 60 percent), is approximated by

(9) $$\Upsilon_{np}(c) = \frac{e^{-((g+1)/s)c}}{s}$$

and the fraction of these dealers ordering n cases by

(10) $$f_{np}(n) = \frac{s^n}{(s+g+1)^{n+1}}$$

The fit of equation 8 to observed values is shown by the solid line in Figure 2.

Equations 7 and 8 were also tested by application to the records of several groups of dealers subject to the normal promotional campaigns. The checks described previously were also made, substituting equations 7 and 8 for equations 3 and 1, respectively. The agreement in all cases was found to be excellent, lending considerable support to the conclusion that equation 7 accurately describes the effect of the selection process in picking dealers for promotion.

The functions discussed in the last four paragraphs were derived from experiments in which *all* dealers were promoted. If the promotional effort had no effect on business, equations 9 and 10 would describe the nonpromoted dealers. Comparison of the observed fractions of nonpromoted dealers ordering a given number of cases with the values calculated from equation 10 therefore gives a basis for estimating the effect of the promotional effort. When this comparison was made, two differences were found:

1. According to equation 10, the ratio of $f_{np}(n)$ to $f_{np}(n+1)$ is $(s+g+1)/s$. When the observed values of these ratios for $n \geqq 1$ were used to determine s, the average number of cases ordered by one dealer per month, the value found was 0.71 of the value expected from study of the promoted dealers.
2. When this value of s was substituted in equation 10 to calculate the values of the fractions ordering n cases, $f_{np}(n)$, the observed values of $f_{np}(n)$ for $n \geqq 1$ were found to be 0.7 times the calculated values.

Adjustment of equation 10 to account for these two effects yields equation 10*a*, shown as a dashed line in Figure 2:

$$f_{np}(n) = \frac{0.7(0.71s)^n}{(0.71s + g + 1)^n} \qquad n \geq 1$$

(10a)

$$f_{np}(0) = (1 - a)\left\{1 - \sum_{n=1}^{\infty} f_{np}(n)\right\}$$

These two effects can be summarized as follows: When a dealer is given no promotion, the probability is 0.3 that he will act as if his characteristic order, c, were zero; moreover, the probability is 0.7 that he will act as if c were 0.71 of his frequency if promoted. The net effect is a reduction in his expected business of 50 percent.

APPLICATIONS

The isolation of the effect of promotion makes it possible to write down the sales resulting from any given level of promotional effort. Suppose there are N dealers, of which Na are to be selected for promotion by the usual means. Then the resulting number of cases ordered will be

$$\begin{aligned} O(a) &= N\left\{a\int_0^{\infty} cY_p(c)\,dc + 0.5(1 - a)\int_0^{\infty} cY_{np}(c)\,dc\right\} \\ &= \frac{Ns}{2}(1 + 2a - a^2) \end{aligned} \tag{11}$$

Since the value of a case is fixed, the resulting business will be

$$B(a) = \frac{Nsv}{2}(1 + 2a - a^2) \tag{12}$$

where v is the value per case.

The best that could be expected from a system of the type used for selection of dealers would be a system which always picked the upper tail of the distribution $Y(c)$ in equation 3. In this case the resulting business would be

$$\begin{aligned} B'(a) &= Nv\left\{\int_{-s\ln a}^{\infty} \frac{c}{s}e^{-c/s}\,dc + 0.5\int_0^{-s\ln a} \frac{c}{s}e^{-c/s}\,dc\right\} \\ &= \frac{Nsv}{2}\{1 + a - a\ln a\} \end{aligned} \tag{13}$$

The poorest reasonable method of selecting dealers for promotion would be random selection, and the resulting business would be

$$B''(a) = \frac{Nsv}{2}(1 + a) \tag{14}$$

The relative efficiency of the present selection method might be defined as the gain in business over that resulting from random selection, compared with the potential gain from use of an ideal method of selection. The efficiency necessarily must depend on a, the level of promotional activity, since any system would be "ideal" if no dealers or if all dealers were promoted. The relative efficiency $E(a)$ is therefore defined as

$$E(a) = \frac{B(a) - B''(a)}{B'(a) - B''(a)} \tag{15}$$

or in this case

$$E(a) = -\frac{(1 - a)}{\ln a} \qquad 0 < a < 1 \tag{16}$$

$E(a)$ is shown in Figure 3.

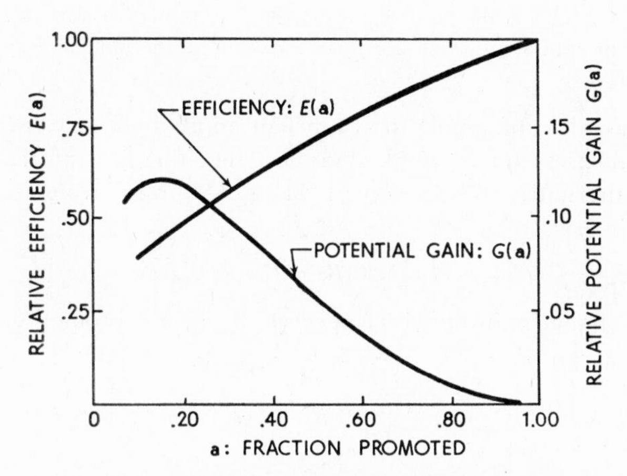

FIGURE 3. Relative efficiency and potential gain.

The relative potential gain from improvement of the selection of dealers is given by

$$\begin{aligned} G(a) &= \frac{B'(a) - B(a)}{B(a)} \\ &= \frac{a(a - 1 - \ln a)}{1 + 2a - a^2} \end{aligned} \tag{17}$$

and is also shown in Figure 3.

Note that both the measure of relative efficiency, $E(a)$, and the measure of relative potential gain, $G(a)$, are independent of the factors influenced by economic conditions: the average number and value of cases, s and v.

CONCLUSION

A theoretical analysis of promotional methods, based on existing data, and without the need for special experiments, yielded measures of the relative efficiency of distribution of promotion and potential gain in sales through better distribution, a measure of the effect of promotion on individual accounts, and a broad view of the whole operation forming an important part of a general theory of company operations.

REMARKS

Some side comments on the development leading to equation 12 may be of interest. The business represented by the equation is, of course, not all profit. Let us suppose the following functions are known:

$C(B)$ = The cost of producing and distributing a volume B of product
$C(a)$ = The cost of promotion of a fraction a of the dealers
$I(B)$ = The capital required to support production of a volume B of output
$I(a)$ = The capital required to support a level of promotional activity represented by a

These are usually obtainable to a sufficient approximation. Assume a minimum desirable return on capital, i, has been set either as a matter of policy or because of alternative uses for capital. Then the "profit" from a volume $B(a)$ is given by

$$P(a) = B(a) - C(B) - C(a) - i\{I(B) + I(a)\} \tag{18}$$

The rate of change of profit with respect to the level of promotional activity a is given by

$$P'(a) = Nsv(1 - a) - \frac{d}{da}\{C(B) + C(a)\} - i\frac{d}{da}\{I(B) + I(a)\} \tag{19}$$

The profit will be maximized when $P'(a) = 0$, or when

$$a = 1 - \left(\frac{1}{Nsv}\right)\left[\frac{d}{da}\{C(B) + C(a)\} + i\frac{d}{da}\{I(B) + I(a)\}\right] \tag{20}$$

The computation of what is normally meant by profit typically does not include an imputed interest charge on capital employed. Maximization of profit as conventionally defined may well be erroneous, however. It is only correct in the very special case when the minimum acceptable return on capital is zero, which is hardly the typical case today. Neglect of imputed interest is sometimes based on the appeal to the fixed volume of capital employed in "the short run." The exceptions to this idea, however, have been more numerous in our experience than the applications.

The limitations of a model of the type discussed here are, of course, great. The model is static; it does not account for time changes introduced by promotional effort. These dynamic consequences are probably small, though, compared with short-run effects in an established enterprise. The model does not tell us why the promotional effort has the effect it does, as a basis for improvement in the quality of this effort; this is a separate question. Finally, this model is not directly applicable to the analysis of new types of promotional activity completely outside the scope of the usual promotional effort. It does provide a solid starting point for such an analysis.

The functional relationship between sales and promotional effort developed here is useful in directing sales promotional activities. It is also of fundamental importance in any general model of the business as a whole. A general model can be extremely valuable in providing quantitative guides to planning basic strategy of the business.

The distribution of expected number of cases purchased, equation 3, is intriguing. One wonders whether the same or similar distributions have been found in similar analyses elsewhere. If so, would a study of this phenomenon lead to a deeper understanding of the mass habits of the buying public?

REFERENCES

Derivations and a variety of examples of applications can be found in:

1. FELLER, W. *Introduction to Probability Theory and Its Applications*, particularly pp. 110–23. New York: John Wiley & Sons, Inc., 1950.

2. FRY, T. C. *Probability and Its Engineering Uses*. New York: D. Van Nostrand Co., Inc., 1928.

16

The authors develop a model for the analysis of advertising campaigns with the sales decay constant, saturation level, and response constant as parameters. Each parameter is explained in detail and graphically illustrated with actual sales data. Procedures for measuring the parameters are briefly discussed. Finally, the optimum total advertising budget and the allocation of this budget among products are determined from the model.

*AN OPERATIONS RESEARCH STUDY OF SALES RESPONSE TO ADVERTISING**

M. L. Vidale aud H. B. Wolfe

OPERATIONS RESEARCH has not as yet found many applications in the field of advertising. Only a few papers [1–6] on the subject have appeared in the literature. It is difficult to obtain reliable experimental data. It is probably true that designing original advertising copy and making *a priori* estimates of the behavior of the buying public are not promising material for operations research; there do exist, however, problems that are of great interest to the advertising man and that can be studied quantitatively. For example:

1. How does one evaluate the effectiveness of an advertising campaign?
2. How should the advertising budget be allocated among different products and media?
3. What criteria determine the size of the advertising budget?

The last two questions cannot be answered without a knowledge of advertising effectiveness; this is where most of the difficulties lie and where research is most needed. Once the relation between sales response and advertising has been established, the optimum budget size and allocation can be determined.

During the past few years the Operations Research Group at Arthur D. Little, Inc., has studied these problems and examined sales promotions for several large industrial concerns. In this paper, we wish to present some generalizations that have been suggested by the results of our experiments.

We shall first describe the type of experimental results we have obtained and then discuss a simple mathematical model consistent with our observations.

---

* Reprinted from *Operations Research*, June, 1957, pp. 370–81.

EXPERIMENTAL RESULTS: ADVERTISING PARAMETERS

In order to measure the sales response of individual products to advertising and to compare the effectiveness of various media, we have performed a large number of controlled experiments in which the intensity and type of promotion were varied. With the cooperation of sales and advertising departments and their advertising agencies, we have been able to run large-scale tests over considerable portions of the U.S. market. The results of the tests have in most cases been significant and reproducible. In the analysis of advertising campaigns, we have found it helpful to describe the interaction of sales and advertising in terms of three parameters:

1. The sales decay constant
2. The saturation level
3. The response constant

We shall introduce these parameters by means of a few sales histories that exemplify them. The relations and the data in the examples are real. However, for reasons of industrial security, it has been necessary to conceal the types of products tested and, in a few cases, to paraphrase the advertising media.

Sales Decay Constant

In the absence of promotion, sales tend to decrease because of product obsolescence, competing advertising, etc. Under relatively constant market conditions the rate of decrease is, in general, constant: that is, a constant percent of sales is lost each year. Figure 1 (p. 216) presents the eight-year sales history of product A, plotted on a semilogarithmic scale. This product exhibits a small seasonality in sales; however, over the years the sales have been decreasing exponentially. Figure 2 (p. 216) presents the sales history of a very seasonal product, *B*. Here again, the monthly sales, averaged over a full year, "decay" at a constant rate.

This behavior, which we have observed in a great number of unpromoted products, leads us to introduce as a parameter the exponential sales decay constant λ; that is, the sales rate at time t of an unpromoted product is given by $S(t) = S(0)\exp(-\lambda t)$. In the examples above the sales decay constants are 0.24 per year and 0.06 per year for products A and B, respectively. As might be expected, the sales decay rate ranges from large values for products that become quickly obsolescent or products in a highly competitive market to almost zero for noncompetitive, well-established products.

Product C (Fig. 3, p. 217) exhibits some interesting features when analyzed with this parameter in mind. The sales of this product were "decaying" at a constant rate ($\lambda = 0.9$ per year) up to the beginning of 1953, when an article favorable to the product appeared in a popular magazine of wide circulation.

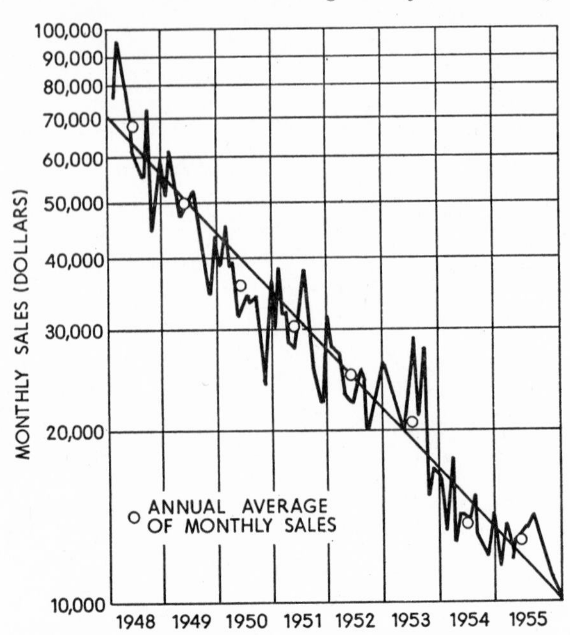

FIGURE 1. Unpromoted product *A*—sales history.

Sales increased by a factor of five within a month. This level of sales, however, was not maintained but began to decrease much more quickly ($\lambda = 4.7$ per year) than the original rate until it reached a new level, double that before the promotion. At this point the sales decay constant returned to the original

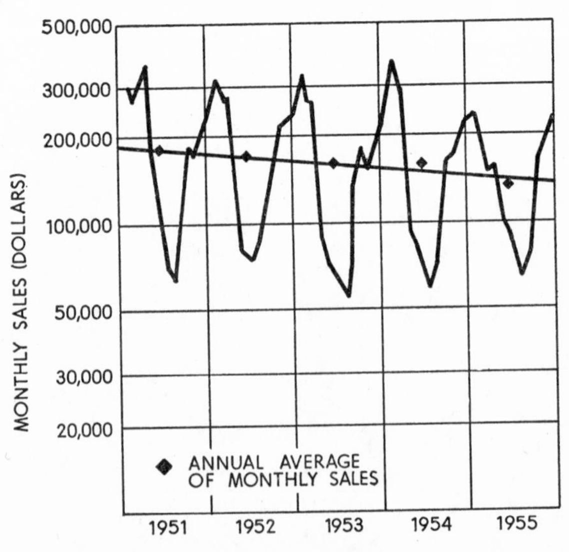

FIGURE 2. Unpromoted product *B*—sales history.

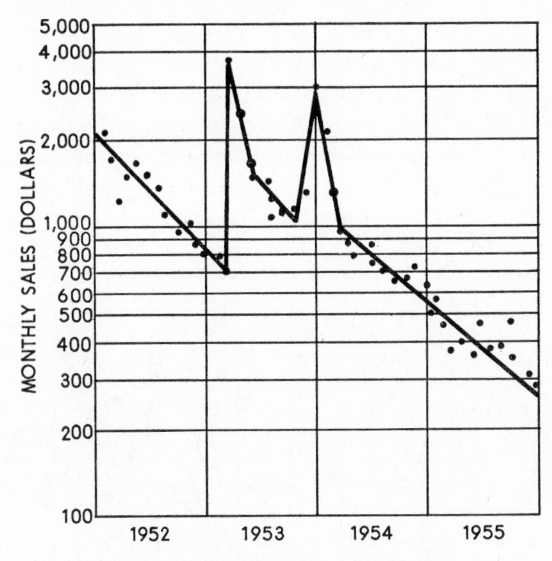

FIGURE 3. Product *C*—sales history.

value of 0.9. Eight months later, the product was mentioned favorably in another popular magazine, and the same phenomenon occurred. Clearly, we are dealing here with two classes of customers: those who were induced to purchase after reading the magazine articles but who soon lost interest in the product; and the "normal" customers, who behaved much like the original customer population. Both articles succeeded in raising the number of "normal" customers.

Saturation Level

The concept of saturation level is illustrated by the sales history of product *D* (Fig. 4). This product was promoted continuously for one year by weekly

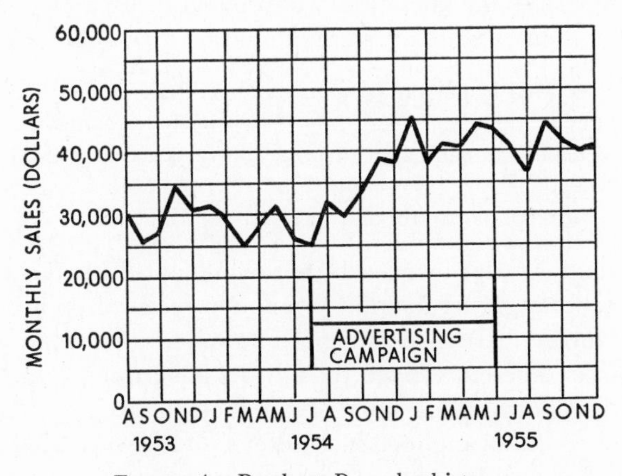

FIGURE 4. Product *D*—sales history.

newspaper advertisements beginning in July, 1954. In the first six months, sales rose 30 percent and then leveled off, although the advertising campaign was continued for another six months. This additional advertising may have helped to maintain sales at the new level, but this effect cannot have been large, because the decay rate both before and after the advertising campaign was small. We conclude that this campaign could have been considerably shorter and equally effective, and that beyond a certain point it lost its value.

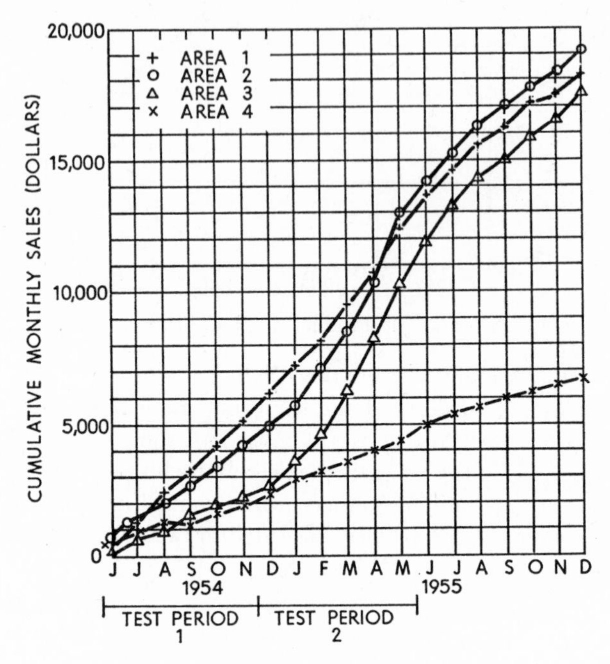

FIGURE 5. Product *E*—sales history.

Figure 5 presents the sales history of product *E*. Because of the complexity of the sales responses, sales are here plotted on a cumulative scale.

1. Area 1 received a spot radio commercial campaign for six months.
2. Beginning at the same time, area 2 received the campaign for 12 months.
3. At the end of the campaign in area 1, area 3 received the campaign for six months.
4. Area 4 was kept as control and received no promotion.

In areas 1 and 2, sales increased approximately 150 percent over those in area 4; the additional six months' promotion received by area 2 did not increase sales further. Area 3 experienced a similar sales increase after the promotion started. Therefore, even though the advertising campaign was postponed for six months, it lost none of its effectiveness.

From the results exemplified in Figures 4 and 5, we are led to describe the interaction of advertising and sales in terms of a second parameter—the saturation level, M, or practical limit of sales that can be generated. This saturation level depends not only on the product being promoted but also on the advertising medium used; it represents the fraction of the market that the particular campaign can capture. This saturation level can often be raised further by other advertising media.

Response Constant

In addition to the decay constant and the saturation level, we need a third parameter to describe the sales behavior of a product. We define the response constant, r, as the sales generated per advertising dollar when $S = 0$. We note that the number of new customers who are potential buyers decreases as sales approach saturation. When advertising is directed indiscriminately to both customers and noncustomers, the effectiveness of each advertising dollar in obtaining new customers also decreases as sales increase. In general, the sales generated per advertising dollar, when sales are at a level S, is given by $r(M - S)/M$, where M is the saturation level.

As an example, for product D the saturation level was $42,000 per month (see Fig. 4). The advertising expenditure was $5,000 per month. In 1954, before the start of the advertising campaign, monthly sales averaged $29,000, or 70 percent of the saturation level. The unsaturated portion, or the percentage of the potential represented by noncustomers, was 30 percent. The new customers converted to the product as a result of the July promotion increased sales by approximately $3,000 per month. The response constant was therefore $r = (\$3{,}000/\text{mo.})/(0.30 \times \$5{,}000) = 2/\text{mo.}$

MEASUREMENT OF PARAMETERS

In the next section, we will present a model of the interaction of advertising and sales, based on the three parameters: sales decay constant, saturation level, and response constant. These parameters differ from product to product and must therefore be determined separately for individual products. The sales decay constant can be measured from the sales data either before or after a promotion. The saturation level and response constant can be determined from a detailed analysis of the sales history or, when necessary, experimentally. We have found that test promotions, when carefully designed with experimental controls and on a sufficiently large scale, give results that are both significant and reproducible, though the degree of accuracy attainable is smaller than ordinarily considered acceptable in many other fields of research. Product advertising, when effective, shows results within days or at most weeks, so proposed advertising programs can be thoroughly pretested. When as large a market share as possible must be captured before competing products are developed and marketed, it may be necessary to forgo pretests. In such cases, rough estimates of the three parameters can be made from a knowledge of past performances of similar products. As the campaign progresses and the estimates of the parameters are improved, the campaign can be modified accordingly.

MATHEMATICAL MODEL

We have seen that the response of sales to a promotional campaign can be described by three parameters: λ, the exponential sales decay constant; M, the saturation level; and r, the response constant.

A mathematical model of sales response to advertising, based on these parameters, is represented by

$$dS/dt = r\,A(t)\,(M - S)/M - \lambda S \tag{1}$$

where S is the rate of sales at time t and $A(t)$ is the rate of advertising expenditure. This equation has the following interpretation: The increase in the rate of sales, dS/dt, is proportional to the intensity of the advertising effort, A, reaching the fraction of potential customers, $(M - S)/M$, less the number of customers that are being lost, λS.

This model has been chosen because it describes in simple mathematical terms our experimental observations. Undoubtedly, the probability of losing customers is decreased by advertising. Further experiments may prove that r and M are altered by changes in market conditions, by competing advertising, and by the introduction of new products. However, every increase in complexity requires the introduction of one or more additional parameters into equation 1. Since this model has been sufficient to describe the observed phenomena to the degree of accuracy allowed by the quality of our experimental data, there seems to be no reason at this time to complicate the picture unnecessarily. As our knowledge of advertising increases, it should be possible to improve this model and to develop more sophisticated theories.

From equation 1, we can derive several results that have proved useful in the design and evaluation of advertising campaigns.

Steady-State Solution

We can determine the advertising effort required to maintain sales at a steady predetermined level by setting $dS/dt = 0$. From equation 1, we then have $A = (\lambda/r)\,SM/(M - S)$. We see that the closer sales are to the saturation level M, and the larger the ratio λ/r, the more expensive it is to maintain the required sales rate.

Solution of Equation 1

For a constant rate, A, of advertising expenditure, maintained for time T, the rate of sales is obtained by integration of equation 1:

$$S(t) = [M/(1 + \lambda M/rA)]\{1 - e^{-(rA/M+\lambda)t}\} + S_0 e^{-r(A/M+\lambda)t} \qquad (t < T) \tag{2}$$

where S_0 is the rate of sales at $t = 0$, the start of the advertising campaign. After advertising has stopped $(t > T)$, sales decrease exponentially:

$$S(t) = S(T)e^{-\lambda(t-T)} \qquad (t > T) \tag{3}$$

The sales response to an advertising campaign of constant intensity and of duration T is shown in Figure 6.

The rate of sales increase is most rapid at $t = 0$; as saturation, M, is approached, this rate is reduced. This means that the first advertising dollar expended is most effective, the second dollar is next most effective, and so on. A second implication of this advertising model is that for equal expenditures, a

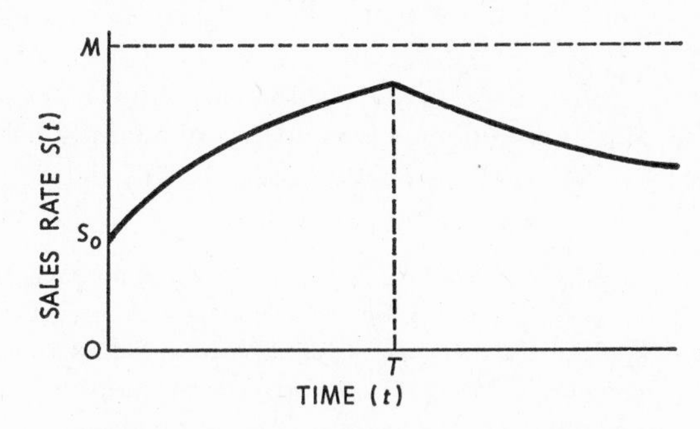

FIGURE 6. Sales response to an advertising campaign of duration T.

protracted advertising campaign is more profitable than a short, intense campaign. We have not yet tested this conclusion experimentally.

ADVERTISING PULSE

Many advertising campaigns are short and very intense. To get an expression for a single-pulse campaign of negligible duration, we can integrate equation 1 to obtain

$$S(t) = Me^{-\lambda t} - (M - S_0)e^{-(ra/M+\lambda)t} \tag{4}$$

where S_0 is the rate of sales immediately preceding the promotion and a is the total advertising expenditure. The immediate sales increase resulting from the promotion is

$$S(0) - S_0 = (M - S_0)(1 - e^{-ra/M}) \tag{5}$$

The total additional sales generated by this campaign are

$$\int_0^{\infty} [S(0) - S_0]\, e^{-\lambda t}\, dt = \frac{M - S_0}{\lambda}(1 - e^{-ra/M})$$

which reduces to $(ra/\lambda)(M - S_0)/M$ for sales well below saturation. The total extra sales generated by the advertising campaign are therefore the immediate sales increase, multiplied by the mean life of the product, λ^{-1}. Also, given a choice of several products, the advertising campaign will generate the most sales for the product with the largest value of $(r/\lambda)(M - S_0)/M$.

ALLOCATION OF ADVERTISING BUDGET

We have discussed experimental results of sales response to advertising and have described a simple mathematical model that adequately fits our observations. Once the parameters are measured for individual products, the problems of advertising budget size and of the allocation of the budget among different products can be considered.

Advertising is a form of investment. Those products should be advertised that will result in a return on capital invested equal to or greater than the returns from other possible investments, such as new equipment and research.

As an example, let us consider the simple case of a family of products that might be advertised by short, intense campaigns. We define the following quantities:

a_k = Total cost of the proposed advertising campaign for product k.
$R_k(t)$ = Additional sales resulting from the advertising campaign.
$C_k(t)$ = Rate of additional expenditures resulting from the advertising campaign. These include (a) the cost of the advertising campaign itself and (b) the cost of manufacturing and distributing the additional items sold.
I_k = Return on capital invested in advertising product k. For example, \$100 at time t_1 is equivalent to \$100 $\exp[I_k(t_2 - t_1)]$ at time t_2.

The sum total of expenditures incurred by the promotion of product k discounted at the rate I_k from the start of the advertising campaign ($t = 0$) is

$$\int_0^\infty C_k(t)\, e^{-I_k t}\, dt$$

The additional sales resulting from the advertising campaign, also discounted at the rate I_k, are

$$\int_0^\infty R_k(t)\, e^{-I_k t}\, dt$$

In order to determine the rate of return on capital invested in the promotion of product k, we equate expenditures and sales increases:

$$\int_0^\infty C_k(t)\, e^{-I_k t}\, dt = \int_0^\infty R_k(t)\, e^{-I_k t}\, dt \tag{6}$$

Under the assumption that production and distribution costs are proportional to sales, we have

$$C_k(t) = f_k\, R_k(t) + a_k \tag{7}$$

where f_k is the ratio of production and distribution costs to selling price. Assuming that the rate of sales of the unpromoted product decays exponentially at the rate λ_k, we have

(8) $$R_k(t) = R_{0k}\, e^{-\lambda_k t}$$

where R_{0k} is the instantaneous sales increase resulting from the campaign. Substituting equations 7 and 8 into equation 6, we obtain

$$a_k + \int_0^\infty f_k\, R_{0k}\, e^{-\lambda_k t}\, e^{-I_k t}\, dt = \int_0^\infty R_{0k}\, e^{-\lambda_k t}\, e^{-I_k t}\, dt$$

Integrating and solving for I_k:

(9) $$I_k = (R_{0k}/a_k)\,(1 - f_k) - \lambda_k$$

It should be noted that the relation between R_{0k} and a_k is not linear, so the rate of return I_k is a function of the intensity of the advertising campaign.

Once the values of I_k are known, one can in principle select the products that may be advertised profitably. The rate of return considered acceptable by management varies considerably from company to company but remains relatively constant in time.

We see that the amount of advertising appropriate to each product, and consequently the total advertising appropriation, can be determined once the I_k's are known.

SUMMARY

In summary, we wish to stress the following points:

1. When carefully designed and executed, advertising experiments give results that are both reliable and reproducible. The degree of accuracy attainable is, however, considerably smaller than would be considered acceptable in many other fields of research. Product advertising gives quick results; the pretesting of proposed product advertising campaigns, therefore, is especially attractive.
2. The response of sales to advertising varies widely from product to product, but some generalizations are possible. The response of individual products to an advertising promotion may be characterized by two parameters: response constant and saturation level. A third parameter, the sales decay constant, gives the rate at which customers are lost.
3. A mathematical model of sales response, based on these three parameters, has proved useful in the analysis of advertising campaigns. By means of this model, one can compute the quantities needed to evaluate and compare alternate promotional campaigns.
4. A knowledge of sales response to advertising for each product permits one to evaluate the return that can be expected from capital invested in advertising for each product. With this information, it is then possible to select profitable advertising programs and to estimate the optimum total size of the advertising budget.

We do not know whether the model of sales response discussed in this paper will prove applicable to all situations; our experience is limited to a few industries, and we have not tested all advertising media. It is our hope that as these studies progress, and as the volume of experimental data grows, it will be possible to refine the model and thus increase its usefulness.

We wish to express our appreciation to Sherman Kingsbury, George E. Kimball, and Frank T. Hulswit, who, in their studies of advertising effectiveness, first developed many of the ideas expressed in this paper and helped to demonstrate the value of the operations research approach to sales problems.

REFERENCES

1. Levinson, Horace C. "Experiences in Commercial Operations Research," *Operations Research*, 1953, p. 220.
2. Koopman, Bernard O. "The Optimum Distribution of Effort," *Operations Research*, 1953, p. 52.
3. Magee, John F. "The Effect of Promotional Effort on Sales," *Journal of Operations Research*, March, 1953, p. 64.
4. Dorfman, Robert, and Steiner, Peter O. "Optimal Advertising and Optimal Quality," *American Economic Review*, 1954, p. 5.
5. Weinberg, R. S. "Multiple Factor Break-Even Analysis," *Operations Research*, 1956, p. 152.
6. Brown, A. A.; Hulswit, Frank T.; and Kettelle, J. D. "A Study of Sales Operations," *Operations Research*, 1956, p. 296.

17

The author depicts a profit-maximizing model which uses the concepts of distributed lags, constant decay rate, and present value. The relevant inputs include (1) sales effect of advertising in the current period, (2) sales in the prior period, (3) the rate at which sales decline in the absence of advertising, and (4) the discount rate. The model is developed for use by a small firm in a relatively large market, but various policy alternatives for monopolistic and oligopolistic market conditions are also presented and discussed.

*A SIMPLE MODEL FOR DETERMINING ADVERTISING APPROPRIATIONS**

Julian L. Simon

THE GENERAL THEORY of choosing the optimum advertising appropriation is clear. The advertiser should equate marginal revenue and marginal cost to maximize the present value of profits from advertising expenditure.

If the sales effect of each advertisement can be established, the theory can be implemented easily. Mail-order advertisers can and do record separately the sales made over the years to each customer, and each customer can be attributed to a particular advertisement. The process of determining how much total revenue each ad produces is then speeded up by estimation of future sales. Mail-order advertisers commonly note that of any group of customers a given proportion "decay" and cease to buy in any year. Stated conversely, another proportion (one minus the decay proportion) is retained from year to year. These proportions generally remain constant, other things being equal, and hence the total revenue that an advertisement will produce can be predicted on the basis of the first period's sales, together with the retention rate.

Mail-order advertisers, therefore, have all the information they need to predict whether any particular tested advertisement will produce revenue above or below the break-even point. All advertisements that promise profitable results are run, and the amount spent for advertising is the sum of the individual advertisement costs. In other words, there is no advertising budget as such. Rather, decisions are made piecemeal for the various advertising opportunities, as in capital budgeting theory.[1]

* Reprinted from *Journal of Marketing Research*, August, 1965, pp. 285–92. The *Journal* is a publication of the American Marketing Association.

[1] For a complete discussion of mail-order advertising expenditure decisions, see [17].

Unlike mail-order firms, the general advertiser does not have sales records with which to trace the purchasing history of individual consumers. Nor can the general advertiser establish with precision which advertising or nonadvertising stimulus created an individual customer. These difficulties have foiled the advertiser's wish for a rational procedure for setting the advertising budget.

Until recently there have only been rule-of-thumb methods for setting budgets, all of which have been discredited [5]. Recently, there have been several rational attacks upon the problem. Kuehn [11] developed a model based on brand loyalty characteristics intended for use in a competitive market share duopoly. Friedman [8], and Mills [13] have each applied game theory logic to the problem. But none of the models has characteristics that make it widely appreciable to a great variety of firms. (A partial explanation is presented in the last section.)

Recently, the concept of distributed lags has been applied to advertising, theoretically by Jastram [9], and Nerlove and Arrow [14], and empirically by Telser [18] and Palda [15]. Using time series analysis, these investigators have shown how to calculate how much of the effect of the advertising expenditure in any period continues into future periods. Using this retention factor and some specific types of advertising response functions, it is possible to calculate the long-term marginal sales effect of the advertising, and from that to estimate how much a given firm should spend to maximize profits.

Promising as this approach is, it depends upon data from several previous years, during which time market conditions may have changed considerably. The time series approach also is very sensitive to the particular type of function that the investigator fits to the data. For example, if the investigator finds that a straight line is the best description of the past relationship between advertising and sales, there is no limit to the amount of advertising which he would estimate might be spent profitably, a patent absurdity. Furthermore, the technique depends crucially upon a constant retention percentage from period to period.

The model described in this article utilizes the concept of distributed lags. It also takes advantage of the assumption that the effect of advertising diminishes at a constant percentage rate from period to period; but it does not depend crucially upon that assumption, as previous work generally does. Neither does it require considerable historical data or time series analysis, except to determine the retention rate, and the retention rate may also be estimated from panel data or in test market experiments. It is these features that make this model simple to use and constitute an advance over previous work.

MODEL FOR GENERAL ADVERTISERS WITH SMALL MARKET SHARES AND A RELATIVELY UNDIFFERENTIATED PRODUCT

We shall assume that the firm for whom we are constructing the model is small enough so that its advertising expenditures will not elicit "defensive" expenditures by other firms; that is, the firm's appropriation may be set as if other firms' advertising will not be changed in response. Furthermore, the small firm's advertising for a product that is not physically differentiated competes for sales against other firms, rather than against the same firm's advertising in other periods. (Later, this assumption will be loosened to deal with larger firms.) Our firm may sell either an expensive durable product (e.g., a washing machine) or a repeat purchase item e.g., bread).

The dependent variable will be net revenue, R, equal to total revenue minus cost of goods sold, delivery costs, and other nonselling variable costs. We shall assume that these deducted production costs are a linear function of output. This assumption is not likely to vitiate our conclusions over the ranges of operation we shall consider.

Let

T = Advertising period ($T = 1, 2, \cdots m$)
t = Revenue period ($t = 1, 2, \cdots n$)
$T = t$
$R_{T,t}$ = Net revenue caused by advertising in period T, realized in period t, undiscounted (gross revenue less all production costs)
$V_{T,t}$ = Present value net revenue
A_T = Advertising expenditure in period T
P_T = Profit from advertising in period T
b = Retention rate, equal to one minus the decay rate of customer purchases from period to period (in absence of further advertising)
p = Discount rate of the cost of money to the firm.

$\sum_{T=1}^{t} R_{T,t}$ = Sum of sales in period t, caused by all prior advertising in periods $1, 2, \ldots t$

By definition, the total sales in period t, $\sum_{T=1}^{t} R_{T,t}$, are the sum of those sales attributable to advertising[2] in period T, plus the sales that would occur in period t even if no advertising occurs in t. The latter may also be thought of as sales in period t caused by advertising in all periods prior to T. Therefore:

$$\sum_{T=1}^{t} R_{T,t} = \sum_{T=1}^{t-1} R_{T,t} + R_{T=t,t} \tag{1}$$

By definition of the retention rate:

$$\sum_{T=1}^{t-1} R_{T,t} = b \sum_{T=1}^{t-1} R_{T,t-1} \tag{2}$$

[2] Assume that we are dealing with a firm in which the sales caused by advertising can be logically partitioned from sales caused by other factors. In some cases, such as cigarettes, advertising may actually be the prime mover of sales.

that is, sales in the present period caused by prior advertising equal sales in the last period diminished by the decay rate. So

$$\sum_{T=1}^{t} R_{T,t} = b \sum_{T=1}^{t-1} R_{T,t-1} + R_{T=t,t} \tag{3}$$

The sales caused in period t by A_t are

$$\sum_{T=1}^{t} R_{T,t} - b \sum_{T=1}^{t-1} R_{T,t-1} \tag{4}$$

It is this core idea upon which the model is built.

It is known that the sales caused in period $t + 1$ by $A_{T=t}$ will equal $R_{T=t,t}$ diminished by the decay rate, $(1 - b)$. Similarly, sales in $t + 2$ will equal those in $t + 1$ diminished by $(1 - b)$, and so on, ad infinitum.

The basic result of this model is then

$$\begin{aligned} \sum_{T=1}^{\infty} R_{T=t,t} = {} & \left(\sum_{T=1}^{T=t} R_{T,t} - b \sum_{T=1}^{t-1} R_{T,t-1}\right) + b\left(\sum_{T=1}^{T=t} R_{T,t} - b \sum_{T=1}^{t-1} R_{T,t-1}\right) \\ & + b^2\left(\sum_{T=1}^{T=t} R_{T,t} - b \sum_{T=1}^{t-1} R_{T,t-1}\right) \cdots + b^{\infty}\left(\sum_{T=1}^{T=t} R_{T,t} - b \sum_{T=1}^{t-1} R_{T,t-1}\right) \end{aligned} \tag{5}$$

In other words, the total sales caused by advertising A_t in all periods equal the total of the sales caused by A_t in each future period; this is true by definition. The sales caused by A_t in each future period equal the total sales in that period, less sales that would have occurred anyway.

Since the terms within each bracket are identical, the entire expression can be simplified to

$$\sum_{t}^{\infty} R_{T=t,t} = \frac{1}{1-b}\left(\sum_{T=1}^{t} R_{T,t} - b \sum_{T=1}^{t-1} R_{T,t-1}\right) \tag{6}$$

So all that is needed to estimate the total sales caused by A_t are sales in $t - 1$, sales in t, and the retention rate.

To allow for the diminished value of a dollar in revenue in the future, as compared to current revenue, we modify with the discount rate. The *present value* of the advertising in the present period, $A_{T=t}$, is then obtained:

$$\sum_{t}^{\infty} V_{T=t,t} = \frac{1}{1-b\rho}\left(\sum_{T=1}^{t} R_{T,t} - b \sum_{T=1}^{t-1} R_{T,t-1}\right) \tag{7}$$

The profit from advertising in the present period is

$$P_T = \sum_{t}^{\infty} V_{T=t,t} - A_{T=t} \tag{8}$$

This enables us to compare the profitability of given advertising levels, assuming we know the sales in each period, the sales that would occur during this period with each given level of advertising, and the retention rate. The most profitable level of advertising can then be selected by inspection. This simple idea is the main finding; apparently, it is the first time it has been so stated.

The profit-maximizing rule can be expressed thus: Advertise until

$$\Delta A_{T=t} = \Delta \sum_{t}^{\infty} V_{T=t,t} \tag{9}$$

To illustrate, assume a firm with

$$\text{Retention rate } b \text{ from year to year} = 0.65$$

$$\text{Last year's sales } \sum_{T=1}^{t-1} R_{T,t-1} = \$1{,}387{,}000$$

$$\text{This year's sales } \sum_{T=t}^{t} R_{T,t} \text{ for } A_T \text{ of } \$564{,}000 = \$1{,}289{,}000$$

$$\text{Discount rate } p = 0.90$$

The value in sales of this year's advertising equals ($1,289,000 − $1,387,-000 × 0.65) + 0.65 ($1,289,000 − $1,387,000 × 0.65) 0.90 + 0.65 × 0.65 ($1,289,000 − $1,387,000 × 0.65) 0.90 × 0.90, etc.

As a shortcut, calculate

$$\left[\frac{1}{1 - 0.90 \times 0.65}\right] (\$1{,}289{,}000 - 0.65 \times \$1{,}387{,}000) = \$929{,}000 \tag{10}$$

This example is based on 1960 data from Palda's [15] study of Lydia Pinkham. Similar computations for years before 1960 are shown in Table 1. The retention rate of 0.65 is an approximation based on Palda's estimates. The discount rate of 0.90 seems appropriate for a small business such as Lydia Pinkham.

A casual inspection of the Lydia Pinkham data reveals that whatever relationship exists between advertising and profit is highly variable. There appears to be some autocorrelated variability from year to year; high years are followed by low years, perhaps because of overstocking and understocking of trade channels. There also appears to be a strong negative trend over time, for which Palda found the negative of disposable income to be the best proxy. If management wished to determine the optimum budget from these data, it could standardize the data on disposable income, or it could make any other adjustments which it believed would make the observations in various years comparable. Notice that this property of the model is not a weakness but is an example of the great flexibility the model possesses.

In any case, it appears quite clear that Lydia Pinkham was underadvertis-

TABLE 1

APPLICATION OF ADVERTISING MODEL TO LYDIA PINKHAM DATA

(1) Year	(2) Sales in t Caused by Prior Advertising, in Thousands of Dollars		(3) Advertising in t, in Thousands of Dollars		(4) Profit from Advertising, in Thousands of Dollars
	$\left[\sum_{T=1}^{t} R_{T,t} - b\sum_{T=1}^{t-1} R_{T,t-1}\right]\left(\frac{1}{1-b\rho}\right)$	$-$	A_T	$=$	$\sum_{t}^{\infty} V_{T=t,t}$
1960	.387 × 2.4		564		365
1959	.484 × 2.4		644		518
1958	.312 × 2.4		639		110
1957	.492 × 2.4		770		411
1956	.596 × 2.4		802		628
1955	.538 × 2.4		789		502
1954	.452 × 2.4		811		274
1953	.683 × 2.4		964		675
1952	.768 × 2.4		920		923
1951	.527 × 2.4		766		499
1950	.497 × 2.4		974		219
1949	.643 × 2.4		981		562
1948	.662 × 2.4		941		648
1947	.519 × 2.4		836		410

NOTE: 2.4 is $1/(1 - 0.90 \times 0.65)$, with $b = 0.65$, based on Palda's estimates. SOURCE: [15, p. 23].

ing in 1960 and previous years. Also, note that different estimates of the retention rate would alter the entire picture.

Estimation of Parameters in the Simple Case

Estimation of the Retention Rate. In the example above, Palda estimated the retention rate with multiple regressions of time series. Telser [18] has also demonstrated this technique with the prewar major cigarette manufacturers. There are difficulties in such estimating procedures; the literature on the subject is huge. The most likely difficulties in this situation are a paucity of historical data and change in market conditions over time. (For example, the retention rate for cigarettes seems to be lower since cancer warnings began [18].)

The decay rate can also be established by experimentation in test markets. Vidale and Wolfe [19], among others, have verified that (constant percentage) decay (retention) rates may be observed and measured when advertising is removed from a test market. In the case of Lydia Pinkham, which uses newspaper advertising very heavily, test market experiments would be unusually easy.

It is also possible to determine the retention rate for individual consumers from panel data. Care is required in proceeding from panels to the crucial aggregate estimates, however. The logical steps are by no means obvious. Estimation of retention rates is neither easy nor perfectly accurate. However, such lack of accuracy is not a flaw of this model. No matter what method of budget setting the advertiser employs, even rule of thumb, he is implicitly dependent on some estimate of retention rates.

It has been assumed that the retention rate continues the same from period to period. Kuehn [12], working with panel data, and Fourt and Woodlock [6] suggest that the decay rate decreases over time as customer buying from the firm becomes more habitual; but Frank [7] argues that if there is any change, it is slight. If b is discovered to change, it will then become a variable to be applied in the calculation for particular periods, with only slight extra difficulty.

Estimation of Present-Period Sales Effect

The model requires an estimate of total sales in the present period that will follow each proposed amount of advertising. In the example given earlier, each of several years was a trial measure of sales accompanying several levels of advertising. However, if the market is not in perfect equilibrium (and it never is), variations will be caused by extrinsic factors. It may be possible to eliminate them by further analysis of trends. Time series data alone will seldom be completely satisfactory.

Test market experimentation can establish with considerable precision the differential sales effect of injections of various quantities of advertising. Several experimental designs have been created for this purpose [10]. Many firms undoubtedly use these techniques, though Du Pont and Ford are unusual in publicizing their procedures [2, 4]. This model requires only that firms be ready to undertake such experimentation, *or* that they be willing to make quantitative estimates of the sales effect of advertising by deduction from readership studies, time series, or other indirect techniques. Statistical decision theory provides a conceptual framework for such estimates.

Many readers will offer the "realistic" objection that it is not "practical" to establish the sales effect of advertising by test market experimentation or similar techniques, and that estimating sales effects using only educated judgment is sheer folly. An even more realistic rejoinder is offered: The advertising appropriation must be set somehow; and in the process, decision makers must employ the kind of data discussed here, whether they employ it explicitly or implicitly, and whether it is based on research or on arbitrary judgment. Explicit estimation is more practical and much safer in the long run.

General Consideration of Estimation Problems

The difficulties in making the estimates called for by this model can be seen in better perspective if the following points are considered:

1. This model requires few parameters to be estimated, because of the model's self-adjusting characteristic. The estimate of total sales in the present period for various levels of advertising sums up all other variables, such as copy effectiveness and shifts in total market size.
2. None of the parameters needs to be estimated judgmentally, as, for example, the relative effectiveness of several firms' advertising that Kuehn's model requires.
3. Every one of the estimates made in this model is also required for any other type of model, even rule-of-thumb estimates. Market share models may apparently not require estimates of one or more of them; but before a market share model can be used for an optimization calculation, it must be converted to absolute dollar terms, and all these parameters must be estimated.
4. The model permits *any* estimate to be inserted flexibly. If, for example, the advertiser believes that his retention rate will change in the future, he can plug in various future values with only slight extra arithmetic complexity.

MODEL FOR A FIRM WITH CONSIDERABLE MONOPOLY POWER

The "Borrowing" Effect

The previous model optimizes the advertising appropriation separately for each period of time. It thereby assumes that what happens in each period of time is independent of every other period. That model is appropriate for a product that has a relatively small share of a highly competitive market. In such a situation, advertising in period T does not compete with the firm's own advertising in period $T + 1$. Rather, it competes only with the advertising of other firms and products in period T. Sales *not* made in period $T = t$ will be picked up by other firms in the same period, rather than by the firm's ads in period $T + 1$. Thus a model that treats each time period as a separate optimization problem is appropriate for perhaps canned goods, candy bars, bicycles, bed sheets, and wristwatches, to name a few.

But when a firm has a highly differentiated product or service to sell, its ads in one period may "borrow" from its ads in another period. This is most likely to be true of goods such as color television sets, *Life* and other magazines, encyclopedias, and services such as dancing instruction, excess hair removal, and special industrial equipment. The existence of a borrowing effect was established empirically for Teflon cookware as a class, in Du Pont's promotional test market experiments [2]. For cases in which a firm has considerable monopoly power, a solution is needed that establishes the optimal sizes of each A_T, $A_{T+1}, \cdots A_m$, taking into account their mutual dependence.

There is also a theoretical possibility that the earlier period's advertising enhances the selling power of the later period's advertising, rather than borrowing from it. If so, it would suggest that the first-period advertising is more valuable than it appears at first and therefore should be larger than otherwise calculated. (Remember that lagged sales are attributed to the advertising that caused them. For a period's advertising to be enhanced by subsequent advertising, the sum total of all the sales it causes, including lagged sales, must be greater than would have been the case in the absence of prior advertising.)

Attention will be given to the borrowing effect, and any possible enhancement effect will be disregarded, because the existing empirical evidence suggests that the sum of the effects is negative (borrowing) rather than positive (enhancement). There is no empirical evidence of an enhancement effect.

Solution to the Borrowing Problem for Established Products

1. It is noted that no economies of scale in advertising exist.[3] If a firm reaches the point in its advertising operations at which it intends to spend roughly the same amount over an extended period of time, it will achieve greatest efficiency by distributing its expenditures evenly over the period. In other words, it is more efficient to spend X dollars in each of years 1, 2, 3, and 4, than to spend $2X$ dollars in years 1 and 3, and nothing in years 2 and 4. Concentration of advertising in the latter fashion is the less efficient strategy, given that there are no economies of scale.

2. If the market for a product has reached a relatively stable size, it can be demonstrated that under most assumptions, advertising expenditure will oscillate around an equilibrium expenditure, and that the oscillations will grow progressively less and approach equilibrium as a limit. We can describe this process in a loose but commonsense way:

a) If a firm has done no previous advertising, its first-period advertising has a virgin field. No prospects have been borrowed by previous advertising. So the optimum first expenditure will be heavy.
b) The heavy advertising in the first period will borrow many customers from the second period, so optimum second-period advertising will be light.
c) Third-period advertising will have a relatively unspoiled field, because second-period expenditures were small. So third-period advertising will be heavier, but not as heavy as in the first period.
d) Fourth-period expenditures will be lighter, because third-period expenditures were heavy and borrowed much from the fourth period. But fourth-period expenditures will be heavier than second-period expenditures, because less was spent in the third period than in the first period.

This series obviously approaches an equilibrium value after some time. Other simple assumptions about how one period borrows from another also suggest that the succeeding period would approach a single expenditure level. Furthermore, diminishing returns suggest that once the equilibrium value has been reached, expenditures should be spread evenly over time.

3. The less one period borrows from another, the more quickly the opti-

[3] For an empirical argument of this proposition, see [16].

mum value approaches equilibrium. In several examples worked out, the series is very close to equilibrium in the third period, or even in the second period.

The foregoing discussion supports an important conclusion: If a firm is already spending substantial sums for advertising a product—enough to constitute a substantial proportion of its equilibrium expenditure—and if the firm's market is relatively stable, the firm can then disregard the fact that one period's advertising may borrow from the next period. The firm can set its advertising appropriation at the long-run equilibrium value, allocate the same amount in each period, and be sure that it is not far from an optimum (so long as copy effectiveness, competition, etc., do not change).

In other words, a firm advertising an established product in a stable market can use the same model described above, even if the firm has considerable monopoly power. New products do not meet the conditions of this section. Early-period expenditures will be somewhat higher than the equilibrium level. But a satisfactory formal model for this situation has not been developed.

The Borrowing Effect

In most monopoly power cases the model that optimizes period by period will be satisfactory. Furthermore, a firm's natural desire to earn profits while it can, and to pay less attention to the uncertain future, also argues for maximizing profits period by period. This attitude is well justified by the changes up or down in the total size of the market, more or less close competition, and a dozen variables that probably would swamp the adjustments a multiperiod model would recommend. This is an added reason why the soundest plan would be to push to the margin in each period, independent of other periods.

MODEL FOR FIRM WITH A SUBSTANTIAL SHARE OF THE MARKET

Consider the case in which our firm is large enough to have an important effect upon the sales and market shares of other competitors, some of whom are, in turn, large enough to affect our firm. Assume sufficient homogeneity of product within the industry so that cross-elasticities of advertising among brands are significantly high. Also assume that consumer shifts *among* brands are large in comparison to the number of new consumers attracted to the industry by advertising. This is the classic case of mature industries treated in advertising optimization literature—frozen orange juice, cigarettes, coffee—markets in which competition is keen for business, rather than dependence upon expansion of the total market for growth.

In stable markets, firms measure their success by market share, and this is why most advertising budget models use market share as the dependent variable. However, in any optimization model, market share must eventually be converted into dollar sales. In this model, advertising is related directly to dollar sales (actually net revenue), rather than proceeding through the market share concept.

The Oligopoly Problem

No one has yet developed a model of less-than-perfect competition that produces satisfactory predictions. Furthermore, it seems likely that there will always be indeterminacies in the oligopoly solution because (1) unlike the competitive situation, an oligopolistic firm has some market power to affect price, and a stake in maintaining price at a high and stable level; and (2) the firm's interest is most often not identical with the interest of the industry as a whole. Management behavior depends upon personal character, state of knowledge, and ways of perceiving competitors' behavior. Therefore the solution to the advertising problem, as well as to the price problem, must include an explicit prediction of competitors' immediate response behavior, a prediction not soluble analytically. To elucidate, consider two well-known advertising optimization models.

1. Kuehn's model [11] implies that a firm assumes that other firms will also optimize in a similar manner. There are two important, though unstated, parts of Kuehn's assumption:

a) The assumption that competitors will optimize profits on some given model is really a prediction, despite its formal elegance. Baumol's recent work suggests that this prediction is most often false [1].

b) Kuehn implicitly assumes that firms will not tacitly reduce their advertising expenditures on some prorated basis in order to raise overall industry profits in which they can all share. In other words, Kuehn's model assumes hard advertising competition. We have neither a priori nor empirical reasons to believe that this is the case in any industries.

2. Models developed by Friedman [8] and Mills [13] assume that competitors will operate on game theoretic principles. These game theory models also assume that competitors will optimize, as does Kuehn's model, and the same objection applies.

There are additional objections to game theory models:

a) Game theory models presuppose an already fixed appropriation. Our very problem is to accomplish the optimum fixing of the appropriation.

b) Game theory gives solutions different from ordinary maximization procedures only in situations where there is an "all-or-nothing" settlement, i.e., where the competitor who outadvertises the other gets *all* the sales. For all consumer products, however, the response functions are continuous. Sales may be divided among competitors in any proportion. In some industrial situations (the sale of airplanes or the negotiation of large contracts), all-or-nothing may be the case. But that type of negotiation is more likely to depend on personal selling than on advertising. (Advertising in presidential elections has a distinct all-or-nothing character: A candidate either wins or loses an entire state, no matter how large or small the voting margin. A game theoretic model may be appropriate for that situation.)

c) Most competitors have relatively stable advertising appropriations, and therefore their actions are relatively predictable for some periods of time. Game theory disregards this fact, thereby throwing away valuable information. Game theory is only the best solution where the competitor's actions are not predictable at all. Most industries contain more than two competitors. The larger the number of competitors, the more likely the variation in their responses to "wash out" in a random fashion.

The advertising planner must accept the disagreeable fact that there is no general, rational solution to the appropriation problem in the oligopoly situation. The solution must depend on the nature of the situation and on the planner's predictions of how the competition will react.

A few broad classes of oligopoly problems can be distinguished and indications of how our model can help given. The most important factors that determine the appropriate solution are:

a) The size of our firm's present appropriation compared with competitors' appropriations.
b) Whether a first approximation, noncompetitive solution indicates that our firm or the competition is overspending or underspending.
c) The toughness of competitive fiber of the firms, or disposition to peaceful cartel behavior.
d) The capital resources of the rivals.
e) The advertising elasticity of demand for the product, barriers to entering the industry, and disposition on the part of the firms to restrict competition.

Differences in production cost and in the efficiency of advertising copy can also be important. Both factors are considered equal for the various firms, though any other assumptions will work just as well.

Example: Situation A. In this situation, both competitors are spending sums of the same magnitude. Our firm's measurements and the model indicate that if the competition continues spending at an unchanged rate, our advertising could be increased profitably. If our advertising is increased, our competitor may either increase or decrease his advertising. Sufficient data are not available to indicate whether the competitor is overspending or underspending at present, given our present budget.

These are possible ramifications:

1. If the competitor is currently overspending (and this is apparently not unusual), or if he is at an optimizing point, our increased budget will decrease his advertising profitability. If he is sensible, he will decrease his budget, in which case we shall again be able to increase our budget and our profit in future periods.

2. If he is overspending or underspending, and if he is slow about altering his appropriation because it is pegged as a constant percentage of sales, or for other reasons, our firm increases its profits.

3. If the competitor is currently overspending or is at his optimizing point, and if our increased expenditures trouble him, he may increase his expenditure and overspend even more. The competitor's overspending will hurt our firm, but it is known from sensitivity analyses by Weinberg [20] and Mills [13] that the overspending will hurt the competition even more. Sooner or later, probably sooner, he will be forced to reduce his expenditures. We may also have to reduce expenditures somewhat, and an equilibrium will then be found.

4. If the competitor is presently underspending, our increase may stimulate him to increase his expenditures considerably, and we may have to retreat somewhat. It is true, of course, that both competitors may operate most profitably if neither one of them increases spending. This cartel solution could be effective if the demand is advertising-inelastic. But this solution violates the antitrust laws.

Example: Situation B. In this situation, considerably less is spent than by the competition. Our copy and cost position are as good as his. Measurements of the effect of our advertising and the model's calculations indicate that we are spending less than we should, given the present competitive situation.

1. If the competitor is presently spending an amount that would be optimum if we continued our old appropriation, and if we increase our spending, he is likely to recognize that he is overspending and consequently reduce his expenditures. This would be wise on his part because, since we are spending much less for advertising, our advertising results are likely to be much better. Hence, overspending will not be proportionally as costly for the smaller firm as for the large firm. In this case, our spending increase will directly and immediately increase our profits.

There seems to be plenty of evidence that dominant firms often recognize that they cannot maintain their huge share of the market against strong competition. Perhaps they sometimes retreat because of antitrust threats. But it is more likely that they recognize the greater selling efficiencies often present for smaller shares of the market.

2. If the dominant competitor is very intent on not retrenching his advertising position, his losses will be much greater in the short run than will the smaller competitor's (as demonstrated by the Weinberg and Mills sensitivity analyses). However, if the dominant competitor has much greater capital resources, he may be able to inflict great enough losses on the competing firm to make it either drop out or operate at a lower level. The dominant competitor may be able to recoup his losses in the long run if he is able to maintain a monopolistic position.

Discussion of Oligopoly Solution

Our model seems to provide satisfactory guidance under most conditions of oligopolistic competitive behavior. Using the model confers the special advantage on a competitor of being able to gauge accurately whether he is currently overspending or underspending. He is then better equipped to venture into oligopolistic competition.

However, there are two cases in which the model breaks down:

1. The solution given by the model can be inferior to collusive agreements to restrict advertising. The competitors as a group would be best off without any expenditures for advertising at all if the size of the market is stable. Furthermore, no model that assumes competition can make a better prediction for this case.

2. If the competitor continues to overadvertise, our optimum solution will be wrong. Such a competitor hurts his firm far more than he hurts our firm, and sooner or later must either learn this error or possibly go bankrupt. Again, no other model will handle this problem satisfactorily.

In general, competitor reaction in advertising probably is not an overwhelming problem even in oligopoly situations. From experience with advertising pharmaceutical drugs, books, and magazine space, most advertisers advertise without too much worry about competition. Even in the classic advertising oligopoly, cigarettes, Telser's findings indicate little oligopolistic advertising interdependence from period to period. For the period and firms investigated, Telser found a negative correlation between advertising outlays [18]. Brems emphasizes the time lag between conception and execution of advertising plans, as well as human inertia and slowness to learn about the selling behavior of competitors as causes of lack of immediate response to changes in competitors' advertising expenditures [3]. The common practice of setting advertising appropriations at a fixed percentage of sales also emphasizes this lack of response to rival spending. Certainly the difficulties of learning exactly what the competition is doing are much greater, and the information less precise, in advertising compared to price behavior. The interval before response makes it possible for a firm to enjoy a profit advantage over the equilibrium situation for a significant length of time. The very fact that advertising budgets of competitors do not seem to gravitate to the same level, unlike their prices, corroborates that advertising expenditure competition is slow and muted.

SUMMARY

The model set forth here is an effort to achieve simplicity and practicality. It requires of a firm only that (1) it must decide on its cost of capital, appropriate to the advertising situation; (2) it must establish the rate(s) at which its sales decay (are retained) over time in the absence of advertising; and (3) it must estimate the functional relationship in any one period between advertising and sales.

This model should work well for established advertisers with considerable independence of movement. It requires adjustment for the first few periods for new products, an adjustment for which no formal model exists. The model also should help the oligopolist, whether or not he wishes to make explicit predictions about rival behavior.

This model does not require any judgmental estimate of the relative effectiveness of the firm's advertising and rivals' advertising, as does Kuehn's model. Neither does this model assume that the firm's advertising effectiveness will be constant from year to year, as does Weinberg's model. Nor does it require any long-term forecasting about the size of the industry market or about competitor behavior.

The major strength of this model is that it is in constant adjustment from period to period; it is automatically sensitive to changing advertising effectiveness (a very important variable in consumer goods industries), changing market sizes, and changing behavior by rivals. The effects of all these variables show up together in the quantity $R_{T=t,t}$ for the current period.

The model works directly with absolute sales data rather than with share-of-market data. Share-of-market models must eventually convert to absolute advertising and sales data, and they raise far more problems than they solve. This model also requires no distinction between repeat purchase probabilities and transfer purchase probabilities, and takes full advantage of a firm's ability to vary its advertising budget to meet changing situations with appropriate optimizing responses.

We have seen that the model has limitations in the oligopoly situation because it cannot forecast the behavior of competitors, and hence it cannot suggest the appropriate response to that forecasted behavior. The model does allow, however, for the inclusion of management's prediction of rival responses. The model's primary mode of dealing with the competitive situation is to remain sensitive to rival behavior and to constantly modify. Since no model can forecast competitive response behavior, the lack of forecast is not a disadvantage of the model.

The model will certainly not meet the exact needs of all firms, or even of any firm, but the advertising planner should be tolerant of small discrepancies and errors in an optimization model. These errors are small when compared to the manner in which most firms really *do* set appropriations, as a recent survey of advertising practices emphasizes [21].

REFERENCES

1. BAUMOL, WILLIAM J. *Business Behavior, Value and Growth.* (New York: Macmillan Co., 1959.)

2. BECKNELL, JAMES C., JR., and MCISAAC, ROBERT W. "Test Marketing Cookware Coated with 'Teflon,'" *Journal of Advertising Research*, September, 1963, pp. 2–8.

3. BREMS, HANS. *Product Equilibrium under Monopolistic Competition*, chaps. xii, xv, and xvi. Cambridge: Harvard University Press, 1951.

4. BROWN, GEORGE H. "Measuring the Sales Effectiveness of Alternate Media," in ADVERTISING RESEARCH FOUNDATION, *Proceedings, 7th Annual Conference* (1961).

5. DEAN, JOEL. *Managerial Economics.* Englewood Cliffs, N.J.: Prentice-Hall, Inc., 1951.
6. FOURT, LOUIS A., and WOODLOCK, JOSEPH W. "Early Prediction of Market Success for New Grocery Products," *Journal of Marketing*, October, 1960, pp. 31–38.
7. FRANK, RONALD E. "Brand Choice as a Probability Process," in RONALD E. FRANK *et al.*, *Quantitative Techniques in Marketing Analysis* (Homewood, Ill.: Richard D. Irwin, Inc., 1963).
8. FRIEDMAN, LAURENCE. "Game-Theory Models in the Allocation of Advertising Expenditures," in FRANK BASS *et al.*, *Mathematical Models and Methods in Marketing* (Homewood, Ill.: Richard D. Irwin, Inc., 1961).
9. JASTRAM, ROY N. "A Treatment of Distributed Lags in the Theory of Advertising Expenditure," *Journal of Marketing*, July, 1955, pp. 36–46.
10. JESSEN, R. J. "A Switch-Over Experimental Design to Measure Advertising Effect," in RONALD E. FRANK *et al.*, *Quantitative Techniques in Marketing Analysis* (Homewood, Ill.: Richard D. Irwin, Inc., 1963).
11. KUEHN, ALFRED A. "A Model for Budgeting Advertising," in FRANK BASS *et al.*, *Mathematical Models and Methods in Marketing* (Homewood, Ill.: Richard D. Irwin, Inc., 1961).
12. KUEHN, ALFRED A. "Consumer Brand Choice—A Learning Process?" in RONALD E. FRANK *et al.*, *Quantitative Techniques in Marketing Analysis* (Homewood, Ill.: Richard D. Irwin, Inc., 1963).
13. MILLS, HARLAND D. "A Study in Promotional Competition," in FRANK BASS *et al.*, *Mathematical Models and Methods in Marketing* (Homewood, Ill.: Richard D. Irwin, Inc., 1961).
14. NERLOVE, MARC, and ARROW, KENNETH J. "Optimal Advertising under Dynamic Conditions," *Economics*, May, 1962, pp. 129–42.
15. PALDA, KRISTIAN S. *The Measurement of Cumulative Advertising Effects.* Englewood Cliffs, N.J.: Prentice-Hall, Inc., 1964.
16. SIMON, JULIAN L. "Are There Economies of Scale in Advertising?" *Journal of Advertising Research*, June, 1965.
17. SIMON, JULIAN L. *How to Start and Operate a Mail-Order Business* (New York: McGraw-Hill Book Co., Inc., 1965).
18. TELSER, LESTER G. "Advertising and Cigarettes," *Journal of Political Economy*, October, 1962.
19. VIDALE, M. L., and WOLFE, H. B. "An Operations Research Study of Sales Response to Advertising," in FRANK BASS *et al.*, *Mathematical Models and Methods in Advertising* (Homewood, Ill.: Richard D. Irwin, Inc., 1961).
20. WEINBERG, ROBERT S. *An Analytical Approach to Advertising Expenditure Strategy.* New York: Association of National Advertisers, 1960.
21. WOLFE, H. B.; BROWN, J. K.; and THOMPSON, G. C. *Measuring Advertising Results.* New York: National Industrial Conference Board, 1962.

18

Statistical data are presented which both support and refute the existence of a time lag in advertising. Following the presentation of this statistical evidence, the author expresses in a mathematical model the relationship between a given period's advertising and sales for the same period to new and former customers, given certain specified assumptions. Once data are introduced into the model, and with certain assumed parameters, the data output confirms the existence of a carry-over effect. Finally, a model for the hypothesis of "cumulated impression" is presented.

*THE CARRY-OVER EFFECT OF ADVERTISING**

Donald S. Tull

THE BELIEF that there is a carry-over (lagged) effect of advertising on sales has had general currency among advertisers for many years. This belief is supported by such statements as ". . . generally speaking, the effect of a given advertising expenditure on sales revenue is distributed over time";[1] and "reaction to advertising is delayed and is sometimes spread over a long period."[2]

Belief in the lagged effect is further evidenced by the fact that many companies have continued to advertise for prolonged periods when incoming orders could not be filled. For instance, during both World War II and the Korean War, many manufacturers who had completely converted to military products continued to advertise their consumer or industrial products. The steel producers did this during World War II and the immediate postwar years, during which time they were rationing steel to customers. The primary justification for continuing to advertise during such periods would appear to be the belief that advertising has a carry-over effect.

Additional evidence could be cited that many advertisers *believe* that there is a carry-over effect, and that some advertisers *act* as if a carry-over exists. The major concern here, however, is to examine relevant evidence concerning whether a carry-over effect *actually* exists.

---

* Reprinted from *Journal of Marketing*, August, 1965, pp. 46–53. The *Journal* is the national quarterly publication of the American Marketing Association.

[1] Roy N. Jastram, "A Treatment of Distributed Lags in the Theory of Advertising Expenditure," *Journal of Marketing*, July, 1955, pp. 36–46.

[2] Joel Dean, "Cyclical Policy on the Advertising Appropriation," *Journal of Marketing*, January, 1951, pp. 265–73.

The first question in such an examination is, "*What are the results of empirical studies on the carry-over effect of advertising?*"

EMPIRICAL STUDIES OF THE CARRY-OVER EFFECT

The available empirical evidence which bears on this problem falls into two general categories, between which the method of investigation is the distinguishing feature. The first category consists of evidence developed through use of the *historical method;* the second is comprised of evidence generated through use of the *statistical method.*

EVIDENCE FROM HISTORICAL STUDIES

The "case history" is a useful and valid approach to the examination of business problems. However, unwarranted conclusions often are reached in case studies for reasons of inadequate investigation, lack of convincing evidence, or both.[3]

The advertising trade press has published many case histories over the years which, directly or indirectly, bear on the question of carry-over effect. Most of these case histories follow a similar pattern: Company *A* advertised and experienced high sales; advertising was reduced; at a later date, sales declined substantially. The conclusion is then reached that the reduction in advertising was the *cause* of the subsequent sales decline.

Most marketing men are inclined to regard these individual case histories as providing no real evidence that the advertising reduction was the primary cause for the subsequent decline in sales. The logical fallacy of *post hoc, ergo propter hoc* is invoked, and the case is dismissed. A reasonably careful investigation of the circumstances of one such case history provides evidence that the reduction in advertising was not the cause of the later sales decline.[4]

Yet such case histories cannot be entirely waved aside and disregarded. From a Bayesian standpoint, they collectively constitute evidence that must be considered in forming a prior judgment concerning the existence of the carry-over effect. This argument resolves to the observation that the case for the existence of a carry-over effect is stronger, given such case histories, than it would be without them.

Packer's Tar Soap

The case of Packer's Tar Soap is one which often has been cited as an example of a reduction in advertising resulting in a later decline in sales.

In the early 1920's, Packer's Tar Soap was one of the leading shampoos

---

[3] Pauline V. Young, *Scientific Social Surveys and Research*, 3d ed., (Englewood Cliffs, N.J.: Prentice-Hall, Inc., 1956), chap. vi.

[4] Donald S. Tull, "A Re-examination of the Causes of the Decline in Sales of Sapolio," *Journal of Business,* April, 1955, pp. 128–37.

TABLE 1

DOMESTIC SALES OF PACKER PRODUCTS, 1919–29
(Sales in Gross)

	Tar Soap		Tar Shampoo		Olive Oil Shampoo	
	Regular Size	*10¢ Size*	*Regular Size*	*10¢ Size*	*Regular Size*	*10¢ Size*
1919	15,684	.....	1,335	.....	.....	.....
1920	17,562	.....	1,872	.....	.....	.....
1921	17,761	.....	2,048	.....	.....	.....
1922	18,730	.....	2,628	.....	.....	.....
1923	20,356	.....	3,188	.....	.....	.....
1924	21,576	.....	3,658	.....	.....	.....
1925	21,550	.....	4,020	.....	.....	.....
1926	19,408	.....	3,383	.....	622	.....
1927	18,481	.....	3,584	.....	1,484	.....
1928	16,999	1,791	4,123	2,265	1,423	2,012
1929	16,974	1,582	5,285	3,928	2,711	3,659

on the market. In the years following World War I, Packer's enjoyed particularly large increases in sales of its product, which had already sold well for over 60 years. Sales more than doubled between 1917 and 1925.

Beginning in 1926, sales of the tar soap started a steady and persistent decline. See Table 1. Several factors could have contributed to these sales

TABLE 2

ADVERTISING EXPENDITURES FOR PACKER PRODUCTS, 1919–29

	Packer's Tar Soap	*Packer's Liquid Shampoos*	*Total*
1919	$ 91,138	....	$ 91,138
1920	107,395	....	107,395
1921	142,937	....	142,937
1922	155,490	....	155,490
1923	183,520	....	183,520
1924	97,690	$ 65,290	162,980
1925	54,450	114,800	169,250
1926	45,400	118,600	164,000
1927	51,500	115,250	166,750
1928	27,100	113,975	141,075
1929	27,736	183,067	210,803

losses. One factor was a substantial reduction in advertising made in 1924, followed by further reductions in succeeding years. See Table 2.

An investigation of the circumstances faced by the company from 1919 through 1929 brings out several possible explanations for the decline in sales of Packer's Tar Soap:

1. Shift in preference from bar shampoos to liquid shampoos
2. Partial boycott by the service wholesalers handling the bar soap

3. Shift in preference from tar shampoos to other kinds of shampoos
4. Decrease in the relative price of competing shampoos
5. Increase in the absolute amount of sales promotion of competing shampoos
6. Introduction of Packer's Olive Oil Shampoo
7. Reduction in advertising of the tar soap

Each of these seven potential reasons for the decline in sales of Packer's Tar Soap has been examined in detail.[5] The investigation indicated that none of the first six possible explanations were major causal factors.

The relationship of advertising, the seventh factor, and sales of the tar soap is shown in Figure 1.

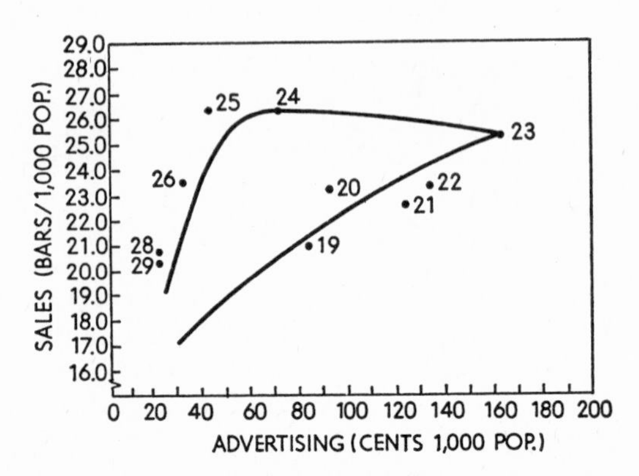

FIGURE 1. Advertising and sales of Packer's Tar Soap, 1919–29.

The evidence with respect to the effect of reduction in advertising is necessarily circumstantial. The most convincing evidence of a causal relationship is provided by comparing sales reductions by geographic area with advertising reduction by geographic area; the two patterns matched closely. On the basis of this and other less direct evidence, the tentative conclusion was drawn that the reductions in advertising initiated in 1924 were causally related to the sales decline starting in 1926.

EVIDENCE FROM STATISTICAL STUDIES

At least six empirical studies have been published which employ a statistical approach to the problem of determining whether prior-period advertising affects later-period sales.

A study concerning the effect of advertising on sales of an ethical drug has been reported by Hollander.[6] The technique of graphic multivariate correlation was used. While the conclusion was drawn that there was a demonstrable carry-over effect, the difficulties encountered in the study raised

[5] Donald S. Tull, "An Examination of the Hypothesis That Advertising Has a Lagged Effect on Sales" (unpublished doctoral dissertation, University of Chicago, 1956).

[6] Sidney Hollander, Jr., "A Rationale for Advertising Expenditures," *Harvard Business Review*, July, 1949, pp. 78–87.

questions about the reliability of the findings. The major problems were in developing suitable indexes for the independent variables and in insuring that these variables were in fact independent. Neither problem was resolved in a fully satisfactory manner.

Nerlove and Waugh carried out a statistical study of the advertising of oranges. Their conclusion was that a lagged effect exists.[7] An interesting finding was that no measurable decay factor could be found for the effect of prior-year advertising on present-year sales for prior periods ranging back as far as 10 years.

Vidale and Wolfe[8] reported that they statistically verified a "sales decay constant" that occurred after advertising was reduced or stopped, but no empirical data are given.

The study by Palda on the Lydia E. Pinkham Company is the most comprehensive of any statistical investigation to date on the carry-over effect.[9] Using the technique of multivariate regression, he tested a large number of models for both goodness of fit and accuracy of prediction. The general model which met both criteria best was one employing Koyck's model of distributed lags. Palda concludes that "using the distributed lag approach, first the existence and then relative importance of the operation of lagged advertising effects is all but confirmed in the case of a successful advertiser."[10]

The most convincing type of evidence is that provided by carefully designed experiments. Unfortunately, the results of two published studies, each employing a crossover experimental design, are conflicting.

A test marketing-advertising experiment for "Teflon" coated cookware was initiated in the fall of 1962 by Du Pont. The conclusion reached was that "there is strong evidence of an advertising 'carry-over effect' from season to season in terms of building market share."[11]

A similar design was employed by the U.S. Department of Agriculture in studying the effect of advertising on the sales of apples. The results were that carry-over effects . . . did not approach statistical significance."[12]

CONCLUSIONS FROM EMPIRICAL EVIDENCE

Only limited empirical evidence about the existence of a carry-over effect in advertising is available. The evidence examined in this paper, while tend-

[7] Marc Nerlove and Frederick V. Waugh, "Advertising without Supply Control: Some Implications of a Study of the Advertising of Oranges," *Journal of Farm Economics*, November, 1961, pp. 813–37.

[8] M. L. Vidale and H. B. Wolfe, "An Operations Research Study of Sales Response to Advertising," *Operations Research*, June, 1957, pp. 370–81.

[9] Kristian S. Palda, *The Measurement of Cumulative Advertising Effect* (Englewood Cliffs, N.J.: Prentice-Hall, Inc., 1964).

[10] *Ibid.*, p. 95.

[11] James C. Becknell, Jr., and Robert W. McIsaac, "Test Marketing Cookware Coated with 'Teflon,' " *Journal of Advertising Research*, September, 1963, pp. 2–8.

[12] Peter L. Henderson, James F. Hind, and Sidney E. Brown, "Sales Effects of Two Campaign Themes," *Journal of Advertising Research*, December, 1961, pp. 2–11.

ing to support the belief that such an effect exists, is persuasive but not conclusive.

In examining the carry-over effect further, it is useful to turn to theoretical models of the relationship of advertising and sales over time.

MATHEMATICAL MODELS OF THE CARRY-OVER EFFECT

Several models relating sales and advertising over time have been described in the marketing literature.[13] In these models the existence of a carry-over effect has been assumed. Exploring the implications of this assumption on advertising budgeting has been the real purpose.

Two simplified mathematical models which examine bases for the existence of the carry-over effect are constructed and presented next. These are exploratory models and, as such, are not intended to be complete, operational representations of the complex realities surrounding an advertising decision.

Simplifying assumptions are made about the relationship of given-period advertising to sales in the same period, the purchase cycle, multiple purchases, customer survival rates, and impression cumulation. Furthermore, the important variables of competitive advertising reaction and share elasticity are not treated.

Brand Loyalty

An early study by Brown and a later study by Kuehn of purchases by members of a consumer panel throw considerable light on the nature of brand loyalty.[14] The findings indicate that degree of brand loyalty varies widely among products and that the purchasers behave in varied ways, from the extreme of those who buy a single brand of the product exclusively to the other extreme of those who seem to choose brands at random. Other groups appear to have a primary preference for one or more brands and a secondary preference for others, or a divided preference for two or more brands, or will use one brand for a period of time and then switch to another.

If advertising is instrumental in introducing the brand to buyers who later develop some degree of loyalty to it, a carry-over effect is initiated. Each repeat purchase of the brand by these buyers may be considered to be the result of earlier advertising. Sales of the brand in the period $n + j$ will be

---

[13] James M. Parrish and John M. Ryan, "A Note on the Determination of Advertising Budgets," *Journal of Marketing*, January, 1953, pp. 277–80; Alfred A. Kuehn, "A Model for Budgeting Advertising," in Frank Bass *et al.*, *Mathematical Models and Methods in Marketing* (Homewood, Ill.: Richard D. Irwin, Inc., 1961); Alfred A. Kuehn, "How Advertising Performance Depends on Other Factors," *Journal of Advertising Research*, March, 1962, pp. 2–10; Jastram, *op. cit.*

[14] George H. Brown, "75% of Chicago Families Buy Shampoo: Brand Loyalty Difficult to Assess," *Advertising Age*, August 11, 1952, pp. 55–58; similar articles by same author in same publication from June 9, 1952, through January 26, 1953; Alfred A. Kuehn, "Consumer Brand Choice as a Learning Process," *Journal of Advertising Research*, December, 1962, pp. 10–17.

higher as a result of advertising in period n than they would have been in the absence of such advertising.

Sales to New Buyers

For purposes of analysis, it is convenient to break the sales of the brand during any one period into two categories: those to new buyers and those to repeat buyers. Total sales during any given period may therefore be defined as

$$Y_n = Y_{n_i} + Y_{n_r} \tag{1.1}$$

where

$$Y_{n_i} = \text{New sales}$$

and

$$Y_{n_r} = \text{Repeat sales}$$

In developing an expression for the relationship between given-period advertising and sales for the same period to new buyers, four assumptions are made:

1. The relationship between the amount of advertising and the level of sales during that same period to new buyers is linear.
2. Each new buyer makes one purchase only during the period.
3. Prior-period advertising does not influence the level of sales to new buyers during the given period.
4. The level of all other variables affecting sales to new buyers during the given period remains constant.

The function defining the level of new sales in a given period may now be written as

$$Y_{n_i} = a + bA_n \tag{1.2}$$

where

Y_{n_i} = Sales to new buyers in period n
a = Amount of new sales which would be made in the absence of advertising
b = Change in sales to new buyers per given increment of advertising
A_n = Amount of advertising in period n

Sales to Repeat Buyers

The new buyers for any period, of course, become the potential repeat buyers of later periods. Assuming that none of the new buyers drops out of the market, the total number of possible repeat buyers in the present period (N) is equal to the summation of all prior-period new buyers.

By again assuming that each purchaser buys only one unit of the product each period, the expression for the total number of possible repeat buyers, and therefore repeat sales, in the present period (N) may be written as

$$\sum_{n=1}^{n=N-1} Y_{n_i} \tag{1.3}$$

Clearly, however, not all prior-period buyers will "survive" as potential repeat buyers. A certain "mortality" will arise from such causes as changes in tastes, income, and age, and deaths. These mortalities will no longer be in the market as buyers of any brand of the product class.

Surviving Buyers

It can be assumed that a fixed percentage, f, of all prior-period new buyers survive each period. In period 2, for example, f percent of the initial purchasers in period 1 will still be in the market for some brand of the product class. In period 3, f percent times f percent of period 1, plus f percent of period 2 new buyers, will remain in the market as potential repeat buyers. As the reader may readily verify by expanding this series for a few periods, the expression for the surviving number of potential repeat buyers in period N is

$$\sum_{n=1}^{n=N-1} f^{N-n} Y_{n_i} \tag{1.4}$$

While this is an expression for the number of potential repeat purchasers in the period N, it gives no indication of the number who will actually make repeat purchases of a given brand during that period.

It seems reasonable to suppose, and there is evidence to suggest, that advertising affects the percentage of potential repeat buyers making repeat purchases.[15] It might well increase the number of buyers who will remain exclusively loyal to a particular brand. In addition, it seems likely that it might affect both the percentage and the division of purchases among those buyers having divided preferences or essentially no preference at all.

Potential and Actual Repeaters

Again, the simplifying assumption of linearity is used. That is, it is assumed that the relationship between the percentage of surviving potential repeat purchasers actually making purchases and the level of advertising is linear over the relevant range of advertising expenditures. The percentage of potential repeat buyers making purchases in any given period may therefore be written as

$$c + dA_n \tag{1.5}$$

---

[15] National Broadcasting Company, *Why Sales Come in Curves* (New York, 1952).

where

c = Percentage of potential repeaters buying in the absence of advertising
d = Change in percentage of repeat purchasers per given increment of advertising
A_n = The amount of advertising in period n

It should be noted that a and b in expression 1.2 refer to *numbers* of buyers, whereas c and d in expression 1.5 refer to a percentage of buyers.

An assumption for these models has been that each buyer buys only one unit of the product each period. By multiplying the number of potential repeat purchasers (expression 1.4) by the percentage of these actually making purchases (expression 1.5), one can find the number of repeat purchasers (Y_{n_r}):

$$Y_{n_r} = (c + dA_n) \sum_{n=1}^{n=N-1} f^{N-n} Y_{n_i} \tag{1.6}$$

where

Y_{n_r} = Repeat sales to repeat purchasers in period n

Total Sales

Expressions for both terms on the right side of equation 1.1 have now been derived. A model giving total sales (the sum of new sales plus repeat sales) is therefore as follows:

$$Y_n = Y_{n_i} + Y_{n_r}$$

$$Y_n = a + bA_n + (c + dA_n) \sum_{n=1}^{n=N-1} f^{N-n} Y_{n_i} \tag{1.7}$$

where

Y_n = Total sales in period n

The results of the operation of the model with a set of assumed values for advertising expenditures and the constants involved are shown in tabular form in Table 3 and graphically in Figure 2.

As shown in Table 3, advertising was assumed to increase by 100 units each period for the first six periods and to decrease by 100 units each period thereafter until it reached zero in the twelfth period. The assumed values for the constants are as follows:

a = Fifty new buyers each period in the absence of advertising
b = Twenty new buyers each period for each 100 units of advertising expended in that period
c = Twenty percent of all potential repeat purchasers to repurchase each period in the absence of advertising
d = The above percentage to increase by 2 percent for each 100 units of advertising expended in the period
f = Ninety-five percent of previous new buyers to survive each period

TABLE 3

OPERATION OF "REPEAT PURCHASE" MODEL*

$$Y_n = a + bA_n + (c + dA_n) \sum_{n=1}^{n=N-1} f^{N-n} Y_{n_i}$$

Period	Units of Advertising A_n	New Sales Y_{n_i} $a + bA_n$	Repeat Sales: Proportion Buying $c + dA_n$	Repeat Sales: Potential Repeat Purchasers $\sum_{n=1}^{n=N-1} f^{N-n} Y_{n_i}$	Repeat Sales Y_{n_r} [(3) × (4)]	Totals Sales Y_N [(2) + (5)]
1	100	70	0.22	...	...	70
2	200	90	0.24	67	16	106
3	300	110	0.26	150	39	149
4	400	130	0.28	247	69	199
5	500	150	0.30	358	107	257
6	600	170	0.32	483	154	324
7	500	150	0.30	620	186	336
8	400	130	0.28	730	204	334
9	300	110	0.26	817	212	322
10	200	90	0.24	881	211	301
11	100	70	0.22	922	203	273
12	..	50	0.20	942	188	233
13	..	50	0.20	942	188	233

* Where $a = 50$, $b = 20$, $c = 0.20$, $d = 0.02$, and $f = 0.95$.

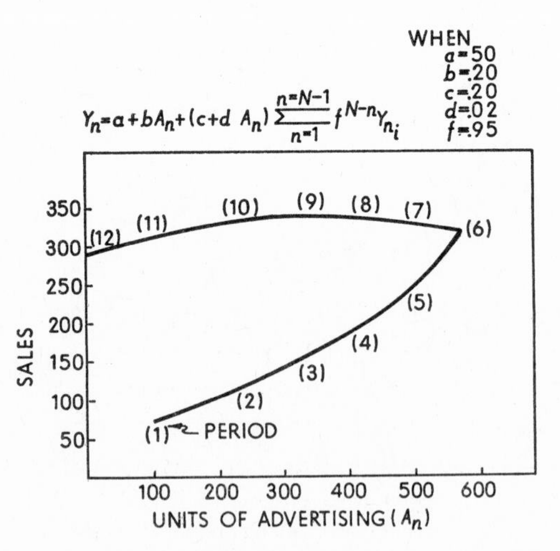

FIGURE 2. Plot of "repeat purchase" model results.

As shown in Figure 2, the model demonstrates the possibility of a lag between the reduction of advertising and the resulting decline in sales. The model predicts an increase in sales for one period after the reduction in advertising. This overall increase in sales resulted from the fact that repeat sales increased by an amount greater than that by which new sales fell.

CUMULATED IMPRESSION MODEL

The psychology of advertising has been the subject of investigation ever since Walter Dill Scott published his treatise on *The Psychology of Advertising* in 1903. Yet, while the advent of motivation research in recent years gives promise of substantial advancements in the field, most of the material written on advertising psychology leans heavily on the findings of psychological experiments that appear to have application in the field.

From the findings of experiments on memory, one can formulate a "cumulative impression" hypothesis (based on the assumption that advertising impressions cumulate over time) that will "explain" why advertising might have a carry-over effect on sales. Lucas and Britt point out:

> Repetition of advertising has advantages in memory other than the increased chance of *recency*. Repetition reinforces and strengthens the impressions made on the audience. Each time an idea is repeated, the impression becomes stronger. Each time an impression is reestablished, it tends to last longer. . . .
>
> Each time an impression is repeated, it becomes stronger in two ways. First, it builds to a higher level than the original by combining the influence of the new with the residue of the old. Second, there is a definite tendency for impressions established through space repetitions to fade more slowly in each successive stage.[16]

To illustrate this, see Figure 3.

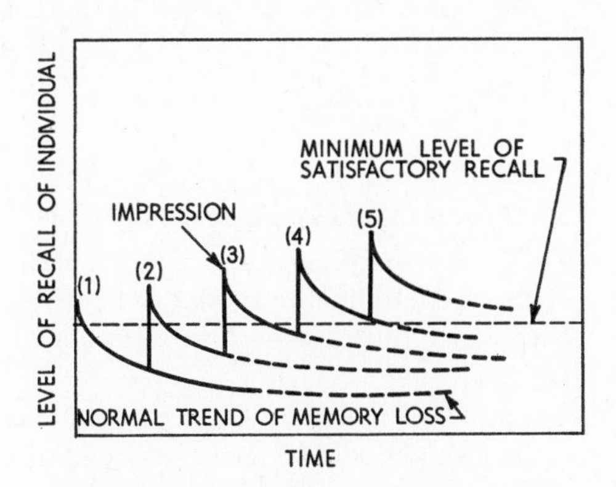

FIGURE 3. Reinforcing effect of impressions on recall.

[16] Darrell Blaine Lucas and Steuart Henderson Britt, *Advertising Psychology and Research* (New York: McGraw-Hill Book Co., Inc., 1950), p. 80.

According to the statement quoted, the level of awareness of brand and of product attributes may be built up over time with advertising. By making the further assumption that the level of sales is a function of brand awareness, present-period sales become a function of both present- and past-period advertising.

If it is assumed that all other variables affecting sales are held constant, a simple mathematical model may be constructed in the following general form:

$$Y_n = F(A_n, A_{n-1}, \ldots, A_{n-j}) \tag{2.1}$$

where

Y_n = Given period sales
A_n = Given period advertising

Advertising-Sales Assumptions

If a linear relationship is assumed, equation 2.1 becomes

$$Y_n = a + b(A_n, A_{n-1}, \ldots, A_{n-j}) \tag{2.2}$$

where

a = Level of sales without advertising
b = Change in given-period sales per increment of cumulated advertising

For further ease of handling, only given-period and immediately-preceding-period advertising are assumed to affect the given-period sales. It is further assumed that the effect of the previous-period advertising on given-period sales will be reduced by a constant decay factor of $1/c$. The model now becomes

$$Y_n = a + b\left(A_n + \frac{A_{n-1}}{c}\right) \tag{2.3}$$

Increasing-Decreasing Results

The operation of the model and the results of first increasing and then decreasing advertising expenditures over time are shown in Table 4 and graphically in Figure 4.

Advertising is increased by increments of 50 units each period to a maximum of 250 units in the fifth period. It is then decreased by decrements of 50 units each period. The carry-over effect is shown by comparing sales for periods 1 and 9, 2 and 8, 3 and 7, and 4 and 6. For each of these pairs of periods the amount of advertising expended was the same. Yet sales are higher in each case on the downward side of the expenditure cycle as a result of carry-over effect. This is shown graphically by the "loop" in Figure 4.

TABLE 4

OPERATION OF "CUMULATED IMPRESSION" MODEL*

$$Y_n = a + b\left(A_n + \frac{A_{n-1}}{c}\right)$$

Period	Advertising A_n	a	$b\left(A_n + \frac{A_{n-1}}{c}\right)$	Sales Y_n
1	50	50	15	65
2	100	50	38	88
3	150	50	60	110
4	200	50	82	132
5	250	50	105	165
6	200	50	98	148
7	150	50	75	125
8	100	50	52	102
9	50	50	30	80

* Where $b = 0.30$, $c = 2.0$.

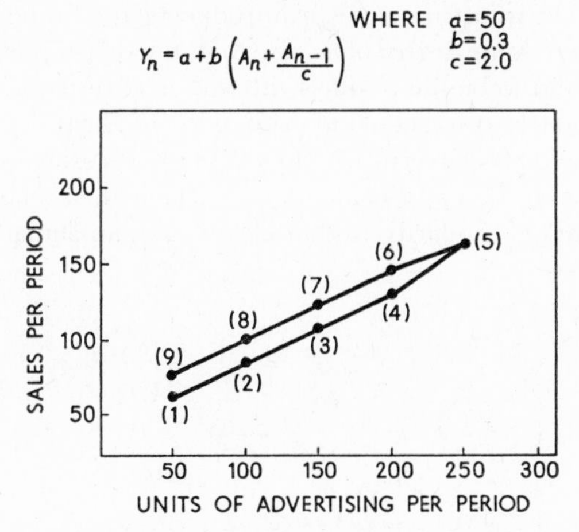

FIGURE 4. Plot of "cumulated impression" model results.

COMBINATION OF THE TWO MODELS

The repeat purchase model, through changing one assumption, may be readily and logically expanded to include the cumulated impression model. In the repeat purchase model, only present-period advertising (A_n) is assumed to affect the number of new buyers and the percentage of potential repeat buyers repurchasing.

A case may be built for the assumption that both the number of new purchasers and the rate of repurchasing by potential repeat buyers depend on both present- and past-period advertising. This assumption may be included in the "repeat purchase" model by substituting

$$A_n + \frac{A_{n-1}}{g}$$

(for example) where A_n now appears.

Combining the two models would of course serve to increase the carry-over effect. The width of the loop resulting from the operation of such a combined model would be greater than that shown in either Figure 2 or Figure 4. Since this effect may be readily foreseen, computations on the operation of such a model are not included.

CONCLUSIONS

At least two reasons indicate that a carry-over effect of advertising on sales may occur. Advertising impressions may cumulate over time to build up brand awareness and finally to persuade the buyer to purchase the brand. In this case, present-period sales are partially a function of past-period advertising. If advertising is instrumental in introducing the brand to a purchaser who later develops some degree of loyalty to it, the repeat purchases he makes may be considered to be the result of the earlier advertising.

Simplified models, constructed to explore the implications of each of these reasons, generate sales-advertising "loops" as advertising is first increased and then decreased. Perhaps incidentally, but nonetheless noteworthy, these loops bear a marked similarity to that observed in an actual case study.

19

This article describes an experiment in which both nonprice and price-related measures of brand performance were simulated. Problems of using the information derived as well as the uses to which the data may be put are discussed. Additional consideration is given to discounted cash flow analysis, which is illustrated and discussed in the context of relevance to advertising campaigns.

*FORECASTING BRAND PERFORMANCE THROUGH SIMULATION EXPERIMENTS**

Edgar A. Pessemier

EVERY MARKETING MANAGER needs practical measures of consumer behavior that reflect the strengths and weaknesses of his brand and competing brands.

However, the dynamic nature of the market, the welter of influences present, and management's inability to exercise a significant degree of control make it difficult to predict the behavior of customers or to accurately judge the results of a marketing policy.

These considerations underline the potential advantages of a research methodology that gathers data about the behavior of *real* customers in a simulated shopping environment. In properly designed simulation experiments, the observed behavior of subjects should yield a great deal of information about their expected behavior under normal market conditions.

THE EXPERIMENTAL PROCEDURE

How can shopping experiments be devised that will encourage subjects to act in the experimental environment in the way they would act on real shopping trips?

First, subjects should be asked to make selections from normal assortments of brands presented in a graphic form that display the characteristics of the merchandise. Second, each subject should be given a personal "stake" in acting according to *his own* system of values relating to the various products and in expressing them in monetary terms.

* Reprinted from *Journal of Marketing*, April, 1964, pp. 41–46. The *Journal* is the national quarterly publication of the American Marketing Association.

In other words, the most important elements influencing behavior in the real market should be retained in the simulated market. Therefore the emphasis must be on attaining a reasonable degree of psychological equivalence between the real and simulated market environments.

To accomplish these objectives in an experimental situation, each individual can be asked to assume that he needs an item from each of several classifications and that he has enough money to "purchase" any item from each classification. Further, he can be told that each set of assortments which he will see represents what is available in the market at the time and that he should select the items he would choose under similar real shopping conditions.

To encourage normal behavior, he should be informed that he will *actually receive the merchandise and change* called for by his purchase decisions on several of the simulated shopping trips made during the series of experiments. On successive simulated shopping trips the price of the brand normally preferred by the individual in each classification would be raised or the price of a nonpreferred brand lowered.

Under the author's direction an extensive series of experiments of the type described above was administered to 320 adults. Fully identified assortments of soap and toothpaste were used throughout, and each subject received about $1.50 in merchandise and change.

A detailed description of the strengths and limitations of the methodology, the results of the study, and potential extensions of the techniques to most other types of consumer goods are presented elsewhere.[1] Selected disguised data will be used here to illustrate measures of consumer behavior which can be helpful in analyzing a brand's competitive position and in planning marketing strategy.

COMPETITIVE STRENGTH OF A BRAND

Customarily, an assessment of the competitive strength of a brand is made in terms of historical sales growth or current market share.

Although these measures have their place, they are not forward-looking and can be misleading for purposes of planning and forecasting. Instead of indicating a brighter future, spectacular sales gains or a large market share may actually point the way to a more difficult period for the brand's marketing management.

To demonstrate this, results from the toothpaste classification used in the shopping experiments are helpful. Brand switching can be encouraged by raising just the price of the brand normally preferred by an individual subject. The purchase behavior of subjects following various increases in the price of their preferred brand is summarized in Table 1.

[1] Edgar A. Pessemier, *Experimental Methods of Analyzing Demand for Branded Consumer Goods with Applications to Problems in Marketing Strategy* (Pullman: Washington State University Press, 1963).

TABLE 1

BRAND MARKET SHARES DURING SIMULATED SHOPPING TRIPS FOLLOWING SELECTED PRICE INCREASES IN SUBJECT'S PREFERRED BRAND—TOOTHPASTE CLASSIFICATION

*Toothpaste Brands**	*Percentage of Subjects Originally Preferring a Brand†*	*Percentage of All Subjects Selecting a Designated Brand When the Price of the Brand Normally Preferred by Each Subject Was Increased*		
		1¢	*3¢*	*5¢*
A	33.8	33.8	31.3	28.4
B	29.7	27.8	24.4	20.0
C	17.2	17.1	20.6	21.3
D	8.4	8.5	10.6	13.1
E	7.2	8.4	8.4	10.3
F	3.7	4.1	4.4	6.3
G‡	...	0.3	0.3	0.6
Total	100.0	100.0	100.0	100.0
Percentage of subjects switching brand		20.0	38.4	54.0

* Brand names disguised for purposes of this discussion. All brands originally priced 31 cents.
† July, 1961, 320 subjects, Pullman, Washington.
‡ A new brand.

As the price of each preferred brand increases, more buyers switch brands. Under these conditions, brands with large market shares tend to be at a disadvantage, and brands with small market shares tend to be at an advantage.

The reason for this result is simple. Unless an offsetting reduction in the *proportion* of buyers lost by a brand can be achieved, the number of brand-switching buyers contributed by the brand will rise as its market share grows. But to be brand switchers, these subjects *must* buy some other brand. Therefore, brands with large market shares tend to contribute large numbers of brand-switching buyers, and the proportion of all brand switchers which they can attract tends to shrink.

An extreme illustration can be seen if only two brands are competing in a market. Brand *X* has 1,000 buyers, 1 percent of whom switch to brand *Y*. Brand *Y* had only 10 buyers, 10 percent of whom switch to brand *X*. At the end of the period, brand *X* would have suffered a net *loss* of nine buyers, even though its buyers displayed far greater brand loyalty. On the other hand, brand *Y* would have a net *gain* of nine buyers, almost twice the number it had at the beginning of the period.

Nonprice Measures of Brand Performance

Several norms can be developed against which observed brand behavior can be judged in the real market or in the simulated market. The ones presented here are dependent on price only to the degree that price changes were used to induce a given level of brand switching.

TABLE 2

NATURAL UNADJUSTED MARKET SHARES* AND NATURAL ADJUSTED MARKET SHARES* FOLLOWING VARIOUS DEGREES OF BRAND SWITCHING—TOOTHPASTE CLASSIFICATION

		Natural Market Share: Price Increase of Subject's Preferred Brand					
		1¢		*3¢*		*5¢*	
Toothpaste Brand†	*Percentage of Subjects Originally Preferring Brand*‡	*Unadjusted*	*Adjusted*	*Unadjusted*	*Adjusted*	*Unadjusted*	*Adjusted*
A.	33.8	29.3	32.5	24.9	31.7	21.5	30.8
B.	29.7	26.1	29.4	22.8	28.8	19.9	28.5
C.	17.2	16.5	17.8	15.9	18.2	15.3	18.5
D.	8.4	9.8	8.7	11.1	9.4	12.3	9.6
E.	7.2	8.8	7.5	10.4	7.8	11.6	8.2
F.	3.7	6.2	4.1	8.5	4.1	10.4	4.4
G§.	....	3.3	....	6.4	....	9.0	....
Total.	100.0	100.0	100.0	100.0	100.0	100.0	100.0
Percentage switching brands.		20.0		38.4		54.0	

$$*\ NUS_i = \frac{1}{n-1}(a - ab_i) + (c_i - ab_i)$$

$$NAS_i = \frac{ab_ib_1}{1-b_1} + \cdots + \frac{ab_ib_n}{1-b_n} + (c_i - ab_i);\ b^2_i = 0;\ \sum_i^n b_i = 1$$

NUS_i = *I*th brand's natural unadjusted market share
NAS_i = *I*th brand's natural adjusted market share
a = Number switching brands
b_i = *I*th brand's market share
c_i = *I*th brand's original number of buyers
n = Number of brands

† Brand names disguised for purposes of this discussion. All brands originally priced 31 cents.
‡ July, 1961, 320 subjects, Pullman, Washington.
§ A new brand.

The first is what may be called a brand's "natural *unadjusted* market share" following a purchase cycle. It is computed on the assumption that all brands lose the same share of their last-period buyers and attract an equal number of the eligible brand-switching buyers. The second norm may be called a brand's "natural *adjusted* market share." All brands are assumed to lose the same proportion of their last-period buyers, *but* a brand's original market share determines its capacity to attract eligible brand-switching buyers.

The results of using these two norms to determine the origin and destination of the numbers of brand-switching buyers observed in the simulation experiments are shown in Table 2.

A brand's competitive ability can be assessed by comparing the standards developed in Table 2 with the performances recorded in Table 1. The computed standards recognize the effect of a brand's original market share but apply the same rules concerning the movement of brand switches to every brand.

A third norm for judging the competitive capacity of a brand is based on the assumption that the existing brand-switching pattern for a classification of goods will continue unchanged. For example, assume that Table 3 shows

TABLE 3

HYPOTHETICAL BRAND-SWITCHING PATTERN WHEN A "NORMAL" NUMBER OF BUYERS SWITCH BRANDS PER PURCHASE CYCLE—TOOTHPASTE CLASSIFICATION *

Last Brand Purchased	*Number of Buyers per Thousand at Beginning of Cycle*	*Probability That the Buyer of a Brand Last Period Will Buy the Designated Brand This Period*						
		A	*B*	*C*	*D*	*E*	*F*	*G*
A	338	0.851	0.024	0.072	0.017	0.026	0.008	0.002
B	297	0.063	0.811	0.042	0.050	0.021	0.010	0.003
C	172	0.074	0.103	0.745	0.006	0.034	0.033	0.005
D	84	0.101	0.037	0.064	0.667	0.070	0.020	0.041
E	72	0.082	0.071	0.005	0.043	0.781	0.012	0.006
F	37	0.073	0.010	0.005	0.002	0.073	0.834	0.003
G†	..	0.091	0.082	0.079	0.030	0.010	0.008	0.700
Number of buyers per thousand at end of purchase cycle		336	275	168	82	87	46	6

* Adopted from experimental data to admit switching *to and from* brand *G*.
† A new brand.

the brand-switching pattern found in a real or experimental market when the usual fraction of all buyers switch brands during one purchase cycle.

The figures in Table 3 at the foot of the column designated for a brand indicate the number of buyers that it would obtain during one purchase cycle. Through the use of these figures as the initial number of buyers for each brand for the next period, the process can be continued for as many periods as necessary.

The net gains or losses over whatever length of time is selected can then be used as a standard by which to judge a brand's competitive capacity *if existing conditions continue* to prevail. The division of the market at the end of each of five purchase cycles is given in Table 4.

TABLE 4

BRANDS' MARKET SHARES PER THOUSAND BUYERS PER PURCHASE CYCLE—CURRENT BRAND-SWITCHING PATTERN CONTINUES TO PREVAIL—TOOTHPASTE CLASSIFICATION

Periods in Future	*Number of Buyers per Thousand Buying Brand*						
	A	*B*	*C*	*D*	*E*	*F*	*G**
1	336	275	168	82	87	46	6
2	333	259	165	80	98	54	11
3	332	247	164	77	106	59	15
4	332	238	163	75	112	62	18
5	332	231	162	75	118	63	19
Initial period	338	297	172	84	72	37	..

* See footnotes * and † to Table 3.

Price-Related Measures of Brand Performance

There are a number of additional fruitful ways that the behavior of subjects in simulated shopping trips can be tabulated. Two important price-related ones will be given before attention is directed toward using the results from simulation experiments for planning and evaluating marketing strategy.

First, it is possible to display data concerning a brand in the form of a demand schedule. The number of buyers a brand will attract with various

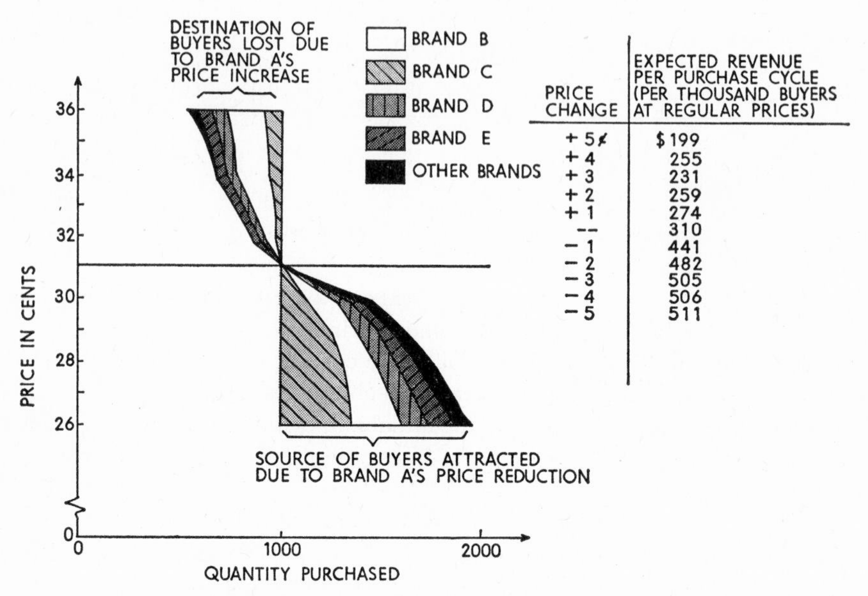

FIGURE 1. Demand characteristics of brand *A* toothpaste.

price decreases or will lose with various price increases can be shown; and in addition, the source or destination of these buyers may also be displayed.

This type of demand schedule is shown in Figure 1 for brand *A* toothpaste, along with the total revenue associated with each price at which brand *A* was offered.

Second, the elasticities of demand for each brand at various price increases and decreases can be displayed. Elasticities of demand observed in the shopping experiments indicate that the price elasticity of a brand depends on its market share and its relative price.

To illustrate this latter effect, results for selected brands of toothpaste *and* soap are shown in Table 5.

These results are not unexpected, if it is assumed that a significant proportion of the individuals preferring each brand have a weak degree of brand loyalty. In that case the brands with large market shares contribute a larger share of brand switchers and have a smaller pool of eligible brand switchers from which to attract buyers.

It is also possible that the low-loyalty, price-conscious brand switchers are likely to be distributed at random among the remaining brands unless a price differential is present to influence their secondary brand preferences.

Therefore, it is fair to conclude that if a brand with a small market share can effectively publicize a price reduction, it can make a *relatively* large gain in market share in comparison with a brand with a large market share that adopted the same policy.

DEVELOPING AND TESTING ALTERNATIVE MARKETING STRATEGIES

With this kind of information about customer behavior available from simulation experiments, a brand manager will want to know how he can use the information to generate, test, and select effective marketing strategies for his brand. If reviewed on a continuing basis with related marketing research data, experimental results should suggest productive lines of action.

For example, they may indicate that prevention of serious competitive inroads is a more efficient strategy for a brand with a large market share than efforts directed toward gaining new buyers. Therefore the manager of such a brand should look for ways to increase customer loyalty to his brand, particularly among those customers who seem most likely to switch in large numbers to one or more competing brands.

On the other hand, strategies designed to attract brand switchers may be more promising for a brand with a small market share.

In each case the study of experimental results will offer helpful clues concerning the forces at work and the likely direction of the market *if* current conditions are permitted to continue. In this latter regard, the marketing manager of a brand should complete the analysis suggested by Table 4 and also assess the effect of various strategies on the results obtained. Doing so will permit him to investigate the desirability, over time, of the various marketing plans he may have under consideration.

If a brand manager has progressed in his study of the market to the point that he has a half dozen or so promising, well-defined strategies under consideration, he should proceed to test the relative effectiveness of each one by comparing the expected discounted net cash flow it will produce with that which will result from no change in the strategy currently being employed.

It is important to use the discounted net cash flow criterion for several reasons. First, marketing activities typically require the expenditure of large sums. Second, the length of time over which a strategy is employed is often long and typically varies from one strategy to another. Third, the time pattern of applying and recovering funds may differ greatly from strategy to strategy. Fourth, the technique of evaluating investments in marketing should be compatible with the firm's overall capital-budgeting procedures.

TABLE 5

BRAND PRICE ELASTICITY RELATED TO A BRAND'S ORIGINAL MARKET SHARE AND THE RELATIVE MAGNITUDE OF THE BRAND'S ORIGINAL PRICE

Brand	Original Price	Original Market Share	Price Elasticity of Demand at Specified Price Change									
			+5¢	+4¢	+3¢	+2¢	+1¢	−1¢	−2¢	−3¢	−4¢	−5¢
Toothpaste:												
A	31¢	33.8	2.81	2.80	3.25	3.30	4.59	14.95	10.24	8.30	6.78	5.90
B	31	29.7	3.79	3.51	4.31	4.24	5.87	22.48	13.95	10.85	9.69	8.52
C	31	17.2	3.49	3.94	4.13	5.64	7.88	40.18	26.40	19.52	17.51	15.38
D	31	8.4	3.90	4.31	5.36	6.31	10.34	55.35	37.64	31.00	31.55	28.78
E	31	7.2	3.77	4.04	4.94	5.39	6.73	64.21	43.17	32.48	32.10	27.90
F	31	3.4	2.07	2.58	3.44	3.87	5.17	79.21	53.38	44.77	43.05	38.57
Toilet soap:												
A	2/31¢	29.4	3.36	3.96	4.61	5.77	8.90	4.59	2.87	2.67	2.58	2.07
B	2/15	22.2	0.51	0.42	0.35	0.53	0.85	14.32	9.89	6.82	5.45	4.64
C	2/25	14.4	2.01	2.05	2.28	2.74	4.57	35.53	18.57	14.00	11.31	10.01

To discover the effect on cash flows over a period of time that results from a particular marketing strategy, it is necessary to determine or estimate the following data for each strategy under consideration.

1. The period-by-period cash expenditures needed.
2. An appropriate opportunity cost of capital to be used as the discount rate.
3. The contribution to "fixed" expenses and profit from an additional unit sold.
4. The period-by-period changes that the strategy will make in the normal brand-switching pattern for the classification. (See Table 3.)
5. The future period at which the analysis will be terminated.
6. The value of each additional buyer obtained in the terminal period.

To make estimates of new switching patterns over a period of time, a marketing manager would refer to how experimental subjects switched brands under "normal" conditions, how they behaved when given larger incentives to switch brands, and how intensively and for what duration the campaign's particular appeals would be employed. Some time might pass before the full effect of the campaign would be felt, and some segments of the market might be more affected than others. All these factors should be incorporated in the sets of brand-switching patterns used to evaluate the strategy.

Brands *X* and *Y*, referred to earlier, may be used for illustrative purposes. Brand *X* retained 99 out of every 100 buyers, and brand *Y* retained 9 out of every 10 buyers. Under continuing "normal" conditions, brand *X*'s original market of 1,000 buyers would drop to 991, 983, 976, 969, and 963 over five purchase cycles; and brand *Y*'s 10 original buyers would increase to 19, 27, 34, 41, and 47 over the same time spans.

Two alternative strategies could be considered for brand *Y*, one calling for a price reduction for one period, and another calling for an advertising campaign extending over two periods with a one-period delay in its effect on sales. The one-month price reduction would increase the 1 percent of the buyers switching from brand *X* to 10 percent, and would eliminate switching from brand *Y* for one period. This would be the sole effect obtained by a price reduction of $20 per unit.

On the other hand, spending $1,000 on an advertising campaign in each of the first two periods would increase the number switching from brand *X* to 6 percent in period 2 and 6 percent in period 3, but would not affect the percentage switching from brand *Y*.

If each unit of brand *Y* contributes $10 over variable cost, the incremental cash flows are as shown in Table 6.

If it were appropriate to terminate the analysis at the end of five periods, the best strategy could be selected with ease. To complete the analysis, the only additional data needed are a cash flow value per additional customer in period 5 and an appropriate rate to discount the net cash flows.

In this numerical illustration a 24 percent annual rate of return is employed for periods of three months' duration, and each additional buyer in period 5 is assigned a value *equivalent* to a $50 cash flow. Under these condi-

TABLE 6

INCREMENTAL NET CASH FLOWS DURING FIVE PERIODS FROM TWO STRATEGIES

Period	*"Normal" Number of Buyers*	*One-Month Price Reduction*			*Two-Month Advertising Campaign*		
		Buyers	*Buyers Gained*	*Net Cash Flow*	*Buyers*	*Buyers Gained*	*Net Cash Flow*
Initial	10	10	..	.....	10	..	.....
1	19	110	91	($1,290)	19	..	($1,000)
2	27	108	81	810	76	41	(590)
3	34	106	72	720	124	90	900
4	41	104	63	630	121	80	800
5	47	103	56	560	118	71	710
Total				$1,430			$ 920

tions a price reduction produces $3,121 discounted net cash flow and the advertising campaign, $3,109.

For practical purposes the two proposals are equally desirable if the rate of return that was used reflected the risk inherent in each strategy.

However, if this is not so, then the nature of the risks must be assessed and accounted for. One method of doing this is to adjust the desired rate of return. The other way is to generate several likely outcomes of a strategy and then weight each one by the likelihood of its occurrence. The latter practice is useful if one or more important possible competitive responses must be considered.

IV

Production Planning and Control

TABLEAU IV

Methodological Analysis

	Descriptive Models for Analysis					*Optimizing Models*			
Methodology / *Article*	*Algebraic or Symbolic (Deterministic)*	*Algebraic or Symbolic (Probabilistic)*	*Matrix Methods*	*Markov Processes*	*Simulation*	*Linear Programming*	*Game Theory*	*Calculus*	*Other*
20. Economic Manufacturing Lot Size								X	
21. A Study of Optimum Assembly Runs	X								
22. An Investigation of Some Quantitative Relationships between Break-Even Point Analysis and Economic Lot-Size Theory									X
23. Planning Transistor Production by Linear Programming						X			
24. The Use of Mathematics in Production and Inventory Control			X						
25. Cost-Volume-Profit Analysis under Conditions of Uncertainty		X							
26. PERT/Cost: The Challenge	X								

PRODUCTION PLANNING AND CONTROL

Production planning is often considered to be little more than a scheduling problem, with the single objective of producing sufficient inventory to meet expected demand. This viewpoint patently ignores two important considerations: costs of placing inventory in a given location at a specified time and physical constraints on output for the given time period. The effect of these considerations is difficult to grasp in an involved production-scheduling operation, but mathematical models are available which may, with relative ease, resolve these considerations.

The following classes of basic production problems may be configured and resolved by various mathematical techniques:

1. *Determination of raw materials requirements*
2. *Determination of production-run length*
3. *Effect of variable sales on production*
4. *Allocation of productive capacity to products*
5. *Planning special contracts*

The first problem is described in article 24. Articles 20, 21, and 22 analyze the second problem. The effect of variable sales is considered in article 25, and an allocation problem involving productive capacity is presented in article 23. Some special considerations relating to PERT/Cost analysis are presented in article 26.

20

There is presented herein a description of the variables which are normally included in economic lot-size formulas, together with the standard formulation of this problem. Thereafter the author modifies the model by considering work-in-process inventories, deriving the new formulation in a step-by-step process. The relation of economic lot size to annual demand is considered, and it is demonstrated that the choice of the appropriate model is dependent upon the type of demand function. Three examples are presented illustrating significant differences between the original and the modified models.

ECONOMIC MANUFACTURING LOT SIZE*

Subodh Bhattacharjee

MANUFACTURING PROCESSES can be broadly divided into two distinct classifications: continuous or intermittent. Where processes are continuous, individual parts move from one operation to another in sequence. No storage of parts is necessary between operations, because each part is transferred to the next operation as soon as it is finished at the present one. Conversely, in the case of intermittent processes, parts are manufactured in batches or lots. One operation on all parts in one batch may have to be finished before the next operation is started. However, it is often possible for two or more operations on the same batch to overlap. We are concerned with only intermittent production in this paper.

The size of the lot produced in one batch has considerable influence on the economic operation of intermittent manufacturing processes. Lot size is often determined arbitrarily. A convenient number such as 500 or 1,000 is selected without due regard to the economics of manufacture.

Many manufacturing costs are not affected by lot size, but those costs that are affected by the size of the lot can be further classified into two categories: fixed costs and variable costs. Fixed costs are defined as those which are constant for a lot and independent of the number of pieces in the lot. On the other hand, the variable costs are those which vary proportionately with the size of the lot.

---

* Reprinted from *Journal of Industrial Engineering*, March–April, 1957, pp. 119–26. The *Journal* is the official publication of the American Institute of Industrial Engineers, Inc., 345 East 47th Street, New York, New York 10017.

The total fixed cost per lot, generally termed "setup cost," is the sum of the make-ready cost of the machines and the clerical cost associated with the lot. The amount of time required for making the machine ready for production is often considerable in comparison to the actual production time and is independent of the number of pieces in the lot. Also, clerical costs required for issuing and expediting a production order are independent of the size of the lot. For any given amount of fixed costs, the smaller the lot size, the larger the fixed expenses allocated to each piece in the lot. In order to keep fixed expenses per piece as small as possible, it is desirable to have the size of the lot be as large as possible.

On the other hand, the costs of storage, rent, insurance, interest on investment, etc., tend to be constant per unit of product and may be classified as variable "holding" costs. If current production exceeds current demands, inventories increase, and these holding costs are increased. The lot size therefore should be as small as possible for the holding cost to be correspondingly small.

There is a lot size for which the total of setup and holding costs is minimum, and this is known as the "economic lot size."

The conventional formula (Camp's formula) [1] for economic lot size is suitable primarily for determining lot size for purchased items. This formula is derived by minimizing the total of the holding costs of purchased parts and the fixed clerical and other costs associated with the processing of a purchase order. It cannot be used to determine economic lot size for manufactured products, especially in those cases where work-in-process inventory is large.

In case of products manufactured in the shop, it is necessary to consider the holding cost of work in process during the course of manufacture. As soon as the production of a batch of product is started, capital, representing the cost of material, is tied up. Also, the value of materials in process is increased more and more as labor cost is added to it by the performance of successive operations. Considerable time is often necessary from the beginning of the process to the delivery of the finished parts to the stock room. The semifinished state of the product during this period is called work in process. The time from the beginning of the process to the delivery to the stock room is known as "lead time."

During the entire period of lead time, capital representing the average value of work in process does not produce any return. Also, expenses for storage, insurance, etc., are incurred for holding the product during work in process. The holding cost of work in process may in certain cases be comparable to and even greatly exceed the holding cost of finished goods. It is therefore necessary to consider the holding cost of work in process, along with the setup cost and holding cost of finished goods, to determine the economic lot size.

The conventional formula used for determining economic purchase quantities does not take into consideration the holding cost of the work-in-process inventory. As such, it cannot be correctly employed for determining economic lot size for products in cases where work-in-process inventory is considerable. The purpose of this paper is to derive a formula for economic lot size which will be applicable when the consideration of work in process is necessary. The use and limitations of the formula will be discussed, and the results obtained will be compared with those obtained from the simpler formula. Also, a criterion will be suggested for deciding when the revised formula should be used.

DERIVATION OF CAMP'S FORMULA

The lot-size formula derived by Camp takes into account the fixed cost per lot, such as setup and other clerical costs, and the holding cost of finished goods inventory. The total annual cost is considered, and its derivative with respect to the lot size (Q) is equated to zero to obtain the lot size corresponding to the minimum total cost.

Let

i = Annual rate for the cost of storage and interest on investment in inventory, expressed as a decimal
c = Total cost per piece in dollars, excluding setup cost
Q = Lot size in number of pieces
Y = Total annual demand in number of pieces
S = Cost of one setup (including clerical and other fixed costs) in dollars

Then

Average quantity in finished stock $= \frac{Q+0}{2} = \frac{Q}{2}$ (assuming a uniform rate of usage)

$$\text{Average annual storage and other costs (holding cost)} = \frac{Q}{2} \cdot i \cdot c$$

$$\text{Number of setups required in one year} = \frac{Y}{Q}$$

$$\text{Annual setup cost} = \frac{Y}{Q} \cdot S$$

$$\text{Total annual cost} = \text{Setup cost} + \text{holding cost}$$

$$= \frac{Y}{Q} \cdot S + \frac{Q}{2} \cdot i \cdot c$$

For minimum cost:

$$\frac{d}{dQ}(\text{Total cost}) = -\frac{Y}{Q^2} \cdot S + \frac{c \cdot i}{2} = 0$$

or

$$Q = \sqrt{\frac{2Y \cdot S}{c \cdot i}} \quad \text{(Camp's formula)} \tag{1}$$

Example

Let

$$\begin{aligned}\text{Total cost per piece excluding setup cost, } c &= \$12\\ \text{Setup cost per lot, } S &= \$50\\ \text{Annual rate of storage and other costs, } i &= 10\% = 0.10\\ \text{Annual demand, } Y &= 12{,}000 \text{ pieces}\end{aligned}$$

Then the economic lot size is

$$Q = \sqrt{\frac{2YS}{Ci}} = \sqrt{\frac{2 \times 12{,}000 \times \$50}{\$12 \times 0.10}} = 1{,}000 \text{ pieces per lot}$$

$$\begin{aligned}\text{Total annual cost} &= \text{Setup cost} + \text{Annual holding for finished goods}\\ &= \frac{12{,}000}{1{,}000} \times \$50 + \frac{1{,}000}{2} \times \$12 \times 0.10 = \$600 + \$600 = \$1{,}200\end{aligned}$$

COMPARISON OF TOTAL COSTS FOR VARIOUS LOT SIZES

Economic lot size is defined as that lot size for which total cost is minimum. In the example above the total cost, which varies with lot size, was \$1,200 when the economic lot size was 1,000 pieces per lot. Any other lot size will result in total cost higher than \$1,200. However, we considered only the setup cost and holding cost for finished goods in arriving at the total cost of \$1,200. The holding cost of work in process during the period of lead time has not yet been considered. It has been stated before that when the value of the work in process is high and the lead time is considerable, the holding cost of the work in process may be considerable. We will compare below total costs, including holding costs for work-in-process inventory, for various lot sizes. It will be of interest to note whether the lot size which corresponds to minimum total cost in this case differs significantly from the economic lot size of 1,000 pieces obtained from Camp's formula. The holding costs for work in process for lot sizes 400, 460, 500, 600, and 1,000 pieces are calculated, and corresponding total costs are given in Table 1.

Holding Costs of Work-in-Process Inventory

Holding costs of work in process depend on the value of work-in-process inventory and length of lead time. In the simplest case the lead time for any lot size can be determined by knowing the total time required to make one piece and the number of pieces in the lot.

That is, if

$$\begin{aligned}L &= \text{Lead time}\\ t &= \text{Total time for making one piece}\\ Q &= \text{Quantity in the lot}\end{aligned}$$

then

$$L = Q \times t$$

Total time for making one piece is obtained by adding the time required for all operations. However, as we shall see later, length of lead time depends on actual scheduling of manufacturing operations. Consequently, holding costs of work in process also depend on efficiency of scheduling. The lengths of lead time for lot sizes illustrated assume proper scheduling and are given below with other cost data.

TABLE 1

Lot Size	*Annual Setup Cost*	+	*Annual Holding Cost of Finished Goods*	+	*Annual Holding Cost for Work in Process*	=	*Total Annual Cost*
1,000	$\frac{12{,}000 \times 50}{1{,}000}$		$\frac{1{,}000 \times 12 \times 0.10}{2}$				
	$ 600	+	$600	+	$2,250	=	$3,450
600	$\frac{12{,}000 \times 50}{600}$		$\frac{600 \times 12 \times 0.10}{2}$				
	$1,000	+	$360	+	$1,350	=	$2,710
500	$\frac{12{,}000 \times 50}{500}$		$\frac{500 \times 12 \times 0.10}{2}$				
	$1,200	+	$300	+	$1,125	=	$2,625
460	$\frac{12{,}000 \times 50}{460}$		$\frac{460 \times 12 \times 0.10}{2}$				
	$1,300	+	$276	+	$1,020	=	$2,596
400	$\frac{12{,}000 \times 50}{400}$		$\frac{400 \times 12 \times 0.10}{2}$				
	$1,500	+	$240	+	$ 900	=	$2,640

The value of work in process is obtained by multiplying unit cost of work in process by the number of pieces in the lot. Unit cost of work in process is equal to the material cost plus labor cost added to the product during manufacture. Let us consider the following data in connection with the same example for which economic lot size was calculated.

Let

Lead time for lot sizes of 1,000 pieces = 2.5 months
600 pieces = 1.5 months
500 pieces = 1.25 months
460 pieces = 1.075 months
400 pieces = 1 month
Unit material cost = $6 per piece
Total cost (excluding setup cost) = $12 per piece
Unit labor cost = Total cost (excluding setup cost) − Unit material cost = $12 − $6 = $6

Average cost per piece of work in process = Material cost + ½(Labor cost) = 6 + ½(6) = \$9

Annual rate of holding cost = 10% per year

Annual demand = 12,000 pieces

Holding costs of work in process = Average cost per piece × Number of pieces in the lot × Manufacturing lead time *in years* × Annual rate of holding costs × Number of lots per year $\left(= \frac{\text{Annual demand}}{\text{Lot size}}\right)$

Holding costs (annual) of work in process for various lot sizes are:

Lot Size	*Annual Holding Costs*
1,000 pieces..........	$\$9 \times 1{,}000 \times \frac{2.5}{12} \times 0.10 \times 12{,}000/1{,}000 = \$2{,}250$
600 pieces..........	$\$9 \times 600 \times \frac{1.5}{12} \times 0.10 \times 12{,}000/600 = 1{,}350$
500 pieces..........	$\$9 \times 500 \times \frac{1.25}{12} \times 0.10 \times 12{,}000/500 = 1{,}125$
460 pieces..........	$\$9 \times 460 \times \frac{1.075}{12} \times 0.10 \times 12{,}000/460 = 1{,}020$
400 pieces..........	$\$9 \times 400 \times \frac{1.00}{12} \times 0.10 \times 12{,}000/400 = 900$

Total Annual Costs

The total annual costs, including holding costs of work in process, holding cost of finished goods, and annual setup costs for lot sizes of 1,000, 600, 500, 460, and 400 pieces are shown in Table 1. It will be noticed that the minimum total cost is obtained for a lot size of approximately 460 pieces.

DETERMINATION OF ECONOMIC LOT SIZE WHEN WORK IN PROCESS IS CONSIDERED

We have observed before that when only setup and holding costs of finished goods are considered, economic lot size can be calculated from Camp's formula:

$$Q = \sqrt{\frac{2YS}{ci}}$$

We can now introduce the holding costs of work-in-process inventory in the total annual variable costs and recalculate the formula for economic lot size.

Let

m = Cost of material at the beginning of process in dollars
c = Total material and labor cost of one part, excluding setup costs, in dollars
i = Annual rate for the cost of storage and interest on investment in inventory, expressed as a decimal

Y = Annual demand in number of pieces
Q = Lot size in number of pieces
t = Total time required for all operations for making one part, expressed in years
L = Lead time in years
S = Cost of one setup in dollars

Lead Time

Then

$$L = Q \times t \text{ years}$$

Cost of Work in Process for Lot Size Q

$$\text{The average cost per piece of work in process} = \text{Material cost} + \tfrac{1}{2}(\text{Labor cost})$$
$$= m + \frac{(c-m)}{2} = \frac{m+c}{2}$$
$$\text{The total cost of work in process} = \frac{Q \times (m+c)}{2}$$

Annual Holding Cost of Work in Process

$$\text{The length of holding time} = \text{Lead time} = L$$
$$\text{Holding cost per unit during lead time} = \text{Lead time} \times \text{Cost of unit in process}$$
$$\times \text{ Annual rate of interest and storage cost} = L \cdot \frac{m+c}{2} \cdot i$$
$$\text{Total holding cost per lot} = \text{Lot size} \times \text{Holding cost per unit} = Q \cdot L \cdot \frac{m+c}{2} \cdot i$$
$$\text{Annual holding cost of work in process} = \text{Holding cost per lot} \times \text{Number of lots}$$
$$\text{per year} = Q \cdot L \cdot \frac{m+c}{2} \cdot i \cdot \frac{Y}{Q} = Q \cdot Q \cdot t \cdot \frac{m+c}{2} \cdot i \cdot \frac{Y}{Q}$$

since

$$L = Q \cdot t = Q \cdot \frac{m+c}{2} \cdot Y \cdot t \cdot i$$

Total Annual Cost

$$\text{Total annual cost} = \text{Annual setup cost} + \text{Annual holding cost for finished goods}$$
$$+ \text{ Annual holding cost for work in process}$$
$$= \frac{Y}{Q} \cdot S + \frac{Q}{2} \cdot c \cdot i + Q \cdot \frac{m+c}{2} \cdot Y \cdot t \cdot i$$

For the total to be minimum for a given Q:

$$\frac{d(\text{total cost})}{dQ} = -\frac{Y}{Q^2} \cdot S + \frac{c}{2} \cdot i + \frac{(m+c)}{2} \cdot Y \cdot t \cdot i = 0$$

Therefore:

$$Q^2 = \frac{YS}{\frac{c \cdot i}{2} + \frac{(m + c)}{2} \cdot Y \cdot t \cdot i}$$

which reduces to

$$Q = \sqrt{\frac{Y \cdot S}{\frac{c \cdot i}{2} + \frac{(m + c)}{2} \cdot Y \cdot t \cdot i}} \tag{2}$$

Lot Size in Terms of Setup and Unit Holding Costs

The above formula can be expressed as

$$Q = \sqrt{\frac{S}{\frac{1}{2Y} \cdot c \cdot i + \frac{(m + c)}{2} \cdot t \cdot i}}$$

where

$\frac{1}{2Y}$ = Average holding time of one unit of finished stock in years

c = Cost per piece

i = Annual holding rate

$\frac{m + c}{2}$ = Average cost per piece of work in process

t = Holding time per piece of work in process in years

But

Holding time × Cost per unit × Annual holding rate = Unit holding cost

Therefore:

$$Q = \sqrt{\frac{\text{Setup cost per lot}}{\text{Unit holding cost for finished goods} + \text{Unit holding cost for work in process}}}$$

RELATION OF ECONOMIC LOT SIZE TO ANNUAL DEMAND

Holding cost of work in process may far exceed that of finished goods. In such cases the first term in the denominator of formula 2, the holding cost of finished goods, may be negligible in comparison to the second term, the holding cost of work in process. Then the formula for economic lot size will reduce to

$$Q = \sqrt{\frac{Y \cdot S}{\frac{(m + c)}{2} \cdot Y \cdot t \cdot i}} = \sqrt{\frac{S}{\frac{(m + c)}{2} \cdot t \cdot i}}$$

$$= \sqrt{\frac{\text{Setup cost per lot}}{\text{Unit holding cost of work in process}}}$$

The lot size in this case is independent of annual demand and is constant so long as the setup costs and the unit holding cost for work in process do not change.

When the unit holding cost of work in process is negligible in comparison to that of finished goods, formula 2 reduces to Camp's formula: $Q = \sqrt{2YS/ci}$. The lot size then becomes proportional to the square root of the annual demand.

When both holding costs of finished goods and work in process are equally important, the economic lot size is given by formula 2 and is smaller than either of the two cases discussed above.

The variation of lot size with annual demand for the three cases can be in-

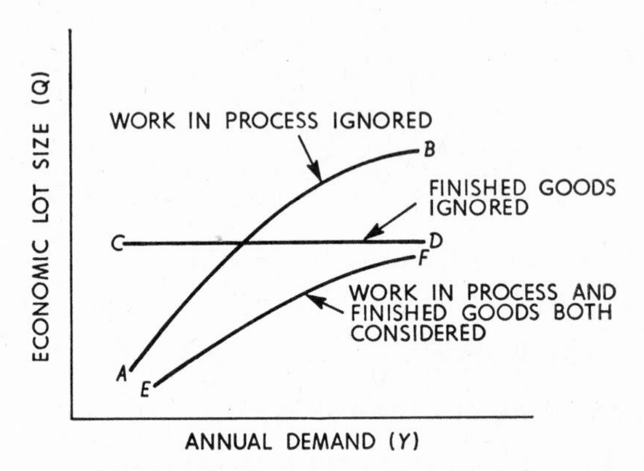

FIGURE 1. Variation of lot sizes for three general cases of treatment.

dicated graphically as shown in Figure 1 [2]. The curve *AB* represents the lot size when work in process is ignored. The line *CD* represents the constant lot size when the holding cost of finished goods is not considered. The curve *EF* represents the lot size when both holding costs of finished goods and work in process are considered.

As annual demand increases, the lot size obtained by considering both work in process and finished goods (*EF*) varies more and more widely from that obtained by ignoring work in process (*AB*). This suggests that the consideration of holding cost of work in process becomes more important for those items which have high annual demand.

CHOICE OF ECONOMIC LOT-SIZE FORMULA

The discussion regarding the nature of variation of lot size with annual demand suggests that under some conditions it is only necessary to consider the holding cost of work in process in the calculation of economic lot size. Under other conditions, lot size obtained from the consideration of holding cost of finished goods alone is sufficiently accurate for practical purposes. In still other cases, it is necessary to consider the holding costs of both work in process and finished goods.

The holding cost of work in process is all that is necessary to consider in calculating lot size for a "fast-moving" item. On the other hand, the holding cost of finished goods need only be taken into account for calculating lot size for a "slow-moving" item. When an item cannot be clearly classified in either category, the holding cost of both work in process and finished goods has to be considered.

Two criteria are proposed for classifying an item as fast moving or slow moving. The first requirement is the comparison of holding costs of work in process and finished goods. The second criterion is the comparison of holding times for work in process inventory and finished goods inventory for a given quantity. An item should be classified as fast moving or slow moving if and only if both criteria are satisfied. In that case the appropriate simple formula should be used for determining the economic lot size. If both requirements are not satisfied, the item should not be classified in either category; and the joint formula, derived in this paper, should be used to determine the economic lot size.

According to the first requirement, an item will be classified as "fast moving" if the unit holding cost of work in process is significantly higher than that of finished goods, that is, the numerical value of $\frac{(m + c)}{2} \cdot t \cdot i$ is greater than that of $\frac{c \cdot i}{2Y}$.

An item will be classified as slow moving if the unit holding cost of work in process is negligible in comparison to that of finished goods. This implies that the numerical value of $\frac{(m + c)}{2} \cdot t \cdot i$ will be negligible compared to that of $\frac{c \cdot i}{2Y}$.

According to the second criterion, an item is fast moving if the length of holding time for a given quantity in the work-in-process stage is longer than the holding time for the same quantity in finished goods inventory. Conversely, an element is slow moving if the length of the holding time for a given quantity in work in process is negligible in comparison to the holding time for the same quantity in finished goods.

EXAMPLES

The classification of items as to fast moving and slow moving and the effect of considering the holding cost of work in process on lot size are illustrated below. The same example which was used to calculate the lot size by Camp's formula is considered. The data are restated as follows:

EXAMPLE 1

$$c = \$12$$
$$m = \$6$$
$$i = 0.10$$
$$Y = 12{,}000$$
$$S = \$50$$
$$L = 2.5/12 \text{ years for } 1{,}000 \text{ pieces}$$
$$t = \frac{L}{Q} = \frac{2.5}{12 \times 1{,}000} \text{ years/piece}$$

Classification of the Item

Criterion 1—holding cost basis:

A. Unit holding cost of work in process $= \dfrac{m + c}{2} \cdot t \cdot i = \dfrac{\$2.25}{12{,}000} = \$0.00019$

B. Unit holding cost of finished goods $= \dfrac{ci}{2Y} = \dfrac{\$0.60}{12{,}000} = \$0.00005$

A is nearly four times *B*, so the item is fast moving.

Criterion 2—holding time basis:

C. Holding time for work in process for 1,000 pieces = 2.5 months

D. Holding time for finished goods for 1,000 pieces (selling time) $= \dfrac{1{,}000}{12{,}000} \times 12$
$= 1$ month

C is greater than *D*, so the item is fast moving.

Lot-Size Calculations

E. Camp's formula—no work in process considered:

$$Q = \sqrt{\frac{2 \cdot Y \cdot S}{c \cdot i}} = 1{,}000 \text{ pieces}$$

F. Revised formula—work in process and finished goods considered:

$$Q = \sqrt{\frac{Y \cdot S}{\dfrac{c \cdot i}{2} + \dfrac{m + c}{2} \cdot Y \cdot t \cdot i}} = \sqrt{\frac{600{,}000}{0.60 + 2.25}} = 460 \text{ pieces}$$

G. Holding cost of finished goods neglected:

$$Q = \sqrt{\frac{Y \cdot S}{\dfrac{m + c}{2} \cdot Y \cdot t \cdot i}} = \sqrt{\frac{600{,}000}{2.25}} = 516 \text{ pieces}$$

The lot size obtained by Camp's formula is very large in comparison to those obtained by the other two formulas. The difference in economic lot size is small whether holding costs for finished goods inventory is considered or not. As calculated in Table 1, total annual cost is minimum for a lot size of nearly 460 pieces. For a fast-moving item, therefore, the economic lot size should be calculated by the revised formula, which takes into account the holding cost of work in process as well as of finished goods inventory. However, sufficiently accurate lot size can be obtained by considering the holding cost of work-in-process inventory alone.

EXAMPLE 2

Let 360 pieces be the annual demand of the same item considered in example 1 in place of 12,000 pieces. All the data will be as in example 1 except the value of Y, which will be changed to $Y = 360$.

Classification of the Item

Criterion 1—holding costs:

A. Unit holding cost of work in process $= \dfrac{m + c}{2} \cdot t \cdot i = \dfrac{\$0.0675}{360} = \$0.00019$

B. Unit holding cost of finished goods $= \dfrac{ci}{2Y} = \dfrac{\$0.60}{360} = \$0.0017$

A is much smaller than *B*, so the item is slow moving.

Criterion 2—holding time:

C. Holding time of work in process (30 pieces) $= Q \cdot t$ (assuming proportionality of lead time)

$$= 30 \times \frac{2.5}{1{,}000} = 0.075$$

month (approximately)

D. Holding time of finished goods (selling time of 30 pieces) = 1 month

C is negligible compared to *D*, so the item is a slow-moving item.

Lot-Size Calculations

E. Camp's formula—no work in process considered:

$$Q = \sqrt{\frac{2Y \cdot S}{c \cdot i}} = \sqrt{\frac{2 \times 360 \times 50}{12 \times 0.10}} = 173 \text{ pieces}$$

F. Revised formula—work in process and finished goods considered:

$$Q = \sqrt{\frac{Y \cdot S}{\frac{c \cdot i}{2} + \frac{(m + c)}{2} \cdot Y \cdot t \cdot i}} = \sqrt{\frac{360 \times 50}{0.60 + 0.0675}} = 165 \text{ pieces}$$

The lot size obtained from the revised formula is very near to that obtained from Camp's formula. In case of a slow-moving item, therefore, Camp's formula can be used—that is, the holding cost for work in process can be neglected—for calculating economic lot size.

EXAMPLE 3

Let the annual demand (Y) of the same item now be 3,000 pieces. All other data will be as in example 1.

Classification of the Item

Criterion 1—holding cost:

A. Unit holding cost of work in process $= \frac{m + c}{2} \cdot t \cdot i = \frac{\$0.562}{3,000} = \$0.00019$

B. Unit holding cost of finished goods $= \frac{c \cdot i}{2 \cdot Y} = \frac{\$0.60}{3,000} = \$0.0002$

A and *B* are of the same order of magnitude, so classification of the item is doubtful.

Criterion 2—holding time:

C. Holding time of work in process (250 pieces) $= Q \cdot t$ (assuming proportionality of lead time) $= 250 \times \frac{2.5}{1,000} = 0.625$ month (approximately)

D. Holding time of finished goods (250 pieces) = 1 month

D is larger than *C*. But the difference is not marked enough to definitely classify the item as slow moving, according to this criterion. The classification of this item is therefore doubtful.

Lot-Size Calculations

E. Camp's formula—work in process neglected:

$$Q = \sqrt{\frac{2Y \cdot S}{c \cdot i}} = \sqrt{\frac{2 \times 3,000 \times 50}{12 \times 0.10}} = 500 \text{ pieces}$$

F. Revised formula—work in process and finished goods both considered:

$$Q = \sqrt{\frac{YS}{\frac{c \cdot i}{2} + \frac{m + c}{2} \cdot Y \cdot t \cdot i}} = \sqrt{\frac{3,000 \times 50}{0.06 + 0.562}} = \sqrt{\frac{150,000}{1.162}} = 360 \text{ pieces}$$

G. Holding cost of finished goods neglected:

$$Q = \sqrt{\frac{YS}{\frac{m + c}{2} \cdot Y \cdot t \cdot i}} = \sqrt{\frac{3,000 \times 50}{0.562}} = 516 \text{ pieces}$$

The lot size obtained by the revised formula (F) is significantly different (approximately 20 percent) from those obtained by other two formulas. It can be shown that total annual cost is lowest for the lot size of 360 pieces. Therefore, economic lot size for items of doubtful classifications should be calculated by the revised formula.

It can be concluded from the above discussion that the consideration of holding cost of work in process is important for fast-moving items and also for items of doubtful classification. Therefore the revised lot-size formula, which takes into account the work in process as well as the finished goods, should be used to calculate economic lot sizes for those items. When the holding cost of work in process is negligible in comparison to that of the finished goods, as in the case of slow-moving items, Camp's formula may be used. On the other hand, the holding cost of finished goods can be neglected when it is very small compared to that of work in process, as in the case of fast-moving items.

INFLUENCE OF SCHEDULING ON LOT SIZE

When the holding cost of work in process is considered, the formula for economic lot size is expressed as

$$Q = \sqrt{\frac{2Y \cdot S}{c \cdot i + \frac{(m + c)}{2} \cdot Y \cdot t \cdot i}}$$

The terms Y, S, m, c, and i are known for any item. The term t has been defined as the total time required to perform all operations on one item.

It was assumed that the next operation is started only after the present one is completed on all parts in the lot. It is obvious that in a manufacturing plant of any size, this practice will not be followed unless the nature of the process determines the timing of operations. For a considerable time during the process, two or more operations may be performed on the same batch simultaneously, thereby reducing the total time of work in process per part.

The following simplified example illustrates the situation.

Let

$$\text{Number of operations} = 3$$

$$\text{Time required per piece per operation} = 0.32 \text{ hours}$$

$$\text{Total time per operation for lot of 1,000 pieces} = 0.32 \times 1{,}000 \text{ hours} = \frac{320}{160}$$

$$= 2 \text{ months (@ 160 hours per month)}$$

The time required between successive operations for handling, etc. = ¼ month

The scheduling of operations is given in Figure 2.

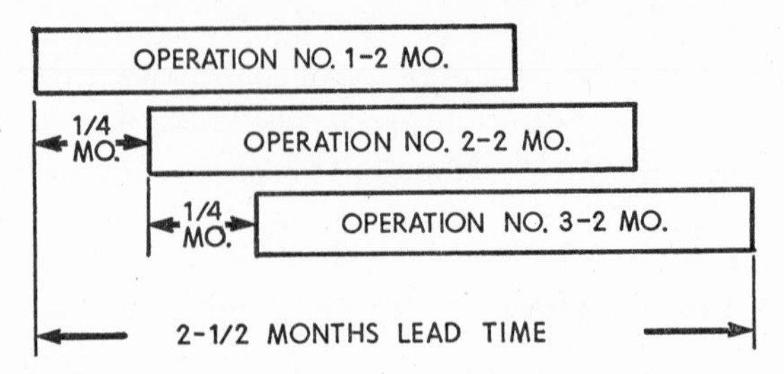

FIGURE 2. Production schedule for a lot of 1,000 pieces.

Lead time, $L = 2.5$ months

$$t = \frac{L}{Q} = \frac{2.5}{1{,}000} m = \frac{2.5 \times 160}{1{,}000} = 0.40 \text{ hours}$$

However, if the operations do not overlap, the total time required per piece for all three operations $= 0.32 \times 3 = 0.96$ hours.

The question may now be asked whether the time per piece obtained from the overlapping schedule for a lot size of 1,000 pieces will remain the same when a lot size of 500 pieces is processed. Let us draw another simple schedule for a lot size of 500 pieces, assuming that one quarter of a month is still necessary between successive operations for handling, etc. The schedule is given in Figure 3:

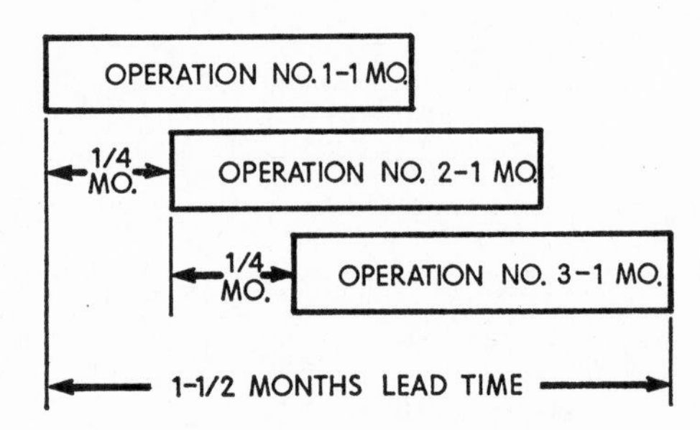

FIGURE 3. Production schedule for a lot size of 500 pieces.

$$L = 1.5 \text{ months} = 240 \text{ hours}$$

$$t = \frac{L}{Q} = \frac{240}{500} = 0.48 \text{ hours}$$

The total time per piece now comes out to be 0.48 hours in place of 0.40 hours as obtained for 1,000 pieces.

The unit holding time for work in process, t, therefore varies with both the effectiveness of scheduling and the size of the lot processed.

When the holding cost of work in process is considered, it is necessary to know the holding time per piece, t, for the work in process in order to calculate the lot size.

In the formula

$$Q = \sqrt{\frac{2Y \cdot S}{c_s \cdot i + (m + c) \cdot Y \cdot t \cdot i}}$$

t cannot be calculated if the correct lot quantity is not known. It is suggested that as a first approximation the lead time should be determined for an estimated lot size. (The actual lead time may be obtained from previous production records of comparable lots or from the actual schedule when it is available.) The time per piece calculated from the lead time of the estimated lot size will be used for the calculation of the economic lot size. If the economic lot size turns out to be much different from the estimated lot size, it can be recalculated using the time per piece, now based on the lot size obtained from the first calculation. Either the first or the second approximation will generally be close enough for practical purposes.

In practice, it appears to be satisfactory to assume that the lead time is directly proportional to the lot size within a small range, that is, to assume that if the lead time for 1,000 pieces is 2½ months, the lead time for 800 pieces is two months. In that case the holding time per piece will be independent of the lot size within that range. The nearer we can estimate the economic lot size, the smaller the initial error will be in calculating t.

Variation of Lot Size with Scheduling and Methods Improvement

From formula 2, it is observed that lot size is increased when the unit holding time, t, for work in process is reduced. The value of t depends on the length of lead time and also on the time required for each operation. Whenever there is scope for improvement, the time t can be reduced by increasing the effectiveness of scheduling and improving the methods of production, either of which will result in an increase in economic lot size [2].

CONCLUSION

Consideration of the holding cost of the work-in-process inventory is often very important in determining the economic lot size for manufactured products. Such consideration is essential in the case of fast-moving items and less important in the case of slow-moving items. In those cases where the unit holding cost of finished goods is negligible in comparison to that of work in process, the lot size becomes independent of the annual demand. On the other hand, when the holding cost of work in process is negligible in comparison to that of the finished goods, Camp's formula gives sufficiently accurate results for practical use. The consideration of both work-in-process holding cost and finished goods holding cost is necessary in intermediate cases for obtaining optimum lot size.

Scheduling of production operations also has considerable effect on the economic lot size. The economic lot size can be increased by efficient scheduling and reduction of operation times through methods improvements.

REFERENCES

1. Alford, L. P., and Bangs, J. R. *Production Handbook*, p. 101. New York: Ronald Press Co., 1944.
2. Raymond, F. E. *Quantity and Economy in Manufacture*, p. 81. New York: McGraw-Hill Book Co., Inc., 1931.
3. Raymond, F. E. "Economic Production Quantities," *ASME Transactions*, January–April, 1928, pp. 65–80.
4. Camp, W. E. "Determining Production Order Quantity," *Management Engineering*, January, 1922, pp. 17–18.
5. Eidmann, F. L. *Economic Control of Engineering and Manufacturing*, pp. 245–49. New York: McGraw-Hill Book Co., Inc., 1931.
6. Koepke, C. A. *Plant Production Control*, pp. 436–51. 2d ed. New York: John Wiley & Sons, Inc., 1951.

21

This article is essentially a case study involving the application of a production-inventory model. The model is developed by separately considering assembly costs (with a learning curve), fabrication costs, materials costs (with price breaks), and inventory costs (raw materials, goods in process, and finished goods—each considered separately). The total annual cost function is then derived, and a brief description of the technique for solving the model using a computer is presented.

*A STUDY OF OPTIMUM ASSEMBLY RUNS**†

Edwin S. Mills and Hartsel G. McClain

DESPITE the extensive theoretical development of the subject during the last decade or so, there is still no surfeit of published studies reporting successful applications of production and inventory control models. This paper reports one such study in which elements of discreteness and choice among alternative productive processes are considered. The plant in which the study was undertaken produces approximately two dozen major electronic equipments, mainly for use in or with commercial aircraft. The main qualitative elements of the problem are as follows:

Most equipments are produced in discrete runs, assembly taking place for a few months, during which inventory accumulates rapidly. Assembly then ceases, and sales are made from inventory for several more months until a new run is started. There is still, however, considerable choice as to the rate of assembly during a run. The assembly of each equipment—a radar set, for example—consists of dozens or hundreds of elementary rated operations: placing and cutting a wire, soldering, fastening a mechanical component, etc. These operations are grouped into subtasks, each of which is assigned to an assembly operator. The rated time for all the operations in a given subtask defines the assembly time cycle for that operator. Choice results from the fact that there are many different ways of grouping operations into subtasks, so that more or fewer operators are employed in the assembly of each equipment.[1] If 10 operators are employed on an assembly line using a one-hour

* Reprinted from *Operations Research*, January–February, 1961, pp. 30–38.

† The study was undertaken in the Aviation Electronics Division of the Bendix Aviation Corporation, Baltimore, Maryland. The authors are indebted to W. A. MacCrehan of that organization for valuable guidance and assistance.

[1] The related "line-balancing" problem was not considered in this study. The procedure described for selecting the appropriate time cycle implies that the line-balancing problem has already been solved for each time cycle considered.

time cycle, output per unit time is naturally much higher than if five operators are employed using a two-hour cycle. Thus, two related decisions must be made simultaneously. Not only must the length of the run be ascertained, but also the time cycle to be employed. The second decision is complicated by the fact that different time cycles have different "learning curves" (which affect production costs) and different time rates of output (which affect inventory costs).

Three distinct classes of activities are involved in the production process. These are materials purchases, parts fabrication, and final assembly. Substantial economies in each activity are associated with long assembly runs. Price breaks are obtained on purchased materials, fewer setups are required, and operator efficiency increases in both fabrication and assembly. The variation of assembly costs with run length is complicated by the following factors:

1. Learning curves are different for different time cycles.
2. Base hourly rates of pay are higher for operators who work on very long time cycles.
3. A system of bonus payments is provided for in the union contract such that, if an operator completes her subtask in less than its rated time, her hourly pay rises proportionately with any increased efficiency.

Inventory charges are based on the cost of materials, goods in process, and finished goods in inventory on the last day of each month. In addition to the usual factors of interest, insurance, taxes, handling, and imputed rental costs, some equipments are subject to a considerable inventory cost from obsolescence and modifications required if a unit spends a considerable time in inventory.

A 12-month sales forecast is made for each equipment when a run is planned. These forecasts are necessarily subject to considerable error. This is partly due to the unexpected placing and canceling of orders by customers. In part, it is also due to unexpected changes in delivery dates when, for example, an airframe manufacturer requests postponement of delivery for six months. No attempt was made to improve these forecasts as part of this project since this would require a major study in itself.

DEVELOPMENT OF THE MODEL

Assembly Costs

It was felt desirable to estimate direct labor assembly costs directly from timecard records of operator performance. From these data, learning curves were estimated for each of three sets of assembly cycles, with rated times of about one-half, one, and two hours. Such a learning curve for a particular time cycle is valid for use with any equipment, since rated operations are common to all equipments. The basic learning curve formula employed was of the common form

$$y = A_k z^{a_k} \tag{1}$$

where y is the percent efficiency reached in the assembly of the zth unit using a k-hour cycle ($k = \frac{1}{2}$, 1, 2), and A_k and a_k are constants to be estimated from the records. Equation 1 was fitted by least squares to data for dozens of runs for each of the three time cycles. The calculations were performed on a digital computer. Some surprise was registered at the fact that the learning curves for the two longer time cycles were everywhere above that for the half-hour cycle, indicating that a higher percent of efficiency is reached on each unit assembled when the long rather than the short cycles are used. It was decided that the following factors explain this result: Operators on longer cycles are higher paid, more experienced, and more skilled; short cycles require more operators on an assembly line, and this increases the risk of delay caused by absence of an operator, presence of a particularly slow operator, interruptions, etc.; operators tend to become bored with short, repetitive cycles.

An efficiency of 100 percent is reached when the subtask is completed in the rated time. The percent of efficiency reached in assembly of the zth unit is simply the ratio of the time required to complete the operation at 100 percent efficiency to the time actually required, all multiplied by 100. Thus, $y = 100\ \mathrm{k}/t_k(z)$, where k is the rated time for the cycle and $t_k(z)$ is the actual assembly time on the zth unit using a k-hour cycle. Then, using equation 1, we find

$$t_k(z) = 100\ k/y = 100\ kz^{-a_k}/A_k$$

The total number of hours required for the operator to reach 100 percent efficiency is

$$T_k(z_k) = \int_0^{z_k} t_k(z)\ dz = \frac{100\ kz_k^{(1-a_k)}}{A_k(1 - ak)}$$

where z_k is the unit on which 100 percent efficiency is reached, i.e., z_k satisfies $t_k(z_k) = k$.

Conversion of this efficiency information into costs requires consideration of the fact that premium rates are paid on base hourly pay rates that do not include fringe benefits and cost-of-living adjustments. Writing W_k for the base hourly wage rate of an operator on a k-hour cycle, and g_k for her fringe benefits per hour, the cost per operator of assembling the first z_k units is

$$(W_k + g_k)\ T_k(z_k) \tag{2}$$

On the next unit, premium pay starts. The hourly pay then becomes

$$kW_k/t_k(z) + g_k$$

for $z > z_k$, since the operator's premium pay is $(100 + r)$ percent of her base pay (W_k) when she reaches $(100 + r)$ percent efficiency, plus g_k. Hence the total cost per operator of the assembly of units z_k to z is

$$\int_{z_k}^{z} \left(\frac{kW_k}{t_k(z)} + g\right) t_k(z)\ dz = kW_k(Z - z_k) + g_k[T_k(Z) - T_k(z_k)] \tag{3}$$

The cost of the first z units is the sum of equations 2 and 3:

$$(4) \qquad \begin{aligned} C_k(Z) &= (W_k + g_k)\, T_k(z_k) + kW_k(Z - z_k) + g[T_k(Z) - T_k(z_k)] \\ &= W_k T_k(z_k) + kW_k(Z - z_k) + g_k T_k(Z) \end{aligned}$$

Equation 4 is the cost per operator of assembling z units. If an equipment has a rated time of H hours, then H/k operators are required, and the total assembly cost is

$$(5) \qquad L_k(Z) = (H/k)\, C_k(Z)$$

For $Z > z_k$, substitution for $T_k(z)$ and collection of terms shows that $L_k(Z)$ has the form

$$(5a) \qquad L_k(Z) = b_{1k} + b_{2k}\, Z + b_{3k}\, Z^{b_{4k}}$$

Fabrication Costs

The study of direct labor costs in parts fabrication was simplified by the fact that mainly machine time is involved, and hence the complication of different assembly cycles did not arise. Records indicated that unit labor costs decline approximately exponentially as run size increases. This suggests fitting to the data a function of the form

$$(6) \qquad C_F(z) = C_F[1 + B_F \exp(-\alpha_F z)]$$

Here C_F is the base or rated cost per equipment of fabricated parts, and $C_F B_F \exp(-\alpha_F z)$ is the starting load which must be added for a run of z units; α_F and B_F were estimated from historical cost records by least squares, and again the calculations were performed on a digital computer. Since equation 6 represents unit costs, $zC_F(z)$ gives total direct labor costs in fabrication for a run of z units. In addition, fabrication involves setup costs of, say, S dollars. Thus, total fabrication costs are

$$(7) \qquad S + zC_F(z) = S + C_F[1 + B_F \exp(-\alpha_F z)]$$

Materials Cost

Price breaks for materials tend to occur at discrete points. However, many different materials are contained in a given equipment, and the price breaks occur at different points for different materials. The result is that the unit cost of materials declines rather smoothly with the length of the run. Some experimentation indicated that this could be represented by the simple piecewise linear function

$$(8) \qquad m(z) = \begin{cases} P_0 z & (z < z_0) \\ [P_0 + (P_0 - P_1)(z - z_0)/(z_0 - z_1)]\, z & (z_0 \leqq z \leqq z_1) \\ P_1 z & (z_1 < z) \end{cases}$$

This means that for runs of less than z_0 units, unit materials cost is P_0 dollars. For runs of more than z_1 units, unit materials cost is P_1 dollars ($P_1 < P_0$, $z_0 < z_1$). In between runs of z_0 and z_1, unit costs falls off linearly from P_0 to P_1.

Summarizing, we can say that total production cost for a run of z units is the sum of assembly, fabrication, and materials costs, represented respectively by equations 5*a*, 7, and 8. We can represent this sum by

$$K_k(z) = L_k(z) + S + zC_F(z) + m(z) \tag{9}$$

Inventory Costs

Subsections 1–3 below consider the inventory costs associated with a run for each major inventory type—raw materials, goods in process, and finished goods.

1. The number of dollar-months of raw material inventory is the value of raw materials used in the run multiplied by the average number of months spent in inventory prior to the commencement of the run. The latter factor is largely determined by scheduling requirements that are independent of the number of units in the run. Hence the average time spent in material inventory is a constant n and

$$nm(z) \tag{10}$$

dollar-months of inventory result.

2. *Goods in Process.* A run of z units takes N months when a k-hour time cycle is used, resulting in P_k units assembled per month. Thus, $NP_k = z$. Using the approximation that production takes place evenly through time during assembly, this means that the $m(z)$ dollars of material spend an average of $N/2 = z/2P_k$ months in process. Thus:

$$m(z)z/2P_k \tag{11}$$

dollar-months of inventory result. During the assembly process, labor value is added to the materials. From equation 5, $L_k(z)$ dollars of labor value are added, and the assembly process requires H hours. (H hours is the rated assembly time per unit of the equipment.) Using the approximation that labor is added at an even rate, the average labor dollar spends $\frac{1}{2}H$ hours or $\frac{1}{320}H$ months (assuming 160 working hours in a month) in process. Thus, for a run of z units the total number of dollar-months of labor-in-process inventory is

$$\tfrac{1}{320}\, H\, L_k(z) \tag{12}$$

3. *Finished Goods.* Units are put into finished goods inventory at a rate of P_k per month during the N months of the run. Since the only sales forecast available is for the 12-month period following the beginning of the run, some assumption concerning the monthly rate of sales must be made. The simplest assumption is that whatever annual sales, x, may result, sales in each month

are $x/12$ units. Since an examination of past sales data revealed no seasonal pattern, this assumption was embodied in the model. Assume further that each run is started when the finished goods inventory of the equipment is exhausted.[2] Then the number of units in finished goods inventory at the end of any month is the cumulated difference between output and sales since the beginning of the run. Since the inventory is exhausted in month j where $\frac{1}{12} jx = z$, the total number of unit-months of finished goods inventory associated with a given run is

$$(P_k - \tfrac{1}{12} x) + \cdots + (NP_k - \tfrac{1}{12} NX) + [NP_k - \tfrac{1}{12} (N+1) x] + \cdots + (NP_k - 12 z/x) = z^2 (6/x - 1/2P_k)$$

This last step follows by eliminating N in the first expression with $NP_k = z$ and summing the separate terms. Each unit of finished goods inventory is valued at the average cost of production, which from equation 9 is $K_k(z)/z$. Hence the total number of dollar-months of finished goods inventory associated with the run is

$$K_k(z)(6/x - 1/2P_k) \tag{13}$$

Summarizing, we can say that the total number of dollar-months of inventory associated with the run is the sum of the materials, goods in process, and finished goods terms represented by formulas 10, 11, 12, and 13. It is assumed that each dollar-month of inventory costs R dollars (100 R is the percentage cost). Thus the total inventory cost associated with the run is

$$I_k(z,x) = R\,[n\, m(z) + m(z)\, z/2P_k + \tfrac{1}{320} H\, L_k(z) + K_k(z)\, z\, (6/x - 1/2P_k)] \tag{14}$$

For some items a special obsolescence cost attaches to finished goods inventory. In an industry such as electronics, where products are subject to rapid technological change, modifications may be required on items that spend more than a very short time in finished goods inventory. This was taken into account by weighting the finished goods term in equation 14 by a factor $\lambda > 1$. Here, $\lambda - 1$ represents the dollar cost of modifications expected to be required per dollar-month of finished goods inventory; λ was estimated purely on the basis of the judgment of personnel concerned.

The sum of equations 9 and 14 gives us the total production and inventory costs associated with a run of z units when a k-hour time cycle is used and annual sales are x units, viz., $K_k(z) + I_k(z,x)$. The decision criterion employed with this model is the minimization of the expected value of annual costs. To convert the above expression to annual costs, we recognize that if

[2] A more general and more common procedure would be to assume that the inventory (or shortages) at the beginning of a run was a random variable and that shortages involve a cost similar in structure to the cost of inventories. Though this is not difficult to include in the model presented here, it was not done in this study. The reason is that for the items covered by the study, delivery can usually be speeded up or delayed a month or so without risk of sales loss. Thus, if the firm tries to start each run approximately when the inventory of the item runs out, this flexibility means that there is little cost to be associated with errors in forecasting demand during the lead time.

annual sales are x units and each run contains z units, then x/z runs are required.[3] Thus the total annual costs are

$$(x/z)[K_k(z) + I_k(z,x)] \tag{15}$$

To obtain the expected value of annual costs, we multiply expression 15 by $f(x)$, the distribution function of sales, and integrate, giving

$$V_k(z) = \int_0^\infty \frac{x}{z}[K_k(z) + I_k(z,x)]f(x)\,dx \tag{16}$$

An inspection of equation 14 makes it clear that x enters equation 15 only linearly. Hence, only the expected value of x, $\bar{x}$, appears in expression 16. In fact, equation 16 can be written

$$\text{(16a)}\quad V_k(z) = (\bar{x}/z)\,K_k(z) + (R\bar{x}/z)[n\,m(z) + m(z)\,z/2P_k + \tfrac{1}{320}\,H\,L_k(z)] + R\,K_k(z)(6 - \bar{x}/2P_k)$$

This means that the optimum z can be found independently of information about any of the moments of $f(x)$ other than its mean.[4] In other words, all that we need to know is that the sales forecast is unbiased so that it can be taken for $\bar{x}$.

PRACTICAL APPLICATION

Equation 16*a* is a rather complex equation to evaluate manually. In the study on which this paper is based, the computations were performed on a Bendix G–15 computer. Once the program had been written out, this proved to be a valuable and inexpensive procedure. The technique used is as follows. For each value of k, a guess is made as to the value of z which minimized $V_k(z)$. The computer then starts from this point and searches for the z which minimizes $V_k(z)$, recording both the z and the minimum cost so found. This yields a minimum-cost run length for each of three time cycles ($k = \frac{1}{2}$, 1, 2). That time cycle is chosen whose minimum cost is least. This procedure yields the optimum run, the optimum time cycle, and the annual costs that can be expected to result. In addition, the computer can tabulate $V_k(z)$ term by term for various values of z in an interval around the optimum value z^*. This makes it possible to show separately the effects on the costs of direct labor, materials, and the three classes of inventory resulting from run lengths different from the optimum. Such information is valuable to man-

---

[3] When x/z is an integer, this procedure seems completely unobjectionable. In general, however, this is not true; and in this case, some assumption about end-of-year inventory is implicit in equation 15. There are two equivalent ways of stating this assumption. One is that only the cost of goods actually sold this year should be imputed to this year's operations. The other is that end-of-year inventory should be valued at its cost of production. Both of these are standard accounting conventions, and both lead to the representation of total annual costs by equation 15.

[4] It should be noted that this result assumes that the probability that $x/12 > P_k$ is negligible.

agement not only for the immediate problem of determining optimum run length but also in making more general decisions concerned with pricing policy, sales promotion, etc. In all the cases so far encountered, $V_k(z)$ has had only one local minimum, so that no problems of multiplicities have been encountered. On the other hand, this appears to result from the particular cost relations which have been used rather than from the structure of the model.

In many cases, it is feasible to find z^*, at least to a good approximation, without the use of a high-speed computer. This depends very greatly on the form of the materials, assembly, and fabrication cost functions included in equation 16. Using the specific forms of these functions introduced above, the following procedure was found to be very accurate and only moderately tedious. First, it was found that z^* almost always lay between the values z_0 and z_1 introduced in the section "Materials Cost." In other words, it was rarely worthwhile to have a run longer than that necessary to exploit all available economies in materials purchasing. Within this interval a guess $\bar{z}$ of z^* is made. This guess is inserted in equation 9, and the total production cost, $K_k(\bar{z})$, is found. This gives the unit production cost, $\bar{K}_k = K_k(\bar{z})/\bar{z}$ of a run of $\bar{z}$ units. Then the true total production cost, $K_k(z)$, which appears twice in equation 16*a*, is replaced by the approximate value $\bar{K}_k\, z$. Since $K_k(z)$ is much the most complicated term in equation 16*a*, this modification greatly simplifies the computations. It is then an easy matter to find the z which minimizes the modified form of equation 16*a*, since the modification involves nothing more complicated than powers of z. The basic idea behind this procedure is to approximate the complicated term $K_k(z)$ in equation 16*a* by one which is much simpler. This means that $K_k(z)$ must be evaluated only once. The accuracy of the approximation depends on the fact that in any small interval around z^* the average cost of production will be about the same as that at z^*. If further accuracy is desired, a second iteration can be undertaken using as a "guess" of z^* the result of the first iteration, just described. It may be necessary to follow this procedure for each value of k in order to determine the optimum time cycle. It would probably not be feasible to do the term-by-term tabulation described above if manual calculation must be employed.

It should also be mentioned that a slight modification of the model makes it possible to consider more complicated materials-ordering, production-run policies. For example, it might be profitable to order at one time the materials for two or more production runs (run splitting). Furthermore, it is sometimes possible to order at one time the materials for several production runs but to have deliveries "spaced" in order to coincide more nearly with the timing of production runs. By introducing one more parameter into equation 16*a*, the profitability of these policies can be investigated.

This model is now being used on a routine basis in the firm for which the study was undertaken. When a run of a major equipment is planned, the estimating department estimates the base assembly and fabrication labor costs and setup costs. The purchasing department estimates the materials cost information described in the section "Materials Cost." Together with several preliminary sales forecasts, this information is inserted in the model equation 16*a*, and the computer tabulates detailed production and inventory costs for a variety of run lengths around the optimum run length for each preliminary sales forecast. On the basis of this and other information, a final sales forecast is made, and the appropriate run length is chosen.

The use of the model has not involved any dramatic change in policies previously followed. Formerly, there was some tendency to "split" runs (i.e., have two short runs separated by a few months) in order to keep finished goods inventory at a low level. The model indicates that this is a false economy since the resulting higher production costs more than offset the lower inventory costs. The savings from this change appear to be in the neighborhood of 5 percent of variable production costs. Aside from this, previous policy does not appear to have been systematically different from that indicated by the model, though individual decisions differ substantially as between the operations research and "intuitive" approaches. In addition to correcting these faults, the model has made the calculation of run lengths more systematic and more efficient. It has had the further desirable effect of focusing management's attention on certain elements—such as the sales forecast—which crucially influence production decisions regardless of the decision-making technique employed.

22

The author asserts that use of a simple break-even analysis can result in error when choosing between alternative production schedules. In order to demonstrate this fact, simplified break-even and production economic lot-size models are described; thereafter a combined model is developed in which are introduced certain hypothetical data. Errors implicit in the break-even model are elicited from an analysis of this combined model, and conditions which are likely to accentuate the effect of these errors are listed.

*AN INVESTIGATION OF SOME QUANTITATIVE RELATIONSHIPS BETWEEN BREAK-EVEN POINT ANALYSIS AND ECONOMIC LOT-SIZE THEORY**

Wayland P. Smith

Two common tools utilized to evaluate the economic potential of alternative ways of performing a specified task are (1) break-even point analysis and (2) economic lot-size theory.

These two techniques have become the basic devices around which many courses in engineering economics have been built over the past 40 years. Most engineering undergraduate students at some time are exposed to these two fundamental methods. Industrial engineers, in particular, find a persistent recurrence of problems that utilize one or the other of these models in their solution.

In retrospect, one wonders why these two schemes have never been combined into one common model. On the other hand, they have primarily been developed to solve two problems that at least on the surface appear to be quite divergent. The purpose of this paper is to show that these problems are

* Reprinted from *Journal of Industrial Engineering*, January–February, 1958, pp. 52–57. The *Journal* is the official publication of the American Institute of Industrial Engineers, Inc., 345 East 47th Street, New York, New York 10017.

not divergent, that they have much in common, and that they are actually very much interrelated. In short, a single mathematical formulation will be developed that relates the two theories.

Before presenting such a combined formulation, a brief review is presented of the two basic techniques in very simple form. The purpose of this review is twofold: (1) to reestablish the assumptions on which these two techniques are based and (2) to establish a common set of symbols that will be helpful for the combined formulation.

A SIMPLIFIED BREAK-EVEN POINT MODEL

The historical development of break-even analysis and the break-even chart would be exceedingly difficult to trace. Like many other techniques, it was simultaneously created and developed by many people with the rapid growth of the scientific management movement during the early years of the 20th century. It was one of the techniques that was quickly exploited.

Certainly, Dr. Walter Rautenstrauch was one of the principal developers and proponents of this technique [7]. It is to be found in practically all books which deal with engineering economy problems [1, 2, 3, 4, 10, 13].

Generally, it is treated in its most simple form for solving short-range problems, and the time-value-of-money aspect of the problem is omitted. This is not always the case, and more sophisticated methods involving different basic assumptions have been developed. One of these is the MAPI formulation [6, 9].

Although many types of problems lend themselves to break-even analysis, a specific type of problem is of concern here—the economic comparison of two alternative methods of performing a task (actually, any number of alternatives can be compared simultaneously by this procedure).

Costs for each alternative are divided into two categories and called either fixed costs or variable costs. The fixed costs are those costs that occur only once during the life of the alternative. Once these costs have been expended, they are not recoverable. Examples of such costs are

1. Setup and teardown cost
2. Cost of special tooling
3. Paper work and clerical cost required to schedule a job

In other words, the fixed costs are those costs that are not incurred by every unit of production. If we were to plot cost versus the number of units produced, these costs would appear as step functions. In the most simple problem, only those fixed costs that occur prior to the first unit of production are included. This is frequently done when the other fixed costs are assumed to be negligible.

Conversely, variable costs are those costs that are incurred by every unit of production. Examples of such costs are

1. Direct labor cost per piece
2. Direct material cost per piece
3. Depreciation

Once both types of costs have been identified for each alternative, it is possible to write a total cost equation for each one of the alternatives in terms of production quantity:

(1) Total cost = (Summation of all fixed costs) + (Production quantity) × (Summation of all variable costs)

where

C_i = Total cost of the ith alternative
f_{xi} = An initial cost of the ith alternative
F_i = Summation of all initial fixed cost for the ith alternative
v_{xi} = A variable cost of the ith alternative
V_i = Summation of all variable cost for the ith alternative
N = The quantity to be produced

then

$C_i = (f_{1i} + f_{2i} + \cdots) + N(v_{1i} + v_{2i} + \cdots)$

or

$$C_i = F_i + NV_i$$

If C_i is plotted against N for each alternative, a simple graphical relationship results (Fig. 1). F_i becomes the y intercept and V_i becomes the slope of the straight line that this equation represents. If the two alternatives have been selected such that the one having the lower F_i has the higher V_i, then the two lines will intersect at some positive value of N. This point is called the break-even point. It represents the quantity at which the total costs are the

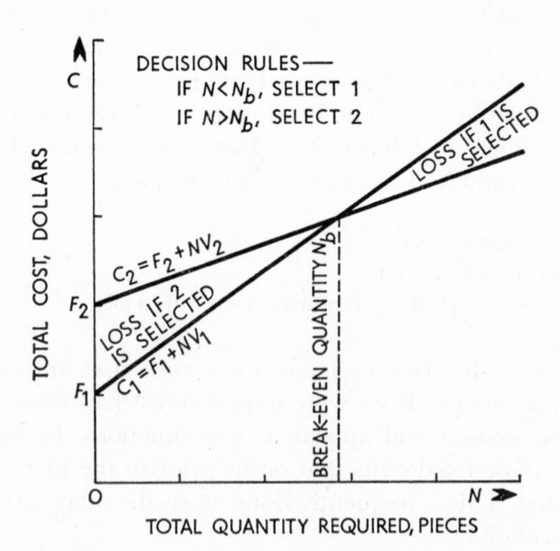

FIGURE 1. A break-even chart for two alternatives.

same for both alternatives. When the demand for the product is greater than this break-even quantity, then the alternative with the lower V_i is more economical. When the required quantity is less than the break-even point, then the alternative with the lower F_i is the more economical.

In a quantitative manner, this analysis tells us what we recognize intuitively—that a production method with relatively low fixed costs and high variable costs will be more economical at lower quantities, while a production with relatively high fixed costs and low variable costs will be more economical at higher quantities.

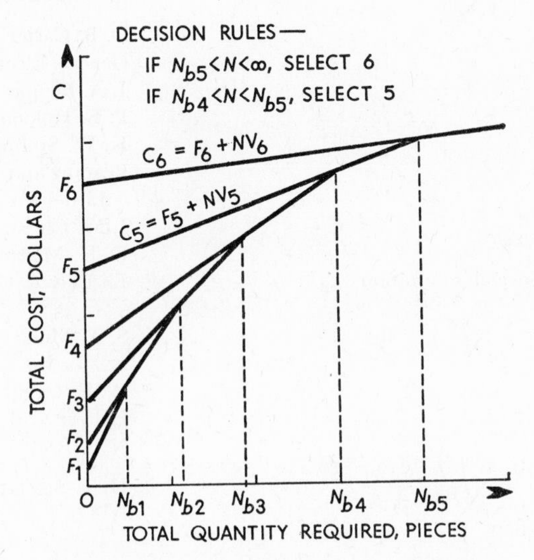

FIGURE 2. Break-even chart for multiple-alternative case.

It also reminds us that no single production method is best for all quantities of production. Since minor and major methods of variation are easy to conceive through changes in machines, tools, men, motion patterns, etc., it should not be too difficult to imagine an almost infinite number of possible production methods from which to choose—each with its own small range of production quantities over which it is more economical than any other alternative (Fig. 2).

A SIMPLIFIED PRODUCTION ECONOMIC LOT-SIZE MODEL

Like break-even analysis, economic lot-size theory was developed during the period from 1910 through 1930. Its historical development has been clearly traced by F. E. Raymond in his monumental treatise on the subject [8]. Since this book tells the story so well and contains a complete bibliog-

TABLE 1

EQUATIONS EMPLOYED TO SHOW THE STAGES IN THE DEVELOPMENT OF FORMULAS FOR ECONOMIC LOT SIZES

First Appearance	*Form*	*Authorities*	*Approximate Date of Record*
1912	Cubic equation not published	G. D. Babcock	1912
1915	$Q = \sqrt{\frac{P \cdot S}{c} \cdot k}$	F. W. Harris	1915
		D. B. Carter	
		General Electric Co.	
		J. A. Bennie	1922
		P. E. Holden	1922
		K. W. Stillman	1923
		Benning and Littlefield	1924
		J. M. Christman	1925
		G. H. Mellen	1925
1917	Special adaptation	Eli Lillv & Co.	1917
1917	$Q = \sqrt{\frac{P \cdot S}{c \cdot i} \cdot k}$	S. A. Morse	1917
		W. E. Camp	1922
		Heltzer Cabot Co.	1924
		N. R. Richardson	1927
	$Q = \sqrt{\frac{P \cdot S \cdot k}{c \cdot (i + f_i)}}$ where f_i = Allowances for insurance, storage costs, etc.	H. T. Stock	1923
		B. Cooper	1926
1918	$Q = \sqrt{\frac{P \cdot S \cdot D'}{c \cdot i(D' - S)} \cdot k}$	G. Pennington	1927
		E. T. Phillips	1927
		W. L. Jones	1929
		J. W. Hallock	1929
1918	$Q = -\frac{P}{c} + \sqrt{\frac{P^2}{c^2} + \frac{P \cdot S \cdot D'}{c \cdot i(D' - S)} \cdot k}$	E. W. Taft	1918
1923	$Q = \sqrt{\frac{P \cdot S \cdot k}{c \cdot i \cdot f_a + \frac{a \cdot b}{h} \cdot k'b}}$	G. Pennington	1927
		F. H. Thompson	1923
		R. C. Davis	1926
		C. N. Neklutin	1929
1924	$Q = \sqrt{\frac{P \cdot S \cdot k}{c \cdot i + (m + c) \cdot t_p \cdot S \cdot i}}$	A. C. Brungardt	1923
		P. N. Lehoczky	1927

raphy, it would be superfluous to repeat it here. However, a table from this text showing the development of economic lot-size formulas has been reproduced here because it is so revealing (see Table 1).

The operations research movement stemming from the success of operations evaluation groups in the various services during World War II has given a rebirth to economic lot-size theory. It is interesting to note, however, that the recent writings of many operations researchers seem oblivious of the work done during the 1920's. At least, there appears to be some hesitancy toward acknowledging this earlier work [5, 11]. Economic lot size as it relates to inventory control has also been treated recently by T. M. Whitin in the theory of inventory management [12].

In the production of goods when the rate of production exceeds the rate of demand, the production must proceed in batches if the maximum production rate of the process is to be fully utilized. Otherwise, a ponderous, growing stockpile will soon exist. The question arises as to the size of these batches or length of the run or the number of batches or lots to be started each year (in other words, four ways of stating the same problem).

In order to achieve the lot size that is most economical, two opposing cost elements must be considered. On the one hand, there are the costs that are incurred for each new lot, namely, setup costs of the process, including necessary scheduling, handling, paper work, etc. These costs are relatively proportional to the number of lots and would tend to make the lot size large. On the other hand, there are the costs incurred due to the storage of items necessitated by the production rate being higher than the demand rate. When long production runs are made, the amount of storage space required and the amount of money involved in inventory would increase. These costs would tend to make the lot size small.

Economic lot-size theory, as does break-even analysis, involves the development of the total cost equation for any specific situation of this kind:

(2)[1] Total cost = (Number of lots) × (Preparation and setup cost) + (Production quantity) × (Sum of all variable costs) + (Average inventory quantity) × (Inventory cost per unit during a given time period) × (Number of time periods during the demand period)

where

C_i = Total cost of the ith alternative
N = Total quantity to be produced
n = Lot-size quantity
F_i = Sum of preparation and setup costs for the ith alternative
V_i = Sum of variable costs for the ith alternative
P_i = Production rate (after setup) for the ith alternative
D = Demand rate
$\frac{n}{2}\left(1 - \frac{D}{P_i}\right)$ = Average inventory quantity (assuming a constant demand rate)
I = Sum of storage and inventory costs per unit during a given time period

[1] This only is true where $P > D$.

Then

$$C_i = \left(\frac{N}{n}\right) F_i + NV_i + \left(\frac{n}{2}\right)\left(1 - \frac{D}{P_i}\right)\left(\frac{N}{D}\right) I$$

or

$$C_i = N\left[\left(\frac{I}{2}\right)\left(\frac{1}{D} - \frac{1}{P_i}\right) n^1 + V_i n^0 + F_i n^{-1}\right]$$

If C_i is plotted against n for a specific alternative, a simple graphical relationship results for any specified value of D. This represents the graphical sum of the three costs in equation 2. (Refer to Fig. 3.)

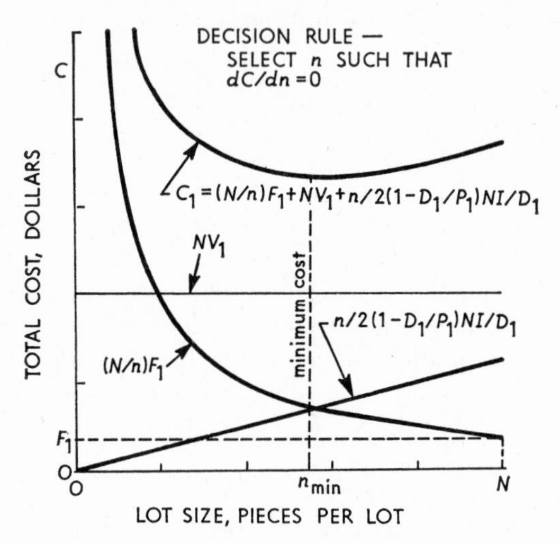

FIGURE 3. Graphic formulation of economic lot for a single alternative.

By setting the first derivative of cost with respect to the lot size equal to zero, it is possible to find the lot size which yields minimum cost:

$$\frac{dC_i}{dn} = 0 = N\left[\frac{I}{2}\left(\frac{1}{D} - \frac{1}{P_i}\right) - \frac{F_i}{n^2}\right] \tag{3}$$

$$n = \sqrt{\frac{2F_i}{I\left(\frac{1}{D} - \frac{1}{P_i}\right)}} \tag{4}$$

If this value of n is substituted back into equation 2, a total cost equation results which is the minimum cost for any value of N:

$$\min_{C_i} = N\left\{\left(\frac{I}{2}\right)\left(\frac{1}{D}-\frac{1}{P_i}\right)\sqrt{\frac{2F_i}{I\left(\frac{1}{D}-\frac{1}{P_i}\right)}} + V_i + F_i\sqrt{\frac{I\left(\frac{1}{D}-\frac{1}{P_i}\right)}{2F_i}}\right\}$$

(5)

$$\min_{C_i} = N\left\{\sqrt{\frac{I\left(\frac{1}{D}-\frac{1}{P_i}\right)F_i}{2}} + V_i + \sqrt{\frac{I\left(\frac{1}{D}-\frac{1}{P_i}\right)F_i}{2}}\right\}$$

$$\min_{C_i} = N\sqrt{2I\left(\frac{1}{D}-\frac{1}{P_i}\right)F_i} + NV_i$$

When this result is compared with equation 1, there is considerable similarity. The variable cost term is identical. The coefficient of the fixed cost term in the economic lot-size formulation is considerably more complex than that of the break-even formulation. In the break-even formulation, this coefficient is unity.

It should be apparent from the foregoing simple formulation of economic lot size that the concept of alternative manufacturing methods is totally ignored. Economic lot-size theory as developed here assumes one and only one manufacturing method. While this may be realistic enough after production methods have been established, it is not realistic at the time the manufacturing method is being established.

Thus, two methods have been explored. Both of these methods purport to select the best method of doing a job. But these two techniques are based upon assumptions that are radically different. *Break-even analysis ignores inventory cost and assumes a single setup, while economic lot-size theory ignores the possibility of different manufacturing methods with their accompanying differences and fixed and variable cost patterns.*

THE COMBINED MODEL

There are two possible ways of approaching combined formulation of break-even analysis and economic lot-size techniques. The simpler case is the discrete case which assumes a limited finite number of possible production alternatives. The more complex case is the continuous one which assumes an infinite number of alternative production methods. The first case selects the optimum method from several stated possibilities. The second case selects the cost pattern of the optimum alternative and then searches for the method which actually matches this cost pattern. Only the first case is discussed in this report.

To fully explore the discrete case, we will examine a problem involving three alternatives, namely, the old problem of whether it is better to use an engine lathe, a turret lathe, or an automatic lathe to perform a specified manufacturing operation.

To make this combined formulation as realistic as possible, the following values have been assumed:

1. Sum of costs that are incurred each time the job is set up (F_i):
   a) Engine lathe, $F_1 = \$1$
   b) Turret lathe, $F_2 = \$30$
   c) Automatic lathe, $F_3 = \$70$
2. Sum of all variable costs, including direct labor, direct material, and manufacturing expense (V_i):
   a) Engine lathe, $V_1 = 20$ cents per unit
   b) Turret lathe, $V_2 = 10$ cents per unit
   c) Automatic lathe, $V_3 = 5$ cents per unit
3. Sum of all storage and inventory costs per unit of production when stored for *one month*. This amount is the same for all three alternatives (I).
   $I = 12.5$ cents per month per unit
4. Production rate (P_i):
   a) Engine lathe, $P_1 = 5{,}000$ pieces per month
   b) Turret lathe, $P_2 = 15{,}000$ pieces per month
   c) Automatic lathe, $P_3 = 45{,}000$ pieces per month

All of these values are inherent in the particular production method and storage system. In a sense, these are fixed values. In addition, we must know or assume values relative to customer demand. We wish to examine what happens at different levels of customer demand.

To make this formulation more realistic, the following levels have been assumed:

5. Demand rate (D):
   Case No. 1, $D_1 = 100$ pieces per month
   Case No. 2, $D_2 = 1{,}000$ pieces per month
   Case No. 3, $D_3 = 5{,}000$ pieces per month

Now, it is possible to calculate the total cost equation for each alternative according to equation 5. This is done in the three steps shown as follows:

Step No. 1 (the basic equation):

Engine lathe:

$$\min_{C_1} = N\sqrt{\frac{1}{4}\left(\frac{1}{D_j} - \frac{1}{5{,}000}\right) 1} + 0.2N \tag{6}$$

Turret lathe:

$$\min_{C_2} = N\sqrt{\frac{1}{4}\left(\frac{1}{D_j} - \frac{1}{15{,}000}\right) 30} + 0.1N \tag{7}$$

Automatic lathe:

$$\min_{C_3} = N\sqrt{\frac{1}{4}\left(\frac{1}{D_j} - \frac{1}{45{,}000}\right) 70} + 0.05N \tag{8}$$

Step No. 2 $\left(\text{let } K_{ji} = \sqrt{\frac{1}{4}\left(\frac{1}{D_j} - \frac{1}{P_i}\right)}\ F_i\right.$, and find the K value for each alternative at each demand rate—nine cases in all):

	D_1	D_2	D_3
K_1	0.049	0.014	0
K_2	0.274	0.084	0.031
K_3	0.42	0.132	0.056

Step No. 3 (substitute K values into equations 6, 7, and 8, and combine terms):

	D_1	D_2	D_3
$\min c_1$	$0.249N$	$0.214N$	$0.2N$
$\min c_2$	$0.374N$	$0.184N$	$0.131N$
$\min c_3$	$0.425N$	$0.182N$	$0.106N$

It is now possible to plot the total minimum cost of each alternative against the demand rate. Figure 4 shows this relationship.

When a smooth curve is drawn through the points for each alternative, three break-even points become apparent. The engine lathe is the most economical method when the demand rate is greater than zero and less than 450 pieces per month. The turret lathe is the most economical when the demand rate is greater than 450 pieces per month and less than 900 pieces per month.

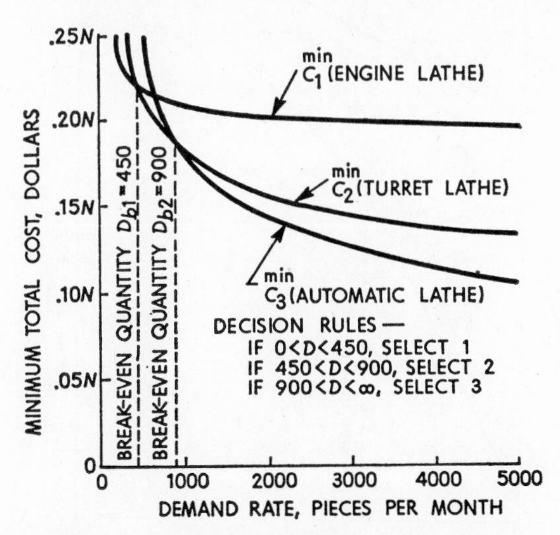

FIGURE 4. Combined formulation for three alternatives.

The automatic lathe is the most economical when the demand rate is greater than 900 pieces per month.

How do these answers compare with those obtained from the typical break-even analysis? In the first place, it should be pointed out that these answers are entirely independent of the total quantity required (N). Thus the answer obtained is much more general. To compare these answers with the standard break-even analysis, it is necessary to assume various values of N.

Substituting known values into equation 1 yields the following total cost equation for each alternative according to the break-even analysis model which has been developed previously:

$$\text{Engine lathe, } C_1 = 1 + 0.2N \quad (9)$$

$$\text{Turret lathe, } C_2 = 30 + 0.1N \quad (10)$$

$$\text{Automatic lathe, } C_3 = 70 + 0.05N \quad (11)$$

When the C_i versus N curves are plotted, three break-even points are once again apparent. The engine lathe is the most economical method when the quantity required is greater than zero and less than 290 pieces. The turret lathe is the most economical method when the quantity required is greater than 290 pieces and less than 800 pieces. The automatic lathe is the most economical when the quantity required is in excess of 800 pieces. This relationship is shown in Figure 5.

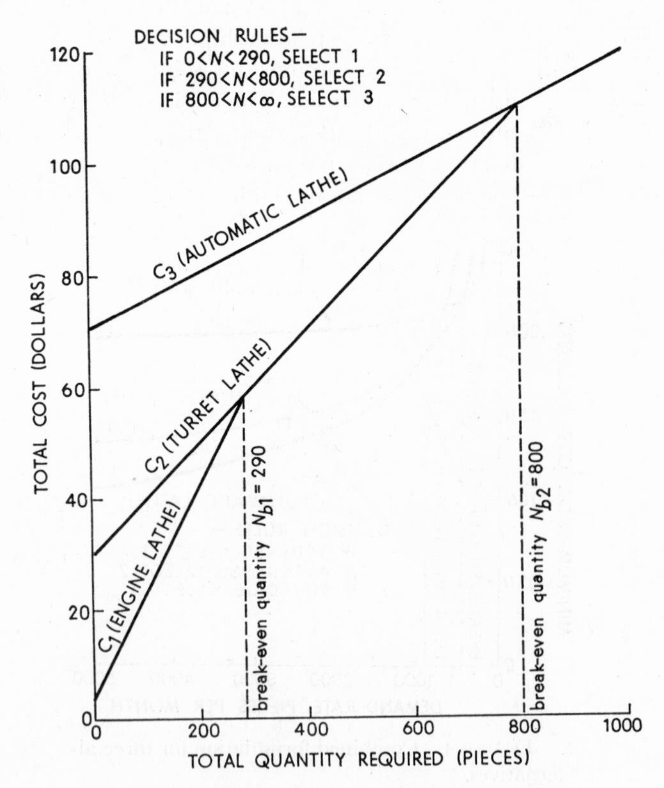

FIGURE 5. Break-even chart for three alternatives.

COMPARISON OF RESULTS

The next problem is to find a convenient and graphic way of portraying the errors that would have been generated in this specific problem if the simple break-even method had been used to solve the problem. Or to state it another way, what savings would have been derived by using the more complicated, combined model in determining the best production method?

A glance at the decision rules which are established in this example by the break-even model and the combined model is revealing because in most situations the two methods result in different courses of action rather than the same course of action. Figure 6 clearly reveals the disparity between the two methods. Table 2 lists the types of errors that can be made. These are shown graphically in Figure 6. In each case the area over which the error can be made is a rough approximation of the probability of this type of error. The actual loss at a specified point in the Figure 6 matrix may be determined from Figure 4.

Generally, a sales forecast would be able to limit to some degree the space in Figure 6 that is actually pertinent. Let us say in this example that we are reasonably certain that the total volume required will be between 1,200 and 2,100 pieces and that the demand rate will be between 200 and 700 pieces per month. If this were the case checking Figure 6, it is apparent that the break-even model would give us the wrong decision over this entire space.

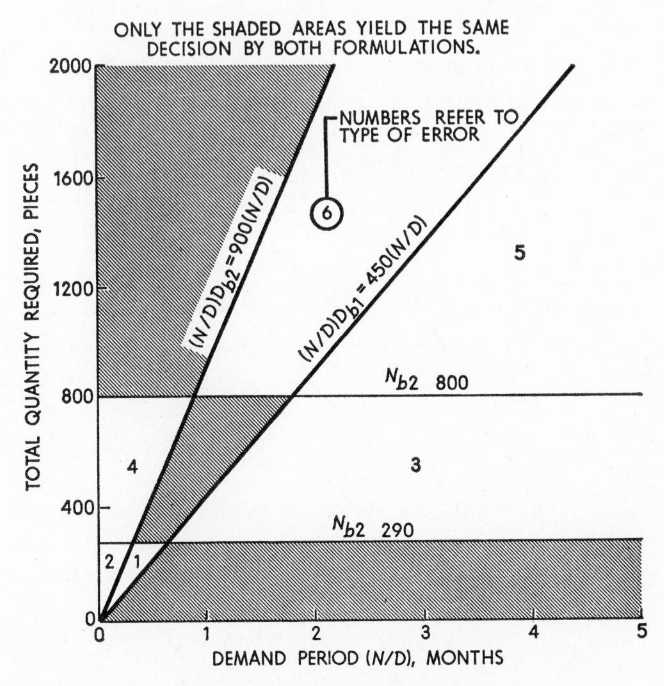

FIGURE 6. Error space diagram.

TABLE 2

TYPES OF ERROR

Type of Error	*Break-Even Model Chooses:*	*Combined Model Chooses:*
1	Engine lathe	Turret lathe
2	Engine lathe	Automatic lathe
3	Turret lathe	Engine lathe
4	Turret lathe	Automatic lathe
5	Automatic lathe	Engine lathe
6	Automatic lathe	Turret lathe

According to the break-even model, we should always use the automatic lathe. According to the combined model, we should either use the engine lathe or the turret lathe, depending on the point in this space that actually occurs.

CONCLUSIONS

1. The use of the simple break-even model to decide between several alternative methods of performing a task can give rise to serious errors.

2. These errors are particularly pronounced when

a) The production rates are considerably higher than the demand rates.
b) The storage and inventory costs are significantly large.
c) There is a substantial difference between the ratio of setup cost and storage cost for the several alternative methods.

3. The combined model is not significantly more difficult to work with when modern computing techniques and equipment are considered.

REFERENCES

1. BULLINGER, C. E. *Engineering Economic Analysis*. New York: McGraw-Hill Book Co., Inc., 1950.
2. EIDMANN, F. L. *Economic Control of Engineering and Manufacturing*. New York: McGraw-Hill Book Co., Inc., 1931.
3. GRANT, E. L. *Principles of Engineering Economy*. New York: Ronald Press Co., 1950.
4. KNOEPPEL, C. E. *Profit Engineering*. New York: McGraw-Hill Book Co., Inc., 1933.
5. LATHROP, JOHN B. "Production Problems Bow to Operations Research," *SAE Journal*, May, 1954, p. 46.
6. ORENSTEEN, R. B. "Topics on the MAPI Formula," *Journal of Industrial Engineering*, November–December, 1956, p. 283.
7. RAUTENSTRAUCH, WALTER, and VILLERS, RAYMOND. *The Economics of Industrial Management*. New York: Funk & Wagnalls Co., 1949.
8. RAYMOND, F. E. *Quantity and Economy in Manufacture*. New York: McGraw-Hill Book Co., Inc., 1931.

9. TERBORGH, GEORGE. *Dynamic Equipment Policy.* New York: McGraw-Hill Book Co., Inc., 1949.

10. THUESEN, H. G. *Engineering Economy.* New York: Prentice-Hall, Inc., 1950.

11. VARNUM, EDWARD C. "The Economic Lot Size," *Tool Engineer*, November, 1956, p. 85.

12. WHITIN, T. M. *The Theory of Inventory Management.* Princeton: Princeton University Press, 1953.

13. WOODS, B. M., and DE GARMO, E. P. *Introduction to Engineering Economy.* 2nd ed. New York: Macmillan Co., 1953.

23

The author develops and describes a linear programming model (in summation form) for a transistor production process. Thereafter the problems of data collection and the results of applying the model in this dynamic environment are discussed.

*PLANNING TRANSISTOR PRODUCTION BY LINEAR PROGRAMMING** †

Spencer B. Smith

THE DIFFICULTIES involved in planning and controlling production of transistors stem from three sources. First, there is little product standardization in the industry, and most sales are to individual-customer specifications. The variety and changing character of customers' needs present a complex, moving target for production. Second, the technology is still in its early stages, and much remains to be learned about how the choice of materials specifications and processing variables affects the distribution of electrical parameters in the final product. Finally, there is considerable stochastic variation in the product, resulting from the use of components of microscopic size and raw materials that require a high degree of purity and are extremely susceptible to contamination. Because of these factors, a substantial part of the total manufacturing cost is incurred by rejection of work in process and mismatch between the electrical characteristics of the output from production and sales requirements.

The purpose of this paper will be to describe a linear programming model of transistor production that was developed to deal with these problems. The model was used to select materials, processing variables, and activity levels, with the objective of satisfying sales and inventory requirements at minimum overall cost. This model was developed in 1958 in the Semiconductor Division, Raytheon Company, and was subsequently used for planning and controlling production of several families of germanium alloy transistors.

---

* Reprinted from *Operations Research*, January, 1965, pp. 132–39.

† This paper is based on work performed by the author while with the Semiconductor Division, Raytheon Company.

THE PRODUCTION PROCESS

A typical production process for germanium alloy transistors starts with germanium dioxide. This white powder is reduced in a hydrogen atmosphere to obtain the germanium element, which is then melted and cooled to form solid bars of metallic germanium. The bars are purified by zone refining; one end of the bar is heated to form a molten zone that is moved slowly along the length of the bar. Most impurities are swept along in the molten zone to be concentrated at one end of the bar, which is then chopped off. Purity is measured by resistivity since impurities serve as current carriers.

The purified germanium is melted in a crucible. A germanium seed is lowered into the melt and slowly withdrawn. The molten germanium adheres to the seed and forms a single crystal as it becomes solid. Controlled amounts of impurity, such as antimony or gallium, are added to the melt to obtain the desired crystal resistivity.

The crystal is sliced with diamond saws, and the slices are ground. They are then scribed and broken into tiny square wafers. These are etched to reduce their thickness to specification and remove surface impurities. Final measurements may be about $0.05 \times 0.05 \times 0.03$ inches.

The wafers are loaded in cavities in graphite jigs. Two indium spheres, a collector and emitter, are also inserted in the cavities, one on each side of the wafer. The jig is then passed through a furnace where the germanium wafer melts and alloys with the two spheres. Upon cooling, a sandwich-like subassembly is produced, which is the heart of the transistor.

The geometry of the two junctions in the subassembly, including alignment, area, parallelism, regularity, and distance apart, has a critical effect on the operating characteristics of the finished transistor. The subassemblies are tested electrically, and if penetration of the indium has been too deep and the fusion areas meet, the subassembly shorts and is rejected. If the test indicates that fusion has not been deep enough, the subassembly may be sent through the furnace again.

The subassembly is mounted on a stem that consists of a base and three leads. The leads are connected to the collector, the emitter, and the wafer by welding, soldering, and bonding. The mount assembly is etched to remove any surface material damaged by the mechanical operations. The subassembly is then encapsulated by welding a metal can to the stem; this provides protection against moisture, shock, and vibration. Finally, the transistor is plated and marked.

In final test, units are extracted from a transistor family to satisfy the specifications of particular product types. The term *transistor family* means transistors made with the same components, physical configuration, and target specifications. Product type refers to the way in which the transistors are defined when they are sold; this may be by industry standard, company standard, or customer specification. All units from a family are first tested automatically for a number of the more important parameters and are sorted into an interim inventory consisting of up to 2,000 categories. From there, they are withdrawn and tested further against the specifications for product types. Tests on 60 different combinations of parameters and test conditions against the specifications for 100 different product types may be performed during the course of a month.

FORMULATING A MODEL

From an economic standpoint, the decision as to which subassemblies to mount, which to refire, and which to scrap is of critical importance. Subassemblies are placed in categories based on the results of electrical testing, and there is a strong correlation between the category of subassemblies mounted and the yields of finished transistors to product types at final test. Furthermore, the cost of the subassembly is small relative to the material and labor costs incurred in subsequent operations, and a substantial saving in assembly and testing costs can be achieved by selecting subassemblies to be mounted in such a way as to minimize the mismatch between production and demand. On the other hand, being too selective in choosing subassemblies could reduce subassembly yield to a point where the increased cost of subassemblies would outweigh the savings in assembly and final test.

Based on these observations, a linear programming model of the feed-mix type was considered that would include various categories of subassemblies as raw materials. This formulation introduced a problem in costing of subassemblies. The furnace produces a distribution of subassemblies to categories. The total cost of subassemblies depends upon the yield to production or the match between the distribution from the furnace and the distribution required for mounting obtained from the linear programming solution. However, once the requirements for mounting are known, the wafer specifications or the furnace controls would be changed to improve the match between the subassemblies produced and those required for mounting. In this way the yield and hence the cost of subassemblies would be changed, rendering the linear programming solution invalid.

This problem was solved by moving the initial cut point for the model back one stage. Firing patterns were defined as particular combinations of wafer resistivity and furnace temperature, and the distribution of subassemblies to categories for each firing pattern was determined. Then, firing by pattern was included as a set of activities in the model.

The interim inventory of transistors also presented problems. Initially, it was planned to consider production into each category of interim inventory and solve for the level of testing out of each category to product types. However, this would require a model restriction on each interim category that withdrawals had to be less than or equal to starting inventory plus production into the category and would require up to 2,000 restrictions.

At the time, we were using the Orchard-Hays revised simplex program on an IBM 704 computer, and the maximum number of restrictions allowed by this program was 255. Furthermore, even if we wrote a program to handle 2,000 restrictions, determining test yields for each of the interim categories to all product types and maintaining these data in the face of constantly changing customer requirements seemed infeasible.

It was decided that an improvement in the characteristics of the product coming into testing was much more important than improvement in the efficiency of testing itself. Therefore, realism in testing was sacrificed, and the model was simplified by the use of an idealized interim inventory of greatly reduced dimensions. Although these were up to 100 product types per family in a given month, as is usually the case a small number, perhaps eight, of these accounted for most of the sales. It was estimated that if production plans were based on satisfying the requirements for these few large-volume types, the requirements for the other smaller volume types could normally be met from fallout. Transistor categories in the idealized interim inventory were defined as the Venn sets of specifications for large-volume product types. For example, if there were three product types, A, B, and C, there could be up to seven transistor categories, that is, transistors passing the specifications for and only for ABC, AB, AC, BC, A, B, and C. Some of the specifications for types were mutually exclusive, further limiting the number of categories.

THE MODEL

The model was designed to determine a monthly production plan that would satisfy the net demand for each product type at minimum overall manufacturing cost.

Symbols used in the model are as follows:

1. Input data:
   a) Demand:
   - D_g = demand for the gth product type in units: sales forecast plus or minus planned change in inventory

   b) Yields:
   - u_{hi} = First-fire yield using the hth firing pattern to the ith subassembly category
   - v_{ij} = Refire yield from the ith subassembly category to the jth subassembly category
   - w_{jk} = Yield of mounting from the jth subassembly category to the kth transistor category

   c) Costs:
   - C_f = Variable cost of first firing one subassembly
   - C_r = Variable cost of refiring one subassembly
   - C_m = Variable cost of main assembly and testing per subassembly mounted
   - Z = Total variable cost for the period

d) Capacities:

K_f = Firing capacity in subassemblies input

K_m = Assembly capacity in subassemblies mounted

2. Variables to be evaluated:

F_h = Quantity of subassemblies first fired using the hth firing pattern

R_i = Quantity of subassemblies refired from the ith category

M_i = Quantity of subassemblies mounted from the ith category

W_{kg} = Allocation from the kth transistor category to satisfy demand for the gth product type

The objective function to be minimized is the sum of cost of firing, refiring, and assembly.

$$Z = C_f \Sigma_h F_h + C_r \Sigma_i R_i + C_m \Sigma_i M_i \quad (1)$$

For each subassembly category, there is a restriction that input from firing and refiring must be greater than or equal to withdrawals for mounting and refiring. Starting inventories are neglected because it was found that in critical subassembly categories they were normally insignificant.

$$\Sigma_h u_{hi} F_h + \Sigma_j v_{ji} R_j \geqq M_i + R_i \quad (2)$$

There is a similar restriction for each transistor category. Production into the category must be greater than or equal to withdrawals to product types. Again, starting inventories are neglected, in this case because they are already deducted from gross demand to obtain net demand by product type.

$$\Sigma_i w_{ik} M_i \geqq \Sigma_g W_{kg} \quad (3)$$

A capacity restriction on firing states that the number of units fired plus the number refired is restricted by the total firing capacity.

$$\Sigma_h F_h + \Sigma_i R_i \leqq K_f \quad (4)$$

Similarly, the number of subassemblies mounted is restricted by the total assembly capacity.

$$\Sigma_i M_i \leqq K_m \quad (5)$$

The final set of restrictions requires that demand for each product type is satisfied; that is, withdrawals from transistor categories to types must equal demand.

$$\Sigma_k W_{kg} = D_g \quad (6)$$

DATA COLLECTION

Obtaining the yield data from subassembly categories to transistor categories presented the largest single problem in implementing the use of linear programming. In dealing with semiconductor devices, laboratory results were often not reproducible on the production line. Furthermore, the type of yield data required was not normally recorded in production. By the time a transistor reached final test, there was no way of knowing what subassembly category it came from. In addition, it was not determined in final test whether a unit would pass the specifications for each major product type, the information needed for establishing yields to the transistor categories used in the model.

The required yields from subassembly to transistor categories were obtained through a series of large-scale production experiments. A tag showing the category the subassembly came from was attached at mounting to one of the leads of each transistor in the experiment. Special procedures were established to test these units to all major product types when they arrived at final test.

In order to enable us to take new product types into account in the program prior to their actual production and to reduce the need for further production experimentation, a method for simulating experiments was developed. Transistors from an actual experiment were extensively tested by parameters, and the results for each unit were recorded on a punched card together with pass or fail information for each major product type. Then, when a new type was to be produced, the cards were sorted against the type's specifications, and a new set of yield data was obtained.

Cost data were available but had to be reorganized in a form suitable for use in the model. For example, the cost of assembly and test per subassembly mounted, C_m, was developed in the following way.

Let

$1 \cdots i \cdots n =$ Operations, mounting through final test
$Y_i =$ Yield of the ith operation in percent
$C_i =$ Variable cost of performing the ith operation per unit of input

Then

$$C_m = C_1 + Y_1C_2 + Y_1Y_2C_3 + \cdots + (Y_1Y_2 \cdots Y_{n-1})C_n$$

$$= C_1 + \sum_{i=2}^{i=n} \left(\prod_{j=1}^{i-1} Y_j\right) C_i \tag{7}$$

OPERATION

For a number of reasons, the first application involved a linear programming model of small dimensions. We intentionally selected a product family with relatively few major product types. In addition, there had been a high degree of mismatch between past production and demand, so there were severe shortages of some types and excess inventories of others. This meant that the number of types with a net demand for the month was further reduced. Finally, the restrictions on production capacity were not used, as the management first wanted to determine the optimum method of manufacture regardless of the capacity that would be required.

As a result, the model for the first program contained only 10 restrictions and 24 variables. The input was punched on 80 cards, and the computer running time was 7.2 minutes. Later applictions to more complex families required larger models and longer running times. However, once insight was gained into the structure of the solution, it was often found possible to produce new optimal programs simply by modifying programs produced for prior months that had similar distributions of demand.

The production plan for the month was prepared directly from the linear programming solution and contained the following:

1. A firing and refiring plan showing (*a*) how many chips to first fire by resistivity range and the furnace temperatures to use, (*b*) how many subassemblies to refire from each subassembly category, and (*c*) the expected final distribution of subassemblies by category.
2. A mounting plan showing how many subassemblies to mount from each category. In cases where subassemblies were common to different families, the plan showed how many subassemblies to mount to each family from each subassembly category.
3. A production plan showing the number of units to be produced by transistor category.

Each month on the day the plan was produced, a meeting was held of all the production and engineering managers concerned. The plan was reviewed in detail and then immediately put into effect.

RESULTS

The first program called for major changes in the method of operation. The furnace temperature was changed to give a different distribution of subassemblies. A wider range of subassemblies was mounted, and this resulted in a larger subassembly yield. Ninety-five thousand subassemblies, which had previously been accumulated as scrap, were mounted. At final test, yield to the most critical product types increased by 80 percent. In other words, total customer demand could be satisfied by producing only 55 percent as many transistors as were required before. The net result was a substantial saving in manufacturing costs.

During this period, semiconductor technology was developing at a rapid pace. The manufacturing system that we modeled was subject to continual innovation involving changes in materials, components, processes, production and testing equipment, and product designs. Frequently, these innovations resulted in sudden changes in yields, making production far different from that expected by the current program. This also made obsolete the yield data used in programming and required us to undertake new production experiments. Sometimes, further changes rendered these experiments obsolete before they were completed.

As a result of these changes, production planning by linear programming was frequently interrupted. Nevertheless, it was continued for several years and extended to other product families. Even when linear programming was not being used directly, the information gained from the experiments and previous linear programming solutions was used in managing production.

CONCLUSION

It has sometimes been stated that linear programming should be applied in stable situations. In this case, it was applied in what was probably the most rapidly changing industry in America. It is true that this dynamic situation made application difficult and intermittent, and that it limited extension of the model and the uses that were made of it. Nevertheless, the project proved to be highly profitable; and this was attributable, at least in part, to the very fact that the technology was new and the managers and engineers responsible had not had a long period of time to make improvements by more traditional methods.

24

The author describes a method of delineating the parts requirements in respect to an assembly unit, both in matrix and in graphic form. Then, given a sales forecast, the total parts requirements are determined from a total requirements factor table by means of matrix multiplications.

*THE USE OF MATHEMATICS IN PRODUCTION AND INVENTORY CONTROL**

Andrew Vazsonyi

IT IS BECOMING increasingly apparent that some new scientific and mathematical theories are now being developed in this country which, in combination with the remarkable performance of electronic data processing machines, will bring about significant changes in current managerial techniques. The field of production and inventory control is particularly amenable to these new theories, as evidenced by the extensive literature devoted to this subject; and therefore, it can be expected that a reorientation of production control methods will be in order in various segments of American industry in the not too distant future. How distant in the future is not known, but it is clear that the tempo of these changes will greatly depend on the degree of integration effected between the production men, the management scientists, and the electronic engineer.

A particularly significant difficulty to be overcome is the successful transmission of information between the production men and the scientist developing new theories of production. While it is not to be expected that operating personnel will find it necessary to delve into the fine details of some of these mathematical techniques, it still is mandatory that a clear concept of the nature of these methods be understood. Unfortunately, there has been very little effort expended in "popularizing" these mathematical concepts; and in fact, there might have been an implication that it is hopeless to transmit to the "layman" the essence of these techniques.

In the course of studying production and inventory control, the author of this paper found it repeatedly necessary to explain his mathematical theory to operating personnel, many of whom had little or no formal training in mathe-

* Reprinted from *Management Science*, October, 1954, pp. 70–85.

matics at the college level. This paper, then, is an outgrowth of these presentations and has a twofold purpose: (1) to present a theory of a very small part of the problem of production and inventory control with the objective of acquainting the reader with the nature of the mathematical methodology and (2) to lay emphasis on a didactic presentation to show the principles involved in explaining these mathematical concepts.

The subject matter to be discussed is what is generally called the preparation of parts requirement lists and production explosion charts.

In order to fix ideas, we paraphrase the problem in question as follows:

> The manufacturing planning program begins with breaking down the sales forecast into the requirements for the detailed subassemblies and parts. A production explosion chart is plotted showing, for a manufacturing unit, first, the breakdown into major assemblies and separate parts, and then at each successive step the further breakdown into subassemblies and parts. Based on this "explosion system" the requirements of all assemblies and subassemblies are determined before any parts manufacturing orders are initiated.[1]

Every production man knows that a great deal is implied in the above statement; however, the statement contains little clue as to what these implications are. The fact of the matter is that many pages of verbal discussions of the subject are required to develop these implications; and in many instances, from the point of view of operating personnel, there is no complete description available in the literature at all. In contrast, we proceed here to develop a statement in terms of mathematical concepts which not only suggest procedures and methods but in fact specifically contain answers to some of the fundamental issues involved in the above statement.

In order to develop such a theory, it is necessary to examine these questions in detail and, step by step, to build a bridge from this above statement to mathematical equations. That such a thing can be done and that it can be useful most likely is a perplexing thought to the reader.

THE CONCEPT OF THE ASSEMBLY PARTS LIST

We begin by considering Figure 1, where a sample assembly parts list is shown—each assembly to be made has a similar sheet. The assembly in question is a "panel" with part No. 435090012. This number is shown on the upper right-hand corner under the words "Makes Assembly." This assembly is made up of seven different articles[2]—bushing, panel blank, etc. The part number of each of these is given on the sheet. Under the heading N. A. QTY. (next assembly quantity), it also is shown how many of these articles are needed. Thus the bushing with part No. 420990309 is required in a quantity of three for each of the panels 435090012.

[1] L. P. Alford and J. R. Bangs, *Production Handbook* (New York: Ronald Press Co., 1944), p. 230, "Breaking Down Requirements."

[2] An "article" might be an assembly, subassembly, or part.

NA QTY	PART NUMBER		DESCRIPTION
	PANEL		ASSEMBLY DESCRIPTION — MAKES ASSEMBLY 435 09 0012
3	42099 0309		BUSHING
1	435 09 0012	1	PANEL BLANK
2	435 09 0012	2	ANGLE
1	435 09 0012	7	ANGLE
5	999 67 C098		RECEPTACLE
10	AN4 26 AD3		RIVET
8	AN4 26 AD4		RIVET

ASSEMBLY PARTS LIST

FIGURE 1. This sheet refers to the assembly "panel" which is assigned the part number 435090012. This panel is made up of seven different articles which could be subassemblies or parts. The panel requires three bushings 420990309, and one panel blank 435090012–1, etc. Each assembly will have a similar sheet. The type of information contained on these sheets will form the basis of our discussion.

The assembly parts list has some other information which for the purpose of our simplified discussion is disregarded.

In order to build a mathematical model, the information in the assembly parts list is to be put in a concise symbolic form. Note first that the information in Figure 1 is redundant; the panel in question has the part No. 435090012; and therefore, this assembly could be identified solely by this number.

Figure 2, then, presents an abbreviated parts list; the names of the articles are no longer listed.

In the remainder of the report, for the sake of brevity, we shall not carry these long part numbers but shall assume that the articles are numbered 1, 2, 3, etc. With these shortcuts, then, a set of assembly parts lists might take the form of Figure 3. This purely hypothetical manufacturing process (which bears no relationship to the one described in Figures 1 and 2) deals with assemblies 1, 2, 4, 5, 7, 8, and 9. Assembly 1 is made up of one of article 3 and two of article 5. Each column of Figure 3 represents a single assembly parts list similar to Figures 1 or 2.

A further saving of words can be effected by saying A instead of article and saying A_1 for article 1, A_2 for article 2, etc. With this notation, then, Figure 3 becomes Figure 4.

The information in Figure 4 can be presented in a somewhat different form using rectangular tables. Such a table is shown in Figure 5. The information is the same as in Figure 4; for instance, it can be seen that A_4 is made up of two A_1's and one A_7. The advantage of the new presentation is that it is conceptually more descriptive. One can talk about a column, describing what an assembly is made of; or one can talk about a row, showing what an assembly goes into. For instance, A_1 is made of one A_3 and two A_5's; A_5 goes into A_1 twice, into A_7 twice, into A_8 once, and into A_9 three times.

The same information is finally presented again in Figure 6. What we did is very simple; we filled in the empty squares with zeros and omitted the A's. This presentation is very simple because we can say that every article goes into every other article—the numbers on the table show how many times. The zeros mean that a particular article does not "really" go into the other article in the ordinary sense; from our point of view, this distinction need not be made.

ARTICLE	435090012
3 OF ARTICLE	420990309
1 OF ARTICLE	435090012-1
2 OF ARTICLE	435090012-2
1 OF ARTICLE	435090012-7
5 OF ARTICLE	99967C098
10 OF ARTICLE	AN426AD3
8 OF ARTICLE	AN426AD4

FIGURE 2. Abbreviated assembly parts list: the names of the various articles are omitted.

For explanation, let us insert an analogy from algebra. We can subtract any two numbers; five less five equals zero. If we did not have zeros, we would have to say that subtraction can be carried out only under certain circumstances. We always would have to watch that the formulas have meaning. Therefore the invention of the zero is an extremely useful thing. It also forms the essential foundation of the concept of arabic numbers as distinct from roman numerals, where zeros do not exist. Anyone who would have the courage to carry through a division in roman numerals would appreciate the point.

ARTICLE

1	2	4	5	7	8	9
1 OF ARTICLE 3	2 OF ARTICLE 6	2 OF ARTICLE 1	3 OF ARTICLE 3	1 OF ARTICLE 1	1 OF ARTICLE 1	3 OF ARTICLE 6
2 OF ARTICLE 5	1 OF ARTICLE 7	1 OF ARTICLE 7	1 OF ARTICLE 6	2 OF ARTICLE 5	1 OF ARTICLE 5	1 OF ARTICLE 8
	2 OF ARTICLE 8					

FIGURE 3. Set of abbreviated assembly parts lists. Each column represents a single assembly parts list. For instance, article 2 is made up of two of article 6, one of article 7, and two of article 8.

A_1	A_2	A_4	A_5	A_7	A_8	A_9
$1A_3$	$2A_6$	$2A_1$	$3A_3$	$1A_1$	$1A_1$	$3A_6$
$2A_5$	$1A_7$	$1A_7$	$1A_6$	$2A_5$	$1A_5$	$1A_8$
	$2A_8$					

FIGURE 4. Set of abbreviated assembly parts lists. The words *article 1* are replaced by A_1, *article 2* by A_2, etc.

	A_1	A_2	A_3	A_4	A_5	A_6	A_7	A_8	A_9
A_1				2			1	1	
A_2									
A_3	1				3				
A_4									
A_5	2						2	1	
A_6		2			1				3
A_7		1		1					
A_8		2							1
A_9									

FIGURE 5. Table of Assembly Parts. The information still is the same as in Figure 4, but the presentation is more systematic. Note that for completeness, *all* the articles are listed in the top now. For instance, A_3 requires no other article, as A_3 is not an *assembly* but a *part*.

	1	2	3	4	5	6	7	8	9
1	0	0	0	2	0	0	1	1	0
2	0	0	0	0	0	0	0	0	0
3	1	0	0	0	3	0	0	0	0
4	0	0	0	0	0	0	0	0	0
5	2	0	0	0	0	0	2	1	0
6	0	2	0	0	1	0	0	0	3
7	0	1	0	1	0	0	0	0	0
8	0	2	0	0	0	0	0	0	1
9	0	0	0	0	0	0	0	0	0

FIGURE 6. Next Assembly Quantity Table. This is a concise mathematical representation of the information contained in the assembly parts lists, and this table will form one of the building blocks of the mathematical theory.

One further point—we have put zeros into the "diagonal" elements[3] of the table. The question of how many A_2's go into A_2 is not a significant one, and we could adopt any convenient system. Later, however, it becomes clear that using zeros makes the mathematics simple. In Figure 6, it can be seen that a row of zeros (e.g., the fourth row) indicates a top assembly; A_4 does not go into anything. A column of zeros indicates a detail part; thus, article 6 does not require anything, since it is not an assembly but a part.

Let us stop for a moment now, as we have in fact reached our first objective; the information contained in the assembly parts lists has been put into an appropriate form for further mathematical discussion. Instead of assembly parts lists, we will talk in terms of the Next Assembly Quantity Table, as represented in Figure 6.

[3] The diagonal elements are formed by the first number of the first row, the second number of the second row, the third number of the third row, etc.

We proceed now to the determination of the parts requirements; that is, we develop a formula which tells us how many of each assembly and each part is required to meet any sales forecast.

THE TOTAL REQUIREMENT FACTOR TABLE

Before we discuss the determination-of-parts requirement, we introduce some visual aids to clarify our concepts. Consider for this purpose Figure 7. It can be seen that A_1 is made up of one A_3 and two A_5's. A_2 is made up of two A_6's, one A_7, and two A_8's, etc. All this information is contained in the Next Assembly Table in a numerical fashion. Suppose now, we want to know all the articles that are required for each A_2.[4] The resultant diagram is shown in Figure 8. This is not very convenient, and so we present the same information in Figure 9 in a different form. Note that each article is shown only once. A_5 goes into A_7 twice, so we have two arrows on the line going from A_5 to A_7. The insert shows that, say, A_5 goes into A_1, A_7, and A_8, twice, once, and twice, respectively. Figure 9 is a pictorial representation of certain columns of the Next Assembly Quantity Table; in order to fix our ideas, it will be called the Gozinto graph for A_2. Similar pictorial representations can be prepared for

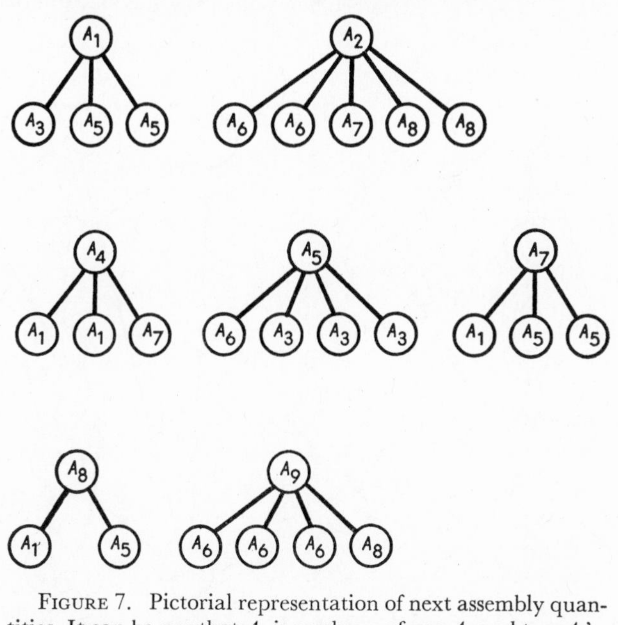

FIGURE 7. Pictorial representation of next assembly quantities. It can be *seen* that A_1 is made up of one A_3 and two A_5's; A_2 is made up of two A_6's, one A_7, and two A_8's. It *cannot* be seen how many assemblies and parts are required *in total*, say, making up an A_2, when it is recognized that A_7 and A_8 are assemblies.

[4] We mean by the statement "articles required for each A_2" all the articles that go directly into A_2, *and* all the articles that go into these, *and so on.*

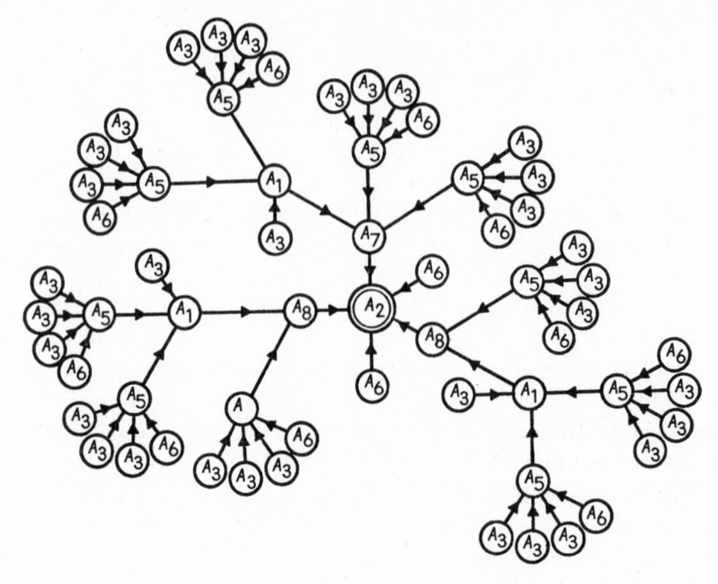

FIGURE 8. Pictorial representation of total requirements. By a direct count, it can be determined how many, say, A_3's are required for each A_2.

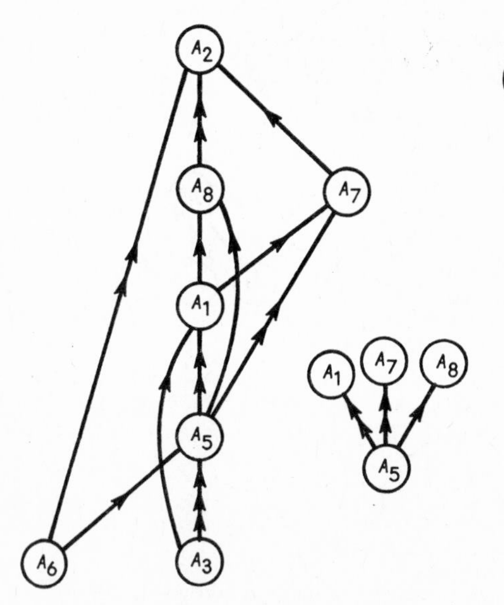

FIGURE 9. The Gozinto graph for A_2 is a pictorial representation of the requirements for A_2. Each article is shown only once. The next assembly quantities are shown by the multiplicity of the arrows. Total requirements cannot be observed directly but can be deduced.

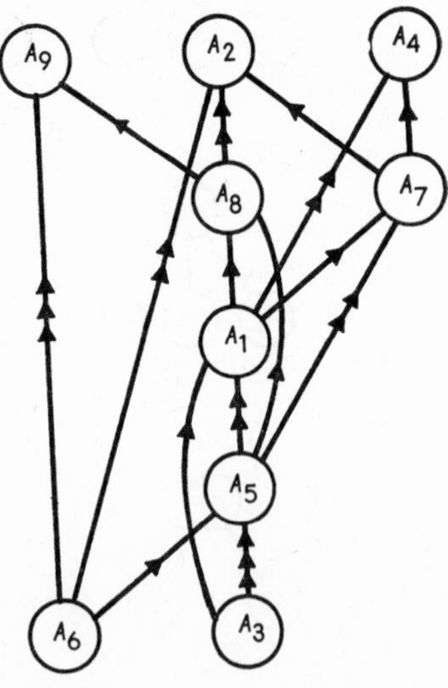

FIGURE 10. The composite Gozinto graph is a pictorial representation of the parts requirements. The next assembly quantities can be observed directly by counting the arrows on each connecting line. Total requirements cannot be observed directly but can be deduced.

A_4 and A_9, and a composite Gozinto graph for all our articles is shown in Figure 10. Figure 9 is much more simple than Figure 8 but contains the same information. However, from one point of view, it is not quite so convenient. How many A_6's are required (in total) for each A_2? In Figure 8, one can answer this question by direct count of the A_6's. In Figure 9, some mental effort is required to answer the same question. However, this is the type of thinking that leads to the result we want, as, when dealing with thousands of assemblies, we are not able to draw these various pictures. Suppose we wanted to figure out how many A_5's are required for each A_2. A_5 goes directly into A_1, A_7, and A_8 (see Figure 9), so we can make the statement that

Total number of A_5's required for each A_2 =
[Number of A_5's going directly into each A_1]
· [Total number of A_1's required for each A_2]
+ [Number of A_5's going directly into each A_7]
· [Total number of A_7's required for each A_2]
+ [Number of A_5's going directly into each A_8]
· [Total number of A_8's required for each A_2]

Note the important difference between these two statements—"Number of A_5's going directly into each A_8" and "Total number of A_5's required for each A_2." The answer to the first statement is the quantity 1, while the answer to the second one is the quantity 3. In our Next Assembly Quantity Table, we have the number of assemblies going directly into each other assembly listed, but we do not have the total number of assemblies required for each other assembly.

Let us contemplate the above statement. It gives a relationship between total number of quantities required and next assembly quantities. It does not tell us how to compute the total number of quantities required from the next assembly quantities, as the various total numbers required and the next assembly quantities appear at both sides of the equation.

The same statement also implies some sort of a rule, as we could also figure a relationship for how many A_5's we need, say, for each A_8. Very likely, this rule could be described in words; however, if one attempted to work out this rule, it would get lengthy and confusing. Clearly, what we need is a concise notation to describe the idea represented. And this is the point where mathematics comes in handy. Consider Diagram 1:

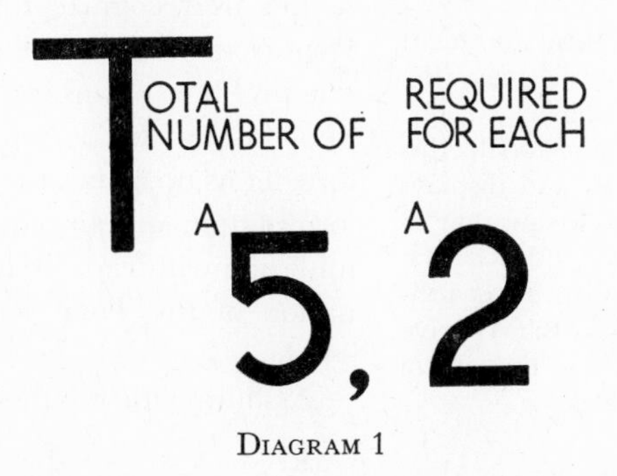

DIAGRAM 1

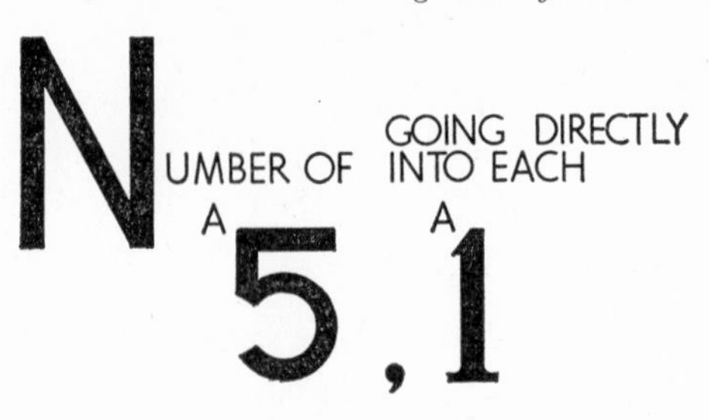

DIAGRAM 2

We have magnified the statement "Total number of A_5's required for each A_2." The way the picture was prepared suggests that instead of the long sentence, we could simply say $T_{5,2}$. Quite similarly, Diagram 2 suggests that instead of saying, "Number of A_5's going directly into each A_1," we should say $N_{5,1}$.

At this point, bear in mind that the notation means nothing more or less than what we said. It is a concise statement of things we have known. However, we can now replace the statement in question with an equation:

$$T_{5,2} = N_{5,1} \cdot T_{1,2} + N_{5,7} \cdot T_{7,2} + N_{5,8} \cdot T_{8,2}$$

We have accomplished, then, our first objective—our specific statement is represented in a shorthand form.

Suppose, for the moment, that we know the answer we are attempting to find—that is, we have computed all the total requirements, which are all the various T's. They can be put in a table, as shown in Figure 11. This table, which we call the Total Requirement Factor Table, or briefly, the T Table, is very similar to the Next Assembly Quantity Table. Just as the latter one shows the N's, the new table shows the capital T's. One can see, for instance, that each A_7 requires one A_1, 13 A_3's, nine A_5's, four A_6's, and one A_7.

	1	2	3	4	5	6	7	8	9
1	1	3	0	3	0	0	1	1	1
2	0	1	0	0	0	0	0	0	0
3	7	33	1	27	3	0	13	10	10
4	0	0	0	1	0	0	0	0	0
5	2	10	0	8	1	0	4	3	3
6	2	12	0	8	1	1	4	3	6
7	0	1	0	1	0	0	1	0	0
8	0	2	0	0	0	0	0	1	1
9	0	0	0	0	0	0	0	0	1

FIGURE 11. Total Requirement Factor Table. Observe, say, the *second* column relating to A_2. The *third* element from the top in this column relates to A_3 and displays the number 33. This means that 33 A_3's are required (in total) for each A_2. This can be confirmed by a direct count from Figure 8. (We have not explained yet how this above table was computed.)

Let us recognize that once the Total Requirement Factor Table is determined, our problem of answering the question of "how many" becomes very simple. Therefore, let us turn our attention to the general formulation of our equation, which formulation will lead directly to the determination of the Total Requirement Factor Table.

Assuming for the moment that we have

already computed all the T's, let us focus our attention, say, on the second column of the T Table. Figure 12 shows the fifth row of the N Table and the second column of the T Table. Consider $T_{5,2}$, that is, the second element of the fifth row. We can say, as is shown by our equation above, that $T_{5,2}$ can be obtained by taking the left-hand side number from the N Table and multiplying it by the top number on the T Table; to this number, we have to add the seventh number from the N Table multiplied by the seventh number from the top of the T Table; finally, we have to add the eighth number from the T Table multiplied by the eighth number of the T Table. This rule can be stated in a more simple form: Multiply the first number in the N Table with the first number in the T Table, multiply the second number with the

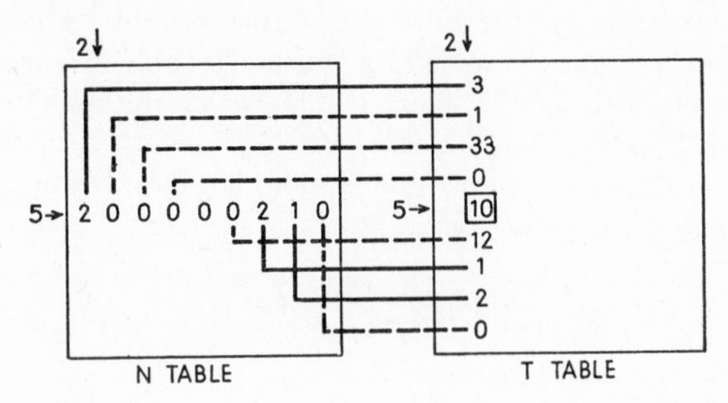

FIGURE 12. Determination of the T Table. Schematic representation of the equation $T_{5,2} = \sum_k N_{5,2} T_{k,2}$. The second number of the fifth row of the T Table equals the "scalar multiple" of the fifth row of the N Table and second column of the T Table: $10 = 2 \times 3 + 0 \times 1 + 0 \times 33 + 0 \times 0 + 0 \times 10 + 0 \times 12 + 2 \times 1 + 1 \times 2 + 0 \times 0$.

second number, the third with the third,and so on, keeping in mind that we are combining a row with a column. This last rule is, of course, the same as the first, but it takes advantage of the zeros we have in the table.

Incidentally, to make this a good rule, we need both $N_{5,5}$ and $T_{2,2}$. The former was defined as zero on page 320, and now we have to define $T_{2,2}$. We are at liberty to use any number, as the question of how many A_2's are required for each A_2 is not a significant one. However, it turns out that in order to make our rules uniform, we have to assign to the diagonals of the T Table the value one. It was precisely the same reason that we assigned the zeros to the diagonals of the N Table on page 324.

Mathematicians have developed a shorthand notation for sums of the kind we are discussing here. They simply write

$$T_{5,2} = \sum_k N_{5,k} T_{k,2}$$

using for summation the Greek capital letter Σ. This equation means exactly the same thing as the former one. The letter k indicates that the product should be computed for all values of k.

It is quite clear that the equation that we have here works not only for $T_{5,2}$ but for any element on the T Table. This can be written in mathematical form as

$$T_{i,j} = \sum_k N_{i,k} \cdot T_{k,j} \quad i \neq j \tag{1}$$

The letters i and j simply mean that i can be any number and that j can be any number, though it is postulated that i must be different from j, as in that case $T_{i,i}$ takes the value one.

Let us try this formula—consider, say, $i = 4$, $j = 2$; the T in question is $T_{4,2}$, the second element in the fourth row of the T Table. According to our rule, we have to combine the fourth row of the N Table (Figure 6) with the second column of the T Table (Figure 11). However, the fourth row of the N Table is a zero. Therefore, we can conclude the $T_{4,2}$ must be zero. This is not surprising, as A_4 is a top assembly and A_2 does not require any A_4's.

Quite similarly, we deduce from

$$T_{9,2} = \sum_k N_{9,k} \cdot T_{k,2}$$

that $T_{9,2}$ equals zero.

Let us continue now the computation of the rest of the elements in the second column of the T Table. We get

$$T_{8,2} = \Sigma_k N_{8,k} \cdot T_{k,2} = N_{8,2} \cdot T_{2,2} + N_{8,9} \cdot T_{9,2} = 2 \times 1 + 1 \times 0 = 2$$[5]

$$T_{7,2} = \Sigma_k N_{7,k} \cdot T_{k,2} = N_{7,2} \cdot T_{2,2} + N_{7,4} \cdot T_{4,2} = 1 \times 1 + 1 \times 0 = 1$$

$$T_{1,2} = \Sigma_k N_{1,k} \cdot T_{k,2} = N_{1,4} \cdot T_{4,2} + N_{1,7} \cdot T_{7,2} + N_{1,8} \cdot T_{8,2} = 2 \times 0 + 1 \times 1 + 1 \times 2 = 3$$

$$T_{5,2} = \Sigma_k N_{5,k} \cdot T_{k,2} = N_{5,1} \cdot T_{1,2} + N_{5,7} \cdot T_{7,2} + N_{5,8} \cdot T_{8,2} = 2 \times 3 + 2 \times 1 + 1 \times 2 = 10$$

$$T_{6,2} = \Sigma_k N_{6,k} \cdot T_{k,2} = N_{6,2} \cdot T_{2,2} + N_{6,5} \cdot T_{5,2} + N_{6,9} \cdot T_{9,2} = 2 \times 1 + 1 \times 10 + 3 \times 0 = 12$$

and finally

$$T_{3,2} = \Sigma_k N_{3,k} \cdot T_{k,2} = N_{3,1} \cdot T_{1,2} + N_{3,5} \cdot T_{5,2} = 1 \times 3 + 3 \times 10 = 33$$

We can see, therefore, that equation 3 indeed allowed us to compute the second column of the T Table. Furthermore, it is clear that equation 3 also can be used to compute all the other numbers on the T Table; therefore, we can conclude that equation 3 does contain the necessary instruction for the determination of the T Table.

One more remark before we discuss our result in detail. It is to be pointed out that the computations had to be done in a very particular *sequence*, since the T's appear on both sides of equation 3. However, this need not be a cause for worry, as one can try to compute the top element in the column; if this is

[5] Note that $T_{2,2} = 1$.

not possible, try the one below, proceed down to the bottom, and then again start on the top. This procedure eventually leads to all the numbers in the column. This method might not be the most efficient, but it always works. A more careful study of the problem can lead to a quicker procedure, but we shall not go into the details here.

THE MATHEMATICAL FORM OF A SALES FORECAST

We have said before that once the Total Requirement Factor Table is determined, the problem of parts requirements is easy to solve. We propose to establish now the necessary mathematical formulism to determine the parts requirements.

In order to fix ideas, let it be supposed that 20 of A_2, 30 of A_4, 80 of A_9, and 50 of A_5 are specified by the sales forecast, and the problem is to determine how many A_5's are required. Clearly, we have

Quantity of A_5's required = (Total number of A_5's required for each A_2) × (Sales forecast of A_2)
+ (Total number of A_5's required for each A_4) × (Sales forecast of A_4)
+ (Total number of A_5's required for each A_9) × (Sales forecast of A_9)
+ (Sales forecast of A_5)

We can put this statement into a mathematical formula. Let S_1, S_2, S_3, $\cdots$, etc., denote the sales forecast for articles A_1, A_2, A_3 $\cdots$, etc.; and let the unknown requirements for A_5 be denoted by X_5. Then

$$X_5 = T_{5,2} \cdot S_2 + T_{5,4} \cdot S_4 + T_{5,9} \cdot S_9 + S_5$$

In our particular numerical case, we get

$$730 = 10 \times 20 + 8 \times 30 + 3 \times 80 + 50$$

Using again the summation notation, the last equation can be written as

$$X_5 = \sum_k T_{5,k} \cdot S_k$$

where advantage is taken of the fact that $T_{5,5}$ equals one. Finally, it is clear that a similar equation holds for any article, and so we write

$$X_i = \sum_k T_{i,k} \cdot S_k \qquad (2)$$

In actual practice, many of the S's are zero, as only some of the articles (say, top assemblies and spares) are shippable.

In order to be sure that we understood our formula, let us try the case when $i = 3$. We get

$$X_3 = \sum_k T_{3,k}S_k = T_{3,2} \cdot S_2 + T_{3,4}S_4 + T_{3,5}S_5 + T_{3,9}S_9$$

and

$$2{,}440 = 33 \times 20 + 27 \times 30 + 3 \times 50 + 10 \times 80$$

showing that 2,440 A_3's are required.

THE FINAL MATHEMATICAL FORMULATION

We have "solved" the problem of parts requirements in terms of the N and T tables, our solution being expressed by equations 1 and 2. As it happens, mathematicians have studied such tables in detail—they call them matrices—and a theory of matrices has been developed. In matrix algebra, rules for the addition, subtraction, multiplication, and division of matrices are developed. We cannot go into the details of such a theory, but we will point out here that equation 1 can be written as

$$[T] = [N][T] + [I]$$

or

$$[T] = \frac{[I]}{[I] - [N]} \tag{3}$$

where $[I]$ is the so-called "unit matrix." Equation 2 can be written as

$$[X] = [T] \times [S] \tag{4}$$

Finally, the two equations can be combined into a single equation:

$$[X] = \frac{[I]}{[I] - [N]} [S] \tag{5}$$

this being the final mathematical formulation of our problem. In order to bring into focus the mathematical methodology, we make now a complete statement using the language of a mathematician:

Consider the manufacture of articles $A_1, A_2, \cdots$ and denote by $N_{i,j}$ the number of A_i's going directly into A_j. Let $S_1, S_2, \cdots$, denote the sales forecast and let $X_1, X_2, \cdots$, denote the (unknown) parts requirements. Then

$$\boxed{[X] = \frac{[I]}{[I] - [N]} [S]}$$

where $[N]$ is the (square) matrix formed by the $N_{i,j}$'s, $[I]$ is the unit matrix, $[S]$ and $[X]$ are the column matrices formed by the S's and X's.

CONCLUDING REMARKS

We have reached the end of our presentation—we have accomplished the transformation of our original verbal statement into a mathematical form. However, let us remind ourselves that we have studied only a very small part of the problem of production and inventory control, and that the practical value of the theory lies in its extension to more complicated problems. As an example, we mention that our principal formula can be generalized to include the problems of scheduling. Instead of the sales forecast, $S_1, S_2, \cdots$, one must deal with the sales forecast *functions*, $S_1(t), S_2(t), \cdots$, where each of these functions describes the sales forecast for individual planning periods such as days, weeks, months, etc. The requirements $X_1, X_2, \cdots$ are replaced by the requirement functions, $X_1(t), X_2(t), \cdots$, designating the requirements for each planning period. The equations relating the $X(t)$'s to the $S(t)$'s become much more complicated as the effect of the various lead times, make spans, inventory policies, etc., all must be incorporated into the mathematics. A more detailed discussion of these problems lies beyond the scope of this paper, and future publications are planned to report on this work. We conclude this paper now by elaborating on some of the advantages offered by the mathematical theory.

1. The mathematical statement deals with clear-cut and precise concepts. For instance, compare the exactness of the ideas involved in matrix multiplication with the vague thoughts represented by the word *explosion*. The mathematical theory leads to a comprehension of matters that cannot be obtained by verbal discussions. A more and more complete mathematical statement of managerial problems and the mathematical solution of these problems will lead to an insight never heretofore realized.

2. A further outcome of the foregoing is the possibility of better ways of transmitting information on certain industrial practices. The writer has been constantly impressed by the great barriers that exist between various operating people and departments. The fact of the matter is that many systems and procedures are too complicated to be adequately described in words; and therefore, transmission of their description becomes very difficult. On the other hand, there is the likelihood that a mathematical formulation can be easily explained, as experienced by (in the rare instances of) lucid publications in scientific and engineering fields. The fact that current operating personnel are not trained along mathematical lines should not be considered an insurmountable obstacle.

3. Once the ideas are represented in mathematical form, specific managerial problems may be answered by manipulating the mathematical formulas with the aid of known mathematical techniques. These mathematical techniques need not be practiced by the operating personnel, as mathematicians well trained along these lines could be employed. It is to be emphasized that the mathematics used are not beyond the usual training of a mathematician with a Bachelor's or a Master's degree.

4. In the introduction, we touched upon the role that electronic computing machines will play in industry. However "intelligent" these machines will be, it still will be necessary to prepare the problems to be solved in a language digestible to the computing machine. Many current procedures are not completely formulated and are transmitted by verbal instructions or examples; clearly, this will not be sufficient for the electronic computing machine. Do

we face the problem here of training our electronic computing machine experts in all ramifications of managerial tasks? A mathematical formulation gives great comfort in solving this problem. For instance, our mathematical formulation of the parts requirement problem can be given to a person trained in the use of electronic computing machines, and he can solve the problem without going into the mass of details related to actual practices.

5. Finally, let us point out that such mathematical theories will lead to the general understanding of some managerial problems that so far have been treated only in an intuitive or haphazard fashion. Each result obtained in a mathematical theory will form a building block in the structure which eventually will form a discipline that truly could be called by the name "management sciences."

25

The traditional treatment of break-even analysis is explained, after which are introduced probability assignments for various sales volumes. Calculation then yields the probabilities of taking a loss, of achieving at least the break-even volume of sales, of exceeding a certain critical profit level, etc. Necessarily, this analysis exposes the risk a firm is willing to take under different sales scheduling, and it becomes a decision factor in the event that expected profits from two or more alternatives are equal (or not significantly different).

*COST-VOLUME-PROFIT ANALYSIS UNDER CONDITIONS OF UNCERTAINTY**

Robert K. Jaedicke and Alexander A. Robichek

COST-VOLUME-PROFIT ANALYSIS is frequently used by management as a basis for choosing among alternatives such decisions as (1) the sales volume required to attain a given level of profits and (2) the most profitable combination of products to produce and sell—examples of decision problems where C-V-P analysis is useful. However, the fact that traditional C-V-P analysis does not include adjustments for risk and uncertainty may, in any given instance, severely limit its usefulness. Some of the limitations can be seen from the following example.

Assume that the firm is considering the introduction of two new products, either of which can be produced by using present facilities. Both products require an increase in annual fixed cost of the same amount, say $400,000. Each product has the same selling price and variable cost per unit, say $10 and $8, respectively; and each requires the same amount of capacity. Using these data, the break-even point of either product is 200,000 units. C-V-P analysis helps to establish the break-even volume of each product, but this analysis does not distinguish the relative desirability of the two products for at least two reasons.

* Reprinted from *Accounting Review*, October, 1964, pp. 917–26.

The first piece of missing information is the *expected* sales volume of each product. Obviously, if the annual sales of *A* are expected to be 300,000 units and of *B* are expected to be 350,000 units, then *B* is clearly preferred to *A* so far as the sales expectation is concerned.

However, assume that the expected annual sales of each product are the same—say 300,000 units. Is it right to conclude that management should be indifferent as far as a choice between *A* and *B* is concerned? The answer is *no, unless* each sales expectation is certain. If both sales estimates are subject to uncertainty, the decision process will be improved if the relative risk associated with each product can some how be brought into the analysis. The discussion which follows suggests some changes which might be made in traditional C-V-P analysis so as to make it a more useful tool in analyzing decision problems under uncertainty.

SOME PROBABILITY CONCEPTS RELATED TO C-V-P ANALYSIS

In the previous section, it was pointed out that the *expected* volume of the annual sales is an important decision variable. Some concepts of probability will be discussed, using the example posed earlier.

The four fundamental relationships used in the example were:

1. The selling price per unit
2. The variable cost per unit
3. The total fixed cost
4. The expected sales volume of each product.

In any given decision problem, all four of these factors can be uncertain. However, it may be that *relative to* the expected sales quantity, the costs and selling prices are quite certain. That is, for analytical purposes the decision maker may be justified in treating several factors as certainty equivalents. Such a procedure simplifies the analysis and will be followed here as a first approximation. In this section of the paper, sales volume will be treated as the only uncertain quantity. Later, all decision factors in the above example will be treated under conditions of uncertainty.

In the example, sales volume is treated as a *random variable.* A random variable can be thought of as an *unknown quantity.* In this case the best decision hinges on the value of the random variable, sales volume of each product. One decision approach which allows for uncertainty is to estimate, for each random variable, the likelihood that the random variable will take on various possible values. Such an estimate is called a subjective probability distribution. The decision would then be made by choosing that course of action which has the highest *expected monetary value.* This approach is illustrated in Table 1.

The expected value of the random variables, sales demand for each product, is calculated by weighting the possible conditional values by their re-

TABLE 1

PROBABILITY DISTRIBUTION FOR PRODUCTS *A* AND *B*

Events (Units Demanded)	*Probability Distribution (Product A)*	*Probability Distribution (Product B)*
50,000	..	0.1
100,000	0.1	0.1
200,000	0.2	0.1
300,000	0.4	0.2
400,000	0.2	0.4
500,000	0.1	0.1
	1.00	1.00

spective probabilities. In other words, the expected value is a weighted average. The calculation is given in Table 2.

Based on an expected value approach, the firm should select product *B* rather than *A*. The expected profits of each possible action are as follows:

Product *A*:

$$\$2(300{,}000 \text{ units}) - \$400{,}000 = \$200{,}000$$

Product *B*:

$$\$2(305{,}000 \text{ units}) - \$400{,}000 = \$210{,}000$$

Several observations are appropriate at this point. First, the respective probabilities for each product, used in Table 1, add to one. Furthermore, the possible demand levels (events) are assumed to be mutually exclusive and also exhaustive. That is, the listing is done in such a way that no two events can happen simultaneously, and any events *not* listed are assumed to have a zero probability of occurring. Herein are three important (basic) concepts of probability analyses.

Secondly, the probability distributions may have been assigned by using historical demand data on similar products, or the weights may be purely subjective in the sense that there are no historical data available. Even if the probability distributions are entirely subjective, this approach still has merit.

TABLE 2

EXPECTED VALUE OF SALES DEMAND FOR PRODUCTS *A* AND *B*

(1) Event	(2) P(A)	(1 × 2)	(3) P(B)	(1 × 3)
50,000	..	......	0.1	5,000
100,000	0.1	10,000	0.1	10,000
200,000	0.2	40,000	0.1	20,000
300,000	0.4	120,000	0.2	60,000
400,000	0.2	80,000	0.4	160,000
500,000	0.1	50,000	0.1	50,000
	1.00		1.00	
Expected value		300,000 units		305,000 units

It allows the estimator to express his uncertainty about the sales estimate. An estimate of sales is necessary to make a decision. Hence the question is *not* whether an estimate must be made but simply a question of the best way to make and express the estimate.

Now, suppose that the expected value of sales for each product is 300,000, as shown in Table 3. In this example, it is easy to see that the firm would *not* be indifferent between products *A* and *B*, even though the expected value of sales is 300,000 units in both cases. In the case of product *A*, for example, there is a 0.1 chance that sales will be only 100,000 units; and in that case a loss of \$200,000 would be incurred (i.e., \$2 × 100,000 units − \$400,000). On the other hand, there is a 0.3 chance that sales will be above 300,000 units, and if this is the case, higher profits are possible with product *A* than with product *B*. Hence the firm's attitude toward risk becomes important. The expected value (or the mean of the distribution) is important, but so is the "spread" in the distribution. Typically, the greater the spread, the greater the risk involved. A quantitative measure of the spread is available in the form of the standard deviation of the distribution, and this concept and its application will be refined later in the paper.

TABLE 3

Demand	*P(A)*	*Expected Value (A)*	*P(B)*	*Expected Value (B)*
100,000 units	0.1	10,000	...	......
200,000 units	0.2	40,000	...	......
300,000 units	0.4	120,000	1.00	300,000
400,000 units	0.2	80,000	...	......
500,000 units	0.1	50,000	...	......
	1.00		1.00	
Expected sales demand		300,000		300,000

THE NORMAL PROBABILITY DISTRIBUTION

The preceding examples were highly simplified, and yet the calculations are relatively long and cumbersome. The possible sales volumes were few in number, and the probability distribution was discrete, that is, a sales volume of 205,762 units was considered an impossible event. The use of a continuous probability distribution is desirable not only because the calculation will usually be simplified but because the distribution may also be a more realistic description of the uncertainty aspects of the situation. The normal probability distribution will be introduced and used in the following analysis, which illustrates the methodology involved. This distribution, although widely used, is not appropriate in all situations. The appropriate distribution depends on the decision problem and should of course be selected accordingly.

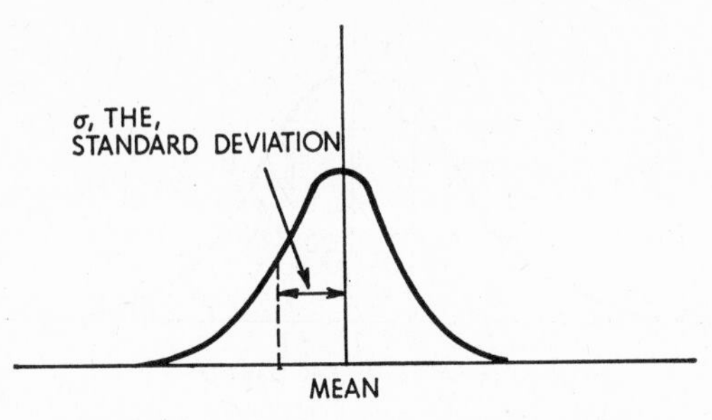

FIGURE 1. The normal probability distribution.

The normal probability distribution is a smooth, symmetric, continuous, bell-shaped curve, as shown in Figure 1. The area under the curve sums to one. The curve reaches a maximum at the mean of the distribution, and one half the area lies on either side of the mean.

On the horizontal axis are plotted the values of the appropriate unknown quantity or random variable; in the examples used here, the unknown quantity is the sales for the coming periods.

A particular normal probability distribution can be completely determined if its mean and its standard deviation, σ, are known. The standard deviation is a measure of the dispersion of the distribution about its mean. The area under any normal distribution is one, but one distribution may be spread out more than another distribution. For example, in Figure 2, both normal distributions have the same area and the same mean. However, in one case the σ is one and in the other case the σ is greater than one. The larger the σ, the more spread-out is the distribution. It should be noted that the standard deviation is not an area but is a measure of the dispersion of the individual observations about the mean of all the observations—it is a distance.

Since the normal probability distribution is continuous rather than discrete, the probability of an event cannot be read directly from the graph. The unknown quantity must be thought of as being in an interval. Assume, for example, that the mean sales for the coming period are estimated to be 10,000

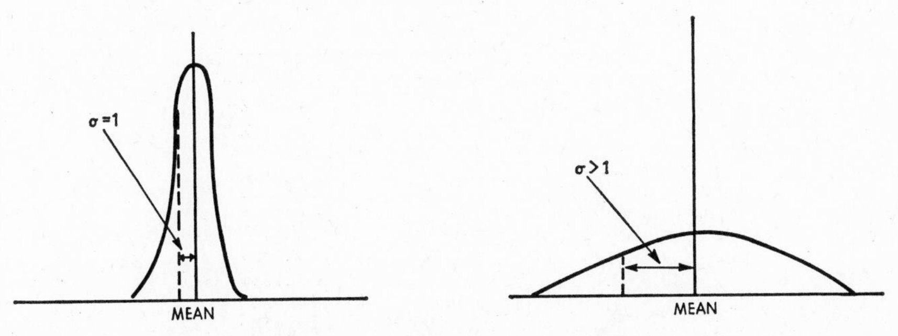

FIGURE 2. Normal probability distributions with different standard deviations.

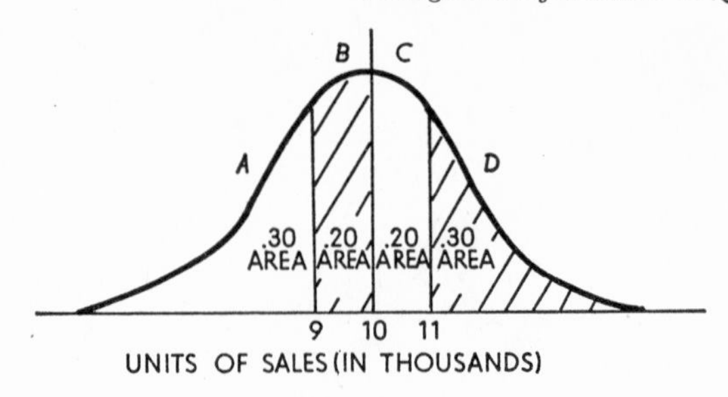

FIGURE 3

units and the normal distribution appears as in Figure 3. Given Figure 3, certain probability statements can be made. For example:

1. The probability of the actual sales being between 10,000 and 11,000 units is 0.20. This is shown by area *C*. Because of the symmetry of the curve, the probability of the sales being between 9,000 and 10,000 is also 0.20. This is shown by shaded area *B*. These probabilities can be given a frequency interpretation. That is, area *C* indicates that the actual sales will be between 10,000 and 11,000 units in about 20 percent of the cases.
2. The probability of the actual sales being greater than 11,000 units is 0.30, as shown by area *D*.
3. The probability of the sales being greater than 9,000 units is 0.70, the sum of areas *B*, *C*, and *D*.

Given a specific normal distribution, it is possible to read probabilities of the type described above directly from a normal probability table.

Another important characteristic of any normal distribution is that approximately 0.50 of the area lies within ± 0.67 standard deviations of the mean; about 0.68 of the area lies within ± 1.0 standard deviations of the mean; 0.95 of the area lies within ± 1.96 standard deviations of the mean.

As was mentioned above, normal probabilities can be read from a normal probability table. A partial table of normal probabilities is given in Table 4.

TABLE 4
AREA UNDER THE NORMAL PROBABILITY FUNCTION

X	*0.00*	*0.05*
0.1	0.4602	0.4404
0.3	0.3821	0.3632
0.5	0.3085	0.2912
0.6	0.2743	0.2578
0.7	0.2420	0.2266
0.8	0.2119	0.1977
0.9	0.1841	0.1711
1.0	0.1587	0.1469
1.1	0.1357	0.1251
1.5	0.0668	0.0606
2.0	0.0228	0.0202

This table is the "right tail" of the distribution; that is, probabilities of the unknown quantity being greater than X standard deviations from the mean are given in the table. For example, the probability of the unknown quantity being greater than the mean plus 0.35σ is 0.3632. The distribution tabulated is a normal distribution with mean zero and standard deviation of one. Such a distribution is known as a standard normal distribution. However, any normal distribution can be standardized and hence, with proper adjustment, Table 4 will serve for any normal distribution.

For example, consider the earlier case where the mean of the distribution is 10,000 units. The distribution was constructed so that the standard deviation is about 2,000 units.[1] To standardize the distribution, use the following formula, where X is the number of standard deviations from the mean:

$$X = \frac{\text{Actual sales} - \text{Mean sales}}{\text{Standard deviation of the distribution}}$$

To calculate the probability of the sales being greater than 11,000 units, first standardize the distribution and then use the table:

$$X = \frac{11{,}000 - 10{,}000}{2{,}000} = 0.50 \text{ standard deviations}$$

The probability of being greater than 0.50 standard deviations from the mean, according to Table 4, is 0.3085. This same approximate result is shown by Figure 3; that is, area D is 0.30.

THE NORMAL DISTRIBUTION USED IN C-V-P ANALYSIS

The normal distribution will now be used in a C-V-P analysis problem, assuming that sales quantity is a random variable. Assume that the per unit selling price is $3,000, the fixed cost is $5.8 million, and the variable cost per unit is $1,750. Break-even sales (in units) are calculated as follows:

$$S_B = \frac{\$5{,}800{,}000}{\$3{,}000 - \$1{,}750} = 4{,}640 \text{ units}$$

Furthermore, suppose that the sales manager estimates that the mean expected sales volume is 5,000 units and that it is equally likely that actual sales will be greater or less than the mean of 5,000 units. Furthermore, assume that the sales manager feels that there is roughly a two-thirds (i.e., 0.667) chance that the actual sales will be within 400 units of the mean. These subjective estimates can be expressed by using a normal distribution with mean $E(Q) =$ 5,000 units and standard deviation $\sigma_q = 400$ units. The reason that σ_q is about 400 units is that, as mentioned earlier, about two-thirds of the area

[1] To see why this normal distribution has a standard deviation of 2,000 units, remember that the probability of sales being greater than 11,000 units is 0.30. Now, examine Table 4, and it can be seen that the probability of a random variable being greater than 0.5 standard deviations from the mean is 0.3085. Hence, 1,000 units is about the same as 0.50 standard deviations. So 2,000 units is about one standard deviation.

under the normal curve (actually 0.68) lies within one standard deviation of the mean. The probability distribution is shown in Figure 4.

The horizontal axis of Figure 4 denotes sales quantity. The probability of an actual sales event taking place is given by the area under the probability

FIGURE 4

distribution. For example, the probability that the sales quantity will exceed 4,640 units (the break-even point) is the shaded area under the probability distribution (the probability of actual sales exceeding 4,640 units).

The probability distribution of Figure 4 can be superimposed on the profit

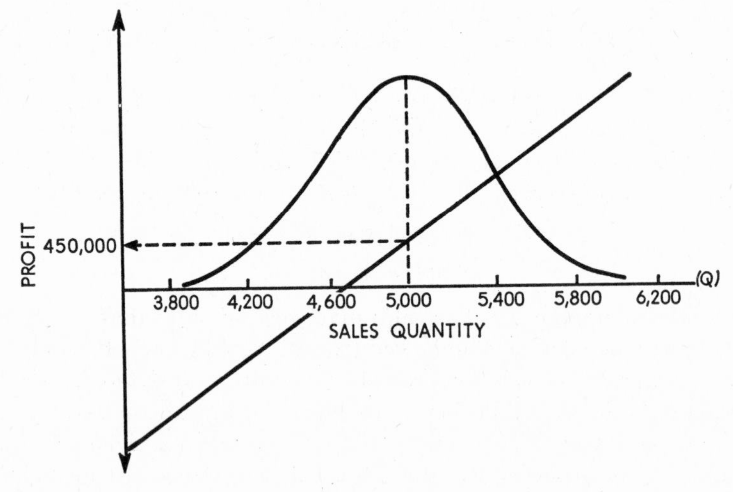

FIGURE 5

portion of the traditional C-V-P; this is done in Figure 5. The values for price, fixed costs, and variable costs are presumed to be known with certainty. Expected profit is given by

$$E(Z) = E(Q)(\text{P-V}) - F = \$450{,}000$$

where

$E(Z)$ = Expected profit
$E(Q)$ = Expected sales
P = Price
V = Variable cost
F = Fixed cost

The standard deviation of the profit (σ_z) is

$$\sigma_Z = \sigma_Q \times \$1{,}250 \text{ contribution per unit} = 400 \text{ units} \times \$1{,}250 = \$500{,}000$$

Since profits are directly related to the volume of sales, and since it is the level of profits which is often the concern of management, it may be desirable to separate the information in Figure 5 which relates to profit. Figure 6 is a

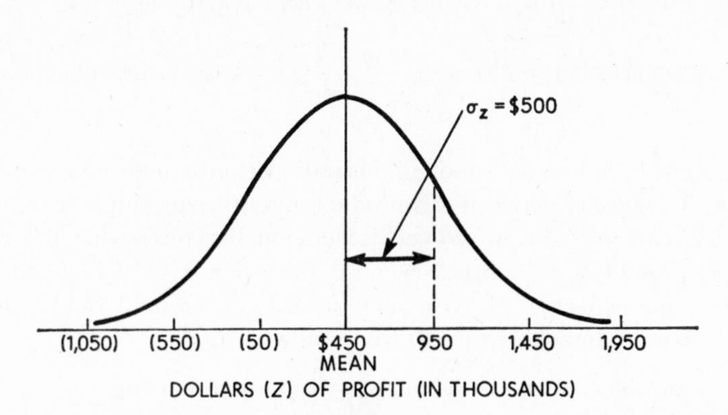

FIGURE 6

graphical illustration of the relationship between profit level and the probability distribution of the profit level. A number of important relationships can now be obtained in probabilistic terms. Since the probability distribution of sales quantity is normal with a mean of 5,000 units and a standard deviation of 400 units, the probability distribution of profits will also be normal with a mean, as shown earlier, of \$450,000 and a standard deviation of \$500,000.

Using the probability distribution shown in Figure 6, the following probabilities can be calculated (using Table 4).

1. *The probability of at least breaking even:* This is the probability of profits being greater than zero and can be calculated by summing the area under the distribution to the right of zero profits. This probability can be calculated as one minus the probability of profits being less than zero. Since the distribution is symmetric, Table 4 can be used to read left-tail as well as right-tail probabilities. Zero profits fall 0.9 standard deviations to the left of the mean, that is:

$$\left(\frac{\$450 - 0}{\$500} = 0.9\right)$$

Hence the probability of profits being less than zero is

$$P(\text{Profits} < 0.9\sigma \text{ from the mean}) = 0.184$$

Therefore:

$$P(\text{Profits} > 0) = 1 - 0.184 = 0.816$$

2. *The probability of profits being greater than $200,000:*

$$\begin{aligned} P\,(\text{Profits} > \$200{,}000) &= 1 - P\left(\text{Profits} < \frac{450 - 200}{500}\,\sigma \text{ from the mean}\right) \\ &= 1 - P\,(\text{Profits} < 0.5\sigma \text{ from the mean}) \\ &= 1 - 0.3085 = 0.692 \end{aligned}$$

3. *The probability of the loss being greater than $300,000:*

$$P\,(\text{Loss} > \$300{,}000) = P\left(\text{Loss} > \frac{450 - (-300)}{500}, \text{ or } 1.5\sigma \text{ from the mean}\right)$$

$$P = 0.067$$

The question of how the above information can be used now arises. The manager, in choosing between this product and other products or other lines of activity, can probably improve his decision by considering the risk involved. He knows that the break-even sales are at a level of 4,640 units. He knows that the expected sales are 5,000 units, which would yield a profit of $450,000. Surely, he would benefit from knowing that

1. The probability of at least reaching breakeven sales is 0.816.
2. The probability of making at least $200,000 profit is 0.692.
3. The probability of making at least $450,000 profit is 0.50.
4. The probability of incurring losses, i.e., not achieving the break-even sales volume, is (1.816, or 0.184).
5. The probability of incurring a $300,000 or greater loss is 0.067, etc.

If the manager is comparing this product with other products, probability analysis combined with C-V-P allows a comparison of the risk involved in each product, as well as a comparison of relative break-even points and expected profits. Given the firm's attitude toward and willingness to assume risk (of losses as well as high profits), the decision of choosing among alternatives should be facilitated by the above analysis.

SEVERAL RELEVANT FACTORS PROBABILISTIC

It is evident from the above discussion that profit, Z, is a function of the quantity of sales in units (Q), the unit selling price (P), the fixed cost (F), and the variable cost (V). Up to this point, P, F, and V were considered only as given constants, so that profit was variable only as a function of changes in sales quantity. In the following discussion, P, F, and V will be treated in a manner similar to Q, i.e., as random variables whose probability distribution is known. Continuing the example from the preceding section, let

Variable	*Expectation (Mean)*	*Standard Deviation*
Sales quantity (Q)	$E(Q') = 5{,}000$ units	$\sigma_{Q'} = 400$ units
Selling price (P)	$E(P') = \$3{,}000$[2]	$\sigma_{P'} = \$50$[2]
Fixed costs (F)	$E(F') = \$5{,}800{,}000$[2]	$\sigma_{F'} = \$100{,}000$[2]
Variable costs (V)	$E(V') = \$1{,}750$[2]	$\sigma_{V'} = \$75$[2]

For purposes of illustration, the random variables will be assumed to be independent, so that no correlation exists between events of the different random variables.[3] In this case the expected profit, $E(Z')$, and the related standard deviation, $\sigma_{Z'}$, can be calculated as follows:

$$E(Z') = E(Q')[E(P') - E(V')] - E(F') = \$450{,}000$$
$$\sigma_{Z'}{}^{4} = \$681{,}500$$

TABLE 5

COMPARISON OF EXPECTED PROFITS, STANDARD DEVIATIONS OF PROFITS, AND SELECT PROBABILISTIC MEASURES*

	Products		
	(1)	*(2)*	*(3)*
Expected profit	$450,000	$450,000	$ 450,000
Standard deviation of profit	$500,000	$681,500	$1,253,000
The probability of:			
a) At least breaking even	0.816	0.745	0.641
b) Profit at least +$250,000	0.655	0.615	0.564
c) Profit at least +$600,000	0.382	0.413	0.456
d) Loss greater than $300,000	0.067	0.136	0.274

* NOTE: The above probabilities, in some cases, cannot be read from Table 4. However, all probabilities come from a more complete version of Table 4.

Note that when factors other than sales are treated as random variables, the expected profit is still $450,000, as in the previous cases. However, the profit's risk as measured by the standard deviation is increased from $500,000 to $681,500. The reason for this is that the variability in all of the components (i.e., sales price, cost, etc.) will add to the variability in the profit. Is this change in the standard deviation significant? The significance of the change is a value judgment based on a comparison of various probabilistic measures and on the firm's attitude toward risk. Using a normal distribution, Table 5

[2] The mean and standard deviation for P, F, and V can be established by using the same method described earlier. That is, the sales manager may estimate a mean selling price of $3,000 per unit; and given the above information, he should feel that there is roughly a two-thirds probability that the actual sales price per unit will be within $50 of this mean estimate.

[3] This assumption is made to facilitate computation in the example. Where correlation among variables is present, the computational procedure must take into account the values of the respective covariances.

[4] For the case of independent variables given here, $\sigma_{Z'}$ is the solution value in the equation

$$\sigma_Z = \sqrt{[\sigma_Q{}^2(\sigma_P{}^2 + \sigma_V{}^2) + E(Q')^2(\sigma_V{}^2 + \sigma_V{}^2) + [E(P') - E(V')]^2\sigma_Q{}^2 + \sigma_F{}^2]}$$

compares expected profits, standard deviations of profits, and select probabilistic measures for three hypothetical products.

In all three situations the proposed products have the same break-even quantity—4,640 units. The first case is the first example discussed, where sales quantity is the only random variable. The second case is the one just discussed; that is, all factors are probabilistic. In the third case the assumed product has the same expected values for selling price, variable cost, fixed cost, and sales volume; but the standard deviations on each of these random variables have been increased to $\sigma_{Q''} = 600$ (instead of 400 units), $\sigma_{P''} =$ \$125 (instead of \$50), $\sigma_{F''} =$ \$200,000 (instead of \$100,000), and $\sigma_{V''} =$ \$150 (instead of \$75).

Table 5 shows the relative "risk" involved in the three new products which have been proposed. The chances of at least breaking even are greatest with product 1. However, even though the standard deviation of the profit on product 3 is over twice that of product 1, the probability of breaking even on product 3 is only 0.17 lower than product 1. Likewise, the probability of earning at least \$250,000 profit is higher for product 1 (which has the lowest σ) than for the other two products.

However, note that the probability of earning profits above the expected value of \$450,000 (for each product) is *greater* for products 2 and 3 than for product 1. If the firm is willing to assume some risk, the chances of high profits are improved with product 3 rather than with products 2 and 1. To offset this, however, the chance of loss is also greatest with product 3. This is to be expected, since product 3 has the highest standard deviation (variability) as far as profit is concerned.

The best alternative cannot be chosen without some statement of the firm's attitude toward risk. However, given a certain attitude, the proper choice should be facilitated by using probability information of the type given in Table 5. As an example, suppose that the firm's position is such that any loss at all may have an adverse effect on its ability to stay in business. Some probability criteria can perhaps be established in order to screen proposals for new products. If, for example, the top management feels that any project which is acceptable must have no greater than a 0.30 probability of incurring a loss, then projects 1 or 2 would be acceptable, but project 3 would not.

On the other hand, the firm's attitude toward risk may be such that the possibility of high profit is attractive, provided the probability of losses can be reasonably controlled. In this case, it may be possible to set a range within which acceptable projects must fall. For example, suppose that the firm is willing to accept projects where the probability of profits being greater than \$600,000 is at least 0.40, provided that the probability of a loss being greater than \$300,000 does not exceed 0.15. In this case, project 2 would be acceptable, but project 3 would not. Given statements of attitude toward risk of this nature, it seems that a probability dimension added to C-V-P analysis would be useful.

SUMMARY AND CONCLUSION

In many cases the choice among alternatives is facilitated greatly by C-V-P analysis. However, traditional C-V-P analysis does not take account of the relative risk of various alternatives. The interaction of costs, selling prices, and volume is important in summarizing the effect of various alternatives on the profits of the firm. The techniques discussed in this paper preserve the traditional analysis but also add another dimension—that is, risk is brought in as another important decision factor. The statement of probabilities with respect to various levels of profits and losses for each alternative should aid the decision maker once his attitude toward risk has been defined.

26

The PERT network is first described, after which PERT/Cost is discussed as an extension of PERT/Time. The methodology of developing a cost framework is examined and extended to PERT/Cost development. Finally, the resource allocation procedure is illustrated by two simple examples.

*PERT/COST: THE CHALLENGE**

Don T. De Coster

EACH DAY that passes sees the growth of new management planning and control tools. Many of these new tools leave the accountant with the unhappy feeling that he should be participating in their use but that he lacks the orientation for active involvement. The desire of the accountant to become involved with these tools is evident from the growth of "management planning and control" chapters in textbooks and the numerous articles dealing with the managerial aspects of accounting output.

One of the newest tools, if evidenced by current publications, is Program Evaluation and Review Technique (PERT). Recently, there have been many discussions, publications, and applications of this technique. PERT's acceptance has been widespread. The accountant must become involved with PERT if he accepts the challenge of Norton Bedford that "the accounting profession has the potential to become one of the great professions if it will accept all phases of measurement and communication of economic data as within its province."[1]

The principal motivating factor in PERT development has been the growth of the concept of systems management within the military services. With programs of unprecedented size, complexity, and breadth, an integrating device has become mandatory. In addition, time is of the essence in weapons system design and development. PERT/Time has been a powerful tool in the kit of managers for planning, coordinating, and integrating these weapon systems.

The culmination of PERT/Time is the network. This network is a pictorial representation of the events and activities that lead to completion of the end objectives. The events represent the beginning and/or ending of ac-

* Reprinted from *Management Services*, May–June, 1964, pp. 13–18.

[1] John L. Carey, *The Accounting Profession: Where Is It Headed?* (New York: American Institute of Certified Public Accountants, 1962), p. 94.

tivities. An *event* is a specific accomplishment or milestone. The *activities* represent things that must be done in going from one event to another. The activity is the time-consuming task. The activities are related to their order of precedence in accomplishing the events. The end result is a network depicting a well-thought-out plan. After the flow of activities and events is mapped, schedule timing can be superimposed. When completion times are included on the activities, the critical path (longest time path) can be determined.

At this point the manager has a tool which needs no further justification. The network presents a clear picture of all the activities and events that must be accomplished before the end objective can be attained. The individuals with responsibility for accomplishment will have discussed all of the relationships, potential drawbacks, and completeness of the plan. When times are imposed upon the plan, the problems of a timely completion are apparent. The activities affecting a timely completion and the schedule's effect on work loads are laid bare for scrutiny. When actual times become available, the updated estimates provide a dynamic control tool to anticipate adverse results. There can be little question that PERT/Time is a tool which, when applied with common sense and vigor, represents a "breakthrough" in management planning and control of the valuable resource of time.

TIME-COST MIX

PERT/Cost is, in reality, an expansion of PERT/Time. With times indicated on the network, it becomes possible to consider alternative plans of action. As the network is being developed, time options are presented which can be considered. Techniques of system stimulation can be employed to ensure that the activities and events will lead to the best climax. The next logical step, with time options available, is to obtain the optimum mix of time and cost. This has led to the attempt to assign costs to the activities on the network. An additional advantage when costs have been assigned to the network for time-cost options is that they can be summed for total cost planning and control.

The development of a system for cost accumulation synchronized with the PERT/Time network must be founded upon objectives consistent with the responsibility of management. In program management the manager is faced with a twofold job. He is charged with the financial planning and control of his firm's resources, while at the same time he is committed to delivery of the end items with a minimum of cost incurrence to the customer.

This was recognized by the developers of PERT/Cost, the National Aeronautics and Space Administration and the Department of Defense, when they visualized it as a three-part system.[2] Basic PERT/Cost is intended to assist the project managers by assigning costs to the working levels in the detail needed for planning schedules and costs, evaluating schedule and cost

[2] Office of the Secretary of Defense and National Aeronautics and Space Administration, *DOD and NASA Guide: PERT/Cost* (Washington, D.C., June, 1962).

performance, and predicting and controlling costs during the operating phase of the program. In addition, there are two supplemental procedures. The time-cost option procedure displays alternative time-cost plans for accomplishing project objectives. The resource allocation procedure determines the lowest cost allocation of resources among individual project tasks to meet the specified project duration. The basic system is to provide total financial planning and control by functional responsibility, while the two supplements are to achieve minimum cost incurrence.

The concept of cost predetermination for planning and control is not new to the accountant. The entire function of budgeting is predicated upon predetermination. Comprehensive budgeting relates income budgets, covering revenues and expenses, to the financial goals of the firm. The expense budgets lead to financial planning and control via projected income, while at the same time the flexible budget and the expense forecasts serve as tools for decision making by relating costs to volume.

PERT/Cost estimates are a new way of looking at the expense budgets. If properly conceived, they can become an integral part of the comprehensive budget program. Yet they differ from conventional expense budgeting in certain respects. From the financial planning and control viewpoint, the PERT/Cost estimates are not concerned with accounting periods. PERT/Cost is activity-oriented. There is a cutting-across of organizational structures and time periods to define "things to be accomplished." The focal point of cost accumulation shifts from the department to the project work package. The annual budget is bypassed to encompass an end item accomplishment. From the detailed decision-making viewpoint, where the flexible budget normally uses volume as the factor of variability, PERT/Cost attempts to use activity time. These two differences will now be examined in more detail.

COST FRAMEWORK

The establishment of a PERT/Cost system begins by developing a framework for gathering cost data and preparing the schedule for all activity levels. The project is defined, then broken down into end item subdivisions, and then into work packages which are assignable to frontline supervision. The integration of the work packages is accomplished through the conventional PERT/Time network. When the interrelationships and time paths have been plotted, the responsible operating and managerial personnel develop cost estimates for each work package.

It is important that both cost and time be planned and controlled from a common framework. From such a framework the managers can obtain an accurate picture of progress and at the same time appraise realistically the consequences of alternative courses of action. The PERT/Time network is this common framework. This imposes upon the network developers the responsibility of carefully defining the activities so that they can represent cost centers as well as the areas of work effort.

The identification of the project objectives in terms of end items is the starting point for network design to be used with PERT/Cost. By using a top-down approach in the development of the network, the total project is fully planned, and all components of the plan are included. Standard units for the breakdown of work below the project level are system, subsystem, task, and subtasks. The work breakdown continues to successively lower levels until the size, complexity, and dollar value of each level is a workable planning and control unit. These subdivisions are end item subdivisions representing horizontal segments of the total project. The final step would be to divide each of these end item subdivisions into the tasks that must be done to complete them, i.e., design, manufacturing, testing, and so forth. This concept is demonstrated in Figure 1.[3] It is this project work breakdown that serves as the input data to the network.

The theoretical optimum level of cost accumulation would be the functional level of each of the end item subdivisions. For example, a cost account would be established for mechanical engineering of the instrumentation, one for manufacturing, and one for testing. The PERT/Cost estimates would then be made for manpower, material, and overhead charges for each of these work packages. It is obvious that a cost accounting system broken down into such intricate detail would comprise numerous accounts. The pragmatic number of account subdivisions will naturally depend upon the detail needed for planning and control, the dollar value of the subdivisions, the activity time on the network, and the machine and personnel capacity available. A practical compromise is often necessary.

PERT/COST COST DEVELOPMENT

Once the network has been established, based upon the project work breakdown, costs can be estimated. If the breakdown has been made satisfactorily, it will serve as both an estimating and an actual cost accumulation vehicle. The proper implementation of PERT/Cost, like budgeting, must rest upon active participation by the responsible executives. This was recognized by the NASA/DOD PERT/Cost Guide when it was recommended that the operating and management personnel develop the cost estimates for each work package.[4] As with budgeting, any accounting work during the estimation period would be of a coordinating nature.

The development of the cost estimates must rest upon a sound philosophical basis consistent with management needs. Presently, there are four approaches to developing the cost estimates:

1. A single-cost estimate of expected actual cost
2. Three-cost estimates combined by formula into expected cost

---

[3] *Ibid.*, p. 28.

[4] *Ibid.*, pp. 109–13.

3. Optimum time-cost curves (used in construction industries and by NASA/DOD Resource Allocation Procedure Supplement)
4. Three separate cost estimates (used in the NASA/DOD Time-Cost Option Procedure Supplement)

Each of these theories of PERT/Cost estimating has as its goal the assigning of the best cost estimates possible to the network. Yet each offers the manager separate, distinct planning capabilities.

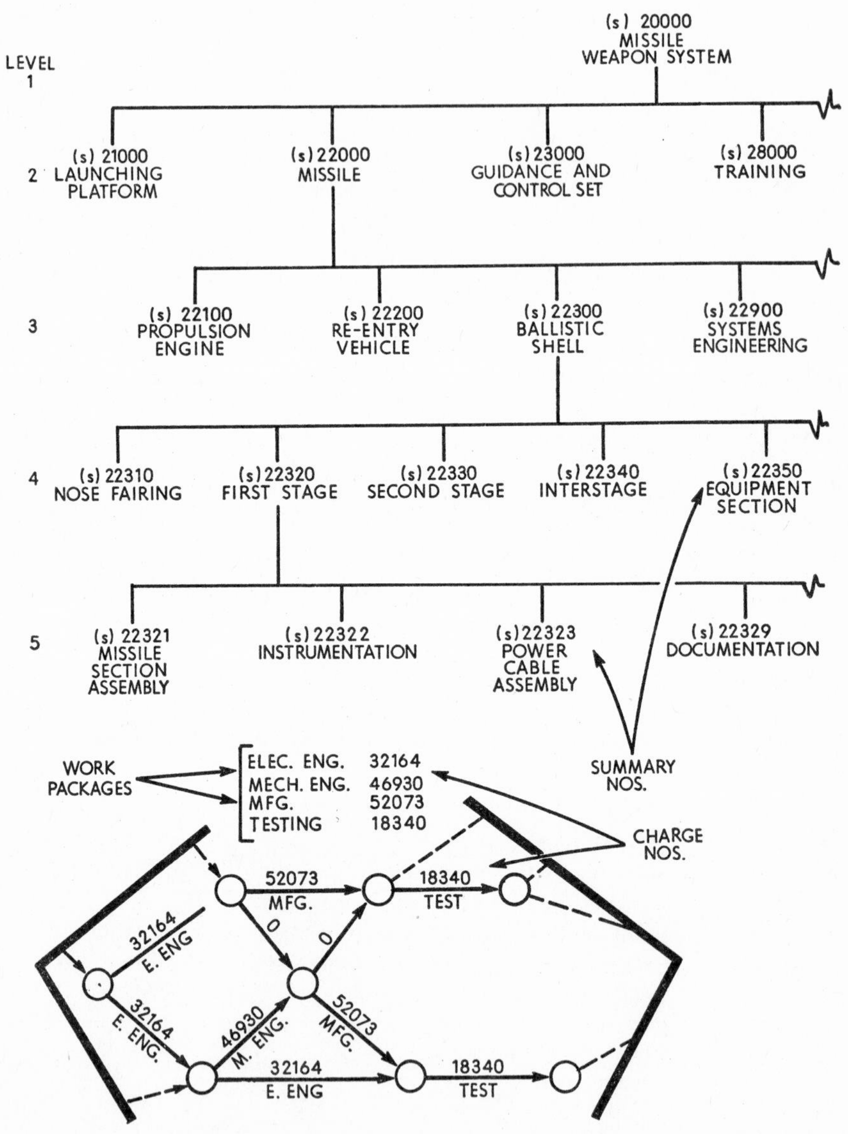

FIGURE 1. Simplified example of a work breakdown structure and account code structure.

A single-cost estimate of expected actual cost is based upon the summation of the cost elements. These estimates are first made by determining the manpower, material, and other resources required to complete each work package. The estimates for the direct costs applicable to the network activities are expressed in terms of expected dollar expenditures. Indirect costs may then be allocated to the individual work package or added to the total cost of the project.

The three-cost-estimate approach has as its goal the determination of the "expected cost." The advantage of the three-cost estimate over the single-cost estimate is that the result is subject to probability analysis. The formula combines an optimistic, most likely, and pessimistic cost estimate. The mean cost for each activity is calculated by the formula

$$C_e = \frac{C_P + 4C_L + C}{6}$$

where C_P is the pessimistic estimate, C_L is the most likely cost, and C_O the optimistic estimate. The standard deviation of the cost distribution can insert probability into the analysis. With this expected cost the manager cannot necessarily assume that he has the optimum cost-time mix. However, if the cost estimates are realistic, the probabilities of achieving the expected cost can be used for project negotiations.

A third approach to cost estimates is the optimum time-cost curve concept. This is differential costing with time as the factor of variability. The intention of this approach is to optimize time and costs by using optimum estimated costs. It assumes there is a direct relationship between time and costs on any activity. This relationship can be expressed by a continuous curve. If a cost curve can be developed similar to Figure 2, many insights can be gained. Network schedules can be modified to obtain the lowest cost commensurate with the customer's delivery desires. Other questions can also be anticipated—questions such as: How long will completion take with a fixed budget? What will the costs be to complete the project within a given time period? In theory, this concept is undoubtedly superior to either the one- or the three-formula estimates, but without complete historical cost data the development of this curve is impractical.

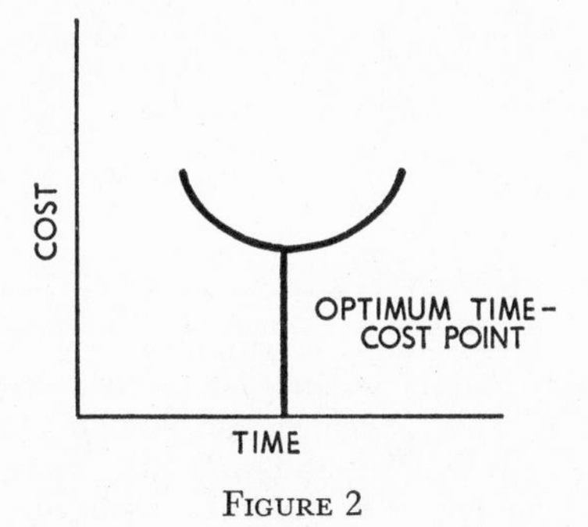

FIGURE 2

Because the development of continuous time-cost curves for all activities is extremely difficult, if not practically impossible, the Resource Allocation Supplement to PERT/Cost was developed. This supplement is a variation of continuous time-cost curves which can be used in planning a small group of *significant* activities representing only a minor portion of the overall project.

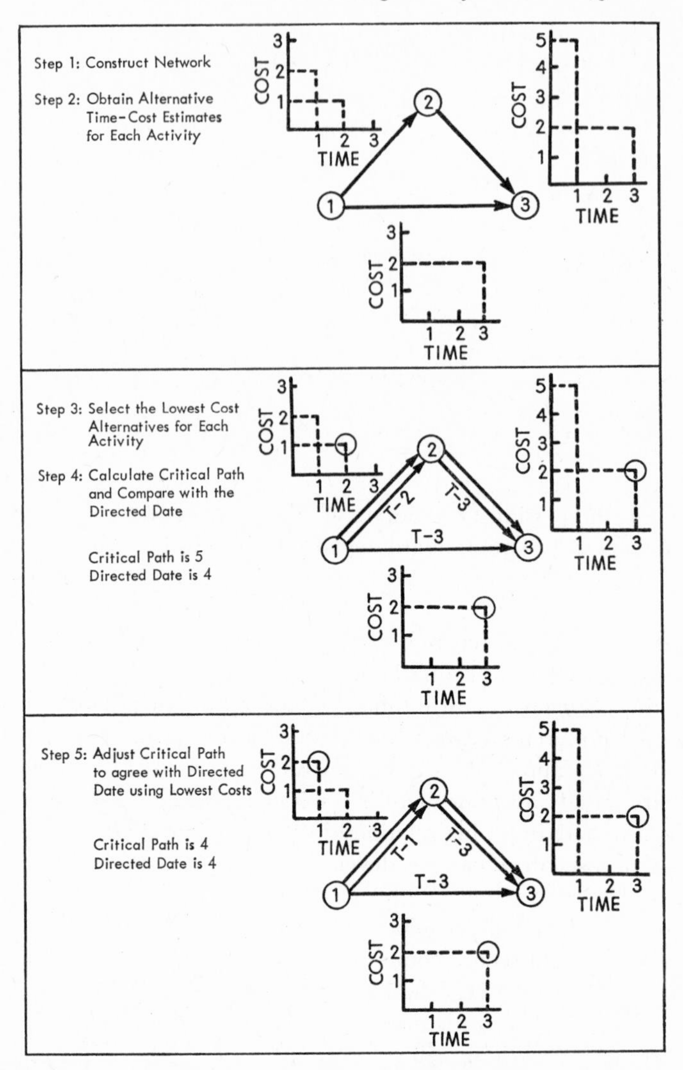

FIGURE 3. A summary of the resource allocation procedure.

In the resource allocation procedure, we can determine how to accomplish a project by a specified date at minimum cost. The critical path here is the path from event 1 to event 2, and from event 2 to event 3, since this will require five days at absolute minimum costs. But the directed date for completing the project is four days from its beginning. Thus, from the time-cost chart, we find that we can cut the time between events 1 and 2 to one day, but we double the cost of this activity. Since shortening the time of the second step in the critical path would cost more, however, we choose to reduce time of the first step to one day.

This method is also based upon the concept that activities are subject to time-cost trade-offs. The steps of this procedure are shown in the diagrams in Figure 3.[4]

[4] *Ibid.*, pp. 109–13.

Another alternate to overcome the practical problem of the continuous cost curve is a linear function based upon two time-cost relationships. The cost and time expenditures are forecast for two conditions: normal and crash. The normal point is the minimum activity cost and the corresponding time. The crash point is defined as the minimum possible time to perform the activity and the related cost. A linear function is assumed to exist between these points. Figure 4 shows this graphically. This method is similar to the high-low point method of fixed and variable cost determination and suffers from the same type of criticism.[5] The problems of realistic estimates, discretionary costs, stairstepped cost functions, incorrect correlation between

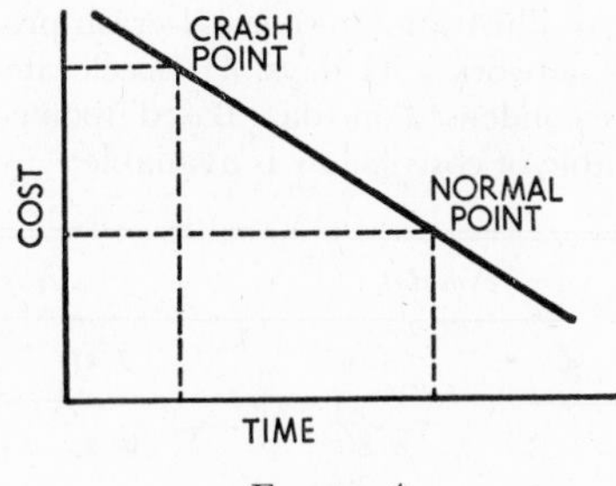

FIGURE 4

time and cost, and external factors are continually present. It is justifiable due to its relative simplicity when the element of nonpredictable error can be permitted. A simplified but typical usage is shown in Figure 5.

The NASA/DOD PERT/Cost Guide presents a time-cost option (called the Time-Cost Option Procedure Supplement) based upon three time estimates. The single estimate of expected cost and the three-cost-estimate formula methods do not indicate whether there may be a substantially more efficient alternative plan. The continuous cost curve concept provides these data[6] but requires considerable sophistication in cost analysis, or else considerable supposition. The time-cost supplement recognizes that a single estimate will normally be used for contract proposals and that additional data are needed to provide information as to the amount of time that might be saved by spending more money or the amount of money that could be saved by extending the contract time. The three time estimates used are:

1. *The most efficient plan:* This is the network plan that will meet the technical requirements of the project utilizing the most efficient use of present resources. This is the plan that would be chosen without budget and time constraints.
2. *The directed-date plan:* This is the network plan developed to meet the technical requirements of the project by the specified completion date.
3. *The shortest time plan:* This is the network plan that will meet the technical requirements of the project in the shortest possible time.

---

[5] Glenn Welsch, *Budgeting: Profit-Planning and Control* (Englewood Cliffs, N.J.: Prentice-Hall, Inc., 1957), pp. 173–74.

[6] See Figure 2.

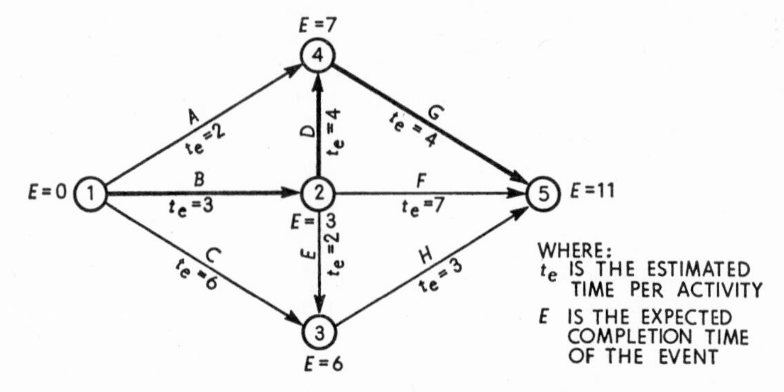

FIGURE 5. An illustration of normal-crash procedure.

The critical path of this network is 11 days. To accelerate the program one day, activities *B*, *G*, or *D* must be condensed one day. Based upon cost curves computed on a normal-crash basis, the table of costs below is available:

Activity	*Normal*		*Crash*		*Acceleration Cost per Day*
	Days	*Cost*	*Days*	*Cost*	
A	2	80	1	130	50
B	3	70	1	190	60
C	6	110	5	135	25
D	4	60	3	100	40
E	2	90	1	100	10
F	7	85	6	115	30
G	4	105	3	175	70
H	3	50	2	70	20
Totals		650		1,015	

Since activity *D* costs \$40 to accelerate, whereas activity *G* costs \$70 and activity *B* \$120, accelerating activity *D* is least expensive. The total cost of completing the program in 10 days is \$690 (\$650 + \$40). By compressing the project one day, activity *F* enters the critical path. To accelerate the program to nine days, the following activities could be reduced: *G* and *F* at a total cost of \$100 or *B* at a cost of \$60. Therefore, for the reduction to nine days the cost would be \$750 (\$650 + \$40 + \$60).

Since the desired plan is the most efficient plan, any study should begin there. This most efficient plan must then be modified to achieve the project's objectives by the specified date. The most efficient plan, when altered to attain the desired delivery date, becomes the directed-date plan. The directed-date plan is then revised to obtain the shortest time plan. The work packages that have not changed in evolving the alternate plans will utilize cost estimates for the most efficient plan. New cost estimates will be necessary only on those work packages that are expected to increase or decrease because of the modifications. With three estimates on these work packages, the customer is apprised of the impact of his decisions during negotiations. Once the customer has made his decision, the appropriate cost estimate can be assigned to the network.

These cost-estimating techniques represent the current approaches to computing forecast costs. When coupled with a sound approach to determining the project work breakdown, forward planning is definitely facilitated. To this point, PERT/Cost is a planning tool, but the loop between planning and control is not closed. For control, there must be comparisons of actual cost expenditures with those estimated during the planning state. The accountant must play an active role when the loop is closed between the planning and control phases. The generation of feedback data consistent with the planning stage calls for a chart of accounts correlated to the PERT network.

THE PERT/COST CHALLENGE

The accountant is charged by management and society with providing financial information for all levels of decision making. If the accountant is to serve the managers effectively, he will have to broaden his influence beyond the confines of historical data to include all areas of the firm and the future. PERT/Cost offers him one challenge in this direction. It can be seen that if PERT/Cost can be coordinated with PERT/Time, the manager has an excellent tool for project planning and control. In addition to financial reporting both on the total cost level and on the individual manager's level, it offers distinct opportunities for decision making during both the planning and the control phases.

The discussions here might lead one to believe that PERT/Cost offers no problems. Unfortunately, this is not the case. Despite the potential, there are basic problems. An enumeration of some of these problems would include:

1. PERT/Cost for decision making in optimizing costs requires a sophistication of cost analysis that is not possessed by some firms.
2. There is a lack of historical information for assigning costs to networks since the concept is new.
3. There is difficulty in making project costs compatible with fiscal practices.
4. The problems of overhead charges, joint costs, and incompatibility of the organizational cost flow with the functional flow are numerous.
5. There is a problem of reconciling the jobs that are using PERT/Cost with those that aren't for fiscal reporting.
6. The personnel and machine capabilities are not always available.
7. Cost accumulation for financial stewardship reports can conflict with the cost centers for PERT/Cost and can therefore create redundant systems.
8. The conversion of project-oriented costs to mesh with annual budget concepts requires additional analysis.

If the problems associated with PERT/Cost can be resolved, PERT with Cost could be considered a major breakthrough, as was PERT with time. The majority of the potential problem areas with PERT/Cost lie in the controller's department. These difficulties present a very real challenge to the controller. PERT/Cost is putting the adaptability of the accountant to the test.

V

Inventory Control

TABLEAU V

Methodological Analysis

Article / Methodology	General Analysis of Basic Concepts	Descriptive Models for Analysis					Optimizing Models			
		Algebraic or Symbolic (Deterministic)	*Algebraic or Symbolic (Probabilistic)*	*Matrix Methods*	*Markov Processes*	*Simulation*	*Linear Programming*	*Game Theory*	*Calculus*	*Other*
27. Inventory Control	X									
28. Some Business Applications of Marginal Analysis—With Particular Reference to Inventory Control	X									
29. A Basis for Strategic Decisions on Inventory Control Operations									X	
30. Markov Chains and Simulations in an Inventory System						X				
31. The Application of Monte Carlo Analysis to an Inventory Problem						X				

INVENTORY CONTROL

Inventory control has traditionally been considered to be one of the compelling preoccupations of the accountant. Particular attention has been directed to cost accounting as one of the major tools to be utilized by accountants in achieving this control. But even here, it is noteworthy that decisions made are often of a subjective nature, even though based upon numerical data. The effect of a decision upon fundamental objectives is seldom quantified; often, only the disclosure that the decision will either increase or decrease a few highly constrained elements of total cost is made.

Inventory models provide a means for evaluating in quantitative terms a broader spectrum of relevant effects of decisions relating to inventory. Thus an optimal solution for given objectives can often be obtained. The objective need not be cost minimization, although that is the criterion frequently applied in most inventory models. Significantly, if cost minimization is the goal, concepts of cost different from that conventionally referred to by the cost accountant must be applied in order to derive the optimal solution.

Articles 27, 28, and 29 discuss the relevant concepts of inventory cost and apply the cost minimization criterion. Simulation is also a powerful tool in inventory problems, especially with the improvement of computer technology. The general concepts applied in simulation models are described in article 31. The effectiveness of this technique is then demonstrated in article 30 in a comparison of simulation results with the solution obtained from an analytic model (Markov process).

27

The basic objectives of inventory control are broadly outlined and discussed. The author then focuses on the problems involved in estimating the cost parameters included in standard inventory models. In particular, each of the several general types of inventory costs are analyzed, and the major items comprising each group are set out and briefly described. Additionally, various procedures for computing safety-stock levels are presented.

*INVENTORY CONTROL**

Robert D. Niemeyer

INVENTORY CONTROL is concerned with establishing and maintaining desired inventory levels. In keeping with this concept, the inventory control techniques that will be discussed are directed toward unit control of inventory rather than the closely related function of accounting for inventory dollars.

Broadly stated, the basic objective of inventory control is to establish and maintain an adequate inventory level at a minimum inventory cost. Achievement of this objective requires solution to two basic problems:

1. Determination of desired inventory levels, weighing inventory costs against such inventory benefits as
   a) Improved customer service that may result in increased sales
   b) Smoother production operations yielding lower production costs
2. Minimization of total inventory costs for a given inventory level, giving consideration to the interaction between
   a) Acquisition costs
   b) Holding costs

An approach to the solution of these basic inventory control problems will be discussed in the following sequence:

1. Methods of control
2. Inventory costs
3. Determination of expected inventory usage
4. Other refinements

There are two primary factors that must be considered in the control of inventories:

1. *How much* of an item is replenished at a time
2. *When* the item is replenished

*Reprinted from *Management Services*, July-August, 1964, pp. 25–31.

These two factors control inventory levels; and through these factors, total inventory costs can be minimized for any given inventory level.

How Much

In discussing this factor, we should first look at the basic sawtooth inventory pattern to visualize the effect of replenishment quantities on inventory levels. This basic pattern is depicted in Charts 1 and 2.

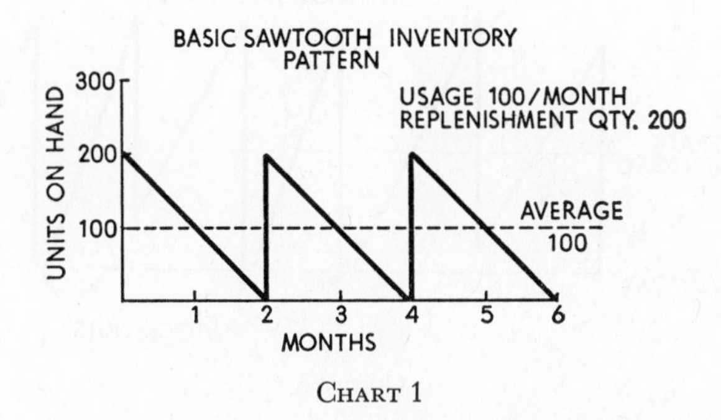

CHART 1

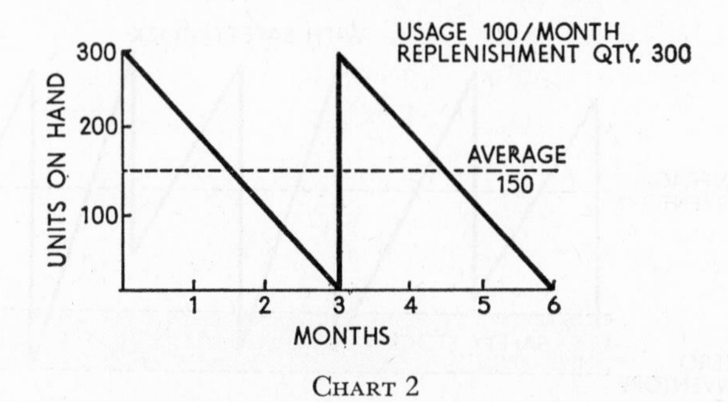

CHART 2

These charts illustrate the effect of replenishment quantities on inventory levels. Stock is replenished in quantities of 200 (Chart 1) and 300 (Chart 2).

In these charts, we have assumed that the *when* factor is controlled so that a replenishment is received when on-hand balance has reached zero. From Chart 1, we can also easily see that the average inventory is 100 and that this amount is also equal to one half of the replenishment quantity. If we increase the order quantity to 300 units, we increase the average inventory to 150 units, as shown on Chart 2.

When

Charts 1 and 2 demonstrate that *how much* is a definite factor in determining inventory levels. Now, consider the *when* factor. On these charts the *when* factor was controlled so that a replenishment was received when the on-hand balance reached zero. However, some replenishment lead time is normally involved, and this factor must be known in solving the *when* problem. Assuming a lead time of one month, we find that on our first chart the items must be ordered at the end of the first month so that replenishment will arrive when on-hand balance reaches zero. This order point could also be

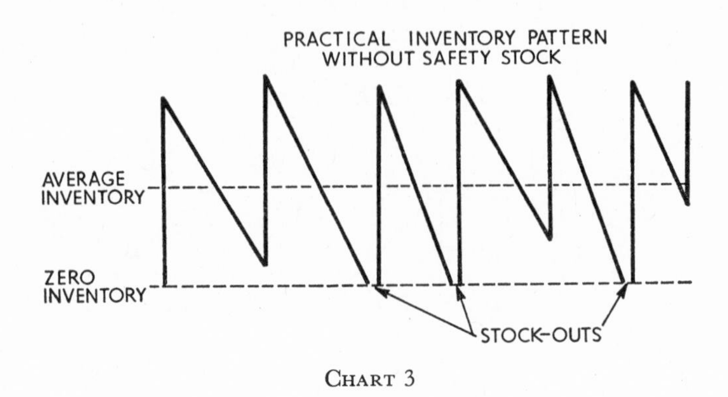

CHART 3

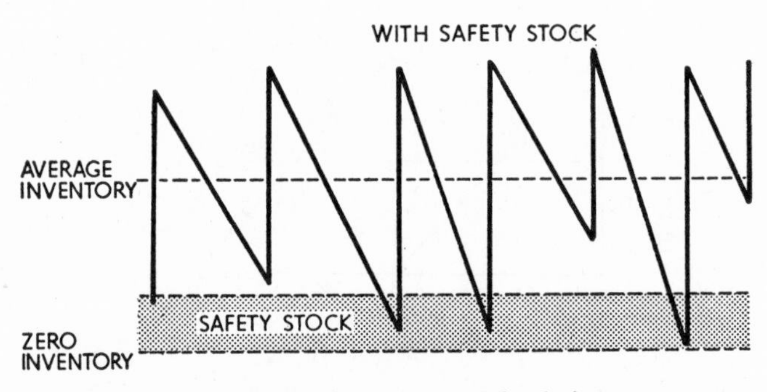

CHART 4. Variations in usage and lead time may cause stock-outs (Chart 3) unless a higher inventory level is maintained (Chart 4) to provide safety stock.

expressed in terms of on-hand balance as 100 units, this quantity representing expected usage during the lead-time period. So we see that lead time and expected usage are both required for determining a reorder point expressed in terms of on-hand balance. However, we have not yet considered just how the *when* factor influences inventory levels. When we do this, we find that the basic sawtooth pattern with usage and other variations would appear as shown on Charts 3 and 4.

In Chart 3 the basic inventory pattern is disrupted by two factors found in practical inventory situations:

1. Usage variations
2. Lead-time variations

As this chart indicates, these factors cause stock-outs when inventories are controlled under the premise that a replenishment will be received when on-hand balance reaches zero.

To provide for these inherent variations, an additional amount of stock must be carried. This additional quantity, or safety stock, thus makes our practical inventory chart appear as it does in Chart 4.

This protection is built into our inventory balance by the *when* factor. Under an order-point system the protection is primarily needed during the replenishment (lead-time) period and is obtained by adding the protection required to the reorder point expressed in terms of on-hand balance. The formula for the reorder point then becomes:

Reorder point = (Expected usage during the lead-time period) + (Safety stock)

This action can probably best be shown with these new factors superimposed on our first basic chart (see Chart 5). In this illustration, we have

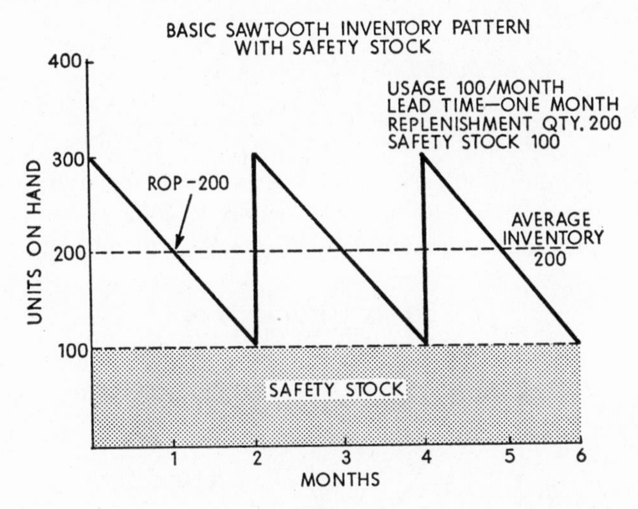

CHART 5. This chart shows what happens to average inventory if the reorder point is calculated with allowance for both expected usage during the lead-time period and safety stock.

assumed a desirable safety stock of 100 units and have accordingly increased the reorder point from 100 to 200 units. Under these conditions the average inventory becomes 200 units. It can also be seen that this average inventory is composed of two elements:

1. One half of replenishment quantity
2. Safety stock

We have now determined a formula for development of average inventory under an order-point system:

Average inventory = (½ Order quantity) + (Safety stock)

This same formula holds approximately true under our practical inventory problem previously charted. Safety stock tends to be on the average a constant amount, while working stocks are composed of replenishment quantities, the average of which is approximately one half of the established replenishment quantity.

Before discussing these principles of basic inventory control further, let us summarize the points that have been covered:

1. Replenishment quantity directly affects average inventory levels.
2. When to replenish stock can be expressed in terms of on-hand units as reorder point.
3. Reorder point = Expected usage during the lead-time period plus safety stock.
4. Average inventory = (½ Replenishment quantity) + (Safety stock).

These basic rules lead normally, then, to the question of determining replenishment and safety-stock quantities since these two factors determine average inventory levels.

Replenishment Quantities

Since replenishment (order) quantities affect average inventory levels, they affect the costs associated with having inventory (holding or carrying costs). The size of replenishment quantity also affects the frequency with which an

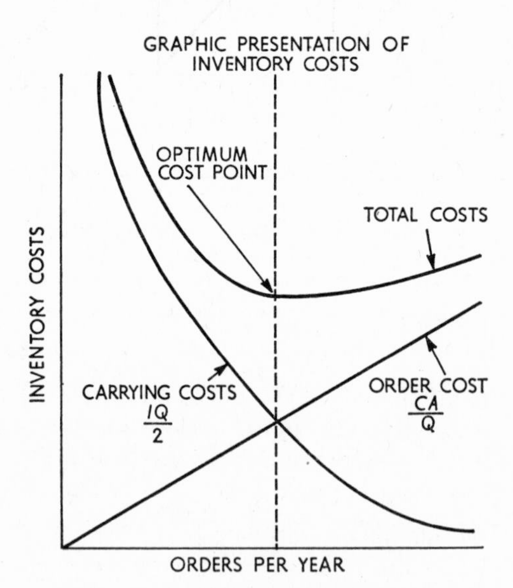

CHART 6. The economic order-quantity formula is based on the relationship between holding and acquisition costs. Total cost is lowest where the lines cross.

item must be reordered. Therefore the replenishment quantity also affects order or acquisition costs, and economic order quantity formulas consider both holding and acquisition cost factors in arriving at the best balanced or least-cost order quantity.

This relationship between the two individual cost lines and the total cost line is shown graphically on Chart 6. It can be seen that the minimum total cost occurs at the same order quantity at which the two individual lines meet. A basic economic order quantity formula can be developed from the relationships as charted.

Let

Q = Economic order quantity in dollars
A = Annual usage in dollars
C = Cost of an order in dollars
I = Inventory carrying cost, as a decimal

Then

$$\text{Order cost line} = \frac{CA}{Q}$$

and

$$\text{Carrying cost line} = \frac{IQ}{2}$$

When these two are equated, we have

$$\frac{CA}{Q} = \frac{IQ}{2}$$

and

$$Q = \sqrt{\frac{2CA}{I}}$$

By additional mathematics, we can also express order quantity in units, as follows:

$$Q\ (\text{Units}) = \sqrt{\frac{2 \times C \times (\text{Annual usage units})}{1 \times (\text{Unit cost})}}$$

For example, if we assume that we annually use 100 units of an item that costs $4 a unit and that we have an order cost of $10 and an inventory carrying cost of 20 percent, our formula becomes

$$\text{Units to order} = \sqrt{\frac{2 \times 10 \times 100}{0.20 \times 4}} = 50$$

Determination of the inventory carrying and order or acquisition costs required for application of this basic formula will be covered in a later portion of this discussion.

This basic formula, developed in the early part of this century, is in fairly widespread use in solving today's problems of inventory control. There are, however, several points that should be made regarding use of this formula.

As we shall discuss a little later, some of the costs required for application of the formula are somewhat difficult to determine precisely. It should be remembered, however, that all factors influencing the answer are under a square root sign, which allows some latitude in the determination of these costs and acts as a sort of "forgiveness factor." In addition, while carrying or acquisition costs may be approximated and the resulting equating of the two not completely precise, the answer should be considerably better than an out-and-out guess or an intuitive approach.

Another limiting factor possibly to be found in the use of the formula is that when constant carrying and acquisition costs are used across a wide range of inventory items, the answers become somewhat impractical at the extreme ends of the range. That is, use of the formula may indicate that an unworkably large amount should be ordered for a low-cost item or that too frequent orders should be placed for a high-cost item. These difficulties can be overcome by actually recognizing the variations in costs for various types of items or, in a more practical way, by limiting the answers at each end of the range.

It can also be pointed out that this basic *EOQ* formula does not consider all variables in the problem, an obvious example being that quantity discounts are not directly recognized. If quantity discounts are a significant factor, the difficulty may be overcome by a simple one-time computation that can be used in determining alternate order quantities from those developed by the formula.

This is done by calculating the additional cost incurred for various increased order quantities and charting these with order quantities down the side, unit cost across the top, and additional cost in the appropriate boxes. Thus the saving by quantity discount can be compared directly with the additional cost incurred because of the larger size of the order, and an intelligent decision can be made accordingly.

Another factor that must be considered in using the formula is that the computation for each order is somewhat complicated. Probably one of the reasons for the considerably extended use of this formula in recent years is the availability of electronic data processing equipment. Such equipment has made it relatively easy to compute *EOQ* amounts at the time of each reorder. There are, however, other methods of applying this basic formula. One practical way is to develop a table of *EOQ* amounts based on various ranges of annual dollar usage. While not completely precise at the extremes of each range, this method is preferable to more arbitrary determination of order quantities. Another method of applying the formula is through the use of a nomograph. An *EOQ* nomograph is a sort of poor man's slide rule and utilizes three equidistant parallel lines with logarithmic scales. The simplest form uses one column for monthly usage in units, the middle scale for order quantity, and the other scale for unit cost. By connecting the appropriate monthly usage with the proper unit cost, the line crosses the middle scale at the economic order quantity. Once a nomograph has been prepared, it can be published in various formats and can even be printed on the back of the requisition form for ready reference.

Safety-Stock Quantities

It has been demonstrated that safety-stock quantities directly affect average inventory holdings. It would then follow that safety-stock levels directly affect inventory holding or carrying costs. Since safety stock is carried to provide protection against stock-outs, the determination of safety-stock quantities requires the balancing of holding costs against outage costs (as differentiated from *EOQ* considerations, where we were balancing holding costs against acquisition costs). As we shall discuss further under the cost portion of this presentation, the cost of an outage is somewhat difficult, if not impossible, to determine precisely. Most approaches to the development of safety-stock quantities take this fact into consideration.

There is probably no widely accepted formula for safety-stock computations as there is for determining economic order quantities. Most approaches do, however, attempt to provide safety stock that will cover *reasonable maximum usage* during the *lead-time period.* Let's take a look at some of the ways this somewhat arbitrary amount may be determined.

One method is tied in with several other inventory refinements, which will be discussed later. The key point in this method is a definition of the *maximum* amount of usage fluctuations (expressed as a percentage) for which protection would be provided. Items for which usage fluctuations are greater than or equal to the maximum considered are given maximum protection. Those for which usage fluctuations are not equal to the maximum are protected for historical actual amounts. Under this method, more consistent use items are given proportionately less safety stock than those with more erratic use patterns.

Another approach—one which requires substantial data and computing facilities—to handle safety-stock computations takes into consideration that most inventory usage patterns follow some standard statistical distribution. On this basis, percentage of outage based on standard statistical factors can be determined. Then, by computing holding costs for various levels of inventory, a chart can be prepared showing cost for various percentages of inventory coverage. Such a chart can be helpful to management in determining just how far it is willing to go in providing inventory protection.

Other safety-stock formulas take into consideration such refinements as the average size of requisition quantities. The formula used by one of the major airlines combines this feature with the statistical approach mentioned above.

In summary, it should be emphasized that considerable judgment enters into safety-stock computations, and that the answer should be designed and tempered to fit the situation. The definition that safety stock should provide protection for *reasonable* maximum usage during the lead-time period is a good guide. It remains, then, to apply some judgment to determine what is reasonable in any given situation.

We have now covered some basic methods of inventory control based on the fixed order quantity approach. Included in these techniques were consideration of certain costs and a requirement for an estimate of future usage. These two items—costs and estimate of future usage—will be discussed next.

INVENTORY COSTS

Major categories of inventory costs are

1. Acquisition costs
2. Holding costs
3. Outage costs

In discussing these costs, it is probably best first to define each item of cost and then to consider some practical means of quantifying these various items.

Acquisition Costs

Costs related to acquisition of purchased items would include the following categories of expense:

1. Requisitioning
2. Purchase order (including expediting)
3. Trucking
4. Receiving
5. Placing in storage
6. Accounting and auditing:
   a) Inventory
   b) Disbursements

Acquisition costs pertaining to company-manufactured pieces include several of the above-mentioned items but also comprehend some different categories, notably setup costs rather than purchase-order costs. A complete list of manufactured-item acquisition costs could include

1. Requisitioning
2. Setup
3. Receiving
4. Placing in storage
5. Accounting and auditing:
   a) Inventory
   b) Product costs

In considering just how much of any of these costs should be applied to inventory control decisions, we again must use some rule-of-thumb or arbitrary methods. To begin with, records frequently are not kept in such a way that the above-mentioned categories of cost are readily accessible. Very often, determination of these costs must be made by special study. Then we have the problem of deciding what degree of variability should be used when these costs are applied in the *EOQ* formula. (This is the only computation reviewed in this presentation where acquisition costs are used.) Welch, in his book *Scientific Inventory Control*, suggests that the effect of a 25 percent change in order rate should be used as a basis for determining acquisition costs. This is a reasonably good approach because some of these costs do not increase in a straight line but rather in a stair-step pattern. This 25 percent rule tends to give some weight to the latter condition. In any event, *all* acquisition costs should *not* be used in the standard *EOQ* formula; but the *variable* portion, determined on some reasonable basis, should be applied.

Holding or Carrying Costs

Holding or carrying costs to be considered in the solution of inventory control problems would include the following items:

1. Interest
2. Insurance
3. Taxes
4. Storage
5. Obsolescence

In arriving at these costs for inventory control solutions, it is probably best to consider only those items meeting the following two tests:

1. Out-of-pocket expenditures
2. Foregone opportunities for profit

An example of the application of these tests would be the consideration of warehouse space costs only to the extent that additional facilities would need to be acquired or that unused space could be rented for profit. These rules would also indicate that interest would be considered from the standpoint of forgone profit opportunity when sufficient capital exists in the business that money need not be borrowed to finance inventories.

Again, as with acquisition costs, holding costs are somewhat difficult to determine precisely because the usual records do not easily identify them. In addition, problems exist with the application of the above-mentioned rules or tests. As a guide to reasonableness of holding costs that may be computed, the following table of representative cost ranges is offered:

Item	*Approximate Range*
Interest	4–10%
Insurance	1– 3
Taxes	1– 3
Storage	0– 3
Obsolescence	4–16
Total	10–35%

This table is a composite taken from various references and tempered with personal experience. Obviously, any extreme situation may fall outside the ranges shown, but the table should be representative of the majority of situations.

Outage Costs

This category of costs is mentioned primarily because it exists, and not because definitive rules can be set forth for computing outage costs. It was noted earlier that outages result in

1. Decreased customer service level, which *may* result in decreased sales
2. Less efficient production operations
3. High costs resulting from "crash" procurements

It is probably obvious that out-ages affect the items named above; the unanswered question in most cases is "How much?" Unless some very direct relationships exist, the cost of an outage is difficult to quantify.

The fact that answers to the determination of outage costs are approximate and arbitrary in nature does not necessarily mean, however, that their significance should be ignored. As was seen in the computation of safety stocks (where these costs apply), knowledge of the cost of alternatives enables the application of enlightened judgment to produce satisfactory answers to the problem of just how great an outage rate is acceptable.

DETERMINATION OF EXPECTED USAGE

All replenishment of inventory requires some sort of forecast for determining expected usage. This forecast can take various forms, including

1. Hunches
2. Visual review of past history
3. Computation of average demand over a past period
4. Exponential smoothing of past demand
5. Tying past demand to a more reliable forecast
6. Relationship with other forecast items

This is obviously only a partial list, but it can serve as a basis for discussing forecasting methods as they relate to inventory control situations.

The first two of these categories have been included not because of their advantages but because of their widespread use. Whenever human judgment is the primary ingredient in inventory usage forecasts, the resulting answers tend to show the influence of overcompensation for the current situation. For example, when usage temporarily increases, much greater quantities are ordered. When usage then seeks its normal trend and declines, a large overstock results. Human reaction to temporary decreases in usage, on the other hand, often results in stock-outs.

The point of this discussion is that an answer arrived at in a methodical, consistent fashion is usually much more reliable over a period of time than an answer obtained by hunch. In fact, in a particular application of some of these inventory control principles, a good portion of the benefit was obtained by replacing a usage forecast based mainly on human judgment by one based on principles *consistently* applied to past usage.

In direct computation of usage forecasts, either the averaging of past demand for a selected period of time or the exponential smoothing of past demand provides an acceptable method. The characteristics of the inventory in question and the facilities available for making the computation should influence the decision as to which method to use. Exponential smoothing gives greater weight to more recent periods and has the advantage of not requiring detailed usage history for each inventory item.

In certain production situations the last two forecasting methods outlined above can be used to advantage. The use of other forecasts can probably best be illustrated by a method that utilizes the explosion of a finished item into its component and piece parts. The demand for the finished item is forecast directly, and the component and piece parts then become a logical extension of that forecast.

OTHER REFINEMENTS

Two inventory control concepts that have been used successfully and have fairly broad application should also be covered in a general discussion of inventory control principles. These two are

1. *A-B-C* approach
2. Use of control limits

A-B-C Approach

This concept is based on the premise that in most inventories approximately 10 percent of the items account for about 85 percent of the annual dollar usage. At the other extreme, about 75 percent of the items account for only about 5 percent of the annual dollar usage. Recognition of this situation and division of the inventory into three groups (*A*, *B*, and *C*) based on annual dollar usage has commonly been called the *A-B-C* method.

These relationships appear to exist in virtually all inventories; and because of this and the advantages of being able to place emphasis on the important items, this approach has begun to be used somewhat more extensively in recent years. In addition to being able to concentrate attention on the items that make the big difference in inventory results, this method also enables several different methods of control to be applied to the same inventory. An alternative to this approach is the use of the same method, but varying decision rules for each group.

In order to utilize this concept, it is first necessary to analyze the inventory to determine the approximate distribution of items so that ranges for

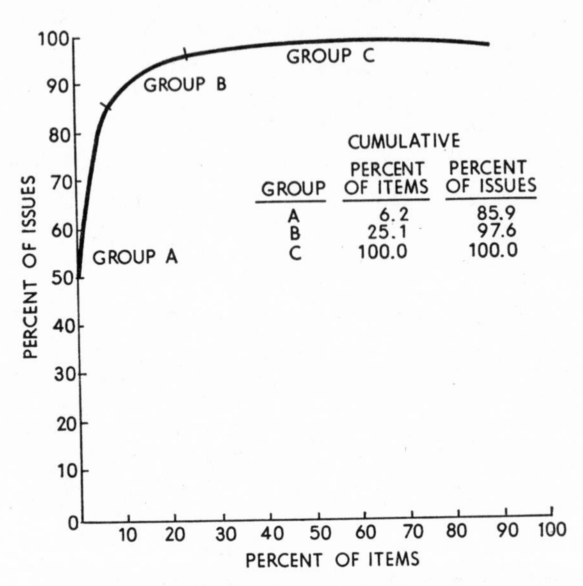

CHART 7. The fact that in all inventories a few items account for most of the dollar usage makes it possible to concentrate the control effort where it is most needed. This is the *A-B-C* approach.

each of the *A-B-C* categories can be set. Chart 7 shows the distribution of inventory usage values based on an actual inventory study. In this particular case, *A* items were determined to be those with annual usage exceeding $1,000, *B* items to include those with annual usage of from $100 to $1,000, and *C* items to have annual usage of less than $100.

Use of Control Limits

This approach, based on statistical quality control concepts, emphasizes the management-by-exception technique. The key assumption in this approach is that there is a "normal," expected usage for an item and that some deviations from this expected usage will occur. Significant usage deviations are determined by control limits, and only upon such occurrences need the item be reviewed. Otherwise, with the item operating within limits, decision rules can be applied mechanically to produce desired results.

This technique can also be combined with the *A-B-C* approach by varying the degree of control for each of the *A-B-C* categories. The tighter control is obviously applied to the *A* items; and because of the more frequent and earlier inspection of usage variances, less safety stock is required for these items. This then meets the requirement of minimizing inventory balances on the 10 percent of the items that account for 85 percent of the annual dollar usage.

Also, because only 10 percent of the items are being more tightly controlled, effort required for inventory administration is minimized.

We have now reviewed some of the basic principles of inventory control. This has not been a complete coverage; instead, emphasis has been placed on the order-point approach because it probably has the widest application in problems of inventory control and is well accepted today. The basic principles reviewed are just that—basic principles. As always, a specific solution must be worked out for the problem at hand. It is hoped that the points discussed will be helpful and can be applied in a practical way to the solution of some of these specific problems.

28

The author asserts that marginal analysis can be applied to the solution of business problems, arguing that the use of calculus in the classical economic purchase quantity problem supports this position; further, he argues that the determination of safety allowances involves marginal analysis (cost savings versus cost increases). Thereafter an overview of important issues in inventory control is presented. Inventory-sales ratios are discussed from both the economist's and the businessman's point of view; problems in estimating cost parameters are examined; four significant criticisms of economic theory are refuted; and the author concludes by suggesting arguments for and against the mathematical approach to inventory control.

*SOME BUSINESS APPLICATIONS OF MARGINAL ANALYSIS—WITH PARTICULAR REFERENCE TO INVENTORY CONTROL**†

T. M. Whitin

INTRODUCTION

AMONG ACCOUNTANTS, businessmen, and economists, a widely held opinion is that marginal analysis is not, and cannot be, applied to business problems. The present article is intended to show some simple situations where marginal analysis is applicable. It is hoped that the description of a few situations where there is a close connection between economic theory and business practice will help dispel the popular conception that economic theory is a futile discipline, although this conception may be found even among economists.

* Reprinted from *Accounting Research*, July, 1952, pp. 205–19.

† This article embodies the results of research sponsored by the Office of Naval Research of the United States.

The inventory control field provides several examples of applied marginal analysis. As this subject is of much interest to economists, accountants, statisticians, and businessmen, these examples may be considered appropriate for illustrative purposes.

Inventory control necessarily involves a balancing of the advantages of storing various additional amounts of different inventory items against the advantages resulting from not storing them. The following two sections illustrate one type of formal analysis of this balancing process. In these sections an inventory control system involving the calculation of "economical purchase quantities" and "safety allowances" is described. This system may be appropriately applied to staple goods inventory problems. Style goods present problems of their own which have been treated elsewhere in detail.[1] For all types of goods, however, the analysis is marginal, the differences being in the specific nature of the advantages and disadvantages of storing the different kinds of items.

THE DETERMINATION OF ECONOMICAL PURCHASE QUANTITIES

After their harrowing experiences during the "inventory depression" of 1921, entrepreneurs placed great emphasis on the importance of keeping inventories at low levels, and a phenomenon called "hand-to-mouth" buying spread throughout the economy. The importance of this phenomenon is evidenced by the existence of several books and periodical articles on the subject.[2] It would probably be correct to say that while inventories were above the "optimum" level, however defined, in 1920, they were considerably below this level in the succeeding years of hand-to-mouth buying.

The fluctuation of inventories has been of great quantitative importance both for individual firms and for the economy as a whole. Abramovitz has recently pointed out that in five business cycles between 1919 and 1938 the increase in inventory accumulation between trough and peak years of business cycles accounted, on average, for about 23 percent of the cyclical growth in gross national product. From peaks to troughs, inventories accounted for 47 percent of the decline in gross national product.[3] The need for reduction of inventory fluctuations led to a search for methods of determining optimum inventory levels. During the years 1925, 1926, and 1927, several authors arrived at essentially the same formula for determining economical purchase quanti-

---

[1] Cf. the author's "Inventory Control in Theory and Practice," *Quarterly Journal of Economics*.

[2] Leverett S. Lyon, *Hand to Mouth Buying* (Washington, D.C.: Brookings Institution, 1929); and Fred E. Clark, "An Analysis to the Causes and Results of Hand-to-Mouth Buying," *Harvard Business Review*, July, 1928, pp. 394–400.

[3] M. Abramovitz, *Inventories and Business Cycles* (New York: National Bureau of Economic Research, 1950), pp. 6–7.

ties.[4] The solution of the purchase quantity problem, combined with a method of determining safety allowances, completely determines the level of inventory.

The economical purchase quantity should be determined in roughly the following manner. Two different sets of cost factors must be considered, namely, those which increase as inventories increase and those which decrease as inventories increase. Among those costs which increase are interest, obsolescence, risk, depreciation, storage, and the like, while the set of decreasing costs includes such items as quantity discounts, freight differentials, and procurement costs.[5] The economic purchase quantity will be that quantity which represents a balancing of these cost factors.[6]

To illustrate by a simplified example, assume (1) that the expense of procurement is a constant amount for each order placed and (2) that interest, risk, depreciation, obsolescence, etc., may be lumped into one percentage figure, expressed as I. Let Y designate the expected yearly sales (in physical units), let Q be the economic purchase quantity (in physical units), let C be the unit cost, and S be the procurement expense involved in making one order (in dollars). Then, total annual variable costs may be expressed as follows:

$$TVC = \frac{QC}{2} I + \frac{Y}{Q} S$$ [7]

In order to determine the Q which minimizes total costs, we differentiate the above expression with respect to Q and set the derivative equal to zero. The following equation is obtained:

$$\frac{IC}{2} - \frac{YS}{Q^2} = 0$$

---

[4] George F. Mellen, "Practical Lot Quantity Formula," *Management and Administration*, September, 1925, p. 155; Ralph C. Davis, "Methods of Finding Minimum-Cost Quantity in Manufacturing," *Manufacturing Industries*, April, 1925, pp. 353–56; H. S. Owen, "How to Maintain Proper Inventory Control," *Industrial Management*, February, 1925, pp. 83–85; *idem*, "The Control of Inventory through the Scientific Determination of Lot Sizes" (in nine installments), *Industrial Management*, Vols. *LXX* and *LXXI*, 1925 and 1926; Benjamin Cooper, "How to Determine Economical Manufacturing Quantities," *Industrial Management*, October, 1926, pp. 228–33; Gordon Pennington, "Simple Formulæ for Inventory Control," *Manufacturing Industries*, March, 1927, pp. 199–203; R. H. Wilson and W. A. Mueller, "A New Method of Stock Control," *Harvard Business Review*, January, 1927, pp. 197–205.

[5] For simplification, it is assumed in the succeeding pages that the cost factors under consideration vary in a linear fashion with inventory changes.

[6] Other factors such as price expectations and sales expectations may act to increase the economic purchase quantity in some cases and to decrease it in others.

[7] In the absence of safety allowances, inventories vary from Q to O. The average value of inventory is therefore $QC/2$ if the new ordering quantity arrives at the same time the old quantity is exhausted. The $QC/2$ times I represents the annual carrying charges. Y/Q represents the number of times a year that orders are placed; therefore, $(Y/Q)S$ represents the total annual procurement expenses.

which results in the solution

$$Q = \sqrt{\frac{2YS}{IC}} \tag{1}$$

This equation states that Q, the economic purchase quantity, varies directly with the square root of expected sales and the square root of procurement expenses, and varies inversely with the square root of the carrying charges.

For those not at ease with the differential calculus, a graphical interpretation may be helpful. On Diagram 1 the horizontal axis represents the purchase quantity in physical units, and the vertical axis represents the annual costs involved in ordering and carrying this quantity. The calculus served as a tool that was helpful in finding the particular purchase quantity that minimized these costs, i.e., the quantity (OM) directly below the minimum point (T) of the curve.

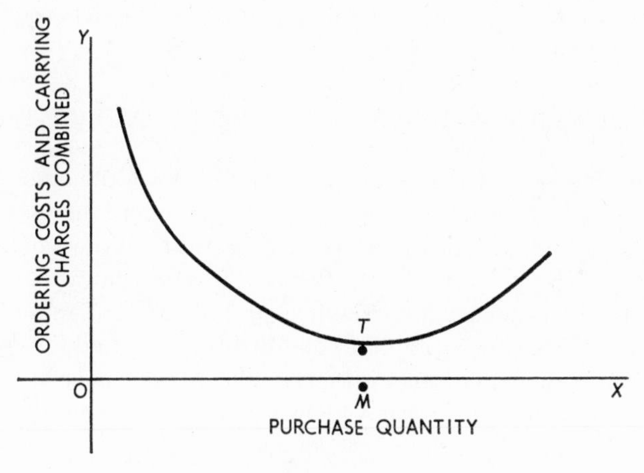

DIAGRAM 1

The problem of determining economical lot sizes in manufacturing is similar to that of finding economic purchase quantities. Here the problem is one of balancing the initial costs for machine and clerical preparation against the costs of carrying the order in stock. If lots of smaller than optimum size are manufactured, the increase in setup costs outweighs the saving in carrying charges; if lots of larger than optimum size are manufactured, the reduction in setup costs is outweighed by the increase in carrying charges. If the letter S in formula 1 above is changed in order to designate setup costs instead of ordering costs, formula 1, as it stands, may be applied to the problem of determining economical lot sizes in manufacturing. In fact, the use of formula 1 by Cleveland's Osborn Manufacturing Company resulted in an 18 percent savings on combined setup costs and carrying charges.[8] The International

[8] W. W. Hannon, "How One Company Determines Economic Lot Sizes," *Factory Management and Maintenance*, September, 1948, pp. 71–73.

Business Machines Corporation has been active in designing practical methods for applying a formula of this type.

The use of the calculus in deriving formula 1 indicates that the analysis is marginal in character. For the marginal unit, carrying charges are exactly offset by the concomitant decrease in ordering costs. It is doubtful whether the users of this type of formulas are concerned about whether or not its use constitutes an application of marginal analysis. Nevertheless, it is important that people who distrust economic theory should be informed of the existence of many such applications of its basic principles. Without altering its marginal nature, the analysis can be extended to handle problems such as quantity discounts and price anticipations.[9]

THE DETERMINATION OF SAFETY ALLOWANCES

Safety allowances, defined as the difference between the amount of goods stocked to satisfy sales during a certain time interval and the mean expected sales for that period, are for the purpose of providing protection against depletion. Determination of the optimal level of these allowances is a second fundamental part of the inventory control problem. If demand and the time interval between the placing of orders and their arrival (lead time) are known with *certainty*, no safety allowance is necessary. However, since in almost every case the levels of demand are not known precisely, it is necessary to have safety allowances. The optimum level of a safety allowance is determined by consideration of the costs and benefits of storing additional units. As units are added to the safety allowance, the probability of depletion[10] is reduced; and hence, costs resulting from depletion are incurred with a smaller probability. At the same time, additional costs, such as interest, depreciation, obsolescence, insurance, risk, and so on, are incurred. At some level of safety allowance the costs of storing an additional unit are balanced by the expected savings through avoidance of depletion. As a net loss results from moving from this level in either direction, this level, for which the probability of depletion brings into balance the expected costs of depletion and carrying charges for the marginal unit, is optimal. If the probability of depletion (or level of satisfaction) is to be kept constant, then the safety allowance must vary with changes in lead time and expected demand distribution. After finding appropriate probability levels for various inventory items, safety allowances should be set at levels which provide this desired amount of protection against depletion.

It should be clear from the above that the process of determining optimal safety allowances is an application of marginal analysis. In fact, analysis of this sort is carried on by some entrepreneurs. Important problems, of both a statistical and a conceptual nature, about how to estimate the parameters in-

[9] Such an extension is made in the author's *Theory of Inventory Management* (Princeton: Princeton University Press, 1953).

[10] "Depletion" here means running out of stock.

volved, remain—as will be discussed below. Nevertheless, the use of "rough-and-ready" approximations for these parameters has produced successful results. In an inventory control plan already in use in several large corporations, it has been found useful to divide inventory items into a few general categories such as "very important," "moderately important," and "unimportant," according to the estimated costs of depletion. Safety allowances are then set in accordance with a scheme: Such a scheme might be, for example, that the business expects to run out of the very important items only once every eight years, the moderately important items once every two years, and the unimportant items once every year. A study at the Bell Telephone Laboratories revealed that if safety allowances are set so that the business expects to run out of each item once a year, a $76,000 inventory is required; if it expects to run out once every 10 years, a $167,000 inventory is required; and if a "never out" system is adopted, a $276,000 inventory is required.[11] Thus the application of even a very crude type of marginal analysis may be accompanied by large savings.

When safety allowances are set so that the entrepreneur expects to run out of stock during only a specified percentage of time periods, it can be shown that the amount of inventory in the safety allowance should be varied with the square root of expected demand, if the expected demand distribution is of a reasonable sort. It has been found particularly appropriate to use the Poisson distribution for small probabilities of depletion.[12] In an example given by Dr. Churchill Eisenhart,[13] the proprietor of a store selling cigar lighters had an opportunity to replenish his stock every Monday. When average weekly demand was 24 lighters, computations showed that a safety allowance of 12, that is, a total Monday stock of 36 lighters, was required if the proprietor was to run out only one week in a hundred; when the average weekly demand increased to 100 units, a safety allowance of 24 was necessary. Thus a quadrupling of sales was accompanied by a doubling of the safety allowance. This square root relationship was brought out clearly by Eisenhart by use of the "direct normal approximation" to the Poisson distribution. In this approximation, K represents the number of units on hand on Monday that reduces the probability of depletion during the week to 1/100. D represents the average weekly demand. Then

$$K = D + 2.326\sqrt{D}$$

The safety allowance $K - D$ is equal to a constant times the square root of D.

Eisenhart assumed that the entrepreneur wanted to run out only one week

[11] R. H. Wilson, "A Universal System of Stock Control," *Purchasing*, March, 1941, p. 85.

[12] This distribution is defined by $p = \frac{e^{-U} U^m}{m'}$, where U is the average demand and p is the probability that m units are demanded, and e is the base of the Naperian logarithmic system.

[13] Churchill Eisenhart, "Some Inventory Problems," National Bureau of Standards, Techniques of Statistical Inference, A22, Lecture 1, January 6, 1948 (hectographed notes).

in a hundred. The desired probability level is dependent on the costs of depletion and the costs of storage, and the probability that brings into balance the advantages and disadvantages of storing the marginal unit can be calculated.

It is interesting to note that a square root relationship between inventories and expected sales held both for purchase quantities and for safety allowances when they are determined in accordance with the inventory control systems described. However, the factors that led to this square root relationship were quite unrelated, the square root relationship in the case of purchase quantities arising because of the nature of the calculus operation involved,[14] while well-known laws of statistics give rise to the square root relationship in the case of safety allowances.

Upon reflection, it seems to be only simple common sense to set safety allowances in such a manner that they are larger (1) the higher the costs of depletion, (2) the longer the delivery time, (3) the larger the expected variations in demand, and (4) the lower the carrying charges. Nevertheless, entrepreneurs often ignore these fundamental considerations, using general rules of thumb that are likely to obscure important interitem differences. Entrepreneurs who have adopted modern inventory control systems that take these differences into account usually have found their efforts well rewarded. An idea of what can be accomplished by the introduction of improved inventory control methods is obtained by examining the claims made by the "Wilson Inventory Management Plan," which involves the determination of economical purchase quantities and safety allowances in the general manner described above: "Experience to date indicates that, in general, the Wilson Plan will either reduce inventories by at least one-third, with no decrease in stockroom service, or reduce the present number of stock-outs per year to one-third of the present number, with no increase in inventory, thus making a tremendous improvement in customer service without increasing operating costs."[15] Interviews with inventory control personnel of the General Foods Corporation and the Westinghouse Electric Corporation, two companies that have purchased the Wilson Plan, have indicated that the management is highly satisfied with it.

Currently, the subject of inventory control is receiving a great deal of attention. Knowledge of the success that has attended the adoption of inventory control plans involving marginal analysis will eventually lead to widespread use of such systems, which will in turn help eliminate the skepticism with which economic analysis is often viewed.

INVENTORY-SALES RATIOS IN THEORY AND PRACTICE

Most businessmen use inventory-sales ratios as an important guide in the control of their businesses. Economic theorists, on the other hand, often neglect to discuss the inventory problems of their "rational entrepreneurs." When

[14] Taking the derivative of a quotient gives rise to a squared term in the denominator.

[15] R. H. Wilson, "Control of Inventories," reprinted from *Bulletin of the Robert Morris Associates*, February, 1949.

they include a consideration of inventories in their analysis, theorists usually assume a constant inventory-sales ratio, whereas data on inventory-sales ratios indicate that they are subject to variation over a wide range. Economic theorists cannot escape from their dilemma by saying that rational (or actual) entrepreneurs *attempt* to maintain a constant ratio. The above sections on the determination of economical purchase quantities and safety allowances indicated that the rational entrepreneur should attempt to vary inventories less than proportionately with expected sales, in many instances proportionately with the square root. Entrepreneurs who use inventory control systems of the sort described above naturally do not attempt to maintain constant inventory-sales ratios; nor, in fact, do entrepreneurs in general. Interviews by the author have not yet revealed a business where the entrepreneur has said that he would not try to increase his turnover rate, that is, decrease his inventory-sales ratio, as sales increase. A study of desired inventory-sales ratios in department stores revealed a decreasing inventory-sales ratio as sales increased for all stores in the sample, as well as for the individual departments in each store.[16] Schmalz's ratios showed that the entrepreneurs attempted to vary their inventories more than proportionately with the square root of sales, although less than proportionately with sales. His data revealed that a quadrupling of sales would effect a tripling of the desired inventory level, whereas the square root assumption would indicate a doubling of the desired level, and the constant inventory-sales ratio assumption would imply a quadrupling of inventories.

J. M. Clark contended that when demand increases, entrepreneurs will attempt to achieve a more than proportionate increase in inventories. Each of Clark's five reasons for this more than proportionate variation can be shown to involve faulty reasoning.[17] A knowledge of the fundamental principles of inventory control should enable economic theorists to make more realistic assumptions about how rational entrepreneurs should behave. These improved assumptions should in turn make actual entrepreneurs more interested in theory and more willing to consider applying it. Thus, more similarity between "rational" entrepreneurs of economic theory and actual entrepreneurs in the economy may be brought about by modification of both theory and practice. As mentioned above, there are several instances where a high degree of harmony between economic theory and business practice has been effected through the adoption of modern inventory control methods.

PROBLEMS INVOLVED IN ESTIMATING INVENTORY CONTROL PARAMETERS

Thus far, the problems involved in making estimates of the various parameters used in inventory control formulas have been ignored. Typical of the sort of information required are (1) estimates of carrying charges, (2) esti-

[16] Carl N. Schmalz, "Standard Departmental Stock-Sales Ratios for Department Stores," *Michigan Business Studies*, Vol. I, No. 4 (1928), pp. 1–16.

[17] The author's "Inventory Control in Theory and Practice."

mates of ordering costs, (3) estimates of the cost of depletion, and (4) estimates of the demand distribution. Perhaps a discussion of some of the difficulties involved in assigning numbers to any of these categories will indicate the type of problems that are commonly encountered.

Estimation of the costs of carrying inventories is essential to an adequate inventory control system. Yet there is room for much disagreement about the level of these charges. Frequently, the answer to questions concerning the costs of carrying inventory is that carrying charges are about 6 percent per year. According to G. T. Trundle:

> As far as we know, and we have studied hundreds of businesses, we have yet to find one case in which this 6 percent was the correct answer. The truth is that few manufacturers are able to answer accurately, considering all factors. . . . We became interested recently in finding out how closely the average executive's idea of the cost of inventory carrying approximated actual costs as we had found them. We sent out hundreds of questionnaires and from the replies were convinced that inventory costs are more often than not an unknown figure.[18]

TABLE 1

	Company A Percentage	*Company B Percentage*	*Company C Percentage*
Interest on capital invested	6.00	6.00	6.00
Taxes	2.50	0.55	2.00
Insurance	0.50	0.20	Included above
Housing	0.50	1.24	0.70
Keeping house in repair	0.25	Included above	
Handling	2.00	3.16	Included above
Taking inventory	0.25	1.03	Included above
Clerical costs	1.00	2.58	4.60
Deterioration, spoilage	3.00		
Repairs	1.00		
Obsolescence	5.00	3.43	4.00
Totals	22.00	18.19	17.30

Three typical replies are found in Table 1.[19] The following statements are typical of economists' estimates of carrying charges:

"Carrying charges for all materials in stock, which charges include insurance, taxes, depreciation, rent, and manual and clerical labour, plus the interest to be earned on the investment probably amount to from 10 percent to 20 percent per annum of the value of the stores."[20]

---

[18] G. T. Trundle, Jr., "Your Inventory a Graveyard?" *Factory Management and Maintenance*, Vol. 94, No. 12 (1936), p. 45.

[19] *Ibid.*

[20] M. Cartmell, *Stores and Materials Control* (New York, 1922), cited in L. P. Alford and J. R. Bangs, *Production Handbook* (New York: Ronald Press Co., 1944), p. 396.

"The carrying-costs of these stocks will seldom be less than 10 percent per annum."[21]

According to Parrish, for stores or stocks in an industrial concern a charge of 25 percent per annum of the cost of the inventory is considered reasonable on active items.[22] (See Table 2.)

In spite of these estimates, figures for total carrying charges of 5 percent to 8 percent have been used in applications of formula 1 above. It is surprising that the results have been good when the carrying charges used in the formula are less than one half what they should be. The explanation might be either that the currently used methods of inventory control are so poor that almost any system would lead to an improvement or that carrying charges are not so high as indicated by the economists' estimates.

TABLE 2

Item	*Percent*
Storage facilities	0.25
Insurance	0.25
Taxes	0.50
Transportation	0.50
Handling and distribution	2.50
Depreciation	5.00
Interest	6.00
Obsolescence	10.00
Total	25.00

Among the elements included in carrying charges is "interest." Should the interest figure represent the actual cost of borrowing? Or should it represent the rate of return on alternative uses of the funds? If the latter, how is this rate to be ascertained? The answer to these questions must be somewhat arbitrary, as rigorous methods for handling these problems do not yet exist. Difficult problems are encountered in estimating "obsolescence" costs. Obsolescence is in many cases dependent on the rate of technological change, which is itself not known with any degree of precision.

The estimation of the costs of placing an order appears to be of a more simple nature than estimating carrying charges. Yet, here also, several problems arise. In the first place, a somewhat arbitrary allocation of overhead costs must be made. Secondly, can the cost per order best be obtained by dividing the total costs of the purchasing department by the total number of orders, or should a process or time and motion study be made? The former method, although the simpler of the two, ignores interitem differences completely. Finally, the total costs involved in placing orders might not vary in a simple manner with the number of orders. The total cost function is not likely to be smooth because of indivisibilities of labor, plant, and other productive factors. Some ordering costs may be unavoidable in the short run but

[21] J. M. Keynes, *The General Theory of Employment, Interest and Money* (New York: Harcourt Brace and Company, 1935), p. 318.

[22] Alford and Bangs, *op. cit.*, p. 397.

avoidable in the long run. For example, a reduction in the number of orders might not reduce total ordering costs significantly unless it was sufficiently large and of sufficiently long duration so that clerks could be laid off.

Estimation of the costs of depletion is perhaps the most difficult of all. Costs of depletion include such items as loss of profits, loss of goodwill, and the costs of idleness of other equipment caused by depletion of the item in question. The loss of profits may depend in a complicated manner upon the length of time the item in question is out of stock;[23] no precise value can be assigned to the amount of goodwill lost; and the process of estimating costs of idleness of equipment is likely to become hopelessly involved because of the high degree of interrelationships between processes in many plants. The problem becomes still worse for nonprofit organizations, for which prices do not exist as a guiding mechanism. For example, if the shortage of an item of military equipment made a training cruise impossible, what value could be assigned to the cruise? Military experts have long sought in vain for the answer to this type of question.

Finally, the estimation of demand distributions is by no means an easy matter. In the case of style goods the problem is accentuated by the fact that there may be no historical data that can be used as a basis for estimating demand. Nevertheless, in spite of the difficulties involved in estimating sales, estimates must be made, regardless of the type of inventory control system employed. An efficient inventory control system is one that makes good use of these estimates, whether or not they are precise. It was mentioned above that the use of inventory control systems based upon rough estimates of carrying charges and extremely crude estimates of the costs of depletion have often effected substantial savings. It is likely that the use of probability distributions will also be successful, even though the precise nature of the distributions is not known. Businessmen have not yet experimented in this direction to any great extent.

A CRITICISM OF TWO RECENT CONTRIBUTIONS TO INVENTORY THEORY

Among economists as well as businessmen,[24] many are quite outspoken in their attacks on economic theory. A recent example of such an attack is *Price Determination: Business Practice versus Economic Theory*, by Wilford J. Eiteman,[25] who offered the following four principal criticisms of conventional economic theory:

---

[23] For example, a firm's competitive position might be affected by the length of time stocks are depleted.

[24] The general opinion that economic theory is useless is so widespread among businessmen that specific reference to these criticisms is unnecessary.

[25] *Michigan Business Reports*, No. 16 (Ann Arbor: University of Michigan Press, January, 1949).

1. Inventories rather than marginal costs and revenues serve as a barometer to indicate when and to what extent prices or output should be changed.[26]
2. No consideration is given in conventional economic theory to the problem of how intensively working capital should be used.[27]
3. Conventional economic theory fails to consider the "time dimension" of demand.[28]
4. Because it is at best uncertainly known, demand should be represented by a "twilight zone" rather than by the line usually used in conventional theory. Eiteman wrote that "If the twilight-zone concept of an average revenue curve is accepted, then all marginal concepts become fantastically unreal," and that the twilight-zone concept "renders obsolete all theory based upon marginal-line analysis."[29]

These four arguments may be answered in the following vein:

1. The inventory aspects of marginal costs and revenues can be, and should be, included in marginal cost and revenue curves. The use of inventories in the determination of price and output is not used *instead of* marginal analysis but is included in it.[30]

2. The clockwork behind the marginal cost and marginal revenue curves can take into consideration the time necessary to turn working capital. The marginal curves apply to some period and may be applied to the period of time necessary to turn working capital over once. The problem has by no means been completely ignored by economic theorists and is treated in most writings on capital theory. For example, Hayek contends that if a firm has its capital rationed and all output prices but no input prices go up, then it will pay the entrepreneur to increase turnover.[31] The calculation of economical lot sizes in manufacturing explicitly takes turnover rates into consideration as the number of times a year that setup costs are incurred is calculated.

3. Before conventional theory can be applied, it must be (although sometimes tacitly) assumed that the diagrams apply to a certain unit period. As correctly indicated by Eiteman, a demand curve has no meaning in the absence of a time dimension. This time dimension is implicit in conventional theory and has been explicitly mentioned by many economists, including Alfred Marshall.[31]

4. There is a notion of probability implicit in the twilight-zone concept. Economists can combine, and in some cases have combined, probability

---

[26] *Ibid.*, p. 36.

[27] *Ibid.*, p. 15.

[28] *Ibid.*, p. 60.

[29] *Ibid.*, pp. 67–68.

[30] In the previous sections of this article the level of inventories in economic purchase quantities, in safety allowances, and in economic manufacturing lot sizes were all determined through use of marginal analysis. The costs and benefits of stocking marginal units were compared in each case. See F. Hayek, "The Ricardo Effect," *Economica*, 1942, pp. 127–52.

[31] Alfred Marshall, *op. cit.*, pp. 330, 338, 379, and *passim*.

analysis and marginal analysis.[32] There are no logical reasons given why the twilight-zone concept should render marginal analysis obsolete.[33]

In the alternative approach suggested by Eiteman, turnover and inventories are the factors that determine prices and control expansion.[34] However, the author is not clear either as to what the goal of his entrepreneur is or what it should be. At one point, it is said that wholesalers and retailers "strive to hold inventories constant";[35] at other points in the text, vague statements occur such as "balance between retail purchases and retail sales,"[36] "normal levels,"[37] "minimum consistent with efficient operations." These statements leave the reader in a state of confusion concerning what the entrepreneurs are trying to do. Another statement that further clouds the issue is: "Thus with profit margins set, the most profitable situation is one minimizing inventories while maximizing deliveries of goods to customers."[38] The maximization of two functions simultaneously is impossible, as has been pointed out in *The Theory of Games and Economic Behaviour*, which states that "A guiding principle cannot be formulated by the requirement of maximizing two (or more) functions at once."[39] Even without this formal criticism, the statement can be shown to be false, for the analysis does not consider ordering costs or setup costs. Economical lot sizes and purchase quantities may be determined by balancing setup costs (ordering costs in the case of wholesalers and retailers) and carrying charges. It is possible to secure too fast as well as too slow a rate of turnover.

Eiteman contended that the twilight-zone concept invalidates marginal analysis. Instead of marginal analysis, he contends that break-even charts are used, and the use of these charts shows that "managers don't believe in equating marginal cost and revenue."[40] The results of break-even chart analysis were compared to the results of conventional theory: "Thus from the same data and under identical assumptions, our alternative theory suggests that outputs will be greater and prices will be lower than they will be according to the conventional theory of monopolistic competition."[41]

A principal cause of the supposed divergence between the results is that the

---

[32] A. J. Nichol, "Probability Analysis in the Theory of Demand, Net Revenue, and Price," *Journal of Political Economy*, 1941, pp. 637–61; *idem*, "Production and the Probabilities of Cost," *Quarterly Journal of Economics*, November, 1942, pp. 68–69.

[33] In the determination of optimum safety allowance levels in the previous chapter, probability analysis was used. However, the analysis was still *marginal* analysis, comparing *expected marginal* revenues that resulted from stocking additional units.

[34] *Ibid.*, p. 84.

[35] *Ibid.*, p. 42.

[36] *Ibid.*, p. 38.

[37] *Ibid.*, p. 41.

[38] Nichol, "Production and the Probabilities of Cost," p. 37.

[39] John von Neumann and Oscar Morgenstern, *The Theory of Games and Economic Behaviour* (Princeton: Princeton University Press, 1944), p. 1.

[40] Eiteman, *op. cit.*, p. 75, n.

[41] *Ibid.*, p. 86.

author contends that when demand increases, the interests of the entrepreneur are best served by increasing output rather than price.[42] He thus (by assumption) rules out a vertical (price) probe into the twilight zone in favor of a horizontal (output) probe. Hence, it is evident that the assumptions underlying the two alternative theories are not identical.

The general conclusion of this section is that Eiteman has neither destroyed the foundations of conventional theory nor proposed an adequate alternative hypothesis. However, his book does serve a useful purpose in emphasizing the importance of inventories to businessmen and the need for economic theorists to probe more deeply into the role of inventories in the economic theory of the firm.

Kenneth E. Boulding's *A Reconstruction of Economics*[43] criticizes the existing theory of the firm for its deficiency in capital theory, contending that the usual marginal analysis totally neglects the balance sheet aspects of business. While it is refreshing to find attention being directed toward the inventory aspects of economy theory, it is regrettable that Boulding's theory is fully as unrealistic as the theory he is "reconstructing," as evidenced by conclusions such as that a firm will not pay dividends until both cash and inventories are completely superfluous.[44] The above sections have indicated that marginal analysis *can* be used to analyze some of the balance sheet aspects of business. The marginal costs involved in ordering and carrying inventories can be and should be incorporated in the marginal curves of the economic theory of the firm.

ARGUMENTS FOR AND AGAINST THE MATHEMATICAL APPROACH TO INVENTORY CONTROL

There has been considerable debate concerning the desirability of applying mathematics to inventory control. Many people do not understand the relationship between mathematical and verbal formulations of problems. They view mathematics as an application of simplified and rigid formulas to complex situations. But mathematical formulations are extremely helpful in explicitly bringing to light assumptions underlying analysis, thus bringing about a better understanding of problems. Entrepreneurs often make decisions on business problems on the basis of experience, judgment, and intuition. Attempts to formalize their decision-making processes often contribute new insights into the problems at hand.

For the most part, the arguments for and against the mathematical approach have been due to a misunderstanding of what it is intended to accomplish. The following quotation is typical of the antimathematical attitude:

---

[42] *Ibid.*, p. 43.

[43] Kenneth E. Boulding, *A Reconstruction of Economics* (London: Chapman and Hall, Ltd., 1950).

[44] That is, until they become "disutilities."

> Dissertations on purchasing have appeared, particularly by those who are perhaps unduly engineeringly minded or mathematically inclined, which devote page after page to the statement, elaboration, and proof of some formula, the value of which is ruined by a very necessary statement, at the end, to the effect that varying conditions alter the character of the formula and that under no condition is it to be taken as a substitute for human judgment. . . . The real significance of all this is that it is but a presage of the sort of thing into which an attempt to measure purchasing efficiency may degenerate.[45]

Apparently, Lewis does not realize that the mathematical approach is not intended as a substitute for judgment. It provides a systematic method for calculating the effects of several variables; it is intended as an *aid* to judgment, not as a *substitute.* Mathematics leads to more precise ways of determining inventory levels than are possible on the basis of intuition. As soon as several variables are present in a problem, most human minds cannot readily estimate the results of their interaction—the mathematical approach is of much aid in this respect. As summed up by one author: "Quite clearly the balancing and appraising of cost factors may be carried out far more effectively if the purchasing agent forms a definite quantitative opinion with respect to each of them instead of merely considering them in vague and intangible terms."[46]

Another argument against the use of mathematics in inventory control is that involved in the problem are many intangibles that cannot be quantified with any degree of precision. While it may be true that it is hard to attach a value to such items as goodwill, the problem is not necessarily made insoluble by this fact. Suppose a choice must be made between inventory plans *A* and *B*. Assume that plan *B* costs more than plan *A* but is worth something in goodwill. Without knowing exactly what the goodwill is worth, the entrepreneur may know whether or not the gain in goodwill resulting from adoption of plan *B* rather than plan *A* is sufficient to compensate for the loss incurred through the higher costs of the plan. In any case the use of mathematical formulas indicates what must be paid for the gain in intangible items.

Arguments of a more valid sort than have thus far been discussed are that proponents of various inventory control formulas do not give adequate consideration to the costs of using them. In many cases, formulas that include the important variables are of a complicated nature, and computations necessary for their use are costly and time-consuming. Even in this case the formulas are not useless. Although carrying out extensive computations of this nature may prove to be uneconomical, nevertheless it is quite possible that useful information of a qualitative nature may be obtained from the formulas. This information will frequently be of sufficient value to justify large expenses on research on the use of mathematics in inventory control. Furthermore, the costs of using inventory control formulas can themselves be included in the

---

[45] Howard T. Lewis, "Purchasing in Relation to Industrial Marketing," *Harvard Business Review*, Vol. 10, 1931–32, pp. 189–90.

[46] John G. McLean, "Determination of Purchase Quantities," *Purchasing*, May, 1941, p. 77.

formulas. In this event the foregoing objection is invalid. However, there is a certain amount of truth in the contention that these costs have been for the most part ignored.

Another argument against the use of mathematics in inventory control is that unless the formulations are extremely complex (and thus uneconomical to use), they are usually based on assumptions not in accord with reality. Against this argument, it may be said that extremely simple formulations have been applied in several instances with success. Furthermore, in some cases the results obtained by oversimplified formulations provide an approximation to the desired results. There is considerable scope for improvement of inventory control by application of relatively simple mathematics.

Mathematical inventory control systems may be expected to involve marginal analysis. The marginalism implicit in the systems discussed in this article has been explained. It should also be clear that systems based on inventory-sales ratios can be in complete harmony with marginal analysis. Improvement in inventory control practice, combined with a marginal analysis that considers more of the relevant variables in a realistic manner, should help bring about a closer correspondence between economic theory and business practice, a correspondence beneficial to both theoreticians and practitioners.

29

The various elements which comprise the total inventory problem are succinctly described, viz., decision variables, item parameters, outcome parameters, cost parameters, assumed operational relationships, linear cost models, cost minimization decision rules, and the efficient surface. These elements are described mathematically both for the general case and for a simple lot-size problem. The author then examines the two basic problems of inventory control—the tactical problem, which is implicitly solved in the inventory formulation per se, and the strategic problem, which consists of choosing a point on the efficient surface. Problems of making this latter choice are discussed, and an alternative approach is described, illustrated, and evaluated.

*A BASIS FOR STRATEGIC DECISIONS ON INVENTORY CONTROL OPERATIONS**†

George J. Feeney

INTRODUCTION

IT IS THE PURPOSE of this paper to suggest that inventory control operations involve two distinct types of problems which may be identified as *tactical* decision problems and *strategic* decision problems. The difference between these two types of problems will be discussed in more detail below. For the moment, it is sufficient to observe that a solution to the tactical problem defines a family of decision rules, while a solution to the strategic problem involves a final selection of some particular member of this family. It will be suggested further that while much attention has been given to the tactical decision problem, the methods typically employed to solve the strategic problem are frequently less than satisfactory. Finally, an alternative approach to strategic decisions on inventory control operations will be outlined. This alternative approach will be illustrated through two specific examples taken from recent experience.

---

* Reprinted from *Management Science*, October, 1955, pp. 69–82.

† Delivered at the seventh national meeting of the Operations Research Society of America, Los Angeles, August 15–17, 1955.

BASIC ELEMENTS OF AN INVENTORY FORMULATION

In order to specify precisely what we mean by the strategic decision problem, it is necessary first to identify the basic elements generally contained in a formulation of the inventory problem. Throughout this section, we will refer to both Table 1, which contains a brief list of these basic elements in general

TABLE 1

BASIC ELEMENTS OF AN INVENTORY FORMULATION

1. Decision variables (order quantity, order point, etc.):

$$X = (x_1, x_2, x_3, \cdots, x_k)$$

2. Item parameters (average usage rate, unit cost, lead time, etc.):

$$P = (p_1, p_2, p_3, \cdots, p_m)$$

3. Outcome variables (average inventory investment, number of orders processed, number of shortages, etc.):

$$Y = (y_1, y_2, y_3, \cdots, y_n)$$

4. Cost parameters (cost per dollar invested, cost per order processed, etc.):

$$C = (c_1, c_2, c_3, \cdots, c_n)$$

5. Assumed operational relationships:

$$\{y_i = f_i(X, P)\} \qquad i = 1, 2, 3, \cdots, n$$

6. Linear cost model:

$$W = \sum_i c_i y_i = \sum_i c_i f_i(X, P)$$

7. Cost-minimizing decision rules:

$$\{x_i^* = R_i(P, C)\}$$

such that

$$\sum_i c_i f_i(X^*, P) = \min_X \sum_i c_i f_i(X, P)$$

8. Efficient surface: In order to satisfy the optimality criterion

$$\sum_i c_i f_i(X^*, P) = \min_X \sum_i c_i f_i(X, P)$$

it is clearly sufficient that the X^* satisfy

$$\sum_i \frac{c_i}{c_n} f_i(X^*, P) = \min_X \sum_i \frac{c_i}{c_n} f_i(X, P)$$

where

$$c_n \neq 0$$

Table 1 (*Continued*)

Thus:

$$\{R_i(P, C) \equiv R_i(P, \hat{C})\} \qquad i = 1, 2, \cdots, k$$

where

$$\hat{C} \equiv \left(\frac{c_1}{c_n}, \frac{c_2}{c_n}, \cdots, \frac{c_{n-1}}{c_n}, 1\right)$$

It follows that the n cost parameters in the decision rule

$$X^* = R(P, C)$$

may be replaced by $n - 1$ cost ratios:

$$X^* = R(P, \hat{C})$$

Since, from item 5

$$\{y_i^* = f_i(X^*, P)\} \qquad i = 1, 2, \cdots, n$$

we may replace X^* by $R(P, \hat{C})$ to form

$$\{y_i^* = f_i[R(P, \hat{C}), P]\} \qquad i = 1, 2, \cdots, n$$

The $n - 1$ cost ratios may be eliminated from these n equations to form

$$\phi(Y^*, P) = 0$$

a surface in the outcome (Y) space containing all points optimal to some set of cost ratios.

---

form, and Table 2, which lists as example the specific form each element assumes in the simplest inventory formulation, the optimum lot-size problem.

Decision Variables

The first element is a set of decision variables identifying those aspects of the situation that can be influenced directly by the decision maker. In general, these might include order quantity, order point, timing of delivery, etc.

In the simple lot-size example, there is only one decision variable, the lot size (order quantity). It will be assumed here that the formulation applies to a *group* of stock items; consequently, the subscript j has been added to each factor which refers to stock items specifically. Thus, x_j identifies the lot size of the jth stock item.

Item Parameters

The second element is a set of parameters descriptive of the individual stock items included in the inventory system. These parameters might define for each stock item such characteristics as the average rate of use per month, the cost per piece, procurement lead time, minimum shipping quantity, etc.

In the lot-size example, there are two item parameters: p_{1_j}, the average monthly usage of the jth stock item; and p_{2_j}, the unit cost of the jth stock item.

TABLE 2

SIMPLE LOT-SIZE PROBLEM

1. Decision variable (lot size):

$$X_j \equiv (x_j), \text{ (}j\text{th stock item)}$$

2. Item parameters (average monthly usage, cost per piece):

$$P_j \equiv (p_{1_j}, p_{2_j}), \text{ (}j\text{th stock item)}$$

3. Outcome variables (total inventory investment, total orders processed per year):

$$Y. \equiv (y_{1\cdot}, y_{2\cdot})$$

4. Cost parameters (annual cost per dollar invested, cost per order processed):

$$C \equiv (c_1, c_2)$$

5. Assumed operational relationships:

$$y_{1_j} = f_1(x_j, p_{1_j}, p_{2_j}) = \frac{x_j p_{2j}}{2}$$

$$y_{2_j} = f_2(x_j, p_{1_j}, p_{2i}) = \frac{12 p_{1i}}{x_j}$$

6. Linear Cost Model:

$$W. = \sum_j W_j = \sum_j (c_1 y_{1_j} + c_2 y_{2_j}) = \sum_j \left(c_2 \frac{12 p_{1_j}}{x_j} + c_1 \frac{x_j p_{2_j}}{2} \right)$$

7. Cost-minimizing decision rule:

$$x_j^* = R(p_{1_j}, p_{2_j}, c_1, c_2) = \sqrt{\frac{24 c_2 p_{1_j}}{c_1 p_{2_j}}}$$

8. Efficient surface:

$$\phi(Y^*, P) = y_{1\cdot} y_{2\cdot} - 6 \left(\sum_j \sqrt{p_{1_j} p_{2_j}} \right)^2 = 0$$

Outcome Variables

The third element contained in most inventory formulations is a set of variables, each descriptive of some aspect of the outcome to the company of inventory control operations. These outcome variables might include the average inventory investment, the number of procurement orders processed per year, the number of stock shortages that occur per year, etc.

In the lot-size example, two outcome variables are employed: $y_{1\cdot}$, the total average inventory investment, (the sum of average inventory investments over all of the individual stock items); and $y_{2\cdot}$, the total number of orders processed per year (summed over all stock items).

Cost Parameters

The fourth element present in an inventory formulation is a set of cost parameters, each corresponding to a particular outcome variable, which measure the cost to the company of each outcome variable at unit level. The first cost parameter might measure the cost associated with average inventory investment at unit level, i.e., cost per dollar invested. Another cost parameter might be the cost per order processed; and similarly, another might be the cost per stock shortage.

The lot-size formulation employs two cost parameters: c_1, the annual cost per dollar invested; and c_2, the cost per order processed.

The four elements described above—decision variables, item parameters, outcome variables, and cost parameters—are the structural elements of the inventory formulation.

Assumed Operational Relationships

The fifth basic element that might be contained in an inventory formulation is a set of assumed operational relationships between the decision variables, the item parameters, and the results variables. These relationships define functionally the outcome expected from any specified set of component decisions over any given set of item parameters. A separate relationship is defined for each outcome variable. Essentially, the operational relationships map the decision space into the outcome space.

The operational relationships employed in the lot-size formulation are well known—y_{1_j}, the average inventory investment in the jth item is assumed to be equal to half the lot size $(x_{2_j}/2)$ times the cost per piece (p_{2_j}). That is, it is assumed that the average inventory investment will be equal to half the value of each order. The number of orders issued per year, y_{2_j}, is assumed to be equal to annual usage $(12p_{1_j})$ divided by the lot size (x_j); that is, the number of orders per year is assumed to be equal to an annual usage divided by lot size.

Notice that these functions define the outcome in terms of each stock item. The overall outcome variables, $y_{1.}$ and $y_{2.}$, are defined as the sum over all stock items of y_{1_j} and y_{2_j}, respectively.

Linear Cost Model

The sixth element we would expect to find in most inventory formulations is a linear cost model. Total variable cost is defined as the sum of the products of the cost parameters and the corresponding outcome variables. Since the outcome variables are themselves defined in terms of the decision variables and the item parameters (through the assumed operational relationships), total variable cost is thus defined for any given values of the decision variables and the item parameters.

In the lot-size example the cost model defines $W.$, the total variable cost, as the sum of the products of the cost parameters and the corresponding outcome variables. Total variable cost is thus defined as the sum over all stock items of the annual cost per dollar invested times the total average inventory investment plus cost per order processed times the total number of orders processed per year. If the corresponding operational relationship is substituted for each outcome variable, this equation then defines total variable cost in terms of the lot-size decision variable and the pair of item parameters.

Cost-Minimizing Decision Rules

The seventh element present in an inventory formulation is a set of cost-minimizing decision rules which define an optimal level for each decision variable as a function of the specific levels of the item parameters and the cost parameters. These rules satisfy the following criterion: For any fixed item parameters and cost parameters, no alternative levels of the decision variables yield a lower total variable cost than the particular levels defined by the decision rules. Since total variable cost is defined as the sum of the products of the individual cost parameters and the corresponding outcome variables, this cost-minimizing criterion may be stated equivalently in another manner: The sum of the products of the cost parameters and the specific outcome levels generated by optimal decision rules must be no greater than the sum of the products of the cost parameters and any *attainable* outcome levels.

In the lot-size example the cost-minimizing decision rule is formed by setting the derivative of total variable costs with respect to lot size equal to zero. This operation yields the known relationship

$$x^*_j = \sqrt{\frac{24c_2p_{1_j}}{c_1p_{2_j}}}$$

Efficient Surface

The minimizing criterion stated above is not changed if both sides of the equation are divided by a constant. Specifically, we might divide each side by c_n, the nth cost parameter. Thus the optimal decision rules which satisfy the original criterion defined in terms of a set of cost parameters must satisfy this second criterion defined in terms of a set of cost *ratios* formed by dividing each cost parameter by a single specified cost parameter. For this reason, we may replace the cost parameters by cost ratios without changing the decision rules. This is significant because there are n cost parameters, but only $n - 1$ cost ratios.

Suppose now that the decision rules are inserted in the assumed operational relationships so that each outcome variable is now defined as some function of the cost ratios and the item parameters. Since there are n outcome variables, this substitution yields n equations which contain the $n - 1$ cost ratios. We may eliminate the $n - 1$ cost ratios from these n equations to form a single equation containing only the outcome variables and the item parameters.

This final equation, $\phi(Y^*, P)$ was derived by substituting the cost-minimizing decision rules in the assumed operational relationships and eliminating the cost ratios from the resulting set of equations. Thus any outcome which satisfies $\phi(Y^*, P)$ must be an optimal outcome for some set of cost ratios. The entire set of points in the outcome space which satisfy $\phi(Y^*, P)$ are thus efficient outcomes in the sense that any such outcome is optimal to some set of costs. This entire set of outcomes satisfying $\phi(Y^*, P)$ we will refer to as the efficient surface.

The nature of the efficient surface may be clarified by reference to the lot-size example.

If, in each of the two operational relationship equations:

$$y_{1.} = \sum_j \frac{x_j p_{2_j}}{2} \tag{1}$$

$$y_{2.} = \sum_j \frac{12 p_{1_j}}{x_j} \tag{2}$$

we substitute the value of x_j, obtained from the decision rule:

$$x_j^* = \sqrt{\frac{24 c_2 p_{1_j}}{c_1 p_{2_j}}} \tag{3}$$

two equations result:

$$y_{1.}^* = \sum_j \left[\sqrt{\frac{24 c_2 p_{1_j}}{c_1 p_{2_j}}} \cdot \frac{p_{2_j}}{2} \right] \tag{4}$$

$$y_{2.}^* = \sum_j \left[\sqrt{\frac{c_1 p_{2_j}}{24 c_2 p_{1_j}}} \cdot 12 p_{1_j} \right] \tag{5}$$

which may be reduced to

$$y_{1.}^* = \sqrt{\frac{c_2}{c_1}} \cdot \sum_j \sqrt{6 p_{1_j} p_{2_j}} \tag{4a}$$

$$y_{2.}^* = \sqrt{\frac{c_1}{c_2}} \cdot \sum_j \sqrt{6 p_{1_j} p_{2_j}} \tag{5a}$$

If the corresponding sides of equations 4*a* and 5*a* are multiplied together, the c_2/c_1 ratio is eliminated in the resulting equation:

$$y_{1.}^* y_{2.}^* = 6 \left[\sum_j \sqrt{p_{1_j} p_{2_j}} \right]^2 \tag{6}$$

or

$$\phi(Y^*, P) = y_{1.}^* y_{2.}^* - 6 \left[\sum_j \sqrt{p_{1_j} p_{2_j}} \right]^2 = 0 \tag{7}$$

Note, further, that if each side of equation 4*a* is divided by the corresponding side of equation 5*a*, an equation

$$\frac{y_{1.}^*}{y_{2.}^*} = \frac{c_2}{c_1} \tag{8}$$

is formed which defines the cost ratio c_2/c_1 corresponding to any specified *optimal* outcome levels $(y_{1.}^*, y_{2.}^*)$

Thus, equation 7 defines the entire set of efficient outcomes (optimal under some set of costs), and equation 8 defines the particular cost ratio corresponding to any particular set of efficient outcome levels.

To illustrate this further, consider a specific situation in which 10,000 stock items are to be controlled using this optimal lot-size rule. Suppose further that $p_{1_j}p_{2_j}$ (average *value* of usage per month) is computed for each stock item and the sum of the square roots is taken; and finally, that the value of the entire term (six times the square of the sum of the square roots) is found to be 15 times 10^9. The efficient surface associated with this system is shown in Figure 1. This curve may be interpreted in the following way:

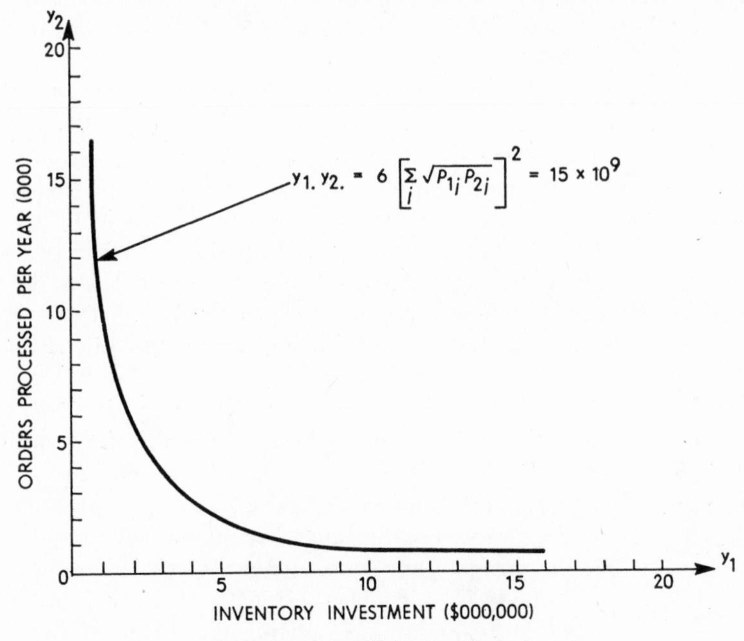

FIGURE 1. Efficient surface.

Any point on the curve is attainable through the decision rule we have just derived and is efficient in the sense that the outcomes associated with that point yield a minimum total variable cost for some cost parameter ratio. Thus any relationship between inventory investment and orders processed per year that lies on this curve may be attained and will be the lowest cost relationship for some set of cost parameters. Conversely, for any given cost parameters used in the decision rules, the resulting outcomes must lie at a point on this efficient surface.

STRATEGIC DECISIONS

At this point, it is possible to specify exactly what we mean by a strategic decision in inventory control operations. From the point of view of this discussion, a strategic decision is a selection of some point on the efficient surface. For example, in the case that we just studied, should the system invest $1 million in inventory and create sufficient capacity to process 15,000 procurement orders per year? Or would it be better to invest $3 million in inventory and process only 5,000 orders per year? Or perhaps $15 million inventory investment with only 1,000 orders processed per year would be best. Any combination of inventory investment level and order-processing level present in the efficient surface is available to the company.

We have called the final selection of a point on this efficient surface a strategic decision because typically such a selection can be made only with reference to the overall objectives and operational restrictions of the company involved.

Notice that the inventory formulation itself does not tell how to make this decision. The formulation does perform a crucial function by defining the efficient set of outcomes and providing a mechanism for attaining these outcomes. In effect, the inventory formulation solves the *tactical* problem of inventory control in the sense that it shows how local decisions may be made on each item individually so as to achieve any efficient outcome in the operation as a whole. But the formulation thus only defines but does not solve the strategic problem—the problem of deciding which particular efficient outcome configuration is best related to the overall objectives and operational restrictions of the company.

Since a tactical solution is unusable until this final selection is made, it appears appropriate to examine carefully the basis for strategic decisions in inventory operations.

How are such decisions commonly made? Since an efficient outcome is one that is optimal under some set of cost ratios, there is a direct correspondence between every point on the efficient surface and every set of cost ratios. Thus the final selection of a point of the efficient surface is equivalent to the final selection of a specific set of cost ratios. Consequently, if one can determine "the actual level" of the various cost parameters, the strategic problem is immediately solved. This is precisely the approach that is commonly used. One sets out to determine such things as how much it costs the company to have money tied up in inventory, how much to process a purchase order, how much to have a stock shortage. These numbers, once found, are inserted in the decision rules, and the strategic problem is solved.

LIMITATIONS OF USUAL APPROACH

It is the contention of this paper that such an approach is frequently, if not always, subject to serious limitations and that an alternative approach may be preferred in many situations. The cost of holding inventory, for example, involves not only the cost to the company of obtaining money but must also take into account the policy restrictions the company places on the extent of indebtedness, which in many cases may be entirely unrelated to the market price for capital funds. Inventory-holding costs must also take into account obsolescence risks as well as the capacity and variable operating costs of storage facilities.

The unit costs of processing purchase orders may depend heavily on the volume of orders actually processed. Thus a curious circular situation results in which the unit cost of ordering depends on the volume of ordering, but the volume of ordering depends on the unit cost that is used in the decision rules. In the case of finished or semifinished material that is being ordered on the company's own manufacturing facilities, order costs must also take into account the effect of different order sizes on plant congestion, and is thus related to the whole production priority system.

If the model includes some consideration of stock shortages, as is generally the case, measurement of the shortage cost parameter offers even greater problems than the previous two. What does it cost the company to delay a customer's shipment or to have material unavailable for internal manufacturing operations? How much does it cost to expedite delivery of material? The list of questions related to the measurement of shortage cost could be extended indefinitely. Only in the simplest operating situation can present techniques satisfactorily answer such complex questions.

What is needed is some method of relating the alternative outcomes defined in the efficient surface to the overall objectives and restrictions with which the company operates. Fortunately, a mechanism exists in every company for carrying out complex analyses of this sort.

ALTERNATIVE APPROACH

This mechanism is the mind of the decision maker himself. We conclude, therefore, that in situations in which it is not possible by direct methods to obtain meaningful measures of the cost parameters contained in the decision rules, the strategic decision might best be made by confronting the executive with a picture of the efficient surface. In essence, we present him with the set of all possible alternatives that have the property of being optimal under some set of costs. If, as is generally the case, the efficient surface is convex, we may make a very strong statement with respect to the properties of these alternatives, namely, that so long as total variable cost is nondecreasing over the range of each of the outcome variables, the efficient surface derived under a linear cost model *must* contain the optimal outcome regardless of the nature of the cost function that is actually employed by the decision maker. That is, even if the cost function is nonlinear and the outcome variables themselves are subject to a multitude of complex restrictions, some point on the efficient surface must provide minimum total variable cost.

Returning to the simple lot-size formulation that was explored earlier, the curve shown in Figure 1 (or some modified form of this curve) might be presented to the executive. He could be told that under the rules that have been developed, any relationship between inventory investment and orders processed per year that lies on this curve can be attained and that regardless of the factors that are actually taken into account, some point on this curve must be the best available outcome for the company. He would be told also that the final selection of a point on this curve as a target for company inventory operations is a decision that he himself must make. This picture might be elaborated through such things as an indication of the outcome attained through existing controls to provide some perspective, and perhaps by an indication of the point or points along the curve that would be selected through a cost accounting study of the underlying cost parameters. We believe that through the use of such an approach the analyst provides the best available basis for executive decision making and avoids the undesirable practice of working beyond the limits of his methodology.

SECOND EXAMPLE

In order to show more precisely how this alternative approach to the strategic decision problem works, we will discuss a second example. Table 3 outlines the basic elements of the formulation which was used in this study. There were two decision variables, the order point (essentially the number of pieces of material on hand and on order at the time a new order should be placed) and the order quantity (the number of pieces to be ordered). The three item parameters employed were the average rate of use per month, the cost per piece, and the procurement lead time in months. Three outcome variables were included: the average inventory investment, number of orders processed per year, and number of shortage delays per year. In this situation, stock was held in central points to meet field requirements. A shortage delay was defined simply as a delay in the shipment of material to the field caused by the unavailability of stock material.

The cost parameters corresponding to these outcome variables were annual cost per dollar invested, cost per order processed, and cost per shortage delay. The assumed operational relationships were as follows: Average inventory investment was assumed to be half of the order size plus the excess of order point over the average amount used during the procurement lead time, all times the cost per piece. The number of orders processed per year was assumed to be 12 times the average monthly rate of use (the annual rate of use) divided by the order quantity. The number of shortage delays per year was assumed to be equal to the expected number of shortage delays per order

TABLE 3

MODIFIED s, S POLICY

1. Decision variables (order point, order quantity):

$$X_j \equiv (x_{1_j}, x_{2_j})$$

2. Item parameters (average monthly usage, cost per piece, lead time):

$$P \equiv (p_{1_j}, p_{2_j}, p_{3_j})$$

3. Outcome variables (average inventory investment, orders processed per year, shortage delays per year):

$$Y_j \equiv (y_{1_j}, y_{2_j}, y_{3_j})$$

4. Cost parameters (cost per dollar invested, cost per order processed, cost per shortage delay):

$$C \equiv (c_1, c_2, c_3)$$

5. Assumed operational relationships:

$$y_{1_j} = f_1(X_j, P_j) = \left(\frac{x_{2_j}}{2} + x_{1_j} - p_{1_j}p_{3_j}\right) p_{2_j}$$

$$y_{2_j} = f_2(X_j, P_j) = \frac{12p_{1_j}}{x_{2_j}}$$

$$y_{3_j} = f_3(X_j, P_j) = \frac{12p_{1_j}}{x_{2_j}} \int_{\xi = x_{1_j}}^{\infty} (\xi - x_{1_j}) n(\xi; p_j p_{31_j}, \sqrt{p_{1_j} p_{3_j}})\, d\xi$$

where

$$n(\xi; \mu, \sigma) = \frac{1}{\sigma\sqrt{2\pi}} e^{-(\xi - \mu)^2/2\sigma^2}$$

6. Linear cost model:

$$W_j \equiv \sum_i c_i f_i (X_j, P_j) = \sum_i c_i y_{i_j}$$

7. Cost-minimizing decision rules:

$$x_{1_j}{}^* = R_1(x_{2_j}{}^*, c_j, P_j)$$
$$x_{2_j}{}^* = R_2(x_{1_j}{}^*, c_j, P_j)$$

8. Efficient surface:

$$\phi(Y.^*, P) = 0$$

cycle times the number of order cycles per year. The expected number of shortage delays was defined under the assumption that usage over the procurement interval is normally distributed with mean equal to the average rate of use times the length of the procurement lead time and standard deviation equal to the square root of the mean.

One further comment should be given with respect to this shortage model. Since shortages were defined in terms of the number of shipments delayed, all usage data had to be expressed in terms of the average size of a shipment to the field.

A linear cost model was assumed, that is, total variable cost was assumed equal to the sum of the products of corresponding outcome levels and cost parameters. Cost-minimizing decision rules were derived in a method similar to that discussed in Whitin's *Theory of Inventory Management.*

In analytic form the equation for optimal order quantity involved the order-point variable, and the equation for optimal order point involved the order-quantity variable. An iterative procedure was used for final determination of each decision variable.

You will notice that throughout Table 3, all variables occur with the subscript j. This, as in the first example, identifies the correspondence of the variable to the jth stock item. In the case we were considering, approximately 60,000 stock items were present. Once the rules were developed, the tactical problem was solved. Given the cost parameters, the rules were completely defined, and a mechanism was available for determining order point and order quantity on each of the 60,000 stock items.

The strategic problem, however, was far from solved. In this particular situation, even under the most painstaking analysis, no satisfactory measurement of the three cost parameters could be obtained. As might be expected, the cost of shortage delays was particularly evasive. Thus, we concluded that an alternative procedure of defining the efficient surface was to be preferred. Because of the complexity of the situation, and because of the oversimplicity of the operational relationships we had assumed, it was felt that an analytic derivation of the efficient surface would be unacceptable. Instead, a method was developed to simulate the actual behaviour of the inventory system to derive the efficient surface synthetically.

SYNTHETIC DERIVATION OF EFFICIENT SURFACE

A group of items was selected randomly from the system. The actual cost, lead time, and monthly usage of these stock items were taken from company records covering a two-year period. A program was written for IBM's 701 computer to simulate the actual behaviour of these items over the two-year period. In essence, the computer used system data to determine average usage (over the previous six months) as well as unit cost and lead time, and employed the decision rule that we had formulated to decide when an order should be placed on each item and how much material should be ordered. The computer kept track of both actual usage and orders placed, and maintained a running balance of stock on hand. Measurements were made simultaneously of the value of inventory investment, the number of orders issued, and the numbers of shortage delays that resulted over the period studied. The program was designed with sufficient flexibility so that the cost ratios present in the decision rules could be varied without difficulty.

Our procedure then was to select particular values for the pair of cost ratios, insert these values in the decision rules, and then simulate the behavior of the inventory system over the two-year period. The upper panel in Figure 2

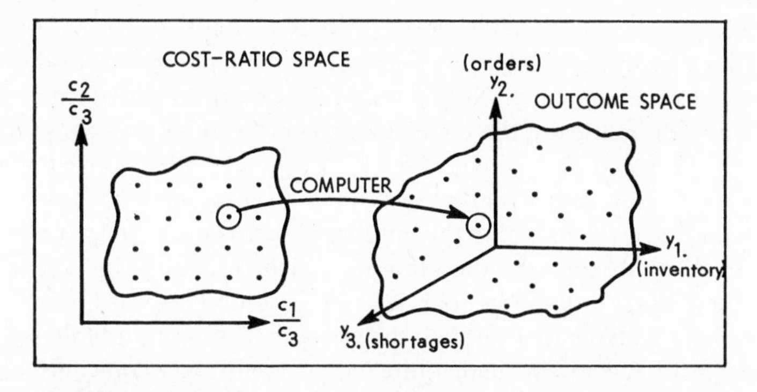

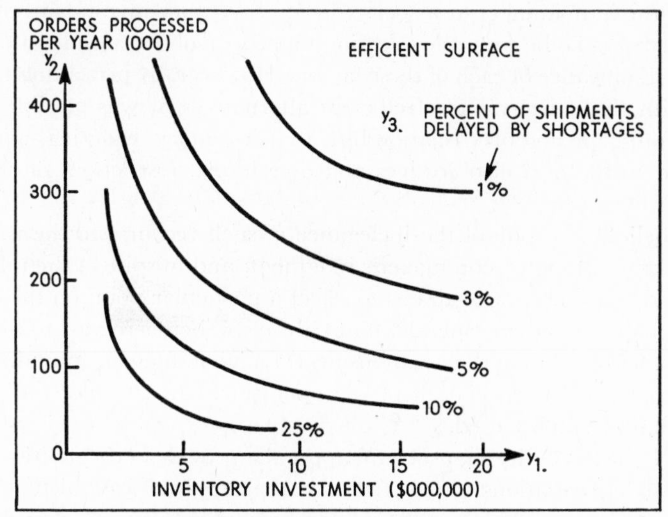

FIGURE 2. Synthetic generation of efficient surface.

shows the process that was followed. A lattice of points in the cost-ratio space was explored in this manner. Corresponding to each point studied, the outcome was observed in terms of the average inventory investment, the numbers of orders processed, and the number of shortage delays.

In this way a group of points on the efficient surface of the outcome space was defined. The lower panel in Figure 2 shows a complete picture of the outcome space as generalized from the particular values obtained. Notice that shortages were defined in terms of the percentage of shipments delayed rather than the absolute number of shortage delays that occurred. This appeared to be a more meaningful representation of the alternative shortage levels.

This lower panel thus shows the entire range of alternative outcomes available to the company under the formulation that was employed. Any given point in this chart could be identified with a particular pair of cost ratios and could thus be attained through the decision rules. At this point, it was possible to confront the principal executive involved with the entire range of alternatives available, so that a decision could be made on inventory control operations which best related the outcome of these operations to the overall objectives of the company. Notice that this picture of the efficient surface shows quite dramatically the conflict between the three outcome variables.

The inventory control system which the company had employed up to that point was of such a nature that it was possible to effect a substantial reduction in inventory investment and in the number of orders processed per year while maintaining approximately the same overall percent of shipments delayed that had occurred in the past. This was the position that was finally selected by the company. Note that through the use of the efficient surface concept the strategic decision could be made quite independently of a conscious measurement of the individual costs associated with inventory investment, ordering, and shortages. To be sure, the selection process involved consideration of the relative significance of each of these factors. However, by presenting the executive with the entire range of efficient alternatives, it was possible to take into account the complex relationships that inventory, ordering, and shortages had to the overall objectives and operational restrictions of this company.

We believe, in spite of the inelegance of such recourse to the unexplicit mechanisms of the decision maker's judgment, and in spite of the reluctance that the decision maker often has to select a particular point on this surface, that such a procedure frequently, if not always, is better related to the actual problems involved than the usual business of having someone hunt down costs without any real appreciation of the operational ramifications of the cost values that are finally used.

Notice the flexibility that such an approach provides. As conditions affecting company operations change, such as the supply of capital funds or the significance of service to customers, appropriate adjustments may be made in the strategic direction of inventory control operations. The decision rules may be modified to free funds or to improve the reliability of stocks with direct reference to the effect such changes will have on the other components of the results vector. The decision maker is shown not only how to free funds that are tied up in inventory but also what the effect will be on shortages and on the level of ordering.

UNSOLVED PROBLEMS

Space has not permitted an examination of some of the *unsolved* problems. For example, almost nothing is known of the transient behavior of inventory systems after a change in the strategic objective. If new cost ratios are inserted in the decision rules, we know only that the system will come to rest at the point in the outcome space which corresponds to these cost ratios. We do not know how the system will behave as it approaches this point or even how long it will take to come within some specified neighborhood of the resting point.

Frequently, such transient behavior is of the greatest significance. To our knowledge, no work on this problem has ever been carried out.

SUMMARY

First, we suggested that inventory control operations involve two separate types of decision problems (1) the tactical problem: how to control the supply of individual stock items in a way that most effectively achieves a particular aggregate outcome; and (2) the strategic problem: how to select among the attainable alternatives the specific outcome which is best related to the overall objectives and operational restrictions of the company.

We have suggested further that while much excellent work has been done on the tactical problem, the typical approach to the strategic problem—involving the search for certain hypothetical costs—frequently leaves much to be desired. Finally, we suggested that for any given formulation it is possible to identify, either analytically or synthetically, the entire set of alternative outcomes that would be best under some cost criterion and that direct executive selection from this set of alternatives frequently appears to bring about a better solution to the strategic decision problem.

30

The author develops two models for optimization in respect to the variables of an inventory problem. Data are substituted into both a Markov chain model and a simulation model. The assessment is made that the Markov chain model is theoretically feasible but that the simulation model is simpler and still provides satisfactory results. General conclusions are also drawn in respect to an inventory system without regard to the type of model used.

*MARKOV CHAINS AND SIMULATIONS IN AN INVENTORY SYSTEM**†

Eliezer Naddor

INVENTORY SYSTEMS are systems in which inventories shortages and replenishments can be controlled through appropriate decisions pertaining to when to replenish and by how much. In general, these systems do not pose special conceptual difficulties (in contrast, say, to the theory of games). In principle, at least, it seems possible to construct a mathematical model for any given inventory system and to use it to find optimal decisions for that system. However, frequently inventory systems are encountered for which it is quite difficult to construct mathematical models which can be used to find optimal decisions. These difficulties arise even in systems with relatively simple properties.[1]

In this article an inventory system is described in which the difficulties of constructing a mathematical model are explored. Only for a very special case of the system can such a model be constructed. This model turns out to be a finite Markov chain with a "reasonable" number of states.[2] The analysis of this special case suggests that the Markov chain approach, though theoretically feasible, is in practice not suitable for the analysis of the general inventory system under study. An alternative method of approach is the use of simulation. This alternative is also explored in this article.

---

* Reprinted from *Journal of Industrial Engineering*, March–April, 1963, pp. 91–98. The *Journal* is the official publication of the American Institute of Industrial Engineers, Inc., 345 East 47th Street, New York, New York 10017.

† The work reported here was in part supported by the Research Laboratories, General Motors Corporation, Warren, Michigan.

[1] See [8], pp. 322–34.

[2] See [1]; [4], pp. 338–96; [5]; [6]; [7], pp. 384–438.

The properties of the inventory system studied in this presentation are described in the following section. This system is an idealized abstraction of the inventory control procedures of General Motors' Parts Division. The study was undertaken to get theoretical insights as to the sensitivity of the system to variables which can be controlled by suitable management decisions.

In section 2 the analysis views the inventory system as a Markov chain, and numerical results are obtained for a few special cases. In section 3 the analysis is based on a simulation of the inventory system, and numerical results are obtained for several special cases including some of the cases which were dealt with in section 2. All the numerical results are summarized in section 4, and several conclusions are reached on the sensitivity of the inventory system. A comparison of the results of sections 2 and 3 indicates that simulation can be used to advantage even though it is possible to obtain exact answers through the application of Markov chains.[3]

1. THE INVENTORY SYSTEM

The policy used in replenishing inventories in the system to be discussed may be called a modified (t, B) policy.[4] Every t units of time a decision with respect to replenishments is made. The amount to be replenished at time i is such as to raise available inventories A_i to a *bank* B_i. No returns are allowed. Thus the quantity P_i ordered for replenishment of inventory may be formally given by

$$P_i = \max(B_i - A_i, 0) \tag{1}$$

The question whether this is a good policy or how to evaluate other policies will not be discussed. We will also not investigate the parameter t in the given policy. We shall assume that it is prescribed and is not subject to control. Furthermore, for ease of discussion, t will be assumed to be one week.

Our analysis will thus only be concerned with the bank B_i, which is subject to control by a decision maker.

The bank may be viewed as composed of several weeks of expected average demand:

$$B_i = N\bar{S}_i \tag{2}$$

In equation 2, N is the number of weeks in the bank, and $\bar{S}_i$ is the average demand as of week i.

Several methods may be used to determine the average demand. In this presentation, only one such method will be studied.[5] The average demand at

[3] A reviewer of this article notes that there is a widespread misconception about the use of simulation, namely, that simulation should be used only when the problem defies analysis by conventional mathematical tools.

[4] See [9], pp. 262–64.

[5] A variation of this method is being used by General Motors' Parts Division. For another method, see [3].

time i will be determined by finding the mean demand over a period of M weeks immediately preceding time i:

$$\bar{S}_i = \left(\sum_{j=i-M+1}^{i} S_j \right) \Big/ M \tag{3}$$

The parameters N and M completely specify how decisions may be reached in the inventory system. Table 1 illustrates this for a case where demand ranges from zero to 300, lead time is two weeks, M is four and N is six.

TABLE 1

i	Q_i	S_i	q_i	$\bar{S}_i$	B_i	A_i	$B_i - A_i$	P_i	R_i
8	...	100	...	...	...	...	...	...	...
9	...	100	...	...	...	...	...	100	...
10	...	100	...	...	...	...	...	100	...
11	400	100	300	100	600	500	100	100	100
12	400	300	100	150	900	300	600	600	100
13	200	100	100	150	900	800	100	100	100
14	200	100	100	150	900	800	100	100	600
15	700	100	600	150	900	800	100	100	100
16	700	100	600	100	600	800	−200	0	100
17	700	200	500	125	750	600	150	150	100
18	600	0	600	100	...	...	...	...	0
19	600	100	500	100	...	...	...	...	150
20	650	100	550	100	...	...	...	...	...
..	...	...	...	...	...	...	...	...	...
..	...	...	...	...	...	...	...	...	...

In the table, we have:

i = Week number
Q_i = Inventory on hand at the beginning of week i
S_i = Demand during week i
q_i = Inventory on hand at end of week i
$\bar{S}_i$ = The average demand as of end of week i, based on equation 3
B_i = The bank as of end of week i, based on equation 2
A_i = The available inventory as of end of week i before ordering replenishment (that is, amounts on hand and on order)
P_i = The replenishment quantity ordered at the end of week i, based on equation 1
R_i = Replenishment added to inventory at end of week i and available at beginning of week $i + 1$

Let L designate lead time in weeks. Then, in addition to equations 1, 2, 3, we also have

$$q_i = Q_i - S_i \tag{4}$$

$$A_i = \begin{cases} q_i & \text{for } L = 0 \\ q_i + \sum_{j=i-L}^{i-1} P_j & \text{for } L > 0 \end{cases} \tag{5}$$

$$R_i = P_{i-L} \tag{6}$$

$$Q_{i+1} = q_i + R_i \tag{7}$$

In this inventory system, M and N are thus the only unknown decision parameters. They are the parameters which management has to specify. Once they have been established, there is no other way to control the inventories, shortages, and replenishments in the inventory system.[6]

Let I_1 designate the expected average amounts in inventory, let I_2 designate the expected average shortages, and let I_3 designate the expected number of replenishments per week.[7] We now proceed to investigate the effect of M and N on I_1, I_2, and I_3, thus finding how sensitive the system is to its decision parameters.

2. MARKOV CHAIN APPROACH

In order to fix ideas and to demonstrate an analytical approach to the problem, a numerical example will be studied.

Demand during a week is assumed to be only for either 100 units or 300 units. It is also assumed that a demand for 100 occurs 70 percent of the time; and for 300, it occurs 10 percent of the time. There is therefore no demand at all 20 percent of the time. We also assume that lead time is zero; that is, any replenishment quantity decided on at the end of week i is immediately added to stock and is available for use at the beginning of week $i + 1$.

Symbolically, these assumptions can be stated as follows: Demand S during a week is a random variable whose probability distribution $P(S)$ is given by $P(0) = 0.20$, $P(100) = 0.70$, $P(200) = 0$, $P(300) = 0.10$. Also, for lead time, $L = 0$.[8]

Let, for example, $N = 2$, and let $M = 2$. The inventory system may then operate as in Table 2. The amounts in inventory may also be described graphically as in Figure 1.

Over the period of 20 weeks, we note that the amounts in inventory at the beginning of each week vary from 100 to 400. The relative frequency of occurrence of these amounts is summarized as follows:

Amount in inventory at beginning of week........	100	200	300	400
Relative frequency of occurrence................	0.10	0.60	0.15	0.15

The average amount at the *beginning* of each week is seen to be 235.

We can also compute the average amount carried in inventory and the average amount short throughout the 20-week period. During the first week, these averages are 66⅔ and 16⅔, respectively; in the second week, they are 400 and 0, respectively; then 350, 0; 250, 0; 200, 0; 66⅔, 16⅔; 250, 0; etc.; so that the overall averages in 20 weeks are 186⅔ and 1⅔, respectively. Simi-

[6] This is only true in our idealized model. In practice, there are usually several other decision parameters subject to control, such as the scheduling period t, lead time L, etc.

[7] I_3 can thus be at most one.

[8] As we shall see, even for this simplified example the Markov chain approach would in general lead to very large transition matrices. Hence, we do not include here a discussion of trends and seasonality in demands nor the case of nonzero lead time. These can be readily included in the simulation approach.

TABLE 2

i	Q_i	S_i	q_i	$\bar{S}_i$	B_i	A_i	$B_i - A_i$	P_i	R_i
0		100							
1	200	300	−100	200	400	−100	500	500	500
2	400	0	400	150	300	400	−100	0	0
3	400	100	300	50	100	300	−200	0	0
4	300	100	200	100	200	200	0	0	0
5	200	0	200	50	100	200	−100	0	0
6	200	300	−100	150	300	−100	400	400	400
7	300	100	200	200	400	200	200	200	200
8	400	100	300	100	200	300	−100	0	0
9	300	100	200	100	200	200	0	0	0
10	200	100	100	100	200	100	100	100	100
11	200	100	100	100	200	100	100	100	100
12	200	0	200	50	100	200	−100	0	0
13	200	100	100	50	100	100	0	0	0
14	100	100	0	100	200	0	200	200	200
15	200	100	100	100	200	100	100	100	100
16	200	100	100	100	200	100	100	100	100
17	200	100	100	100	200	100	100	100	100
18	200	0	200	50	100	200	−100	0	0
19	200	100	100	50	100	100	0	0	0
20	100	100	0	100	200	0	200	200	200

larly, we can compute the average number of replenishments per week. In 20 weeks, 10 replenishments have been scheduled, so that the average number of replenishments per week is 0.5.

We now consider the question of finding the expected values of the relative frequencies, $F(Q)$, and averages, I_1, I_2, I_3. We first study the relative frequencies of the amounts in inventory at the beginning of each week.

From equations 1 to 7 for $L = 0$, $N = 2$, $M = 2$, we get the following results:

$$
\begin{aligned}
Q_{i+1} &= q_i + R_i = q_i + P_i = q_i + \max\,[B_i - A_i, 0] \\
&= q_i + \max\,[2(S_{i-1} + S_i)/2 - q_i, 0] \\
&= \max\,[S_{i-1} + S_i, q_i] \\
&= \max\,[S_{i-1} + S_i, Q_i - S_i]
\end{aligned}
\tag{8}
$$

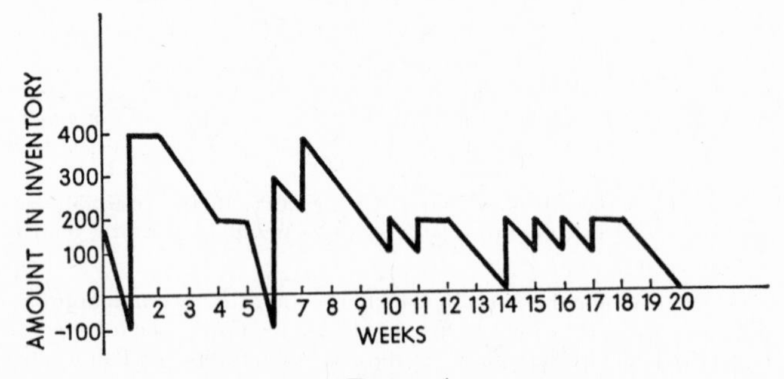

FIGURE 1

Equation 8 implies that the transition from an amount Q_i to an amount Q_{i+1} depends both on S_{i-1} and on S_i. This result suggests defining a Markov chain state as the couple (S_{i-1}, Q) from which we can go the state (S_i, Q_{i+1}). This transition now depends only on the occurrence of S_i, the probabilities of which are known. How many such states are there? In general, there will be very many; but in the present example, it is relatively simple to show that only the following 14 states should be considered:

State	*1*	*2*	*3*	*4*	*5*	*6*	*7*	*8*	*9*	*10*	*11*	*12*	*13*	*14*
S_{i-1}......	0	0	0	0	0	0	100	100	100	100	100	300	300	300
Q_i......	100	200	300	400	500	600	100	200	300	400	500	300	400	600

Using these definitions, Table 2 can then be viewed as representing the following states: 8, 13, 4, 9, 8, 2, 12, 10, 9, 8, 8, 8, 2, 7, 8, 8, 8, 8, 2, 7.

The transition matrix can now be stated as shown in Table 3.

TABLE 3

TRANSITION MATRIX

State	*1*	*2*	*3*	*4*	*5*	*6*	*7*	*8*	*9*	*10*	*11*	*12*	*13*	*14*
1....	0.2	0	0	0	0	0	0.7	0	0	0	0	0.1	0	0
2....	0	0.2	0	0	0	0	0.7*	0	0	0	0	0.1	0	0
3....	0	0	0.2	0	0	0	0	0.7	0	0	0	0.1	0	0
4....	0	0	0	0.2	0	0	0	0	0.7*	0	0	0.1	0	0
5....	0	0	0	0	0.2	0	0	0	0	0.7	0	0.1	0	0
6....	0	0	0	0	0	0.2	0	0	0	0	0.7	0.1	0	0
7....	0.2	0	0	0	0	0	0	0.7*	0	0	0	0	0.1	0
8....	0	0.2*	0	0	0	0	0	0.7*	0	0	0	0	0.1*	0
9....	0	0	0.2	0	0	0	0	0.7*	0	0	0	0	0.1	0
10....	0	0	0	0	0	0	0	0	0.7*	0	0	0	0.1	0
11....	0	0	0	0	0.2	0	0	0	0	0.7	0	0	0.1	0
12....	0	0	0.2	0	0	0	0	0	0	0.7*	0	0	0	0.1
13....	0	0	0	0.2*	0	0	0	0	0	0.7	0	0	0	0.1
14....	0	0	0	0	0	0.2	0	0	0	0	0.7	0	0	0.1

The transitions that occurred in Table 2 are represented by asterisks in the transition matrix. It can readily be seen that the other transitions with positive probabilities in the matrix can also occur, but none other.

The transition matrix can now be used to find the steady-state probabilities of the occurrence of the various states.

Let p_j designate the steady-state probability of being in state j. Clearly, then:

$$p_j = \sum_{\kappa} a_{kj} p_k \tag{9}$$

where a_{kj} is the transition probability of going from state k to state j. Also, of course:

$$\sum_j p_j = 1 \tag{10}$$

Applying equations 9 and 10 to the transition matrix leads to the following equations[9] for the p_j:

$$\begin{aligned} p_1 &= 0.2p_1 + 0.2p_7 \\ p_2 &= 0.2p_2 + 0.2p_8 \\ &\vdots \\ p_{14} &= 0.1p_{12} + 0.1p_{13} + 0.1p_{14} \\ p_1 + p_2 + &\cdots + p_{14} = 1 \end{aligned}$$

Solving these equations for the p_j's, we get the results:

State j	1	2	3	4	5	6	7	8	9	10	11	12	13	14
p_j	0.024	0.113	0.023	0.035	0.002	0.002	0.96	0.451	0.074	0.071	0.009	0.020	0.070	0.010

By adding the appropriate probabilities, we can now find the expected values, $F(Q)$, of the occurrence of amounts in inventory Q at the beginning of each week:

Q	100	200	300	400	500	600
$F(Q)$	0.120	0.564	0.117	0.176	0.011	0.012

The expected average amounts of inventories and shortages in the system can readily be determined from

$$I_1 = \sum_{Q=100}^{600} \left\{ \sum_{s=0}^{Q} (Q - S/2)P(S) + \sum_{s=Q+100}^{300} [Q^2/(2S)]P(S) \right\} F(Q) \tag{11}$$

$$I_2 = \sum_{Q=100}^{600} \sum_{S=Q+100}^{300} [(S - Q)^2/(2S)]P(S)F(Q) \tag{12}$$

By substituting the values of $P(S)$ and $F(Q)$, we get $I_1 = 194.838$ and $I_2 = 1.738$.

The expected number of replenishments per week can be computed from

$$I_3 = \sum_j \sum_S p_j P(S) b_{js} \tag{13}$$

where b_{js} is the probability that replenishment is scheduled when the system is in state j and a demand S occurs (b_{js} is either one or zero).

In the above example the b_{js} can readily be seen to be as in Table 4. Applying equation 13, and using the values of p_j and b_{js}, we get $I_3 = 0.5624$. We may now summarize the results for $N = 2$ and $M = 2$.

In order to find the expected averages of inventories, shortages, and

[9] There will be 15 equations and 14 unknowns. The 15 equations are not independent, of course.

TABLE 4

j \ S	0	100	300
1	0	1	1
2	0	0	1
3	0	0	1
4	0	0	1
5	0	0	1
6	0	0	0
7	0	1	1
8	0	1	1
9	0	0	1
10	0	0	1
11	0	0	1
12	0	1	1
13	0	1	1
14	0	0	1

replenishments, 14 different states have to be recognized. These lead to the six possible amounts in inventory at the beginning of each week with appropriate probabilities. The knowledge of the probabilities immediately gives the expected averages of inventories and shortages: $I_1 = 194.838$ and $I_2 = 1.738$. Similarly, we also get the expected number of replenishments per week of $I_3 = 0.5624$.

Suppose now that $N = 2$ and $M = 1$. Following the reasoning of equation 8, we get

$$Q_{i+1} = \cdots = q_i + \max\,[2(S_i/1) - q_i, 0] \\ = \max\,[2S_i, Q_i - S_i] \tag{14}$$

Here, then, we can define a Markov chain state as the amount Q_i. It is again relatively simple to show that only the following states should be considered:

State	1	2	3	4	5
Q_i	200	300	400	500	600

And the transition matrix becomes as shown in Table 5. The expected values,

TABLE 5

State	1	2	3	4	5
1	0.9	0	0	0	0.1
2	0.7	0.2	0	0	0.1
3	0	0.7	0.2	0	0.1
4	0	0	0.7	0.2	0.1
5	0	0	0	0.7	0.3

$F(Q)$, can be readily computed as before:

State	1	2	3	4	5
Q	200	300	400	500	600
$F(Q)$	0.586	0.084	0.096	0.109	0.125

Using equations 11 and 12, we now get $I_1 = 261.277$ and $I_2 = 0.977$. The values of b_{js} are now as shown in Table 6. Hence, by equation 13, where now $p_j = F(Q)$, we have $I_3 = 0.5102$.

TABLE 6

j \ S	0	100	300
1	0	1	1
2	0	0	1
3	0	0	1
4	0	0	1
5	0	0	1

A similar approach can be used for several other values of N and M, such as $N = 1$, $M = 1$; $N = 1$, $M = 2$; $N = 3$, $M = 1$. However, for other values the transition matrices become very large. The size of transition matrices for various values of M and N are as shown in Table 7.[10]

TABLE 7

N \ M	1	2	3
1	3	11	72
2	5	14	135
3	9	36	81

The size of the transition matrices becomes larger by several orders of magnitude when lead time is not zero. It thus appears that the use of the Markov chain approach to the inventory problem at hand seems to be rather limited. An alternative approach, that of simulation, is discussed in the following section. However, before proceeding with the simulation approach, it seems worthwhile to summarize the results obtained thus far and to add results which have been obtained using the Markov chain approach. This is done in Table 8.

[10] It can be shown that the approximate size of the transition matrix is $NMn^M/(N, M)$ where n is the number of different demands and (N, M) is the largest common denominator of N and M.

TABLE 8

N M	1 1	2 1	3 1	1 2	2 2	1 ∞	2 ∞	3 ∞
$F(Q = 50)$				0.141				
$F(Q = 100)$	0.766			0.638	0.120	1.000		
$F(Q = 150)$				0.025				
$F(Q = 200)$	0.109	0.586		0.146	0.563		1.000	
$F(Q = 300)$	0.125	0.084	0.449	0.050	0.118			1.000
$F(Q = 400)$		0.096	0.064		0.176			
$F(Q = 500)$		0.109	0.073		0.011			
$F(Q = 600)$		0.125	0.084		0.012			
$F(Q = 700)$			0.069					
$F(Q = 800)$			0.109					
$F(Q = 900)$			0.125					
$\bar{Q}$	135.900	310.300	514.100	118.800	243.100	100.000	200.000	300.000
I_1	91.189	261.277	464.100	76.093	194.838	56.667	151.667	250.000
I_2	5.289	0.977	0.000	7.293	1.738	6.667	1.667	0.000
I_3	0.636	0.414	0.414	0.691	0.562	0.800	0.800	0.800

The results for $N = 2$, $M = 2$ and for $N = 2$, $M = 1$ were obtained earlier in this article. In a similar way, we can obtain the results for $N = 1$, $M = 1$; $N = 2$, $M = 1$; and $N = 1$, $M = 2$. To obtain the results when M approaches infinity, we note by equation 3 that $S_i = S = 100$. Hence the bank is always constant: $B = 100N$, so that also $Q_i = 100N$.

The value of $\bar{Q}$ in Table 8 is the average amount in inventory at the beginning of each week:

$$\bar{Q} = \Sigma QF(Q)$$

3. SIMULATION APPROACH

The simulation approach to the analysis of the inventory systems will be based on computations similar to those of Table 2. The methods of approach will be demonstrated for the two cases $N = 1$, $M = 2$ and $N = 2$, $M = 2$ considered in the previous section.

Table 9 contains all the computations necessary for the simulations and will be explained column by column. Columns 1 to 3 pertain to both case $N = 1$, $M = 2$ and case $N = 2$, $M = 2$; columns 4 to 9 pertain to the first case; columns 10 to 15 pertain to the second.

Column 1: Week number. Here a total of 50 weeks has been simulated (this total is sometimes referred to as the run size).

Column 2: Demand during the week. Two principles have been used in generating and using demands in the simulations.[11]

First principle: The distribution of simulated demands should be *identical* with the theoretical distribution of demands.

Second principle: The same simulated demands will be used for all cases under review.

[11] It seems intuitively obvious that the use of these principles would reduce the size of runs needed to obtain results within given tolerances. Some research work in this area will be included in [2].

TABLE 9

1	2	3	4	5	6	7	8	9	10	11	12	13	14	15
i	S_i	$\bar{S}_i$	B_i	Q_i	q_i	I_{1_i}	I_{2_i}	I_{3_i}	B_i	Q_i	q_i	I_{1_i}	I_{2_i}	I_{3_i}
1....	100	100	100	100	0	50	0	1	200	200	100	150	0	1
2....	300	200	200	100	−200	17	67	1	400	200	−100	67	17	1
3....	0	150	150	200	200	200	0	0	300	400	400	400	0	0
4....	100	50	50	200	100	150	0	0	100	400	300	350	0	0
5....	0	50	50	100	100	100	0	0	100	300	300	300	0	0
6....	100	50	50	100	0	50	0	1	100	300	200	250	0	0
7....	100	100	100	50	−50	12	12	1	200	200	100	150	0	1
8....	100	100	100	100	0	50	0	1	200	200	100	150	0	1
9....	100	100	100	100	0	50	0	1	200	200	100	150	0	1
10....	100	100	100	100	0	50	0	1	200	200	100	150	0	1
11....	0	50	50	100	100	100	0	0	100	200	200	200	0	0
12....	100	50	50	100	0	50	0	1	100	200	100	150	0	0
13....	0	50	50	50	50	50	0	0	100	100	100	100	0	0
14....	100	50	50	50	−50	12	12	1	100	100	0	50	0	1
15....	100	100	100	50	−50	12	12	1	200	100	0	50	0	1
16....	100	100	100	100	0	50	0	1	200	200	100	150	0	1
17....	100	100	100	100	0	50	0	1	200	200	100	150	0	1
18....	100	100	100	100	0	50	0	1	200	200	100	150	0	1
19....	100	100	100	100	0	50	0	1	200	200	100	150	0	1
20....	100	100	100	100	0	50	0	1	200	200	100	150	0	1
21....	300	200	200	100	−200	17	67	1	400	200	−100	67	17	1
22....	100	200	200	200	100	150	0	1	400	400	300	350	0	1
23....	100	100	100	200	100	150	0	0	200	400	300	350	0	0
24....	100	100	100	100	0	50	0	1	200	300	200	250	0	0
25....	0	50	50	100	100	100	0	0	100	200	200	200	0	0
26....	300	150	150	100	−200	17	67	1	300	200	−100	67	17	1
27....	100	200	200	150	50	100	0	1	400	300	200	250	0	1
28....	100	100	100	200	100	150	0	0	200	400	300	350	0	0
29....	0	50	50	100	100	100	0	0	100	300	300	300	0	0
30....	100	50	50	100	0	50	0	1	100	300	200	250	0	0
31....	100	100	100	50	−50	12	12	1	200	200	100	150	0	1
32....	100	100	100	100	0	50	0	1	200	200	100	150	0	1
33....	100	100	100	100	0	50	0	1	200	200	100	150	0	1
34....	100	100	100	100	0	50	0	1	200	200	100	150	0	1
35....	100	100	100	100	0	50	0	1	200	200	100	150	0	1
36....	0	50	50	100	100	100	0	0	100	200	200	200	0	0
37....	100	50	50	100	0	50	0	1	100	200	100	150	0	0
38....	100	100	100	50	−50	12	12	1	200	100	0	50	0	1
39....	0	50	50	100	100	100	0	0	100	200	200	200	0	0
40....	0	0	0	100	100	100	0	0	0	200	200	200	0	0
41....	100	50	50	100	0	50	0	1	100	200	100	150	0	0
42....	100	100	100	50	−50	12	12	1	200	100	0	50	0	1
43....	300	200	200	100	−200	17	67	1	400	200	−100	67	17	1
44....	100	200	200	200	100	150	0	1	400	400	300	350	0	1
45....	300	200	200	200	−100	67	17	1	400	400	100	250	0	1
46....	100	200	200	200	100	150	0	1	400	400	300	350	0	1
47....	0	50	50	200	200	200	0	0	100	400	400	400	0	0
48....	100	50	50	200	100	150	0	0	100	400	300	350	0	0
49....	100	100	100	100	0	50	0	1	200	300	200	250	0	0
50....	100	100	100	100	0	50	0	1	200	200	100	150	0	1

To satisfy the first principle for the period of 50 weeks, demands for zero units were simulated for 10 weeks, demands for 100 units for 35 weeks, and demands for 300 units for 5 weeks. The assignment of demands to specific weeks was then made at random.

To satisfy the second principle, the demands of column 2 were used both for the case $N = 1$, $M = 2$ (to get from column 5 to column 6) and for the case $N = 2$, $M = 2$ (to get from column 11 to column 12).

Column 3: The average demand, $\bar{S}_i = (S_{i-1} + S_i)/2$. Computations for all i (except $i = 1$) are straightforward. To compute $\bar{S}_1$, it has been assumed that[12] $S_0 = \bar{S} = 100$.

[12] For larger M, one would assume that $S_0 = S_{-1} = \cdots = S_{-M+2} = \bar{S}$.

Columns 4 and 10: The bank, $B_i = N\bar{S}_i$. For column 4 we have $B_i = \bar{S}_i$, so that columns 3 and 4 are identical. For column 10, $B_i = 2\bar{S}_i$.

Columns 5 and 11: Amount on hand at beginning of week.

Since lead time is zero, then by equations 1, 5, 6, 7:

$$Q_{i+1} = q_i + \max (B_i - q_i, 0) = \max (B_i, q_i) \tag{15}$$

Computing Q_i for all i (except $i = 1$) can thus be done by equation 15. For $i = 1$, we assume for all cases $Q_1 = NS = 100N$. Hence, in column 5, $Q_1 = 100$, and in column 11, $Q_1 = 200$.

Columns 6 and 12: Amount on hand at end of week, $q_i = Q_i - S_i$.

Columns 7 and 13: The average amount carried in inventory:

$$I_{1_i} = \begin{cases} Q_i - S_i/2 & \text{when } q_i \geqq 0 \\ Q_i^2/(2S_i) & \text{when } q_i < 0 \end{cases} \tag{16}$$

Columns 8 and 14: The average shortage:

$$I_{2_i} = \begin{cases} 0 & \text{when } q_i \geqq 0 \\ q_i^2/(2S_i) & \text{when } q_i < 0 \end{cases} \tag{17}$$

Columns 9 and 15: A scheduled replenishment:

$$I_{3_i} = \begin{cases} 1 & \text{when } q_i < B_i \\ 0 & \text{when } q_i \geqq B_i \end{cases} \tag{18}$$

The results of these simulations and a few others are summarized in Table 10. The probabilities of the occurrence of the various Q's can be obtained from columns 5 and 11 in Table 9. For $N = 1$, column 5 gives $Q = 50$ seven times, $Q = 100$ thirty-two times, $Q = 150$ once, $Q = 200$ ten times; hence the corresponding probabilities 0.14, 0.64, 0.02, 0.20 in Table 10. The values of $\bar{Q}$, I_1, I_2, I_3 are the corresponding averages of the Q_i, I_{1i}, I_{2i}, and I_{3i} for the 50-week period.

4. SUMMARY AND CONCLUSIONS

The main results of the analysis of sections 2 and 3 are summarized in Table 11.

It appears that the following conclusions pertaining to the inventory system studied may be drawn:

1. As N increases, then the amounts in inventory increase, shortages decrease, and the number of replenishments per week decrease. However, the larger the M, the less marked are the increases and decreases. When M approaches infinity, the number of replenishments per week is a constant.[13]
2. As M increases, then the amounts in inventory decrease, and the number of replenishments per week increase. Shortages, on the other hand, first increase and then decrease.
3. The system is more sensitive to the parameter N than to the parameter M.

---

[13] This constant is the probability of nonzero demands during the week.

TABLE 10

N	*1*	*2*	*3*	*1*	*2*	*3*	*1*	*2*	*3*	*1*	*2*	*3*
M	*1*	*1*	*1*	*2*	*2*	*2*	*3*	*3*	*3*	*4*	*4*	*4*
$P(Q = 33)$							0.02					
$P(Q = 50)$				0.14						0.08		
$P(Q = 67)$							0.30	0.02				
$P(Q = 75)$										0.28		
$P(Q = 100)$	0.74			0.64	0.10		0.36		0.02	0.26	0.06	
$P(Q = 125)$										0.16		
$P(Q = 133)$							0.08	0.22				
$P(Q = 150)$				0.02		0.02				0.16	0.28	0.06
$P(Q = 167)$							0.22	0.04				
$P(Q = 200)$	0.14	0.54		0.20	0.56	0.08		0.32	0.20	0.06	0.28	
$P(Q = 225)$												0.24
$P(Q = 233)$							0.02	0.06				
$P(Q = 250)$											0.14	
$P(Q = 267)$								0.10				
$P(Q = 275)$												0.04
$P(Q = 300)$	0.12	0.10	0.46		0.14	0.46			0.36		0.18	0.26
$P(Q = 333)$								0.18				
$P(Q = 367)$								0.04				
$P(Q = 375)$												0.14
$P(Q = 400)$		0.10	0.04		0.20	0.10			0.16		0.16	0.02
$P(Q = 450)$						0.02						0.16
$P(Q = 467)$								0.02				
$P(Q = 500)$		0.14	0.04			0.12			0.20			0.02
$P(Q = 600)$		0.12	0.10			0.20			0.04			0.06
$P(Q = 700)$			0.10						0.02			
$P(Q = 800)$			0.14									
$P(Q = 900)$			0.12									
$\bar{Q}$	138.00	320.00	524.00	114.00	244.00	386.00	108.70	226.00	352.00	107.00	217.00	330.50
I_1	93.70	271.00	474.00	71.20	195.30	336.00	66.70	177.80	302.30	64.70	169.00	281.30
I_2	5.70	1.00	0.00	7.20	1.30	0.00	8.00	1.80	0.30	7.70	2.00	0.80
I_3	0.62	0.48	0.42	0.72	0.58	0.52	0.76	0.66	0.54	0.80	0.72	0.70

TABLE 11

		$M = 1$		$M = 2$		$M = 3$		$M = 4$		...	$M = \infty$	
		Markov Chain	*Simulation*	*Markov Chain*	*Simulation*	*Markov Chain*	*Simulation*	*Markov Chain*	*Simulation*		*Markov Chain*	*Simulation*
$N = 1$	$\bar{Q}$	135.90	138.00	118.80	114.00		108.70		107.00		100.00	
	I_1	91.20	93.70	76.10	71.20		66.70		64.70		56.70	
	I_2	5.20	5.70	7.30	7.20		8.00		7.70		6.70	
	I_3	0.64	0.62	0.69	0.72		0.76		0.80		0.80	
$N = 2$	$\bar{Q}$	310.30	320.00	243.10	244.00		226.00		217.00		200.00	
	I_1	261.30	271.00	194.80	195.30		177.80		169.00		151.70	
	I_2	1.00	1.00	1.70	1.30		1.80		2.00		1.70	
	I_3	0.51	0.48	0.56	0.58		0.66		0.72		0.80	
$N = 3$	$\bar{Q}$	514.10	524.00		386.00		352.00		330.50		300.00	
	I_1	464.10	474.00		336.00		302.30		281.30		250.00	
	I_2	0.00	0.00		0.00		0.30		0.80		0.00	
	I_3	0.41	0.42		0.52		0.54		0.70		0.80	

4. No conclusions can be drawn as to the optimal N and M without a knowledge of the appropriate costs. If the cost of shortage is large, then N should be large; the choice of M would then depend on the relative costs of carrying inventory and making replenishments.
5. For similar cases (that is, for the same N and M) the simulation results are very close to the analytical results, even though only 50 weeks have been simulated.
6. The simulation approach, while being as good as the Markov chain approach in predicting the effect of various parameters, is better than the Markov chain approach in its applicability to a wider range of parameters.

REFERENCES

1. Arrow, Kenneth J.; Karlin, S.; and Scarf, H. *Studies in the Mathematical Theory of Inventory and Production.* Stanford: Stanford University Press, 1958.
2. Brenner, Michael E. A doctoral dissertation in preparation, Johns Hopkins University.
3. Brown, R. G. "Less Risk in Inventory Estimates," *Harvard Business Review*, July–August, 1959, pp. 104–16.
4. Feller, William. *An Introduction to Probability Theory and Its Applications.* 2d ed. New York: John Wiley & Sons, Inc., 1959.
5. Gaver, D. P. "Base Stock Level Inventory Control," *Operations Research*, November–December, 1959, pp. 689–703.
6. Hadley, G., and Whitin, T. M. "A Family of Inventory Models," *Management Science*, July, 1961, pp. 351–71.
7. Kemeny, John G.; Mirkil, H., Snell, J.; and Thompson, D. *Finite Mathematical Structures.* Englewood Cliffs, N.J.: Prentice-Hall, Inc., 1959.
8. Naddor, Eliezer. "Elements of Inventory Systems," chap. xii in C. D. Flagle, W. H. Huggins, and R. H. Roy (eds.), *Operations Research and Systems Engineering* (Baltimore: Johns Hopkins Press, 1960).
9. Naddor, Eliezer. "Evaluation of Inventory Control," in J. Banbury and J. Maitland (eds.), *Proceedings of the Second International Conference on Operational Research* (London: English Universities Press, 1961), pp. 255–67.

31

The author begins his discussion by defining all relevant variables and by classifying the types of decisions to be made. He then provides a specific numerical example of the application of Monte Carlo analysis, in which both demand and lead time are permitted to vary between time periods. Reference is made to the use of the computer as a random number generator in creating a random demand schedule.

*THE APPLICATION OF MONTE CARLO ANALYSIS TO AN INVENTORY PROBLEM**

Donald L. Raun

INTRODUCTION

ALL INVENTORY SITUATIONS have certain general characteristics, each involving some aspects of cost, service, and usage. One characteristic is that as an inventory increases, the cost of storing those goods will also increase, but the cost resulting from an inability to fill orders will decrease. Hence, one aspect of the inventory problem is to find an inventory level which minimizes the sum of the expected holding and shortage costs. Our objective, then, is to consider a set of decisions which will minimize total cost and provide an acceptable level of goods to satisfy the anticipated or expected demand rate.

The purpose of this discussion is to introduce the reader to the application of the Monte Carlo method to inventory problems involving uncertainty of demand and/or lead time. We will make no effort to cover here a wide variety of problems since it is obvious that each inventory problem will differ somewhat in its specific structure and use of quantitative methods necessary for control and management decisions. The level of mathematical sophistication will depend upon the unique characteristics of each situation and will dictate how far one needs to go in using the refined mathematical methods available.

A general statement defining the Monte Carlo technique would be that it

* Reprinted from *Accounting Review*, October, 1963, pp. 754–58.

is a process whereby data are generated by the use of some random number generator, such as a random number table. We then use this random sampling to play a game, so to speak, with nature or a man-made system in which an experiment is simulated. In essence, the Monte Carlo method consists of simulating the real world to determine some probabilistic property of a population of events by the use of random sampling applied to the various components of the events. This statement will be clarified by illustration of a simple problem of the College Book Company.

There are many variables to consider in the inventory problem, and a general breakdown would include the following:

1. The general cost structure:
   a) The cost of obtaining goods.
   b) The cost of holding goods in stock over a fixed period of time.
   c) The cost of shortage, which is the cost associated with either a delay in meeting a given demand or simply the physical inability to meet all the demand at a given instant of time.
2. Demand and order variables:
   a) Demand may vary, as indicated by Table 1.

TABLE 1

ANALYSIS OF ACTUAL DEMAND SCHEDULE IN PAST

Units Demanded per Week	*Frequency Distribution*		*Probability Distribution*	
X	*f*	Σf	$\%P(\leq X)$	*X*
0	1	..	2.5	....
1	5	6	12.5	15.0
2	7	13	17.5	32.5
3	6	19	15.0	47.5
4	5	24	12.5	60.0
5	6	30	15.0	75.0
6	4	34	10.0	85.0
7	2	36	5.0	90.0
8	0	..	0	90.0
9	2	38	5.0	95.0
10	2	40	5.0	100.0

   b) The time between placing an order and receiving an order is not easily established (lead time).

The general decisions may be classified into two types of problems:

1. Quantity and order time must be determined.
2. The *time* required between placing and receiving an order (lead time) is *fixed*, and the problem is therefore to determine the quantity to be ordered.

In order to avoid the trial-and-error method, we can make use of the Monte Carlo technique to study a representation of the real situation.

THE CASE PROBLEM

The case example to be studied here concerns the purchase and sales of leather briefcases ordered from Mexico City by the College Book Company. The objective is to discuss ordering policy and inventory level based on the model resulting from the simulation, or generation, of a random weekly briefcase demand and the time between ordering new stock and receiving it (lead time). Table 1 presents an analysis of the actual demand for briefcases of the College Book Company in the past. Table 2 presents the relevant data in regard to the problem. Table 3 presents an analysis of the actual time experienced between placing the order and receiving the merchandise from the supplier.

TABLE 2

RELEVANT DATA

Symbol	
P, sales price per unit	$8
C, cost per unit	$5
D, annual demand	300 units
S, ordering cost per order	$2
C_1, carrying cost percent per year (based upon cost, C)	25%
C_2, stock-out cost per unit (gross margin lost)	$3

TABLE 3

ANALYSIS OF ACTUAL LEAD TIME IN PAST

	Lead Time in Weeks			
	Frequency Distribution		*Probability Distribution*	
Lead Time t	f	Σf	%	$(P \leq t)$
1	0	0	...	....
2	1	1	2.5	....
3	2	3	5.0	7.5
4	5	8	12.5	20.0
5	7	15	17.5	37.5
6	7	22	17.5	55.0
7	6	28	15.0	70.0
8	6	34	15.0	85.0
9	4	38	10.0	95.0
10	2	40	5.0	100.0

The application of the Monte Carlo technique may be briefly described by the following five-step sequence. The results of the analysis are presented in Table 6 (p. 424) and Chart 1 (p. 424).

Step 1

First, we must set up the distribution of demand and lead time, assigning the appropriate set of random numbers. You will note that in Table 4 the

TABLE 4

Demand				*Lead Time*			
(*x*) *Demand per Week*	*Frequency*	*Cumulative f*	*Assigned Random Numbers*	(*t*) *Weeks*	*Frequency*	*Cumulative*	*Assigned Random Numbers*
0	1	..	01–03	1	0	0	.....
1	5	6	04–15	2	1	1	01–03
2	7	13	16–33	3	2	3	04–08
3	6	19	34–48	4	5	8	09–20
4	5	24	49–60	5	7	15	21–38
5	6	30	61–75	6	7	22	39–55
6	4	34	76–85	7	6	28	56–70
7	2	36	86–90	8	6	34	71–85
8	0	..	.....	9	4	38	86–95
9	2	38	91–95	10	2	40	96–00
10	2	40	96–00	..	.	..	.....

random number intervals are inclusive and selected on the basis of the percentages of the individual frequencies to the total demand. For example, in 5 percent of the cases above, lead time was 10 weeks, so 5 percent (or 5 of the 100 random numbers) have been assigned to this event: 96, 97, 98, 99, 00. (See Tables 1 and 3.)

Step 2

Second, we refer to a random number table to determine the lead time for each of the 20 sample simulations in Table 5. We select a two-digit number from the random number table and place it in the lead-time column of Table 5. (Two-digit random numbers are selected since only two-digit numbers have been assigned to represent events in Table 4.) A sample size of 20 is used here to demonstrate the method outlined, noting that in general a much larger sample would be used.

Step 3

Next, we refer back to the lead-time portion of Table 4 and corresponding to the random number in parentheses enter the appropriate lead time in weeks.

For example, consider line 1, where the random number in parentheses is (50); referring to Table 4, we find that the number 50 lies in the random number interval 39–55, so we enter in Table 5 the number 6 next to (50).

TABLE 5

SUMMARY OF THE RANDOMLY GENERATED DEMAND

		Weekly Demand (X) during Lead Time										
Line	*Lead Time*	*1*	*2*	*3*	*4*	*5*	*6*	*7*	*8*	*9*	*10*	*T Total*
1......	(50)6	(29)2*	(82)6*	(08)1*	(43)3*	(17)2*	(19)2*					16
2......	(52)6	(40)3*	(62)5*	(49)4*	(27)2*	(50)4*	(77)6*					24
3......	(68)7	(71)5*	(60)4*	(47)3*	(21)2*	(38)3*	(28)2*	(40)3*				22
4......	(29)5	(38)3*	(08)1*	(05)1*	(22)2*	(70)5*						12
5......	(23)5	(58)4*	(21)2*	(92)9*	(70)5*	(52)4*						24
6......	(40)6	(33)2*	(28)2*	(10)1*	(56)4*	(61)5*	(39)3*					17
7......	(14)4	(11)1*	(96)10*	(01)0*	(81)6*							17
8......	(96)10	(44)4*	(54)4*	(62)5*	(27)2*	(29)2*	(03)0*	(62)5*	(17)2*	(92)9*	(30)2*	35
9......	(94)9	(38)3*	(12)1*	(38)3*	(07)1*	(56)4*	(17)2*	(91)9*	(83)6*	(81)6*		35
10......	(54)6	(55)4*	(60)4*	(05)1*	(21)2*	(92)9*	(08)1*					21
11......	(37)5	(20)2*	(72)5*	(73)5*	(26)2*	(15)1*						15
12......	(42)6	(74)5*	(14)1*	(28)2*	(21)5*	(72)5*	(33)2*					20
13......	(22)5	(52)4*	(74)5*	(41)3*	(89)7*	(28)2*						21
14......	(28)5	(66)5*	(45)3*	(13)1*	(87)7*	(46)3*						19
15......	(07)3	(49)4*	(16)2*	(36)3*								9
16......	(42)6	(76)6*	(68)5*	(91)9*	(97)10*	(85)6*	(56)4*					40
17......	(33)5	(84)6*	(39)3*	(78)6*	(78)6*	(01)0*						21
18......	(96)10	(41)3*	(65)5*	(37)3*	(26)2*	(64)5*	(45)3*	(01)0*	(23)2*	(64)5*	(58)5*	33
19......	(25)5	(17)2*	(05)1*	(94)9*	(59)4*	(66)5*						21
20......	(05)3	(25)2*	(24)2*	(95)9*								13

( ) Numbers from 01 to 100 selected at random from a random numbers table.
* Random demand selected by matching the specific random number in ( ) with the random numbers in Table 4.

This simply indicates that the simulated lead time for this sample observation is six weeks.

Step 4

For each week during the lead-time periods established in step 3, draw a *two-digit* random number to determine weekly sales. (See figures in parentheses in the columns headed "Weekly Demand.") Reference is made next to the *Demand* portion of Table 4 to find the starred (*) numbers in Table 5 determined by the random number in the parentheses. In this manner, we simulate the demand for each respective week during the lead time.

Step 5

Enter in the Total column the total demand for each lead-time period.

The result of the inventory demand and lead-time simulation by employing the random number method is translated into Table 6 and Chart 1.

Chart 1 gives us a graphic representation of the data in Table 6. Readings on the vertical axis are probabilities; and on the horizontal axis, we have usage during lead time. For any given order point, we know the probability of demand exceeding that point. For example, referring to Table 6, if we were to select an order point of 35, there would be a 5 percent probability that the demand during the lead time would be greater than 35 (probability of $T >$

TABLE 6

SIMULATED RANDOM DEMAND DURING LEAD TIME*

Demand in Units T	*Frequency f*	*If R Is*	*Probability of T < R Cumulative*	*Probability of T > R*
0–5	0	5	0	1.00
6–10	1	10	0.05	0.95
11–15	3	15	0.20	0.80
16–20	5	20	0.45	0.55
21–25	7	25	0.80	0.20
26–30	0	30	. . .	. . .
31–35	3	35	0.95	0.05
36–40	1	40	1.00	0.00

*Tabulated demand (*T*) based on 20 sampled lead-time events (*R* is the reorder point).

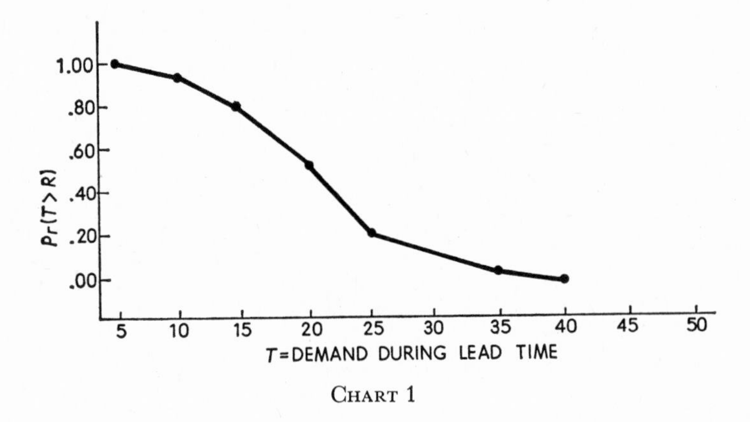

CHART 1

R is 0.05). In other words, with an order point set at 35 units, 5 percent of the time our reorder point would not meet the demand for merchandise.

DETERMINING THE OPTIMUM ORDER POINT

The usual treatment in inventory problems is to ignore the presence of variability in either one or both of the factors of demand and lead time. Such treatment may result in ordering decisions being either too early or too late, with the consequent inventory levels being too high or too low. The above application of Monte Carlo analysis is an attempt to recognize the presence of variability in demand and lead time and to generate or simulate this variability.

To minimize expected costs or maximize profits, we should establish the order point at the level where the ratio of the probability of an overage to the probability of a shortage is equal to the ratio of shortage cost to overage cost.[1]

In our case

C_2 = Cost of being short by one unit = Gross profit loss = \$3 per unit
C_1 = Cost of being over by one unit = Inventory carrying costs per unit = 25% × \$5 = \$1.25

The critical probability:

$$\frac{C_2}{C_1 + C_2} = \frac{3.00}{1.25 + 3.00} = 70\%$$

Referring to Table 6, the $T < R$ probability which is closest to the critical probability is 80 percent; therefore the best choice would be an order point of 25 units; this choice would tend to minimize total costs.

If profits are to be maximized, the expected profits obtainable through stocking an additional unit must be equal to the expected losses or costs of that unit.

If expected profits are greater than expected costs, stocking an additional unit is to the management's advantage; if expected profits are less than expected costs, it is not profitable to stock the additional unit.

In our case, if we stock 35 units, 10 units in excess of the optimum, our inventory costs would increase as follows:

10 × \$5 × 25% = \$12.50 Increased cost

Our potential additional profits would be

10 Units × \$3 × 15% = \$4.50 Potential increased revenue

The incremental cost, \$12.50, is greater than the incremental revenue, \$4.50. It again appears that the optimum order point is 25 units. The quantity to order requires further consideration.

CONCLUSION

The Monte Carlo process itself is very simple, but the mathematical sophistication associated with the inventory analysis, as indicated in the references at the end of the case, can be quite complex. The accuracy of the method increases with the number of trials, or size of sample, so that con-

---

[1]
$$\frac{3.00}{1.25} = \frac{x}{1.00 - x}$$
$$1.25x = 3(1.00 - x)$$
$$1.25x = 3.00 - 3x$$
$$1.25x + 3x = 3.00$$
$$4.25x = 3.00$$
$$x = \frac{3.00}{4.25} = \frac{C_2}{C_1 + C_2} = \frac{3.00}{1.25 + 3.00}$$
$$x = 0.70$$

sideration of the cost to run the simulation does loom into importance as a practical consideration in each case.

Again, it should be pointed out that the computer can be used, incorporating the Monte Carlo technique, to automatically generate a random demand schedule such as was manually determined in Table 5 (see Table 7).

TABLE 7

IBM 7090 COMPUTER SIMULATION: SIMULATED RANDOM DEMAND DURING LEAD TIME *

Demand in Units T	*If* R *Is*	*Probability of* $T < R$ *Cumulative*
0–5	5	0.0000
6–10	10	0.0379
11–15	15	0.1267
16–20	20	0.2954
21–25	25	0.5389
26–30	30	0.7295
31–35	35	0.8732
36–40	40	0.9630
41–45	45	0.9930
46–50	50	0.9970
51–55	55	1.0000

* Tabulated demand (T) based on 1,000 sampled lead-time events. It should be noted that with the larger sample of 1,000 and the use of the computer, employing the same method, the optimum order point is actually 30 units. The critical probability of 0.70 is closest to the 0.7295, probability of $T < R$. In this case a sample of 100 lead-time events, using the 7090, gave the same results.

R is the reorder point.

The Monte Carlo technique is simply a method of simulating, or generating, a schedule of events which would be expected to occur in a random fashion. The College Book Company case has demonstrated the details of the Monte Carlo technique in regard to inventory problems involving uncertainty of demand and/or lead time. Possibly the reader can visualize other problem areas in which the Monte Carlo technique may be applicable if a random occurrence exists, such as the number of sales of an item per day, week, or month; the hourly schedule of work load of a machine; the daily collection of accounts receivable; or the schedule of maintenance requirements.

BIBLIOGRAPHY

BOWMAN, E. H., and FETTER, R. B. *Analysis for Production Management.* Homewood, Ill.: Richard D. Irwin, Inc., 1957.

BROWN, ROBERT G. *Statistical Forecasting for Inventory Control.* New York: McGraw-Hill Book Co., Inc., 1959.

CHURCHMAN, C. W.; ACKOFF, R. L.; and ARNOFF, E. L. *Introduction to Operations Research.* New York: John Wiley & Sons, Inc., 1957.

FETTER, R. B., and DALLECK, W. C. *Decision Models for Inventory Management.* Homewood, Ill.: Richard D. Irwin, Inc., 1961.

HOLT, C. C.; MODIGLIANI, FRANCO; NORTH, JOHN; and SIMON, HERBERT A. *Planning Production, Inventories, and Work Force.* Englewood Cliffs, N.J.: Prentice-Hall, Inc., 1960.

MEYER, HERBERT A. *Symposium on Monte Carlo Methods.* New York: John Wiley & Sons, Inc., 1956.

MORRIS, WILLIAM T. *Engineering Economy.* Homewood, Ill.: Richard D. Irwin, Inc., 1960.

SAATY, T. O. *Mathematical Methods of Operations Research.* New York: McGraw-Hill Book Co., Inc., 1959.

VI

Operations Budgeting

TABLEAU VI

Methodological Analysis

Article \ *Methodology*	*Descriptive Models for Analysis*					*Statistical Theory*	
	Algebraic or Symbolic (Deterministic)	*Algebraic or Symbolic (Probabilistic)*	*Matrix Methods*	*Markov Processes*	*Simulation*	*Sampling*	*Regression and Correlation Analysis*
32. Operational Analysis—Statistical Approach							X
33. Statistical Techniques for Financial Planning and Forecasting							X
34. Improving Separation of Fixed and Variable Expenses							X
35. Cost Finding through Multiple Correlation Analysis							X
36. The Learning Curve—A Basic Cost Projection Tool	X						
37. Learning Curve Techniques for More Profitable Contracts	X						

OPERATIONS BUDGETING

Operations budgeting (budgeting, profit planning, or short-range projections) is not necessarily a model for the optimization of objectives, although it can be used for this purpose (see Section VIII). Rather, an operations budget usually represents a firm's plan for the short run, given that certain variables will behave in a prescribed manner. Implicit in this objective is the problem of predicting sales and of determining the functional relationships between costs and levels of operations. Although these determinations have been made, with apparent success, for many years without the use of mathematical and statistical techniques, there is an accumulating quantity of evidence that these techniques may be of substantial value in improving business projections.

Regression analysis is a statistical technique used principally to provide a basis for predictions. The functional relationship between costs and volume, or between profit and sales, can be estimated using this type of quantitative analysis. Articles 32, 33, 34, and 35 discuss the concepts involved and present examples for these situations.

The learning curve is another quantitative tool applicable to the problem of projecting costs for a particular job or for certain production or assembly runs. Parameters required are determined on a statistical basis. The learning curve technique is described and applied in articles 36 and 37.

It should be noted that data used in models of the three preceding sections (III, IV, and V) may also be useful in preparing the operations budget, and decisions derived from the preceding models necessarily must be considered when structuring the operations budget.

32

This discussion illustrates the application of regression analysis (linear and hyperbolic) to the determination of the relationships between several relevant business variables. These combinations of variables include the following: net return on sales and volume, period costs and time, period costs and volume, and nonperiod costs and volume. Using the relationships thus established, a cost projection model is developed.

*OPERATIONAL ANALYSIS—STATISTICAL APPROACH**

Charles B. Allen

THE BEST BUSINESS MANAGERS can never be fully informed on what lies in the future. It is impossible to forecast or evaluate the multitude of internal and external factors that will affect business in tomorrow's environment. The achievement of American industry in spite of these limitations is a tribute to the foresight and acumen of its industrial leaders. However, the increasing complexity of business activity requires increasing assistance in the resolution of the problems it produces.

The accounting profession, and especially cost accountants, should be the principal agents in reducing industrial operational possibilities to quantitative form. To become full partners in the direction of business, they must contribute dynamic analyses of management action, presented in understandable form. They should consider the static function of the record keeper of secondary importance.

Among the questions which confront business executives, the heaviest barrage usually relates to the financial results of operations. What will be the relation between profit and volume? What volume will maintain a given profit, or what profit will result from a given volume? Where will volume and sales mixture give the greatest net return? Where is the critical or break-even area, and how will it change with sales composition, volume, and costs? These questions are all posed in the future tense. This paper will describe one method of projecting operational analyses to provide a forward-looking answer to these questions.

This procedure is a refinement and extension of a previous investigation along similar lines.[1] It is proposed to construct an econometric model of the

---

* Reprinted from *NACA Bulletin*, published by the National Association of Accountants, December, 1953, pp. 459–76.

[1] Charles B. Allen, "Today's Picture of Tomorrow's Business," *Cost and Management*, July–August, 1950.

operating structure of a fictitious company, estimated from previous mathematical relations, adjusting the future projection by the past trend. This technique should be generally applicable to manufacturing companies which measure operating action in either sales dollars or sales units. At least some of the principles employed should be basic to any type of economic activity.

STARTING DATA ASSEMBLY AND FOLLOWING EARLY LEADS

For the purposes of illustrating this method, it is presumed that the reader is employed by A-N-Y Manufacturing Co., Inc. The financial situation of the company has weakened in the past few years, and you are asked to analyze the cause of the increasingly unsatisfactory results of its operations. In beginning the study, it is decided that unessential details of bookkeeping niceties should be ignored and an examination of the net results of operations made. It is always necessary to establish an accounting control over the analysis, to provide for subsequent inquiry into the details of broad results.

Data relating to A-N-Y Manufacturing Co., Inc., are shown in Exhibit 1. A representative period must be covered to provide a range of operating patterns over expected levels of operation. The 36 monthly periods shown might be 1949 through 1951, if this is the desired structure for analysis. These data also presume an annual two-week vacation shutdown in July. Sales dollars and sales units have been shown, although only one of these measures is required for the type of analysis to be performed. The units produced are presumed to be a mixture of several hundreds slightly different items, selling in different price ranges.

In beginning the investigation, it is necessary to explore many possibilities before discovering leads to the most useful relationships. Many such dead ends will accumulate as scrap in the accountant's working papers. The examination of data subsequently abandoned should not be considered unproductive. It serves to make eliminations which constructively narrow the field of possible economic relationships.

Although the work papers will not be reproduced here, there were several comparisons of this sort, yielding negative results in A-N-Y Manufacturing Co., Inc., operations. For example, scatter charts of sales prices compared to unit costs showed only random fluctuations, as did a plot of sales prices and volumes. Sales price trends were typical with a decline in late 1949, a substantial recovery to the Korean conflict in 1950, and fairly uniform averages in 1951 from O.P.S. action. There was no evidence of any seasonal trend.

SIGNIFICANT RELATIONSHIP OF RETURN TO VOLUME —BUT WHAT CURVE?

Still another phase of the preliminary investigation contrasted net return on sales with volume. This aroused instinctive interest. The initial scatter

EXHIBIT 1

A-N-Y MANUFACTURING CO., INC.
CONDENSED OPERATING DATA, THREE YEARS BY MONTHS

Month	*Sales Units*	*Sales Dollars (Thousands)*	*Percent Return on Sales (before Taxes)*	*Profit or Loss (before Taxes) (Thousands)*	*Total Costs (Thousands)*
1	4,400	$452	7.45%	$34	$418
2	3,500	346	1.00*	3*	349
3	2,200	240	3.10*	7*	247
4	2,000	220	4.18*	9*	229
5	1,700	176	9.65*	17*	193
6	3,300	347	5.78	20	327
7	2,800	280	.20	1	279
8	3,800	386	6.01	23	363
9	3,700	378	6.40	24	354
10	3,300	332	1.20	4	328
11	3,700	377	8.20	31	346
12	3,800	380	3.10	12	368
13	5,400	550	8.00	44	506
14	5,600	567	8.80	50	517
15	4,000	410	7.40	30	380
16	5,200	538	9.00	48	490
17	4,700	484	6.60	32	452
18	3,500	377	6.00	23	354
19	2,600	253	8.85*	22*	275
20	5,100	510	7.40	38	472
21	3,900	406	4.45	18	388
22	3,700	391	5.10	20	371
23	4,000	416	6.00	25	391
24	5,800	600	9.80	59	541
25	5,100	524	6.75	35	489
26	5,000	511	5.70	29	482
27	4,100	429	2.80	12	417
28	4,300	435	3.40	15	420
29	4,700	488	5.40	26	462
30	4,500	464	5.30	25	439
31	3,100	318	4.66*	15*	333
32	3,700	385	2.60	10	375
33	4,400	463	4.30	20	443
34	4,200	430	3.90	17	413
35	4,600	476	3.10	15	461
36	4,300	444	2.10	9	435

* Indicates loss.

chart of the selected data from Exhibit 1, shown on the chart offered as Exhibit 2, disclosed enough apparent relation to warrant further study. First, the mathematical method of least squares was applied to determine the average relationship between return on sales and volume according to an equation in

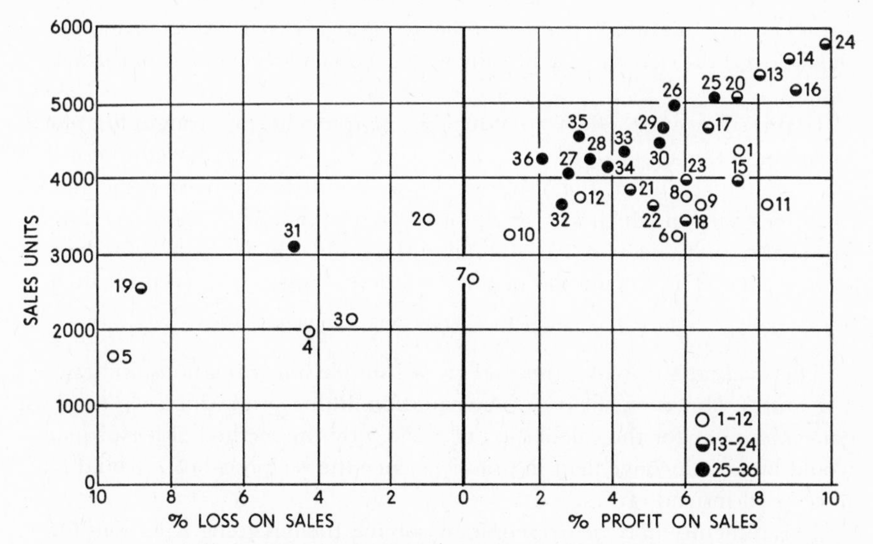

EXHIBIT 2. A-N-Y Manufacturing Co., Inc., Profit or loss as percent of sales dollars compared to sales units, three years by months.

which X represents percent return on sales and Y represents sales units, of the form:

$$Y = a + bX$$

or, as calculated:

$$Y = 3381 + 168X$$

This equation means that the average sales units required to produce any desired profit percentage is determined by adding the break-even volume (3,381 units) to the desired percentage multiplied by 168 units. The standard error of this estimate (S_y) is ± 558 units. The equation, with its substituted values, can be restated as

$$X = \frac{Y - 3{,}381}{168}$$

As so restated, it means that average percent return on sales dollars is determined by dividing the difference between actual and break-even volume, or 3,381 units, by a constant factor of 168 units. The standard error of this estimate is ± 2.47 percent. Obviously, the 168 in the relation is the volume in units required to produce a 1 percent change in net profit. The break-even-volume in units is 3,381 units.

However, if the straight line equation is plotted on the scatter chart, Exhibit 2 (which represents the data from Exhibit 1), it does not fit well. The plotted points on the left of the average line are somewhat below it, while those on the right are above it. Perhaps another relationship will more closely approximate the relationship of return on sales to volume. Reference to other curves which might be adopted indicates that a hyperbola or a log curve should bend the straight line just the way necessary to get closer to the actual data.

In this connection, efforts to reduce the data to a linear (straight line) form to facilitate the application of the method of least squares showed that if $1/Y$ were plotted against X, the result was linear. In other words, an inspection of a scatter chart on which $1/Y$ was plotted against X showed that the relationship between these two variables might reasonably be represented by a straight line. The calculation of this equation for the data given resulted in

$$1/Y = a - bX = 0.0003283 - 0.0000159X$$

This evaluates the constants and gives a simple linear relationship between $1/Y$ and X. However, the use of the equation in this form, which was the most convenient one for the calculation of a and b by the method of least squares, would be very inconvenient in practice, since the reciprocal of Y would have to be used instead of Y.

This difficulty may be overcome by solving the foregoing equations for Y, which gives

$$Y = \frac{1}{a - bX} = \frac{1}{0.0003283 - 0.0000159X}$$

Dividing both the numerator and the denominator of the fraction on the right-hand side of the equation by 0.0000159, the coefficient of X, we get

$$Y = \frac{62893}{20.64 - X}$$

Then, dividing both the numerator and the denominator of the fraction on the right-hand side of the last given equation by 20.64, we get

$$Y = \frac{3046}{1 - X/20.64}$$

which, solved for X is

$$X = 20.64\left(1 - \frac{3046}{Y}\right)$$

These equations are somewhat more complicated than those first introduced ($Y = abX$ and $1/Y = a - bX$) because the equations immediately above are for hyperbolas while the earlier ones are equations of straight lines (provided that the dependent variable in $1/Y = a - bX$ be considered as $1/Y$). However, the hyberbolic equations give a relationship between Y (sales units) and X (percent return) which may be readily interpreted. It will be seen that sales units required to produce any desired profit percentage are determined above by dividing the break-even volume (3,046 units) by one minus the ratio of the desired profit percentage to 20.64. Average percent return may be determined by multiplying the constant 20.64 by a ratio that is one minus the ratio of break-even volume (3,046 units) to actual volume.

It will be noted that in these latter equations, 3,046 units is the break-even volume instead of the 3,381 units shown before. The 20.64 is the maximum value of X, the average rate of return on sales, since the hyperbolic equation as solved for X shows that to be the asymptotic value of X when Y becomes indefinitely large. The operating structure we are working with thus places a limit of 20.64 percent on net profit on sales, regardless of increases in volume, by reason of the fact that there is a point at which unit fixed cost disappears, with a sufficiently large increase in volume.

It can be shown statistically that one of these relationships most nearly fits the data or "describes" the underlying relationship—in this case, that of return on sales to volume. The coefficient of determination for the straight line equation is +0.666; the index of determination for the hyperbola is +0.7213. This indicates that 67 percent and 72 percent, respectively, of the changes in profits or loss as a percent of sales are due to or associated with changes in volume. Accordingly, the hyperbola is closer to the actual data. The log curve for this data was also calculated in the form of the equation, $\log Y = a + bX$, but further space is not devoted here to this relation because its index of determination was smaller than that for the hyperbola.

AN UNDERLYING FACT AND A NECESSARY COST CLASSIFICATION

The equations and graphs for the straight line and the hyperbola are summarized in Exhibit 3. The curve representing the average variation of net return with volume in units has established the hyperbola as the better mathe-

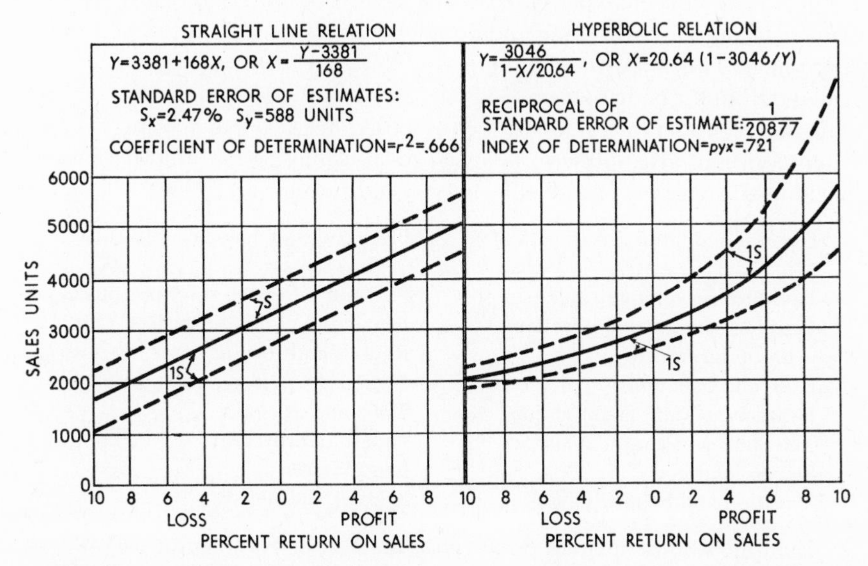

EXHIBIT 3. A-N-Y Manufacturing Co., Inc., Percent return on sales dollars compared to volume of sales units, average relationships, three-year period.

matical model of these two variables. Net return increases at an increasing rate with increasing volume. It also decreases at an increasing rate. This curve can be logically established as typical in manufacturing activity, particularly heavy industry.

But the purely statistical approach has severe limitations. It uses historical data only. The averaging process tends to freeze the operating picture instead of emphasizing its fluidity. Trends are concealed. The extent of correlation is not great enough to be useful in managerial decisions. Accordingly, this analysis must be considered as a preliminary study of the past rather than a final result in the form of a tool for use in the future.

The hyperbolic relation has a certain fascination and is surely significant. However, a little more imagination and realistic thinking are required. To paraphrase Lord Keynes, it is the amalgam of logic, intuition, and a wide knowledge of facts which may not be precise that results in economic interpretation. Traditionally, logically, or mathematically, fixed costs are a major key to operating losses and determine where profitable operations become unprofitable. Obviously, if all costs were variable (assuming selling price at least equaled costs), there could be no losses. Since fixed costs are constant over short periods of time, they may well be the principal factor causing profit variation. It is evident that the value of X must depend on variation of unit fixed costs with volume. Also, it is known that the curve of fixed costs per unit is a hyperbola. This looks like the fundamental underlying reason for the previously discovered hyperbolic relationship between net return and volume.

We are not quite set to go straight ahead on this perception. Before investigating further, logic compels consideration of a classification of costs compatible with this concept—period costs and volume costs. Period costs are those which accumulate with time and do not necessarily relate to cost accounting groupings. They may or may not be considered overhead. They must be considered from the point of view of a going concern, the operations of which may fluctuate considerably, and will be presumed necessary to continued operations. Without attempting to be exhaustive, it may be said that period costs include all or a part of the following expenditures or accruals:

- General and administrative salaries
- Miscellaneous salaries and wages
- Payroll taxes on applicable payrolls
- Pension, compensation, welfare, or group insurance
- Dues and donations
- Depreciation and amortization
- Telephone, telegraph, teletype
- Selling salaries
- Vacation and holiday pay
- Property, state income, and franchise taxes
- Fire and other necessary insurance
- Legal and auditing expenses
- Rentals and royalties
- Stationery, postage, office supplies
- Traveling expenses
- Patent amortization
- Bond interest
- Repairs and renewals

Exhibit 4 shows the total period costs for A-N-Y Manufacturing Co., Inc., as defined above. The difference between total costs, as shown in Exhibit 1, and period costs is grouped into what is shown as volume costs in Exhibit 4.

EXHIBIT 4

A-N-Y MANUFACTURING CO., INC.
SEGREGATION OF PERIOD AND VOLUME COSTS, THREE YEARS BY MONTHS
Thousands of Dollars (000 Omitted)

Month	*Total Costs* *	*Segregation*	
		Period Costs	*Volume Costs*
1	$418	$50	$368
2	349	45	304
3	247	47	200
4	229	42	187
5	193	41	152
6	327	38	289
7	279	31	248
8	363	37	326
9	354	39	315
10	328	43	285
11	346	41	305
12	368	48	320
13	506	53	453
14	517	49	468
15	380	42	338
16	490	51	439
17	452	48	404
18	354	52	302
19	275	39	236
20	472	46	426
21	388	48	340
22	371	42	329
23	391	47	344
24	541	49	492
25	489	49	440
26	482	47	435
27	417	53	364
28	420	48	372
29	462	52	410
30	439	51	388
31	333	47	286
32	375	51	324
33	443	55	388
34	413	53	360
35	461	56	405
36	435	51	384

* Excludes federal income and excess profits taxes.
SOURCE: From Exhibit 1.
Period costs are presumed to have been determined by element (see text) and carried forward to this schedule.
Volume costs are determined by deduction of period from total costs.

EXHIBIT 5

A-N-Y MANUFACTURING CO., INC.
PERIOD AND VOLUME COSTS
PER SALES UNITS AND SALES DOLLARS,
THREE YEARS BY MONTHS

	Period Costs		*Volume Costs*	
Month	*Per Sales Dollar*	*Per Sales Unit*	*Per Sales Dollar*	*Per Sales Unit*
1	11.1¢	$11.40	81.4¢	$83.60
2	13.0	12.90	87.9	86.90
3	19.6	21.40	83.3	90.80
4	19.1	21.00	85.0	93.50
5	23.3	24.10	86.4	89.30
6	11.0	11.50	83.3	87.50
7	11.1	11.10	88.6	88.70
8	9.6	9.70	84.5	85.70
9	10.3	10.50	83.3	85.10
10	13.0	13.00	85.8	86.30
11	10.9	11.10	80.9	82.40
12	12.6	12.60	84.2	84.20
13	9.6	9.80	82.4	83.90
14	8.6	8.80	82.5	83.60
15	10.2	10.50	82.4	84.50
16	9.5	9.80	81.6	84.50
17	9.9	10.20	83.5	86.00
18	13.8	14.90	80.1	86.30
19	15.4	15.00	93.3	90.80
20	9.0	9.00	83.5	83.60
21	11.8	12.30	83.7	87.20
22	10.7	11.40	84.1	89.00
23	11.3	11.80	82.7	86.00
24	8.2	8.40	82.0	84.80
25	9.4	9.60	84.0	86.30
26	9.2	9.40	85.1	86.90
27	12.4	12.90	84.8	88.70
28	11.0	11.20	85.5	86.60
29	10.7	11.10	84.0	87.20
30	11.0	11.30	83.6	86.30
31	14.8	15.20	89.9	92.30
32	13.2	13.80	84.2	87.50
33	11.9	12.50	83.8	88.10
34	12.3	12.60	83.7	85.70
35	11.8	12.20	85.1	88.10
36	11.5	11.90	86.5	89.30

For subsequent inquiry into volume costs, Exhibit 5 shows these two cost groupings as cost per sales dollar and per sales unit.

WHAT STUDY OF PERIOD COSTS?

The hyperbolic behavior of costs which accumulate with time is not a new concept. However, it has not been expressed in the terms of this mathematical model. An examination of the left-hand portion of Exhibit 6 shows a definite

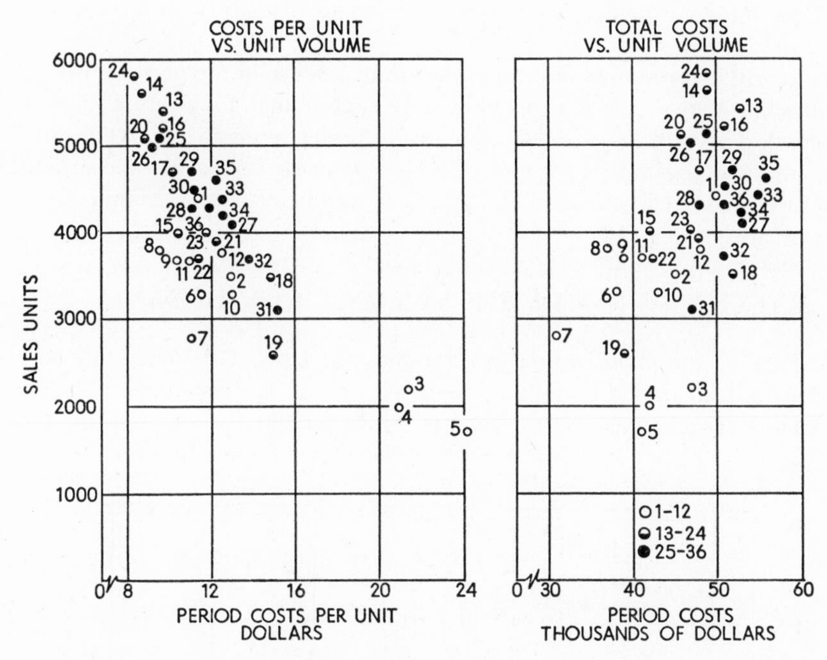

EXHIBIT 6. A-N-Y Manufacturing Co., Inc., review of period costs, three years by months.

tendency for period costs per unit to vary hyperbolically with volume for A-N-Y Manufacturing Co., Inc., as could be shown mathematically. This part of the chart should be examined in the light of the fact that the X scale from 0 to 8 has been condensed. Visualization of the chart without this condensation would show that the curve approximates the simplest form of hyperbola, which is known as an equilateral hyperbola.

The right-hand portion of this chart shows total period costs plotted against volume. It should be noted that condensation of the X scale from 0 to 30 greatly accentuates the apparent amount of the variations. As would be expected, the variations can be considered random. A further study of the chart indicates a definite progression in the level of period costs, comparing one time period with another. They appear to be increasing uniformly, regardless of volume. This may be easier to see in graphic form than in the tabulation in

Exhibit 4. Simple averaging shows the following monthly period costs for each of the three years reviewed:

Months 1–12	$42,000
Months 13–24	47,000
Months 25–36	51,000

It has previously been noted that period costs per unit give a definite hyperbolic relation. It has now been shown that these costs per unit, and in total, show a consistently advancing trend. A little further analysis of the elements of these expenses should point the way to estimating these period costs for the next 12 months.

It will be presumed that an appropriate analysis of the period costs indicates that they should approximate $55,000 per month for a future 12-month period. This will be used subsequently to project costs in estimating future operational possibilities. As such, it will become the keystone of the structure of an econometric model of the operating results of A-N-Y Manufacturing Co., Inc.

WHAT THE STUDY OF VOLUME COSTS INDICATES

Turning the investigation to the remaining costs, little more can be expected. If all period costs have been segregated, the remainder should be variable costs, depending on volume. However, this is not quite the case. Exhibit 7, which should be examined in the light of the fact that the variations

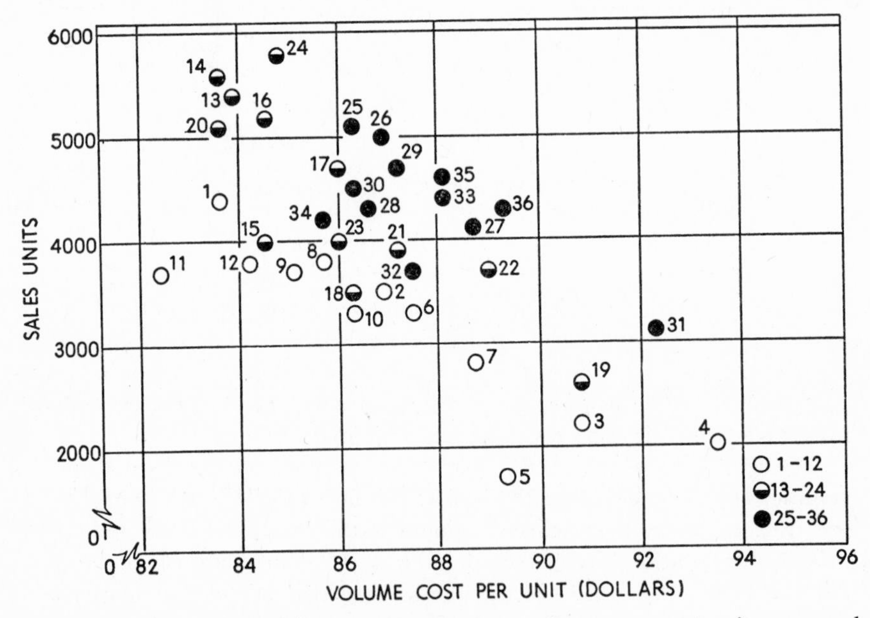

EXHIBIT 7. A-N-Y Manufacturing Co., Inc., volume costs per unit compared with unit sales volume, three years by months.

are greatly accentuated by condensing the X scale from 0 to 82, shows volume costs per unit, as tabulated in Exhibit 5, plotted against sales units. Of course, we would not expect exactly a straight line vertically down the chart, showing an equal unit volume cost regardless of volume. Nevertheless, it is surprising to note from the location of plotted points that volume costs per unit seem actually to decrease with increasing volume. The effect is not nearly so large as for period costs, but there is definitely a measurable variation, in excess of normal probability.

The reasons for this are cloudy, although there are a number of possibilities apparent. It may be due in part to the residual effect of incompletely segregated period costs. The most conspicuous controllable element in manufacturing costs is labor—salaries and wages paid for productive effort. When volume drops, it is very human to stretch six hours' work to eight. Conversely, when there is a large backlog of work, there is a real possibility of achieving a little extra productivity by the simple and normal acceptance by operators of the challenge represented by work to be done. Also, many of the tools, operating supplies, and other elements entering into volume costs progress in steps rather than in direct proportion to quantities processed. The net result is that total volume costs vary with volume but at different rates for different operating ranges.

A careful examination of Exhibit 7, buttressed by the knowledge already gained of the mathematical model of manufacturing costs, is quite revealing. It shows that volume costs per unit vary with volume, decreasing with increasing volume. Also, each group of 12 monthly unit costs seems to be at a higher level, indicating an upward movement in these volume costs.

Although the mathematics involved has been eliminated from this paper, it can be shown that again the hyperbolic relation expresses the variation between unit volume costs and volume in units as shown in Exhibit 7. If volume cost were completely variable, the volume costs per unit as a function of volume would be represented by a vertical straight line. However, to the extent that fixed cost components are present, a hyperbolic function is added to the linear one, the sum of the two being hyperbolic. This is shown in Exhibit 8, interpretation of which should be tempered by the realization that the range of values for unit volume cost is very small. Here again, the steady advance of these costs can be seen from the higher level of the succeeding curves.

It is quite difficult to estimate the future trend of this group of costs. An analysis can be made of the principal elements in the cost grouping. It will be assumed that a further slight increase seems quite probable, although it is difficult to evaluate the amount. The hyperbolic form is somewhat clumsy to use, and the lack of precision in the estimate makes it unnecessary. Trial and error indicates that an appropriate volume cost per unit can be postulated by decreasing an arbitrary base cost. In this case the expected volume costs per unit, using the symbol Vu for this, may be expressed as follows:

$$Vu = \$102 - \$3 \text{ per thousand units}$$

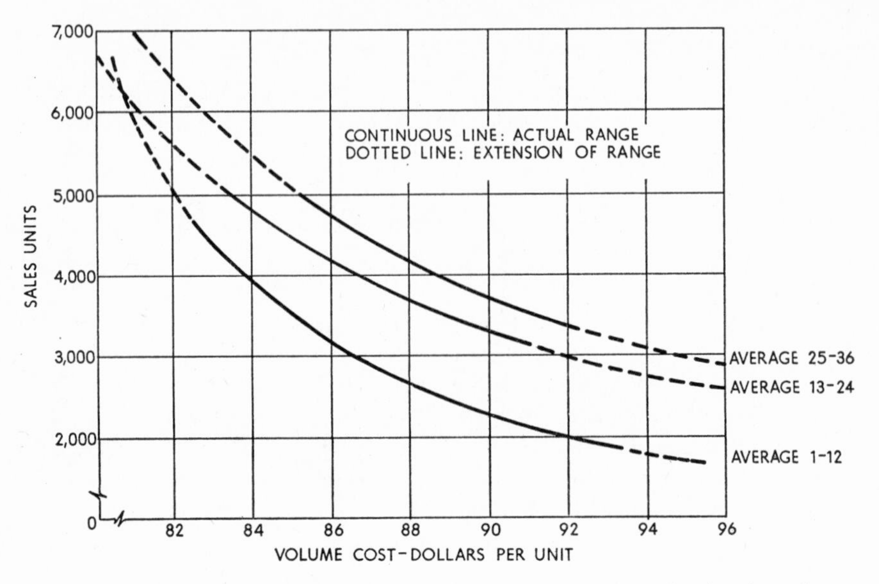

EXHIBIT 8. A-N-Y Manufacturing Co., Inc., volume costs and unit sales volume, average relationships, three 12-month periods.

The above is a linear equation, which is sufficiently accurate for the purpose at hand. The unit costs for various volume levels calculated from this equation are

Volume in Units	*Unit Volume Cost*
2,000	$96
3,000	93
4,000	90
5,000	87
6,000	84

COST MODEL, SALES ASSUMPTIONS—AND TWO MANAGEMENT TOOLS

A projection of costs can now be made. Period costs are estimated (as indicated earlier) to be $55,000 per month. Unit period costs are thus $55 divided by sales volume in thousands. Unit volume costs, using the formula immediately above, are $102 less the product of $3 and the sales volume in thousands. Total unit costs (Y) will be the sum of these two results:

$$\frac{\$55}{X} + \$102 - \$3X$$

where X equals sales volume in thousands.

This combination results in a hyperbola $\left(Y = \frac{55}{X}\right)$ superimposed on a straight line ($Y = 102 - 3X$), the curve thus being hyperbolic. The hyperbolic nature of the curve is quite pronounced in the range considered, since it is a region of high curvature. This may be readily visualized by plotting the curve from $X = 0$ to $X = 50{,}000$ units.

This can be portrayed very simply in graphic form (based on the \$55,000 volume costs and the \$102 value for *Vu* in the equation for unit volume costs), as in Exhibit 9, which summarizes the following table:

Volume in Units	*Total Costs per 1,000 Units*	*Period Costs per 1,000 Units*	*Volume Costs per 1,000 Units*
2,000	\$123.50	\$27.50	\$96
3,000	111.33	18.33	93
4,000	103.75	13.75	90
5,000	98.00	11.00	87
6,000	93.17	9.17	84

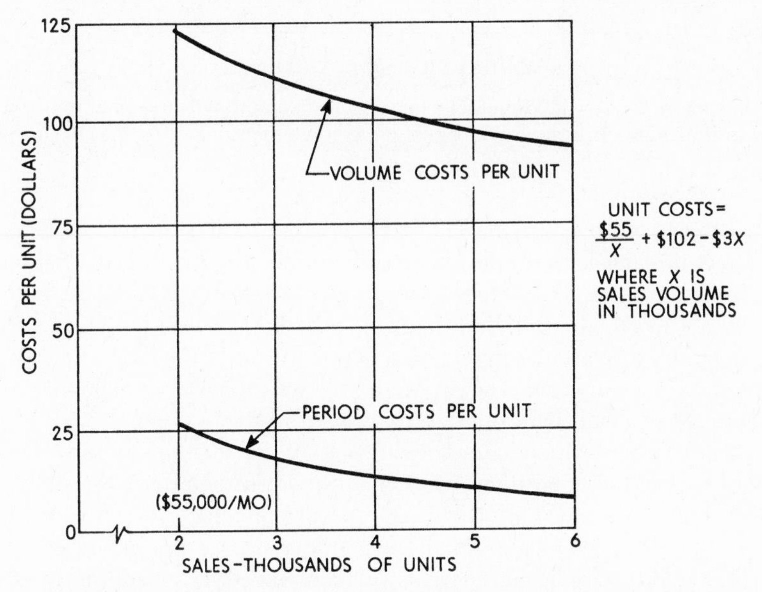

EXHIBIT 9. A-N-Y Manufacturing Co., Inc., projected unit costs, period and volume costs per unit for various sales levels.

Up to this point, most of the survey work is not in a form which would be presented to management. We can now shape such a presentation. Having built a cost structure, it remains only to superimpose various sales unit mixtures resulting in different levels of average sales prices. The same analysis could be made for various profit-volume ratios. In the case of A-N-Y Manufacturing Co., Inc., it is presumed that these sales prices will be \$95, \$100, \$105, and \$110. This can be a pure assumption, using the historical record as a guide, or may be constructed from various product mixes in the sales pattern.

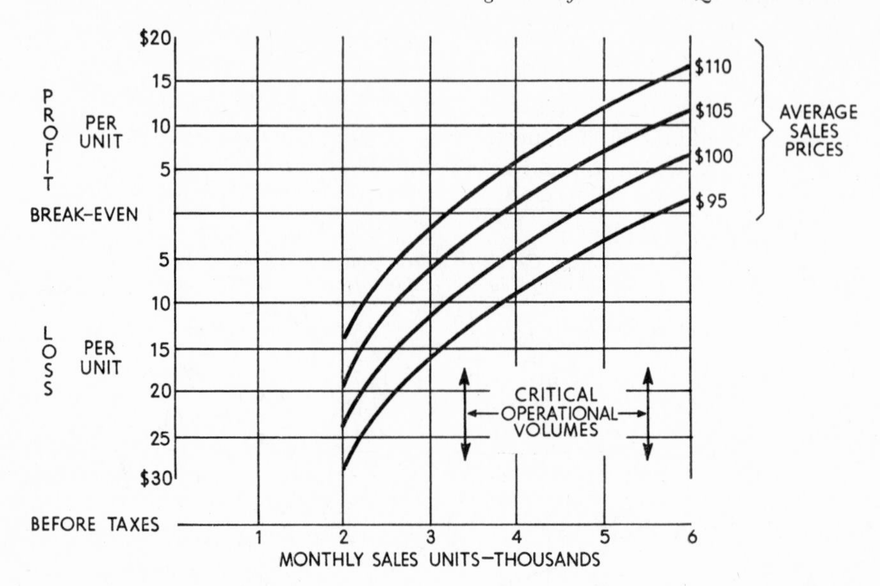

EXHIBIT 10. A-N-Y Manufacturing Co., Inc., monthly operational possibilities for an immediate future period, based on average sales mix, $95 to $110 per sales unit.*

Exhibit 10 has been prepared by deducting the costs shown in the previous section of this article from the average sales prices just mentioned and plotting net profits or losses. From this chart the executives of A-N-Y Manufacturing Co., Inc., can visualize a broad range of operating possibilities. It is clear that this chart relies on an underlying cost picture for the immediate future, which is known. Hence the results of any change which management can make in its operating plans can be evaluated quite accurately.

Of course, the fictitious company used as a test case in this laboratory study is not in a healthy condition. There may be several alternatives available to A-N-Y Manufacturing Co., Inc. If competitive and government control conditions permit, price increases may be considered. It is the period costs—the inexorable time-cost accumulations—which have weakened the operating structure and increased the break-even point from about 50 percent of capacity to perhaps 70 percent, dependent on sales mix. If the increase in these costs can be checked or the costs reduced, a considerable change can be produced in net operating results.

With our new tools, however difficult and painstaking their derivation, it is only a matter of simple arithmetic to provide a relatively accurate answer to the questions raised initially. We have determined the interrelation of costs, sales prices, volume, and profits. By substituting theoretical requirements in these mathematical equations, we can provide the answers.

Increases in volume have a very important effect on the net operating re-

* Adapted from "Profit Graphs," Sec. 2, *Cost Accountants' Handbook* (New York: Ronald Press Co., 1945), pp. 108 *et seq.*)

sults of A-N-Y Manufacturing Co., Inc. Assuming no change in average sales prices, the net change in costs with volume will be carried through directly to net operating results. This change in cost can be read from the total cost curve in Exhibit 9. However, for management's convenience, it may be preferable to restate the relationship in the combined chart and table shown as Exhibit

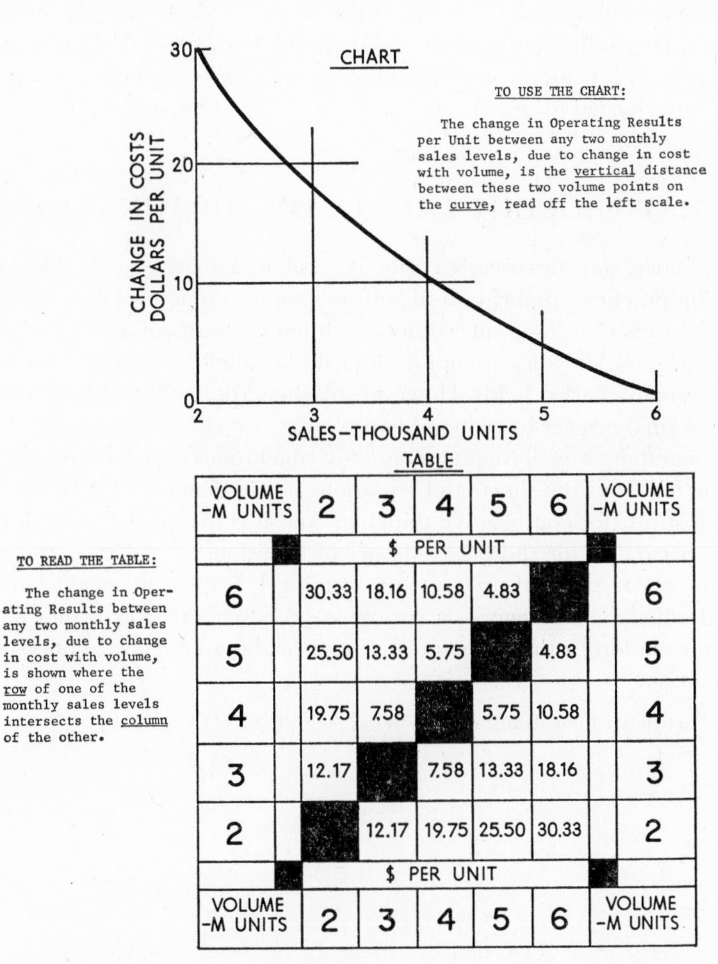

TABLE

VOLUME -M UNITS	2	3	4	5	6	VOLUME -M UNITS
	$ PER UNIT					
6	30.33	18.16	10.58	4.83		6
5	25.50	13.33	5.75		4.83	5
4	19.75	7.58		5.75	10.58	4
3	12.17		7.58	13.33	18.16	3
2		12.17	19.75	25.50	30.33	2
	$ PER UNIT					
VOLUME -M UNITS	2	3	4	5	6	VOLUME -M UNITS

EXHIBIT 11. A-N-Y Manufacturing Co., Inc., effect of change in volume on net operating results (before taxes) due to change in cost with volume.

11. The curve at the top of this chart is merely a replot of the total cost curve as constructed in Exhibit 9, except that zero has been substituted for the $93.17 line (cost at 6,000 units) to concentrate attention on the slope of this curve rather than its absolute level. The table in the lower portion of Exhibit 11 shows the values between specific volume levels. These values are merely the differences in total costs for the various volumes, as shown above in the

table introduced into the text in connection with construction of a cost model (see p. 447).

Of course, such a chart and table are not as precise as may be implied from the exactness of the amounts shown therein. As they are based on cost projections, the degree of accuracy is only relative. However, they will provide a general guide and a concrete estimate and evaluation of the underlying relation. Depending on how far the management of A-N-Y Manufacturing Co., Inc., wishes to go, other similar relationships can be segregated and separately charted for executive use. Exhibit 11 is only one example of what may be done.

SO THAT THOUGHT CAN FLY ON THE WINGS OF FACT

In essence, statistics merely symbolize real, imaginative, and logical thinking. The practical application of statistics to economic problems can be effectively used by accountants without an intensive mathematical background. People who use statistics are not necessarily statisticians—applications can be made in many varied fields. However, mathematics and statistics can rarely supply a final answer to economic problems.

Logical thought will frequently modify conclusions drawn from the models constructed from the shorthand equations of mathematics. No formula will ever substitute for constructive thinking. And it is the mental struggle which acts as a catalyst for those rare flashes of intuition, crystallizing the understanding of complicated processes or, seemingly, leaping to conclusions without intermediate inferences or reasoning.[2] Mathematics, as a safe point of departure in forecasting events to come, provides an anchor to unrestrained imagination.

[2] See article on Louis Bean, *Business Week*, August 18, 1951.

33

Three hypothetical cases, each of increasing difficulty, are presented in this article. The first involves the forecasting of sales using regression analysis and the mathematical description of other variables such as total expense, overhead rate, profit rate, etc. The second case introduces an additional department and generalizes the mathematical formulation. The final case postulates several divisions with several departments in each division, and multiple regression analysis is applied separately to each division. Each case is expressed in terms of equations relating direct labor and expenses.

*STATISTICAL TECHNIQUES FOR FINANCIAL PLANNING AND FORECASTING**

Andrew Vazsonyi

A MONTH seldom goes by without a conference being held somewhere in this country in which businessmen are exposed to some new scientific method of business management. Similarly, business periodicals contain a continuous stream of articles on operations research, linear programming, statistical decision theory, or the use of giant electronic computers. Many of these conferences and articles are aimed at scientists, not businessmen. Consequently, businessmen often find it difficult to understand the theories advanced by the authors or speakers. It is not surprising, therefore, that a certain amount of skepticism and even apprehension is developing on the part of some businessmen when exposed to these new scientific methods. The fact that many of the theories are full of mathematics and statistics makes it even more difficult.

The purpose of this paper is to present, in simple language, a new method that has been found useful in financial planning. In particular, we are going to describe a statistical method of accounting which can save a great deal of clerical work and which can significantly increase visibility in managerial planning.

Let us recognize that accountants face a dilemma when preparing budgets and forecasts. We are accustomed to considering accounting as a very exact sort of procedure which deals with dollars and cents. However, in forecasting or budgeting, one deals with uncertainties, and the accountant is asked to build a structure of dollar figures based on these uncertainties. From uncer-

* Reprinted from *Controller*, May, 1957, pp. 216–48.

tain forecasts, exact accounting calculations for revenues, expenses, profits, etc., are carried out to the last dollar and cent. This is generally accomplished through the expense of a great deal of clerical effort.

In spite of the fact that it is tacitly understood that these forecasts do not have accuracies down to the last penny, traditional accounting is not capable of providing shortcuts just because high accuracy is not possible. The method we shall describe in this paper takes full advantage of the inherent inaccuracies contained in forecasts. For instance, the relationships between direct and indirect expenses are developed as statistical relationships which are inherently inexact. As will be seen, capitalizing on the fact that there are always inaccuracies in forecasting, one can obtain significant simplifications in budgeting and forecasting procedures.

In order to present this material, we could follow two alternative approaches. One would be to describe in detail an actual application (how the method is being used) and show specific benefits obtained. The advantage of this kind of approach is that it can be very realistic. The disadvantage, however, is that it is difficult to disengage the details from the fundamentals; and consequently, it is hard to present basic principles. An alternate approach—and this is the one we will follow—is to present the forecasting method through illustrative examples of hypothetical business firms. We shall begin by describing our forecasting technique in a very simple form of organization and then move on to more complicated situations. Through the discussion of an idealized business, the basic principles can be clearly described and subsequently applied to more realistic situations.

Accepting this method of presentation, we will describe budgeting and forecasting in the Alpha Corporation, which is a very simple sort of corporation indeed. Then we will discuss the Beta Corporation, which is somewhat more complicated; and finally, we will describe forecasting in the hypothetical Gamma Corporation. At the end of the paper, we will relate the principles of this budgeting and forecasting system to a real-life business situation.

BUDGETING AND FORECASTING IN THE ALPHA CORPORATION[1]

The Alpha Corporation bills its customers at a flat rate per dollar of direct labor. The customer sets up rules as to what labor can be considered direct or

[1] Explanation of principal symbols:

a, b = Factors in regression equation 12
a_1, b_1 = Factors in regression equation 35
a_2, b_2 = Factors in regression equation 36
A_1, A_2, A_3, B, B_1 = Factors in regression equations 39 and 47
c_1 = Cost of operating department 1
c_2 = Cost of operating department 2
c_3 = Cost of operating department 3
C = Total expense (cost); also, corporate costs for Beta Corporation
C_1 = Total divisional cost for division 1 of Gamma Corporation
C_c = Corporate costs for Gamma Corporation

indirect. For instance, clerical people or supervisors are not considered as direct labor. Also, it is recognized that some of the employes of the Alpha Corporation work on many different contracts, and it is impractical to keep track of their time every minute. Consequently, the corporation follows the rule that only labor performed in excess of half a day is recorded against a contract, and the rest of the labor is accounted for as indirect labor. (The important thing is that there are definite rules in deciding whether or not a

TABLE 1

COST ANALYSIS FOR THE ALPHA CORPORATION

	Direct Labor	*Indirect Labor*	*Overhead*
January	24,000	16,000	67%
February	23,000	22,000	96
March	24,000	19,000	79
April	26,000	20,000	77
May	32,000	21,000	66
June	20,000	17,000	85
July	26,000	10,000	88
August	22,000	16,000	84
September	28,000	19,000	65
October	24,000	17,000	71
November	30,000	18,000	60
December	22,000	19,000	56

man is considered a direct or an indirect charge.) In a more general sense, we could say that the corporation incurs certain expenses that can be directly charged to the customer's order—and then some other expenses that are not chargeable directly. To be more specific, in Table 1 we show an illustrative record for the year of 1955. This table shows a monthly record of direct labor in dollars; and also, it shows indirect expense.

e = Expense (indirect labor)
e_1 = Direct expense in department 1
e_2 = Direct expense in department 2
E = General and administrative expense
E_1 = Divisional overhead expenses for division 1 of Gamma Corporation
E_c = General and administrative expenses for Gamma Corporation
f_0, f_1, f_2, f_3 = Factors in equation 49
L = Direct labor
L_1 = Direct labor in department 1
L_2 = Direct labor in department 2
O_r = Overhead rate
P = (Gross) profit
P_c = Corporate revenue for Gamma Corporation
P_r = Profit rate
r = Overhead rate charged to customer
r_1 = Overhead rate charged in department 1
r_2 = Overhead rate charged in department 2
R = Revenue
R_1 = Departmental revenue for department 1 in Gamma Corporation
R_c = Corporate revenue for Gamma Corporation

The management of the Alpha Corporation is relying on these data in developing forecasts for the future course of business. The marketing research department predicts the level of business for the Alpha Corporation, and the management wants to have a multitude of questions answered. Management would like to predict gross profits and to know what the profit would be depending on alternate possible billing rates. It would like to know what the profit is going to be after taxes. It would like to know what dividends it can pay to stockholders. As there are no inventories in the Alpha Corporation, it does not need to worry about inventory-carrying costs or obsolescence. As there is no substantial equipment here, there is no need to study investments, depreciation, capital gains, and many other things.

In a real-life situation, of course, most of these questions and many others would have to be answered. However, as previously stated, we are dealing with a highly idealized type of corporation, and we are interested only for the moment in answering certain specific questions.

Decrease of Overhead

First of all, we want to forecast the gross profit, assuming that there are alternate forecasts for the level of business. An analysis of past data in Table 1 indicates that the overhead decreases as the level of business increases. In order to forecast costs and profits, it is necessary to put this decrease of overhead into some sort of simple rule.

Now, here is a place where mathematics may be useful. Figure 1 presents a chart in which the horizontal axis is the direct labor in thousands of dollars taken from Table 1 and the vertical axis is the indirect labor in thousands of dollars. Each little cross in Figure 1 represents the accounting data from

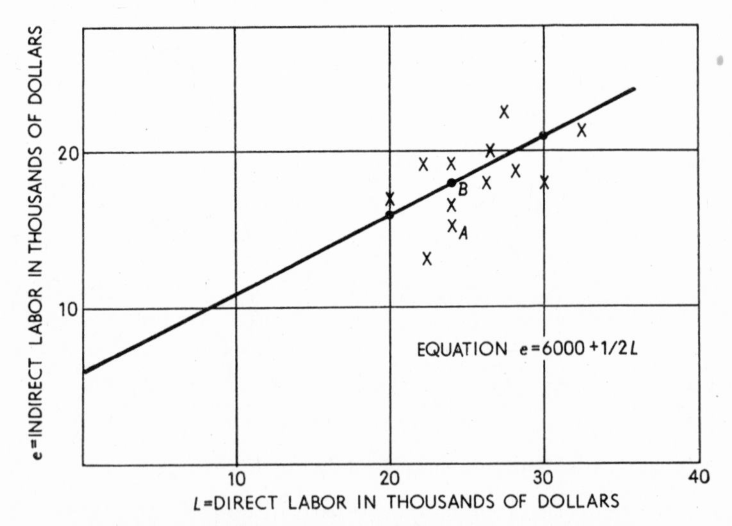

FIGURE 1. Indirect expenses in the Alpha Corporation.

Table 1 for a single month. For instance, point A represents the month of January, as during this month direct labor was set up at \$24,000, and indirect labor was \$16,000. We see then that the accounting data are represented by a group of crosses in Figure 1, and our problem is to develop a summarized mathematical representation of these data. In the language of the statistician, we wish to determine the regression line expressing the indirect labor as a function of the direct labor.

This is a problem that statisticians have studied for a long time, and the technique of least squares has been developed to solve such problems. Without going into details, we may say that the problem is to put a straight line through the crosses in such a way that this straight line goes close to these crosses. When such a straight line is obtained, we can write the equation of the straight line in this example in the following form:

$$e = 6{,}000 + 0.5L \tag{1}$$

In this equation, L denotes the direct labor, and e denotes the expense, or the indirect labor. The formula says that in order to get the expense we need to determine the direct labor, take half of it, and add \$6,000. For instance, if the direct labor, L, is \$24,000, we need to take half of this, which is \$12,000, and add \$6,000, arriving at the indirect labor of \$18,000.

This is represented in Figure 1 by point B. We recognize that our formula does not give exactly the expense for the month of January because, instead of \$16,000, it gives the value \$18,000. However, we note from the diagram that when direct labor is \$14,000, there may be three different amounts of indirect labor: \$16,000, \$17,000, and \$19,000. Our formula gives only a sort of average value. Thus, we see that our mathematical equation represents an idealized summarization of our data; and as far as forecasts are concerned, this equation may be used to compute future expenses. Let us remember that this mathematical equation does not give any information that we do not have in Table 1. In fact, the mathematical equation contains only a part of the information since, for instance, it does not tell how far the actual indirect labor expenses may vary from this idealized equation. But as far as the future is concerned, we cannot tell when these variations will occur; and therefore, we feel that for forecasts the use of this equation may be adequate.

Total Expense Involved

The next thing we want to put into mathematical language is the formula for forecasting the total expense in the Alpha Corporation. This is obtained by adding the direct labor and the expense, or in mathematical form:

$$C = e + L \tag{2}$$

We can combine this last equation with our first equation and get an alternate expression for the total cost in the Alpha Corporation:

$$C = 6{,}000 + 0.5L + L = 6{,}000 + 1.5L \tag{3}$$

We can then see that the total cost for the corporation is forecast by taking the direct labor cost, multiplying it by 1.5, and adding \$6,000. In Figure 2, we show this total cost equation as represented by a straight line.

Expressing the Revenue

Now that we have an equation for the total cost, we can proceed to the next problem of forecasting the revenue. Let us say that the corporation bills the

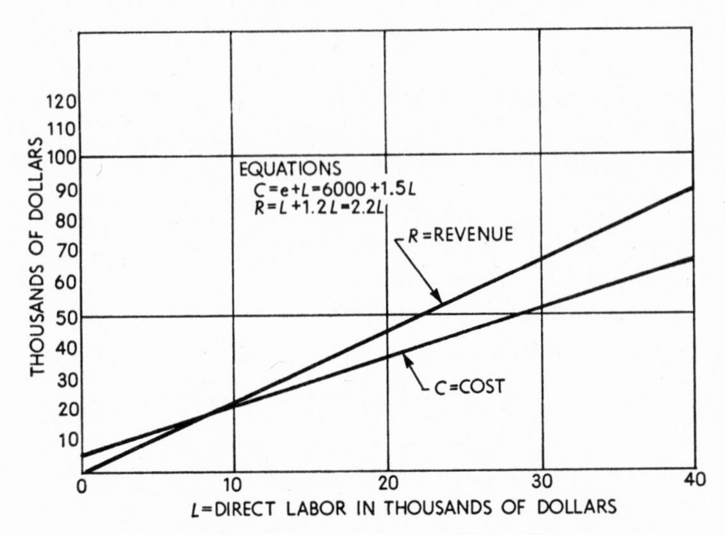

FIGURE 2. Cost and revenue for the Alpha Corporation.

customer for direct labor plus 120 percent overhead. We can say that the revenue is expressed by

$$R = L + 1.2L = 2.2L \tag{4}$$

We observe that the revenue is obtained by taking the direct labor and multiplying it by the factor 2.2. The revenue associated with the direct labor, L, is represented by a second straight line in Figure 2. The difference between the revenue and the cost is the gross profit. This can be written in mathematical form as

$$P = R - C \tag{5}$$

It will be convenient to express the profit for any value of the direct labor, and so we take our equation 5 and substitute in the expression for the revenue from equation 4 and for the cost from equation 3, and get

$$P = 2.2L - (6{,}000 + 1.5L) \tag{6}$$

This can be written as

$$P = 0.7L - 6{,}000 \tag{7}$$

We see that the profit is forecast by taking 0.7 times the direct labor and by subtracting \$6,000, as shown graphically in Figure 3. For instance, if the labor is \$20,000, then the profit is \$14,000 less \$6,000, or \$8,000. The break-even point is obtained when the profit is zero, or when

$$L = \frac{6{,}000}{0.7} = 8{,}600 \tag{8}$$

We can verify in Figure 3 that the break-even point is indeed at a direct labor cost of \$8,600.

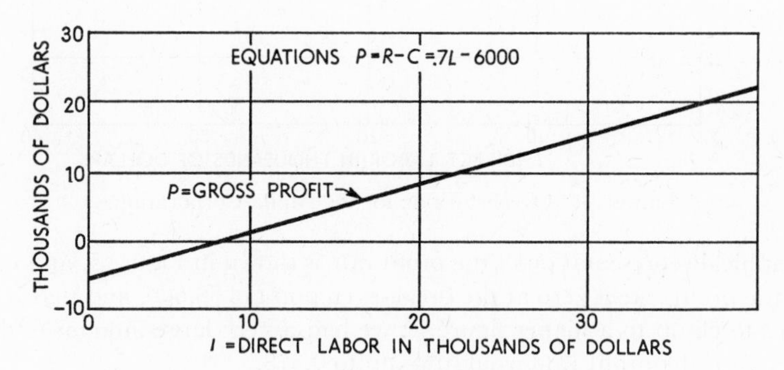

FIGURE 3. Profit for the Alpha Corporation.

Overhead Rate

Now we can ask the question: What is the formula for the overhead rate? We obtain the overhead rate by taking the expense divided by direct labor, or

$$O_r = \frac{e}{L} \tag{9}$$

We can take our equation 1 and write

$$O_r = \frac{6{,}000 + 0.5L}{L} = 0.5 + \frac{6{,}000}{L} \tag{10}$$

This is the expression for the overhead rate. A graphical representation of the overhead rate is shown in Figure 4. For instance, when the direct labor is \$20,000, we forecast an overhead rate of 80 percent, which is shown as 0.8. The diagram clearly shows that as direct labor goes up, the overhead rate decreases. If we had a very large amount of direct labor, the overhead rate would decrease to 50 percent.

Profit Rate

What is the profit rate for the Alpha Corporation? The profit rate is obtained by taking the profit and dividing it by the revenue, or

$$P_r = \frac{P}{R} = \frac{0.7L - 6{,}000}{2.2L} = 0.318 - \frac{2{,}730}{L} \tag{11}$$

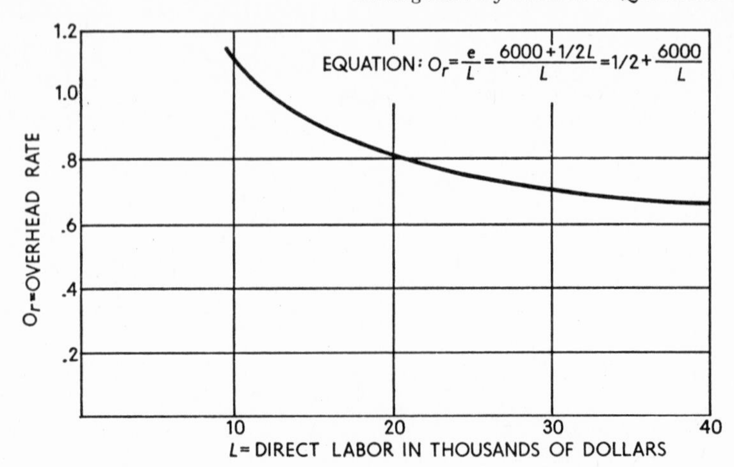

FIGURE 4. Overhead rate for the Alpha Corporation.

A graphical representation of the profit rate is shown in Figure 5, and we see that the profit rate is zero at the break-even point of $8,600, and that it then begins to climb to a higher figure. If we had a very large amount of direct labor, then the profit rate would rise up to 0.318.

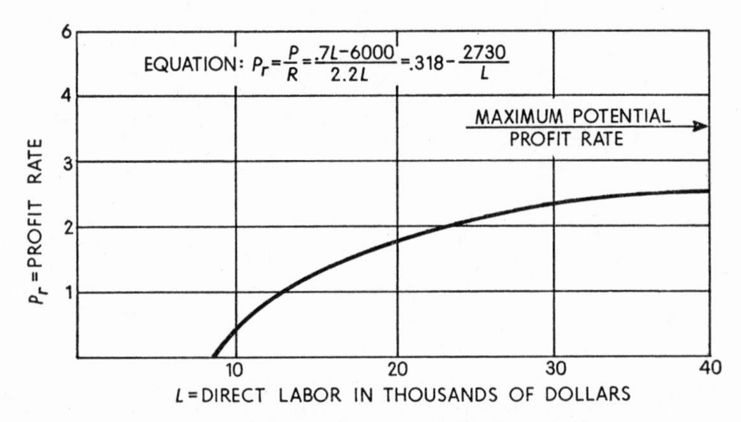

FIGURE 5. Profit rate for the Alpha Corporation.

The point we are trying to make here is really a very simple one. The mathematical formula expressing the expense as a function of the direct labor is a simple and convenient way of forecasting costs and profits. Of course, one wants to compute the overhead rate, and this is a simple computation, as indicated by equation 10.

Allowing for Change

One of the peculiar traits of scientists is that they try to describe a phenomenon in a general sort of fashion. Our equation for the Alpha Corporation says that the expense is forecast by taking one half of the direct labor and adding \$6,000. If we had another corporation with this simple sort of a sales structure, we would expect that these particular numbers in the formula would change. The advantage of mathematics is that this contingency of having these numbers change can be taken care of in a very simple way. We write that indirect labor or expense can be given by the following equation:

$$e = a + bL \tag{12}$$

In this equation, L is again the direct labor; and on the left-hand side, e is again the expense. However, you will note that instead of writing \$6,000, the letter a is written; and instead of writing that we need to take one half of the direct labor, the letter b is written. This is the algebraic notation expressing the fact that the expense is a straight line function of the direct labor. Now, we can express the total cost as

$$C = L + e = a + (b + 1)L \tag{13}$$

In our original equation 3, we had instead of a the \$6,000 figure; and instead of the $b + 1$, we had $0.5 + 1$, which is, of course, 1.5. Now that we have the cost expressed in algebraic form, let us proceed to express the revenue. We say that r is the overhead rate charged to the customer; revenue is shown as

$$R = (1 + r)L \tag{14}$$

(Compare this with equation 4, where r is 1.2 and $r + 1$ is 2.2.) We can compute the gross profit as the difference between the revenue and the cost, and get the equation

$$P = R - C = (r - b)L - a \tag{15a}$$

For the Alpha Corporation, we had $a = 6{,}000$ and $b = 0.5$; and therefore, in that case the profit is given by

$$P = (r - 0.5)L - 6{,}000 \tag{15b}$$

We recognize here that for different values of r (which correspond to the different overhead rates), we get, of course, different profit values. In Figure 6, we show these profit possibilities by different straight lines, each line corresponding to a different overhead rate. This is a financial planning chart for the management of the Alpha Corporation. Depending on the direct labor predicted and the overhead rate proposed, one can forecast profits to be realized.

Let us obtain now the general expression for forecasting the overhead rate. We know that this can be computed by taking the expense and dividing it by the direct labor. Therefore:

$$O_r = \frac{e}{L} = \frac{a + bL}{L} = b + \frac{a}{L} \tag{16}$$

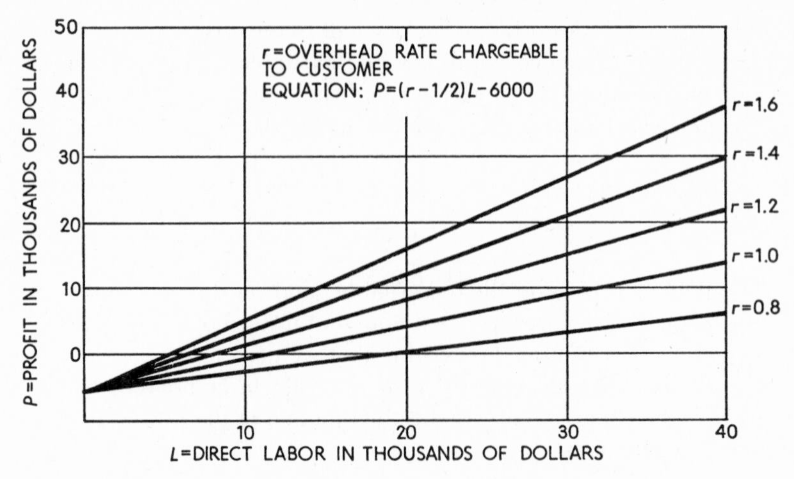

FIGURE 6. Profit possibilities for the Alpha Corporation.

(This is similar to equation 10, which gives the overhead rate for the Alpha Corporation.) We can compute the profit rate by dividing profit by the revenue and so get

$$P_r = \frac{P}{R} = \frac{(r - b)L - a}{rL} = \left(1 - \frac{b}{r}\right) - \frac{a}{rL} \tag{17}$$

For instance, for the Alpha Corporation, $b = 0.5$ and $a = 6{,}000$, and so the profit rate is given by

$$P_r = \left(1 - \frac{0.5}{r}\right) - \frac{6{,}000}{rL} \tag{18}$$

In *Figure* 7, we show a graphical representation of this equation. When the customer is charged 120 percent overhead, $r = 1.2$, and we get our profit

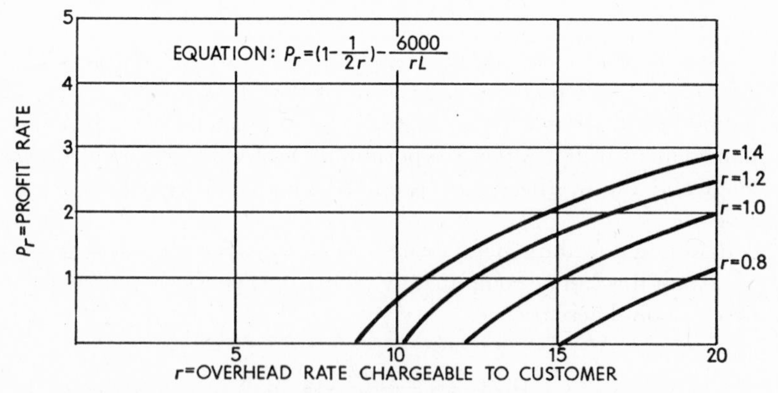

FIGURE 7. Profit rate possibilities for the Alpha Corporation.

rate curve shown in Figure 4. Figure 7 can be useful for planning purposes, as it shows how the profit rate changes if the billing rate is changed.

BUDGETING AND FORECASTING IN THE BETA CORPORATION

The Beta Corporation is somewhat more complicated than the Alpha Corporation, but it is still highly idealized. There are only two departments, department 1 and department 2, and each of these departments has direct and indirect expense. For each of the departments, we can set up a system for forecasting overhead in the same way as was done for the Alpha Corporation. However, in the Beta Corporation, there is in addition general and adminis-

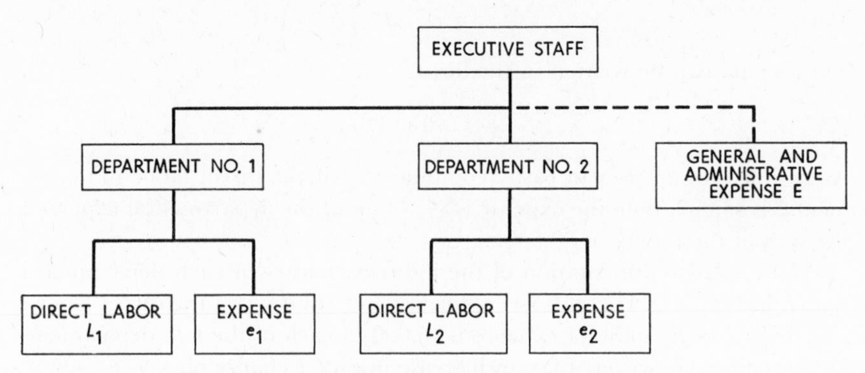

FIGURE 8. Organization of the Beta Corporation.

trative expense which cannot be directly associated with either department 1 or department 2. The graphical representation shown in Figure 8 might be used to portray this forecasting problem. We show direct labor and expense in each of the departments; then, in a separate box, we show general and administrative expenses—which is where all expenses are charged which cannot be directly associated with either department 1 or department 2.

Departmental Expense

We denote by L_1 the direct labor in department 1 and by e_1 the expense in department 1. By carrying out a regression analysis similar to the one we did for the Alpha Corporation, we find that the expense in department 1 can be forecast with the aid of the following formula:

$$e_1 = 1{,}000 + 0.5L_1 \tag{19}$$

For instance, if the direct labor, L_1, is \$15,000, then the expense, e_1, is \$8,500; the cost of operating department 1 can be computed by adding the direct labor and the expense, or

$$e_1 = e_1 + L_1 \tag{20}$$

With the aid of equation 19, this can be written as

(21) $$c_1 = 1{,}000 + 1.5L_1$$

To illustrate this, if the direct labor, L_1, is \$15,000, then the operating cost of department 1 is \$23,500.

Quite similarly, for department 2, the expense, e_2, can be computed as

(22) $$e_2 = 3{,}000 + 0.3L_2$$

where L_2 denotes the direct labor in department 2. The operating costs of department 2 can be computed by adding direct labor and expense. Therefore the operating cost, c_2, of department 2 is given by

(23) $$c_2 = e_2 + L_2$$

This, again, can be written in the form

(24) $$c_2 = 3{,}000 + 1.3L_2$$

As an illustration, we can easily compute that if the direct labor in department 2 is \$5,000, then the expense is \$4,500; and the departmental expense is the sum of these two, or \$9,500.

A graphical representation of the indirect charges in each department is shown in Figure 9. It can be seen, for instance, that when the direct labor is \$10,000, then the indirect expense is \$6,000 in each of the two departments. We recognize, however, that an increase in direct charge of, say, \$1,000 increases expenses in department 1 by \$500, but in department 2 by \$300. The incremental increase in expenses is lower in department 2 than in department 1, though the fixed expense is lower in department 1 than in department 2.

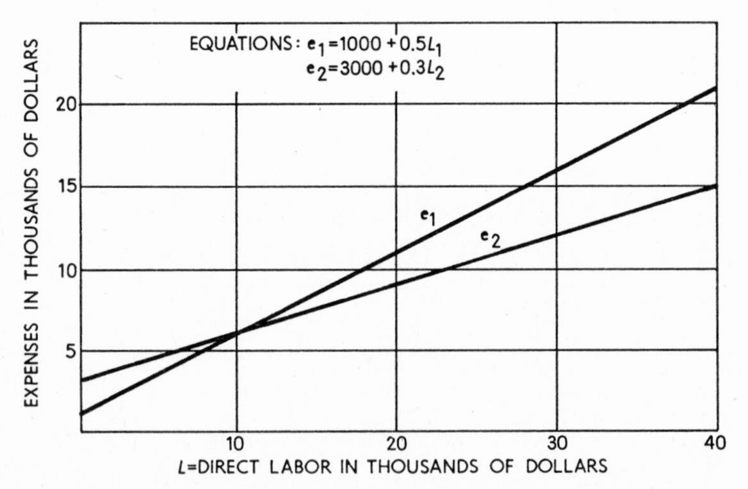

FIGURE 9. Departmental expenses in the Beta Corporation.

General and Administrative Expense

So far, we have established ways of forecasting expenses in department 1 and department 2, but we have not set up the computation for the general and administrative expenses. In Table 2, general and administration expenses for the Beta Corporation are shown for the past 16 months. The first column shows c_1, or the expenses in department 1; the second column shows c_2, or the

TABLE 2

GENERAL AND ADMINISTRATIVE EXPENSES FOR THE BETA CORPORATION

Period	In Thousands		
	c_1	c_2	E*
1	20	6	10,000
2	20	16	11,000
3	16	12	9,000
4	20	10	9,000
5	22	14	12,000
6	18	16	13,000
7	16	15	10,000
8	24	6	6,000
9	24	10	12,000
10	16	14	11,000
11	20	10	11,000
12	26	8	8,000
13	22	4	10,000
14	18	10	11,000
15	22	6	9,000
16	20	14	11,000

* $E = 0.20c_1 + 0.30c_2 + 3{,}000$.

expenses in department 2; and the third column shows E, the general and administrative expenses. The question is how to relate these general and administrative expenses to the departmental costs, c_1 and c_2.

Let us note from Table 2 that in the accounting periods 1, 2, 4, and 16, departmental expenses for the first department are \$20,000. In the same accounting periods the departmental expenses in department 2 vary, and are \$6,000, \$16,000, \$10,000, or \$14,000, respectively. We now prepare a graphical representation, as in Figure 10. The small crosses show the variation in general and administrative expenses for those accounting periods where the departmental expenses in department 1 are \$20,000. We can approximate the general and administrative expenses with the aid of a straight line as shown in Figure 8, and write

$$E = 0.30c_2 + 7{,}000 \tag{25}$$

Let us now take the accounting periods 4, 9, 11, and 14. In these periods the departmental expenses in Department 2 are \$10,000. We prepare a dia-

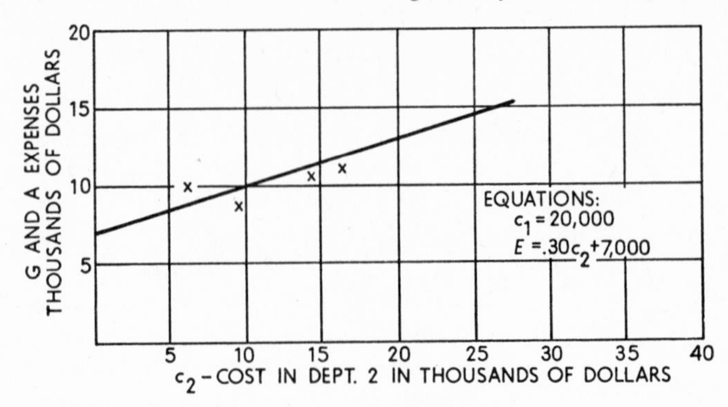

FIGURE 10. General and administrative expenses—Beta Corporation.

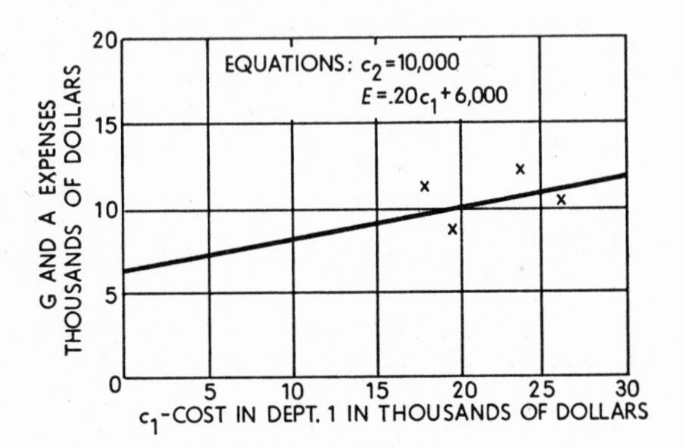

FIGURE 11. General and administrative expenses—Beta Corporation.

gram as shown in Figure 11. This diagram represents general and administrative expenses for the Beta Corporation for those accounting periods when the departmental costs in department 2 are \$10,000. We can again approximate general and administrative expenses with the aid of a straight line and use the formula

$$E = 0.20c_1 + 6,000 \tag{26}$$

Such a formula is useful in forecasting general and administrative expenses for a few accounting periods; that is, it will work only when departmental costs in department 1 are \$20,000 or when departmental costs in department 2 are \$10,000.

Formula for All Periods

The question now is: How can we get a formula that will handle all accounting periods? The first step in the preparation of such a formula is shown

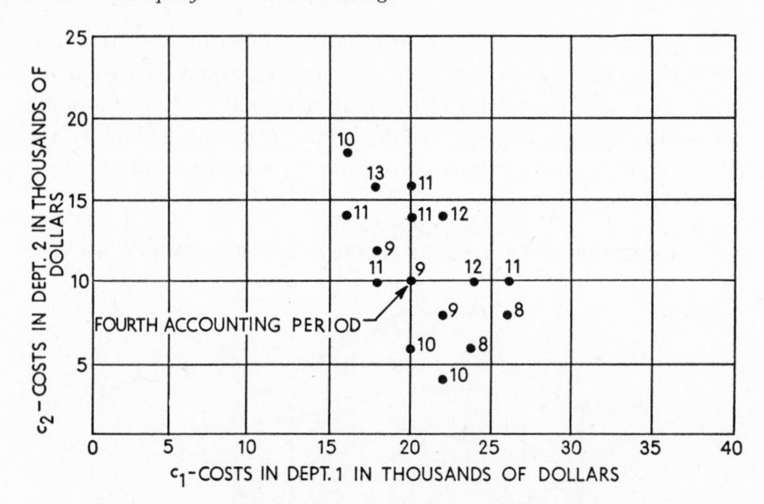

FIGURE 12. General and administrative expenses—Beta Corporation (the number shows general and administrative expenses in thousands of dollars).

in Figure 12. Here the horizontal axis is the cost in department 1, and the vertical axis is the cost in department 2. Each dot in Figure 12 represents one accounting period. Next to each dot is shown a number which gives the general and administrative expense for that particular accounting period. For instance, we notice in Table 2 that in the fourth accounting period, departmental costs in department 1 are $20,000, departmental costs in department 2 are $10,000, and general and administrative expenses are $9,000. This particular accounting period is pointed out by the arrow in Figure 12. A better geometrical representation of this situation is shown in Figure 13, where each accounting period is represented by a dot,

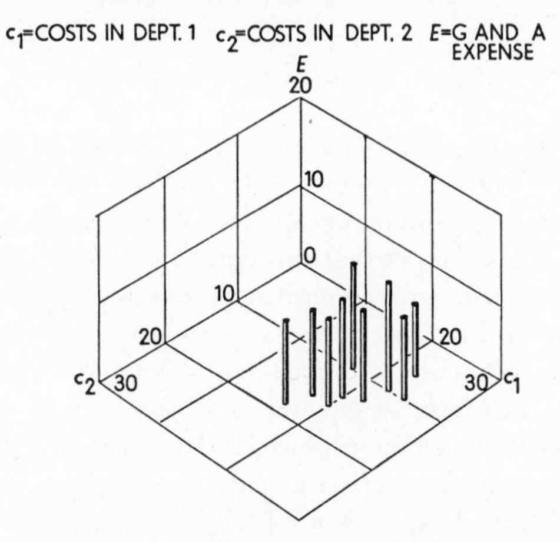

FIGURE 13. General and administrative expenses—Beta Corporation.

but the general and administrative expense is shown by a vertical rod with the length scaled to the general and administrative expense for each accounting period. We have now a dot in three-dimensional space corresponding to each accounting period, and our problem is to express these data by a mathematical formula. A convenient way to do this is shown in Figure 14, where the

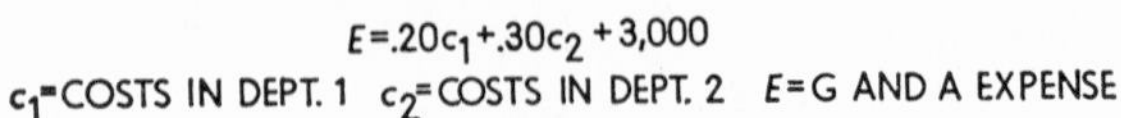

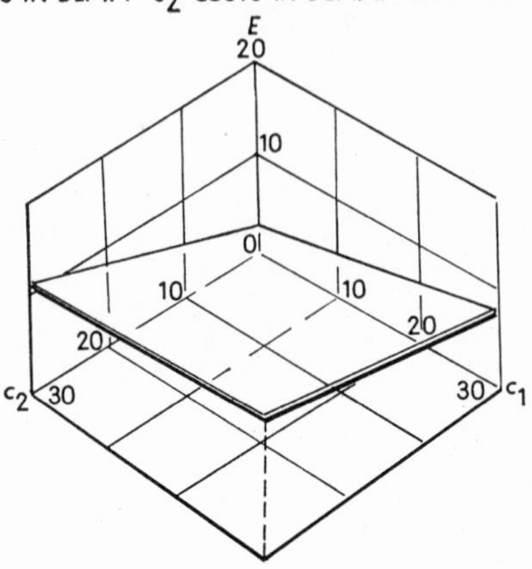

FIGURE 14. General and administrative expenses—Beta Corporation.

plane is adjusted so that it goes close to each of the dots in our three-dimensional space. We say that this plane approximates general and administrative expenses for the Beta Corporation. With the use of analytic geometry, one can compute points on this plane with the aid of the following equation:

$$E = 0.20c_1 + 0.30c_2 + 3{,}000 \quad (27)$$

Considerations in Computing

This is, then, the equation that we use to forecast general and administrative expenses for the Beta Corporation. In the language of the statistician, we have here a regression equation between the costs c_1 and c_2 and the expense E. A simple computation shows that this equation includes as special cases the previous equations, where we computed general and administrative expenses under the condition that departmental costs in department 1 were \$20,000 or when departmental costs in department 2 were \$10,000. In addition, this formula allows us to forecast general and administrative expenses for any other accounting period. For instance, if departmental costs are \$16,000 in department 1 and \$6,000 in department 2, then we can compute that the general and administrative expenses are \$8,000.

Let us notice here that if departmental expenses in department 1 go up by \$1,000, then general and administrative expenses will go up by \$200. However, if departmental costs in department 2 go up by $1,000, then the general and administrative expenses go up by $300. This means, then, that an increment of expenses in department 2 involves a greater increase in general and administrative expenses than an incremental increase in department 1.

Suppose the direct labor cost is $15,000 in department 1 and $5,000 in department 2. What would the general and administrative expense be? We have already computed that costs in department 1 would be $23,500 and costs in department 2 would be $9,500. Therefore, from equation 27, we find that the general and administrative expenses are $10,550.

Our graphical representation shown in Figure 14 is somewhat inconvenient because it is a three-dimensional representation. An alternate way of representing the general and administrative expenses formula is shown in Figure 15. The horizontal axis shows costs in department 1; the vertical axis

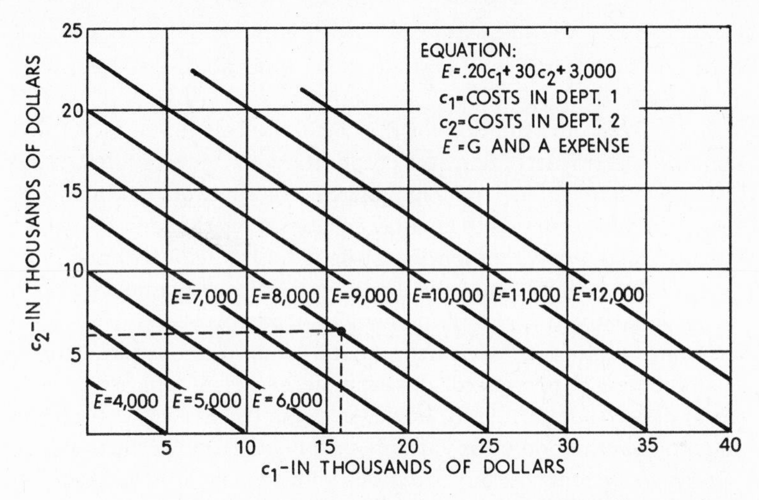

FIGURE 15. General and administrative expenses—Beta Corporation.

shows costs in department 2. Each of the straight lines represents a fixed general and administrative expense line for the Beta Corporation. For instance, we can see from the diagram that if costs in department 1 are $16,000 and costs in department 2 are $6,000, then the general and administrative expense is $8,000. This is a more convenient graphical way of summarizing general and administrative expenses for the Beta Corporation.

Total Corporate Costs

Let us forecast the total corporate costs. This is done by adding the costs in department 1, those in department 2, and finally, the general and administrative expenses. If we denote by C the corporate costs for Beta Corporation, we have

$$C = c_1 + c_2 + E \tag{28}$$

We can use our expression for the general and administrative costs, equation 27, and get

(29) $$C = 1.2c_1 + 1.3c_2 + 3{,}000$$

This is the formula for forecasting corporate costs in the Beta Corporation. For instance, in the case mentioned before, costs in department 1 were \$23,500, and costs in department 2 were \$9,500. From equation 29, we find that corporate costs for the Beta Corporation are \$43,550.

We can also express corporate costs with the aid of the direct labor cost by using our equations 21 and 24. We get

(30) $$C = 1.2(1{,}000 + 1.5L_1) + 1.3(3{,}000 + 1.3L_2) + 3{,}000$$

which can be written in the form

(31) $$C = 1.8L_1 + 1.69L_2 + 8{,}100$$

For instance, if direct labor in department 1 is \$15,000 and direct labor in department 2 is \$5,000, the total cost for the corporation is \$43,550, which, of course, agrees with the previous computation.

We notice from our equation for the corporate cost that a \$1,000 increase in labor in department 1 increases corporate costs by \$1,800. A \$1,000 increase in direct labor in department 2 increases corporate costs by \$1,690. We could say, therefore, that incremental corporate overhead is 80 percent for department 1 and 69 percent for department 2. On the other hand, it follows from equations 19 and 22 that the incremental departmental overhead is 50 percent in department 1 and 30 percent in department 2. Furthermore, we can see from equation 27 that incremental general and administrative expenses amount to 20 percent for departmental costs in department 1 and 30 percent in department 2. Let us, however, remind ourselves that these incremental costs represent only the variable part of overhead. As far as total costs are concerned, we must use our equations in full to take into account the fixed part of the overhead costs.

Profit Picture

Let us look now at the profit picture of the Beta Corporation. First, let us forecast the revenue. Suppose department 1 has such contracts that for each \$1,000 of direct labor, \$3,000 is billed. On the other hand, department 2 collects only \$2,500 for each \$1,000 of direct labor. In mathematical form the revenue for the Beta Corporation is given by

(32) $$R = 3L_1 + 2.5L_2$$

For instance, if direct labor is \$15,000 in department 1 and \$5,000 in department 2, then the corporate revenue is \$57,500. The gross profit is obtained by taking the revenue less the corporate cost. Mathematically, this can be expressed as

(33) $$P = R - C$$

With the aid of our expressions for corporate cost and corporate revenue, this can be written as

$$P = 3L_1 + 2.5L_2 - (1.8L_1 + 1.69L_2 + 8{,}100) \tag{34a}$$

or as

$$P = 1.2L_1 + 0.81L_2 - 8{,}100 \tag{34b}$$

A graphical representation of this profit is shown in Figure 16. The horizontal axis is direct labor in department 1; the vertical axis is direct labor in department 2. Along each of the straight lines the profit is fixed. For instance, if direct labor is \$16,000 in department 1 and \$5,000 in department 2, then

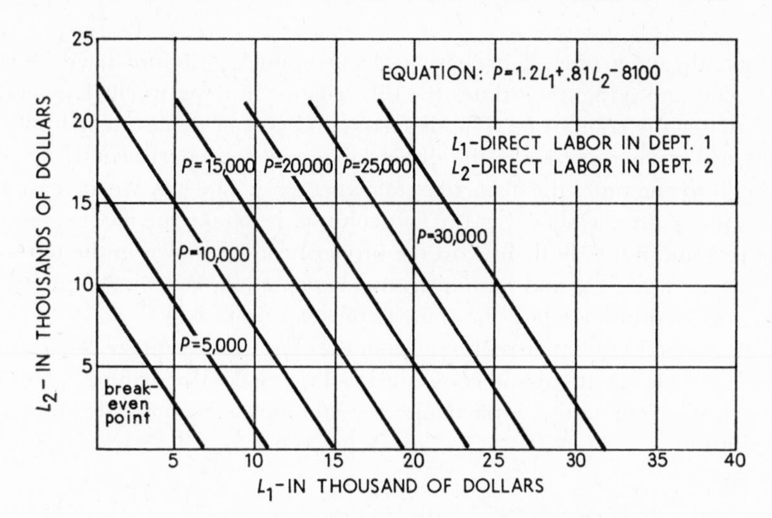

FIGURE 16. Profit for the Beta Corporation.

the profit is \$15,000. We realize that an increase of \$1,000 of direct labor in department 1 results in an increase of profit of \$1,200, whereas the same increase in direct labor in department 2 leads to an increase of profit of \$810. For instance, if management has to make a decision where to put an additional \$1,000 of labor, then this increase should be introduced in department 1, as this will result in a higher profit.

Another Method of Presentation

So far, we have used either graphical or mathematical representation to describe forecasting in the Beta Corporation. Now, we want to discuss another method of presentation which can be more convenient, particularly when the forecasting problem becomes more complex.

In Table 3, we show a description of the forecasting method for the Beta Corporation. Each accounting entity shown in the first column can be computed with the aid of the accounting information listed in the top row. For

TABLE 3

COST AND PROFIT TABLE FOR THE BETA CORPORATION

	I	L_1	L_2	e_1	e_2	c_1	c_2	E	R	C
e_1	1,000	0.5								
c_1		+1		+1						
e_2	3,000		0.3							
c_2			+1		+1					
E	3,000					0.2	0.3			
C						+1	+1	+1		
R		3	2.5							
P									+1	−1

instance, the departmental expense in department 1, e_1, is forecasted by taking \$1,000 and adding 0.5 times the direct labor in department 1, which is listed under the column L_1. The departmental cost in department 1 can be forecast by taking one times the direct labor cost in department 1, L_1, and adding it to one times the departmental expense, e_1. The way we forecast any accounting entity, as shown in the first column, is to take the numbers in the same row and multiply them with the proper heading shown in the top row. For instance, general and administrative expenses, E, can be computed by taking 3,000 times one plus 0.2 times c_1 plus 0.3 times c_2.

Here, then, is a tabular representation that has the advantage that it summarizes all our equations and computational methods. We shall see later that this sort of representation is particularly useful in more complicated forecasting problems.

Forecasting under General Conditions

Before we leave our hypothetical Beta Corporation, we develop the forecasting system for a corporation of this type under more general conditions. We assume again that this type of corporation has two departments, and also general and administrative expenses, but we do not assume a particular rate of overhead in each of these departments or for the corporation. We say that expenses in department 1 can be computed from the equation

$$e_1 = a_1 + b_1 L_1 \tag{35}$$

and expenses in the second department can be computed from

$$e_2 = a_2 + b_2 L_2 \tag{36}$$

Departmental costs for department 1 can be computed from

$$c_1 = e_1 + L_1 = a_1 + (1 + b_1)L_1 \tag{37}$$

and departmental costs for department 2 can be computed from

$$c_2 = e_2 + L_2 = a_2 + (1 + b_2)L_2 \tag{38}$$

General and administrative expenses are related to departmental costs with the aid of the formula

$$E = A_1c_1 + A_2c_2 + B \tag{39}$$

Total corporate costs are forecast by

$$C = c_1 + c_2 + E \tag{40}$$

This can also be written as

$$C = [(1 + b_1)(1 + A_1)L_1 + (1 + b_2)(1 + A_2)L_2] + [B + a_1(1 + A_1) + a_2(1 + A_2)] \tag{41}$$

We recognize here that the first term is the variable cost related to direct labor charges in the departments, and the second is a fixed cost term. We assume again that the customer is billed at a fixed rate for each direct labor charge. We say that this chargeable overhead rate is r_1 for department 1 and r_2 for department 2. This means that total corporate revenue is given by

$$R = (1 + r_1)L_1 + (1 + r_2)L_2 \tag{42}$$

The profit is computed by taking the revenue less the cost, or

$$P = R - C \tag{43}$$

This profit can be written now as

$$P = [(1 + r_1) - (1 + b_1)(1 + A_1)]L_1 + [(1 + r_2) - (1 + b_2)(1 + A_2)]L_2 - [B + a_1(1 + a_1) + a_2(1 + A_2)] \tag{44}$$

We recognize that the first two terms represent the variable part of the profit, whereas the last term is a constant. This last equation is a generalization of the profit equation shown by equation 34b.

A good way of summarizing our many equations is presented in Table 4.

TABLE 4

COST AND PROFIT TABLE FOR CORPORATIONS SIMILAR TO THE BETA CORPORATION

	I	L_1	L_2	e_1	e_2	c_1	c_2	E	R	C
e_1	a_1	b_1								
c_1		+1		+1						
e_2	a_2		b_2							
c_2			+1		+1					
E	B					A_1	A_2			
C						+1	+1	+1		
R		$1 + r_1$	$1 + r_2$							
P									+1	−1

The rules of forecasting the accounting entities shown in the first column are again the same as in Table 3. For instance, corporate costs, C, can be computed by taking one times departmental cost, c_1, plus one times departmental cost, c_2, plus one times the corporate expense, E. This is a convenient means of depicting the cost accounting system in a corporation which is of the same type as the Beta Corporation.

BUDGETING AND FORECASTING IN THE GAMMA CORPORATION

Now we know enough mathematics to consider a more complicated corporate structure. As shown in Figure 17, the Gamma Corporation has three

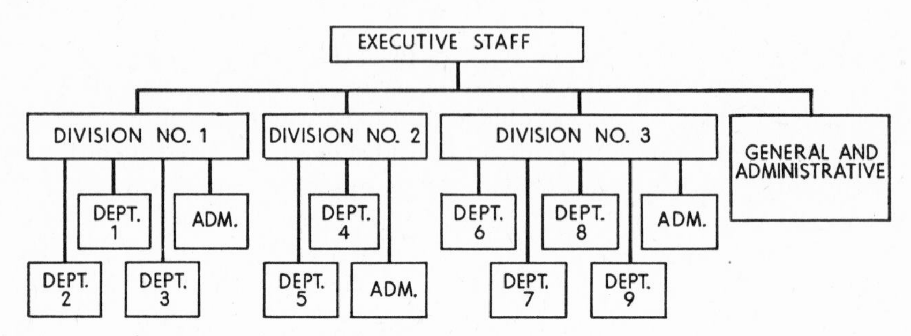

FIGURE 17. Organization chart for the Gamma Corporation.

divisions, and each of these divisions has several departments. There is direct labor and expense in each of these departments, just as in the Alpha and Beta corporations. In addition, there are administrative expenses in each of the three divisions. Finally, we have general and administrative expenses on the corporate level.

Computation of Costs

In order to develop a forecasting system, we follow the method we used in the Alpha and Beta corporations. Let us say that in department i, direct labor costs are L_i. This is a new trick in our mathematical nomenclature. The small letter i denotes that our notation refers to department 1, or department 2, all the way up to department 9—or as the mathematician would say, i can take the value of one to nine. Then we can say that departmental expenses are to be forecasted with the aid of a straight line formula, or

$$e_i = a_i + b_i L_i \tag{45}$$

Departmental costs are obtained by adding direct labor to expenses, and so we get

$$c_i = e_i + L_i = a_i + (1 + b_i)L_i \tag{46}$$

We now have the departmental costs for each of the departments, and we can proceed to determine divisional expense, say, for the first division. It will be recalled that in the Beta Corporation we did this sort of computation; but in that case, we had only two departments, whereas here we have three. What is needed here is, in statistical terms, a "multiple regression analysis." The equation for the divisional expense gets more complicated and can be written in the following form:

$$E_1 = A_1c_1 + A_2c_2 + A_3c_3 + B_1 \tag{47}$$

Total divisional costs are obtained by adding the departmental costs to the divisional expense. For instance, the divisional cost for division 1 is given by the equation

$$C_1 = c_1 + c_2 + c_3 + E_1 \tag{48}$$

Quite similarly, we can develop divisional costs for division 2 and division 3.

The next problem is to develop an equation for the general and administrative expenses for the Gamma Corporation. These will be related to the divisional costs. Following our previous examples, we say that the general and administrative expenses for the Gamma Corporation can be forecast with the aid of the equation

$$E_c = f_0 + f_1C_1 + f_2C_2 + f_3C_3 \tag{49}$$

where f_0, f_1, f_2, and f_3 are constants similar to the ones appearing in equation 27. Corporate costs are obtained by adding divisional costs and general and administrative costs, or

$$C_c = C_1 + C_2 + C_3 + E_c \tag{50}$$

Corporate Revenue and Profit

The corporate revenue can be computed by adding the revenues for each of the departments. We denote the revenue for department 1 by R_1, for department 2 by R_2, and so on, and then express the corporate revenue by the equation

$$R_c = R_1 + R_2 + R_3 + \cdots + R_9 \tag{51}$$

We again assume that each department bills its customers at a fixed rate of the direct labor; and therefore, we say that the corporate revenue is given by

$$R_c = (1 + r_1)L_1 + (1 + r_2)L_2 + (1 + r_3)L_3 + \cdots + (1 + r_9)L_9 \tag{52}$$

On the right-hand side, we have nine terms corresponding to the revenues in each of the departments.

Finally, the profit for the Gamma Corporation is obtained by taking the corporate revenue less the corporate cost, or

$$P_c = R_c - C_c \tag{53}$$

CONCLUDING REMARKS

It can now be seen that we have developed here a system of equations relating direct labor and expenses in the idealized corporations, Alpha, Beta, and Gamma. These equations form the basis of a forecasting system to be used in these corporations. A real business firm of medium size is currently adapting this forecasting system to its financial planning.

The main difficulty with the existing forecasting system is that it takes two to three months to complete a forecast, and this is considered wholly inadequate for financial planning. The management decided to review this forecasting system and consider the possibility of employing an electronic computer with the intent of shortening the preparation time of two to three months.

After a brief study of the forecasting system, it appeared that there were so many individual decisions made in the course of the computations that it would have been impractical to prepare the forecast on an electronic computer. Consequently, it was necessary to look for some alternate method of approach. A careful analysis of the past accounting data made it apparent that the statistical regression analysis described in this paper was particularly suitable to the needs of this corporation. With an analysis of the past data, it was possible to select some major direct and indirect accounts which could be related by regression equations similar to the ones described in this paper. These equations were found sufficiently accurate to meet the forecasting needs of the corporation.

Application of these equations results in vast simplifications in financial calculations and reduces sharply the clerical labor required. Furthermore, the equations can be programmed on an electronic computer; and consequently, the forecast can be prepared with the aid of a computer. Not only is it now possible to complete a forecast in a time period of two weeks, but the forecast can be prepared at substantially less cost.

We believe that the budgeting and forecasting system herein described has many other applications in business and industry. We recognize, though, that the factors to be related in applying the regression analysis technique may vary in each individual case.

34

Scatter diagrams are described with specific indication of their limitations. Emphasis is directed to the importance of the choice of the independent variable, illustrated by an example relating one set of dependent cost data to two different independent variables. It is acknowledged that more than one base, or independent variable, may be appropriate within a single department because of the existence of semivariable expenses. Refinements provided by price level changes, efficiency variations, changes in equipment, etc., are also discussed.

IMPROVING SEPARATION OF FIXED AND VARIABLE EXPENSES*

R. S. Gynther

THE SEPARATION of semivariable expenses into their fixed and variable components is a task confronting more and more accountants and controllers as more and more use is made of flexible budgeting; direct costing; break-even analysis; differential cost analysis for pricing, policies, etc.; fixed and variable expense absorption rates in standard costing; and other managerial aids. In order to enable these tools to be used with great reliance, it is essential that much care be given to this task of separating fixed and variable expenses. Each one of these tools is totally dependent on the accuracy with which this division takes place, especially in those cases where many semivariable items exist. Admittedly, it is the manufacturer who can make the most use of flexible budgets, but they should also be used by wholesalers and retailers for the control of administrative, selling, and distribution expenses. This means that the separation of semivariable expenses is a matter in which all should be interested, even if no use is made of direct costing, break-even analysis, and differential cost analysis.

It is not enough to wander through a chart of accounts saying, "This one is fixed, this is variable, this is fixed, etc.," merely classifying some accounts as fixed or variable because they are predominantly so. Such a procedure does not give accurate formulas for flexible budgets,[1] it usually overstates the total

* Reprinted from *NAA Bulletin*, published by the National Association of Accountants, June, 1963, pp. 29–38.

[1] As Glenn A. Welsch says in the *NACA Bulletin* for May, 1953 ("The Fixed-Flexible Budget—A Study in Integration"): "The Flexible Budget consists of a series of formulas, one series for each department. Each series has a formula for each amount in the department or cost center. The formula for each amount indicates a fixed amount and/or a variable rate."

of fixed expenses in break-even analysis,[2] and it thus usually understates the variable cost per product unit—an action which can result in the taking of unprofitable business in the short run.

Accurate separation is not usually a simple task. This short paper is written in the hope that exposition of an accurate method may be of some assistance. The procedures recommended were applied for several years in practice.

WHY THE USE OF SCATTER CHARTS?

From the literature on the subject, it would seem that the most popular separation technique is the scatter chart method. This is confirmed on page 11 of NAA Accounting Practice Report No. 10, "Separating and Using Costs as Fixed and Variable,"[3] where we are told that this method is used by "the greater number of companies" (out of the 58 practice descriptions which that report summarizes). However, statisticians would agree that the scatter chart

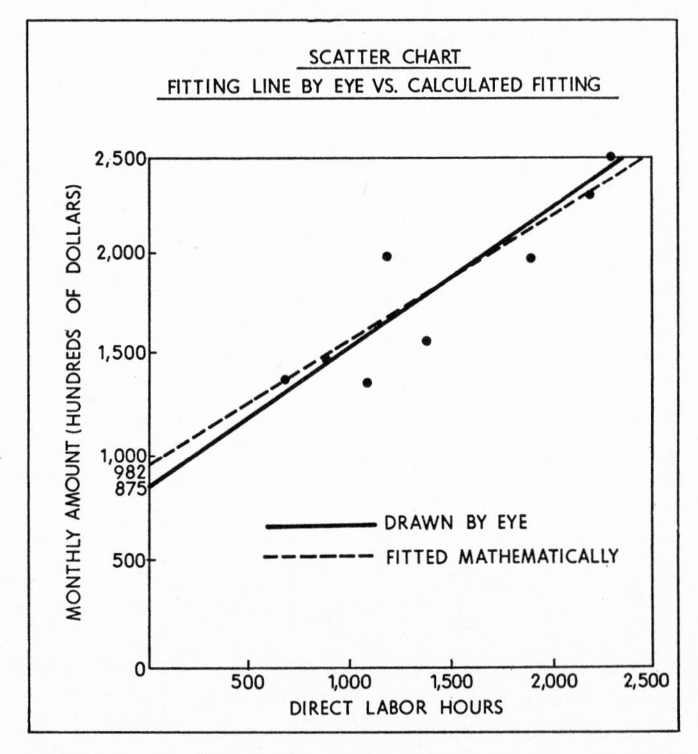

Exhibit 1. Scatter chart—fitting by eye versus calculated fitting.

[2] A deliberate action by some consulting accountants in order to move the break-even point to a high and more "conservative" position.

[3] Sec. 3, *NAA Bulletin*, June, 1960.

method is not an extremely accurate method. We are told on page 12 of the same report that "mention of the method of the least squares as helpful in confirming the accuracy of or revising less exact determinations appears a number of times and one contributor illustrates its use." This is a step in the right direction. The contributor referred to illustrated the use of the technique by quoting a case in which a scatter chart gave him $875 as the fixed content of an expense, corrected to $982 after using the method of the least squares.

How could such an error (12 percent) occur? The scatter chart in Exhibit 1 (using the same data as in the case quoted) shows how easy it is to read off incorrect information. The heavy line is the line of best fit which the contributor fitted to the scatter chart by eye, thus giving the fixed expense amount of $875 on the *Y*-axis. The dotted line is the accurate line he should have drawn if his eye had been perfect. This gives the correct fixed expense amount of $982, which can be confirmed by a calculation of the method of least squares.[4]

To draw the correct line of best fit on this scatter chart by eye is not an easy task, and all sorts of lines would be drawn between the plotted points by different people in order to depict the average slope of the points. This means, in turn, that different accountants would come up with all sorts of different fixed expense portions for this particular expense (and hence different variable rates, too) if they merely resorted to the scatter chart method.

If scatter charts are capable of revealing such inaccurate information (depending upon the eye of the operator), why then is it that they are used so often? Why is it that the method of least squares is not used in every case? It is because of the calculations involved in the method of least squares, and because the scatter chart method is understood by those who have not been exposed to the statistical method. However, the accuracy that results makes the method of least squares desirable. Although calculations are required for each item of expense of a semivariable nature, they usually need to be carried out only once or twice a year. In these days of slide rules, calculators, and computers, this should not be a difficulty.

NEED FOR SATISFACTORY VARIABLE COST BASE

There is another factor affecting the extent and accuracy of the practice of separating fixed and variable expenses. The absence from the literature of advice on the selection of a suitable unit (volume) to which to relate the variable expenses may have turned some people away from the separation of fixed and variable portions of semivariable expenses or may have been the cause of use of incorrect bases. If incorrect volume bases are used, inaccurate results will follow whether the method of least squares, scatter charts, or any other lesser used separation method is employed.

Glenn A. Welsch, in his excellent book, *Budgeting: Profit-Planning and Con-*

---

[4] For those interested, this method is demonstrated later in this paper. For this particular calculation, please refer to p. 13 of NAA Accounting Practice Report No. 10.

trol,[5] is extremely helpful in this regard; and after discussing the departments which have "more than one type of output" and certain service departments which "do not lend themselves to exact units of measurement," he concludes his discussion with the statement that "Cost variability is frequently meaningless because an incorrect factor is being used, showing low correlation between cost and activity."[6] In NAA Accounting Practice Report No. 10, in connection with this matter of selecting the correct volume factor, we find:

> The tools (i.e., scatter charts or method of least squares, etc.) are used to discover the presence of a fixed element in a cost and to disclose its size and the variability of the remainder, all in terms of operating volumes on which the data used are based, normally volumes of the present or immediate past or future. The employment of the tools requires correlation of volume in physical terms, such as units produced or labor hours, with costs in dollars for items or groups of items.[7]

In both of the above quotations, we see the word *correlation* used. In practice, the author of this paper has found that the use of statistical correlation analysis is essential in discovering the correct volume base to be used before attempting to separate the fixed and variable elements of many items of expense which are semivariable in nature. As correlation analysis and the method of the least squares involve similar calculations, they dovetail one into the other. After completing the initial correlation analysis (where necessary), very little extra work is needed to reveal the fixed and variable portions of the expense item in question. Again, with some semivariable items which can be related to only one possible volume, the carrying-out of correlation analysis shows that only a low degree of direct correlation exists; and therefore, little reliance for control purposes can be placed on the flexible budget formula subsequently calculated by using this one available volume factor.

It was found in practice that after the initial correlation analysis has been carried out and the correct volume unit discovered and measured for a particular semivariable expense item, there was little need for such further analysis while circumstances remained unaltered. However, as most relevant calculations were made once or twice a year, when using the method of least squares to establish flexible budget formula, it was an easy matter to check on the various correlation coefficients from time to time.

It is true that "simple correlation techniques such as scatter charts . . . may be of some value in selecting a suitable volume index."[8] It is admitted that any absence of correlation between any semivariable (or completely variable) expense and a selected volume base will be revealed by a scatter chart; but once more, it is left to the eye of the individual to gauge the degree of correlation which exists. If two or more possible volume bases exist, a com-

---

[5] Englewood Cliffs, N.J.: Prentice-Hall, Inc., 1957, pp. 168–69.

[6] *Ibid.*, p. 169.

[7] NAA Accounting Practice Report No. 10, p. 8.

[8] NACA Research Report, *The Analysis of Cost-Volume-Profit Relationships*, (Combined Research Series 16, 17, and 18 (1949–50), p. 9.

parison of scatter charts, each based on a different volume, will not always make obvious the volume unit to be used. On the other hand, statistical correlation analysis gives a measure which simplifies the selection of the volume unit and which indicates the degree to which reliance can be placed on the results of the subsequent separation analysis carried out, using the volume unit selected.

In the scatter chart in Exhibit 1, perfect correlation between the expense concerned and direct labor hours would have been indicated by the plotted points occurring in a straight line. Although the points in this illustration do tend in one direction, they certainly are far from a straight line. This would indicate that a search should be made for a volume unit other than direct labor hours, i.e., one with which the variable portion of this expense varies more directly. It could be that such a unit would be machine hours or units produced or some other volume factor in the department concerned.

AN EXAMPLE

In order to illustrate clearly the two points made in this article, a simple numerical example is given. An examination of certain refinements to underlying data is delayed until after this explanatory example has been discussed.

A flexible budget is to be established to assist in the control of selling expenses each month. An examination of the expense items produces the following results:

Item	*Fixed Portion*	+	*Variable Portion*
Salaries	$1,200		Nil
Salesmen—retainers	2,000		Nil
Salesmen—commissions	Nil		4% on sales values
Advertising	5,000		Nil
Traveling expenses	?		?

The traveling expense item cannot be split up into its fixed and variable portions by observation or engineering analysis. Statistical aids are to be used. The traveling expenses incurred over the past 12 months are:

January	$3,000
February	3,200
March	2,800
April	3,400
May	3,100
June	3,200
July	2,900
August	3,300
September	3,500
October	3,400
November	3,200
December	3,400

It is thought that the variable portion of these might vary in accordance either with movements in number of calls made on customers each month or with the value of orders received each month. These are regarded as the two most likely volume bases for this expense item in this particular company. Records reveal the following details of these bases for the same period:

	Calls Made	*Orders Received*
January	410	$53,000
February	420	65,000
March	380	48,000
April	460	73,000
May	430	62,000
June	450	67,000
July	390	60,000
August	470	76,000
September	480	82,000
October	490	62,000
November	440	64,000
December	460	80,000

One of these volumes will give a better formula than the other. Which one is it—and just how accurate will the formula be? Neither of these questions can be answered from mere observation. It is doubtful if a scatter chart could tell which of the two bases is the better in this case. So we resort to correlation analysis in the first instance in order to determine which volume base will be used in the flexible budget formula.

In Exhibit 2 the coefficient of correlation between traveling expenses and the number of calls made is calculated. In order to cater to those who have not been exposed to this type of statistical analysis, a simple method is used, and symbols are avoided. Many will be able to apply more sophisticated calculation methods.

In Exhibit 3 the coefficient of correlation between traveling expenses and the value of orders received is calculated. A comparison between the two coefficients can then be made.

Perfect direct correlation would be evidenced by a correlation coefficient of one. The coefficient of 0.946 revealed in Exhibit 2 is closer to one than the coefficient of 0.86 in Exhibit 3. This means that we have proved that the variable section of traveling expenses varies more directly with movements in the number of calls made than with the value of orders received. To explain this a little further, we could examine the relative coefficients of determination which are obtained by squaring the coefficients of correlation and expressing the answer as a percentage in each case. Here the coefficients of determination are 90.5 percent for calls made and only 75 percent for orders received. This means that we can say that approximately 90.5 percent of the movements in the variable portion of traveling expenses are caused

1	2	3	4	5	6	7	8
Month	*Traveling Expenses ($00's)*	*Deviation from Average*	*Deviation²*	*Calls Made (0's)*	*Deviation from Average*	*Deviation²*	*Product of Deviations (3 × 6)*
January	30	−2	4	41	−3	9	6
February	32	...	...	42	−2	4	...
March	28	−4	16	38	−6	36	24
April	34	2	4	46	2	4	4
May	31	−1	1	43	−1	1	1
June	32	...	...	45	1	1	...
July	29	−3	9	39	−5	25	15
August	33	1	1	47	3	9	3
September	35	3	9	48	4	16	12
October	34	2	4	49	5	25	10
November	32	...	...	44	...	...	...
December	34	2	4	46	2	4	4
Totals	384		52	528		134	79
Arithmetic average	32			44			

$$\text{Coefficient of correlation} = \frac{\text{The product of the deviations}}{\text{Number of months} \times \text{Standard deviation of traveling-expense series} \times \text{Standard deviation of calls-made series}}$$

$$= \frac{79}{12 \times \sqrt{\frac{52}{12}} \times \sqrt{\frac{134}{12}}} = 0.946 \text{ (approximately)}$$

EXHIBIT 2. Correlation of traveling expense with calls made.

by fluctuations in the number of calls made and that the remaining 9.5 percent of movements are caused by other factors.

Now that the volume unit has been determined, i.e., number of calls made, it is an easy matter to calculate the fixed and variable portions of traveling expenses, as most of the calculations required from the method of least squares analysis have been made already. From Exhibit 2 (Exhibit 3 is now redundant), we obtain the following:

$$\text{Variable traveling expenses} = \frac{\text{Sum of product of deviations } (xy)}{\text{Sum of deviations}^2 \text{ of calls } (x^2)}$$

$$= \frac{\$79\ (000)}{134\ (00)} = \$5.89552 \text{ per call}$$

Therefore the fixed portion of traveling expenses is

$$\$3{,}200 - (\$5.89552 \times 440) = \$606$$

So in the flexible budget for selling expenses that we were constructing previously, we may now show for the traveling expenses item $606 in the column headed "Fixed Portion" and $5.89552 per call made in the column headed "Variable Portion."

1	*2*	*3*	*4*	*5*	*6*	*7*	*8*
Months	*Traveling Expenses ($00's)*	*Deviation from Average*	*Deviation²*	*Orders Received ($000's)*	*Deviation from Average*	*Deviation²*	*Product of Deviations (3 × 6)*
January	30	−2	4	53	−13	169	26
February	32	...	...	65	−1	1	...
March	28	−4	16	48	−18	324	72
April	34	2	4	73	7	49	14
May	31	−1	1	62	−4	16	4
June	32	...	...	67	1	1	...
July	29	−3	9	60	−6	36	18
August	33	1	1	76	10	100	10
September	35	3	9	82	16	256	48
October	34	2	4	62	−4	16	−8
November	32	...	...	64	−2	4	...
December	34	2	4	80	14	196	28
Totals	384		52	792		1,168	212
Arithmetic average	32			66			

Coefficient of correlation (computed in the same manner as in Exhibit 2) $= \dfrac{212}{12 \times \sqrt{\dfrac{52}{12}} \times \sqrt{\dfrac{1{,}168}{12}}} = 0.86$ (approximately)

EXHIBIT 3. Correlation of traveling expense with orders received.

All of this may seem to the casual reader to be a lot of work for just one item, but please remember that the correlation coefficients need be calculated only once with most expense items of a semivariable nature and that to prepare a scatter chart for each such item can be more time-consuming than the method of least-squares calculations made with mechanical assistance.

ONLY ONE DEPARTMENTAL EXPENSE VOLUME BASE?

Some authors suggest that in the setting-up of a flexible budget, only one volume base should be used for all the variable expenses incurred within any one department. Glenn A. Welsch says, "in the case of departments having more than one type of output some common expression of activity must be established as a base or factor of variability. For example, one productive department may use direct labor hours, another productive department may use direct machine hours, and the repair department direct repair hours."[9]

This is certainly an ideal situation if it exists, as this volume unit is probably the one being used to absorb manufacturing overheads into the articles

[9] *Budgeting: Profit-Planning and Control*, p. 168.

being produced. However, my experience has been that the variable portion of some semivariable expense items has been found to bear little relationship to the common departmental volume base. While this base might be used to absorb all overhead expenses into the product, it is useless, for control purposes in a flexible budget, to use a formula which is based on a volume with which the expense item has very little correlation. Subsequent variances between an actual expense figure and the budget figure calculated from such a formula would have little meaning and could not be acted upon.

This experience is confirmed by an extract from the NACA Research Report, "The Analysis of Cost-Volume-Profit Relationships": "In some cases it is desirable to use separate units for different expenses incurred in a single cost center. For example, a company interviewed had found that in one cost center maintenance expense varies with the number of hours machines are operated but in the same cost center consumption of supplies varies with the number of yards of product produced."[10]

For the purposes of break-even analysis, all variable expenses must be related to some overall volume for the whole company; and for the absorption of variable expenses into products, they are related to some overall volume for each department. However, in each case the original division of expenses into the fixed and variable classifications must first be carried out in the manner described above, i.e., using the most suitable volume unit for each expense item. This is an important point which is often overlooked in practice and which is glossed over in much of the literature.

REFINEMENTS TO UNDERLYING FIGURES

Earlier, before the example given, it was indicated that certain refinements of data are necessary. These are now discussed. All apply, irrespective of the method used to separate the fixed and variable portions of any semivariable expense item, i.e., whether scatter charts, methods of the least squares, or any other method is used:

1. As variable expenses tend to vary with some physical volume, a base unit other than one expressed in dollars should be sought if possible. A volume base expressed in dollars—e.g., sales, orders received, direct labor cost, etc.,—is subject to price fluctuations; and in most cases, these are not reflected in the expense being examined.

2. Similarly, the expenses themselves could have been subject to price level changes over the period for which experience is reviewed. All past costs should be brought to current costs by using some suitable index, before commencing any work on the separation of elements. If this is not done, the fixed and variable portions arrived at will be a cross between current and past costs and will not, therefore, be accurate for future control or any other purpose. If it is found that the only suitable volume base is one expressed in dollars, then

[10] Pp. 56–57.

similar action will need be taken here, too, before commencing the preparation of a scatter chart or with the method of the least squares, etc. In any case the fixed and variable expense figures obtained by any separation procedure will need to be adjusted if future price level changes are expected.

3. Even when using some physical unit as the volume base, it must be remembered that these can be affected by efficiency factors. Where unusual inefficiency (or efficiency) is known to exist in any item included in the analysis work, this should first be adjusted if accurate answers are to be obtained. Similarly, any abnormal expense figures, such as those which have occurred during floods, strikes, etc., should be omitted from the calculations. If this is not done, incorrect bias will be included in the results.

4. Individuals responsible for each expense should be in accord with the expense formula calculated to measure it. The principles of responsibility accounting should apply as usual. It is necessary, therefore, for the volume unit selected to be one which is not only understood but also well known and easily measured and recorded. To incur much additional expense in the mere recording of some exotic volume, in order to accomplish separation of cost elements, would defeat the purpose of the whole exercise.

5. Care must be taken to ensure that data which applied to old methods of organization, production, and equipment, etc., are not included in the calculations.

6. As fixed expenses, including the fixed portions of semivariable expenses, tend to increase in a steps-and-stairs fashion as capacity increases, only data which relate to the same capacity range as the expected capacity of the department should be included in the fixed-variable separation analysis work. This can be a most important consideration with many items of expense—e.g., indirect labor.

7. The larger the sample of data included in the analysis work, the more accurate the result tends to be. This still assumes, of course, that only suitable and/or adjusted data are included.

ANOMALY OF NEGATIVE FIXED COST

When using the method of least squares, it sometimes happens that the calculations reveal a minus quantity for the fixed portion of an expense item. While this could indicate an error of some kind (either in the selection of the data included in the analysis work or in the calculations themselves), it often is quite in order—although difficult to explain to some levels of management. It occurs when an item of expense tends to increase at an increasing rate as capacity is extended. Examples could be selling expenses or overtime payments.

When plotted on a chart, such expense items in these circumstances are revealed as an upward-curving line. As the analysis work should include only data typical of the expected capacity, it will embrace items from one section of the curve only. The slope of this section of the curve is such that, if extedned back to the *Y*-axis, it will meet it below the origin of the chart, thus giving the minus quantity calculated. This does not mean that a profit would be earned if the capacity were reduced to zero. It merely means that for the purpose of calculating the budgeted expenses for any capacity within the expected range, accuracy will be obtained by including a minus fixed expense amount in the flexible budget formula. An example of this is shown in Exhibit 4.

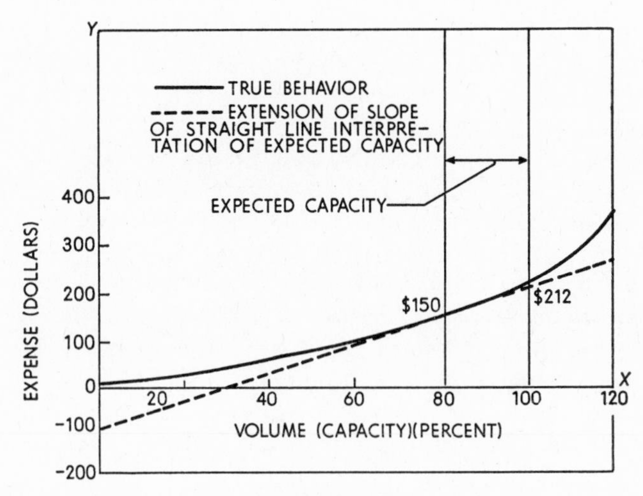

EXHIBIT 4. Occurrence of negative value for fixed costs.

In this example, it is expected that the company will operate at between 80 percent and 100 percent of capacity and that the expense in question will increase from $150 to $212 over this capacity interval. Although the expense will be increasing at a slightly increasing rate over this range, the general slope can be expressed as a straight line, which, when extended back to the *Y*-axis, gives a minus fixed cost of $100.

BETTER METHODS JUSTIFIED

The purpose of this paper has been to plead for the use of more accurate statistical methods in lieu of the popular scatter chart in the separation of fixed and variable portions of semivariable expenses, and for their use in the selection of volume bases in lieu of *ad hoc* selection methods.

To prepare scatter charts in detail takes much time. This time, in most cases, could be devoted to better and more accurate use of the calculation of objective data. Rough scatter charts have their place in the giving of a general impression and in the narrowing-down of the field to be given more detailed analysis work.

This has been the experience of the author in practice. It would seem that the more refined methods outlined are warranted in order to place reliance on control and decision-making tools such as flexible budgets, manufacturing expense variances in standard costing, direct costing, differential cost analysis, and break-even analysis.

35

In this article, multiple correlation analysis is used to determine the number of hours applied per unit (repair job) for several products when only one type of labor exists; the analysis also generates a reason for unproductive time. The general conditions for which multiple correlation is a useful analytic tool are then discussed.

COST FINDING THROUGH MULTIPLE CORRELATION ANALYSIS*†

Paul R. McClenon

MULTIPLE CORRELATION ANALYSIS will not seriously compete with established costing practices but under some circumstances will prove useful for developing cost estimates not determinable by other means. This paper presents a simple example in order to give accountants a glimpse of the technique and to enable them to recognize potential applications. Consultation with a statistician or a good textbook is urged.

Statistical analysts have long been acquainted with multiple correlation, but few accountants recognize it as a device for estimating unit costs. If total dollar costs for a number of time periods are known, along with quantity information about the various items which are related to the total cost, then multiple correlation analysis can furnish individual unit costs. The simplified illustration in this paper is followed by a brief discussion of the circumstances under which the technique may be useful, as well as by a description of the analytical process itself.

AN ILLUSTRATIVE NEED FOR COST INFORMATION

Your company has a small equipment repair shop which performs various kinds of overhauls, including office machines as needed. You have been approached by another company in town with a request that your shop undertake to overhaul the neighbor's electric calculating machines. Your shop has

* Reprinted from *Accounting Review*, July, 1963, pp. 540–47.

† Any views expressed in this paper are those of the author. They should not be interpreted as reflecting the views of the RAND Corporation or the official opinion or policy of any of its governmental or private research sponsors. Papers are reproduced by the RAND Corporation as a courtesy to members of its staff.

one standing job order for "overhaul of typewriters, adding machines, and calculators"; and there are two men who work primarily on this job order. The prospective customer wants to contract for a flat fee for each machine plus needed parts. This approach is satisfactory to your company, and you can establish the fee when you have a good estimate of the direct labor cost. You ask for a review of the recent accounting records. Your analyst points out that in recent weeks there has apparently been a trend toward quicker completion of jobs, on the basis of the facts shown in Table 1.

TABLE 1

Week	*Productive Hours*	*Units Finished*	*Hours per Unit*
1	64	20	3.2
2	64	22	2.9
3	53	19	2.8
4	54	20	2.7
5	51	19	2.7
6	57	22	2.6
7	53	21	2.5
8	49	20	2.4
	445	163	2.7

You call in the foreman of the shop to see whether a price based on an estimated three hours per machine will be reasonable. The foreman says that he thinks five hours would be more reasonable, because calculators are the hardest machines to work on. He thinks they usually take at least half a day to overhaul, but no detailed records have been thought necessary.

You don't want to undergo significant risk of loss on the proposed contract, but neither do you want to charge too much; the prospective customer has done favors for your company, and a valuable neighborly relationship has developed.

How can you find the approximate direct labor cost by machine type? A

TABLE 2

	Machines Overhauled			
Week	*Adding Machines*	*Type-writers*	*Calcu-lators*	*Total Hours*
1	5	7	8	64
2	7	9	6	64
3	9	5	5	53
4	9	7	4	54
5	8	8	3	51
6	9	10	3	57
7	9	10	2	53
8	9	10	1	49
	65	66	32	445

program of careful observation or record keeping starting now will not supply an answer in time. If your shop can supply quantity records by type of machine, you can use the information to estimate the time required for each kind. Assume that you get the data shown in Table 2.

A POSSIBLE HYPOTHESIS

The foreman has already suggested that calculators take about five hours each. If this is accepted as a good estimate, the total time of the past eight weeks may have been spent somewhat as follows:

Direct time:	
Calculators, 32 @ 5 hours	160 hours
Other machines, 131 @ 2 hours	262
Indirect time, 8 weeks @ 3 hours	24
Approximate total	446 hours

Is there any way to tell whether this is a good set of estimates? One way is to see if these estimates explain the observed actual situation in each of the eight weeks for which we have information. A comparison of the total hours which would be expected (if these estimates were reliable) with the hours actually reported is given in Table 3.

TABLE 3

	Hours		
Week	*Estimated*	*Actual*	*Difference*
1	67	64	3
2	65	64	1
3	56	53	3
4	55	54	1
5	50	51	−1
6	56	57	−1
7	51	53	−2
8	46	49	−3
	446	445	1

AN EVEN CLOSER FIT

A review of the above differences and of the record of completion by machine type suggests that an even closer set of estimates could be made if it were assumed that typewriters take a little longer than adding machines to overhaul, and that the foreman overstated the difficulty of calculators somewhat. A little trial-and-error work along these lines might suggest that the total reported time for the eight weeks was made up about as follows:

Direct time:	
65 adding machines @ 2 hours	130 hours
66 typewriters @ 2½ hours	165
32 calculators @ 4 hours	128
Indirect time, 8 weeks @ 2½ hours	22
	445 hours

These estimates, when applied to the information on a week-by-week basis, come fairly close to describing the time actually reported. (See Table 4.)

TABLE 4

Year	*Hours*		
	Estimated	*Actual*	*Difference*
1	62.25	64	−1.75
2	63.25	64	−0.75
3	53.25	53	0.25
4	54.25	54	0.25
5	50.75	51	−0.25
6	57.75	57	0.75
7	53.75	53	0.75
8	49.75	49	0.75
	445.00	445	0.00

These differences are quite small, but one can see that they could be further reduced. The estimates seem to get too high as the number of calculators in the mix gets lower; should we try 4½ hours for calculators? To do so, we would have to reduce the estimate for one or both of the other machines or for the estimated provision for nonproductive time.

HOW SHOULD WE SELECT THE BEST ANSWER?

Repetitive trials entail a lot of arithmetic, and we don't even have an obvious way to decide how to adjust from one trial to the next or how to decide when to be satisfied. We need a criterion for judging the effectiveness of a proposed set of estimates in explaining what actually occurred. The situation is very much like the one we often meet when we have made a scatter diagram for observed cost-value relationships. How, in such cases, can we select the *best* line to represent the relationship? The fairly well accepted technique for calculating a *regression line* through such a scatter diagram is called the *least squares* method. It minimizes the squares of the differences between the estimated and the actual costs. In determining a line through a cost-volume scatter diagram, we need to select two values: an estimated overhead constant and a direct cost per unit.

For the service shop time problem, we can use a similar approach, for which we need four values: one (which may, if appropriate, be estimated to be zero, but which may in fact be fairly high) which represents any constant unproductive time charge or "overhead," and a direct time allowance for each of the three kinds of machines. The standard statistical technique for multiple correlation analysis will, if applied to the available data, supply the four needed values on a least squares basis. The specific computation shown in the Appendix furnishes these explanations of the actual time charges of the past eight weeks:

Direct time:
Adding machines, 65 @ 1.456 hours . . . . 94.64 hours
Typewriters, 66 @ 2.407 hours 158.86
Calculators, 32 @ 4.016 hours 128.51
Indirect time, 8 weeks @ 7.878 hours 63.02
Total estimated time . . . . 445.03 hours

Application of these unit estimates to the actual quantity information on a week-by-week basis comes very close to "predicting" the actual hours reported each week.

The detailed display in Table 5 is rounded to hundredths of hours at each entry; the biggest difference is about 10 minutes.

TABLE 5

	Estimated Hours					
Week	*Adding Machines*	*Typewriters*	*Calculators*	*Nonproductive*	*Total*	*Actual Hours*
1	7.28	16.85	32.13	7.88	64.14	64
2	10.19	21.66	24.10	7.88	63.83	64
3	13.10	12.04	20.08	7.88	53.10	53
4	13.10	16.85	16.06	7.88	53.89	54
5	11.65	19.26	12.05	7.88	50.84	51
6	13.10	24.07	12.05	7.88	57.10	57
7	13.10	24.07	8.03	7.88	53.08	53
8	13.10	24.07	4.02	7.88	49.07	49
	94.62	158.87	128.52	63.04	445.05	445

MEANING OF THESE RESULTS

When the observed actual total time is explained this way, we almost have to accept the unit estimates as the basis for any proposed decision. The overhaul of a calculator apparently takes just about four hours. But this same set of time estimates shows an overhead of almost eight hours per week on this job order. Management improvement on this point may be indicated; at present, this loss factor should also be considered in establishing a price to charge for the service to be rendered the neighbor company.

RELIABILITY OF THE ESTIMATES

Any set of numbers may be subjected to correlation analysis in much the same fashion as for the data used in this example. Least squares estimates of unit costs, of time standards, and of other types can be derived from historical data. If the computational work is done correctly, the estimated values will be better than (in that the sum of the squared differences obtained will be less than those obtained from) any other set of estimates. But sometimes the best isn't very good. A regression line used to represent the trend through a scatter diagram was mentioned earlier. If the individual readings on a scatter diagram are widely dispersed, we can still determine the line of best fit, but we recognize that the wide scatter shows a poor correlation; in such cases, we recognize a considerable uncertainty in using the line for estimating. Real situations will never give as nearly "perfect" results as those in the artificial illustration used here.

Statisticians like us to judge the reliability of estimates by determining for each the *standard error* associated with it. We are then expected to recognize that the specific estimate is within a band of uncertainty whose width is determined by the standard error of the estimate and the degree of confidence desired. Some accountants find such statistical concepts hard to deal with. It is here suggested that we can defer the formal recognition of statistical measures of reliability. As an early step in the long-range program to get better acquainted with statistical tools, we can try to use estimates on the basis of pragmatic standards of reliability. We should recognize the desirability of trying to understand the statistician's way of deciding about the limitations of his results. But we are well advised to get acquainted with the benefits before we worry unduly about limitations.

POSSIBLE APPLICATIONS

Under what circumstances can correlation analysis be useful to accountants? Let there be no misunderstanding on one basic point. This paper does not suggest that statistical analysis of data is able to supply better information than can job engineering or regular cost accounting techniques. What is suggested here is that there are circumstances where these preferred techniques were not used, where some data are available, and where decisions must be made promptly; in those instances, correlation analysis may be useful.

Unit costs may be desired where more than one type of product is in one cost pool. If total costs for the group as well as quantities for each of the product types are known, then correlation analysis can furnish least squares estimates of unit costs by types. The illustration given above shows how this is done. (Dollars of cost could be substituted for hours of productive labor without any impact on the analytical approach.) Such unit cost estimates may be useful in making pricing decisions or make-or-buy decisions, or simply in deciding whether more expensive analysis is worthwhile.

Suppose, for example, that a shop produces three kinds of castings which are quite similar but which require slightly different finishing processes. All three are produced in one cost center. If the official accounting records show a rising trend in unit prices, is the change based on a change in efficiency or simply on a shift in product mix? Individual unit prices, derived by multiple correlation analysis, can shed useful light on this question. (Analysis of actual operations could, of course, also shed useful light. Analysis of existing data may be cheaper and may supply explanations adequate to remove the need for more thorough investigations.)

Multiple correlation analysis can furnish useful unit cost estimates only if certain prerequisites are available. One thing needed is a reasonable quantity of data. (The illustration in this paper used data for only eight weeks in the interest of displaying in the Appendix all the details and enabling the reader to duplicate the computations if desired. Such a small sample cannot usually give results which can be used with much confidence.)

Another prerequisite is reason to believe that all the data used are in fact from one "universe." In other words, all available clues about the unit costs to be determined should be considered before there is resort to this sort of analysis. If there has been any known change in costs (such as an engineering change or a relevant price change) during the period covered by the available data, there would be little reason to compute estimated "average" unit costs.

One important requirement relates to work in process. The available quantity information (usually units completed or shipped) must be related to costs incurred. If the work in process is significant and its composition by product type fluctuates, then it may be desirable to modify the available quantity data to show "equivalent" quantities in the periods when the costs were incurred. The difficulty of doing this job well limits multiple correlation's utility; it will mostly be helpful where work in process is insignificant.

DESCRIPTION OF THE TECHNIQUE EMPLOYED

The basic procedure followed in deriving the estimates used in the illustrative case presented above are here described. The Technical Appendix displays the detailed steps for the benefit of those who like to follow specific examples.

The analysis starts with the assumption that there are fairly stable unit costs (in the illustration, costs in terms of hours required) which are as yet unknown but are to be found. We make a statement (using these unknown unit costs) in a form which is almost a definition: "The total cost in any period is made up of the overhead plus the unit cost of each product type times the number of units of that type." We recognize that we have available a number (eight in the illustration) of different observations, in each of which this basic statement should be true. Adding all the observations together furnishes what is called the first "normal equation." When we want to find four unknown values, we need four different equations using them. As many normal equations as are needed can be created by multiplying each observation by one of the known quantities during the process of summation. In our illustrative case, we create four normal equations which summarize the total hours and the actual quantities completed by types in terms of the four unknown values. Simultaneous solution of the equations gives the desired unknown values.

The direct solution of a system of simultaneous equations can be readily described by using *determinants;* these are square arrays of numbers which represent many factors multiplied together. A computer can, at this point, be helpful. (With four unknowns, direct solution requires the evaluation of two determinants of 16 elements each. The evaluation of each of the determinants involves 24 separate multiplications of four factors each. Then the products must be correctly combined, half being positive and half negative. Without a computer, one would not usually use this approach, even though the work for the second, third, and fourth unknowns will be a little easier.)

For manual solution an algebraic sleight-of-hand technique—illustrated in the Appendix—may be used to reduce the number of equations and unknowns. And for manual work, it may often help to round the available data into small numbers. (Costs may, for example, be shown in hundred or thousands of dollars in order to save arithmetic.) Manual work almost demands the use of special clerical techniques for checking; a crossfooting approach is illustrated.

CONCLUSION—ANOTHER USEFUL TOOL

This paper has tried to show that analyses of multiple correlation might, under some circumstances, supply cost estimates which could not be obtained from the same data by traditional accounting techniques. Multiple correlation analysis is therefore a possibly useful tool. But some tools are sharp, and novices should be careful with them. Accountants should obtain adequate assistance from statistics textbooks or from trained statisticians in deriving cost estimates of this sort. Employed reasonably, this tool may furnish information useful for management planning and decision making.

TECHNICAL APPENDIX

The following material displays the procedures followed in obtaining the four costs used in the attached article. There is no need to read this except to help understand the detailed processes; most testbooks also include examples.

Assign Symbols

Unknowns to be found:

W = Indirect time or "overhead" (in hours) per week
X = Time (in hours) for overhauling an adding machine
Y = Time (in hours) for overhauling a typewriter
Z = Time (in hours) for overhauling a calculator

Data available:

A = Adding machines overhauled in the week
B = Typewriters overhauled in the week
C = Calculators overhauled in the week
T = Total hours reported on this work for the week

Normal Equations

The basic truth:

$$T = XA + YB + ZC + W$$

Adding eight observations gives

$$\Sigma T = X\Sigma A + Y\Sigma B + Z\Sigma C + 8W \tag{1}$$

Multiplication during the summation process gives

$$\Sigma AT = X\Sigma A^2 + Y\Sigma AB + Z\Sigma AC + W\Sigma A \tag{2}$$
$$\Sigma BT = X\Sigma AB + Y\Sigma B^2 + Z\Sigma BC + W\Sigma B \tag{3}$$
$$\Sigma CT = X\Sigma AC + Y\Sigma BC + Z\Sigma C^2 + W\Sigma C \tag{4}$$

Finding the Summations

BASIC ARRAY

Week	*A*	*B*	*C*	*T*	*Check*
1	5	7	8	64	84
2	7	9	6	64	86
3	9	5	5	53	72
4	9	7	4	54	74
5	8	8	3	51	70
6	9	10	3	57	79
7	9	10	2	53	74
8	9	10	1	49	69
	65	66	32	445	608

MULTIPLICATION BY *A*

Week	A^2	*AB*	*AC*	*AT*	*A-Check*
1	25	35	40	320	420
2	49	63	42	448	602
3	81	45	45	477	648
4	81	63	36	486	666
5	64	64	24	408	560
6	81	90	27	513	711
7	81	90	18	447	666
8	81	90	9	441	621
	543	540	241	3,570	4,894

MULTIPLICATION BY *B*

Week	*AB*	B^2	*BC*	*BT*	*B-Check*
1		49	56	448	588
2		81	54	576	774
3		25	25	265	360
4		49	28	378	518
5		64	24	408	560
6		100	30	570	790
7		100	20	530	740
8		100	10	490	690
	540	568	247	3,665	5,020

MULTIPLICATION BY C

Week	*AC*	*BC*	C^2	*CT*	*C-Check*
1.			64	512	672
2.			36	384	516
3.			25	265	360
4.			16	216	296
5.			9	153	210
6.			9	171	237
7.			4	106	148
8.			1	49	69
	241	247	164	1,856	2,508

Substitute Values

$$
\begin{aligned}
&(1) \quad & 445 &= 65X + 66Y + 32Z + 8W \\
&(2) \quad & 3{,}570 &= 543X + 430Y + 241Z + 65W \\
&(3) \quad & 3{,}665 &= 540X + 568Y + 247Z + 66W \\
&(4) \quad & 1{,}865 &= 241X + 247Y + 164Z + 32W
\end{aligned}
$$

Obtaining Summations of Deviations When Gross Summations Are Known

1. Let A = actual quantity, A' = mean quantity, and a = deviation from mean.
2. By definition, $a = A - A'$.
3. Consider the typical term needed: Σab:

$$\Sigma ab = \Sigma[(A - A')(B - B')]$$

4. Expand the right-hand expression:

$$\Sigma ab = \Sigma(AB - A'B - AB' + A'B')$$

5. Simplify by bringing the known arithmetic means outside the summation:

$$\Sigma ab = \Sigma AB - A'\Sigma B - B'\Sigma A + NA'B'$$

6. By definition of the mean: $\Sigma A = NA'$, $\Sigma B = NB'$, and we can rewrite the expression:

$$\Sigma ab = \Sigma AB - \frac{\Sigma A \Sigma B}{N} - \frac{\Sigma A \Sigma B}{N} + \frac{\Sigma A \Sigma B}{N}$$

7. The last two terms cancel each other, and we can say

$$
\begin{aligned}
\Sigma ab &= \Sigma AB - \frac{\Sigma A \Sigma B}{N} = \Sigma AB - B'\Sigma A \\
&= \Sigma AB - A'\Sigma B
\end{aligned}
$$

8. The foregoing is a generally useful expression. In the special case where $a = b$, we have

$$\Sigma a^2 = \Sigma A^2 - A'\Sigma A$$

Three "Normal" Equations in Terms of Deviations

$$\begin{aligned}
&(1) \quad \Sigma at = X\Sigma a^2 + Y\Sigma ab + Z\Sigma ac \\
&(2) \quad \Sigma bt = X\Sigma ab + Y\Sigma b + Z\Sigma bc \\
&(3) \quad \Sigma ct = X\Sigma ac + Y\Sigma bc + Z\Sigma c
\end{aligned}$$

Finding Numeric Values for Three Equations

First, find arithmetic means:

$$A' = 65 \div 8 = 8\tfrac{1}{8} \qquad C' = 32 \div 8 = 4$$
$$B' = 66 \div 8 = 8\tfrac{1}{4} \qquad T' = 445 \div 8 = 55\tfrac{5}{8}$$

Multiplied by A:

				Check
$\Sigma A^2 = 543$	$\Sigma AB = 540$	$\Sigma AC = 241$	$\Sigma AT = 3570$	4894
$A'\Sigma A = 528\frac{1}{8}$	$A'\Sigma B = 536\frac{1}{4}$	$A'\Sigma C = 260$	$A'\Sigma T = 3615\frac{5}{8}$	4940
$\Sigma a^2 = 14\frac{7}{8}$	$\Sigma ab = 3\frac{3}{4}$	$\Sigma ac = -19$	$\Sigma at = -45\frac{5}{8}$	−46

Multiplied by B:

				Check
$\Sigma AB = 540$	$\Sigma B^2 = 568$	$\Sigma BC = 247$	$\Sigma BT = 3665$	5020
$B'\Sigma A = 536\frac{1}{4}$	$B'\Sigma B = 554\frac{1}{2}$	$B'\Sigma B = 264$	$B'\Sigma T = 3671\frac{1}{4}$	5016
$\Sigma ab = 3\frac{3}{4}$	$\Sigma b^2 = 23\frac{1}{2}$	$\Sigma bc = -17$	$\Sigma bt = -6\frac{1}{4}$	4

Multiplied by C:

				Check
$\Sigma AC = 241$	$\Sigma BC = 247$	$\Sigma C^2 = 164$	$\Sigma CT = 1856$	2508
$C'\Sigma A = 260$	$C'\Sigma B = 264$	$C'\Sigma C = 128$	$C'\Sigma T = 1780$	2432
$\Sigma ac = -19$	$\Sigma bc = -17$	$\Sigma c = 36$	$\Sigma ct = 76$	76

Substitute Values in Three Equations

$$\begin{aligned}
&(1) \quad -45\tfrac{5}{8} = 14\tfrac{7}{8}X + 3\tfrac{3}{4}Y - 19Z \\
&(2) \quad -6\tfrac{1}{4} = 3\tfrac{3}{4}X + 23\tfrac{1}{2}Y - 17Z \\
&(3) \quad -76 = -19X - 17Y + 36Z
\end{aligned}$$

Direct Solution

a)	$2023X +$	$510Y - 2584Z =$	$-6{,}205$	(equation 1 times 136)
b)	$570X +$	$3572Y - 2584Z =$	-950	(equation 2 times 152)
c)	$1453X -$	$3062Y =$	$-5{,}255$	(equation *a* minus equation *b*)
d)	$135X +$	$846Y - 612Z =$	-225	(equation 2 times 36)

$$
\begin{array}{lllll}
e) & -323X - & 289Y + 612Z = & 1{,}292 & \text{(equation 3 times 17)} \\
f) & -188X + & 557Y \quad = & 1{,}067 & \text{(equation } d \text{ plus equation } e) \\
g) & 809{,}321X - 1{,}705{,}534Y & = & 2{,}927{,}035 & \text{(equation } c \text{ times 557)} \\
h) & -575{,}656X + 1{,}705{,}534Y & = & 3{,}267{,}154 & \text{(equation } f \text{ times 3062)} \\
i) & 233{,}665X & = & 340{,}119 & \text{(equation } g \text{ plus equation } h)
\end{array}
$$

Therefore:

$$
\begin{aligned}
X &= 1.45558 \\
Y &= 2.40691 \\
Z &= 4.01589
\end{aligned}
$$

(Detailed steps are not shown for last two; using value established for X, the work is easier.)

Back to the Four Normal Equations

Solve for the constant W:

$$
(1)\quad
\begin{aligned}
445 &= 65X + 66Y + 322 + 8W \\
445 &= 94.61 + 158.86 + 128.51 + 8W \\
63.02 &= 8W \\
7.8775 &= W
\end{aligned}
$$

Substitute all four values in the second normal equation:

$$
(2)\quad
\begin{aligned}
\Sigma AT &= X\Sigma A^2 + Y\Sigma AB + Z\Sigma AC + W\Sigma A \\
3570 &= 543X + 540Y + 241Z + 65W \\
3569.9 &= 790.3 + 1299.8 + 967.8 + 512.0
\end{aligned}
$$

36

The author discusses traditional cost projection techniques, including methods based upon recent experience data, similar parts data, and engineering standards and references. He then discusses the nature and applicability of learning curve theory to cost projection problems, and describes the learning curve formula and the computation of parameters from actual data.

*THE LEARNING CURVE—A BASIC COST PROJECTION TOOL**

Marvin L. Taylor

ANYONE MANAGING an enterprise, whether it be a one-man operation or a large corporation, is faced with the common problem of projecting costs. When it is realized that a business exists to earn a profit and that every sound decision must serve this purpose, it becomes easy to appreciate the importance of cost projections as a basis for decision making. Since this is a universal problem, it is not surprising that several methods of projecting costs have been developed and are in regular use in business today. These techniques are so common that they are sometimes used without being recognized or considered "cost projections." Nevertheless, the answers developed predict the effect of management decisions and actions, and so are true projections.

For many years, there have been three traditional techniques used for cost projection:

1. *Recent experience data:* Companies in mass production industries have developed tested methods of determining the costs of their operations. Examination of these costs and correction for known changes to come, plus an allowance for contingencies, permit very accurate forecasts of future costs of producing the same part.
2. *Similar parts data:* If an old part on which costs are available is similar to a new one on which a projected cost is desired, we can make dependable predictions by examining the cost of the similar part and adjusting for known changes and contingencies. Projections based on similar parts are slightly more hazardous than those based on the same part.
3. *Engineering standards and references:* When no data on the exact or a similar part are available, cost projections can still be made by analyzing the operations

* Reprinted from *NAA Bulletin*, published by the National Association of Accountants, February, 1961, pp. 21–26.

called for and applying tested standards to the operations. This technique is regularly used in job shop operations and in the construction industry.

Upon examination of these accepted methods of cost projection, it becomes apparent that the use of recent experience data on the same part or the use of similar parts data is ideally suited to mass production industries. Such projections assume a basis of dependable and consistent data. The use of engineering standards and references, on the other hand, obviously meets the needs of the construction companies or others which must make one item or a very small number of items of a complex nature.

THE LEARNING CURVE THEORY

Some industries fall into an area between mass and single-item production. For example, the aircraft industry produces relatively small numbers of very complicated items. Cost projections under these conditions require consideration of a fourth element, not necessary when dealing with mass or single-item production problems. This fourth element has been termed "learning."

Historically, the idea of an improvement or learning curve was first published in 1936 by T. P. Wright. A number of writers have published articles on the subject since. Of note is the work of J. R. Crawford of Lockheed Aircraft Company and a publication of the Stanford Research Institute entitled "Stanford Learning Curve." Data have been collected by the Air Force over a number of years which support the learning curve theory as applied to large airframe sections. Application of the theory to comparatively small machining and assembly jobs is a more recent development.

"Learning" is the expression of the thought that "every time you do a job, you will do it better than the last time." This idea is the entire key to the learning curve theory of cost projection. At this time, we should answer some questions concerning this idea.

DOES LEARNING ACTUALLY EXIST?

In answering the question of the reality of learning, first let us examine our own personal reaction to the thought. Each one of us feels that each time we do a job, we do it a little better than the last time; so on a personal basis, we find no rejection of this theory. Considering the question on a national level, we find again that, as far back as records are available, this country has constantly improved its rate of productivity; so here again, we find confirmation of the idea that every time you do a job, you do it a little better.

Looking now at a specific industry, we find that the manufacture of cans has continued to improve with the same basic equipment and methods from a speed of about 250 cans per minute in 1940 to a speed of over 500 cans per minute in 1955. The same trend has continued in this industry since 1906, so that it seems evident that "learning" has existed in this industry over an extended period of time and is continuing today.

Therefore, we can make the assumption that learning will continue indefinitely, provided the forces that result in learning continue to be applied.

WHAT ARE THE FORCES THAT RESULT IN LEARNING?

When we think of the forces that cause learning, it must be in terms of the basic thought already stated, "Every time you do a job, you do it a little better." The forces that affect learning include:

1. *Man on the job:* By this, we mean the individual who physically performs an operation to produce a product. It is obvious that this man's training, experience, and skill will have an effect on learning. Not quite so obvious but of significant importance are all the related personnel whose coordinated efforts are required to complete an operation: The material-handling and supply people affect learning; inspection personnel can at times have a dominant effect; maintenance and service personnel are a part of the total job.
2. *Supervision and staff:* By this, we mean the direct supervisors on the floor who concentrate on the seven basics of foremanship—men, material, machines, cost, quality, safety, and housekeeping—as well as the higher echelons of management and related staffs. The work of this group as it plans for the proper coordination of effort and provides solutions to problems has a definite effect on learning.
3. *Methods:* How our work is performed has an obvious effect on learning. Since the items we make are newly created designs at the start of a program, it is to be expected that the original concept of "how to do it" is imperfect. The original tooling, facilities, and processes require review and alteration to more effective methods as a program gets under way. The "convenience tool" developed on the floor can have a significant effect on learning. Continuing reevaluation to adjust to changing work load and techniques is essential to learning.
4. *Production rate:* When a program is scheduled at a predictable rate over a reasonably long period of time, significant learning will be achieved as the job gathers momentum. Most rapid improvement will occur when the production unit is fully loaded.
5. *Lot size:* When an item, because of its nature or schedule, must be batched and run as a group, the advantages of continuous production are lost. Even so, attention to setup time, cycle time, splits, storage and handling, and the other factors entering into economic lot size will result in learning through control of lot size.

These are forces which, if applied continuously, will result in continuous learning.

THE LEARNING CURVE FORMULA

The idea that "every time you do a job, you do it a little better" requires further refinement to be of maximum use. The idea must be expressed in numbers if it is to have any practical value in cost projections.

People with a knowledge of mathematics can help us on this problem. However, in so doing, we find that the basic idea must be restricted; instead of talking about doing any job a little better each time we do it, the idea must be narrowed to "*every time you double the quantity, the unit hours will be reduced by a fixed percentage.*" When we define "learning" in this manner, we can write a formula to express the idea[1] which, when plotted on arithmetical graph paper, appears as shown in Exhibit 1.

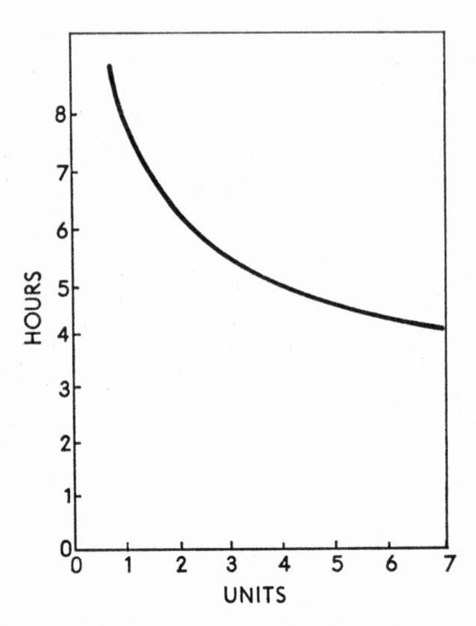

EXHIBIT 1. The learning curve—arithmetical graph paper.

HOURS
10 9 8 7 6 5 4 3 2 1
1 2 3 4 5 6 7
UNITS

EXHIBIT 2. The learning curve—log-log graph paper.

The hours will drop very rapidly at first and later reach a point at which reduction is very slow as the number of units increases. The very same formula when plotted on log-log paper is shown in Exhibit 2.[2] The use of log-log paper has two important advantages:

1. It permits easy determination of learning rate when actual data are plotted.
2. It provides a graphical means of observing the actual learning rate in comparison with the projected rate and so verifying the accuracy of the projection.

---

[1] For those interested, the formula is $Y = KX^{-N}$, where Y = unit hours, K = hours for the first unit, X = unit number, and N = expression of learning. The most bothersome element of this formula is the exponential (X^{-N}). Although it can be translated into numbers by use of logarithms, this tedious and unnecessary job can be avoided by using tables which show all of the values of X and N that are likely to be needed.

[2] The mathematical proof is simple:
Step 1. Basic formula: $Y = KX^{-N}$.
Step 2. Take log of both sides: $\log Y = \log K - N \log X$.
Step 3. Write formula for straight line: $Y = MX + B$.
Step 4. The equations in steps 2 and 3 are of the same form; therefore, it follows that formula 1 will be a straight line when plotted on log-log paper.

Experience in the use of logarithms is not required in making cost projections. The one point of importance here is that the learning curve formula is a straight line on log-log paper.

APPROVAL TO APPLICATION

Now we should gain some idea of the effect of this formula. Let us assume that we know a job will improve at an 80 percent rate and that 100 hours will be required to produce the first unit. The learning curve formula says, "every time we double the quantity, the unit hours will be reduced by a fixed percentage." Exhibit 3 shows the results.

	Quantity		*Unit Hours*
	1		100.0
Doubled, it becomes	2	Unit hours × 80% become	80.0
" " "	4	" " " " "	64.0
" " "	8	" " " " "	51.2
" " "	16	" " " " "	40.9
" " "	32	" " " " "	32.7
" " "	64	" " " " "	26.2
" " "	128	" " " " "	20.9
" " "	256	" " " " "	16.8
" " "	512	" " " " "	13.5
" " "	1,024	" " " " "	10.7

EXHIBIT 3. Effect of an 80 percent learning curve.

It may seem a little startling to seriously expect to achieve a reduction from 100 hours down to 10.7 hours per unit in 1,024 units. However, actual case records show that improvement of this magnitude can be expected.

Once a learning curve has been constructed for a particular program, management has a graphic tool that provides the normal advantages derived from routine cost projections. By merely reading from the charts, answers can be readily obtained to questions such as

1. What will the unit hours be at unit *X*? At unit *Y*?
2. What will the cumulative average hours per unit be at unit *X*?
3. At what unit will the program break even?

GROWING ACCEPTANCE

The learning curve theory has proved itself to be a valuable cost projection tool in industries that fall into an area between mass production and single-item production. With the wide acceptance of this method, particularly in the aircraft field, the learning curve must be ranked with our traditional cost projection techniques.

37

The application of the learning curve technique to budgeting is illustrated with a specific numerical example. This analysis includes the determination of the break-even sales price for the contract, the manpower needed for the established production schedule, and the forecasting of work-in-process inventories.

*LEARNING CURVE TECHNIQUES FOR MORE PROFITABLE CONTRACTS**

Ronald Brenneck

THE LEARNING CURVE has proved to be an invaluable tool for pricing purposes. It is of equal importance in conveying to production personnel what is expected of them and to top management the probability of production achieving these goals. When management has committed itself to manufacture a product for a given sales price, the agreement must be translated into a workable measure of production task, namely, direct labor hours allowed per unit. It is important at this point that management use a consistent mathematical approach in evaluating the actual experience in relationship to quotation hours. The learning curve is just such a tool, which can provide many of the answers to management's questions if valid information is available for analysis. Examples can be readily cited. When a portion of a given contract is complete, profit measurement in the form of break-even analyses is required. It provides information to management as to how the shop must be budgeted in order to achieve the overall goal of a normal profit. This budget should be presented to the manufacturing division of a company in the form of a learning curve. The production staff should be provided with a breakdown of manpower requirements by division or department to achieve the requirement set forth by the budget curve. This will enable the production department to evaluate its work load in relation to other contracts in process, so that the personnel department may be advised if additional employees may be needed to accomplish the task. An important by-product of manpower requirements analysis is the evaluation of inventory in process, so that

* Reprinted from *NAA Bulletin*, published by the National Association of Accountants, July, 1959, pp. 59–69.

management can provide proper financing to carry the contract to completion without undue strain on the financial resources of the company.

FOR CONTRACT SALES PRICES AND PRODUCTION COST GOALS

The average unit direct labor hours built into a unit selling price are usually based on a learning curve positioned on the graph by estimated standard hours factored for realization either at unit 1 or some subsequent unit on the curve. By realization, we mean the ratio of standard hours to the anticipated actual production hours at a given unit expressed as a percentage. The unit number at which this realization is set is determined by management's evaluation based on past experience as to what performance can be expected of the production staff for the task at hand. Take, for example, the data shown in Table 1.

The goal to be achieved was 55 percent realization, based on a standard of 35 hours per unit by unit 100. This point was then backed up an 80 percent learning curve to arrive at projected hours for the first unit. Using learning curve formulas, the average quotation hours for 50 units amounted to 125 hours per unit.

These calculations can be summarized as follows (Exhibit 1):

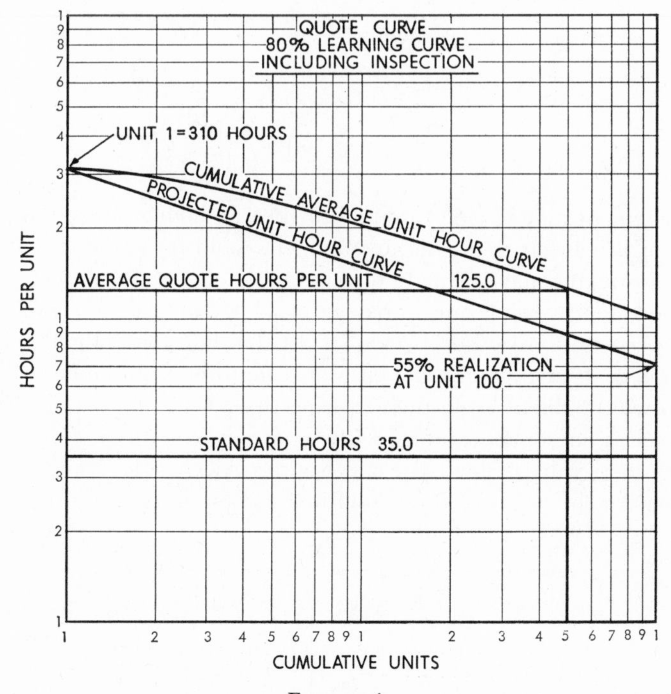

EXHIBIT 1.

TABLE 1

UNIT PRICE BREAKDOWN FOR 50 UNITS

Direct labor hours		125.0
Direct labor amount	$2.50	$ 312.50
Factory burden	3.50	437.50
Direct material		467.50
Outside production		120.00
Engineering and tool maintenance	0.90	112.50
Factory cost	$6.90	$ 1,450.00
Selling and administrative expense	0.58	72.50
Total cost	$7.48	$ 1,522.50
Profit		152.25
Unit selling price		$ 1,674.75
Total contract value		$83,737.50

1. $\text{Projected hours at unit 100} = \dfrac{\text{Standard hours}}{\text{Percent realization}} = \dfrac{35}{55} = 63.6$ Production hours

   $+ 10\%$ Inspection $= 6.4$

   70.0

2. $$\text{Unit hours at unit 1} = \frac{\text{Unit hours at unit 100}}{\text{Unit value at 100 for an 80\% curve}} = \frac{70}{0.226} = 310$$

3. $$\text{Average hours per unit for 50 units} = \frac{\text{Unit hours at unit 1} \times \text{Cumulative factor for 50 units on 80\% learning curve}}{50}$$

or

$$\text{Average unit hours} = \frac{310 \times 20.12}{50} = 125 \text{ hours per unit}$$

Management may decide to establish the 125-hour unit average as shop budget, or if it is felt that a tighter budget should be set for incentive purposes, adjustments may be made to these hours. Once the budget hours are established, the learning curve may be used to calculate budget hours by unit for presentation to shop personnel. In the shop the budget is allocated by division or department on the basis of manpower requirements, the detail of which will be discussed in the following pages.

As soon as one or more units of the contract have been completed, it is necessary to reevaluate the quote curve with respect to slope and position on the graph. In the example the actual hours for the first eight units were as follows:

Unit No.	*Actual Hours*	*Unit No.*	*Actual Hours*
1	550	5	245
2	350	6	210
3	315	7	215
4	280	8	190

The actual hours indicate either that the task—i.e., standard hours—was underestimated or that the shop may not be able to achieve the required performance. The slope of the actual experience indicates a 70 percent curve to be a better approximation of shop performance when plotted on a graph.

While the shop required more hours to make the first units than anticipated, the rate of improvement indicates that better realization will be attained by the end of the contract than the original quote curve. In this case, however, the higher rate of improvement is not enough to offset the excessive hours for the first units on an overall contract basis. It may be management's

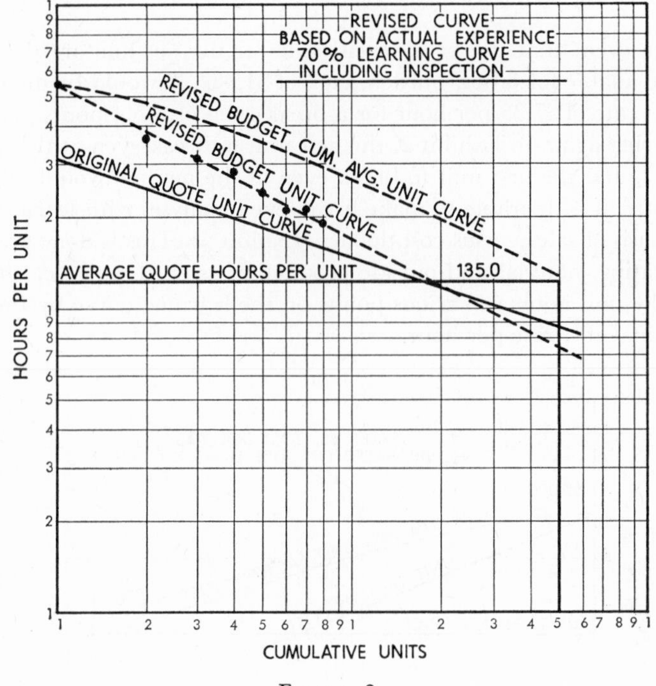

EXHIBIT 2.

decision to reestablish the budget curve hours to the newly established trend, or even less, in an effort to make the shop absorb all the excessive hours by the end of the contract. In the example the trend indicated by the actual experience would then establish the revised budget curve.

Once the budget curve is established, management can be provided with important information relative to the financial outcome of the contract. In the example the budget cumulative average unit hour curve intersects unit 50 at 135 hours per unit (Exhibit 2), or 10 hours per unit over the quote hours. On the basis of a $6.90 factory cost rate per hour, the loss of profit would amount to $69 per unit, or $3,450 for the contract. The first unit to make the quoted profit, the intersection of the average unit quote hour line with the projected unit curve line, would be unit 18. The intersection of the budget cumulative average unit curve line with the average unit quote hour line indicates that the total order quantity would have to be increased to 59 units in order to make quotation profit on a contract basis. Frequently, management wants to know the first unit to break even on the unit price. The break-even hours can be calculated as follows:

Unit selling price	$1,674.75
Less: Material outside production	587.50
Dollars available for labor, burden, engineering, etc.	$1,087.25

Unit hours to break even at the gross line ($1,087.25 ÷ $6.90 rate per hour) 157.6

In the event that the break-even hours at the net line are desired, the dollars available for labor, burden, etc., of $1,087.25 would be divided by a total cost rate of $7.25 per hour for a break-even of 145.4 hours per unit.

Referring again to Exhibit 2, the first unit to break even at the gross line is unit 12, and the first unit to break even at the net line would be unit 14. Frequently, it is desirable to make break-even analyses with learning curves on the basis of sales versus cost dollars (Exhibit 3). This is done graphically by indicating material and outside production as fixed expense, and multiplying the unit hours at various points on the learning curve by the factory cost or total cost rate per hour.

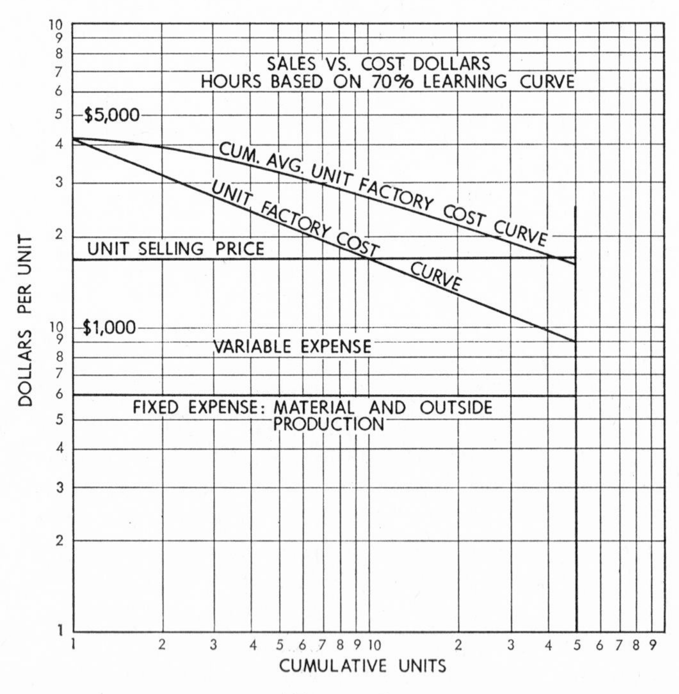

EXHIBIT 3.

In the example the sales dollars do not offset the factory cost dollars until unit 34. It is important to note that the unit factory cost curve would not be a 70 percent learning curve if the actual slope were to be measured. It is closer to being a 76 percent learning rate. The curve decreased in slope in conversion from hours to dollars, due to the addition of material and outside production as a constant. In actual practice, material does follow a curve to some extent, due to improved usage of material, reduction of scrap, and outside production costs decrease due to vendor improvement. However, to simplify calculations, this is generally not taken into account.

FOR ARRIVING AT MANPOWER REQUIREMENTS

Once a shop budget curve has been established by management, it is necessary to determine the manpower required to maintain the proposed production schedules. The following information is needed to make this analysis:

1. Shop budget learning curve
2. Releasing policy for details and lot-ordered subassemblies
3. Delivery schedule for shipment of end item

This procedure may best be illustrated by an example (Exhibit 4). Assume an 80 percent assembly budget curve with unit 1 of 40,000 hours, and an 80

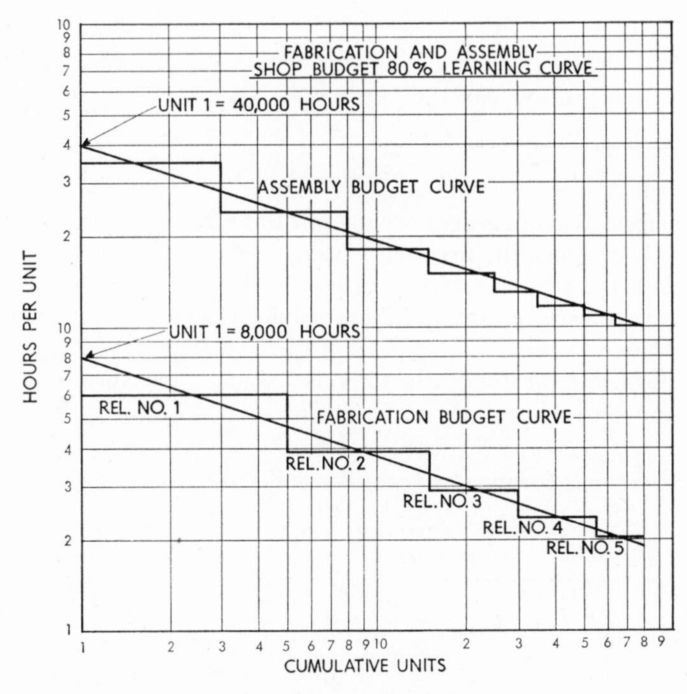

EXHIBIT 4.

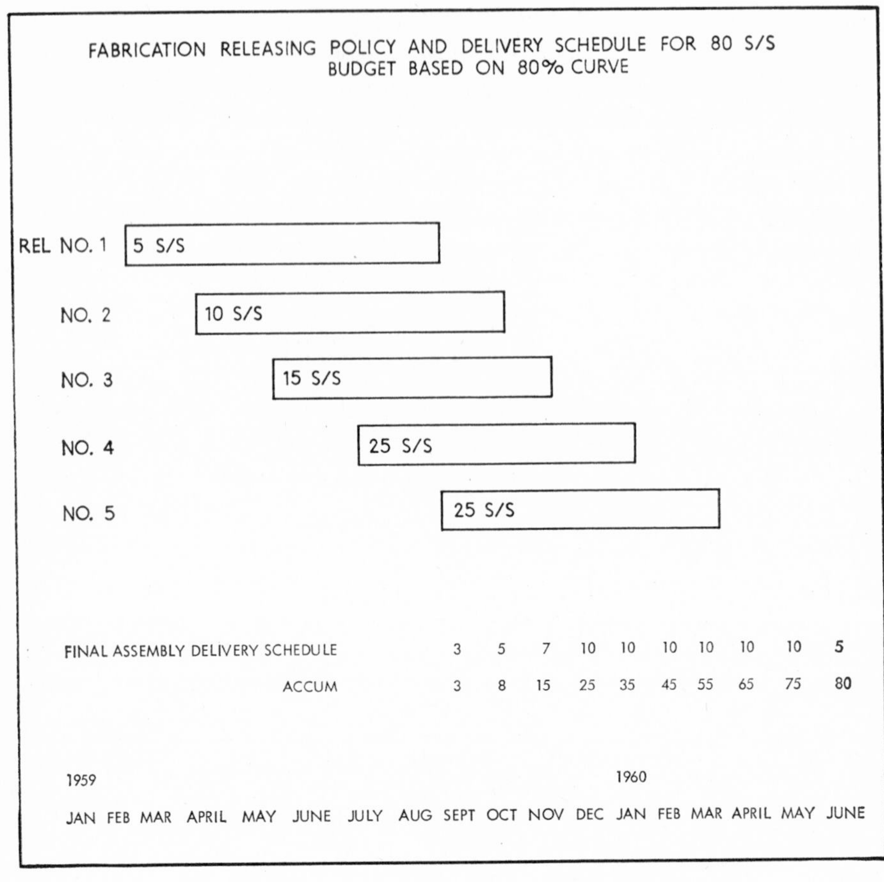

EXHIBIT 5.

percent fabrication budget curve with unit 1 at 8,000 hours. If the total order quantity is 80 units, the first step is to determine, from the fabrication releasing policy, the number of releases to be made for this contract, the number of ship sets for each release, and the scheduled start and completion date for each release.

If the schedule for this contract is as in Exhibit 5, the fabrication releasing can be summarized as shown in Table 2.

TABLE 2

Release No.	*Quantity to Be Released*	*Release Period*	
		Start Date	*Completion Date*
1	5S/S	4/59	8/59
2	10S/S	5/59	10/59
3	15S/S	6/59	11/59
4	25S/S	7/59	1/60
5	25S/S	9/59	3/60

The next step is to determine from the fabrication budget curve the total projected hours for each release. These hours may be calculated if learning curve tables are available. If the tables are not available, the midpoint theory may be used to approximate the average unit hours for each release. This assumes that the numerical midpoint of a given quantity divides the area above and below the curve equally. Applying this principle to the fabrication budget curve in Exhibit 5, the hours would be allocated as indicated in Table 3.

TABLE 3

Release No.	*Midpoint (Cumulative Unit)*	*Unit Hours at Midpoint*	*Total Release Hours*
1	2.5	5,900 × 5	29,500
2	10.0	3,775 × 10	37,750
3	22.5	2,900 × 15	43,500
4	42.5	2,350 × 25	58,750
5	67.5	2,040 × 25	51,000

Once the total hours for each release have been determined, the next step is to allocate these hours by month for each release period. Several methods have been developed to distribute direct labor hours for a contract by month or week. Probably the most widely used method of distribution is that of the *S* curve. Its name is derived from the shape of a curve formed by plotting cumulative direct labor hour input to a contract by week or month. The number of periods over which this curve is formed depends on the delivery schedule for the given contract and the amount of lead time required to support the schedule. Any *S* curve can be expressed in terms of a cumulative percent of hours charged monthly to the total contract hours.

TABLE 4

Month of Production	*Actual Direct Labor Hours Charged per Month*	*Percent of Monthly Hours to Total Hours*	*Cumulative Percent to Total*
1	2,360	8	8
2	5,900	20	28
3	9,145	31	59
4	8,850	30	89
5	3,245	11	100
	29,500	100	

Table 4 provides a set of illustrative data. The cumulative percents, when plotted on a graph, will take the characteristic shape of an *S* curve. Many companies have analyzed their direct labor hour experience in this manner and have compiled tables of percentage breakdowns for various periods. In Exhibit 6 a portion of one of these tables is shown

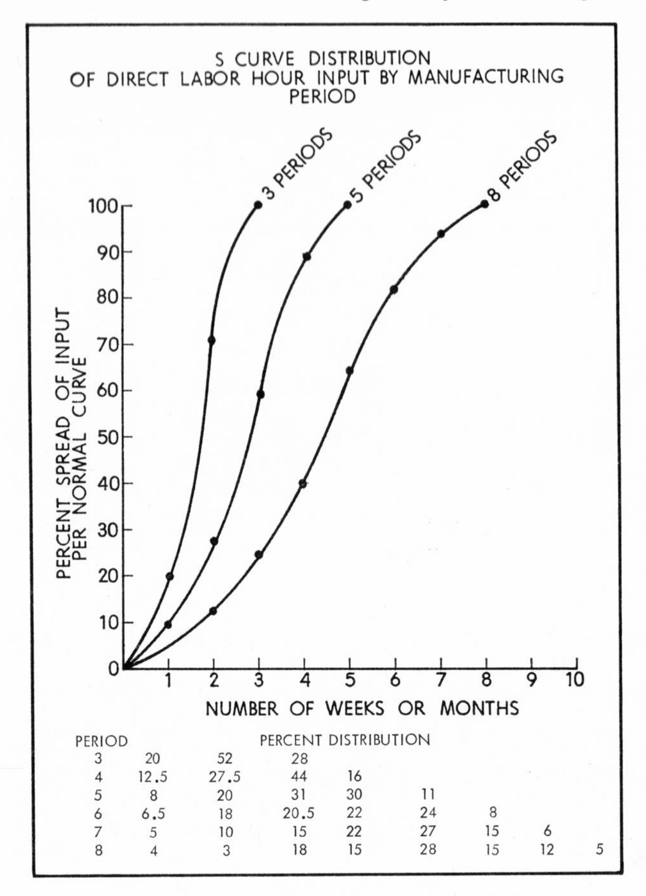

PERIOD	PERCENT DISTRIBUTION							
3	20	52	28					
4	12.5	27.5	44	16				
5	8	20	31	30	11			
6	6.5	18	20.5	22	24	8		
7	5	10	15	22	27	15	6	
8	4	3	18	15	28	15	12	5

EXHIBIT 6.

with periods varying from three to eight months. The percentage distributions for the 3-, 6-, and 10-month periods have been plotted so that the shapes of the curves can be seen. As one would expect, the greater the number of periods, the more gradual the direct labor hour acceleration required in order to maintain production schedules.

The tables shown in Exhibit 6 were used to break down fabrication release hours by month in the following manner:

	Production Month					
	April	*May*	*June*	*July*	*August*	*Total*
Percent distribution from *S* curve table (five-month period)........	8	20	31	30	11	100%
Direct labor hours* (Breakdown by month)....	2,360	5,900	9,145	8,850	3,245	29,500

* Release No. 1. The same calculation was made for the subsequent releases according to the number of months involved.

Once the hours for each release have been distributed by month according to period of manufacture, the total fabrication hours per month can be converted to manpower required on a 40-hour-week basis, by dividing total hours by 172 hours, resulting in equivalent men required per month. This may be further broken down to manpower required for each fabricating department by using percentages from standard hours (Table 5).

TABLE 5

DETAIL AND LOT ORDERED ASSEMBLY INPUT BY MONTH ON THE *S* CURVE WITH CONVERSION TO MANPOWER REQUIREMENTS

Month	*Release No. 1*	*Release No. 2*	*Release No. 3*	*Release No. 4*	*Release No. 5*	*Total Fabrication Hours/Month*	*Manpower Required (172 Hours/Month)*
January							
February							
March							
April	2,360					2,360.0	14
May	5,900	2,453.8				8,353.8	49
June	9,145	4,907.5	2,827.5			16,880.0	98
July	8,850	7,738.7	5,655.0	2,937.5		25,181.2	146
August	3,245	12,080.0	8,917.5	5,875.0		30,117.5	175
September		7,550.0	13,920.0	8,812.5	2,550	32,832.5	191
October		3,020.0	8,700.0	12,925.0	5,100	29,745.0	173
November			3,480.0	15,862.5	7,650	26,992.5	157
December				8,812.5	11,220	20,032.5	117
January				3,525.0	13,770	17,295.0	101
February					7,650	7,650.0	44
March					3,060	3,060.0	18
April							
May							
June							
	29,500	37,750.0	43,500.0	58,750.0	51,000	220,500.0	

In order to determine assembly hour input by month (Table 6), it is necessary to approximate the time from the start of the smallest subassembly for any given unit up to final shipment. In the example, this time was estimated to be three months. The total assembly hours for each month's shipments are arrived at by using midpoints on the assembly curve, following the same procedure as was used for fabrication. The hours for each month are then distributed over the three-month period using the *S*-curve distribution.

This type of analysis provides management with a monthly forecast of direct labor hours for the entire contract and a manpower requirement for each month of manufacture in order to maintain proposed production schedules. The procedure in the example is simplified for brevity of explanation. In practice, provision should be made for spare parts, multishift operations,

TABLE 6. ASSEMBLY HOUR INPUT BY MONTH AND MANPOWER REQUIREMENTS
(Hours for Scheduled Monthly Shipments Spread on Three-Month Cycle)
(20 Percent, 52 Percent, 28 Percent)

Scheduled Shipment Month	*3 September*	*5 October*	*7 November*	*10 December*	*10 January*	*10 February*	*10 March*	*10 April*	*10 May*	*5 June*	*Total Assembly Hours/ Month*	*Manpower Required (172 Hours/ Month)*
June												
July	21,000										21,000	122
August	54,600	23,500									78,100	454
September	29,400	61,100	25,900								116,400	677
October		32,900	67,340	30,800							131,040	762
November			36,260	80,080	27,200						143,540	835
December				43,120	70,720	24,800					138,640	806
January					38,080	64,480	23,000				125,560	730
February						34,720	59,800	21,800			116,320	676
March							32,200	56,680	20,600		109,480	637
April								30,520	53,560	10,000	94,080	547
May									28,840	26,000	54,840	319
June										14,000	14,000	81
	105,000	117,500	129,500	154,000	136,000	124,000	115,000	109,000	103,000	50,000	1,143,000	

	Fabrication Hours	*Assembly Hours*	*Total Hours*	*Manpower Required, Fabrication*	*Manpower Required, Assembly*	*Total Manpower Required*
April	2,360.0		2,360.0	14		14
May	8,353.8		8,353.8	49		49
June	16,880.0		16,880.0	98		98
July	25,181.2	21,000	46,181.2	146	122	268
August	30,117.5	78,100	108,217.5	175	454	629
September	32,832.5	116,400	149,232.5	191	677	868
October	29,745.0	131,040	160,785.0	173	762	935
November	26,992.5	143,540	170,532.5	157	835	992
December	20,032.5	138,640	158,672.5	117	806	923
January	17,295.0	125,560	142,855.0	101	730	831
February	7,650.0	116,320	123,970.0	44	676	720
March	3,060.0	109,480	112,540.0	18	637	655
April		94,080	94,080.0		547	547
May		54,840	54,840.0		319	319
June		14,000	14,000.0		81	81
	220,500.0	1,143,000	1,363,500.0			

absenteeism, rework, and any major design changes that would require substantial work in addition to the basic task.

FOR EVALUATION OF INVENTORY IN PROCESS

The forecasting of inventory in process (see Table 8, p. 514) is one of the most important uses of the learning curve, as viewed by the financial division of any company. One of the main considerations in bidding on a contract for any type of manufacturing is whether the company can finance the work in process required to meet the proposed delivery schedules. In recent years the availability of progress payments on military contracts has enabled many companies to carry inventories for contracts which they might otherwise be unable to accept. Progress payments, i.e., partial billings, provide for monthly payments amounting to a percentage of the total cost input for any given month. There is usually a limitation of the aggregate progress payment amount based on a percentage of the contract price. Even though progress payments may be available for a given contract, a portion of the inventory must still be financed by the manufacturer until the date of final settlement. Thus, inventory evaluation is essential for financing, whether the contract be military or commercial.

The first step in evaluation of inventory in process is to obtain the forecast of direct labor hours per month for a given contract. This is readily available from the manpower requirements calculation previously discussed. Using the hours previously developed in the manpower requirements calculations, (Table 6), with the quotation price breakdown shown in Table 7, the monthly

TABLE 7

		Per Unit	*Total Contract*
Fabrication hours		2,756.3	220,500.0
Assembly hours		14,287.5	1,143,000.0
Total direct labor hours		17,043.8	1,363,500.0
Direct labor amount	$2.50	$ 42,609.50	$ 3,408,760.00
Factory burden	3.50	59,653.30	4,772,264.00
Direct material and outside production		20,000.00	1,600,000.00
Engineering and tool maintenance	0.90	15,339.08	1,227,126.00
Factory cost	$6.90	$137,601.88	$11,008,150.00
Selling and administration expense		6,880.09	550,407.20
Total cost		$144,481.97	$11,555,557.20
Profit		14,448.20	1,155,855.72
Unit selling price		$158,930.17	$12,714,412.92

inventory can be calculated for this example. (See Table 8.)

The first column of Table 8, indicating the forecast direct labor by month, is taken from the summary in Table 6. These hours are then extended by a factory cost rate per hour of $6.90, as shown in the second column. Material and outside production in the third column are allocated by month on the same basis as for fabrication hours. Some adjustment is made to the allocation

TABLE 8

CALCULATION OF INVENTORY IN PROCESS
BY CONVERSION OF MANPOWER FORECAST TO FACTORY COST DOLLARS

Manufacturing Month	(1) *Hours per Month*	(2) *× Factory Cost Rate/Hour, $6.90*	(3) *Add Material and Outside Production*	(4) *Total Factory Cost/Month*	(5) *Less Cost/Sales*	(6) *Monthly Inventory in Process*	(7) *Accumulated Inventory in Process*
April, 1959	2,360.0	$ 16,284.00	$ 16,000	$ 32,284.00	....	$ 32,284.00	$ 32,284.00
May	8,353.8	57,641.22	64,000	121,641.22	....	121,641.22	153,925.22
June	16,880.0	116,472.00	128,000	244,472.00	....	244,472.00	398,397.22
July	46,181.2	318,650.28	176,000	494,650.28	....	494.650.28	893,047.50
August	108,217.5	746,700.75	224,000	970,700.75	....	970,700.75	1,863,748.25
September	149,232.5	1,029,704.25	240,000	1,269,704.25	412,805.63	856,898.62	2,720,646.87
October	160,785.0	1,109,416.50	224,000	1,333,416.50	688,009.38	645,407.12	3,366,053.99
November	170,532.5	1,176,674.25	192,000	1,368,674.25	963,213.13	405,461.12	3,771,515.11
December	158,672.5	1,094,840.25	128,000	1,222,840.25	1,376,018.75	(153,178.50)	3,618,336.61
January, 1960	142,855.0	985,699.50	64,000	1,049,699.50	1,376,018.75	(326,319.25)	3,292,017.36
February	123,970.0	855,393.00	48,000	903,393.00	1,376,018.75	(472,625.75)	2,819,391.61
March	112,540.0	776,526.00	32,000	808,526.00	1,376,018.75	(567,492.75)	2,251,898.86
April	94,080.0	649,152.00	32,000	681,152.00	1,376,018.75	(694,866.75)	1,557,032.11
May	54,840.0	378,396.00	16,000	394,396.00	1,376,018.75	(981,622.75)	575,409.36
June	14,000.0	96,600.00	16,000	112,600.00	688,009.36	(575,409.36)	
	1,363,500.0	$9,408,150.00	$1,600,000	$11,008,150.00	$11,008,150.00		

for equipment items, i.e., assembly materials which continue to be charged to work in process up through the last month of shipment. Column 4 represents total charges to production work in process for each month. We can then determine the inventories if we apply the familiar accounting principle that total input less cost of sales equals inventory. The cost of sales, as shown in column 5, is determined for each month by multiplying the average unit factory cost by the number of scheduled shipments for the month. The difference between columns 4 and 5 then represents the monthly inventory in process, as shown in column 6, and the accumulative inventory in process in column 7.

This calculation of inventory in process can be used to great advantage in the financing of a contract. In the example an inventory buildup prior to shipment of the first unit is $1,863,748.25, or approximately 17 percent of the total cost to be incurred on the contract. On a commercial contract basis, all of this money would have to be financed by the manufacturer. If this contract were subject to progress payments, the manufacturer would still have to provide about $600,000 (assuming a partial billing allowance of 70 percent). The maximum inventory to be provided for of $3,771,515.11 occurs when approximately 20 percent of the contract has been shipped. The value of this type of analysis is entirely dependent on the accuracy of the basic learning curve. If the projection is too optimistic, the inventories will be understated; and the converse, of course, is also true.

This is a general approach to the evaluation of inventory for a proposed contract and no doubt can be refined substantially to fit the needs of each product line and manufacturer as well.

This article was written for the purpose of illustrating a few of the many specialized uses of the learning curve available to the accountant. The applications to budget analysis, profit measurement, man loading, and inventory evaluation are perhaps some of the more important uses. The fact that a company uses these and other learning curve techniques to the best advantage should surely be reflected in its profit and loss statements.

VII

Capital Budgeting

TABLEAU VII

Methodological Analysis

Article \ *Methodology*	*Descriptive Models for Analysis*					*Optimizing Models*			
	Algebraic or Symbolic (Deterministic)	*Algebraic or Symbolic (Probabilistic)*	*Matrix Methods*	*Markov Processes*	*Simulation*	*Linear Programming*	*Game Theory*	*Calculus*	*Other*
38. A Contribution to the Theory of Capital Budgeting—The Multi-Investment Case								X	
39. Risk Analysis in Capital Investment		X							
40. How to Use Decision Trees in Capital Investment		X							
41. Capital Budgeting and Game Theory							X		
42. Practical Application of the Theory of Games to Complex Managerial Decisions							X		

CAPITAL BUDGETING

Capital budgeting, which frequently involves large monetary commitments, is normally conceived to be one of the most important areas requiring managerial judgment; however, the inherent presence of this subjective element does not preclude the use of mathematical and statistical analyses in refining the bases for these decisions. Projections of future revenues and associated costs must be made, as in operations budgeting; consequently, the techniques available for use in operations budgeting also remain operative in capital budgeting (see Section VI). Additional analysis is required, however, in capital budgeting due to the long-run nature and additional uncertainty which normally relates to new investments. Techniques available (in addition to standard present value analyses, return on investment, payback period, etc.) include probabilistic analyses, game theory, and other analytic models.

The cost-of-capital approach is extensively treated in most discussions of capital budgeting; accordingly, it is not repeated here. However, some authors have hypothesized that the presently accepted financial criterion of cost of capital as a cutoff rate of return may not be generally applicable. Accordingly, one exposition of this fundamental limitation has been included (article 38). The remaining articles are devoted to technique-oriented analyses of practical business circumstances. A method for computing a probability distribution for the rate of return on a new investment is presented in article 39; decision trees, a method for outlining possible outcomes for an assumed probabilistic relationship, are illustrated in article 40; and finally, game theory as a basis for choice among alternatives is evaluated and illustrated in articles 41 and 42.

38

The notion of the cost of capital as the basic cutoff rate for investment decisions is first explored, after which an analysis is presented disclosing that the cutoff rate is higher than the cost of capital when more than one project is under consideration. The latter position is illustrated and proved mathematically.

*A CONTRIBUTION TO THE THEORY OF CAPITAL BUDGETING—THE MULTI-INVESTMENT CASE**†

Pao L. Cheng and John P. Shelton

THIS PAPER IS intended to contribute to the theory of capital budgeting by showing conclusively that although the cost of capital (as generally defined) is the correct cutoff point for one investment decision, it is not correct when more than one is being considered. When several investments are simultaneously evaluated, the required rate of return should be higher than the cost of capital. The authors propose for the multi-investment case, instead of using the cost of capital as a hurdle rate, the following decision rule: Rank projects according to their rate of return, then consider each sequentially and accept the project if its contribution to the percentage increase in profits (taking into consideration all previously accepted projects) exceeds the percentage increase in equity capital required for that project.

INTRODUCTION: THE INCREASED ATTENTION PAID TO CAPITAL BUDGETING AND THE COST OF CAPITAL AS A HURDLE RATE

Capital budgeting has become an important part of the theory of corporation finance in the decade since the 1951 publication of Joel Dean's book,

* Reprinted from *Journal of Finance*, December, 1963, pp. 622–36.

† The authors are grateful for financial assistance to support this study furnished by the Faculty Research Grant of the University of Massachusetts and by the Bureau of Business and Economic Research at the University of California at Los Angeles, and to the Ford Foundation for bringing them together at a summer program in the Application of Mathematics to Business held at Ann Arbor, Michigan.

Capital Budgeting.[1] Illustrative of the increased significance of capital budgeting and its related topic, the cost of capital, is the fact that Guthmann and Dougall, in their textbook *Corporate Financial Policy*, which has long been a standard reference, did not have the words *cost of capital* or *capital budgeting* in the index of the third (1955) edition. Yet the fourth edition, published in 1962, devoted a chapter to this concept.

Despite the increased attention paid to this subject in the past decade, many aspects of the theory are still not settled.[2] There is a disagreement, for example, on how a firm should calculate an investment's rate of return, or whether the cost of capital should be evaluated before or after taxes.[3] However, we believe that all theorists who have studied capital budgeting agree on one issue; namely, investment projects should be accepted so long as the rate of return exceeds the cost of capital. (A necessary premise of this theorem is that the firm is trying to maximize the wealth of its stockholders. In the truest sense, this means the sum of market value plus dividends received; in practice, a firm has, at best, limited control over market behavior, so the firm may accept as its proximate goal the maximization of earnings per share. If, for simplification, we assume that price is an increasing function of earnings so long as the capital structure proportions are unchanged, maximizing earnings per share and maximizing market value are identical goals.) This view is the basis for the decision rule that the cost of capital should be used as the cutoff point or hurdle rate for allocating funds where there are many investment projects. This is stated in many articles or texts on capital budgeting; we cite one.

Ezra Solomon, in "Measuring a Company's Cost of Capital," reprinted in *The Management of Corporate Capital*, says:

> The determination of a company's capital budget is an intricate process that requires several simultaneous decisions by management: the total extent of capital expenditures, the form these expenditures will take, and the forms of financing to be used in meeting these expenditures. A rational solution to these complex problems involves three steps:
>
> 1. Each available expenditure proposal must be measured for the rate of return it promises. When these measured proposals are ranked in descending order of prospective yield, this list provides management with an explicit picture of the company's potential demand for capital funds.
>
> 2. Each available source of capital must be measured for its "cost" to stockholders. "Cost" in this context refers to the minimum rate of return that is required to justify the active investment of each succeeding increment of these available funds. When this

---

[1] Joel Dean, *Capital Budgeting* (New York: Columbia University Press, 1951).

[2] Though this article is confined to clarifying one aspect of capital-budgeting theory, for a discussion of the problems encountered in applying capital-budgeting theory to business practice, see Frank E. Norton, "Administrative Organization in Capital Budgeting," *Journal of Business*, October, 1955, pp. 291–95; and W. Warren Haynes and Martin B. Solomon, Jr., "A Misplaced Emphasis in Capital Budgeting," *Quarterly Review of Economics and Business*, February, 1962, pp. 39–46.

[3] Analyses of most of the issues in capital budgeting are found in Ezra Solomon (ed.), *The Management of Corporate Capital* (Glencoe, Ill.: Free Press, 1959).

listing of amounts and expected costs is arrayed in ascending order of cost, it provides management with an explicit picture of the potential supply and cost of funds available to the company.

3. A comparison of these two schedules provides an exclusive and correct solution to the capital budgeting problem. Successive proposals should be accepted from within the descending array as long as the prospective yield from each is higher than the cost of obtaining the increment of funds required for its financing. The first proposal for which capital cost equals or exceeds prospective yields should be rejected and so should all proposals promising a smaller yield.[4]

Since the concept of the cost of capital as a hurdle rate for selecting from an array of investment projects is so commonly accepted and citations are so widely available, we only list further references.[5]

ANALYSIS: THE COST OF CAPITAL IS NOT THE HURDLE RATE WHEN MORE THAN ONE PROJECT IS BEING CONSIDERED FOR SIMULTANEOUS INVESTMENT

Despite the fact that the cost of capital is the proper hurdle rate for one investment decision considered by itself, it is imprecise to apply the cost of capital as a cutoff point for determining which projects to accept and which to reject when the firm has more than one investment opportunity under consideration. This point, which has been overlooked in the discussion of capital budgeting, is the contribution of this paper.

We will demonstrate the proof of this point in three ways. First, we give a numerical illustration; second, we generalize by a graphical analysis; finally, we support our conclusion by mathematical proof.

To illustrate our point by a numerical example, let us focus on the specific issue that is involved; namely, that earnings per share will not necessarily be maximized if a firm undertakes all investment projects that have a prospect of yielding more than the cost of capital.[6] For this purpose, we choose an illustration designed to eliminate the areas of disagreement about the cost of capital and how it is measured, or the rate of return and how it is calculated.

Despite our desire to avoid issues tangential to the thrust of this paper, it helps before going further to provide an explicit and generally acceptable

---

[4] *Ibid.*, p. 128.

[5] See, e.g., Harold Bierman and Seymour Smidt, *The Capital Budgeting Decision* (New York: Macmillan Co., 1960), p. 45; Dean, *op. cit.*, chap. iv, p. 63; Pearson Hunt, Charles Williams, and Gordon Donaldson, *Basic Business Finance* (Homewood, Ill.: Richard D. Irwin, Inc., 1961), pp. 622–25; Robert W. Johnson, *Financial Management* (Boston: Allyn and Bacon, Inc., 1959), pp. 133 and 148; and H. G. Guthmann and H. E. Dougall, *Corporate Financial Policy* (4th ed.; Englewood Cliffs, N.J.: Prentice-Hall, Inc., 1962), p. 121.

[6] This conclusion does not hinge on the fact that returns from investments, being hostages of the future, are uncertain. It is true even if it develops that each project returns the amount forecast for it. Or to put it another way, we are not arguing that given a cost of capital of, say, 10 percent, projects should not be accepted unless they yield at least 15 percent in order to hedge against bad estimates.

definition of the cost of capital. We hope the reader will see the validity of the analysis even if the definition cited here is not completely acceptable to him. Ezra Solomon, in "Measuring a Company's Cost of Capital," acknowledges, "The cost of capital . . . is a difficult concept and one about which little agreement exists in practice," but he then suggests four possible criteria and concludes:

> The fourth, and in the opinion of this writer, the only valid criterion for the cost of new equity capital is a refinement of the E/P ratio. Instead of E, the current earnings per share, the numerator should measure management's best estimate of what average future earnings would be if the proposed capital expenditure were not made. We shall refer to this concept as E_A. Assuming that underwriting and flotation costs are zero, the ratio E_A/P is the best conceptual measure of the cost of new equity capital, and the use of this criterion as the cut off rate for new capital expenditures financed solely by new common stock is the only one that will insure the optimum capital-budgeting decision.[7]

Now for the numerical illustration. Assume a firm has only common stock in its capital structure; the firm pays in dividends all that it earns each year so that further financing cannot be done except by selling more common stock; two projects are being considered, both of which have an expected annual rate of return into infinity; if neither project is undertaken, profits are expected to continue at the present level. (As will be shown in our graphical and mathematical proofs, these specific assumptions do not deprive the illustration of its generality so far as the issue we are raising is concerned.) Assume this firm has a price-earnings ratio of 15 for its common stock and this price-earnings ratio remains constant. Under the circumstances, E/P and E_A/P (to use Solomon's terminology) are the same, and the cost of capital by either criterion is 6⅔ percent.

Assume each project requires \$600,000 investment and the best estimate of future annual net profit is \$200,000 on one project and \$45,000 on the other; these constitute annual rates of return of 33 percent and 7.5 percent, both exceeding the cost of capital.[8] As shown in Table 1, earnings per share (or the

---

[7] Solomon, *op. cit.*, p. 130.

[8] It is realistic to assume that estimates of future returns from projects only at the stage of consideration by a corporation's management would have little influence on the market price of the stock because investors do not know, or are skeptical, of the anticipated returns. In practice, the Securities and Exchange Commission forbids estimates of future income in prospect and has enjoined firms that attempt, in conjunction with a new issue, to release stories in the financial press about prospective profits; this is improper conditioning of the market. Consequently, in the numerical illustration, we assume the market does not anticipate the decision to undertake the new projects and raise the stock price, so we keep the cost of capital at 6⅔ percent. However, our analysis does not hinge on whether investors anticipate, or fail to anticipate, corporate expansion. If, for example, the firm in our illustration is suddenly regarded as having a more prosperous future and the price goes to 20 times earnings, the cost of capital, which is now 5 percent, will still be too low to serve as an optimizing hurdle rate when several investments are being considered at one time. No matter what price the stock sells for, the cost of capital associated with that price will not be the correct hurdle rate for multiproject considerations.

TABLE 1

Example: Assume a corporation has a 100 percent equity capital structure with 100,000 shares outstanding. Assume also the following:

Current earnings per share	$4
Current market price of shares	$60
Earnings-price ratio	6⅔% (*P/E* ratio of 15)

The above implies that the corporation has net income of $400,000 and that this is expected to continue in the next period before the installation of any capital projects. The corporation is considering two capital projects (not mutually exclusive), one involving an estimated cost of $600,000 and an expected rate of return of 33⅓ percent (or an expected additional net income of $200,000) and the other also requiring $600,000 but with an expected rate of return of 7.5 percent (or an expected additional net income of $45,000). Both projects have a rate of return larger than the after-tax cost of capital of 6⅔ percent.

Though the firm believes the income estimates are reliable, the investing public has little foreknowledge or is skeptical until earnings actually develop, so the price at the time of raising new capital reflects profits that are known and experienced, not promised.

Should the corporation approve both projects?

Case 1: Both projects approved simultaneously and financed by issuing enough additional shares at $60 a share. This results in the following:

Total additional shares	20,000
Total shares outstanding	120,000
Total expected net income	$645,000
Expected earnings per share	$5.375

Case 2: Only the first project is approved:

Total additional shares	10,000
Total shares outstanding	110,000
Total expected net income	$600,000
Expected earnings per share	$5.456

market price, given the prior assumption) are not maximized if the firm undertakes both projects at one time. The existing owners of the corporation will be better off if the firm does not undertake the second project. As seen in Table 2, earnings per share will be maximized if the firm undertakes the second project at a subsequent time after the first project has had a chance to show up as an increment to earnings per share, thus raising the market price

TABLE 2

BOTH PROJECTS APPROVED BUT ONE AT A TIME

Expected earnings per share after the first project	$5.456
Expected market price of share, at 15 times its earnings	$81.84
Number of shares required for the second project at the new market price	7,331
Total expected net income	$645,000
Total shares outstanding	117,331
Expected earnings per share after both projects are launched	$5.50

of the stock. In this sense, if a group of projects are each considered separately and taken one at a time, with sufficient delay between each one for the prior one to have its impact on earnings per share and the price of the stock, then the cost of capital is the theoretically proper cut-off rate for investment projects if the firm seeks to maximize earnings per share, but this becomes merely a repeated illustration of the single-investment case.

Much that has been written on capital budgeting avoids the question of treating the cost of capital as a hurdle rate, when many projects are ranked, by restricting the advice to one project. A good example of the analysis being restricted to one investment comes from the article "The Cost of Capital, Corporation Finance, and the Theory of Investment," by Modigliani and Miller: "Under this approach any investment project and its concomitant financing plan must pass only the following test: Will the project, as financed, raise the market value of the firm's shares? If so, it is worth undertaking; if not, its return is less than the marginal cost of capital to the firm."[9]

It is clear that anyone who confines the use of the cost of capital in capital budgeting to a single investment project is being theoretically precise. However, we believe that such advice in practice is of limited value because few large corporations would be considering only one capital project per year or per six months. Thus the existing theorem is valid only in the special case; the analysis developed in this paper applies to the more general case. There has been no warning, unfortunately, that the same principle which applies to a single project cannot be used where several projects have been ranked. In fact, many authors, when writing about capital budgeting, have explicitly stated that the use of cost of capital as a hurdle rate for many projects was a valid inference from the fact that it will work for one project. Our point is simply this: For most firms, capital budgeting involves consideration of more than one project; and therefore, for these firms the advice of using the cost of capital as a hurdle rate for determining which projects to accept and which to reject is not valid.

Before we consider this point in graphical and mathematical generality, it may be helpful to ask: (1) Why is the cost of capital not a satisfactory hurdle rate for many projects when it suffices for one? (2) What generalization can be made that is theoretically precise regarding a cutoff point for accepting or rejecting projects when a firm is considering more than one investment?[10]

---

[9] Franco Modigliani and Merton H. Miller, "The Cost of Capital, Corporation Finance, and the Theory of Investment," reprinted in Solomon, *op. cit.*, p. 152.

[10] Let us warn against another unwarranted conclusion that may be fostered by the numerical example. From Table 1, it might be inferred that the reason earnings per share were not maximized by investing in both projects, even though each had a rate of return greater than the cost of capital, was because the "demand schedule" for capital was sharply discontinuous, dropping from 33 to 7.5 percent. Though, in practice, we expect that discontinuities do prevail, and even though the existence of discontinuities reinforces our point, this condition is not necessary for the conclusion. Actually, as shown in the graphical and mathematical proofs, the cost of capital is not a precisely accurate cutoff point even if the demand schedule for capital is a smooth, continuous function.

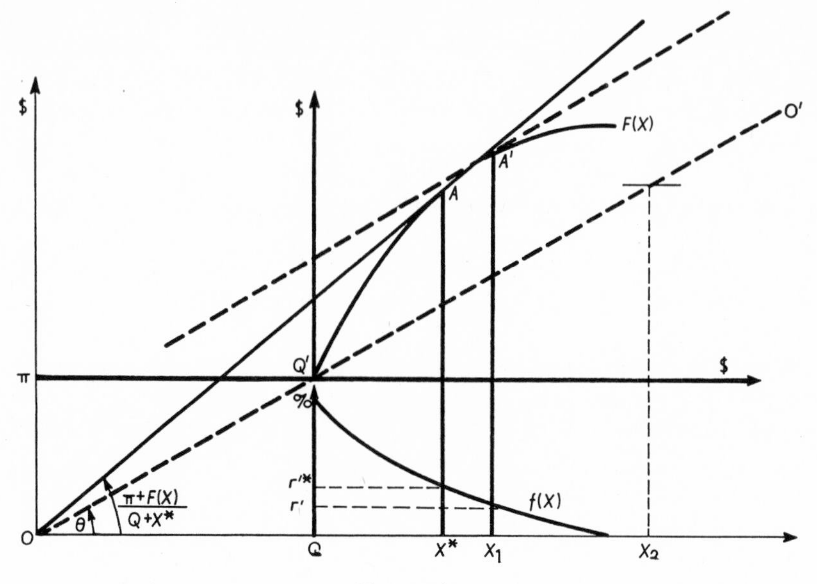

FIGURE 1.

When many projects are being considered, there is a whole range of prospective cumulative profits, one for each successive investment. This is the curve denoted $F(X)$ in Figure 1. To our knowledge, no theorist has argued that the goal of the firm should be to maximize this function, since that would mean taking on any project that promised even one cent of profit. All have recognized that what the firm should maximize is market value, which in our illustration is achieved by maximizing earnings per share, which can be achieved by drawing a line from zero tangent to $F(X)$ in Figure 1. We shall return to this later, but the difficulty is that it was erroneously, though understandably, assumed that earnings per share would be maximized when the marginal change in the total profit function matched the earnings-price ratio. But this will not, in truth, maximize earnings per share.

Assuming the projects are being considered in order of their profitability, earnings per share will be thrust upward with more vigor by the projects ranked near the top of the profitability ladder, that is, the first ones considered. Typically, the projects near the cost of capital will not further elevate the earnings per share attained by the superior projects. Since the goal is to stop investment when earnings per share are at their maximum, this will frequently mean that some projects should not be included, even though their return is greater than the cost of capital. In effect, this avoids dilution of earnings per share that would result from including some projects lower in the profit array, even though they yield more than the current cost of capital.

What generalization can be made, then, if the firm is considering more than one project? There is no simple generalization, such as that the cutoff point should be 3 percent, say, higher than the cost of capital; but each situation has to be considered in terms of the firm's existing investments and their return, the firm's cost of capital, and the size and potential return of each incremental investment under consideration, taken one at a time. A firm should calculate the effect of each project on the amount of capital required and the change of earnings per share from that project alone. The order of assessing the projects should be from the ones with the highest expected rate of return, proceeding down the ladder of projects as ranked by potential return. If a firm follows this procedure, one generalization can be made: The firm will always increase earnings per share if the percentage increase in profits from any investment project exceeds the percentage increase in equity capital required to finance that project. Thus, if some projects which come close to the cost-of-capital hurdle rate require a great deal of incremental investment, it may turn out that their percentage contribution to profits (including the profits from more lucrative projected investments) is smaller than their proportionate increase in capital required; and therefore, earnings per share will be maximized by rejecting these investments, even though they promise a return which exceeds the cost of capital.

To illustrate our argument graphically, assume that a corporation has a set capital structure consisting of a proportion of μ in equity (valued at market price) and the balance $(1 - \mu)$ in debt. At this point the reader may want to note three things: (1) Our phraseology aims at achieving generality; if he prefers to fold the numerical illustration into the graphical analysis, he will want to have equity equal one and debt equal zero. (2) The corporation could also have preferred stock in its capital structure, but the presentation is thereby complicated without gain of understanding, so we deal with this in a subsequent footnote. (3) Why should the common stock be calculated at market, not book value? There are several reasons for this choice; it is the one most capital theorists prefer; it coincides with the assumption we are making that the goal of the firm is to maximize the wealth of the stockholder, which is achieved if the price-earnings ratio is constant, by maximizing earnings per share; and finally, this approach lends itself to the graphical construction we propose.

Let r be the annual expected rate of return for a proposed project, after taxes, and net of interest cost. Then the after-tax rate of return on equity, r', is simply $r' = r/\mu$. For example, if $r = 0.10$, $\mu = 0.6$, and $(1 - \mu) = 0.4$, then the project has a rate of return on equity, r', of $0.10/0.60 = 16\frac{2}{3}$ percent.

Let us now denote:

π = Total current net profit
E = Current earnings per share
P = Current market price of shares
Q = Current market valuation of the equity securities of the corporation, or total current number of shares outstanding multiplied by P
X = Additional equity capital needed in financing new capital

projects, which implies that X/μ is the total long-term capital needed in financing the capital projects

$r' = f(X)$ = The rate of return on equity (after interest and taxes) from new capital projects ranked in descending order of their respective r'; $f(X)$ then may be considered as the expected marginal rate of return on additional equity X

$F(X) = \int_0^x f(X)\, dX$ = The total expected additional net profit per period from the new capital projects

Consider the situation of the firm depicted in Figure 1. At the initial point of time, it is expecting future annual profits to be at the level π (if it makes no further net investment), and the market value of its equity is represented by 0_Q. (NOTE: The vertical axis measures dollars of net profit, the horizontal axis measures the dollar value of the firm's common stock.) Given this situation, angle Θ represents π/Q; or if we divide each part of this ratio by the number of common shares, this is the earnings-price ratio on the common stock.

Now, as our illustration progresses, the firm considers a list of prospective investments, each requiring some additional capital and ranked in order of prospective rate of return. Total profits will rise from the level of π depending on how many projects are undertaken.[11] The increase in profits is marked in the graph by the curve $F(X)$, which is the cumulative profit from all investments, beginning at Q' and rising at a decreasing rate, as is consistent with a diminishing marginal rate of return on equity.

To further illustrate the issues presented in this paper, we superimpose a curve $f(X)$ and place it in the segment of the graph to the right of Q. This latter curve represents the marginal rate of return on equity for new capital projects and is thus the derivative of $F(X)$, the cumulative profit curve.

Now the firm has to decide which investments to accept or reject. Conceivably, it could undertake all investments that yield any net profit, which would be where the $f(X)$ curve was just above zero and $F(X)$ was at its maximum height. But no student of capital budgeting would recommend this. As we understand the current status of capital-budgeting theory, the recommended policy would be to accept new investments to an amount represented by QX_1. At this point the marginal increase in profit, per dollar of equity invested, just equals the earnings-price ratio, which represents the firm's hurdle rate or cutoff point. The equality is demonstrated thus. A line is drawn parallel to the line $00'$ and is found to be just tangent to $F(X)$ at the point A'. Since the parallel dotted line has the slope Θ, at the point of tangency the cost of capital and the marginal rate of return are equal. By dropping a perpendicular line from A', we see that associated with this amount of investment is the marginal rate of r'.

The point of this paper is that the firm is not maximizing for its stockholders by pressing investment to QX_1 but should instead stop at QX^*, where

[11] $F(X)$ could conceivably rise from any level, depending upon what the firm considers to be the expected profit per period from the existing amount of equity.

$F(X)$ is at the value A. At this point the angle representing the earnings per share ratio is maximized. Or putting it another way, the optimum level of investment is QX^* because at that point r'^* is equal to $AX^*/0X^*$, the maximum slope one can find from points on $F(X)$ to 0. One more way to look at this is to think of the horizontal axis as representing the number of common shares (where the price is constant). Then the slope from a point on $F(X)$ to 0 becomes earnings per share, and this is the value to be maximized if we assume the price of the common stock is, at the time new funds are made available, fixed by the market's prior evaluation of the company.

To complete the story told in Figure 1, the reader will be helped if he considers the graph as being time-dated or a presentation of comparative statics. Assume the firm invests only the amount QX^*, which brings $F(X)$ to A and therefore rejects projects below the hurdle rate r'^*. Since we posit that the price-earnings ratio is unaffected by the new investments, as soon as profits flow from these investments the market value of all the common stock will now rise to the amount $0X_2$, which is where the new profits AX^* match the vertical distance of the line $00'$, representing the earnings-price ratio that prevails.

To translate from the graph toward reality, what has happened is that the firm has accepted projects that yield more than the cost of capital, and this profitable investment policy pushes up the market price of the stock. Pushing the investment beyond the amount represented by QX^* would have added proportionately more to the number of shares that would have been sold than it would have to the profit. The maximum earnings per share and market value for the stockholders is achieved by accepting investments only if the marginal rate of return is r'^* and its associated total profits are AX^*, because at this point the angle $\pi + F(X)/\text{market value of equity}$ is maximized. This policy uses a higher cutoff point than r', which most capital-budgeting theory recommends.

By adding subscripts denoting time intervals to Solomon's notation, we can summarize our argument another way. Let E_{A1} represent anticipated earnings if no new projects are financed, and E_{A2} anticipated earnings after the investments are completed and operating. Let P_1 and P_2 be the stock prices at those times, respectively. If the market applies a constant capitalization rate to profits, then E_{A1}/P_1 will equal E_{A2}/P_2. But at the time new capital is raised, the pertinent relationship is E_{A2}/P_1, and this will be greater than the other rate.[12] Traditionally, economists ignore temporary deviations from

[12] One of the referees who evaluated this paper stated our position succinctly, so we take the liberty of quoting him: "[The essence of the argument] is that the marginal rate of return on *a* project must beat E_A/P if subsequent earnings per share are to rise. Further, this rule should be applied to *each* and *every* project. But as projects are adopted, E_A changes, and therefore the E_A/P that must be beaten changes. Thus, with respect to their example, the first project must beat $4 divided by $60. Since the marginal rate of return, in fact, beats this ratio, subsequent earnings rise—in fact, they rise to $5.45. This means that the ratio the *second* project has to beat is $5.45 divided by $60. Since this ratio is larger than the marginal rate of return on the second project, subsequent earnings do not rise but instead fall to $5.37. In short, if one changes E_AP as incremental projects are adopted, one will never add a project that decreases earnings per share."

equilibrium values in order to focus on long-run relationships. Thus, capital-budgeting theory has either chosen to assume that the market price adjusts instantaneously to projected investments, or if it does not, the deviation is merely a short-run phenomenon that can be ignored. Though short-run displacements can usually be overlooked in economic analysis, it is a mistake to do so in capital budgeting, because the number of new shares that have to be sold when the project is financed is determined by the price at the time of financing. And the number of shares added to the firm's capital becomes a permanent, long-run feature that is not eliminated when the market adjusts price to the new profits.

In the illustrative example, the authors provided a realistic tone by assuming that the investors would be less informed about prospective investment opportunities than the firm's management. However, it is important to repeat that the analysis in this paper does not hinge on the special case where investors underestimate future earnings. So far as the analysis offered in this paper is concerned, investors can make any estimate they wish about future earnings. Our analysis applies as well to companies noted for growth and priced accordingly, such as IBM, as to firms with little growth prospects and consequently less favorable price-earnings ratios, such as railroads. Whatever the price of the stock at the time the investment decision is being made, the firm will not maximize its stockholders' wealth if it uses E/P (or E_A/P) as the hurdle rate when more than one project is being considered. No matter how future earnings are capitalized at the time of the investment decision, our analysis shows that the optimum hurdle rate when more than one project is considered is implied by the "sequential solution." This will always involve less investment than the cutoff rate advocated in current doctrine. The doctrine, as currently advocated, is valid only in the special case when one project is being considered. Whatever price the stock sells for, our solution implies the correct cutoff rate when more than one project is being undertaken; current doctrine leads to a different solution.

Mathematically, we want to maximize

$$y = \frac{\pi + F(X)}{Q + X}$$

where y is the expected future rate of return per equity dollar or, equivalently, future expected share prices (assuming a constant price-earnings ratio). By setting the first derivative of this equation equal to zero, we have

$$(Q + X)F'(X) = \pi + F(X) = 0$$

$$F'(X) = \frac{\pi + F(X)}{Q + X}$$

or

$$f(X) = \frac{\pi + F(X)}{Q + X}$$

or

$$r'^{*} = y$$

which means that the optimum hurdle rate r'^* is obtained when r', the marginal rate of return from new capital projects per dollar of additional equity, is equal to y, the future expected rate of return per total equity dollar, the latter denominator including the original as well as additional equity.

It is now clear that the cost of equity capital (after taxes), E/P or π/Q, is equal to $\pi + F(X)/Q + X$ if and only if $F(X)/X = \pi/Q$, since $F(X)/X \neq 0$. More importantly, since $F(X)/X > \pi/Q$ before the traditional cutoff point (or hurdle rate) π/Q, it is obvious that $\pi + F(X)/Q + X > \pi/Q$ or $r'^* > \pi/Q$. This proves that our concept of the optimum hurdle rate r'^* is reached before the traditional cost of equity capital π/Q.[13]

Throughout this paper, we have focused on one issue, namely, that the cost of capital is not a satisfactory hurdle rate when more than one investment project is being considered, and we have tried to bypass many controversial aspects of capital-budgeting theory. In this sense, we feel more comfortable if the reader thinks, as he follows the proofs, of the simplified problem described in the numerical illustration, although the proofs permit generalization. However, near the conclusion we briefly anticipate some questions that might be raised.

What if one assumes the cost of equity capital as the ratio of dividends divided by market price, and the goal of the firm is to maximize dividends instead of earnings? Our response to this—as to all this series of questions—is, first, that this view is not widely held among capital-budgeting theorists for reasons that are sound but too lengthly to repeat here. However, if dividends are a positive function of earnings per share, then the analysis is still valid.

What if one assumes that all the prospective investment projects will be financed by debt, and there will be no downward shift in the price-earnings ratio as a result of the increased debt, so the cost of capital is merely the interest rate? In this case, projects should be taken on so long as they yield more than interest cost. But the view that the interest rate measures the cost of capital is denied by virtually all students of the subject. In any event, the possibility of using all debt for the new investment projects is, by definition, outside the framework of our analysis. We assumed new projects would be financed in the same proportion of debt and equity as the firm currently has. This could be justified as assuming the firm has found the capital structure proportions that optimize or "satisfice" for it and does not want to change this ratio. Our reason, however, for doing this was to avoid getting entangled in discussion of how the cost of capital might change as capital structure changes. All students of this matter who believe that for a given capital structure there is really only one cost of capital (and we think these comprise

[13] One might wish to know how r'^* would be evaluated if there are preferred stocks in the capital structure. Let us assume a corporation that has $(1 - \mu_p - \mu_c)$ as the proportion of debt in the capital structure, and μ_p and μ_c as the proportions for preferred and common stocks (including earned surplus), respectively. Let r be defined as previously. Then, $r/\mu_p + \mu_c = r_{pc}$ is the rate of return on preferred stocks and equity. Now, let d_p be the preferred stock dividend rate; we have $r' = r_{pc} - d_p\mu_p/\mu_c$, the rate of return on equity from the capital projects. We then can proceed as previously by setting $f(X) = r'$, etc.

the great majority of those who have written on the subject) will find our analysis valid.

What if one assumes new projects are financed solely from retained earnings and imputes to these a zero cost of capital? Again, this view has little stature, for reasons too long to develop here; furthermore, this would lead to taking on projects that leave the stockholder less wealthy than if the firm had evaluated retained earnings as having an opportunity cost to the stockholder comparable to newly raised equity and had paid out in dividends any funds not necessary to finance investments yielding more than our optimum hurdle rate, r'^*.

What if the new projects are financed solely from depreciation charges? If the depreciation matched obsolescence, all depreciation charges would have to be invested merely to keep profits at their prior level by replacing obsolete or worn-out plant facilities, so there would be nothing available for net new investment. If the charges are greater than physical or technological obsolescence, then in reality they represent "hidden retained earnings," and again the stockholders' wealth will be maximized if the firm does not invest beyond the optimum hurdle rate.[14]

Finally, we must consider the case of a rising marginal cost of equity capital instead of the constant one we have considered up to now. Let us denote $g(X)$ the marginal cost; then the traditional cutoff point would be established at $g(X) = f(X)$. Does this decision rule maximize the share prices such as $y' = \pi + F(X)/S + S'$, where

$$\begin{aligned} y' &= \text{The expected share prices} \\ S &= \text{The number of existing shares} \\ S' &= \text{The number of additional shares} \\ \pi + F(X) &= \text{The total expected net profit} \end{aligned}$$

Note, however, S' is no longer a linear function of X, because as X increases, increasingly more shares must be issued to raise the same amount of X. We need not elaborate here; suffice it to point out that the maximum of y' would meet the condition $g(X) = f(X)$ only by coincidence.

CONCLUSION

The purpose of this paper has been to show that the cost of capital, though it is the proper hurdle rate for evaluating one project, does not provide the

[14] Another way to evaluate financing from depreciation charges is to treat an amount of depreciation, D, as a portion of the principal recovered from the firm's total existing investment in capital equipment. D, conceptually, could be used to retire an amount of debt-and-equity mix in proportions $(1 - \mu)$ and μ. If this were done, the firm's condition would be at a point of lower π and smaller Q than at the beginning, depending upon the firm's estimate of profit, without reinvesting the depreciation. This point is (Q_D, π_D), with $Q_D = (Q - D\mu)$ and $\pi_D = (\pi - W)$, where W is the estimated decline in profit if D is not reinvested. Graphically, we can now draw $F(X)$, beginning at (Q_D, π_D), and treat D as if it were external funds with proportions $(1 - \mu)$ and μ. From this point the analysis would be the same, except that when X^* is determined, only $(X^* - D\mu)$ amount of equity need be raised externally. In short, funds from depreciation, like any other funds, are scarce and should be allocated in the most efficient manner.

correct cutoff point when more than one project (involving different marginal rates of return) is under consideration. The literature on capital budgeting, prior to this paper, has either erred by stating that the cost of capital can be used as the hurdle rate for screening many projects, or has been confined to the one-project case—which is probably unrealistic for most large firms—and given no warning that the same cutoff rate cannot be used when multi-projects are evaluated.

The optimum hurdle rate is higher than the cost of capital by an amount which depends on each investment ladder. This is because additional projects require additional capital, and even for some projects that will yield more than the cost of capital the percentage increase in profitability they generate—considering the profit the firm would have attained as it moved down the ladder of returns—is less than the percentage increase in equity capital required.

39

This discussion indicates that present value analysis, while often useful, is not sufficient for many investment decisions, and describes some of the methods of accommodating uncertainty data conditions (improved forecasts, empirical adjustments, higher cutoff rates, three-level estimates, and selected probabilities). A new approach is suggested which involves a determination of the probability distribution of the rate of return on an investment. In this procedure a probability distribution for each major variable which affects net return is first established, after which rates of return for random combinations of these variables may be determined—presumably by a computer. The probability distribution for the rate of return may then be constructed. A comparison is drawn between this and the conventional method, and an example of the evaluation of alternatives using the simulation approach is also presented.

*RISK ANALYSIS IN CAPITAL INVESTMENT**

David B. Hertz

OF ALL THE DECISIONS that business executives must make, none is more challenging—and none has received more attention—than choosing among alternative capital investment opportunities. What makes this kind of decision so demanding, of course, is not the problem of projecting return on investment under any given set of assumptions. The difficulty is in the assumptions and in their impact. Each assumption involves its own degree—often a high degree—of uncertainty; and taken together, these combined uncertainties can multiply into a total uncertainty of critical proportions. This is where the element of risk enters, and it is in the evaluation of risk that the executive has been able to get little help from currently available tools and techniques.

There is a way to help the executive sharpen his key capital investment decisions by providing him with a realistic measurement of the risks involved. Armed with this measurement, which evaluates for him the risk at each possible level of return, he is then in a position to measure more knowledgeably alternative courses of action against corporate objectives.

NEED FOR NEW CONCEPT

The evaluation of a capital investment project starts with the principle that the productivity of capital is measured by the rate of return we expect to

* Reprinted from *Harvard Business Review*, January-February, 1964, pp. 95–106.

receive over some future period. A dollar received next year is worth less to us than a dollar in hand today. Expenditures three years hence are less costly than expenditures of equal magnitude two years from now. For this reason, we cannot calculate the rate of return realistically unless we take into account (1) when the sums involved in an investment are spent and (2) when the returns are received.

Comparing alternative investments is thus complicated by the fact that they usually differ not only in size but also in the length of time over which expenditures will have to be made and benefits returned.

It is these facts of investment life that long ago made apparent the shortcomings of approaches that simply averaged expenditures and benefits, or lumped them, as in the number-of-years-to-pay-out method. These shortcomings stimulated students of decision making to explore more precise methods for determining whether one investment would leave a company better off in the long run than would another course of action.

It is not surprising, then, that much effort has been applied to the development of ways to improve our ability to discriminate among investment alternatives. The focus of all of these investigations has been to sharpen the definition of the value of capital investments to the company. The controversy and furor that once came out in the business press over the most appropriate way of calculating these values has largely been resolved in favor of the discounted cash flow method as a reasonable means of measuring the rate of return that can be expected in the future from an investment made today.

Thus, we have methods which in general are more or less elaborate mathematical formulas for comparing the outcomes of various investments and the combinations of the variables that will affect the investments.[1] As these techniques have progressed, the mathematics involved has become more and more precise, so that we can now calculate discounted returns to a fraction of a percent.

But the sophisticated businessman knows that behind these precise calculations are data which are not that precise. At best, the rate-of-return information he is provided with is based on an average of different opinions with varying reliabilities and different ranges of probability. When the expected returns on two investments are close, he is likely to be influenced by "intangibles"—a precarious pursuit at best. Even when the figures for two investments are quite far apart and the choice seems clear, there lurk in the back of the businessman's mind memories of the Edsel and other ill-fated ventures.

In short, the decision maker realizes that there is something more he ought to know, something in addition to the expected rate of return. He suspects

---

[1] See for example, Joel Dean, *Capital Budgeting* (New York: Columbia University Press, 1951); *Return on Capital as a Guide to Managerial Decisions*, National Association of Accountants Research Report No. 35 (December 1, 1959); and Bruce F. Young, "Overcoming Obstacles to Use of Discounted Cash Flow for Investment Shares," *NAA Bulletin*, March, 1963, p. 15.

that what is missing has to do with the nature of the data on which the expected rate of return is calculated, and with the way those data are processed. It has something to do with uncertainty, with possibilities and probabilities extending across a wide range of rewards and risks.

The Achilles Heel

The fatal weakness of past approaches thus has nothing to do with the mathematics of rate-of-return calculation. We have pushed along this path so far that the precision of our calculation is, if anything, somewhat illusory. The fact is that no matter what mathematics is used, each of the variables entering into the calculation of rate of return is subject to a high level of uncertainty. For example, the useful life of a new piece of capital equipment is rarely known in advance with any degree of certainty. It may be affected by variations in obsolescence or deterioration, and relatively small changes in use life can lead to large changes in return. Yet an expected value for the life of the equipment—based on a great deal of data from which a single best possible forecast has been developed—is entered into the rate-of-return calculation. The same is done for the other factors that have a significant bearing on the decision at hand.

Let us look at how this works out in a simple case—one in which the odds appear to be all in favor of a particular decision.

The executives of a food company must decide whether to launch a new packaged cereal. They have come to the conclusion that five factors are the determining variables: *advertising and promotion expense*, *total cereal market*, *share of market for this product*, *operating costs*, and *new capital investment*. On the basis of the "most likely" estimate for each of these variables, the picture looks very bright—a healthy 30 percent return. This future, however, depends on each of the most likely estimates coming true in the actual case. If each of these educated guesses has, for example, a 60 percent chance of being correct, there is only an 8 percent chance that *all five* will be correct ($0.60 \times 0.60 \times 0.60 \times 0.60 \times 0.60$). So the "expected" return is actually dependent on a rather unlikely coincidence. The decision maker needs to know a great deal more about the *other* values used to make each of the five estimates and about what he stands to gain or lose from various combinations of these values.

This simple example illustrates that the rate of return actually depends on a specific combination of values of a great many different variables. But only the expected levels of ranges (e.g., worst, average, best; or pessimistic, most likely, optimistic) of these variables are used in formal mathematical ways to provide the figures given to management. Thus, predicting a single most likely rate of return gives precise numbers that do not tell the whole story.

The expected rate of return represents only a few points on a continuous curve of possible combinations of future happenings. It is a bit like trying to predict the outcome in a dice game by saying that the most likely outcome is a seven. The description is incomplete because it does not tell us about all the other things that could happen. In Exhibit 1, for instance, we see the odds on throws of only two dice having six sides. Now, suppose that each die has 100 sides and there are eight of them! This is a situation more comparable to business investment, where the company's market share might become any one of 100 different sizes and where there are eight different factors (pricing, promotion, and so on) that can affect the outcome.

Nor is this the only trouble. Our willingness to bet on a roll of the dice depends not only on the odds but also on the stakes. Since the probability of rolling a seven is 1 in 6, we might be quite willing to risk a few dollars on that outcome at suitable odds. But would we be equally willing to wager $10,000 or $100,000 at those same odds, or even at better odds? In short, risk is in-

EXHIBIT 1. Describing uncertainty—a throw of the dice.

fluenced both by the odds on various events occurring and by the magnitude of the rewards or penalties which are involved when they do occur. To illustrate again, suppose that a company is considering an investment of $1 million. The "best estimate" of the probable return is $200,000 a year. It could well be that this estimate is the average of three possible returns—a 1-in-3 chance of getting no return at all, a 1-in-3 chance of getting $200,000 per year, a 1-in-3 chance of getting $400,000 per year. Suppose that getting no return at all would put the company out of business. Then, by accepting this proposal, management is taking a 1-in-3 chance of going bankrupt.

If only the best estimate analysis is used, management might go ahead, however, unaware that it is taking a big chance. If all of the available information were examined, management might prefer an alternative proposal with a smaller but more certain (i.e., less variable) expectation.

Such considerations have led almost all advocates of the use of modern capital investment index calculations to plead for a recognition of the elements of uncertainty. Perhaps Ross G. Walker sums up current thinking when he speaks of "the almost impenetrable mists of any forecast."[2]

How can the executive penetrate the mists of uncertainty that surround the choices among alternatives?

[2] "The Judgment Factor in Investment Decisions," *Harvard Business Review*, March-April, 1961, p. 99.

Limited Improvements

A number of efforts to cope with uncertainty have been successful up to a point, but all seem to fall short of the mark in one way or another:

1. *More Accurate Forecasts.* Reducing the error in estimates is a worthy objective. But no matter how many estimates of the future go into a capital investment decision, when all is said and done, the future is still the future. Therefore, however well we forecast, we are still left with the certain knowledge that we cannot eliminate all uncertainty.

2. *Empirical Adjustments.* Adjusting the factors influencing the outcome of a decision is subject to serious difficulties. We would like to adjust them so as to cut down the likelihood that we will make a "bad" investment, but how can we do that without at the same time spoiling our chances to make a "good" one? And in any case, what is the basis for adjustment? We adjust not for uncertainty but for bias.

For example, construction estimates are often exceeded. If a company's history of construction costs is that 90 percent of its estimates have been exceeded by 15 percent, then in a capital estimate there is every justification for increasing the value of this factor by 15 percent. This is a matter of improving the accuracy of the estimate.

But suppose that new-product sales estimates have been exceeded by more than 75 percent in one fourth of all historical cases, and have not reached 50 percent of the estimate in one sixth of all such cases. Penalties for overestimating are very tangible, and so management is apt to reduce the sales estimate to cover the one case in six—thereby reducing the calculated rate of return. In doing so, it is possibly missing some of its best opportunities.

3. *Revising Cutoff Rates.* Selecting higher cutoff rates for protecting against uncertainty is attempting much the same thing. Management would like to have a possibility of return in proportion to the risk it takes. Where there is much uncertainty involved in the various estimates of sales, costs, prices, and so on, a high calculated return from the investment provides some incentive for taking the risk. This is, in fact, a perfectly sound position. The trouble is that the decision maker still needs to know explicitly what risks he is taking—and what the odds are on achieving the expected return.

4. *Three-Level Estimates.* A start at spelling out risks is sometimes made by taking the high, medium, and low values of the estimated factors and calculating rates of return based on various combinations of the pessimistic, average, and optimistic estimates. These calculations give a picture of the range of possible results but do not tell the executive whether the pessimistic result is more likely than the optimistic one—or, in fact, whether the average result is much more likely to occur than either of the extremes. So although this is a step in the right direction, it still does not give a clear enough picture for comparing alternatives.

5. *Selected Probabilities.* Various methods have been used to include the probabilities of specific factors in the return calculation. L. C. Grant discusses

a program for forecasting discounted cash flow rates of return where the service life is subject to obsolescence and deterioration. He calculates the odds that the investment will terminate at any time after it is made depending on the probability distribution of the service life factor. After calculating these factors for each year through maximum service life, he then determines an overall expected rate of return.[3]

Edward G. Bennion suggests the use of game theory to take into account alternative market growth rates as they would determine rate of return for various alternatives. He uses the estimated probabilities that specific growth rates will occur to develop optimum strategies. Bennion points out:

> Forecasting can result in a negative contribution to capital budget decisions unless it goes further than merely providing a single most probable prediction. . . . [With] an estimated probability coefficient for the forecast, plus knowledge of the payoffs for the company's alternative investments and calculation of indifference probabilities . . . the margin of error may be substantially reduced, and the businessman can tell just how far off his forecast may be before it leads him to a wrong decision.[4]

Note that both of these methods yield an expected return, each based on only one uncertain input factor—service life in the first case, market growth in the second. Both are helpful, and both tend to improve the clarity with which the executive can view investment alternatives. But neither sharpens up the range of "risk taken" or "return hoped for" sufficiently to help very much in the complex decisions of capital planning.

SHARPENING THE PICTURE

Since every one of the many factors that enter into the evaluation of a specific decision is subject to some uncertainty, the executive needs a helpful portrayal of the effects that the uncertainty surrounding each of the significant factors has on the returns he is likely to achieve. Therefore the method we have developed at McKinsey & Company, Inc., combines the variabilities inherent in all the relevant factors. Our objective is to give a clear picture of the relative risk and the probable odds of coming out ahead or behind in the light of uncertain foreknowledge.

A simulation of the way these factors may combine as the future unfolds is the key to extracting the maximum information from the available forecasts. In fact, the approach is very simple, using a computer to do the necessary arithmetic. (Recently, a computer program to do this was suggested by S. W. Hess and H. A. Quigley for chemical process investments.[5])

---

[3] "Monitoring Capital Investments," *Financial Executive*, April, 1963, p. 19.

[4] "Capital Budgeting and Game Theory," *Harvard Business Review*, November-December, 1956, p. 123.

[5] "Analysis of Risk in Investments Using Monte Carlo Techniques" *Statistics and Numerical Methods in Chemical Engineering* (Chemical Engineering Symposium Series, No. 42) (New York: American Institute of Chemical Engineering, 1963), p. 55.

To carry out the analysis, a company must follow three steps:

1. Estimate the range of values for each of the factors (e.g., range of selling price, sales growth rate, and so on) and within that range the likelihood of occurrence of each value.
2. Select at random from the distribution of values for each factor one particular value. Then combine the values for all of the factors and compute the rate return (or present value) from that combination. For instance, the lowest in the range of prices might be combined with the highest in the range of growth rate and other factors. (The fact that the factors are dependent should be taken into account, as we shall see later.)
3. Do this over and over again to define and evaluate the odds of the occurrence of each possible rate of return. Since there are literally millions of possible combinations of values, we need to test the likelihood that various specific returns on the investment will occur. This is like finding out by recording the results of a great many throws what percent of sevens or other combinations we may expect in tossing dice. The result will be a listing of the rates of return we might achieve, ranging from a loss (if the factors go against us) to whatever maximum gain is possible with the estimates that have been made.

   For each of these rates the chances that it may occur are determined. (Note that a specific return can usually be achieved through more than one combination of events. The more combinations for a given rate, the higher the chances of achieving it—as with sevens in tossing dice.) The average expectation is the average of the values of all outcomes weighted by the chances of each occurring.

   The variability of outcome values from the average is also determined. This is important since, all other factors being equal, management would presumably prefer lower variability for the same return if given the choice. This concept has already been applied to investment portfolios.[6]

When the expected return and variability of each of a series of investments have been determined, the same techniques may be used to examine the effectiveness of various combinations of them in meeting management objectives.

PRACTICAL TEST

To see how this new approach works in practice, let us take the experience of a management that has already analyzed a specific investment proposal by conventional techniques. Taking the same investment schedule and the same expected values actually used, we can find what results the new method would produce and compare them with the results obtained when conventional methods were applied. As we shall see, the new picture of risks and returns is different from the old one. Yet the differences are attributable in no way to changes in the basic data—*only to the increased sensitivity of the method to management's uncertainties about the key factors.*

[6] See Harry Markowitz, *Portfolio Selection: Efficient Diversification of Investments* (New York: John Wiley & Sons, Inc., 1959); Donald E. Fararr, *The Investment Decision under Uncertainty* (Englewood Cliffs, N.J.: Prentice-Hall, Inc., 1962); William F. Sharpe, "A Simplified Model for Portfolio Analysis," *Management Science*, January, 1963, p. 277.

Investment Proposal

In this case a medium-size industrial chemical producer is considering a \$10 million extension to its processing plant. The estimated service life of the facility is 10 years; the engineers expect to be able to utilize 250,000 tons of processed material worth \$510 per ton at an average processing cost of \$435 per ton. Is this investment a good bet? In fact, what is the return that the company may expect? What are the risks? We need to make the best and fullest use we can of all the market research and financial analyses that have been developed, so as to give management a clear picture of this project in an uncertain world.

The key input factors management has decided to use are:

1. Market size
2. Selling prices
3. Market growth rate
4. Share of market (which results in physical sales volume)
5. Investment required
6. Residual value of investment
7. Operating costs
8. Fixed costs
9. Useful life of facilities

These factors are typical of those in many company projects that must be analyzed and combined to obtain a measure of the attractiveness of a proposed capital facilities investment.

Obtaining Estimates

How do we make the recommended type of analysis of this proposal?

Our aim is to develop for each of the nine factors listed a frequency distribution or probability curve. The information we need includes the possible range of values for each factor, the average, and some ideas as to the likelihood that the various possible values will be reached. It has been our experience that for major capital proposals, managements usually make a significant investment in time and funds to pinpoint information about each of the relevant factors. An objective analysis of the values to be assigned to each can, with little additional effort, yield a subjective probability distribution.

Specifically, it is necessary to probe and question each of the experts involved—to find out, for example, whether the estimated cost of production really can be said to be exactly a certain value or whether, as is more likely, it should be estimated to lie within a certain range of values. It is that range which is ignored in the analysis management usually makes. The range is relatively easy to determine; if a guess has to be made—as it often does—it is easier to guess with some accuracy a range rather than a specific single value. We have found from past experience at McKinsey & Company, Inc., that a series of meetings with management personnel to discuss such distributions is most helpful in getting at realistic answers to the a priori questions. (The term *realistic answers* implies all the information management does *not* have as well as all that it does have.)

The ranges are directly related to the degree of confidence that the estimator has in his estimate. Thus, certain estimates may be known to be quite accurate. They would be represented by probability distributions stating, for instance, that there is only one chance in 10 that the actual value will be different from the best estimate by more than 10 percent. Others may have as much as 100 percent ranges above and below the best estimate.

Thus, we treat the factor of selling price for the finished product by asking executives who are responsible for the original estimates these questions:

1. Given that $510 is the expected sales price, what is the probability that the price will exceed $550?
2. Is there any chance that the price will exceed $650?
3. How likely is it that the price will drop below $475?

Managements must ask similar questions for each of the other factors until they can construct a curve for each. Experience shows that this is not as difficult as it might sound. Often, information on the degree of variation in factors is readily available. For instance, historical information on variations in the price of a commodity is readily available. Similarly, management can estimate the variability of sales from industry sales records. Even for factors that have no history, such as operating costs for a new product, the person who makes the "average" estimate must have some idea of the degree of confidence he has in his prediction; and therefore, he is usually only too glad to express his feelings. Likewise, the less confidence he has in his estimate, the greater will be the range of possible values that the variable will assume.

This last point is likely to trouble businessmen. Does it really make sense to seek estimates of variations? It cannot be emphasized too strongly that the less certainty there is in an "average" estimate, *the more important it is to consider the possible variation in that estimate.*

Further, an estimate of the variation possible in a factor, no matter how judgmental it may be, is always better than a simple "average" estimate, since it includes more information about what is known and what is not known. It is, in fact, this very *lack* of knowledge which may distinguish one investment possibility from another, so that for rational decision making it *must* be taken into account.

This lack of knowledge is in itself important information about the proposed investment. To throw any information away simply because it is highly uncertain is a serious error in analysis which the new approach is designed to correct.

Computer Runs

The next step in the proposed approach is to determine the returns that will result from random combinations of the factors involved. This requires realistic restrictions, such as not allowing the total market to vary more than some reasonable amount from year to year. Of course, any method of rating the return which is suitable to the company may be used at this point; in the actual case, management preferred discounted cash flow for the reasons cited earlier, so that method is followed here.

A computer can be used to carry out the trials for the simulation method in very little time and at very little expense. Thus, for one trial actually made in this case, 3,600 discounted cash flow calculations, each based on a selection of the nine input factors, were run in two minutes at a cost of $15 for computer time. The resulting rate-of-return probabilities were read out immediately and graphed. The process is shown schematically in Exhibit 2.

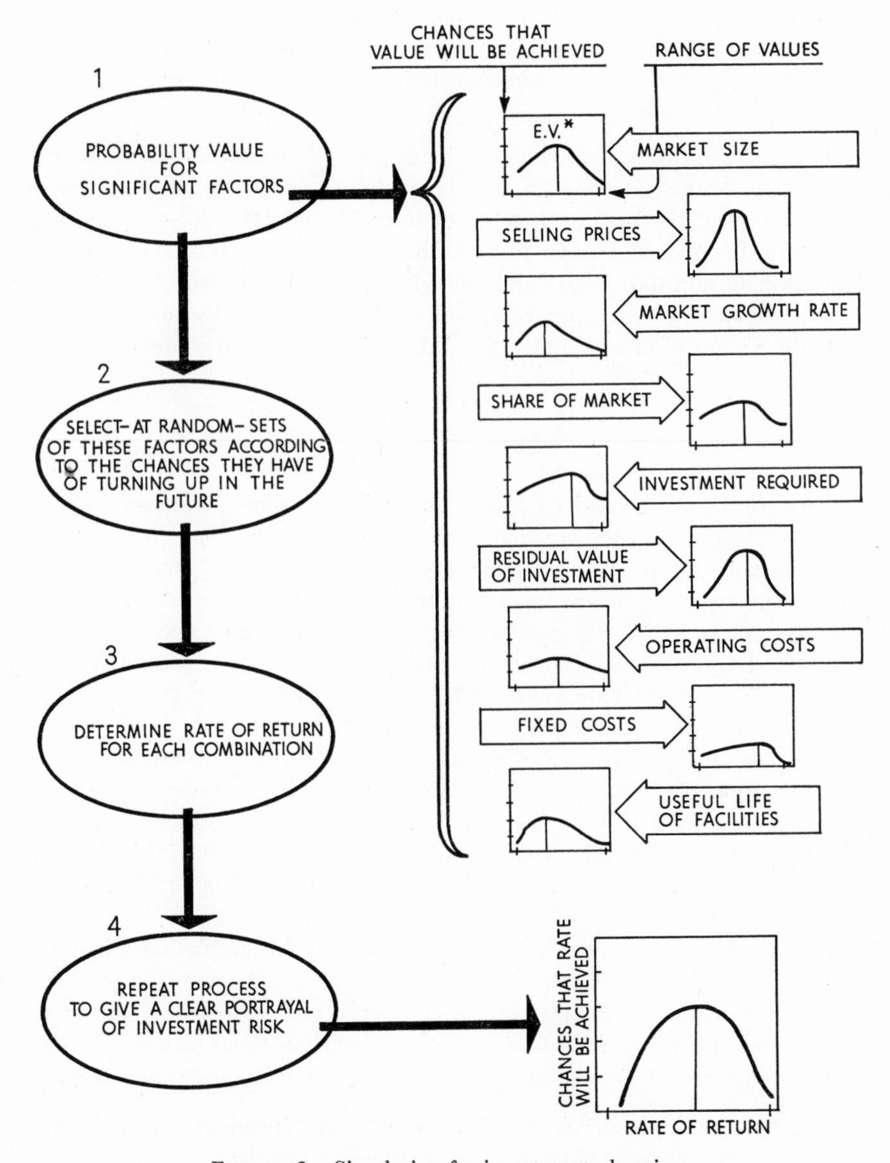

EXHIBIT 2. Simulation for investment planning.

* Expected value equals highest point of curve.

Data Comparisons

The nine input factors described earlier fall into three categories:

1. *Market analyses:* Included are market size, market growth rate, the firm's share of the market, and selling prices. For a given combination of these factors, sales revenue may be determined.
2. *Investment cost analyses:* Being tied to the kinds of service life and operating cost characteristics expected, these are subject to various kinds of error and uncertainty; for instance, automation progress makes service life uncertain.
3. *Operating and fixed costs:* These also are subject to uncertainty but are perhaps the easiest to estimate.

These categories are not independent; and for realistic results, our approach allows the various factors to be tied together. Thus, if price determines the total market, we first select from a probability distribution the price for the specific computer run and then use for the total market a probability distribution that is logically related to the price selected.

We are now ready to compare the values obtained under the new approach with the values obtained under the old. This comparison is shown in Exhibit 3.

Valuable Results

How do the results under the new and old approaches compare?

In this case, management had been informed, on the basis of the "one best estimate" approach, that the expected return was 25.2 percent before taxes. When we ran the new set of data through the computer program, however, we got an expected return of only 14.6 percent before taxes. This surprising difference not only is due to the fact that under the new approach we use a range of values; it also reflects the fact that we have weighted each value in the range by the chances of its occurrence.

Our new analysis thus may help management to avoid an unwise investment. In fact, the general result of carefully weighing the information and lack of information in the manner I have suggested is to indicate the true nature of otherwise seemingly satisfactory investment proposals. If this practice were followed by managements, much regretted overcapacity might be avoided.

The computer program developed to carry out the simulation allows for easy insertion of new variables. In fact, some programs have previously been suggested that take variability into account.[7] But most programs do not allow for dependence relationships between the various input factors. Further, the program used here permits the choice of a value for price from one dis-

---

[7] See Frederick S. Hillier, "The Derivation of Probabilistic Information for the Evaluation of Risky Investments," *Management Science*, April, 1963, p. 443.

	Conventional "Best Estimate" Approach	*New Approach*
MARKET ANALYSES		
1. Market size:		
Expected value (in tons)	250,000	250,000
Range	......	100,000–340,000
2. Selling prices:		
Expected value (in dollars/ton)	$510	$510
Range	......	$385–$575
3. Market growth rate:		
Expected value	3%	3%
Range	......	0%–6%
4. Eventual share of market:		
Expected value	12%	12%
Range	......	3%–17%
INVESTMENT COST ANALYSES		
5. Total investment required:		
Expected value (in millions)	$9.5	$9.5
Range	......	$7–$10.5
6. Useful life of facilities:		
Expected value (in years)	10	10
Range	......	5–15
7. Residual value (at 10 years):		
Expected value (in millions)	$4.5	$4.5
Range	......	$3.5–$5.0
OTHER COSTS		
8. Operating costs:		
Expected value (in dollars/ton)	$435	$435
Range	......	$370–$545
9. Fixed costs:		
Expected value (in thousands)	$300	$300
Range	......	$250–$375

NOTE: Range figures in right-hand column represent approximately 1 percent to 99 percent probabilities. That is, there is only a 1-in-100 chance that the value actually achieved will be respectively greater or less than the range.

EXHIBIT 3. Comparison of expected values under old and new approaches.

tribution, which value determines a particular probability distribution (from among several) that will be used to determine the value for sales volume. To show how this important technique works, suppose we have a wheel, as in roulette, with the numbers from zero to 15 representing one price for the product or material, the numbers 16–30 representing a second price, the numbers 31–45 a third price, and so on. For each of these segments, we would have a different range of expected market volumes; e.g., $150,000–$200,000 for the first, $100,000–$150,000 for the second, $75,000–$100,000 for the third, and so forth. Now, suppose that we spin the wheel and the ball falls in 37. This would mean that we pick a sales volume in the $75,000–$100,000 range. If the ball goes in 11, we have a different price, and we turn to the $150,000–$200,000 range for a price.

Most significant, perhaps, is the fact that the program allows management to ascertain the sensitivity of the results to each or all of the input factors. Simply by running the program with changes in the distribution of an input factor, it is possible to determine the effect of added or changed information (or of the lack of information). It may turn out that fairly large changes in some factors do not significantly affect the outcomes. In this case, as a matter of fact, management was particularly concerned about the difficulty in estimating market growth. Running the program with variations in this factor quickly demonstrated to us that for average annual growths from 3 percent and 5 percent, there was no significant difference in the expected outcome.

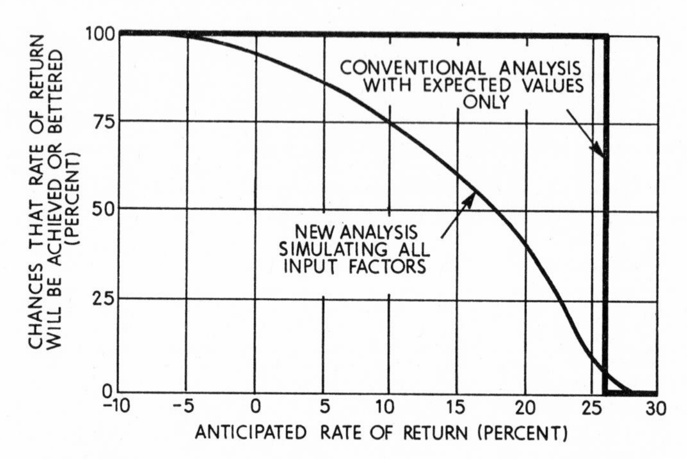

EXHIBIT 4. Anticipated rates of return under old and new approaches.

In addition, let us see what the implications are of the detailed knowledge the simulation method gives us. Under the method using single expected values, management arrives only at a hoped-for expectation of 25.2 percent after taxes (which, as we have seen, is wrong unless there is no variability in the various input factors—a highly unlikely event). On the other hand, with the method we propose, the uncertainties are clearly portrayed:

Percent Return	*Probability of Achieving at Least the Return Shown*
0%	96.5%
5	80.6
10	75.2
15	53.8
20	43.0
25	12.6
30	0.0

This profile is shown in Exhibit 4. Note the contrast with the profile obtained under the conventional approach. This concept has been used also for evaluation of new-product introductions, acquisitions of new businesses, and plant modernization.

COMPARING OPPORTUNITIES

From a decision-making point of view, one of the most significant advantages of the new method of determining rate of return is that it allows management to discriminate between measures of (1) expected return based on weighted probabilities of all possible returns, (2) variability of return, and (3) risks.

To visualize this advantage, let us take an example which is based on another actual case but simplified for purposes of explanation. The example involves two investments under consideration, *A* and *B*.

When the investments are analyzed, the data tabulated and plotted in Exhibit 5 are obtained.

	Investment A	*Investment B*
Amount of investment	$10,000,000	$10,000,000
Life of investment (in years)	10	10
Expected annual net cash inflow	$ 1,300,000	$ 1,400,000
Variability of cash inflow:		
One chance in 50 of being *greater* than	$ 1,700,000	$ 3,400,000
One chance in 50 of being *less** than	$ 0	($600,000)
Expected return on investment	5%	6.8%
Variability of return on investment:		
One chance in 50 of being *greater* than	7%	15.5%
One chance in 50 of being *less** than	3%	(4%)
Risk of investment:		
Chances of a loss	Negligible	1 in 10
Expected size of loss		$ 200,000

* In the case of negative figures (indicated by parentheses), "less than" means "worse than."

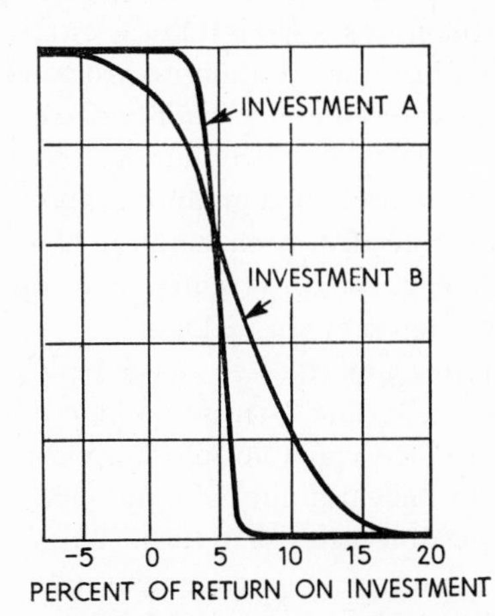

EXHIBIT 5. Comparison of two investment opportunities (Selected Statistics).

1. Investment *B* has a higher expected return than investment *A*.
2. Investment *B* also has substantially more variability than investment *A*. There is a good chance that investment *B* will earn a return which is quite different from the expected return of 6.8 percent, possibly as high as 15 percent or as low as a loss of 5 percent. Investment *A* is not likely to vary greatly from the expected 5 percent return.
3. Investment *B* involves far more risk than does investment *A*. There is virtually no chance of incurring a loss on investment *A*. However, there is one chance in 10 of losing money on investment *B*. If such a loss occurs, its expected size is approximately $200,000.

Clearly, the new method of evaluating investments provides management with far more information on which to base a decision. Investment decisions made only on the basis of maximum expected return are not unequivocally the best decisions.

CONCLUSION

The question management faces in selecting capital investments is first and foremost: What information is needed to clarify the key differences among various alternatives? There is agreement as to the basic factors that should be considered—markets, prices, costs, and so on. And the way the future return on the investment should be calculated, if not agreed on, is at least limited to a few methods, any of which can be consistently used in a given company. If the input variables turn out as estimated, any of the methods customarily used to rate investments should provide satisfactory (if not necessarily maximum) returns.

In actual practice, however, the conventional methods do *not* work out satisfactorily. Why? The reason, as we have seen earlier in this article, and as every executive and economist knows, is that the estimates used in making the advance calculations are just that—estimates. More accurate estimates would be helpful; but at best, the residual uncertainty can easily make a mockery of corporate hopes. Nevertheless, there is a solution. To collect realistic estimates for the key factors means to find out a great deal about them. Hence the kind of uncertainty that is involved in each estimate can be evaluated ahead of time. Using this knowledge of uncertainty, executives can maximize the value of the information for decision making.

The value of computer programs in developing clear portrayals of the uncertainty and risk surrounding alternative investments has been proved. Such programs can produce valuable information about the sensitivity of the possible outcomes to the variability of input factors and to the likelihood of achieving various possible rates of return. This information can be extremely important as a backup to management judgment. To have calculations of the odds on all possible outcomes lends some assurance to the decision makers that the available information has been used with maximum efficiency.

This simulation approach has the inherent advantage of simplicity. It requires only an extension of the input estimates (to the best of our ability) in terms of probabilities. No projection should be pinpointed unless we are *certain* of it.

The discipline of thinking through the uncertainties of the problem will in itself help to ensure improvement in making investment choices. For to understand uncertainty and risk is to understand the key business problem—and the key business opportunity. Since the new approach can be applied on a continuing basis to each capital alternative as it comes up for consideration and progresses toward fruition, gradual progress may be expected in improving the estimation of the probabilities of variation.

Lastly, the courage to act boldly in the face of apparent uncertainty can be greatly bolstered by the clarity of portrayal of the risks and possible rewards. To achieve these lasting results requires only a slight effort beyond what most companies already exert in studying capital investments.

40

The author presents a case study of the application of the decision-tree concept to capital budgeting. Of course, the identification of the problem and alternatives remains a necessary first operation. Unique steps relative to the decision-tree technique per se involve outlining the major choices, determining costs and feasibilities, and constructing the preliminary drawing. It is then pointed out that the input data required are determined from probabilistic estimates and cash flow analyses. Thereafter the procedures used in evaluating each alternative are examined in detail (numeric data are provided), and the final analysis is compared with the standard present value technique.

*HOW TO USE DECISION TREES IN CAPITAL INVESTMENT**

John F. Magee

The decision-tree approach was described in the July-August issue of *Harvard Business Review*[1] as a way of displaying the anatomy of a business investment decision and of showing the interplay among a present decision, chance events, competitors' moves, and possible future decisions and their consequences. We saw the values of decision trees in exploring a variety of problems—new-product introduction, plant modernization, research and development strategy, outlays for new facilities, and others.

In this article, I will discuss how to go about using the decision-tree concept—the skills needed, organization of the analysis, and data required. A case example of a business investment question will serve as a vehicle for discussing aspects of the practical use of decision trees. As this example will illustrate, the new approach leads to different and improved answers to investment analysis questions. It enables management to take more direct account of

1. The impact of possible future decisions
2. The impact of uncertainty
3. The relative values of present and future profits
4. The comparative advantages of varying levels of expected profit and corporate flexibility

* Reprinted from *Harvard Business Review*, September-October, 1964, pp. 79–96.

[1] John F. Magee, "Decision Trees for Decision Making," *Harvard Business Review*, July-August, 1964, p. 126.

PLAN OF ATTACK

Our case example involves a company situation which, though fictitious, incorporates a number of elements of cases I have actually worked with.

The management of Prism Paints, Inc., must decide what to do with one of its manufacturing plants which, though adequate in size, is technically obsolete and unable to supply the quality of products required in the current market. Since the plant in question is rather small by modern standards and it is argued that a plant of its size is at an economic disadvantage, there is considerable managerial controversy over the proper course of action—whether to modernize the operation by construction of better facilities at that location or to scrap the existing plant and supply the area involved from the company's facilities elsewhere—e.g., plants in adjacent states.

The possible alternatives involve significantly different capital expenditures and appear to lead to substantial differences in operating economy as well. Underlying the controversy over what to do is a concern for future product in the area served by the plant.

In this and other cases the key steps in building and using a decision tree for investment project analysis are:

1. *Identification of the problem and alternatives:* The information about the investment opportunity may come from a number of sources, including market analysis, operations research and engineering analysis, research and development work, trend studies, competitive intelligence, and executive imagination. Experience indicates that the more intimate the executive is with his analytical support, the more alternatives can be seen. An analysis team combining some of the key disciplines needed for the problem is very useful if the decision to be made is a major one.
2. *Layout of the decision tree:* This is the formulation of the structure of alternatives underlying the investment decision.
3. *Obtaining the data needed:* Analyses of various sorts are usually required to estimate cash flows and probabilities of uncertain events. This is another function of the analysis team, if such a team exists.
4. *Evaluating alternative courses:* Evaluations frequently lead to a restatement of the problem and a reformulation of the decision tree. A good evaluation will test which alternatives appear desirable in light of the standards used. It will show whether apparent conclusions are sensitive to changes in doubtful or controversial estimates. It will examine the effect of choosing alternate standards, which in turn may lead to revision of standards, further analysis, or reformulation.

Let us examine each of these steps in this article. We can then compare the decision-tree approach with other approaches, review various problems and questions that may arise, and see how the Bayesian method of probabilities analysis can be combined with decision trees to analyze the worth of further research or market analysis for a project.

IDENTIFYING ALTERNATIVES

Experience has demonstrated the importance in investment studies of identifying what alternatives, what freedom of action, and what uncertainties exist now and in the future; of estimating the costs, demand volumes, prices, and competitive action anticipated under alternatives; and of narrowing down estimates of the probabilities or likelihood of uncertain events. All future possibilities cannot be identified, of course, but experience shows a reasonable job can be done. The better the job of identifying and estimating, the more intelligently can the investment decision be made.

Marketing analysis, operations research, engineering analysis, and financial analysis have vital roles in investment analysis. To be most effective, however, they should be integrated; that is, management should use them *in combination* to explore alternatives and to open up new possibilities.

Those engaged in the analysis should be encouraged to express doubts and uncertainties and to express estimates of costs, technical feasibility, or forecasts of market conditions in terms of *ranges* or *probabilities*. Much as management might wish the uncertainties would go away, undue criticism of the analyst for being imprecise or insufficiently firm in his estimates will only force the uncertainties and the risks underground. The purpose of the investment analysis is to help management identify alternatives and bring out the facts about them.

Innumerable examples could be given of how staff analyses have helped in the identification of alternatives in various companies. I shall mention just a few in order to indicate the *range* of possibilities:

One company needed a 10-year forecast of the size and character of the market for new laborsaving equipment. The forecast was made by combining the results obtained—first, by an industry sector analysis to estimate how individual industries might be expected to grow in response to primary consumer demand and secondary industrial investment activity; second, by a productivity analysis to estimate productivity increases and labor substitutions needed if demand estimates were to be achieved; and third, by technical analysis of industry operations to see where labor substitutions of the greatest magnitude were most likely to occur. And out of this came a picture with both a range and a depth that otherwise would have been lacking.

A chemical manufacturer faced the need to expand capacity to meet growing near-term demand. Additions to capacity were extremely expensive, and the manufacturer was uncertain about the longer term load on the plant. Analysis showed that the manufacturer had other alternatives—e.g., revised scheduling procedures combined with a moderate investment in warehouse space would yield an effective increase in production capacity at modest fixed investment but at some increase in operating cost. Again, the result of the investigation was a broadening in the range of choice for management.

In a study of U.S. Mint facilities investment the analysis team investigated a series of alternative combinations of plant sizes and multiple-shift operations, to show the trade-off between operating cost and investment required, that is, the savings in operational expenses that could be achieved by increases in outlays for new facilities. In addition, the costs of excess capacity, overtime, and occasional extra shifts were analyzed to determine the justifiable amount of excess capacity to handle short-term fluctuations in coinage demand.[2]

A proposed field order- and sales-recording system being considered by the management of one company was only marginally attractive. The major part of the investment was in field recording equipment, of which only about half was to be in use more than half the time because of peak-load problems. Investment for handling the peak could be cut, but only with higher operating costs and some congestion. A team of analysts incorporating several types of skill was able to suggest an equipment redesign which permitted more intensive use of expensive electronic gear at peak periods, cut total investment by 25 percent, and made the investment attractive. The original design engineers were unfamiliar with the size of the peak load and its financial impact, so they had not tried to design around it. The analysis team, in turn, might have missed the redesign alternative if it had not included men with engineering experience.

Analysts trained in marketing, operations research, engineering, and finance have a real contribution to make. However, these disciplines need to

Too often, the analysis and decision process on a new investment opportunity seems to look like this (the detailed form, of course, depending on the specifics of the project):

There may be some interaction between market analysis and production engineering or between production engineering and financial analysis, but not a great deal. The type of interaction management should ask for instead looks more like this:

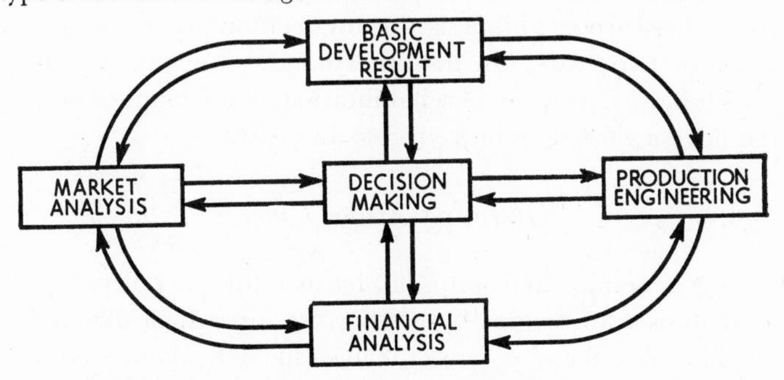

EXHIBIT 1. Use of functional specialists in investment analysis.

[2] Hearing before a subcommittee of the Committee on Banking and Currency, U.S. Senate, on S.874, March 26, 1963, concerning additional Mint facilities.

be integrated in the project analysis if management is to get a clear picture of the available alternatives and their consequences. Exhibit 1 is a schematic portrayal of the right and wrong ways to think of this process.

Returning to the problem of Prism Paints, let us assume that management assigns the plant investment question to a group made up of an operations research man, a marketing researcher, and an engineer with practical experience and imagination in process-plant design and costing. This team works closely with the company treasurer to investigate alternatives. It also meets regularly with other members of top management to review progress and policy problems.

LAYOUT OF THE TREE

Any significant problem can be examined at several levels of detail. The problem in laying out the decision tree is to strike the right level, the one which permits executives to consider major future alternatives without becoming so concerned with detail and refinement that the critical issues are clouded. The illustrations of trees in this and the preceding article indicate the general level of detail that seems reasonable in many typical circumstances.

What time span should be covered for the tree as a whole? The layout of alternatives might go on interminably and be carried out over an indefinite future time. Roughly, the practical time span or "horizon" to consider should extend at least to the point where the distinguishing effect of the initial alternative with the longest life is liquidated, or where, as a practical matter, the differences between the initial alternatives can be assumed to remain fixed.

The time span over which the analysis must extend will vary for *particular decisions*. For some decisions, it will be a year or two; for others, 10 years or longer. The launching of a new product is an example of the short-horizon type; the net effect of introducing the product, if successful, would last a good deal longer, but it can be characterized as a stream of income continuing for some period at some consistent level and hence does not need to be portrayed on the tree. There are no visible significant decisions to be considered beyond the first one or two years. On the other hand, plant investment questions, such as Prism Paints' problem of rehabilitating an old plant or building a new one, often have a time span of from 5 to 15 years.

Outlining Major Choices

With these generalizations in mind, let us return to our case. Let us suppose the analysis team begins by getting the forecast of demand shown in Exhibit 2. The central curve shows the most likely demand estimate, starting at $9 million in the early years of operation, rising to $12 million in five years, and reaching $18 million at the end of a decade. The lower curve, starting at $6 million and growing to $10 million, is the pessimistic estimate. The upper curve represents the most optimistic estimate of the rate of market growth.

The team's examination of the demand estimates indicates that there are three basic patterns of operation offering promise:

Program *A:* To modernize the plant in question and expand elsewhere
Program *B:* To close the plant in question and expand elsewhere
Program *C:* To modernize and expand the plant in question

The management, in discussions, points out that one or two major changes in the manufacturing and distribution pattern over the course of the next 10 years will be all the company wishes to make, if that many.

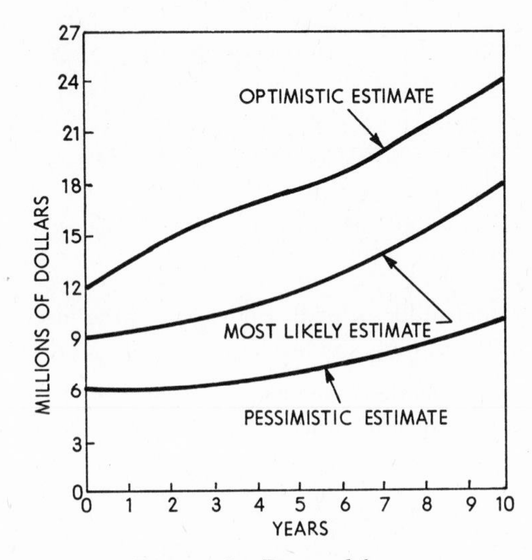

EXHIBIT 2. Demand forecasts.

As a practical matter, experience also indicates that breaking up a question into two to four decision stages (with the associated uncertainty alternatives) is reasonable. Thinking out the decision at least through a second decision stage enriches the analysis considerably over a conventional single-stage consideration; but after about four or possibly five stages, the analysis will bog down in complexity and lack of data. This means that the two, three, or four levels or stages of decision points must be the major significant points of choice as now seen. It means that the time between stages will vary in a given problem and, of course, will vary from one problem to another, depending on the overall span of time under consideration.

Costs and Feasibility

As a next step, the analysis team refines the alternatives and makes cost analyses of operations under these systems at different demand levels. Costs are worked out by calculating the best choice of warehouse locations, assignment of warehouses to plants for service, choice of item-stocking policy,

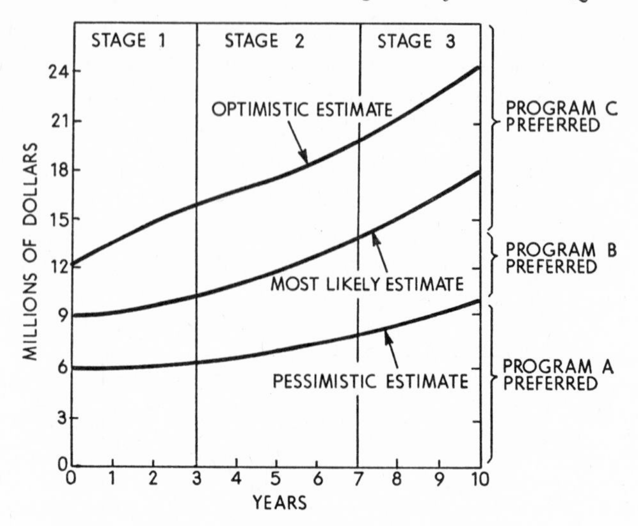

EXHIBIT 3. Effect of demand on preference for alternative patterns.

transportation method, and so forth, under the three alternate patterns of plant operation and volume of demand. Analysis shows that

1. Program *A* is less expensive when demand is less than $10 million annually.
2. Program *B* is less expensive when demand is between $10 million and $14 million annually.
3. Program *C* is less expensive when demand is over $14 million annually.

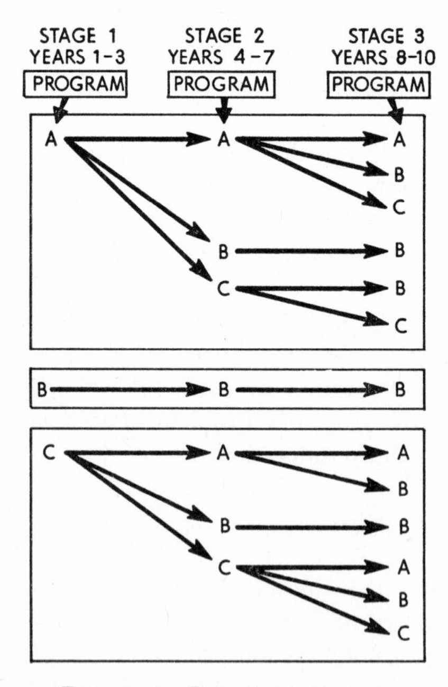

EXHIBIT 4. Program sequences.

It is decided, therefore, to break up the total time span under consideration into three periods—the first three years, the middle four years, and the period from the eighth year onward—as illustrated in Exhibit 3. During the first stage, demand is likely to be at a level where program *A* would be preferred; during stage 2, demand is likely to be in a range where program *B* would be preferred thereafter, demand is likely to be high enough so that program *C* would be preferred.

In theory, there are 27 plans over time that might be considered, although in practice some are out of the question. For example, Prism

Paints' management may conclude that if program *B* were adopted, it would be impractical to go to *A* or *C* and to reopen the plant in question.

The possibilities can be reduced for practical purposes to 13 feasible program sequences, each with its own pattern of investment and operating cost. For example, it is possible to begin to follow program *A*, and at a later time—say, eight years later—convert to program *C* at some cost of sunk investment, rearrangement, and excess operating expense. The 13 feasible sequences are shown in Exhibit 4.

Preliminary Drawing

If the company were sure of the sales volumes and operating costs 5 and 10 years hence, it could choose the particular program for plant construction that would make profits largest, after giving weight in some fashion (for example, by discounting future cash flows) to the relative value of present and future profits. Perhaps if sales do develop as projected, program *C* is the least expensive over the next decade. But what if sales do not develop as well as, or grow even faster than, forecast? The task of the team is to allow for the relative flexibility of various programs as a factor in meeting uncertain product demand. The choice made now will decide what later alternatives are still feasible. For example, as mentioned earlier, if program *B* is chosen, the company will have to live with it for some time. What immediate choice is the best one in view of the interrelationships among the immediate choice, demand levels, and future alternatives?

Exhibit 5 gives a preliminary sketch of the decision tree which shows the interaction between programs *A*, *B*, and *C* concerning plant facilities and the levels of demand in the company's market area. Some of the alternatives are not carried out to complete detail but are indicated by the dashed lines. The portion of the tree shown represents 10 of the 13 alternative patterns, many of which would be repeated in the portions of the tree that are not shown.

OBTAINING DATA NEEDED

In my view, the appropriate standard for corporate investment decisions is the maximization of expected wealth, or of discounted expected cash profit where future cash profit is discounted to present value at a discount rate equivalent to the market "cost of capital" of enterprises of similarly uncertain future.[3] I recognize, of course, that not all businessmen agree with this standard. Those who do not agree can use the principles to be described, but they will want to adjust them to suit their own criteria. Just bear in mind that in *this* illustration which I am presenting, the yield figures to be shown on the decision tree are not accounting profits but cash flows.

The numbers or values needed at each stage under the standard of maximum expected cash profit are

[3] Magee, *op. cit.*, p. 133.

1. The probabilities of each of the alternative uncertain outcomes—in Exhibit 5, for instance, the probabilities that demand will be low, medium, or high during years 1 through 3.
2. The cash flow associated with each combination of decision alternative and chance outcome.
3. Where the time span of the stage is significant—of the order of a few months or more—an estimate of the discount rate to be applied to deferred cash flows in the stage or to the future "position value" of the outcome. (See the discussion of rollback in my previous article.[4])

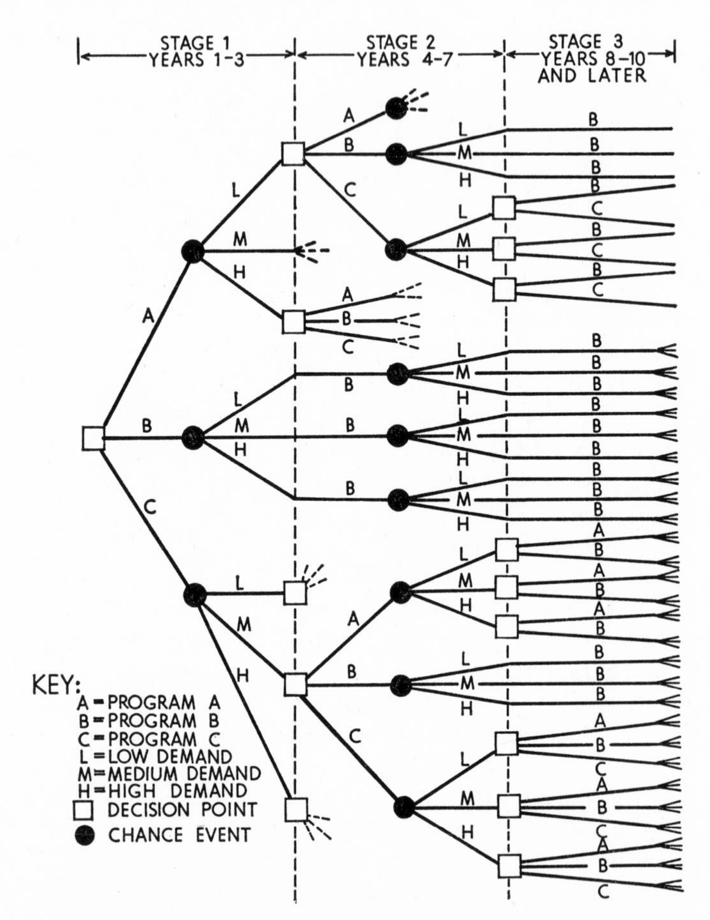

EXHIBIT 5. Preliminary decision tree for Prism Paints, Inc.

Probability Estimates

The probabilities of the uncertain alternatives may sometimes be estimated objectively from research. For example, the likelihood of surges or

[4] *Ibid.*, p. 132.

slumps in demand may be estimated objectively from a statistical analysis of demand variations, or the possibility that the market for a proposed product will be one size or another may be estimated from survey data. At other times the probabilities may have to be estimated subjectively from the intuition of an experienced operator or staff man. For example, the likelihood that a development project will succeed may be estimated from the intuitive judgment of two or three skilled engineers or research managers.

What is gained by trying to make subjective estimates of probabilities where limited objective information exists? Why not make the decision on feel, hunch, or intuition in the first place? For one thing, the estimation of elemental probabilities (and other values) permits various parties to the decision to see the basis for each other's conclusions. For another, it permits the executive to make use of the intuitions and skills of subordinate operators as staff

		Stage 2 If Stage 1 Is:			*Stage 3 If Stage 2 Is:*		
Level of Demand	*Stage 1*	*Low*	*Medium*	*High*	*Low*	*Medium*	*High*
Low (under $10 million)	0.50	0.35	0.15	....	0.20	0.05	....
Medium ($10–$14 million)	0.43	0.50	0.45	0.40	0.60	0.35	0.20
High (over $14 million)	0.07	0.15	0.40	0.60	0.20	0.60	0.80
Total	1.00	1.00	1.00	1.00	1.00	1.00	1.00

EXHIBIT 6. Probabilities that demand will be low, medium, or high.

members without abdicating his position as the decision maker. Further, it permits analysis of the impact of variations in the estimate—what is called *sensitivity analysis*—in the conclusion. Finally, as noted later, it provides a means for measuring the value of further work to sharpen up the estimates. This step is called *Bayesian analysis.*

Let us assume that the need for these estimates is felt by the managers in our Prism Paints case. Accordingly, the team analyzes evidence on market demand and the data underlying the demand forecasts (see Exhibit 2) to estimate how likely it is that demand will fall in the low, medium, or high range in each of the three stages of the analysis. The team concludes that these estimates must be made in relation to demand in the preceding stage. That is, if demand is high in stage 1, that will certainly influence the likelihood that demand will be high in stage 2. These estimates, for each stage, are summarized in Exhibit 6.

Cash Flows

The cash flows are characteristically estimated from the types of marketing, operations, engineering, and financial analyses mentioned earlier. Where the stage covers a considerable time span—one or more years—the schedule should show the cash flow at least on an annual basis.

In our Prism Paints case, distribution analyses show that the relative operating profitability of the alternatives facing management can be expressed by net annual cash flows as follows (in millions of dollars):

	Demand Level		
	Low	*Medium*	*High*
Program *A*	$1.5	$1.8	$1.5
Program *B*	1.0	2.0	2.8
Program *C*	0.5	1.5	3.3

Initial investment to implement program *A* is estimated to be $12 million, compared with $14.75 million for program *B* or $14 million for program *C*. Program *A* could thereafter be converted to *B* at a cost of $6 million, or to *C* for $8 million. Program *C* could be converted to *A* for $4 million, or to *B* for $6 million.

The management of Prism Paints establishes a desired return on investment or cost of capital of 14 percent per year. This is the rate to be used to reduce future cash flows to a present value for comparative purposes.

EVALUATING ALTERNATIVES

We can now construct the complete decision tree for Prism Paints' plant investment problem. The tree is shown in Exhibit 7 (ignore for a moment the numbers outside the boxes and circles).

Part *A* shows how the three alternatives at the initial decision, when combined with the possible market conditions in the period one to three years ahead, can lead to six decision situations at the beginning of the second stage in addition to the closedown situation (program *B*). The remaining parts (*B* through *D*) show how three of these decision situations may develop over the course of the subsequent years.

(The trees for the four situations not illustrated in Exhibit 7 would be quite similar in design.)

To evaluate the data in the decision tree, we follow three steps:

Step 1: Evaluate each of the alternatives at the final-stage decision points. Select the alternative with the largest net present value. Assign this value to the position.

For instance, in stage 3 of decision No. 1 (see Exhibit 7*B*), the expected value of each alternative for the uppermost decision can be calculated as shown in Exhibit 8. The alternative with the largest net present value ($12.8 million) is program *A*. Therefore, program *A* would be chosen *if* this decision at stage 3 *were* to be made *now*.

Step 2: Evaluate each decision alternative at the next preceding stage.

This is accomplished by calculating the expected discounted present value

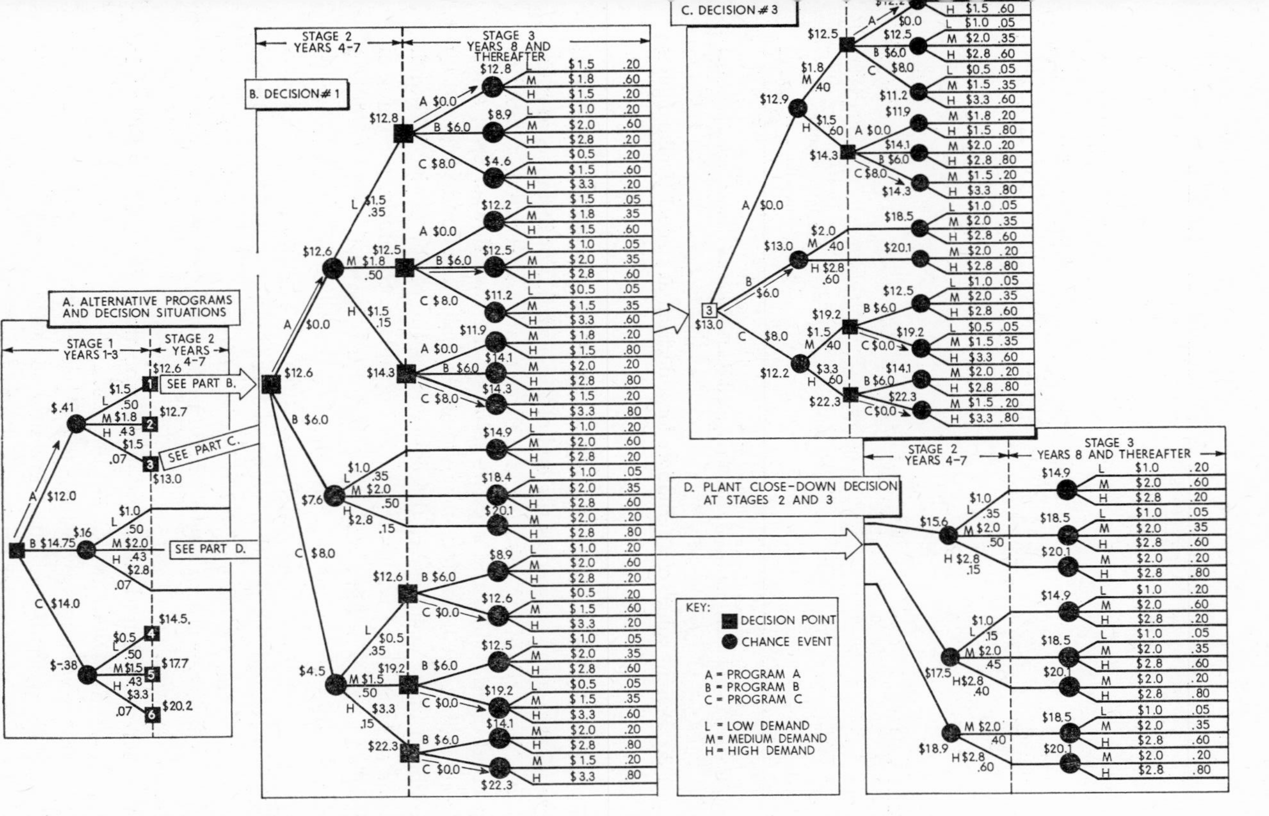

EXHIBIT 7. Complete decision trees for Prism Paints, Inc.

NOTE: Choices at each decision point are indicated by the letters *A*, *B*, or *C*. Figures following these choices represent the investment required. Possible levels of demand (low, medium, high) are indicated at each chance-event point by the letters *L*, *M*, and *H*. Two sets of numbers go with each market level—a dollar figure showing cash flow and a decimal representing the estimated likelihood that the level will occur. The numbers outside the black decision-point boxes and the black chance-event circles represent present value (in millions of dollars). The arrow at a decision box points to the alternative with greatest present value.

Alternative	*Market size*	*Likeli-hood (1)*	*Cash Flow per Year (2)*	*Period*	*Present Value Factor* (3)*		*Total Present Value (1) × (2) × (3)*
Program *A*.	L	0.20	$1.5	Indefinite	7.6		$ 2.3
	M	0.60	1.8	Indefinite	7.6		8.2
	H	0.20	1.5	Indefinite	7.6		2.3
						Total.	$12.8
						Less investment. . .	0.0
						Net present value.	$12.8
Program *B*.	L	0.20	1.0	Indefinite	7.6		$ 1.5
	M	0.60	2.0	Indefinite	7.6		9.1
	H	0.20	2.8	Indefinite	7.6		4.3
						Total.	$14.9
						Less investment. . .	6.0
						Net present value	$ 8.9
Program *C*.	L	0.20	0.5	Indefinite	7.6		$ 0.8
	M	0.60	1.5	Indefinite	7.6		6.8
	H	0.20	3.3	Indefinite	7.6		5.0
						Total	$12.6
						Less investment. . .	8.0
						Net present value	$ 4.6

* The value of $1 per year, received for an indefinite period and discounted at 14 percent per year on a semi-annual basis, is $7.60. Thus, 7.6 times the annual cash flow is the present value of the cash flow discounted at 14 percent per year.

EXHIBIT 8. Present values of alternatives for a decision at stage 3 (Dollar figures in millions).

of the cash flow during the stage, including the value of the following state as if it were a lump sum received at the end of the period. For instance, at stage 2, decision No. 1 (Exhibit 7*B*), there are three chance alternatives related to market conditions. When the present value of the cash flow of each alternative—including the following stage values—is calculated and weighted by the likelihood of its occurrence, the expected value of the choice is found. The value of program *A* is found to be $12.6 million. Similarly, the value of *B* is found to be $7.6 million, and the value of *C* is found to be $4.5 million. The mathematics of this step are the same as described in my July-August article. On this basis the preferred choice at decision No. 1, stage 2, is therefore program *A*, and the position value of Decision No. 1 is $12.6 million.[5]

Step 3: By repeated application of this process—the process of rollback (referred to in my previous article)—to each stage of decisions, the value of each alternative at the first stage can be found.

In Exhibit 7*A*, we find these values for the three programs at stage 1: *A*, $410,000; *B*, $160,000; and *C*, −$380,000.

These are the amounts by which the expected present value cash flow exceeds or falls short of the initial investment called for under each alternative. The cash flows under programs *A* and *B* and more than sufficient to earn the required 14 percent on the investment; the cash flow from program *C* is insufficient.

[5] *Ibid.*, p. 132.

Program *A* is the preferred choice because it has the greatest value. This does not mean, however, that Prism Paints must live with program *A* indefinitely. If the market grows rapidly to high levels, management can shift to program *B* (closing the plant, expanding elsewhere) at the intermediate point. Otherwise, management can choose depending on the rate of market development during the next seven years or so.

Actually, of course, during the years ahead, management will learn more about the market, and conceivably other changes will take place. Thus the *immediate* choice among *A*, *B*, and *C* is all that must be made now. However, the immediate decision is made with a proper eye to its impact on future developments and possible later decisions—with a recognition of the "futurity" of the current decision.

COMPARING OTHER METHODS

Does the use of the decision-tree approach make any difference? Let us compare the result of the Prism Paints analysis with the results of other more conventional discounted cash flow techniques.

One common method is to evaluate each fixed alternative under the "most likely" cash flow using present value techniques. This gives us (in millions of dollars):

		Cash Flow per Year		
	Investment	*Years 1–3*	*Years 4–7*	*Year 8 and Thereafter*
Program *A*	$12.00	$1.5	$1.8	$1.5
Program *B*	14.75	1.0	2.0	2.8
Program *C*	14.00	0.5	1.5	3.3

This approach yields net present values as follows (when the cash flows are discounted at 14 percent per year): program *A*, zero; program *B*, $1.3 million; and program *C*, $2.1 million.

It would appear that program *C* is the preferred; this ignores the possibility that the market may not in fact develop as fully at the "most likely" levels.

Another approach is to calculate the net *expected* present value, with the cash flows weighted by the estimated likelihood of their occurrence. This technique, applied to the Prism Paints data, yields the following net present values: program *A*, $126,000; program *B*, $160,000; and program *C*, −$380,000.

This approach seems to show program *B* as somewhat superior to *A*. This is due to the fact that the technique does not take into account the opportunity, if *A* is chosen, to modify the distribution plan later. As the decision-tree analysis shows, the flexibility implicit in program *A* makes it significantly superior.

The decision-tree analysis brings out the impact both of uncertainty and of possible future decisions, conditioned on future developments. To emphasize a point made earlier, the analysis *could* be made without actually drawing a tree, i.e., by simply listing the alternatives and stages for computation instead; but in practice, the visual form has real value in helping managers understand and discuss an investment problem.

SPECIAL PROBLEMS

In the Prism Paints case example, I have used "discrete" chance events for illustrative convenience. A discrete chance event is one where there is some number of clear-cut chance outcomes, each with its probability of happening. For instance, the toss of a coin is a discrete chance event.

In many practical cases, however, the chance events are in fact continuous; a whole range of answers is possible. There may be an estimated probability distribution associated with this range. The daily temperature is an example of a continuous chance event. There is an expected value for any locale and any time of year, though the actual value can be anywhere in a wide range. Using a probability distribution related to temperature, you can speak of the chance that the temperature will be between 75 and 80 degrees, below 65 degrees, and so forth.

Continuous-chance variables can be handled readily using the decision-tree technique. There are two ways:

1. In the Prism Paints case, we arbitrarily sliced the continuous-chance variable (future market levels) into the form of discrete chance levels—low, medium, and high. This approach often is adequate. It oversimplifies but (in many cases) not so much so as to add serious error.
2. We can calculate the values of the decision alternatives at any stage as related to the full range of the prior chance outcomes. In this way, we can fix the part of the range of possible outcomes for which any alternative is best. In some cases, straight calculation is all that is needed; in other cases, simulation methods are useful (for example, where the relationship between the chance variable and the cash flow following some decision alternative is a complex one).

Another problem is that of many chance variables. In the Prism Paints example, I have used market level as the single-chance variable at each stage; but in some problems, there are several uncertain variables at each stage. These might include, for example, total demand, share of market, costs, yield, or results of a development or promotion program. Any one or all of them might be so uncertain that a range of probabilities should be used.

Uncertainty connected with several variables can be handled readily. One useful way is the Monte Carlo method, a form of simulation.

At each stage—still working back from the last stage—values of the chance variables are picked at random, and the value of each decision alternative is worked out. Through repeated application, the expected values and probability distributions for each decision alternative emerge. The best alternative is chosen, and the rollback principle is applied to carry out the Monte Carlo analysis, if needed, at the next preceding stage.

Finally, there is the calculation problem. The limiting factor in drawing up a complex decision-tree analysis is not the task of computation but the capacity of the analysts to imagine alternatives and think out the implications of the various possible choices. Even so, computer calculation is often useful, and it has one important advantage: It makes it easier to analyze the sensitivity of the end conclusion to changes in key investment or cash flow figures or in probability estimates. If the conclusion as to what to do now is not too sensitive to changes in certain estimates, these can be estimated roughly. If the conclusion is very sensitive to changes in certain numbers, these are the ones where further research may be in order.

USE OF BAYESIAN METHOD

One alternative that frequently exists but may not be considered is further research or investigation. This does not mean procrastination but an intensive look by a fresh and objective team of men. Such a look may be especially valuable where the existing basis for decision is a series of semi-independent studies by staff groups committed to a position. It may mean carrying a research or development program one step further, or making a marketing study to try to narrow the range of market uncertainty. The concepts of Bayesian statistics[6] give a means for building in subsequent information to modify estimates of probabilities. The Bayesian method also gives a means for estimating the value of further investigation.

In the previous article in this series, we discussed the investment issue facing Stygian Chemical Industries, Ltd.—whether to build a small plant or a large one, in view of the uncertainty concerning the size of the market. The key issue facing management was whether to gamble on the size of the market and build a large plant immediately or to build a small plant with the possibility of expanding it later. That example lends itself particularly well to the present question, so I shall go back to it now.

Perfect Foresight?

Using discounted expected cash profit as the criterion, and discounting future cash flows at a 10 percent rate per year, we found in the previous article that the appropriate decision for Stygian appeared to be the large-plant alternative. The discounted expected value of that alternative was \$1.47 million, compared with a \$1.18 million value for building the small plant.[7]

---

[6] See, for example, Robert Schlaifer, *Probability and Statistics for Business Decisions* (New York: McGraw-Hill Book Co., Inc., 1959).

[7] Magee, *op. cit.*, pp. 133–34.

Suppose the company considers now the possibility of doing some further research—for example, making an independent technical-economic or marketing study to estimate more carefully what the long-term market penetration possibilities are. The marketing study, properly and thoroughly done, will be expensive; it will cost $100,000. Should the company contract for the research?

First, what would perfect foresight be worth? If management *knew* the market would be large, it would build the large plant. If it *knew* the market would be small in the long run, it would build the small plant. The value of knowing for sure whether the market is large or not can be calculated as follows:

1. Assuming one of the anticipated market conditions occurs and the preferred strategy for it is followed, calculate the present value of the cash flow which will come to the company (subtracting the cost of plant investment).
2. The discount rate used depends on management's judgment of the situation. For our illustration here, let us assume a 10 percent annual discount rate on future cash flows.
3. Multiply the present value thus obtained by management's present estimate of the probability that the market condition will actually occur.
4. Repeat the procedure for the other market conditions anticipated.

Market Situation (Demand)	*Preferred Strategy*	*Present Value* of Preferred Strategy (1)*	*Present Estimate of Likelihood (2)*	*Value of Perfect Foresight (1) × (2)*
High average	Big plant	$3.7	0.60	$2.22
High initial, low average	Small plant	1.5	0.10	0.15
Low average	Small plant	1.4	0.30	0.42
Total				$2.79

* The present value of the cash flow, discounted at 10 percent annually, including plant investment, and assuming the specified market condition occurred and preferred strategy was followed.

EXHIBIT 9. Calculations for determining value of perfect foreknowledge (Dollar figures in millions).

These calculations are carried out in Exhibit 9. They give us, in effect, a kind of average of the discounted cash flows weighted by the likelihood of their occurrence, if management knew in advance how big the market would be. This result ($2.79 million) is greater than the discounted expected value of the preferred large-plant alternative ($1.47 million) by $1.32 million. Thus the value of perfect foresight compared with present uncertainty is $1.32 million.

New Alternatives

This estimate suggests that there is a sizable potential payoff from good research in reducing the likelihood of a mistake, by narrowing down uncertainty in the market estimates and thus increasing the expected profit from the action taken. Let us suppose management has confidence in the research team, though considering it conservative. Management estimates that

1. If the market actually turns out to be large and demand is high from the outset, the chance the research will show a positive result is 70 percent. (By "positive result," I mean a high estimated demand.)
2. If demand is high initially but tapers off to a low level, the research effort might be misled, and there is a 50 percent chance it will err and report a positive finding.
3. If, however, demand is low, the chance of a positive result is quite small—about 5 percent.

From these estimates, it is possible to calculate that

1. If the research result is positive, the chance of a high average demand is 0.87; an initially high, low subsequent demand is 0.10; a low average demand is 0.03.
2. If the research result is negative, the chance of a high average demand is 0.35; an initially high, low subsequent demand is 0.10; a low average demand is 0.55.
3. The advance estimate of a positive finding is 0.485. (The difference between the estimate of 0.485 that the research will show a large demand and management's estimate of 0.60 that the demand will be large is a measure of management's estimate of the research organization's degree of conservatism.)

For those interested in technique, the method of calculating the foregoing data is shown in Exhibit 10.

Let HH signify a high average demand; HL signify an initially high, but low subsequent demand; and LL signify a low average demand.

Let F represent a positive result from the research and N a negative result.

Then:

$$P(HH/F) = \frac{P(F/HH)P(HH)}{P(F/HH)P(HH) + P(F/HL)P(HL) + P(F/LL)P(LL)}$$

$$= \frac{0.7 \times 0.6}{(0.7 \times 0.6) + (0.5 \times 0.1) + (0.05 \times 0.30)} = 0.87$$

The probabilities $P(HL/F)$, $P(LL/F)$, $P(HH/N)$, $P(HL/N)$, $P(LL/N)$ can be obtained similarly.

The chance of the research showing a positive result is

$$P(F) = P(F/HH)P(HH) + P(F/HL)P(HL) + P(F/LL)P(LL) = 0.485$$

Exhibit 10. Method of obtaining estimates of research reliability.

Now, management has three alternatives: (1) to build a large plant; (2) to build a small plant, with the later possible option of expansion at decision No. 2; or (3) to commission the research. If the third alternative is chosen, then, depending on the outcome of the investigation, the decision alternatives are 1′ and 2′ at decision No 3 (see Exhibit 11) if the research outcome is favorable; or 1″ and 2″ at decision No. 4 if the research outcome is unfavorable. These correspond to the original alternatives: (1) building a large plant or (2) building a small plant.

While the modified decision tree looks a good deal more complex, careful examination will show that the portion following decision No. 3 and the portion following decision No. 4 are each duplicates of the original decision tree,

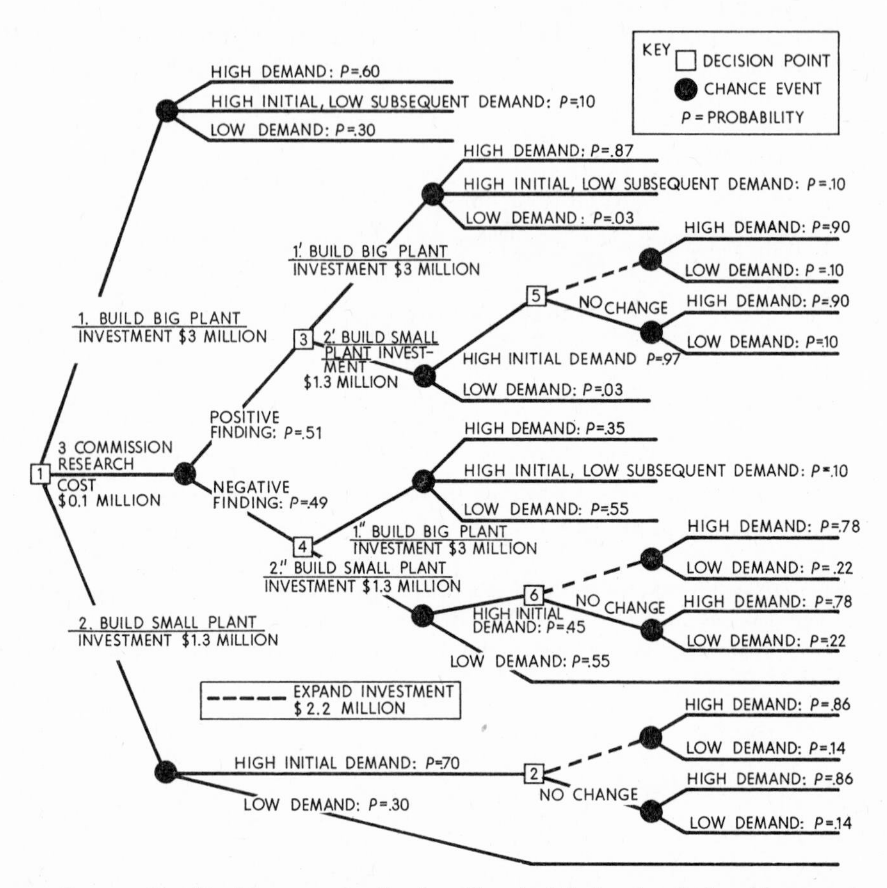

EXHIBIT 11. Decision tree for Stygian Chemical Industries, Ltd., with research alternative.

with just the probability estimates changed. The probability estimates are changed, as earlier described, to reflect the results of the research and its estimated reliability.

Maximizing Expected Value

The calculation of position values associated with the various decision points can be carried out just as shown in my July-August article. Using discounted expected value as the criterion and a discount rate of 10 percent annually, one finds that

1. If management were at decision No. 3 (research carried out, positive finding), the indicated decision would be to build the big plant, and the discounted expected value—the position value—would be $3.1 million.
2. If management were at decision No. 4 (research carried out, negative finding), the indicated decision would be to build the small plant and hold to it, whether initial demand were high or low. The discounted expected value, or position value, would be $2.6 million.

The expected value of alternative 3 at decision No. 1, therefore, can be calculated as

0.49 × $3.1 million	$1.5 million
Plus 0.51 × $2.6 million	$1.3 million
	$2.8 million
Less cost of research	0.1 million
Net expected value, alternative 3	$2.7 million

The discounted expected profits from alternatives 1 and 2 are unaffected by the introduction of the third alternative. So alternative 3, with a value of $2.7 million, is clearly superior to the previously indicated choice, alternative 1, with an expected value of $1.5 million.

The research increases the expected value of the endeavor by $1.2 million. It accomplishes this by reducing the uncertainty surrounding the demand estimates. It is interesting to note that the expected value of the endeavor will be increased significantly *no matter how the research comes out.*

CONCLUSION

Use of the decision-tree concept as a basis for investment analysis, evaluation, and decision is a means for making explicit the process which must be at least intuitively present in good investment decision making. It allows for, indeed encourages, revision of the issue and maximum use of analysis, experience, and judgment. It helps force out into the open those differences in assumptions or standards of value that underlie differences in judgment or choice. It keeps the executive from being trapped in the formalisms of a rigid capital evaluation procedure in which there is little room for feedback, redefinition, or interplay between analysis and decision.

The decision-tree approach will strike some businessmen as complex. Certainly, it is more complicated than rule-of-thumb approaches; but of course, any realistic method would be. In reality, a decision tree need be only as complex as the decision itself. If the decision is a simple choice among alternatives, then the decision tree reduces to a single-stage analysis, i.e., the use of the present-value technique applied to alternative cash flows. If the situation is more complicated, more stages and alternatives are necessary to reflect that fact.

Explicit use of the decision-tree concept will help force a consideration of alternatives, define problems for investigation, and clarify for the executive the nature of the risks he faces and the estimates he must make. The concept can thereby contribute to the quality of decisions which executives, and only executives, must make.

41

Introductory commentary cautions against the use of forecasts—particularly a selected single index—in making investment decisions. A simple example is set up in game theory format, and indifference probabilities for the economic forecasts are computed. These probabilities are then compared with the forecast probabilities in order to determine the best alternative. The degree of forecast accuracy is also established within tolerable limits. Problems involving timing and investment priority are briefly discussed, and the differences between theoretical game theory and the technique described are examined.

CAPITAL BUDGETING AND GAME THEORY*

Edward G. Bennion

THE PURPOSE of this article is to do two things: (1) to suggest a more rational approach to capital budgeting, which is a perennial and imperfectly solved problem for business; and (2) to test the applicability of game theory to the kind of decisions which are involved in capital budgeting.

In a sense, this is singling out a particular problem and a particular technique. However, the problem happens to be one of the most important and least clarified of the top-level issues faced by businessmen, just as the technique happens to be one of the most intriguing and least understood of the statistical devices which have recently been presented to businessmen as aids to top-level decision making. In combination, they offer an unusual opportunity to push progress ahead in an area where it is needed and at the same time put some realism into a methodology whose value may be overestimated at its present stage of development.

ROLE OF FORECASTS

The whole subject of capital budgeting is, of course, too big and complicated to be critically examined within the scope of one brief article. But perhaps some new light can be thrown on one important problem aspect: the relationship that should obtain between the budget and the economic forecast.

It hardly seems necessary to prove that economic forecasts play a significant—sometimes an almost determining—role in shaping the businessman's investment decisions. The traditional explanation is simple:

* Reprinted from *Harvard Business Review*, November–December, 1956, pp. 115–23.

1. In order to decide how much a company should invest or what kinds of assets it should acquire, we need a sales forecast for the firm—to establish its anticipated level of activity.
2. But the firm's sales forecast cannot be made without some estimate of what the industry is going to do. And the industry's sales forecast, in turn, depends in large measure on the predicted level of activity in the economy as a whole.
3. Q.E.D.—the capital budget of any individual firm has a unique and important relation to the general economic forecast.

Unreliable Guide

If it is obvious that forecasts are necessary, it is still more obvious that they are likely to be unreliable.

It is impossible to make an economic forecast in which full confidence can be placed. No matter what refinements of techniques are employed, there still remain at least some *exogenous variables*—i.e., variables, such as defense expenditures, the error limits of whose predicted values cannot be scientifically measured.

It is thus not even possible to say with certainty how likely our forecast is to be right. We may be brash enough to label a forecast as "most probable," but this implies an ability on our part to pin an approximate probability coefficient on a forecast: one if it is a virtual certainty, zero if it is next to an impossibility, or some other coefficient between these extremes. But again, since we have no precise way of measuring the probability of our exogenous variables behaving as we assume them to do, there is no assurance that the *estimated* probability coefficient for our forecast is anything like 100 percent correct.

In spite of such drawbacks, businessmen are willing to pay for having general economic forecasts made and to use them in deciding among alternative investment opportunities for capital funds. For example, the more certain is prosperity, the wiser it will usually be to invest in new plant and equipment; whereas the more certain is depression or recession, the safer it looks to invest in government bonds or other securities. In other words, the businessman uses economic forecasts to assess the relative advantages of investing in fixed or liquid assets, in the light of the expected business cycle phase.

Common Error

At this point the businessman stands before us, his economic forecast in one hand, his proposed investment alternatives in the other. His next step is the one where he is most apt to go wrong. When some one phase of the business cycle is forecast as "most probable," it is likely to look logical to him to go ahead and put his funds into whichever investment alternative maximizes profit in the phase expected.

Looking at the situation superficially, this step appears to be quite sensible. But actually, a businessman armed with only a single most probable forecast is in no position to make a wise investment decision—*unless* his forecast is 100 percent correct; and this, as we have seen, is an impossibility.

A New Approach

In the following pages a more rational way to use an economic forecast is suggested. Furthermore, adoption of the method proposed here permits the businessman to learn the answer to another question over which he probably has spent some sleepless nights if he has ever known responsibility for making a decision on the capital budget. *Just how far off can the forecast be before it leads to a "wrong" investment decision?*

Because the fundamentals of this new approach are most easily grasped if a specific problem is attacked, let us see how it can be applied in concrete cases. We shall look first at a simplified hypothetical case and then at a case based on actual experience (slightly disguised). For the sake of the clearest possible focus on the problems involved, no explicit reference will be made to the role of game theory while we are working out their solution. Following their presentation, however, we will meet the theory head on and discover in the process that we have already drawn from it just about as much as is possible.

SIMPLIFIED CASE

This first case, although hypothetical, is not unrealistic. Further, it has the advantage of reducing the problem and method of solution to the simplest possible proportions.

Alternative Investments

The specific issue of whether to invest in plant or securities is a good one for illustrative purposes because it can be defined so sharply. Suppose we have even more exact information than most businessmen generally assemble before exercising their judgment to reach an investment decision. Under these circumstances, we might know that

1. The most probable forecast is for a recession.
2. In recession, investment in plant will yield 1 percent as compared with a 4 percent yield for securities.
3. In prosperity, plant will yield 17 percent, while securities will yield 5 percent.

Placing these data in diagram form, we get the following 2 × 2 matrix:

Management Investment Alternatives	Cycle-Phase Alternatives: Recession	Cycle-Phase Alternatives: Prosperity
Securities	4%	5%
Plant	1%	17%

Under this condition, no businessman worth his salt is going to want to settle for securities—but how can he justify any other course, given his forecast of a probable recession?

More Data Needed

To begin with, our businessman needs to recognize that the data so far placed at his disposal, rather than limiting his choice, do not provide the basis for a decision at all. Two further questions first require an answer:

1. How probable is the "most probable" forecast? To answer this, the forecast needs to be completed by assigning a *probability coefficient* to each cycle phase considered.
2. How probable does a recession have to be before the earnings prospects of the more conservative choice look just as attractive as the returns available from adopting a bolder course of action? In other words, what are the *indifference probabilities* of recession and prosperity, given the rate of return each will yield?

Probability Coefficients

Establishing probability coefficients on the economic forecast is a job we can relinquish, more than willingly, to the company economist. We are not concerned here with what kind of crystal ball he gazes into, but rather with how top management uses his findings, whatever they may be. So, in order to get on with our problem, let us simply suppose that our forecaster thinks the chances of recession are 6 out of 10 and so has assigned a probability coefficient of 0.6 to his predictions for a recession (which automatically means 0.4 for prosperity).

Indifference Probabilities

The handling of indifference probabilities is not going to be quite so simple, but it can be done readily enough by anyone who can recall his high school course in algebra (he does not have to be blessed with total recall, either):

Suppose we say, in elementary algebraic terms, that the recession probability coefficient equals R and the prosperity probability coefficient equals P. In that event, we know from our matrix figures that over any period:

$$4R + 5P = \text{Return on securities} \tag{1}$$
$$1R + 17P = \text{Return on plant} \tag{2}$$

From this, it is clear that the return on securities will be the same as the return on plant when

$$4R + 5P = 1R + 17P \tag{3}$$

Solving this last equation for R in terms of P, we get

$$R = 4P \tag{4}$$

Since the sum of the probability coefficients ($R + P$) has to equal one, we can say that $R = (1 - P)$ and substitute $(1 - P)$ for R in equation 4:

$$1 - P = 4P \tag{5}$$
$$P = 0.2 \tag{6}$$
$$R = 0.8$$

This merely means that if the probabilities of a recession and prosperity are 0.8 and 0.2, respectively, then the chances are that the company will be just as well off investing in securities as in plant, and vice versa. In other words, it appears to be a matter of *indifference* which alternative is chosen.

Assembling the Data

For the sake of convenience, let us reassemble all our information in the compact easy-to-read form of a matrix:

Management Investment Alternatives	Cycle-Phase Alternatives: Recession	Prosperity
Securities	4%	5%
Plant	1%	17%

Indifference probabilities: $R = 0.8$ $P = 0.2$
Forecasted probabilities: $\hat{R} = 0.6$ $\hat{P} = 0.4$

Here, at last, our businessman has all the information he needs to decide what course of action maximizes his chances for success. So long as the forecasted probability coefficient for a recession is not equal to or greater than the indifference probability coefficient for this phase of the business cycle, the businessman can know that he is not making an *avoidable* mistake by playing for high stakes and building a plant. *The alternative to choose is the one that has a higher forecasted probability than indifference probability.*

Advantage Gained

The little technique outlined above thus does two things:

1. It makes clear that the best-paying investment alternative in the most probable situation is not necessarily the alternative that management should choose.
2. With indifference probabilities, it is possible for us to see what margin of error is permissible in any estimated probabilities before these estimates result in an erroneous decision.

ACTUAL CASE

With this much understanding of the 2×2 matrix, we are now in a position to apply indifference probabilities to our actual but more complicated case.

An integrated petroleum company anticipates the need for refinery in country A, has determined that Alpha City is the best location, but is uncertain as to the appropriate size.

Operating at approximate capacity, internal economies of scale exist up to a refinery size of R barrels per day (B/D).

However, once sales exceed Z barrels per day (with $Z < R$), further economies could best be effected by building a second refinery elsewhere. This puts a ceiling of Z barrels per day on the Alpha City unit.[1]

Whatever size refinery is built, it can be completed in 1960. It is also agreed that depreciation and obsolescence will make the refinery valueless by 1974.

As an aid in determining the size required in 1960, it is known that consumption growth is highly correlated with industrial output.

Unfortunately, there is less than perfect unanimity as to the expected growth rate of industrial output between the present and 1960. The economics department has forecasted a rate of 2.5 percent, the foreign government officially estimates a rate of 5 percent, and the company top management wonders what would happen if the growth rate turned out to be 7.5 percent.

Careful analysis leads to the conclusion that a growth rate of 2.5 percent requires a refinery of X barrels per day capacity; that a growth rate of 5 percent necessitates a refinery of Y barrels per day capacity; and that a growth rate of 7.5 percent requires a refinery of Z barrels per day capacity, this last being our previously established ceiling size.

Pending further study, all agree to work on the assumption of a zero growth rate after 1960.

To evaluate the three alternative refineries, anticipated integrated income (covering refining, marketing, producing, and transportation) will be computed for each facility under each growth rate, and the percent return on integrated investment will then be calculated and compared.[2]

Matrix and Probabilities

With three sizes of refineries to consider, and three growth rates, we will get a 3×3 matrix on this problem. The figures on the diagram, representing

[1] This ceiling decision, it might be noted, involves the solution to a problem to which linear programming conceivably might aptly be applied. Taking this solution as given obviously does not mean it is necessarily easy to come by. See Alexander Henderson and Robert Schlaifer, "Mathematical Programing: Better Information for Better Decision Making," *Harvard Business Review*, May–June, 1954, p. 73.

[2] While the matrix figures of this case are based on careful engineering estimates, this venture is still in an experimental stage and hence does not constitute a part of the budget procedure of Standard Oil Company (New Jersey), with which I am associated.

return on integrated investment, are more or less what common sense tells us to expect. For example, the small *X* B/D refinery shows the highest rate of return if the growth rate is a low 2.5 percent, bringing in an 8.8 percent return against only a 2 percent for the large *Z* B/D unit with its much higher cost of investment. On the other hand, if the growth rate should reach a high of 7.5 percent, the large *Z* B/D refinery can return an average of 12.6 percent, while the small *X* B/D facility with its limited output is tied to its 8.8 percent ceiling yield.

But filling in the matrix does more than verify our commonsense conclusions. It also equips us to see *how much* better one refinery is than another under each possible condition.

		Pre-1960 Growth Rate Alternatives		
		Low 2.5%	Moderate 5.0%	High 7.5%
Refinery Investment Alternatives	*Z* B/D	2.0%	7.3%	12.6%
	Y B/D	3.7%	11.0%	11.0%
	X B/D	8.8%	8.8%	8.8%

Indifference probabilities: $L = 0.301$ $M = 0.114$ $H = 0.585$
Forecasted probabilities: $\hat{L} = 0.333$ $\hat{M} = 0.333$ $\hat{H} = 0.333$

The indifference probabilities here were calculated by the same algebraic procedures as were followed in our previous example. The forecasted probabilities simply reflect the fact that no one in the company could decide which of the three forecasts was most likely, and therefore each was treated as equally "valid" (i.e., chances of 1 out of 3, or 0.33⅓).

The Solution

A quick look at our diagram now reveals that the extra-large *Z* B/D refinery should be ruled out, since its return will be greater only under a 7.5 percent growth rate, and the real probability for a 7.5 percent growth rate is too small to justify considering that alternative. (Remember that an alternative cannot be chosen unless its forecasted or estimated true probability is equal to or above the indifference probability.)

On the other hand, both the *X* B/D and *Y* B/D refineries are still in the running. So, with two possibilities still remaining, new indifference probability calculations are needed in order that we may choose between them.

Suppose (as before) we use the letter L to represent the indifference probability for the low 2.5 percent growth rate; M for the moderate 5 percent rate; and H for the high 7.5 percent figure. In this event, we read off the matrix that

(1) $3.7L + 11.0M + 11.0H =$ Return on the *Y* B/D refinery
(2) $8.8L + 8.8M + 8.8H =$ Return on the *X* B/D refinery

From this, it is clear that the return on *Y* B/D will be the same as the return on *X* B/D when

(3) $$3.7L + 11.0M + 11.0H = 8.8L + 8.8M + 8.8H$$

Solving this equation in terms of L, we get

(4) $$L = 0.43\ (M + H)$$

This means that if the estimated true probability of a 2.5 percent growth rate is greater than 0.43 of the combined estimated true probabilities of the 5 percent and the 7.5 percent growth rates, the *X* B/D refinery is a better bet than the *Y* B/D refinery. This has to be true because the *X* B/D refinery is the best-paying alternative, given the 2.5 percent growth rate.

Since the estimated true probability for the 2.5 percent growth rate is actually 0.33, which is slightly greater than $0.43 \times (0.33 + 0.33)$, we would conclude that the *X* B/D refinery is a little better bet than the *Y* B/D refinery, with the *Z* B/D refinery showing a very poor third.

A Changed Assumption

Now that we have reached an answer to the problem as originally stated, let us (realistically if provokingly) proceed to alter some of our assumptions and see just what this will do to our choice.

Suppose that top management, having injected the 7.5 percent growth rate into the original problem for comparative purposes, concludes that probability of a 7.5 percent growth rate is really nil and that the probabilities of the 2.5 percent and 5 percent growth rates are each 0.5. The indifference equation then becomes

$$3.7L + 11.0M = 8.8L + 8.8M$$

or

$$L = 0.43M$$

Since the estimated true probability of 0.50 for the 2.5 percent growth rate is, in this instance, a great deal bigger than 0.43×0.50, we would conclude that the *X* B/D refinery is a lot better bet than the *Y* B/D refinery and that no one in his right mind would even consider building a *Z* B/D unit.

Thus, we come to the same general conclusion as before, only a bit more cocky, as a result of writing off the 7.5 percent growth rate and distributing its former probability in such a way as to make the 2.5 percent and 5 percent growth rates equally probable.

A Radical Revision

It is clear, however, that the above conclusion is suspect unless we expect no economic growth in country A after 1960. If we do expect further growth, the *X* B/D refinery loses much of its dollar-sign allure. It will not be large enough to take advantage of country A's expanding economy and so can never return any more than 8.8 percent on investment.

In contrast, the *Z* B/D refinery will show an increasing rate of return as A's expanding market permits it to produce more and more per year, perhaps ultimately reaching its capacity. Thus, instead of spurning the *Z* B/D refinery (as in our last example), we must acknowledge its potential attractiveness—provided A's economy does not get stalled after 1960, as was previously assumed.

With this possibility in mind, let us make some alterations in our problem and see what we should do. There are two new conditions:

1. After 1960, it is now agreed, the growth rate of country A will be a steady 2.5 percent each year.
2. It would be possible to build an *X* B/D or *Y* B/D refinery that would be expansible to *Z* B/D; such units would cost more than nonexpansible facilities but less than two separate refineries with a combined *Z* B/D capacity.

At this point, our real problem becomes one of deciding whether to build a *Z* B/D refinery or an *X* B/D or a *Y* B/D refinery expansible to *Z* B/D. It may be helpful, first, to consider how the figures in this new matrix should differ from those presented earlier.

Most of the figures are higher than before, reflecting the fact that average earnings are increased by higher sales toward the end of the productive life of each unit.

To a limited extent, the higher investment costs of the two expansible units operate as a drag on their earnings. Thus, two of the figures happen to be lower than before, and the expansible refineries have a lower maximum return than is possible with a *Z* B/D unit.

On the whole, the figures in the matrix tend to be squeezed closer together; i.e., they no longer range between such wide extremes.

Now our revised matrix reads like this:

Refinery Investment Alternatives	Pre-1960 Growth Rate Alternatives: Low 2.5%	Moderate 5.0%	High 7.5%
Z B/D	4.6%	9.9%	12.6%
Expansible *Y* B/D	7.2%	10.5%	11.1%
Expansible *X* B/D	8.0%	9.7%	10.4%

Indifference probabilities: $L = 0.338$ $M = 0.129$ $H = 0.533$

Forecasted probabilities: $\hat{L} = 0.333$ $\hat{M} = 0.333$ $\hat{H} = 0.333$

Again, we work our algebraic equations to find the indifference probabilities, while the forecasted probabilities result, as before, from assigning equal weight to each forecast.

In this instance the expansible *Y* B/D refinery is a shoo-in. This can be intuitively seen by recognizing that the *Y* B/D refinery is the best-paying one given the 5 percent growth rate, and this growth rate is the only one with an *indifference* probability lower than its *estimated true* probability. By somewhat similar reasoning the *Z* B/D refinery is distinctly the worst choice.

The new matrix also reveals another significant conclusion. One does not have to be a mathematician to perceive, just from inspection, that the cost of a poor decision here is a good deal lower than it was for our earlier versions of this problem. The result, of course, flows from the fact that the differences in the row and column vectors have been greatly narrowed. The *absolute* cost of a mistake is by no means insignificant; but *relatively*, it is much less than in the previous matrix. This piece of information is in itself of considerable value. At a minimum, it will help the budget maker to do less agonized tossing in his bed.

More Tinkering

Just for fun, let us tinker with our problem once more before dropping it, and again assume that management rejects as of nil probability the growth rate of 7.5 percent between the present and 1960, giving the 2.5 percent and 5 percent growth rates equal probabilities (i.e., chances of one out of two, or 0.5).

This eliminates the top row and right column of the 3×3 matrix, leaving it 2×2.

The indifference probabilities equation for the *X B/D* and *Y B/D* refineries then becomes

$$8.0L + 9.7M = 7.2L + 10.5M$$

or

$$L = M$$

This means that the *indifference* probabilities for both L and M are 0.5.

These, however, are also the values for the *estimated real* probabilities for the 2.5 percent and 5 percent growth rates.

Consequently, we have here the unusual case in which the *X* B/D and *Y* B/D refineries are equally good bets, with the *Z* B/D refinery being no bet at all.

No matter which way we look at the problem, therefore, the *Z* B/D refinery is the poorest choice. But under one probability assessment the expansible *Y* B/D refinery is a better choice than the expansible *X* B/D refinery; under the other the expansible *X* and *Y* B/D refineries are toss-ups. This conclusion is, of course, decidedly different from that reached for the previous matrix, in which the influence of post-1960 growth was ignored.

OTHER BUDGET QUESTIONS

So far, we have managed to explore only one small corner of the capital budget domain. Let us look at some further problem areas.

Problem of Timing

Our new technique can also be put to work on a timing problem. Since all but one of the figures in the following matrix have been chosen somewhat arbitrarily (although the choices can easily be defended), they call for no explanation. The only exception is the 9.6 percent prosperity return for the *Y* B/D refinery which appears in the lower right-hand corner; this is the *weighted average* return from this investment under the three possible rates of growth, assuming equal probability for each.

		Pre-1960 Cycle-Phase Alternatives		
		Depression	Recession	Prosperity
Management Investment Alternatives	Government Bonds	3.5%	3.0%	2.5%
	Other Securities	2.0%	5.0%	3.0%
	Y B/D Refinery	−2.0%	3.0%	9.6%
	Indifference probabilities:	$D = 0.43$	$R = 0.24$	$P = 0.33$

It would be a tedious repetition of now familiar principles to attempt to bleed this matrix dry. Let us content ourselves, therefore, with just one reasonable (and relatively simple) interpretation.

Since depression is comparable to the 1937–38 decline in this country, we might well reject this as being of nil probability in the period between now and 1960.

Should we do so, the left column of the 3 × 3 matrix would be eliminated, as would the top row, since government bonds would not be a logical investment except under depressed conditions.

In the remaining 2 × 2 matrix, the indifference equation for other securities and our *Y* B/D refinery then becomes

$$5.0R + 3.0P = 3.0R + 9.6P$$

or

$$P = 0.3R$$

In other words, unless we think the true probability of a recession is something more than twice as great as that of prosperity, the construction of the *Y* B/D refinery ought not to be deferred.

Investment Priorities

Whenever more than one investment alternative is available, there arises the problem of assigning an order of priority among them. To assess and compare each possible project, the method followed in the previous problem can be used to advantage again:

1. Using a 2 × 2 matrix, calculate indifference probabilities for investing in securities and in plant (or other assets to be used in the company's own business).
2. Repeat this process for each contemplated internal use of company funds. The top row will be the same in all of these matrices, but the bottom rows will not in general be the same. Consequently, the indifference probabilities for the numerous matrices may vary widely. Any company project with an indifference probability coefficient for prosperity that is lower than the estimated true prosperity probability coefficient is a good bet.
3. Instead of arraying the projects in order of descending return *for the most probable cycle phase* (which would incur all the defects already shown to exist in tying investment decisions to a single most probable forecast), array them in order of descending *weighted average* return—weighted according to the estimated probabilities of recession and prosperity or of different rates of growth.

In general, this procedure will *not* result in the same priority order for projects as the method commonly employed, but it is a better method of evaluating all the alternative uses for funds. This is because it avoids the frequently fatal mistake of betting on whatever venture seems to look most profitable, given only a single most probable forecast.

If desirable projects turn out to be more numerous than company resources can finance, the management must then decide whether it wants to borrow or not. If external financing should be ruled out, the marginal project must be the one with the lowest weighted average return which just exhausts available funds. On the other hand, if all desirable projects do not exhaust available funds, the marginal project is the one whose indifference coefficient for prosperity is just equal to the estimated true prosperity coefficient. The excess funds should be temporarily invested in securities.

ALMOST A GAME

Now, finally, we are ready to have that initial promise redeemed—i.e., that the role of game theory would be explained and be evaluated. Actually, as anyone who has met this theory before will recognize, it has already been introduced! All our matrices have been "games," although, in playing some of them, we have had to construe a few of the rules pretty loosely.

The two players in most of our games have been the businessman and the business cycle. Each has had either two or three "strategies." For the former, there have been different types of investment alternatives; for the latter, there have been different cycle phases. Indeed, the indifference probabilities calculated by the businessman for depression, recession, and prosperity have an exact parallel in game theory. Those probabilities constitute what would be known as the "business cycle probabilities"—namely, the percentage of the time that the business cycle should provide each of its phases in a random manner to hold the businessman's gains down to a minimum.

Can it be said, then, that our method for deciding on the capital budget marks an extension of game theory concepts to the field of business and economics? In the strictest sense, the answer must be no. Ours is not a rigorous game—it does not meet all the conditions requisite for such a game.

In game theory proper, the opposing players are assumed to be completely selfish and intelligent. Charity and stupidity are unknown to either. Clearly, the business cycle, however malevolent it may sometimes seem, does not meet these requirements. It is as impersonal as nature. In fact, what we really are doing in problems like ours is playing games with nature. Thus the indifference probabilities in our last matrix are actually *nature*'s probabilities. They tell us that if nature were malevolent, it could minimize its "losses" to the businessman by providing depression, recession, and prosperity, in a random manner, 43 percent, 24 percent, and 33 percent of the time, respectively.

If the businessman were confronting an opponent who could maximize gains and minimize losses by a deliberate choice of strategies, then there would be additional calculations to make and prohibitions to observe. For example, in order to keep a selfish and intelligent antagonist from guessing what he might do and benefiting by the knowledge, the businessman might have to figure out several strategies for himself and then use them randomly. Thus, again in our last matrix, the *businessman*'s odds are such that he should invest in government bonds, other securities, and the *Y* B/D refinery, in a random manner, 90 percent, 2 percent, and 8 percent of the time, respectively. Otherwise, faced with a malevolent nature, he would fail to maximize his gains.

It takes some stretching to make a choice of strategies out of a range of possibilities, yet a range of possibilities is all we can get out of nature (as contrasted with a willful opponent); and in the case of some business problems, we cannot even get that. Moreover, nature, alias the business cycle, may have some strategies on the matrix that no sensible antagonist would use at all because under all conditions other strategies would give him higher gains or lower payoffs.

Consequently, our games with nature are not of the "purer," more rigorous type. Our version represents a departure by virtue of recognizing four additional facts: (1) Nature is not malevolent; (2) the odds of a malevolent nature are really the indifference probabilities of the businessman with respect to his alternative courses of action; (3) any time the estimated odds of nature's strategies differ from the businessman's indifference odds, there is a best strategy for the businessman; and (4) this best strategy, as well as the degree of its "bestness," depends on the relationship between the estimated and indifference odds.

However, any readers who are interested in further pursuing the rules of game theory proper can do so handily by consulting J. D. Williams, *The Compleat Strategyst.*[3] Anyone who can add and subtract can follow this pleasant and often humorous exposition, whereas most other books on the subject call for more advanced mathematical learning.[4]

Other Economic "Games"

If capital budgeting can only borrow from game theory but not take it over in its entirety, what about any other business applications? It should be possible to find in the businessman's competitive world a variety of situations that resemble orthodox games—i.e., where the opponents are not noted for their charity toward each other.

The existence of many such parallels is obvious; but unfortunately, game theory in its present state of development is not far enough advanced to handle most of them. (Originated by von Neumann, the theory first achieved a wide audience when he and Morgenstern published their book in 1944.[5]) Thus, game theory still does not deal effectively with situations where there are more than two players or where the loser's losses and the winner's gains do not cancel out.

For example, the most common realistic game cited in economic literature is a duopolistic (two-seller) situation in which each of the duopolists has alternative strategies and seeks the strategy that will maximize his profits.[6] This may be a realistic example, but it is certainly one of limited existence. The businessman may not have a large number of competitors, but he usually has at least several. However, to consider several competitors plunges us into games involving more than two players, and here the theory as it now stands leaves much to be desired.

Another possible realistic game on the two-person level is where the oppo-

---

[3] New York: McGraw-Hill Book Co., Inc., 1954.

[4] John von Neumann and Oscar Morgenstern, *The Theory of Games and Economic Behavior* (Princeton: Princeton University Press, 1944); J. C. C. McKinsey, *Introduction to the Theory of Games* (New York: McGraw-Hill Book Co., Inc., 1952); David Blackwell and M. A. Girshick, *Theory of Games and Statistical Decisions* (New York: John Wiley & Sons, Inc., 1954).

[5] See n. 4.

[6] See L. Hurwicz, "The Theory of Economic Behavior," in George J. Stigler and Kenneth E. Boulding (eds.), *A.E.A. Readings in Price Theory* (Homewood, Ill.: Richard D. Irwin, Inc., 1952), Vol. VI.

nents are the businessman and the trade union. But this sort of game is likely to be one in which the solution may harm or benefit both players, or harm one player more than it benefits the other. This throws us into games with a nonzero-sum payoff, where the theory again leaves much to be desired.

To say that game theory, in its more rigorous sense, still has no significant business applications does not of course mean that claims for its *potential* have been exaggerated. The day of orthodox game theory may well be on its way, just as the day of linear programming has already arrived in some measure.[7] Meanwhile, businessmen may wish to acquaint themselves with the theory and be on the watch for any practical uses it may have.

CONCLUSION

To summarize briefly, we have seen that forecasting can result in a negative contribution to capital budget decisions unless it goes further than merely providing a single most probable prediction. Without an estimated probability coefficient for the forecast, plus knowledge of the payoffs for the company's alternative investments and calculation of indifference probabilities, the best decision on the capital budget cannot be reached.

Even with these aids, the best decision cannot be known for certain, but the margin of error may be substantially reduced, and the businessman can tell just how far off his forecast may be before it leads him to the wrong decision. It is in assessing this margin of error, along with the necessarily quantitative statement of alternative payoffs, that some of the concepts of game theory make their particular contribution to the problem.

[7] See Henderson and Schlaifer, *op. cit.*

42

An elementary introduction to game theory is briefly provided, after which several different business problems ostensibly amenable to game theory analysis are described in a summary manner. Then the elements involved in configuring this type of problem in game theory format are discussed. Based upon this description, an extensive illustration of a capital-budgeting decision is presented.

*PRACTICAL APPLICATION OF THE THEORY OF GAMES TO COMPLEX MANAGERIAL DECISIONS**

Spencer A. Weart

FREQUENTLY, in the management of even the smallest industrial enterprise, complex decisions must be made. Such decisions require that numerous factors must be weighted, one combination of variables equated against all other possible combinations, and a final answer found by some abstruse mental solution of what is really an integral or differential equation. All of this quasi-mathematical process is lumped under the heading of "business judgment," and rarely can the manager trace back the actual steps by which he arrived at his decision in a marginal case, and seldom can he formulate the equations in mathematical terms, despite their real existence. At this point, I hasten to say that managerial decisions never can be purely mathematical, because of the impossibility of assigning exact numbers to intangibles. But the mental torture of evaluating the factors can be reduced or eliminated by analyzing a problem and expressing it in a form that permits a yes or no decision, instead of a *yes-but* or *no-but*.

The procedure for doing this is spelled out in a complicated mathematical manner in the *theory of games*. There is, however, a simple, practical method for applying this interesting theory to complex managerial problems, reducing them to ordinary terms for an easy, reliable, obvious decision.

---

* Reprinted from *Journal of Industrial Engineering*, July–August, 1957, pp. 203–9. The *Journal* is the official publication of the American Institute of Industrial Engineers, Inc., 345 East 47th Street, New York, New York 10017.

THEORY OF GAMES

The theory of games is usually considered to have originated in the late 1920's with the mathematician John von Neumann, who was the first to show that all games could be expressed in the form of a matrix, that is, a diagram or grid, in which one set of factors is arrayed vertically, another set horizontally, and values assigned or computed for each intersection. For example:

SHOULD I CARRY AN UMBRELLA?

Variable / *Choice*	*It Rains*	*It Does Not Rain*
Carry	Do not get wet	Do not get wet
Do not carry	Get wet	Do not get wet

In only one of the four possible values is there a possibility of an unfavorable result, which may explain why few people carry umbrellas. But this is only part of the problem, for now the relative weighting of each variable must be considered—what it costs to own and carry an umbrella, and what it costs if I get wet. When mathematical values are assigned to each of the variables, we might get this, for example:

SHOULD I CARRY AN UMBRELLA?[1]

Variable / *Choice*	*It Rains*	*It Does Not Rain*
Carry	$0.50	$0.60
Do not carry	1.25	0.00

A mathematician will tell you that this matrix figures out[2] at 25 to 2, with a game value of $0.55½; namely, out of every 27 times, on 25 of them I should carry an umbrella, and if I do, I will be $0.55½ better off each time I am right. Now, such a conclusion is really very surprising, and it would appear that the world should teem with umbrella toters. One reason it does not is that we have not taken into account the chances of its raining while I am outside. If the weather map is such that the chances of rain are 1 to 5, and if my

[1] For those who wonder where the values come from, the following may suffice: cost of owning a $5 umbrella, lost after 10 times carried, 50 cents; cost of carrying an umbrella when it does not rain, the above 50 cents plus 10 cents checking charge; cost of getting suit pressed, $1.25.

[2] Those interested in pursuing the mathematics further are referred to *The Compleat Strategyst*, by J. D. Williams (New York: McGraw-Hill Book Co., Inc., 1954), for an elementary but sufficient explanation of how this is done. Those wishing a more complete mathematical discussion are referred to *Introduction to the Theory of Games*, by J. C. C. McKinsey (New York: McGraw-Hill Book Co., Inc., 1952), which has a quite complete bibliography for those wishing to go still further.

expectation of being outside is 1 to 10, then the odds against being caught outside in the rain are 1 to 50, and the matrix would be:

SHOULD I CARRY AN UMBRELLA?

Choice \ *Variable*	*It Rains*	*It Does Not Rain*
Carry	$0.50	$0.60
Do not carry*	$0.02½	0.00

* Method of applying the odds is explained later.

This time the diagram states unequivocably that I should never carry an umbrella, for whether it rains or not my loss is less if I do not have the umbrella. Since this is more nearly the average situation in real life, few people carry umbrellas in average weather.

In brief, all of the foregoing is a simple application of game theory to what is known as a 2 × 2 game, there being two choices and two variables. If there were three variables, the game would be called 2 × 3, and so on, to 2 × *n*. In practice, most business decisions have only two choices, or can be reduced to only two choices—*do* or *do not*, but there are more than two, or *n*, variable factors. It so happens that the 2 × *n* game lends itself to a very simple graphic and arithmetical solution.[3] Where there are three or more choices, no easy solution is available without resorting to more involved mathematics, or perhaps to a lengthy process of trial and error. Occasionally, this may be necessary;[4] but in business, it is a rare problem that cannot be reduced to a yes or no choice, and hence a 2 × *n* format.

There are, of course, marginal cases where the answer may not always appear to be the simple yes or no demanded by the 2 × *n* form. The decision cannot be *yes-but*, but it could perhaps be a yes handled in a different manner. Should the unprofitable store be continued open, or should it be closed? There is another possibility—it might be burned down for the insurance, and with the new working capital thereby gained, reopened, that is, continued—illegal, perhaps, but nonetheless a possible choice. The answer need not always be a dense black or glaring white, for sometimes a gray answer may be wisest. However, in game theory, each gray can become another choice. If there are more than two possible choices, they can be considered sequentially, but it may be simpler to admit that the game is of a variety higher than 2 × *n*.

Assume the question of where a national headquarters office should be located. Should it be in New York City, Chicago, Boston? The choices are three, and the measurable variables can be many—travel costs to plants, state income taxes, office rent, clerical personnel availability, for example. This situation should not be forced into a 2 × *n* mold but should be worked

[3] The procedure is explained later under the caption "An Example" (p. 592).

[4] Games of the 3 × *n* type can be solved by a three-dimensional graph, but 4 × *n* and higher types really require the solution of matrices.

out according to the more complicated rules of $3 \times n$. If there were five candidate cities, a $5 \times n$ diagram would be best. Care is necessary to assure that the problem is not really one of linear programming—the best distribution, for example, of a known limited resource to satisfy a known limited demand. Such problems do not belong to game theory, which is only concerned with the *if* questions—what is the effect *if* this or that happens?

A large field of managerial decisions to which no mathematical procedure is applicable is that of human relations. Definite numerical values cannot be assigned to the intangibles of whether or not Jones will make a good sales manager, of whether or not to let the union have that seniority clause. Here the manager is left to his well-scratched crystal ball. But the fact that game theory does not give an answer to everything need not discourage its use where applicable.

There are innumerable business problems of the $2 \times n$ type, of which the following are representative.

Should a New Plant Be Built to Serve a Certain Market?

There are a number of often conflicting variables: the effect upon present plant overhead through decreased volume—the saving in freight—the reduction or increase in inventories, and in labor or material costs—the cost of newly borrowed funds. While it is not difficult to compute the net gain or loss for a given set of conditions, many contingencies must be faced: If the sales volume does not increase, as hoped? If freight rates rise? If a competitor also builds a plant in that area?

A similar problem is whether two plants should be combined, or one plant divided into two.

Should a Certain Product Be Discontinued or Added?

Among others, the variables may be the effects on competing lines, on manufacturing overhead, on sales of nearly similar company products. Even if difficult to assign exact quantities, the values certainly will range within relatively narrow finite limits. Computations can be made to show what will happen under various possibilities.

A corollary problem would be the raising or lowering of the selling price of one item or line.

Should a Company Be Purchased?

Here the variables are many indeed, for frequent unknowns enter into any calculation based upon an assumed static set of conditions. The proper and safe procedure is to set up a game theory diagram and determine the worst that could happen: the loss of sales, the carrying of an idle plant, the necessity for increased overhead.

A related problem is whether or not a subsidiary company or plant should be sold.

All of the foregoing are essentially yes or no problems, and the decision, once made, is all too frequently irrevocable. But whereas the number of choices is only two, the number of variables is truly *n*—the effect on sales, on competitors, on profits, on operating expenses, and so on, presents a complex of variables, each with its own importance as to weighting, each with its own influence, each contributing its mass, or its little but still not insignificant mite, to the pot which must somehow be cooked up into a decision by the manager. A practical application of game theory can bring order out of this mixture and array the facts so that an obvious, but otherwise hidden, solution will become visible.

THE PROCEDURE

Before the basic principles of game theory can be applied, the problem must be clearly defined in terms of its variables, reducing each variable to one plain, self-contained question. For example, if a 4½-ounce size of a certain product is discontinued, what will be the effect upon *each* of (1) sales of the retained 3-ounce size, (2) sales of the retained 6-ounce size, (3) sales of competitors' 4½-ounce sizes, and (4) factory overhead, to name only several. It is not correct procedure to try to consider simultaneously even these few factors.

The proper method is use of the technique of pure research, which holds all but one of the variables constant and then determines the effect of fluctuations in the one, and only one, variable under study at the moment. A complex problem will become at least to some degree simplified, for the limits of the individual variable are assuredly known, and usually clear. In the 4½-ounce size problem, the worst that can happen in variable 3 is that competition will get all the previous 4½-ounce sales; the best that can happen is that they will get none of them. Once the maximum and minimum are known, a little thought will quickly lead to a logical, practical figure at some position between the limits. The point here made is that an independent and isolated analysis occurs, disregarding, for example, what might happen to the 6-ounce sales.

Each variable, in turn, is studied in its own separate, distinct fashion, and the potential gain or loss under the strictly circumscribed set of conditions is established. Values must be in terms of comparable units, the dollar being most suitable. A few variables may be found for which no monetary or definite arithmetical value can be set. Such are few indeed and, where encountered, must be left for later consideration, at which time it may be found that they are nongoverning and can be ignored.

Wherever applicable, odds can be applied before determining the final unit value of the variable. In the umbrella example the odds of being caught outside in the rain were 1 to 50. That is, the penalty of an unfortunate choice is only one fiftieth of the amount first indicated, for the occurrence will happen only once in 50 times. The amount entered in the diagram is properly computed at only this fraction of the otherwise effective value.

After each variable situation has been independently evaluated, all variables are lined up side by side, as in the umbrella example, with still only two choices, but with many additional variables extending to the right. Here is where game theory really begins to apply, and hence the advisability of restricting the number of choices to two, or at most three, so as to permit a simple mathematical solution.

The final step in pure game theory is determination of the controlling variables, or computation of the correct odds and game value for the specified set of circumstances. The conclusion will be that "the odds are thus and so in favor of (against) making thus and so much profit." This is a noteworthy answer in itself and one which many a perplexed manager might well be glad to learn. Even though his final decision might be based upon some (relatively rare) intangible not susceptible of definition in monetary terms, yet this answer would at least have eliminated all other variables, after considering them all simultaneously, each weighted in proper proportion, and giving in one answer the composite result. With this answer the customary mathematical aspects of game theory would terminate, but *the practical application is merely about to start.*

In business, human nature and our economic system being what they are, managers are usually seeking the most favorable results. In game terminology, this would be a *saddle point* (a pure strategy or sure-fire choice) and high game value; or, if this is impossible, then the most favorable odds, and again a high game value. Where there is no sure choice, game theory terminology calls the answer a *mixed strategy*. Nature being what it is, the initial computations frequently, even usually, are disappointing, and show either or both unfavorable or too low odds, and low game value. The investment of $100,000 in an increased sales force is hardly worthwhile if the chances are only 2 out of 7 that $5,000 can thereby be gained. The first computation, which was the final step in game theory, is only a sort of opening gambit.

The variables must be inspected one by one, after an unfavorable answer, to see which are responsible for the unwanted results. When found, each such variable must be searched once again to see if it contains within itself some element which alone caused the discouraging results. That increase in the sales force—half the unfavorable expense increase was for a California branch—what if no branch were opened, but the territory merely traveled? A new look with a jaundiced eye may pinpoint the part of the program which is causing the bad odds or the low game value—out with it! The part must be sacrificed to retain at least part of the merits of the whole. Conversely, an increase in some expense may tip the balance favorably.

After the search, the isolation of the cause, the reevaluation of variables, comes the new computation of odds and game value; or, if lucky, the finding of the one sure, correct choice. If unlucky, and results are still not favorable enough, then the process must be repeated, and if necessary, repeated again. Finally, the time will come when all possible changes have been exhausted, and the computed results must be accepted. If favorable enough, management's choice is simple—proceed with the plan. If not favorable, the plan must be abandoned, and lucky the manager who otherwise might have proceeded on pure hunches. A complex problem, with its seemingly infinite variations, has been reduced to simple odds for a given stake, asking the manager only whether the game, at such odds, is worth the gamble. The manager then can hazard the risk in the knowledge that if wrong this time, in the long run he must win.

It is important that the manager know the principles of game theory and that he help in defining and setting up the problem, but it is not essential that he make the computations himself. In the case of games of $3 \times n$ and higher order the average executive has neither the mathematical inclination nor the time to work out the solution. Just as the computation of values for each variable and choice is left to engineers and accountants, so is the solution of the diagram, once set up, best left to these assistants or to the mathematician. There is no objection to the manager figuring the answer himself, but it is really a task for the technician, not the executive. If the latter works through a simple example, he will have sufficient knowledge to exercise top-level judgment.

An Example

An example will be helpful in showing how the procedure may be employed in a practical application. While the variables will differ according to the nature of the problem, the procedure always will be the same.

The example is based upon a problem which vexed a long-established Connecticut manufacturer, John Smith & Sons Company. Smith, among a variety of other household appliances, produces a kerosene cookstove, of simple design, and a meat chopper, both of which are popular in Latin-American countries among low-income families. Among these markets, Puerto Rico is not the least in importance. There is, of course, competition from several other American manufacturers and an increasingly strong potential threat of kerosene cookstove imports from West Germany. There is no foreign threat to the meat chopper line. There is a tariff on imports into the United States and Puerto Rico of cookstoves, and Smith is somewhat hopeful that a quota may be imposed on American imports but is not too sanguine about its happening soon.

Smith has heard a lot about how various mainland manufacturers have recently set up plants in Puerto Rico, and thinks that perhaps it should build a plant there to supply at least that local market with both the stove and meat chopper; production in Connecticut would be correspondingly decreased. Calculations show that a plant of practical size could sell its output locally and that a $1 million investment would net the company $140,000 annually.[5] Hence the idea seems quite attractive, especially since the company has idle funds of this amount now invested in government bonds which return only $20,000 per year. The base of the computations as to expected net income is that the Connecticut buildings made idle can be sold and that present conditions as to competition, industry, and tariffs will remain unchanged.

But Smith now is faced with the problem of finding, in dollars per year return on investment, whether or not the return is sufficient to warrant the risks of the venture if certain changes do occur. Smith must undertake what amounts to solving a series of simultaneous equations to find one final figure. The variables are these:

1. Effect upon present Connecticut plant if the vacated space is not sold as expected.
2. Effect upon a Puerto Rico plant if the industrywide volume of kerosene cookstoves decreases. There is some indication that this product may be losing its popularity, being replaced by other types of stoves which Smith does not make nor intend to make.
3. Effect upon Smith's Puerto Rican sales of these and other Smith products if a plant is built there.
4. Effect upon Smith's Puerto Rican sales if Smith does not build a plant there, but a competitor does.
5. Effect upon a Puerto Rican plant, if established, if imports of cookstoves from Europe should continue to increase.

While there are other intangible factors, Smith feels that the foregoing are the important points and that the problems of personnel, local management, etc., can be coped with. Smith already has had experience in starting Latin-American plants and is aware of the intangible problems, which it considers minor.

In terms of game theory, the problem is a 2 × 6 matrix. The 2 represents the choice of *build or not build*, since there is no other possible choice. The 6 represents the above five variables, plus the original expected condition. The matrix, or diagram, has as its initial variable column the data representing the assumed or expected conditions on which the original profitability computations were made:[6]

Variable / *Choice*	*Expected Condition*
Build	140
Not build	20

[5] All income or loss data in the example are considered as being prior to deductions for federal income tax.

[6] Data in all diagrams are shown in terms of thousands of dollars per year.

The 20 for the *not build* choice represents the return that otherwise would accrue from present funds if not invested in the new plant.

Game theory employs the independent analysis of each variable, unrelated to the others at this stage, so each point is considered in turn. We need not be concerned with the computations, which are merely handled by customary accounting and engineering analysis procedures, and will indicate only the answers.

Effect of Not Selling Plant

If the cook stove and meat chopper volume are removed from the Connecticut plant, remaining products must absorb any residual fixed overhead, and this has already been taken into account in the $140,000 profit above computed. But while the vacated plant space, an isolated building, probably can be sold, the property is not especially desirable, and Smith might find that it is unable to sell. Smith then would be required to maintain, insure, and otherwise carry the property indefinitely. This would cost $32,000 annually, so that if not sold, the net annual profit would be only $108,000. The situation as to this variable diagrams as follows:

Variable / *Choice*	*Property Not Sold*
Build	108
Not build	20

Effect of Industry Decline

If the industry volume in kerosene cookstoves should decrease, independently of the effect of imports, operations in a new Puerto Rican plant would in time, of necessity, be curtailed. A reasonable assumption is that within the next decade this might be as much as 50 percent, in which case the unabsorbed fixed overhead there would amount to an estimated $23,000, thereby reducing the expected profit to $117,000. The diagram as to this situation is then:

Variable / *Choice*	*Industry Decline*
Build	117
Not build	20

Effect upon Puerto Rico Sales

While Smith now does a substantial volume in both kerosene cookstoves and meat choppers in Puerto Rico, so do several competitors. It appears to be undeniable that a local plant would have a beneficial effect upon Smith's sales by diverting a substantial part of competitors' volume to Smith. Also, the demand in the region, especially for meat choppers, is growing, and a local plant is much more likely to acquire a larger share of the increase than a remote mainland plant. If Smith builds, it is highly unlikely that a competitor will do so also. The estimates show that an additional $24,000 of profits can be expected within a few years, or that the profits would be $164,000 instead of $140,000. On the other hand, it is not likely that this additional profit can be secured if the Puerto Rico plant is not built, so that the *not build* decision would lose this potential profit of $24,000, less bond income, or a net loss of $4,000. Another diagram thus can be drawn:

Choice \ *Variable*	*Puerto Rico Sales*
Build	164
Not build	−4

Effect if Competitor Builds

If Smith does not build a Puerto Rican plant but a competitor does, then the reverse effect of the foregoing can be expected. By the same logic as before, Smith would lose the profit which it now makes on the volume which would be lost to competition. A probable loss of profit, including unabsorbed fixed overhead at the Connecticut plant, is computed at $36,000, less the bond income, or a net loss of $16,000. The effect of both Smith and a competitor building is ignored, because in practice the first builder will exclude all others. This situation diagrams thus:

Choice \ *Variable*	*Competitor Builds*
Build	140
Not build	−16

Effect of Imports

The biggest unknown in the entire picture is imports. West Germany is making a drive to reenter its former Latin-American markets and is a serious threat to American producers of kerosene cookstoves, even if not of meat choppers. If imports should succeed in getting 80 percent or more of the cookstove market, as there is a real chance they might, the effect upon the new Puerto Rico plant would be nearly disastrous. If imports did increase to this serious extent, the Puerto Rico operation, instead of showing $140,000 profit, could be expected to show a \$15,000 loss. Since best judgment indicates that the probability of a quota being imposed to restrict imports below the 80 percent of market level are at best 1 to 3, this loss statistically is diagrammed at three times as much, or \$45,000:

Choice \ Variable	*Imports Increase*
Build	−45
Not build	20

The various factors have now been considered independently, and the next step is to combine them:

Choice \ Variable	*Expected Conditions*	*Property Not Sold*	*Industry Decline*	*Puerto Rico Sales Increase*	*Competitor Builds*	*Imports Increase*
Build	140	108	117	164	140	−45
Not build	20	20	20	−4	−16	20

The matrix is now complete, and the next step is to compute the odds. There is a simple method for doing this in $2 \times n$ games. First, the diagram is scanned for a saddle point—a value which is the minimum in its row and the maximum in its column.[7] If there were one, this would show the dominant variable and choice. The best possible choice would be that for the row in which the saddle point lay, for this would be the least profit that could be made under any circumstance. The only question then would be the managerial decision as to whether this profit was enough. Since there is no such easy answer in this case, we proceed to solve graphically, as in Figure 1. In this figure, for each variable n the proper values are indicated on the *build* or *not build* vertical line, and a line is drawn between the points.[8] The highest point on the lowest bounding lines indicates the governing variables. All others can be discarded. The odds and game value are computed on these two variables only—*competitor builds*, and *imports increase:*

Build	140	−45
Not build	−16	20

The method of computation consists of merely subtracting the right-hand figure from the left:

[7] Strictly speaking, a *saddle point* is that value which is the largest of the minimums in any row (maxmin) and at the same time is the smallest of the maximums in any column (minmax).

[8] Those mathematically inclined will at once recognize this as being merely the plotting of the equations $y = 140x + 20(1 - x)$, etc., in which x represents the *build* choice, and hence $(1 - x)$ the *not build* choice and y the payoff for this variable. The range of x is, of course, from zero to one.

Build. 185
Not build. . . . . −36

Disregard the sign, reverse the figures, and the odds are as follows:

Build. 36
Not build. 185

That is, out of every 221 chances, only 36 times should Smith build; or the odds are 36 to 185 against building successfully. The game value is computed by applying these odds to either variable (as a check, the answer must be the same for each):

$$\frac{(36 \times 140) + (185 \times -16)}{36 + 185} = 9+$$

Smith has only 36 chances out of 221 of being sure of making at least $9,000 per year out of a $1 million investment if the plant is built—quite a different

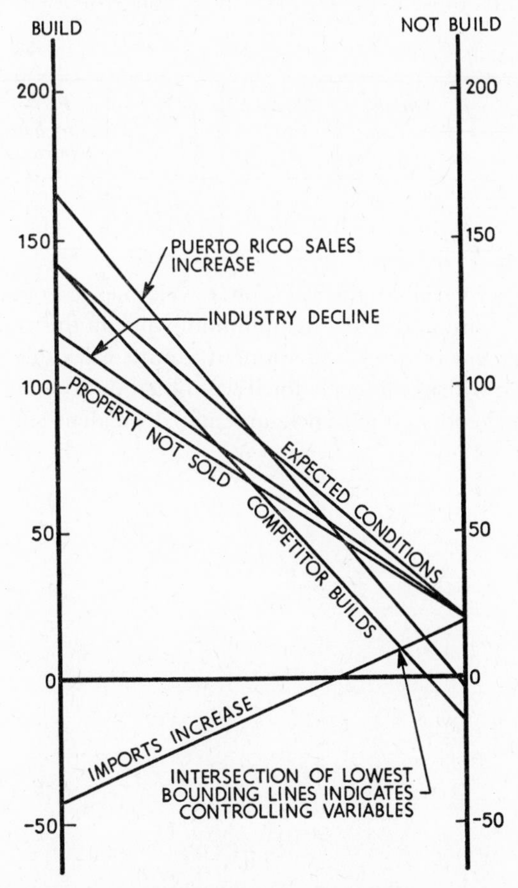

FIGURE 1. Graphic solution of 2 × *n* game to find controlling variables.

story from the $140,000 return under the expected conditions. Should the project be abandoned? Not at all. This is only the first trial run.

The next step is to inspect the diagram to find the reasons underlying the unhappy results. It is at once plain that the only losses in the *not build* row are caused by the failure to have a plant of any kind in Puerto Rico. That is, a plant there would no doubt keep out a competitor, forestalling any diversion of sales to him, and also have a beneficial effect on the sales of all Smith products. It is also evident that the only loss in the *build* row arises from the threat of imports of kerosene cookstoves.

The solution is clear—have a plant in Puerto Rico, but do not make cookstoves there, only meat choppers. Smith then starts a new round of computations along preceding lines to determine the feasibility of having a smaller Puerto Rican plant manufacturing meat choppers only. This is found to be possible from an operating point of view, with a smaller investment of $750,000 and a smaller $96,000 profit under expected conditions. The resulting diagram omits those variables exclusively concerned with kerosene cookstoves:

Choice \ *Variable*	*Expected Conditions*	*Property Not Sold*	*Puerto Rico Sales Increase*	*Competitor Builds*
Build	96	75	113	96
Not build	15	15	15	−2

Since, for every variable, the *build* row is well in excess of the *not build* row, the choice is obvious; and since the minimum value in this row, $75,000, represents a 10 percent return on investment, Smith will build the plant. The decision is made with confidence, for it was based on true business judgment assisted by logic and mathematics, and not dependent solely on hunches.

VIII

Integrated Planning Models

TABLEAU VIII

Methodological Analysis

Methodology / *Article*	*General Analysis of Basic Concepts*	*Descriptive Models for Analysis*					*Optimizing Models*			
		Algebraic or Symbolic (Deterministic)	*Algebraic or Symbolic (Probabilistic)*	*Matrix Methods*	*Markov Processes*	*Simulation*	*Linear Programming*	*Game Theory*	*Calculus*	*Other*
43. General Systems Theory—The Skeleton of Science	X									
44. Mathematical Models in Business Accounting		X								
45. Input-Output Accounting for Business				X						
46. Budgeting Models and System Simulation						X				
47. A Linear Programming Model for Budgeting and Financial Planning							X			
48. A Mathematical Model for Integrated Business Systems				X						

INTEGRATED PLANNING MODELS

The development of comprehensive models, especially in economic theory, has become increasingly widespread in recent years. Whether the complexity of the problem, lack of knowledge concerning the opportunities implicit in such models, or the static inertia of the accounting profession has retarded the development and implementation of these comprehensive models one can only speculate. Some of the reasons for the late development of these models may be inferred from article 43, in which are described two alternative approaches for the development of general systems theory. The remaining articles then illustrate several more specific applications of comprehensive, or integrated, systems models which have been developed in recent years.

A general definition of an accounting model is presented in article 44. An input-output model is illustrated in article 45, with the firm representing the entire producing sector. Simulation as it might be applied to an overall budget model is depicted in article 46. A linear programming budget model for a single time period is illustrated and discussed in article 47. To complete this somewhat kaleidoscopic review, a mathematical model designed to analyze the business enterprise's information system itself is presented in article 48.

The above models appear at first glance to be separate and distinct; yet all are analogous in that each attempts to relate the model to the entire firm. While, of course, they cannot describe or solve all problems of business, these models should promote increased understanding of the multidimensional consequences of the many interacting business variables.

43

Systems theory is examined from two points of view—(1) that which isolates general phenomena common to distinct disciplines, from which are constructed general theoretical models relative to these phenomena; and (2) that which arranges empirical fields in a hierarchy of complexity of organization of their "unit" of behavior, from which are developed levels of abstraction for each. The author discusses the implications of both approaches.

GENERAL SYSTEMS THEORY—THE SKELETON OF SCIENCE*

Kenneth E. Boulding

GENERAL SYSTEMS THEORY[1] is a name which has come into use to describe a level of theoretical model building which lies somewhere between the highly generalized constructions of pure mathematics and the specific theories of the specialized disciplines. Mathematics attempts to organize highly general relationships into a coherent system—a system, however, which does not have any necessary connections with the "real" world around us. It studies all thinkable relationships abstracted from any concrete situation or body of empirical knowledge. It is not even confined to "quantitative" relationships narrowly defined—indeed, the developments of a mathematics of quality and structure is already on the way, even though it is not as far advanced as the "classical" mathematics of quantity and number. Nevertheless, because in a sense mathematics contains all theories, it contains none; it is the language of theory, but it does not give us the content. At the other extreme, we have the separate disciplines and sciences with their separate bodies of theory. Each discipline corresponds to a certain segment of the empirical world, and each develops theories which have particular applicability to its own empirical segment. Physics, chemistry, biology, psychology, sociology, economics, and so on all carve out for themselves certain elements of the experience of man and develop theories and patterns of activity (research) which yield

---

* Reprinted from *Management Science*, April, 1956, pp. 197–208.

[1] The name and many of the ideas are to be credited to L. von Bertalanffy, who is not, however, to be held accountable for the ideas of the present author! For a general discussion of Bertalanffy's ideas, see "General System Theory: A New Approach to Unity of Science," *Human Biology*, December, 1951, pp. 303-61.

satisfaction in understanding and which are appropriate to their special segments.

In recent years, increasing need has been felt for a body of systematic theoretical constructs which will discuss the general relationships of the empirical world. This is the quest of general systems theory. It does not seek, of course, to establish a single, self-contained "general theory of practically everything" which will replace all the special theories of particular disciplines. Such a theory would be almost without content, for we always pay for generality by sacrificing content, and all we can say about practically everything is almost nothing. Somewhere, however, between the specific that has no meaning and the general that has no content, there must be, for each purpose and at each level of abstraction, an optimum degree of generality. It is the contention of the general systems theorists that this optimum degree of generality in theory is not always reached by the particular sciences. The objectives of general systems theory, then, can be set out with varying degrees of ambition and confidence. At a low level of ambition but with a high degree of confidence, it aims to point out similarities in the theoretical constructions of different disciplines, where these exist, and to develop theoretical models having applicability to at least two different fields of study. At a higher level of ambition but with perhaps a lower degree of confidence, it hopes to develop something like a "spectrum" of theories—a "system of systems" which may perform the function of a *Gestalt* in theoretical construction. Such *Gestalt*'s in special fields have been of great value in directing research toward the gaps which they reveal. Thus the periodic table of elements in chemistry directed research for many decades toward the discovery of unknown elements to fill gaps in the table until the table was completely filled. Similarly, a system of systems might be of value in directing the attention of theorists toward gaps in theoretical models and might even be of value in pointing toward methods of filling them.

The need for general systems theory is accentuated by the present sociological situation in science. Knowledge is not something which exists and grows in the abstract. It is a function of human organisms and of social organization. Knowledge, that is to say, is always what somebody knows: The most perfect transcript of knowledge in writing is not knowledge if nobody knows it. Knowledge, however, grows by the receipt of meaningful information—that is, by the intake of messages by a knower which are capable of reorganizing his knowledge. We will quietly duck the question as to what reorganizations constitute "growth" of knowledge by defining "semantic growth" of knowledge as those reorganizations which can profitably be talked about, in writing or speech, by the right people. Science, that is to say, is what can be talked about profitably by scientists in their role as scientists. The crisis of science today arises because of the increasing difficulty of such profitable talk among scientists as a whole. Specialization has outrun trade, communication between the disciplines becomes increasingly difficult, and the republic of learning is breaking up into isolated subcultures with only tenuous lines of communication between them—a situation which threatens intellectual civil war. The reason for this breakup in the body of knowledge is that in the course of specialization the receptors of information themselves become specialized. Hence, physicists only talk to physicists, economists to economists—worse still, nuclear physicists only talk to nuclear physicists and econometricians to econometricians. One wonders sometimes if science will not grind to a stop in an assemblage of walled-in hermits, each mumbling to himself words in a private language that only he can understand. In these days the arts may have beaten the sciences to this desert of mutual unintelligibility, but that may be merely because the swift intuitions of art reach the future faster than the plodding legwork of the scientist. The more science breaks into subgroups, and the less communication is possible among the disciplines, however, the greater chance there is that the total growth of knowledge is being slowed down by the loss of relevant communications. The spread of specialized deafness means that someone who ought to know something that someone else knows isn't able to find it out for lack of generalized ears.

It is one of the main objectives of general systems theory to develop these generalized ears and, by developing a framework of general theory, to enable one specialist to catch relevant communications from others. Thus the economist who realizes the strong formal similarity between utility theory in economics and field theory in physics[2] is probably in a better position to learn from the physicists than one who does not. Similarly, a specialist who works with the growth concept—whether the crystallographer, the virologist, the cytologist, the physiologist, the psychologist, the sociologist, or the economist—will be more sensitive to the contributions of other fields if he is aware of the many similarities of the growth process in widely different empirical fields.

There is not much doubt about the demand for general systems theory under one brand name or another. It is a little more embarrassing to inquire into the supply. Does any of it exist; and if so, where? What is the chance of getting more of it; and if so, how? The situation might be described as promising and in ferment, though it is not wholly clear what is being promised or brewed. Something which might be called an "interdisciplinary movement" has been abroad for some time. The first signs of this are usually the development of hybrid disciplines. Thus, physical chemistry emerged in the third quarter of the 19th century, social psychology in the second quarter of the 20th. In the physical and biological sciences the list of hybrid disciplines is now quite long—biophysics, biochemistry, astrophysics are all well established. In the social sciences, social anthropology is fairly well established; economic psychology and economic sociology are just beginning. There are signs, even, that political economy, which died in infancy some hundred years ago, may have a rebirth.

In recent years, there has been an additional development of great interest in the form of "multisexual" interdisciplines. The hybrid disciplines, as their

[2] See A. G. Pikler, "Utility Theories in Field Physics and Mathematical Economics," *British Journal for the Philosophy of Science*, Vol. V, 1955, pp. 47 and 303.

hyphenated names indicate, come from two respectable and honest academic parents. The newer interdisciplines have a much more varied and occasionally even obscure ancestry, and result from the reorganization of material from many different fields of study. Cybernetics, for instance, comes out of electrical engineering, neurophysiology, physics, biology, with even a dash of economics. Information theory, which originated in communications engineering, has important applications in many fields stretching from biology to the social sciences. Organization theory comes out of economics, sociology, engineering, physiology; and management science itself is an equally multidisciplinary product.

On the more empirical and practical side the interdisciplinary movement is reflected in the development of interdepartmental institutes of many kinds Some of these find their basis of unity in the empirical field which they study such as institutes of industrial relations, of public administration, of international affairs, and so on. Others are organized around the application of a common methodology to many different fields and problems, such as the Survey Research Center and the Group Dynamics Center at the University of Michigan. Even more important than these visible developments, perhaps, though harder to perceive and identify, is a growing dissatisfaction in many departments, especially at the level of graduate study, with the existing traditional theoretical backgrounds for the empirical studies which form the major part of the output of Ph.D. theses. To take but a single example from the field with which I am most familiar, it is traditional for studies of labor relations, money and banking, and foreign investment to come out of departments of economics. Many of the needed theoretical models and frameworks in these fields, however, do not come out of "economic theory" as this is usually taught, but from sociology, social psychology, and cultural anthropology. Students in the department of economics, however, rarely get a chance to become acquainted with these theoretical models, which may be relevant to their studies; and they become impatient with economic theory, much of which may not be relevant.

It is clear that there is a good deal of interdisciplinary excitement abroad. If this excitement is to be productive, however, it must operate within a certain framework of coherence. It is all too easy for the interdisciplinary to degenerate into the undisciplined. If the interdisciplinary movement, therefore, is not to lose that sense of form and structure which is the "discipline" involved in the various separate disciplines, it should develop a structure of its own. This I conceive to be the great task of general systems theory. For the rest of this paper, therefore, I propose to look at some possible ways in which general systems theory might be structured.

Two possible approaches to the organization of general systems theory suggest themselves, which are to be thought of as complementary rather than competitive, or at least as two roads each of which is worth exploring. The first approach is to look over the empirical universe and to pick out certain general *phenomena* which are found in many different disciplines and to seek to build up general theoretical models relevant to these phenomena. The second approach is to arrange the empirical fields in a hierarchy of complexity of organization of their basic "individual" or unit of behavior and to try to develop a level of abstraction appropriate to each.

Some examples of the first approach will serve to clarify it, without pretending to be exhaustive. In almost all disciplines, for instance, we find examples of populations—aggregates of individuals conforming to a common definition, to which individuals are added (born) and subtracted (die), and in which the age of the individual is a relevant and identifiable variable. These populations exhibit dynamic movements of their own, which can frequently be described by fairly simple systems of difference equations. The populations of different species also exhibit dynamic interactions among themselves, as in the theory of Volterra. Models of population change and interaction cut across a great many different fields—ecological systems in biology, capital theory in economics which deals with populations of "goods," social ecology, and even certain problems of statistical mechanics. In all these fields, population change, both in absolute numbers and in structure, can be discussed in terms of birth and survival functions relating numbers of births and of deaths in specific age groups to various aspects of the system. In all these fields the interaction of population can be discussed in terms of competitive, complementary, or parasitic relationships among populations of different species, whether the species consist of animals, commodities, social classes, or molecules.

Another phenomenon of almost universal significance for all disciplines is that of the interaction of an "individual" of some kind with its environment. Every discipline studies some kind of individual—electron, atom, molecule, crystal, virus, cell, plant, animal, man, family, tribe, state, church, firm, corporation, university, and so on. Each of these individuals exhibits "behavior," action, or change, and this behavior is considered to be related in some way to the environment of the individual—that is, with other individuals with which it comes into contact or into some relationship. Each individual is thought of as consisting of a structure or complex of individuals of the order immediately below it—atoms are an arrangement of protons and electrons; molecules of atoms; cells of molecules; plants, animals, and men of cells; social organizations of men. The behavior of each individual is "explained" by the structure and arrangement of the lower individuals of which it is composed, or by certain principles of equilibrium or homeostasis according to which certain "states" of the individual are "preferred." Behavior is described in terms of the restoration of these preferred states when they are disturbed by changes in the environment.

Another phenomenon of universal significance is growth. Growth theory is in a sense a subdivision of the theory of individual behavior, growth being one important aspect of behavior. Nevertheless, there are important differences between equilibrium theory and growth theory, which perhaps warrant giving growth theory a special category. There is hardly a science in which the growth phenomenon does not have some importance; and though there is a great difference in complexity between the growth of crystals, embryos, and societies, many of the principles and concepts which are important at the lower levels are also illuminating at higher levels. Some growth phenomena can be dealt with in terms of relatively simple population models, the solution of which yields growth curves of single variables. At the more complex levels, structural problems become dominant, and the complex interrelationships between growth and form are the focus of interest. All growth phenomena are sufficiently alike, however, to suggest that a general theory of growth is by no means an impossibility.[3]

Another aspect of the theory of the individual and also of interrelationships among individuals which might be singled out for special treatment is the theory of information and communication. The information concept as developed by Shannon has had interesting applications outside its original field of electrical engineering. It is not adequate, of course, to deal with problems involving the semantic level of communication. At the biological level, however, the information concept may serve to develop general notions of structuredness and abstract measures of organization which give us, as it were, a third basic dimension beyond mass and energy. Communication and information processes are found in a wide variety of empirical situations and are unquestionably essential in the development of organization, both in the biological and in the social world.

These various approaches to general systems through various aspects of the empirical world may lead ultimately to something like a general field theory of the dynamics of action and interaction. This, however, is a long way ahead.

A second possible approach to general systems theory is through the arrangement of theoretical systems and constructs in a hierarchy of complexity roughly corresponding to the complexity of the individuals of the various empirical fields. This approach is more systematic than the first, leading toward a system of systems. It may not replace the first entirely, however, as there may always be important theoretical concepts and constructs lying outside the systematic framework. I suggest below a possible arrangement of "levels" of theoretical discourse.

1. The first level is that of the static structure. It might be called the level of *frameworks*. This is the geography and anatomy of the universe—the pattern of electrons around a nucleus; the pattern of atoms in a molecular formula; the arrangement of atoms in a crystal; the anatomy of the gene, the cell, the plant, the animal; the mapping of the earth, the solar system, the astronomical universe. The accurate description of these frameworks is the beginning of organized theoretical knowledge in almost any field, for without accuracy in this description of static relationships, no accurate functional or dynamic theory is possible. Thus the Copernican revolution was really the discovery of

---

[3] See Kenneth E. Boulding, "Towards a General Theory of Growth," *Canadian Journal of Economics and Political Science*, August 19, 1953, pp. 326–40.

a new static framework for the solar system which permitted a simpler description of its dynamics.

2. The next level of systematic analysis is that of the simple dynamic system with predetermined, necessary motions. This might be called the level of *clockworks.* The solar system itself is, of course, the great clock of the universe from man's point of view, and the deliciously exact predictions of the astronomers are a testimony to the excellence of the clock which they study. Simple machines such as the lever and the pulley, even quite complicated machines like steam engines and dynamos, fall mostly under this category. The greater part of the theoretical structure of physics, of chemistry, and even of economics falls into this category. Two special cases might be noted. Simple equilibrium systems really fall into the dynamic category, as every equilibrium system must be considered as a limiting case of a dynamic system, and its stability cannot be determined except from the properties of its parent dynamic system. Stochastic dynamic systems leading to equilibriums, for all their complexity, also fall into this group of systems; such is the modern view of the atom and even of the molecule, each position or part of the system being given with a certain degree of probability, the whole nevertheless exhibiting a determinate structure. Two types of analytical method are important here, which we may call, with the usage of the economists, comparative statics and true dynamics. In comparative statics, we compare two equilibrium positions of the system under different values for the basic parameters. These equilibrium positions are usually expressed as the solution of a set of simultaneous equations. The method of comparative statics is to compare the solutions when the parameters of the equations are changed. Most simple mechanical problems are solved in this way. In true dynamics, on the other hand, we exhibit the system as a set of difference or differential equations, which are then solved in the form of an explicit function of each variable with time. Such a system may reach a position of stationary equilibrium, or it may not—there are plenty of examples of explosive dynamic systems, a very simple one being the growth of a sum at compound interest! Most physical and chemical reactions and most social systems do in fact exhibit a tendency to equilibrium—otherwise, the world would have exploded or imploded long ago.

3. The next level is that of the control mechanism or cybernetic system, which might be nicknamed the level of the *thermostat.* This differs from the simple stable equilibrium system mainly in the fact that the transmission and interpretation of information are an essential part of the system. As a result of this, the equilibrium position is not merely determined by the equations of the system, but the system will move to the maintenance of any *given* equilibrium, within limits. Thus the thermostat will maintain *any* temperature at which it can be set; the equilibrium temperature of the system is not determined solely by its equations. The trick here, of course, is that the essential variable of the dynamic system is the *difference* between an "observed" or "recorded" value of the maintained variable and its "ideal" value. If this difference is not zero, the system moves so as to diminish it; thus the furnace

sends up heat when the temperature as recorded is "too cold" and is turned off when the recorded temperature is "too hot." The homeostasis model, which is of such importance in physiology, is an example of a cybernetic mechanism, and such mechanisms exist through the whole empirical world of the biologist and the social scientist.

4. The fourth level is that of the "open system," or self-maintaining structure. This is the level at which life begins to differentiate itself from not-life: It might be called the level of the *cell*. Something like an open system exists, of course, even in physicochemical equilibrium systems; atomic structures maintain themselves in the midst of a throughput of electrons, molecular structures maintain themselves in the midst of a throughput of atoms. Flames and rivers likewise are essentially open systems of a very simple kind. As we pass up the scale of complexity of organization toward living systems, however, the property of self-maintenance of structure in the midst of a throughput of material becomes of dominant importance. An atom or a molecule can presumably exist without throughput: The existence of even the simplest living organism is inconceivable without ingestion, excretion, and metabolic exchange. Closely connected with the property of self-maintenance is the property of self-reproduction. It may be, indeed, that self-reproduction is a more primitive or "lower level" system than the open system, and that the gene and the virus, for instance, may be able to reproduce themselves without being open systems. It is not perhaps an important question at what point in the scale of increasing complexity "life" begins. What is clear, however, is that by the time we have got to systems which both reproduce themselves and maintain themselves in the midst of a throughput of material and energy, we have something to which it would be hard to deny the title of "life."

5. The fifth level might be called the genetic-societal level; it is typified by the *plant*, and it dominates the empirical world of the botanist. The outstanding characteristics of these systems are, first, a division of labor among cells to form a cell society with differentiated and mutually dependent parts (roots, leaves, seeds, etc.); and second, a sharp differentiation between the genotype and the phenotype, associated with the phenomenon of equifinal or "blueprinted" growth. At this level, there are no highly specialized sense organs, and information receptors are diffuse and incapable of much throughput of information—it is doubtful whether a tree can distinguish much more than light from dark, long days from short days, cold from hot.

6. As we move upward from the plant world toward the animal kingdom, we gradually pass over into a new level, the "animal" level, characterized by increased mobility, teleological behavior, and self-awareness. Here, we have the development of specialized information receptors (eyes, ears, etc.) leading to an enormous increase in the intake of information; we have also a great development of nervous systems, leading ultimately to the brain as an organizer of the information intake into a knowledge structure or "image." Increasingly, as we ascend the scale of animal life, behavior is response not to a specific stimulus but to an "image" or knowledge structure or view of the

environment as a whole. This image is of course determined ultimately by information received into the organism; the relation between the receipt of information and the building-up of an image, however, is exceedingly complex. It is not a simple piling-up or accumulation of information received, although this frequently happens, but a structuring of information into something essentially different from the information itself. After the image structure is well established, most information received produces very little change in the image—it goes through the loose structure, as it were, without hitting it, much as a subatomic particle might go through an atom without hitting anything. Sometimes, however, the information is "captured" by the image and added to it; and sometimes the information hits some kind of a "nucleus" of the image, and a reorganization takes place, with far-reaching and radical changes in behavior in apparent response to what seems like a very small stimulus. The difficulties in the prediction of the behavior of these systems arises largely because of this intervention of the image between the stimulus and the response.

7. The next level is the "human" level, that is, of the individual human being considered as a system. In addition to all, or nearly all, of the characteristics of animal systems, man possesses self-consciousness, which is something different from mere awareness. His image, besides being much more complex than that even of the higher animals, has a self-reflexive quality—he not only knows, but he knows that he knows. This property is probably bound up with the phenomenon of language and symbolism. It is the capacity for speech—the ability to produce, absorb, and interpret *symbols*, as opposed to mere signs like the warning cry of an animal—which most clearly marks man off from his humbler brethren. Man is distinguished from the animals also by a much more elaborate image of time and relationship; man is probably the only organization that knows that it dies, that contemplates in its behavior a whole life span, and more than a life span. Man exists not only in time and space but in history, and his behavior is profoundly affected by his view of the time process in which he stands.

8. Because of the vital importance for the individual man of symbolic images and behavior based on them, it is not easy to separate clearly the level of the individual human organism from the next level, that of social organizations. In spite of the occasional stories of feral children raised by animals, man isolated from his fellows is practically unknown. So essential is the symbolic image in human behavior that one suspects that a truly isolated man would not be "human" in the usually accepted sense, though he would be potentially human. Nevertheless, it is convenient for some purposes to distinguish the individual human as a system from the social systems which surround him; and in this sense, social organizations may be said to constitute another level of organization. The unit of such systems is not perhaps the person—the individual human as such—but the "role"—that part of the person which is concerned with the organization or situation in question; and it is tempting to define social organizations, or almost any social system, as a set

of roles tied together with channels of communication. The interrelations of role and the person, however, can never be completely neglected—a square person in a round role may become a little rounder, but he also makes the role squarer, and the perception of a role is affected by the personalities of those who have occupied it in the past. At this level, we must concern ourselves with the content and meaning of messages, the nature and dimensions of value systems, the transcription of images into a historical record, the subtle symbolizations of art, music, and poetry, and the complex gamut of human emotion. The empirical universe here is human life and society in all its complexity and richness.

9. To complete the structure of systems, we should add a final turret for transcendental systems, even if we may be accused at this point of having built Babel to the clouds. There are, however, the ultimates and absolutes and the inescapable unknowables, and they also exhibit systematic structure and relationship. It will be a sad day for man when nobody is allowed to ask questions that do not have any answers.

One advantage of exhibiting a hierarchy of systems in this way is that it gives us some idea of the present gaps in both theoretical and empirical knowledge. Adequate theoretical models extend up to about the fourth level and not much beyond. Empirical knowledge is deficient at practically all levels. Thus, at the level of the static structure, fairly adequate descriptive models are available for geography, chemistry, geology, anatomy, and descriptive social science. Even at this simplest level, however, the problem of the adequate description of complex structures is still far from solved. The theory of indexing and cataloging, for instance, is only in its infancy. Librarians are fairly good at cataloging books, chemists have begun to catalog structural formulas, and anthropologists have begun to catalog culture trials. The cataloging of events, ideas, theories, statistics, and empirical data has hardly begun. The very multiplication of records, however, as time goes on will force us into much more adequate cataloging and reference systems than we now have. This is perhaps the major unsolved theoretical problem at the level of the static structure. In the empirical field, there are still great areas where static structures are very imperfectly known, although knowledge is advancing rapidly, thanks to new probing devices such as the electron microscope. The anatomy of that part of the empirical world which lies between the large molecule and the cell, however, is still obscure at many points. It is precisely this area, however—which includes, for instance, the gene and the virus—that holds the secret of life; and until its anatomy is made clear, the nature of the functional systems which are involved will inevitably be obscure.

The level of the "clockwork" is the level of "classical" natural science, especially physics and astronomy, and is probably the most completely developed level in the present state of knowledge, especially if we extend the concept to include the field theory and stochastic models of modern physics. Even here, however, there are important gaps, especially at the higher empirical levels. There is much yet to be known about the sheer mechanics of cells and nervous systems, of brains and of societies.

Beyond the second level, adequate theoretical models get scarcer. The last few years have seen great developments at the third and fourth levels. The theory of control mechanisms ("thermostats") has established itself as the new discipline of cybernetics, and the theory of self-maintaining systems, or "open systems," likewise has made rapid strides. We could hardly maintain, however, that much more than a beginning had been made in these fields. We know very little about the cybernetics of genes and genetic systems, for instance, and still less about the control mechanisms involved in the mental and social world. Similarly, the processes of self-maintenance remain essentially mysterious at many points; and although the theoretical possibility of constructing a self-maintaining machine which would be a true open system has been suggested, we seem to be a long way from the actual construction of such a mechanical similitude of life.

Beyond the fourth level, it may be doubted whether we have as yet even the rudiments of theoretical systems. The intricate machinery of growth by which the genetic complex organizes the matter around it is almost a complete mystery. Up to now, whatever the future may hold, only God can make a tree. In the face of living systems, we are almost helpless; we can occasionally cooperate with systems which we do not understand; we cannot even begin to reproduce them. The ambiguous status of medicine, hovering as it does uneasily between magic and science, is a testimony to the state of systematic knowledge in this area. As we move up the scale, the absence of the appropriate theoretical systems becomes even more noticeable. We can hardly conceive ourselves constructing a system which would be in any recognizable sense "aware," much less self-conscious. Nevertheless, as we move toward the human and societal level, a curious thing happens: The fact that we have, as it were, an inside track, and that we ourselves *are* the systems which we are studying, enables us to utilize systems which we do not really understand. It is almost inconceivable that we should make a machine that would make a poem; nevertheless, poems *are* made by fools like us by processes which are largely hidden from us. The kind of knowledge and skill that we have at the symbolic level is very different from that which we have at lower levels—it is like, shall we say, the know-how of the gene as compared with the know-how of the biologist. Nevertheless, it is a real kind of knowledge, and it is the source of creative achievements of man as artist, writer, architect, and composer.

Perhaps one of the most valuable uses of the above scheme is to prevent us from accepting as final a level of theoretical analysis which is below the level of the empirical world which we are investigating. Because, in a sense, each level incorporates all those below it, much valuable information and insights can be obtained by applying low-level systems to high-level subject matter. Thus, most of the theoretical schemes of the social sciences are still at level 2, just rising now to 3, although the subject matter clearly involves level 8.

Economics, for instance, is still largely a "mechanics of utility and self-interest," in Jevons' masterly phrase. Its theoretical and mathematical base is drawn largely from the level of simple equilibrium theory and dynamic mechanisms. It has hardly begun to use concepts such as information which are appropriate at level 3, and makes no use of higher level systems. Furthermore, with this crude apparatus, it has achieved a modicum of success, in the sense that anybody trying to manipulate an economic system is almost certain to be better off if he knows some economics than if he doesn't. Nevertheless, at some point, progress in economics is going to depend on its ability to break out of these low-level systems, useful as they are as first approximations, and utilize systems which are more directly appropriate to its universe—when, of course, these systems are discovered. Many other examples could be given—the wholly inappropriate use in psychoanalytic theory, for instance, of the concept of energy, and the long inability of psychology to break loose from a sterile stimulus-response model.

Finally, the above scheme might serve as a mild word of warning even to management science. This new discipline represents an important breakaway from overly simple mechanical models in the theory of organization and control. Its emphasis on communication systems and organizational structure, on principles of homeostasis and growth, on decision processes under uncertainty, is carrying us far beyond the simple models of maximizing behavior of even 10 years ago. This advance in the level of theoretical analysis is bound to lead to more powerful and fruitful systems. Nevertheless, we must never quite forget that even these advances do not carry us much beyond the third and fourth levels, and that in dealing with human personalities and organizations, we are dealing with systems in the empirical world far beyond our ability to formulate. We should not be wholly surprised, therefore, if our simpler systems, for all their importance and validity, occasionally let us down.

I chose the subtitle of my paper with some eye to its possible overtones of meaning. General systems theory is the skeleton of science in the sense that it aims to provide a framework or structure of systems on which to hang the flesh and blood of particular disciplines and particular subject matters in an orderly and coherent corpus of knowledge. It is also, however, something of a skeleton in a cupboard—the cupboard in this case being the unwillingness of science to admit the very low level of its successes in systematization, and its tendency to shut the door on problems and subject matters which do not fit easily into simple mechanical schemes. Science, for all its successes, still has a very long way to go. General systems theory may at times be an embarrassment in pointing out how very far we still have to go and in deflating excessive philosophical claims for overly simple systems. It also may be helpful, however, in pointing out to some extent *where* we have to go. The skeleton must come out of the cupboard before its dry bones can live.

44

The author is careful to distinguish an accounting model from an economic model. He examines the former in a manner which illustrates the importance of the choice of the independent and the dependent variables (forecasting model). A chart which depicts the relationships between the defined accounting identities is then presented. Finally, a combined accounting-economic model is developed for use in determining an optimal asset and capital structure for a hypothetical trading firm.

MATHEMATICAL MODELS IN BUSINESS ACCOUNTING*

Richard Mattessich

IF ECONOMISTS trace their activity of model building to Cantillon and Quesnay,[1] then accountants may well defend their priority rights in this at present highly fashionable occupation by going back to their still more hoary ancestors, Pacioli and Massari, or even centuries beyond them. It is, however, not a priority right with which we are concerned but the fact that model building is not at all a new activity. It has dominated accounting since the first bookkeeper opened his cash book. The term *model* and the formal activity of expressing such a model by means of a system of simultaneous equations are, of course, of more recent origin. As we all know, it has lately come into high vogue in many social sciences,[2] among which economics seems to be an especially fertile soil.

We cannot deny that this conscious and systematic application of mathematical models to certain branches of economic science opened new paths and perspectives, not without enriching our insight into many a problem. It therefore seems to be comprehensible if accountants, too, try to dabble and experiment in this apparently promising field. Indeed, the term *model* also has recently found increasing application in accounting literature.[3] In spite

* Reprinted from *Accounting Review*, July, 1958, pp. 472–81.

[1] See Joseph A. Schumpeter, *History of Economic Analysis* (New York: Oxford University Press, 1954), p. 562.

[2] See Kenneth J. Arrow, "Mathematical Models in the Social Sciences," in D. Lerner and H. D. Lasswell (eds.), *The Policy Sciences* (Stanford: Stanford University Press, 1951), pp. 129–54.

[3] "Often thought as being confined to investigations in mathematical and developed sciences, models are essential to systematic work in any field dealing with complex problems involving relations between facts and objectives. Business or governmental budgets, systems of accounts, audit working papers, more or less suitably adapted to particular situa-

(or perhaps just because) of this, some clarification on accounting models and their relations to economic models seems to be justified.

Allen writes, for instance: "The whole structure of accounting is an *economic* model,"[4] while Boulding says with regard to the requirements of an economic model:

> Mere classification, however, is not enough. We want to know not only "what" but "why" and "how." It is not enough to have a good system of definitions, even a good system of accounts and measurements. We also want to know something about the causal factors involved in economic systems. . . . The construction of economic "models" is an attempt to give some answers to the question of the determinants of the economic system—some answer that is, to the "why and how" questions.[5]

Obviously, the models which Allen presents in his paper do not live up to Boulding's request of telling us something "about the causal factors"; they are based merely on definitional equations and lack any behavior equations[6] which, according to Boulding, would be an indispensable element for an economic model. From the purely mathematical standpoint, however, one can hardly deny to Allen's equation system the name of model. We therefore suggest a distinction between pure *accounting models* (those which are based on definitional equations only) and *economic models* in the sense of Boulding's exposition. Accounting models, though consisting merely of identities, have important analytic functions and can also be incorporated into economic models, as we shall demonstrate herein.

We may regard an accounting model as a set of simultaneous definitional equations which are based on flows and their systems.[7]

To illustrate this, we have construed a comparatively simple balance sheet

---

tions, are models indispensable to orderly solutions of complex problems" (E. L. Kohler, *A Dictionary for Accountants* [New York: Prentice-Hall, Inc., 1952], p. 272).

See also, for example, M. Allais, *Les Fondements comptables de la macro-économique* (Paris: Presses Universitaires de France, 1954), pp. 9, 10, 82, 83; Charles B. Allen, "Introduction to Model Building on Account Data," *NACA Bulletin*, June, 1955, Sec. 1, pp. 1320–33; F. S. Bray, *Four Essays in Accounting Theory* (London: Oxford University Press, 1953), p. 62; *idem, The Interpretation of Accounts* (London: Oxford University Press, 1957), pp. 107–11; Ernest H. Weinwurm, "Improving Accounting Measures for Management: The Concept of Homogeneity in Accounting Data," *Accounting Research*, July, 1957, p. 264.

[4] Allen, *op. cit.*, pp. 1320–21 (our italics).

[5] Kenneth E. Boulding, *Economic Analysis* (3d ed.; New York: Harper & Bros., 1955), p. 287.

[6] Boulding distinguishes only between *identities* (=definitional equations) and *behavior equations* (in the broad sense) (*op. cit.*, pp. 288–89), while other authors specify between *definitional*, *technological*, *institutional*, and *behavior equations* (in the narrower sense); see, for instance L. Klein, *Econometrics* (Evanston, Ill.: Row, Peterson & Co., 1953), pp. 4, 5,. 10, 15, etc. See also C. F. Christ, "On Econometric Models of the U.S. Economy," in *Income and Wealth*, Series VI (London: Bowes & Bowes, 1957), p. 2; and E. F. Beach, *Economic Models* (New York: John Wiley & Sons, Inc., 1957), p. 31; the latter work is an introductory exposition of economic and econometric models and can be best recommended to accountants —even to those with only elementary mathematical knowledge—who are interested in gaining greater insight into this important field.

[7] For a logical formal definition of *flows* and *flow systems*, see our paper "Towards a General and Axiomatic Foundation of Accountancy," *Accounting Research*, October, 1957, pp. 328–55.

at the *beginning* of an arbitrary accounting period M. This balance sheet can easily be converted into a set of equations (1–12). Another corresponding set of equations represents the balance sheet at the *end* of period M (13–24). To connect these two sets, we need a third set of equations (25–40) which reflects the changes *during* the period M and thereby includes the income statement for this period (see also Graph 1, p. 620). In an ordinary business accounting system, such changes would be based on the individual entries during the period. It will, however, soon be obvious that such a model could require a few hundred or even thousand of variables and, although theoretically possible, would be of little practical value. We have therefore chosen an example out of *forecast accounting*,[8] an area in which the prospects for a practical application of accounting models are much better, mainly due to the more limited number of variables. This limitation arises out of the absence of individual entries, for only the net changes of the various accounts are here of any significance. Such changes can usually be budgeted. Once this has been done, these net changes constitute the data for our independent variables, and the dependent variables can then be determined by solving all simultaneous equations (1–40). Our interest in this paper in the more general and fundamental mathematical formulation does not mean that we are suggesting the substitution of the traditional procedure by a purely mathematical one.[9] We do suggest, however, that our approach may provide a

---

[8] For the mathematical model of an *ordinary* accounting system, the so far independent but now dependent variables representing changes Δa_{110}, Δa_{121}, . . . , Δa_{610}, etc. (for our example, see equations 25–40 and Table 3 items 14–27), would have to be broken down into individual entries, e.g., by the equations:

$$\begin{aligned} \Delta a_{110} &= a^{(1)}{}_{110} + a^{(2)}{}_{110} + a^{(3)}{}_{110} + \cdots + a^{(m)}{}_{110} \\ \Delta a_{121} &= a^{(1)}{}_{121} + a^{(2)}{}_{121} + a^{(3)}{}_{121} + \cdots + a^{(n)}{}_{121} \\ &\vdots \\ \Delta a_{610} &= a^{(1)}{}_{610} + a^{(2)}{}_{610} + a^{(3)}{}_{610} + \cdots + a^{(s)}{}_{610} \end{aligned}$$

etc., whereby the symbols with superscripts represent the individual entries. The latter now constitute the independent variables, for we must realize that a variable is independent only within its defined range (see also Kohler, *op. cit.*, p. 220). If we extend this range, variables so far considered to be independent become dependent, and new independent ones emerge. Should a further extension be required (e.g., to include behavior functions in such a model) it will be obvious that even some or all of the individual entries might lose their independent character. The terms *endogenous* and *exogenous* variables might appear more illuminating in this connection and may be substituted for the expressions *dependent* and *independent* variables, respectively.

Finally, the condition of accounting equilibrium, implicit in the above set of equations—supplementing generally the mathematical model to represent an *ordinary* accounting system—could be stated as follows:

$$\sum_{i=1}^{m} a^{(i)}{}_{110} + \sum_{j=1}^{n} a^{(j)}{}_{121} + \cdots + \sum_{p=1}^{s} a^{(p)}{}_{610}, \text{ etc.} = 0$$

[9] Such substitutions are of course made when electronics equipments are applied to accounting problems. This is another reason why accountants cannot afford to disregard studies of the mathematical and logical foundations of accountancy.

deeper insight into the foundations on which accounting rests. This no doubt will facilitate the coordination and integration of accounting problems with various economic relations nowadays presented in a more rigorous mathematical form.

The balance sheet in Table 1 supplies us with the following equations:[10]

TABLE 1

BALANCE SHEET OF N. N. AT THE BEGINNING OF PERIOD M

Assets			
Current Assets:			
Cash		a'_{110}	
Receivables (minus)	a'_{121}		
Allowance for doubtful accounts	a'_{122}	a'_{120}	
Inventory		a'_{130}	a'_{100}
Fixed Assets:			
Equipment		a'_{210}	
Building (minus)	a'_{221}		
Allowance for depreciation	a'_{222}	a'_{220}	a'_{200}
Total Assets			A'

Liabilities and Capital			
Current Liabilities:			
Bank overdraft	a'_{311}		
Payables	a'_{312}	a'_{310}	
Other Liabilities:			
Mortgage	a'_{321}		
Bonds	a'_{322}	a'_{320}	
Total Liabilities			a'_{300}
Owners Equity:			
Stock capital		a'_{410}	
Earned surplus:			
At the beginning of $M-1$	a'_{421}		
Accumulated during $M-1$	a'_{422}	a'_{420}	a'_{400}
Total Capital			C'

$$A' = -C' \tag{1}$$
$$A' = a'_{100} + a'_{200} \tag{2}$$
$$a'_{100} = a'_{110} + a'_{120} + a'_{130} \tag{3}$$
$$a'_{120} = a'_{121} + a'_{122} \tag{4}$$
$$a'_{200} = a'_{210} + a'_{220} \tag{5}$$
$$a'_{220} = a'_{221} + a'_{222} \tag{6}$$
$$C' = a'_{300} + a'_{400} \tag{7}$$
$$a'_{300} = a'_{310} + a'_{320} \tag{8}$$
$$a'_{310} = a'_{311} + a'_{312} \tag{9}$$
$$a'_{320} = a'_{321} + a'_{322} \tag{10}$$
$$a'_{400} = a'_{410} + a'_{420} \tag{11}$$
$$a'_{420} = a'_{421} + a'_{422} \tag{12}$$

In a similar way, we may set up for the balance sheet at the end of period M the corresponding equations:

$$A = -C \tag{13}$$
$$A = a_{100} + a_{200} \tag{14}$$
$$a_{100} = a_{110} + a_{120} + a_{130} \tag{15}$$
$$a_{120} = a_{121} + a_{122} \tag{16}$$
$$a_{200} = a_{210} + a_{220} \tag{17}$$
$$a_{220} = a_{221} + a_{222} \tag{18}$$
$$C = a_{300} + a_{400} \tag{19}$$

[10] The *magnitude* (but not necessarily the sign of the algebraic symbol) of a variable representing a debit balance or debit sum will be positive; that representing a credit balance or credit sum will be negative.

(20) $a_{300} = a_{310} + a_{320}$
(21) $a_{310} = a_{311} + a_{312}$
(22) $a_{320} = a_{321} + a_{322}$
(23) $a_{400} = a_{410} + a_{420}$
(24) $a_{420} = a_{421} + a_{422}$

We introduce next (1) the changes of the different accounts during the period M with Δa_{110}, Δa_{121}, · · · , etc. and (2) the income statement for the period M (see Table 2).

TABLE 2

INCOME STATEMENT OF N. N. FOR THE PERIOD M

Sales		a_{510}	
Cost of goods sold:			
Inventory at beginning of M	a'_{130}		
Plus: Purchases	a_{521}		
Minus: Inventory at end of M	a_{130}	a_{520}	
Gross profit		a_{500}	
Expenses		a_{600}	
Net Income for Period M			a_{422}

We have to be aware that the item a_{600} (expenses) includes among others the (negative) net change of the allowance for doubtful accounts, Δa_{122}, and the (negative) net change of the allowance for depreciation, Δa_{222}, provided we assume that transfers from the allowance for doubtful accounts to receivables and from the allowance for depreciation to building are here, in contrast to actual practice, nonexistent—the latter might, in such a model, be justified by equations 27 and 30 (see below) which ultimately compensate for all such transfers. We may therefore set up a further equation (see also equation 40 below):

$$a_{600} = \Delta a_{122} + \Delta a_{222} + a_{610}$$

in which a_{610} may be called *other expenses*. It is due to this formulation that the right sides of equations 27 and 30 are presented as differences and not as sums.

Hence, we may set up the following equations (*dividends are neglected*):

(25) $a_{110} = a'_{110} + \Delta a_{110}$
(26) $a_{121} = a'_{121} + \Delta a_{121}$
(27) $a_{122} = a'_{122} - \Delta a_{122}$
(28) $a_{210} = a'_{210} + \Delta a_{210}$
(29) $a_{221} = a'_{221} + \Delta a_{221}$
(30) $a_{222} = a'_{222} - \Delta a_{222}$
(31) $a_{311} = a'_{311} + \Delta a_{311}$
(32) $a_{312} = a'_{312} + \Delta a_{312}$
(33) $a_{321} = a'_{321} + \Delta a_{321}$
(34) $a_{322} = a'_{322} + \Delta a_{322}$
(35) $a_{410} = a'_{410} + \Delta a_{410}$
(36) $a_{421} = a'_{420}$
(37) $a_{422} = a_{500} + a_{600}$

(38) $a_{500} = a_{510} + a_{520}$

(39) $a_{520} = a'_{130} + a_{521} - a_{130}$

(40) $a_{600} = \Delta a_{122} + \Delta a_{222} + a_{610}$

Equation 39 could have been written $a_{520} = \Delta a_{130} + a_{521}$; however, the reason why Δa_{130} is not to be found among our variables (see Tables 3 and 4

TABLE 3

INDEPENDENT VARIABLES
(Magnitudes Assumed)

1. a'_{110} =	100	10. a'_{321} =	− 500	19. Δa_{221} =	200
2. a'_{121} =	520	11. a'_{322} =	− 800	20. Δa_{222} =	20
3. a'_{122} =	− 50	12. a'_{410} =	−1,000	21. Δa_{312} =	− 20
4. a'_{130} =	400	13. a'_{421} =	− 200	22. Δa_{321} =	50
5. a'_{210} =	800	14. Δa_{110} =	− 10	23. Δa_{322} =	0
6. a'_{221} =	2,000	15. Δa_{121} =	− 15	24. Δa_{410} =	0
7. a'_{222} =	− 500	16. Δa_{122} =	20	25. a_{510} =	−2,000
8. a'_{311} =	− 100	17. a_{130} =	600	26. a_{521} =	1,500
9. a'_{312} =	− 300	18. Δa_{210} =	250	27. a_{610} =	200

TABLE 4

DEPENDENT VARIABLES
(Magnitudes Derived from Table 3 and Equations 1–40)

28. a'_{100} =	970	41. a_{110} =	90	55. a_{320} =	−1,250
29. a'_{120} =	470	42. a_{120} =	435	56. a_{321} =	− 450
30. a'_{200} =	2,300	43. a_{121} =	505	57. a_{322} =	− 800
31. a'_{220} =	1,500	44. a_{122} =	− 70	58. a_{400} =	−2,030
32. A' =	3,270	45. a_{200} =	2,730	59. a_{410} =	−1,000
33. a'_{300} =	−1,700	46. a_{210} =	1,050	60. a_{420} =	−1,030
34. a'_{310} =	− 400	47. a_{220} =	1,680	61. a_{421} =	− 570
35. a'_{320} =	−1,300	48. a_{221} =	2,200	62. a_{422} =	− 460
36. a'_{400} =	−1,570	49. a_{222} =	− 520	63. a_{500} =	− 700
37. a'_{420} =	− 570	50. A =	3,855	64. a_{520} =	1,300
38. a'_{422} =	− 370	51. a_{300} =	−1,825	65. a_{600} =	240
39. C' =	−3,270	52. a_{310} =	− 575	66. C =	−3,855
40. a_{100} =	1,125	53. a_{311} =	− 255	67. Δa_{311} =	− 155
		54. a_{312} =	− 320		

as well as Graph 1) will be obvious to anyone who is familiar with accounting practices on this continent.

In principle, every pure accounting model can be schematically represented as in Graph 1.[11] These "identity charts," showing the definitional equations of the systems, should not be confused with "flow charts,"[12] which are designed to illustrate the different accounting channels but do not necessarily reflect the equations of the models.

We now have an accounting *model* which becomes a *theory* as soon as "a

[11] For such a schematic illustration of a macroaccounting model (identity chart), see Allais, *op. cit.*, pp. 44–47.

[12] For "flow charts," see, for example, Fiske and Becket (eds.), *Industrial Accountants Handbook* (New York: Prentice-Hall, Inc., 1954), p. 308; see also Blocker and Weltmer, *Cost Accounting* (New York: McGraw-Hill Book Co., Inc., 1954), Exhibits 55, 57, 83, etc.

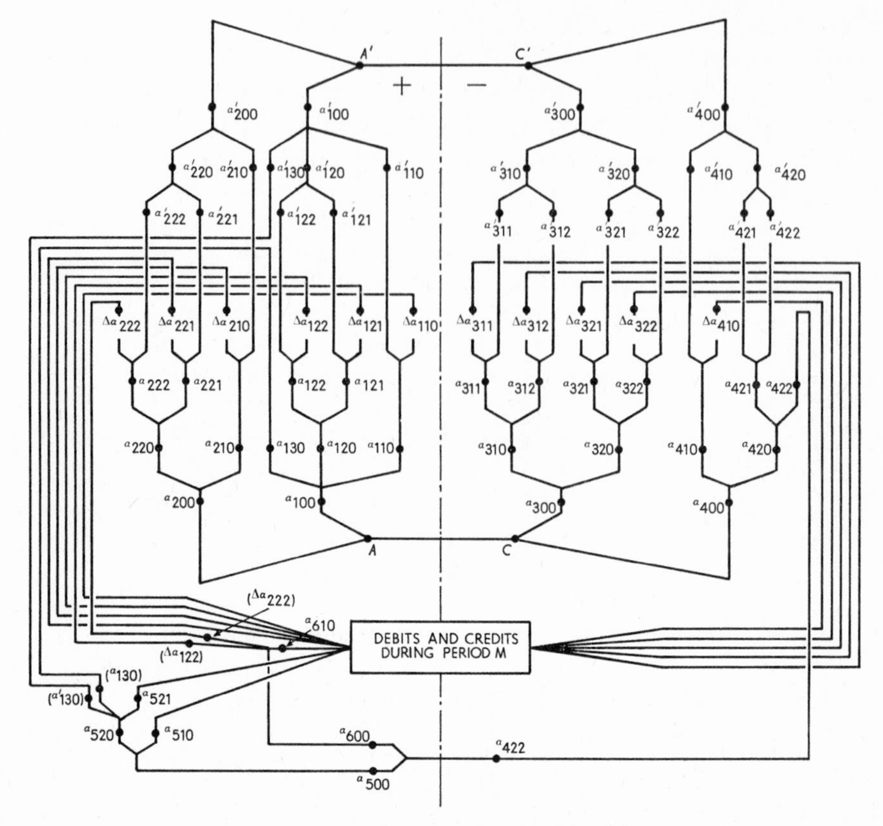

GRAPH 1. Chart of accounting identities.

segment of the real world has been mapped into it."[13] We will carry this out by including assumed data for all—from our model's point of view—*independent* (or predetermined) variables (see Table 3). By inserting these data into our system of equations (1–40) we can derive the pertinent magnitudes of the *dependent* variables (see Table 4).

Besides showing the magnitudes of the variables, Tables 3 and 4 illustrate which of the variables have to be considered independent and which dependent. In most of the cases, this will be quite obvious. There are, however, a few dependent variables which might require some explanation. For instance, it might not be immediately obvious to some accountants why the variables 38 (a'_{422}, net income of period $M - 1$), and 67 (Δa_{311}, change in the bank overdraft account during M), are presented as dependent instead of independent variables.

In the first instance, we may regard the beginning balance sheet (equations 1–12) as an accounting model for itself, in which case the (unknown) net

[13] See Coombs, Raiffa, and Thrall, "Some Views on Mathematical Models and Measurement Theory," in Thrall, Coombs, and Davis (eds.), *Decision Processes* (New York: John Wiley & Sons, Inc., 1954), p. 25.

income for period $M - 1$ will have to be determined as the balance (a'_{422}) of the balance sheet, in the same way as we determine it in a single-entry accounting system from incomplete data. Otherwise, our model would be overdetermined. The second instance is more complicated, because Δa_{311} does not necessarily need to be *the* dependent variable; it may just as well be Δa_{110}, Δa_{312}, or even any other variable among those representing changes during period M. We have chosen Δa_{311}, as it is the variable most likely to be the one dependent on the others, whose magnitudes are determined exogenously, that is, by other than mere bookkeeping incidents. However, as soon as the limit of the bank overdraft is reached, Δa_{311} becomes an independent variable; and, for example, Δa_{110} or Δa_{312} becomes the dependent one (depending on what is decided: to weaken the cash position or to postpone payments to accounts payable). Here the mathematical model reveals connections which are usually disregarded. Therefore, we are afraid that the logic behind this argument will not become entirely clear to many until after they have calculated and constructed their own accounting model. It may, however, facilitate an understanding—and at the same time point to *an area where such models might constitute a tool superior to the traditional approach*—by thinking of an example in which the counterentries to the individual debits and credits are not known, as, for instance, in budgeting and forecast accounting.

Basically, every (traditional) accounting system is mathematically overdetermined; but through the mechanism of double entry, this overdetermination works as a welcome check, while in absence of this mechanism (as in our model), this overdetermination can easily lead to contradictions and incorrect results. Therefore, to avoid overdetermination, at least one of these otherwise independent—we almost want to say semidependent—variables has to be chosen as a buffer. This seems to us the simplest way to adumbrate the interdependence of all variables causing changes during the pertinent period.

Our accounting models, though quite comprehensive, belong of course still to the most primitive mathematical models. They have, however, an enormous advantage over more complex ones; namely, they reproduce reality with a higher accuracy than most economic models do. That means their predictions[14] about the real world are usually more reliable. A bookkeeper who "predicts" that according to his entries in the petty cashbook there should be $100 in the safe, and is then able to verify this by actual count, can be said to have operated a model predicting and depicting reality[15] to the highest possible degree.

The greatest prospects of accounting models, however, seem to lie in their combination with economic models. The unification of accounting identities with behavior equations, so far applied only in macroeconomic models,

---

[14] "One role of mathematical models is to provide a logic route to go from characteristics of the real world to predictions about it." (Thrall, Coombs, and Davis, *op. cit.*, p. 35).

[15] Or at least a certain aspect of reality.

promises also for business accounting a new field of experimentation and application. Thus, we may actually not be too far away from that part of our field of knowledge which L. R. Chenault called some time ago "accountometrics."[16]

For the purpose of demonstration, we have developed an example from the area of managerial decision making with regard to the capital and asset structure.

We assume a trading firm with the following simple balance sheet:

Balance Sheet of B. B. as at T. T.

Cash	c	Liabilities	d
Inventory	s	Owners Equity	e
Total Assets	A	Total Capital	C

We further presume the management to be operating with the following two ratios in order to control the asset and capital structure, respectively:

$$x = \frac{\text{Cash}}{\text{Inventory}}$$

$$y = \frac{\text{Liabilities}}{\text{Owners' equity}}$$

In addition, we need three more concepts:

p = A profit rate of the enterprise (e.g., the marginal efficiency of capital)
l = The liquidity preference (of management)
i = The interest rate for outside capital (liabilities)

Now, we may set up the model consisting of the following equations:

$$A = -C \tag{1}$$

$$A = c + s \tag{2}$$

$$C = d + e \tag{3}$$

$$x = \frac{c}{s} \tag{4}$$

$$y = \frac{d}{e} \tag{5}$$

and

$$x = F(p, l) \tag{6}$$

$$y = G(p, i) \tag{7}$$

Equations 6 and 7 constitute our behavior relations, reflecting the reaction of the management to changes in p, l, and i. We say x is a function (F) of the profit rate and the liquidity preference, and y is another function (G) of the profit rate and the interest rate. These functions have to be determined (econometrically) from past experience. Instead of stating these two assumed

[16] "Business Behavior and the Theory of the Firm," *Accounting Review*, October, 1954, p. 651.

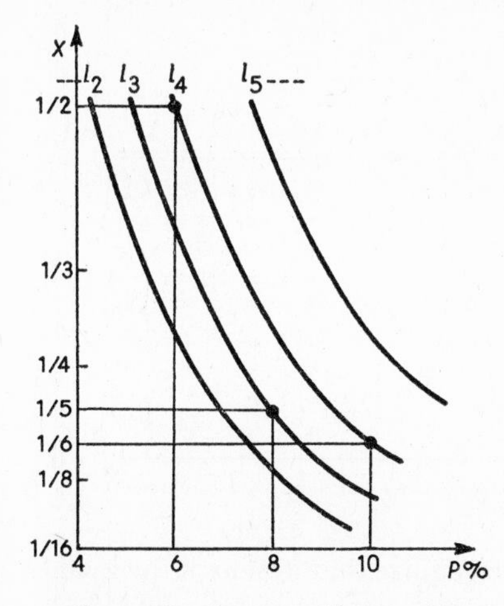

GRAPH 2. Representing sections of function F.

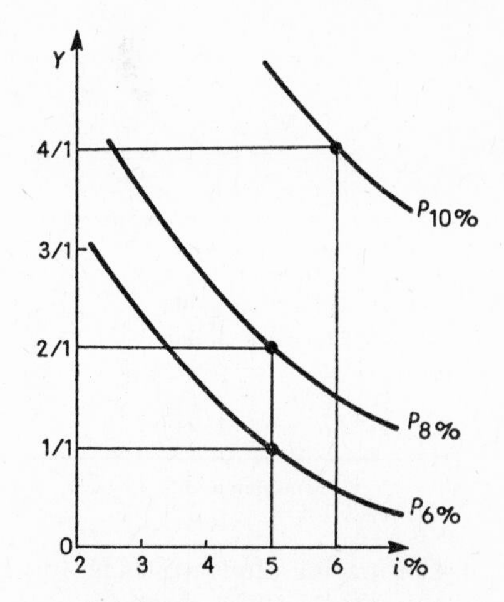

GRAPH 3. Representing sections of function G.

functions algebraically, we have illustrated them (for various liquidity preferences, profit rates, and interest rates) in Graphs 2 and 3.

Our independent variables are now p, i, l, and e (assuming a fixed owners' equity); our dependent ones are A, C, s, d, c, x, and y (as many as we have independent equations in our model; this means that the system is uniquely determined).

Again, we may assume certain magnitudes for the independent variables—but this time, in order to illustrate clearly the changes, three alternatives will be used (see Table 5)—and derive from them the corresponding dependent variables (see Table 6).

TABLE 5

INDEPENDENT VARIABLES*
(Magnitudes Assumed)

	Alternative I	*Alternative II*	*Alternative III*
(1)	$e' = -10{,}000$	$e'' = -10{,}000$	$e''' = -10{,}000$
(2)	$p' = 8\%$	$p'' = 6\%$	$p''' = 10\%$
(3)	$i' = 5\%$	$i'' = 5\%$	$i''' = 6\%$
(4)	$l' = l_3$	$l'' = l_4$	$l''' = l_4$

* The magnitudes of e, C, and d are negative, which indicates that these symbols represent *credit* balances.

Comparing alternatives I and II, the solutions shown in Table 6 demonstrate that the reduction in the profit rate and the application of a more cautious investment policy (higher liquidity preference in alternative II) will lead to a considerable decrease in borrowing and a reduction in inventory investment, while the cash position improves absolutely.

TABLE 6

DEPENDENT VARIABLES*
(Magnitudes Derived from Table 5 and Equations 1–7)

Alternative I		*Alternative II*		*Alternative III*	
(5) $x' =$	1:5	$x'' =$	1:2	$x''' =$	1:6
(6) $y' =$	2:1	$y'' =$	1:1	$y''' =$	4:1
(7) $C' =$	−30,000	$C'' =$	−20,000	$C''' =$	−50,000
(8) $A' =$	30,000	$A'' =$	20,000	$A''' =$	50,000
(9) $d' =$	−20,000	$d'' =$	−10,000	$d''' =$	−40,000
(10) $c' =$	5,000	$c'' =$	6,667	$c''' =$	7,143
(11) $s' =$	25,000	$s'' =$	13,333	$s''' =$	42,857

* The magnitudes of e, C, and d are negative, which indicates that these symbols represent *credit* balances.

Comparing alternatives II and III, we recognize that although the investment *policy* is still relatively cautious (l_4 still holds), the borrowing will increase considerably, whereby the greatest part of it will be used for investment in inventory; this—in spite of the increased interest rate—is due to the comparatively heavy increase in the profit rate.

Another branch using mathematical models and bordering on accountancy is *operations research;* it has developed "inventory models" in order to facilitate and optimize decisions concerning inventory levels. A considerable literature has been accumulated,[17] and progressive accountants will at least have to get a general idea of this new area of economic science. Another promising econometric study somewhat related to our subject is presently carried on in England: "There are now studies in progress at the National Institute of Economic and Social Research in London dealing with the accountants of more than three thousand companies for the period 1948–1953. These accounts will be standardized, transferred to punch cards and, in the course of time, entirely analysed."[18]

Finally, we should not fail to mention the increasing significance which the application of matrices assumes in accountancy. Matrices not only facilitate the formulation of accounting axioms, theorems, and their proofs[19] but have found use already as models in solving various cost accounting problems.[20]

[17] For an illuminating introduction to the building of inventory models, see C. W. Churchman, R. L. Ackoff, and R. L. Arnoff, *Introduction to Operations Research* (New York: John Wiley & Sons, Inc., 1957), pp. 199–273; a comprehensive bibliography to elementary inventory models is offered in pp. 232–34.

[18] S. J. Prais, "Some Problems in the Econometric Analysis of Company Accounts," Report of the Aix-en-Provence Meeting, *Econometrica*, July, 1957, p. 481.

[19] See Mattessich, *op. cit.*, pp. 331–45 and 349–53.

[20] "Matrices can—with regard to their application in accounting—be comprised as tables into which indirectly or directly numerical data are inserted. In this way one obtains not only clear representations of flows (of quantities or values) with a deliberate number of recurrences of transformations, of production-combinations, of capacity limitations, but one is also able to represent causal relations completely considering all influential factors. From such tables—according to the rules of matrix algebra—it is possible to derive

We may conclude from all this that there lies a vast, almost unplowed area before the accountant. It is up to him either to grasp his chance or to pass it by. If he decides on the former, he will certainly help to push accountancy over that threshold which leads to the realm of science.

However, at the end of a paper like this a word of warning still has to be uttered. We ought to be aware that models "are proposals for an unspecified social space. . . . They may hold in some instances of social space and they may not hold in others."[21] "Somehow we still seem to be constructing fairly formal, incompletely interpreted 'models,' rather than fully specified (or interpreted) 'theories' which stand a chance (even in principle) of being refuted by empirical data. Our acts belie our words."[22] In the light of these words of Papandreou's remarkable pioneering work, the present paper may increase in significance when studied in connection with our recently published article.[23] Here, we have models; there, we have the beginning of a whole theory. But before accountants can develop a fully specified theory, they must have a clear vision of the models—and their characteristics—which should organically grow out of such a theory. This requires some experimentation and might, as we hope, justify an attempt like the present one.

---

new tables whereby this process of derivation corresponds to certain unique economic events. From these two qualities—the principles of ordering and combining matrices— result the following advantages of matrix calculus vis-à-vis the classical methods of industrial accounting:

"1. It enables a concise and uniform representation of various accounting problems and their solutions with the help of well developed mathematical methods. So, for instance, cost accounting problems, control of rentability through variances and linear programming can be very simply represented by means of matrix formulation.

"2. In many cases, it permits the settlement of the greatest part of the calculation beforehand, and to store the results in a matrix.

"3. By taking into consideration the causal relations and interrelations of the firm, it offers an effective tool for short and long run forecasts.

"4. It supplies, for a wide range of problems, uniform and simple procedures of calculation for which programmes are already prepared at large scale for electronics equipment."

Translated from the German: O. Pichler, "Antwort zu: Welche Vorteile bietet die Anwendung des Matrizenkalküls gegenüber den klassischen Methoden des industriellen Rechnungswesens?" in *Untersuchungsforschung* (*Journal for Operations Research*), edited by S. Sagoroff and A. Adam (Würzburg, Germany: Physica-Verlag, 1956), Vol. I/2, p. 94.

See also O. Pichler, "Anwendung der Matrizenrechnung auf betriebswirtschaftliche Aufgaben," *Ingenieur Archiv*, 1953, pp. 119–40; and K. Wenke, "Kostenanalyse mit Matrizen," *Zeitschrift für Betriebswirtschaftslehre*, 1956, pp. 558–76.

[21] Andreas G. Papandreou, *Economics as a Science* (Chicago: Lippincott, 1958), p. 118.

[22] *Ibid.*, p. 8.

[23] Mattessich, *op. cit.*, pp. 328–55.

45

Following a brief introduction to the standard input-output model, the author defines an accounting input-output model in terms of balance sheet classes as endogenous variables and the nominal accounts as a single exogenous variable. Data from published financial statements are substituted into the model, and the "interdependence coefficients" are computed and explained. The stability of the system is then tested using other data from the same company. It was established that two endogenous variables—(1) current and other nonfixed assets and (2) equities—appear to be computed with acceptable accuracy; however, the fixed asset measurements did not appear to be satisfactory.

*INPUT-OUTPUT ACCOUNTING FOR BUSINESS**†

Allen B. Richards

IN RECENT YEARS, attention has been directed to the formalizing of accounting systems through the use of mathematical models and concepts.[1] In addition, the integration and similarities of social and business accounting systems have been discussed.[2] In both cases the relation between Leontief input-output analysis and the usual business accounting system has been indicated. Professor Mattessich specifically mentioned input-output analysis and its general relationship to conventional accounting systems.[3] Powelson also indicated the similarity between the two. However, to the best of my knowledge, a direct translation of a business accounting system into an input-output framework has not been made.

The purpose of this paper is twofold: (1) to illustrate the relationship be-

* Reprinted from *Accounting Review*, July, 1960, pp. 429–36.

† The author is indebted to Robert Rebholtz and Charles Filice for their assistance in the initial stages of the study. He is also grateful to Professors Richard Mattessich and Harold O. Carter for their comments and suggestions on the completed paper.

[1] Richard Mattessich, "Towards a General and Axiomatic Foundation of Accountancy," *Accounting Research*, October, 1957, pp. 328–55; *idem*, "Mathematical Models in Business Accounting," *Accounting Review*, July, 1958, pp. 472–81.

[2] Richard Mattessich, "The Constellation of Accountancy and Economics," *Accounting Review*, October, 1956; John P. Powelson, *Economic Accounting* (New York: McGraw-Hill Book Co., Inc., 1955); A. C. Littleton, "Accounting Rediscovered," *Accounting Review*, April, 1958.

[3] Mattessich, "Towards a General and Axiomatic Foundation of Accountancy," p. 332.

tween input-output and business accounting by translating a conventional accounting system into a Leontief input-output framework with the use of actual accounting data and (2) to indicate how input-output accounting may be used as a tool for financial analysis and planning.

The data used in this study are the financial data of Swift & Company, as given in Moody's, for the years 1951 through 1957.

INPUT-OUTPUT MODEL

Leontief input-output analysis is a mathematical method which specifies the quantitative interrelationships of several variables. In essence, it is a system of simultaneous equations in which all variables may or may not be functionally related. If all the variables are functionally related, the system is called a "closed" input-output model. If at least one variable is not functionally related to the rest—i.e., it is determined outside the system—then the system is called an "open" model. Once the parameters of the system have been determined, the model is then used to investigate and analyze various operations of the system.

The usual input-output analysis specifies the interrelationships of various sectors of an economy.[4] Input-output accounting derives its name from the fact that the analysis relates the outputs of economic sectors to the inputs of economic sectors. In the usual closed models of the economy, each sector's output is functionally related to the inputs (purchases) of all other sectors (including itself). A two-sector closed model is given in system 1:

$$\begin{aligned} X_1 &= x_{11} + x_{12} \\ X_2 &= x_{21} + x_{22} \end{aligned} \tag{1}$$

Here, X_1 is the total output of sector 1, X_2 the total output of sector 2, and x_{ij} $(i, j = 1, 2)$ the input or purchases of the jth sector from the ith sector.

A two-sector "open" model is given in system 2:

$$\begin{aligned} X_1 &= x_{11} + x_{12} + Y_1 \\ X_2 &= x_{21} + x_{22} + Y_2 \end{aligned} \tag{2}$$

In this case the X's and x_{ij}'s are interpreted as before, but the Y_i's $(i = 1, 2)$ represent the "final demand" sectors which are exogenous to the system; i.e., they are determined by factors outside the system of equations. Y_1 is the final demand for sector 1 products, and Y_2 is the final demand for sector 2 products.

In the accounting model, debits and credits correspond to inputs and outputs of the sectors. The input-output model would state that the debits and

[4] Wassily Leontief, *The Structure of the American Economy, 1919–1939* (2d ed.; New York: Oxford University Press, 1951); W. Duane Evans and Marvin Hoffenberg, "The Interindustry Relations Study for 1947," *Review of Economics and Statistics,*———1952, pp. 97–142; Hollis B. Chenery, "Interregional and International Input-Output Analysis," in Tibor Barna (ed.), *The Structural Independence of the Economy* (New York: John Wiley & Sons, Inc., 19—), pp. 339–56; Harold O. Carter, "Regional Input-Output Analysis of Agriculture and Industry" (unpublished Ph.D. thesis, Iowa State College Library, 1958).

credits to all the accounts of an enterprise are interdependent and can be quantitatively expressed by a system of equations. Such a system is given in equations 3:

$$(3) \qquad \begin{aligned} X_1 &= x_{11} + x_{12} + Y_1 \\ X_2 &= x_{21} + x_{22} + Y_2 \end{aligned}$$

In this system X_i represents the total debit to account X_i during the accounting period, x_{ij} $(i, j = 1, 2)$ represents that portion of the debit to account i which is credited to account j, and Y_i $(i = 1, 2)$ represents the remaining part of the debit to i that is credited to those accounts independent of the system.[5] Although debits and credits are made to the independent accounts, these accounts are not considered functionally related to the rest of the system. This is an example of an "open" system. If this had been a closed system, the Y's would have been considered x's and another equation added to express the dependence of the Y's on the rest of the accounts.

The above is called the static input-output model because the system does not take specific account of capital formation. The above input-output model is a flow system expressing the interdependence of flows into and out of the respective accounts. It does not provide a picture of the actual level of the individual accounts at any one moment of time, as a balance sheet would, but rather indicates the changes that would take place in the system when the exogenous accounts are altered.

The most important assumption of input-output analysis is concerned with the relation between the credit to an endogenous account and the total debit to this account. This assumption can be expressed by the following equation:

$$(4) \qquad x_{ij} = a_{ij}X_j + c_{ij}$$

where a_{ij} and c_{ij} are constants.

This assumption states that each credit to a given account is some fixed proportion of the total debits to the account plus a constant error (c_{ij}).

In all empirical work the additional assumption is made that c_{ij} is equal to zero. Therefore, a_{ij} can be measured from a single observation of the ratio between x_{ij} (the individual credit) and X_j (the total debit). The a_{ij} is usually referred to as an input-output coefficient. The a_{ij} then becomes

$$(5) \qquad a_{ij} = x_{ij}/X_j$$

Substituting equation 5, assuming c_{ij} is zero, into equations 3 and rearranging the terms gives

$$(6) \qquad \begin{aligned} X_1 - a_{11}X_1 - a_{12}X_2 &= Y_1 \\ X_2 - a_{21}X_1 - a_{22}X_2 &= Y_2 \end{aligned}$$

---

[5] The reader will note that the variables in equations 3 are not defined as analogous to the *meaning* of "input" and "output" of an accounting system. To be strictly comparable, the variables would have to be defined in reverse order, i.e., debits = inputs and credits = outputs. The variables were defined in the present manner in order to explicitly set forth sales (a credit as the key element in the forecasting system.

or in matrix notation, $X - AX = Y$, where X is a vector of account debits, A is a matrix of input-output coefficients, and Y is a vector of exogenous accounts, as yet unspecified.

With specified exogenous accounts, Y_1 and Y_2, and the constant input-output coefficients, a_{ij}, equations 6 can be solved for the total debits X_1 and X_2. The solution, in matrix notation, is

$$X = (I - A)^{-1}Y \tag{7}$$

The elements A_{ij} of the inverse matrix $(I - A)^{-1}$ are "interdependence" coefficients. These coefficients specify the total debit to account i which results from a unit debit to account j *and* a unit credit to the exogenous account Y.

Once the "interdependence" coefficients have been obtained, the system of equations may then be used to predict flows into and out of the various accounts which arise when particular levels of the exogenous accounts are specified. For example, specifying a particular value for vector Y in equation 7 results in a solution for the value of X in this equation. Thus a total credit to account Y results in a total debit to account X of $(I - A)^{-1}Y$. The system also permits determination of the magnitude of the relationship among the various accounts.

THE SWIFT MODEL

This particular study used four endogenous accounts and one exogenous account.[6] These accounts are:

1.0 Current and other nonfixed assets
2.0 Fixed assets—net
3.0 All equity accounts
4.0 Balance account[7]
5.0 Operations account[8]

The system of equations used is found below:

$$\begin{aligned} X_1 &= x_{11} + x_{12} + x_{13} + x_{14} + Y_1 \\ X_2 &= x_{21} + x_{22} + x_{23} + x_{24} + Y_2 \\ X_3 &= x_{31} + x_{32} + x_{33} + x_{34} + Y_3 \\ X_4 &= x_{41} + x_{42} + x_{43} + x_{44} + Y_4 \end{aligned} \tag{8}$$

---

[6] This small number of accounts was used because the data were obtained from financial reports; and consequently, many of the transactions had to be arbitrarily assigned to various accounts.

[7] The "balance account" is a fictitious account which represents debits and credits to the balance of the accounts. For example, an increase in the balance of current assets from one year to the next is represented by a debit to the balance account and a credit to the current asset account. The net effect is that all account balances are transferred out of their accounts and into the fictitious balance account.

[8] The "operations account" is a consolidation of the operating accounts normally found in a business accounting system.

In this system:

X_1 = Total debit to current and other nonfixed assets
X_2 = Total debit to fixed assets including the depreciation account
X_3 = Total debit to the equities
X_4 = Total debit to the "balance account"
x_{ij} = That portion of the total debit to account i that is credited to account j, $(i, j = 1, 2, 3, 4)$
Y_i = That portion of the total debit to account i that is credited to the "operations account" $(i = 1, \ldots, 4)$[9]

Table 1 shows the debits and credits for 1955 in the input-output framework. The figure in each cell represents a debit to the row account and a credit to the column account. Thus, in 1955, Swift had a credit to the operating accounts and a debit to current and other nonfixed assets of $2,408,-596,000. This was largely the sales figure for the year, which is a credit to sales (operations) and a debit to cash or accounts receivable (current assets). The $2,400,478 figure in the first row and column largely represents collections of accounts receivable. In the normal accounting system, this would be a debit to cash and a credit to accounts receivable. In the model, it becomes an element in the first row and column of the input-output matrix.

The small letters above the numbers indicate the position of the number in

TABLE 1

INPUT-OUTPUT MODEL OF SWIFT & COMPANY ACCOUNTING SYSTEM FOR 1955
(Actual Data in Thousands of Dollars)

Debits \ Credits	*Current and Other Nonfixed Assets 1.0*	*Fixed Assets, Net 2.0*	*Equities 3.0*	*Balance 4.0*	*Operations 5.0*	*Total Debits*
1.0 Current and other nonfixed assets........	(x_{11}) 2,400,478	(x_{12}) 3,268	(x_{13}) 1,718,061	(x_{14}) 417	(Y_1) 2,408,596	(X_1) 6,530,820
2.0 Fixed assets, net..........	(x_{21}) 36,900	(x_{22}) 9,687	(x_{23}) 993	(x_{24}) 10,645	(Y_2) 1,981	(X_2) 60,206
3.0 Equities.......	(x_{31}) 1,832,254	(x_{32}) 0	(x_{33}) 14,814	(x_{34}) 49,160	(Y_3) 0	(X_3) 1,896,228
4.0 Balance........	(x_{41}) 31,097	(x_{42}) 27,491	(x_{43}) 1,632	(x_{44}) 0	(Y_4) 2	(X_4) 60,222
5.0 Operations.....	2,230,091	19,760	160,728			2,410,579
Total credits....	6,530,820	60,206	1,896,228	60,222	2,410,579	

[9] Thus, Y_1 represents the credit to operating accounts *resulting from a debit to current and other assets;* Y_2 represents the credit to operating accounts *resulting from a debit* to fixed assets, etc.

equations 8 and the relationship between these equations and Table 1. Since the operations account is the exogenous account, an equation representing row 5 in Table 1 is not included in the system of equations 8. It is assumed that the transactions (debits and credits) in the operating accounts are determined by such outside factors as the demand for the company's products, sales efforts, efficiencies in the operating plants, and other activities which are external to the system of accounts. The balance sheet accounts are assumed, however, to depend entirely upon changes in the operating accounts and interactions among themselves.[10]

From Table 1 the direct input-output coefficients, a_{ij}, can be computed.[11] These are computed by dividing the numbers in each column by the column total. These are the x_{ij}/X_j shown in equation 5. In order to obtain as much stability in the coefficients as possible, the actual coefficients used in the calculations were the simple means of the coefficients computed for 1953, 1955, and 1957. The actual coefficients are given in system 9, which is system 8 with the a_{ij}'s substituted for the z_{ij}'s and the terms rearranged:

$$\begin{aligned}(1-0.3693)X_1 - 0.0583X_2 - 0.8932X_3 - 0.3122X_4 &= Y_1\\ -0.0046X_1 + (1-0.2146)X_2 - 0.0005X_3 - 0.2311X_4 &= Y_2\\ -0.2843X_1 - 0.0025X_2 + (1-0.0071)X_3 - 0.4567X_4 &= Y_3\\ -0.0032X_1 - 0.3982X_2 - 0.0073X_3 + (1-0)X_4 &= Y_4\end{aligned} \tag{9}$$

or in matrix form:

$$\overset{(I-A)}{\begin{bmatrix} 0.6307 & -0.0583 & -0.8932 & -0.3122\\ -0.0046 & 0.7854 & -0.0005 & -0.2311\\ -0.2843 & -0.0025 & 0.9929 & -0.4567\\ -0.0032 & -0.3982 & -0.0073 & 1.0000\end{bmatrix}} \begin{bmatrix}X_1\\X_2\\X_3\\X_4\end{bmatrix} = \begin{bmatrix}Y_1\\Y_2\\Y_3\\Y_4\end{bmatrix} \tag{10}$$

Inverting the *I–A* matrix results in the following system of equations:

$$\begin{aligned}X_1 &= 2.7166Y_1 + 1.3698Y_2 + 2.4609Y_3 + 2.2889Y_4\\ X_2 &= 0.0233Y_1 + 1.4548Y_2 + 0.0243Y_3 + 0.3546Y_4\\ X_3 &= 0.7889Y_1 + 0.6666Y_2 + 1.7257Y_3 + 1.1885Y_4\\ X_4 &= 0.0237Y_1 + 0.5885Y_2 + 0.0300Y_3 + 1.1571Y_4\end{aligned} \tag{11}$$

The coefficients of equations 11, A_{ij}, are called "interdependence" coefficients and may be interpreted as follows: $1 credit to operations *and* debit to current assets results in a *final total debit* to current assets of $2.72; or a $1 credit to operations *and* debit to fixed assets results in a *final total debit* to current assets of $1.37.

System 11, the input-output system, specifies the quantitative relation among the four endogenous (balance sheet) accounts for *any* specified level of

[10] Certain of the balance sheet accounts are also influenced by outside factors. For example, fixed assets are influenced by investment decisions which are independent of the system of accounts. Partial consideration of these decisions is obtained through the balance account. A dynamic input-output model, however, would directly handle capital formation.

[11] See equation 5.

the exogenous account. It shows the way in which the balance sheet accounts are interrelated in the normal course of business operations. It presents a picture of the expected flows into and out of the balance sheet accounts for a given year.

For example, say company sales were expected to be \$4 for the year, an adjustment in the fixed assets of \$2 was to be credited to operations, and a decline in some equity account resulted in a credit to operations of \$1.

The first transaction indicates Y_1 is equal to \$4. The second indicates Y_2 is equal to \$2. The third transaction indicates Y_3 is equal to \$1. It is assumed that Y_4 is zero. Entering these figures into the equations of system 11 gives system 12:

$$
\begin{aligned}
X_1 &= 2.7166(4) + 1.3698(2) + 2.4609(1) + 2.2889(0) \\
X_2 &= 0.0233(4) + 1.4548(2) + 0.0243(1) + 0.3546(0) \\
X_3 &= 0.7889(4) + 0.6666(2) + 1.7257(1) + 1.1885(0) \\
X_4 &= 0.0237(4) + 0.5885(2) + 0.0300(1) + 1.1571(0)
\end{aligned}
\tag{12}
$$

Multiplying and adding the products gives the following *total debits* to the four accounts ($X_1, \ldots, X_4$):

$$
X_1 = 16.0669 \qquad X_3 = 6.2145
$$
$$
X_2 = 3.0271 \qquad X_4 = 1.3018
$$

In this case a \$7 increase (credit) in the operations account resulted in a \$16 increase in current assets, a \$3 increase in fixed assets, a \$6 decrease in equities, and a \$1 debit to the total balance of all accounts. The net additions to or subtractions from the individual balance sheet accounts may be obtained by additional computations with the original matrix. Thus a picture is obtained of the account flows generated by a specified level of operations. These flows are the direct result of the original entry as well as the indirect result of the functional interdependence of the accounts as specified by the system of equations.

STABILITY OF THE SYSTEM

In order to test for stability in the input-output coefficients[12] and to indicate the forecasting ability of the system, operating data for Swift & Company for the years 1951 through 1957 were entered into the system and the total debits to the four endogenous accounts obtained. These results were then compared with the actual data for the given period. The results are found in Figures 1 and 2. Figure 1 shows very little difference between the computed and actual debits to the current asset and equity accounts. The coefficients for these accounts appear to be quite stable from year to year. Figure 2, however, indicates much less stability in the balance and fixed assets coefficients. Part of the instability in these accounts results from unusual entries in the accounts—e.g., adjustments of prior years' transactions and varying

[12] The coefficients which were obtained as simple means of the coefficients for 1953, 1955, and 1957.

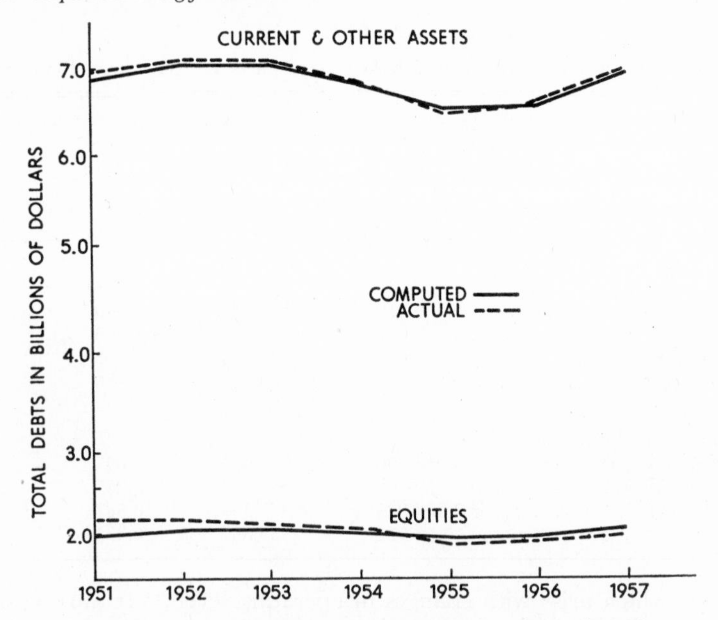

FIGURE 1. A comparison of actual and estimated debits to current and other nonfixed assets and equities, 1951–57.

asset retirements. Table 2 shows the error in both absolute and percentage terms for 1955 and 1957. Very little error existed in estimating the 1955 data. But in 1957, there was a serious error in estimating the balance and fixed assets accounts.

PLANNING WITH THE SYSTEM

Once the input-output system has been obtained and found reasonably accurate in estimating flow values, it can be used to analyze changes in the

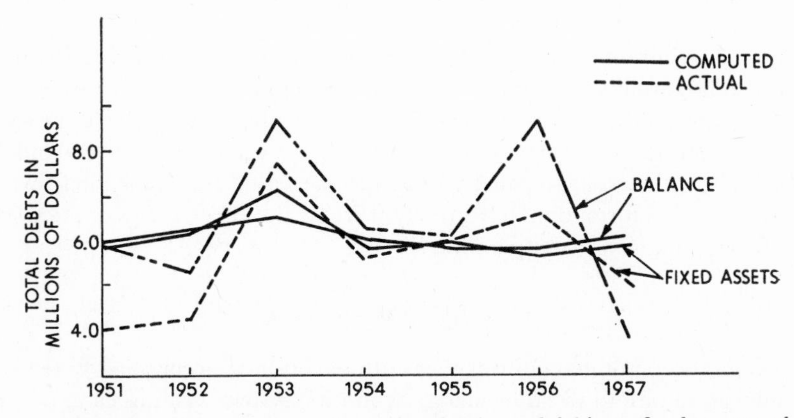

FIGURE 2. A comparison of actual and estimated debits to fixed assets and balance accounts, 1951–57.

TABLE 2

A COMPARISON OF THE ESTIMATED AND ACTUAL DEBITS TO ACCOUNTS, 1955 AND 1957

Accounts	*Estimated* (Thousands of Dollars)	*Actual* (Thousands of Dollars)	*Estimated Less Actual* (Thousands of Dollars)	*Error as Percent of Actual*
		1955		
1.0 Current and other non-fixed assets	6,545,910	6,530,820	15,090	0.2
2.0 Fixed assets	59,003	60,206	−1,203	2.0
3.0 Equities	1,901,464	1,896,228	5,236	0.3
4.0 Balance	58,252	60,222	1,970	3.3
		1957		
1.0 Current and other non-fixed assets	6,914,350	6,907,653	6,697	0.1
2.0 Fixed assets	59,304	51,017	8,287	16.2
3.0 Equities	2,007,925	1,977,358	30,567	1.5
4.0 Balance	60,322	39,887	20,435	51.2

accounts which arise with changes in operating levels.[13] It thus becomes a planning device. For example, the levels of debits (or credits) to each account that are consistent with specified credits (debits) to the operating accounts may be desired. Also, it may be useful to know what kind of capital flows will be generated by an expected level of sales. These and other changes in the accounts can be estimated by the equations. In addition, the financial position of the firm can be estimated for some expected level of sales. The changes in the account balances estimated by the system when added to or subtracted from the initial balances estimates the new financial position of the firm.

This pilot study indicates the need for further work on the input-output system to fully assess its usefulness for financial planning and analysis. Analysis with the aid of the system depends upon the validity of the assumptions, particularly on the stability of the input-output coefficients. One method which may improve the accuracy of the coefficients is to estimate the functional relationships for a number of years using only actual operating data. This means that special adjustments to the accounts would be left out of the analysis. In addition, expansion of the system to include the accounts individually or in less aggregated groups and the use of a dynamic model which handles capital formation may greatly increase the effectiveness of the system for financial analysis and planning.

SUMMARY

As has been pointed out by other authors, business accounting systems are similar in nature to social or macroaccounting systems. In this case, business

[13] See the example presented in system 11.

accounting data were put into a Leontief input-output framework and changes in the accounts predicted by the system. It was found that the estimated changes were very close to actual changes for two accounts and somewhat variable for the other two accounts. The input-output system provides a method whereby management can predict changes in the level of the balance sheet accounts which arise from some level of operations, analyze the dollar flows into and out of accounts, or investigate the impact on the accounting system and level of accounts brought about by changes in operating levels and conditions. The framework, common to all firms, also provides a uniform procedure for aggregating firm data and thus is a method of consistently establishing an interfirm analysis for an industry or an inter-industry analysis for the economy. In order fully to assess the value of the system for financial analysis and planning, a more detailed and expanded system is needed. This would require analysis of the individual accounts and their relationship to each other under normal operating conditions. Changes in operating or accounting procedure, as well as technological changes, would influence the applicability of the system and the specification of the coefficients.

46

The relationship of enterprise goals to budgeting is considered in detail, and the applicability of mathematical models to this problem is effectively dealt with. Simulation as a technique of constructing a model is then described. Finally, a traditional budget is defined in mathematical terms, and a number of practical applications are suggested.

*BUDGETING MODELS AND SYSTEM SIMULATION**†

Richard Mattessich

EXPOSITION OF THE PROBLEM

PERIODIC budgeting, as practiced in industry and taught in the accounting curriculum, combines estimates by individual departments in a process of coordinative aggregation. The purpose is to supply management with a financial plan for future operations.

Frequently, budgeting is charged with the more ambitious task of "finding the most profitable course"[1] for an enterprise. If this means selecting a combination of managerial policies which *optimizes* the long-term profit of the enterprise, the above definition of the purpose of this discipline seems to overstate the potential of traditional budgeting activity. It makes the layman believe that this area of accounting is in a position to determine *optimal solutions.* Undoubtedly, this is not the case since budgeting traditionally neither applies any algorism to optimize the long-term profit function nor provides any means for determining and comparing *all* the alternatives resulting from the *innumerable* factor and policy combinations feasible for an enterprise. If it means, however, finding a policy that yields a prospective profit considered to be *satisfactory*, the above definition is acceptable (provided the term *satisfactory* is interpreted in the Simonian meaning of the best acceptable solution within a limited range of alternatives. Herbert A. Simon calls such a pro-

---

* Reprinted from *Accounting Review*, July, 1961, pp. 384–97.

† The author wishes to acknowledge gratefully (*a*) the financial support of the Management Science Group—Berkeley (Ford Foundation funds) during the summer of 1960 to this project, (*b*) the stimulating discussions under the eminent leadership of Professor C. W. Churchman, and (*c*) the advice and comments he has received from Professors C. Devine, M. Moonitz, and J. Wheeler.

[1] J. B. Heckert and J. D. Wilson, *Business Budgeting and Control* (2d ed.; New York: The Ronald Press), p. 14.

cedure "satisficing" as opposed to the more demanding operation of "optimizing"[2]).

With the application of mathematical-scientific approaches to management problems and the progressive use of automatic data processing, the question arises: In what way can future periodic budgeting be improved? Before a quest for reform can be considered, it is necessary to make a distinction between the immediate future and the long run. There is no doubt that *ultimately* it will be desirable to "optimize" within our budgeting models, but only as long as the mechanism for optimization does not restrict the budgeting procedures in other directions or impose upon them other oversimplifications. The optimization model which has been proposed in the award-winning dissertation by Stedry[3] is a meritorious attempt to find a starting point for the development of managerial models in budgeting; it is a pioneering effort which, considering the lack of "operational research" procedures in accounting, cannot be praised highly enough, though there is still much room for improvement. On the other hand, we must not overrate the immediate *practical* usefulness of this approach on a large scale (for further details, see notes 13 and 15); like most managerial optimization models, it suffers under the serious handicap of being restricted to a single department or limited area of operations, thus enabling us only to *suboptimize* without any hope for *overall optimization* of the whole enterprise. It therefore seems opportune to develop a less ambitious approach which, however, has the advantage of applying to the *whole* enterprise and which eventually may be utilized in combining suboptimization models for individual departments. One purpose of this paper is to stimulate experimentation and simulation with "aggregation models." The concrete example presented in the third section is a first attempt at formalizing such a model and therefore constitutes an illustration rather than an ultimate solution; hence, suggestions for further improvement are invited.

As established before, traditional budgeting already offers a primitive procedure of "satisficing" a goal function. It suffers, however, from the shortcoming of including too small a number of possible alternatives from which to choose in determining the "most satisfactory" solution. Besides, we all recognize that the traditional budget, even if it is a flexible budget, is very difficult to adjust to suddenly changing conditions; it is at best "flexible" only with regard to a changing sales or production volume. Our present proposal therefore rests on the simple assumption that a model which permits the calculation of a larger number of alternatives based on more numerous "flexible" variables and eventually changing parameters would yield a better approximation to the ideal but unattainable optimum solution. This

---

[2] Herbert A. Simon, "Theories of Decision-Making in Economics and Behavioral Science," *American Economic Review*, June, 1959, p. 264. See also J. G. March and Herbert A. Simon, *Organizations* (New York, 1958), pp. 140–41, 169.

[3] Andrew C. Stedry, *Budget Control and Cost Behavior* (Englewood Cliffs, N.J.: Prentice-Hall, Inc., 1960), pp. 113–43.

could be made possible by means of electronic computers and system simulation (discussed in the next section). To construct a model for such a task requires the translation of a traditional budgeting system into algebraic terms. This has not been done before, since accountants are accustomed to present their knowledge through particular examples and individual illustrations, a practice that explains the overemphasis on technicalities and the abounding use of illustrative tables with long figure columns in textbooks of accounting and related fields. The "general" formulations of the accountant rest mainly on verbal descriptions, and past attempts to break this habit were not successful largely because of the conservative attitude of accountants. The present situation appears more promising as more and more accountants realize that soon they will be working in a highly mathematical atmosphere whether they desire it or not. It also must be borne in mind that a few decades ago, modern algebraic notations (e.g., sigma and matrix notations) were not applied at all, at least not in the economic sciences. It is due to these notational devices that a concise and yet general presentation is made possible.

To some operations analysts the mere translation of accounting models into mathematical terminology, without a calculus for determining an optimum, might appear to be a rather pedestrian task. We are convinced, however, that as long as accounting methods are acceptable to the industry, the mere change to a mathematical formulation will be advantageous for several reasons:

1. It can be considered a prerequisite for applying electronic data processing to certain accounting problems.[4]
2. It articulates the structure of the accounting models and illuminates accounting methods from a new point of view, revealing many facets so far neglected or unobserved.
3. It enables a *general* and hence more scientific presentation of many accounting methods.
4. It facilitates the exploration of new areas, thereby accelerating the advancement of accounting; the example chosen for this paper will particularly emphasize this point.
5. Finally, it leads to more sophisticated methods and might help to lay the foundation for close cooperation of accounting with other areas of management science.

Therefore, we will attempt to develop a concise but fairly general frame for traditional budgeting and explore the possibility of extending or modifying

[4] For those who appeal to G. Clarkson and H. Simon's statement that "We are beginning to learn that models do not have to be stated in mathematical or numerical form to permit us to simulate their behavior with electronic computers" ("Simulation and Group Behavior," *American Economic Review*, December, 1960, p. 923; [cf. Herbert A. Simon, *The New Science of Management Decision* (New York, 1960), pp. 22, 24–25]), we may reply that even if mathematics in the narrow sense of the word can be relinquished, symbolic logic will have to be substituted for it. Therefore, if we promote the acquisition of mathematical knowledge by accountants, we refer to it in the broadest sense of the term and include the achievements of modern logic as well.

such a model for the purpose of determining "satisfactory" if not "optimal" managerial plans.

Such an approach has the advantage of using traditional budgeting as a basis for developing a more refined and perhaps a more scientific treatment of the problem.

THE MEANING OF SIMULATION

Whether accounting is considered to be a part of management science will depend to a great extent on the effort accountants make in absorbing tools and techniques of management science and in incorporating them into their own conceptual apparatus. So far, in spite of recognizable endeavors, the vocabulary of management science still constitutes a foreign language to many accountants; and before embarking upon construction of a budgeting model for *simulation* purposes, it becomes advisable to subject the concept of "system simulation" and its use by management scientists to some investigation.

For a long time, social scientists have envied physicists and chemists their vast opportunity of experimentation. This, it is true, has not been their only object of envy; but considering the broad experimental basis on which the achievements of the natural sciences rest, it is still a major target of envy. Everyday life, no doubt, supplied social scientists with *surrogate* experimental material, the cognitive value of which should by no means be underrated;[5] but it usually forces relinquishment of the most important features of the experiment: control of certain variables and arbitrary repetition, a limitation which holds in particular for economics and business administration. In practice, neither the whole economy nor an individual firm lends itself to experimentation in the true sense of the word.

The advent of electronic data processing systems, however, seems to have opened the door to experimental ventures—and adventures—for the economic sciences, mainly through the channel of "system simulation." Such experiments are, of course, of a different nature than those of the physicist, as they do not deal with the medium of reality itself but only with its mathematical structure; they do, however, enable the mental reproduction of a large number of alternative situations and thus help to determine *satisfactory* if not approximately optimal solutions. As Malcolm says:

> System Simulation has the most useful property of permitting the researcher and management to experiment with and test policy, procedure and organization changes in much the same way as the aeronautical engineer tests his design ideas in the laboratory or in the "wind tunnel." Thus we might think of System Simulation as a sort of "management Wind Tunnel" which is used to pretest many suggested changes and

---

[5] Joseph A. Schumpeter, *History of Economic Analysis* (New York: Oxford University Press, 1954), p. 16 (*vide* his citation of Leon Walras).

eliminate much needless "experimentation" with the "real" people, machines and facilities.[6]

In contrast to the "wind tunnel," the simulation models of the management scientist are analytical or analog models which frequently incorporate probability concepts. Where the latter holds—particularly in cases which hinge on a statistical distribution whose structure is not exactly known—a special simulation approach has been developed under the name of the Monte Carlo method.[7] The frequently encountered identification of the term *simulation method* with the expression *Monte Carlo method* does not seem justified, however, since the former implies a much more comprehensive concept than the latter. Not every simulation model relies on a "simulated probability distribution"; the following example of a budgeting system for simulation purposes may be taken as a case in point. For problems which cannot be forced into the straitjacket of an optimization model, or for optimization problems of a forbiddingly complex mathematical structure, *approximate solutions* may be found by simulation, that is, by determining and scanning an array of alternative combinations and selecting that with the most favorable outcome. This, of course, is a fairly crude approach since "the result of a simulation is always the answer to a specific numerical problem without any insight into why that is the answer or how the answer would be influenced by a change in any of the data."[8]

Nevertheless, simulation may have some appeal to accountants; and indeed, the traditional approach to periodic budgeting can, with some imagination, be regarded as a simulation model. It is true that this model so far has not appeared in mathematical attire, just as it is undeniable that the array of alternatives calculated is usually restricted to a small number only. The test for the existence of a simulation approach, however, is the selection of a satisfactory solution from alternatives, even if it is reflected in the preparatory work to the budget rather than in the coordinative level of the budgeting model itself. On this coordinative level the "flexible" budget could be interpreted as a series of alternatives; here the purpose of calculating conditions under various output levels serves primarily to adjust the budget for suddenly changing output conditions, while changes in the product mix, wage rates, material prices, and other costs are rarely given consideration. By simulating the firm through a budgeting model, it should be feasible to extend the flexibility into these other directions. Therefore a major purpose of the proposed project is to provide for a *multidimensional variability or flexibility* of the budget. According to the needs, certain alternatives could be printed

[6] D. C. Malcolm, Foreword to *Report of System Simulation Symposium* (New York, 1957), p. v.

[7] D. W. Miller and M. K. Starr, *Executive Decisions and Operations Research* (Englewood Cliffs, N.J.: Prentice-Hall, Inc., 1960), pp. 152–55.

[8] Robert Dorfman, "Operations Research," *American Economic Review*, September, 1960, p. 604.

out at the beginning of the budgeting period, while other alternatives would be quickly available through a stored computer program into which data for the changed variables or parameters could be inserted.[9]

TRADITIONAL BUDGETING AS A MATHEMATICAL MODEL

Budgeting, as traditionally practiced, is frequently regarded as "accounting for the future." Even if thereby no individual double entries are recorded, the coordination of financial flows is carried out with reference to the classificational device of accounts. Some time ago, we hinted at the possibility and eventual usefulness of presenting accounting in form of a system of simultaneous definitional equations.[10] This is what Dorfman[11] calls the "first" or "straightforward descriptive aspect" of model building; although it is an indispensable step, it no doubt results in "an essentially tautological and sterile description of the problem." In budgeting, however, the second aspect —the state of "creative hypothesizing"—is, at least in principle, also materialized, though it may be a matter of controversy whether the hypotheses of customary budgeting constitute a satisfactory and creative achievement. Yet the question arises whether budgeting may not be the most fertile soil of accounting for planting meaningful mathematical models. It is therefore not surprising that the problem of budgeting (in the broadest sense of the word) has been attacked *mathematically* from various points of view. The oldest, occasionally encountered, and most elaborate approach is the construction of "flow models" for the whole firm. It is true that the hypotheses used in some of these models might be considered as being less crude than those of traditional budgeting; but apart from the fact that their aim might be considered as going beyond the task of a purely financial plan, it is, from the viewpoint of actual practice, not too successful an approach and for the time being has been restricted to business games. It may well be the most promising method of the future; but in spite of intensive experimentation by many research groups, so far the immense number of variables and the magnitude of the task of determining a host of unwieldy parameters have prevented results which give hope of any *wide* and immediate application in the area of indus-

---

[9] For the reader who wants to inform himself in greater detail about many facets of system simulation, we recommend "Simulation: A Symposium" (three articles by G. H. Orcutt, M. Shubik, and G. Clarkson and H. Simon), *American Economic Review*, December, 1960, pp. 893–932; and the reports of the first and second *System Simulation Symposium* (sponsored by American Institute of Industrial Engineers, Institute of Management Science, and Operations Research Society of America) (New York, 1958 and 1960).

[10] Richard Mattessich, "Towards an Axiomatization of Accountancy, with an Introduction to the Matrix Formulation of Accounting Systems," *Accounting Research*, October, 1957, pp. 328–55; and "Mathematical Models in Business Accounting," *Accounting Review*, July, 958, pp. 472–81.

[11] Dorfman, *loc. cit.*

trial budgeting.[12] The second approach can be called a "behavioral model" and is restricted to the control task of budgeting. It is contained in the first part of Stedry's thesis,[13] and its originality may warrant further study by the reader.

Stedry makes a rigorous distinction between budgeting for control purposes and budgeting for planning purposes. Out of this distinction follows the third approach (also developed by Stedry and mentioned previously), which consists of a linear programming model for maximizing the profit function of an individual department. Such "planning" models might be incorporated into the aggregation model suggested below but are not by necessity an integral part of it; it is conceivable that budgeting on the departmental level may continue in the traditional way, while only the budgeting activity on the coordinative level uses a mathematical model. Even then, a multitude of alternatives is feasible.

Fundamentally, there is no difference between the following budgeting model and other simulation models of management science. The main criticism against such an approach, therefore, cannot be found on the methodological plane but must be sought on the level of hypotheses formulation. It is as easy for accountants to demonstrate that their traditional approach is nothing but the application of various models (translatable into mathematical terms) as it is difficult for them to refute the reproach that their models are too simple and their hypotheses too crude. The main weapon in their defense, of course, lies in the counterargument that "too simple" and "too crude" are very relative concepts; and what may appear to the theoretician crude might be considered by the man in practice, who has to weigh costs against benefits, as fairly satisfactory. Therefore, this challenge becomes critical only in the moment when the hypothesis becomes so crude and the model so full of "gaps" that it must be considered meaningless. In the following model, we have used those hypotheses generally accepted in budgeting textbooks as well as in actual practice. Our answer is therefore highly pragmatic, if we justify our approach with the evidence that these hypotheses are used in thousands of enterprises all over the world. Their present acceptance is certainly enough justification for using them as a *starting point* for the construction of a framework which, due to its general formulation, should be flexible enough to be adaptable to more refined hypotheses.

This model, fully spelled out, consists of several hundred simultaneous equations and is intended for experimental use in various enterprises. To avoid overburdening this paper with so many equations, we present here

---

[12] However, a project of such a "flow model" or "management control system" has been undertaken on a large scale by the Systems Development Corporation (Santa Monica). So far, only one aspect of management control has been investigated—the effect of using particular decision rules—through a mathematical model constituting a huge queuing network. Theoretically, this is a fascinating approach and no doubt will bear fruit in the *long run*. *Vide* J. B. Heyne, "Planning for Research in Management Control Systems," Technical Memorandum 546, Systems Development Corporation, October, 1960, p. 30.

[13] Stedry, *op. cit.*, pp. 17–42.

only the most important equations, primarily those which represent in a *succinct* way the tables occasionally encountered in textbooks of budgeting[14] in a fairly general form.

We may point out that in order to understand the presentation of the budgeting model in symbolic form, no knowledge of higher mathematics is required; some familiarity with algebra and the handling of the sigma notation should prove sufficient. The sigma notation is shortly explained in the following and can easily be mastered by practicing the writing of summations in the new, but perhaps unaccustomed way. Thereby, it is well to remember that the various sub- or superscripts refer to different "dimensions" and that we are here concerned with four dimensions: the product, the cost item, the department, and the time. Only the very last part, in which we have tried to connect our model with Stedry's departmental optimization approach, requires some familiarity with maximization under constraints. In order to make the explanation of these equations as concise as possible, a key of symbols with short explanations precedes the equations. It should be mentioned that the list of all variables is actually much longer but is abbreviated through a device explained as follows.

Assume, in a factory producing furniture, that the subscript i refers to the product chairs No. 3487, the subject j to the labor of carpenters at the wage rate of $2 per hour, and the subscript d to the polishing department. Furthermore, assume that the symbol L represents the total labor hours in the factory (during the period anticipated); then, L_i represents the labor hours to be devoted to product i—in this case to chairs No. 3487—and L_j expresses the carpenter labor hours to be required and L_d the labor hours expected in the polishing department. It is important to recognize that, first, these subscripts can be generalized (e.g., $i = 1, \cdots, n$; $j = 1, \cdots, r$; and $d = 1, \cdots, u$); that means they do not any more refer to a certain product, cost item, or department, respectively, but to *any* of the n products, the r cost items, or the u departments, respectively; and second, that various combinations of these subscripts are possible, like L_{ij} (labor hours of work j for product i), or L_{jd} (labor hours of work j in department d), or L_{ijd} (labor hours of work j in department d required for product i), or L_{id} (labor hours in department d required for product i), etc. Hence the reader must be aware that L_i and L_{ij} or L_d *are different variables.* Consequently, the following formulation:

$$L = \sum_i L_i = \sum_i \sum_j L_{ij} \sum_i \sum_j \sum_d L_{ijd}$$
$$= \sum_i \sum_d L_{id} = \sum_d L_d = \sum_j L_j$$

expresses the fact that the total of the labor hours (anticipated in the budgeting period) is equal to the sum of all subtotals of labor hours required for the

[14] Glenn A. Welsch, *Budgeting: Profit-Planning and Control* (Englewood Cliffs, N. J.: Prentice-Hall, Inc., 1957).

various products ($i = 1, \cdots, u$); is also equal to the sum total of all labor hours required for the individual products specified according to the various cost items ($j = 1, \cdots, r$); is furthermore equal to the sum total of all labor hours required for the individual products specified according to both cost items and departments, etc.

The sigma notation, as used here, is one of the most valuable tools of modern algebra and very easy to learn; it may be unfamiliar at first, but after a little practice it proves to be a very *simple* tool but highly useful, especially in accounting, where summations or aggregations occur continuously.

The reader will notice that to our three *dimensions:* product item ($i = 1, \cdots, n$), cost items ($j = 1, \cdots, r$), and department ($d = 1, \cdots, u$ for producing departments and $h = 1, \cdots, e$ for service departments), time is added as a fourth dimension (using the superscript t for various budgeting periods—omitted when misunderstandings are not likely—or τ for subperiods like *months* as used in the present model).

SOME EXPLANATIONS OF THE SYMBOLIC PRESENTATION

The following does not identify each individual symbol but gives a general notion of the basic symbols to which, according to the specification desired, the following subscripts and superscripts will have to be added. If, in a formula, no sub- or superscript is attached to a symbol, the pertinent variable or parameter refers to the entire production or sales activity of the enterprise and the whole budgeting period.

Subscripts

i Indicates the kind of product ($i = 1, \cdots, n$).
j Indicates the kind of cost item ($j = 1, \cdots, r$).
d Indicates the kind of producing department ($d = 1, \cdots, u$).
h Indicates the kind of service department ($h = 1, \cdots, e$).
d and h are mutually exclusive and refer to the same dimension.

Superscripts

t Indicates the budgeting period. In cases where no doubt can arise, the omission of the superscript t means that the pertinent symbol *refers to the whole budgeting period* in case the symbol represents a flow concept, or it *refers to the end of the budgeting period* in case the symbol represents a stock concept. Accordingly, $t - 1$ *refers to the whole period preceding* the budget period in case of a flow concept, and the end of the preceding period (= *the beginning of the budgeting period*) in case of a stock concept.

τ Refers to a whole subperiod of the budgeting period (usually a certain month, $\tau = 1, \cdots, 12$) in case of a flow concept, or to the end of this subperiod in case of a stock concept. Accordingly, $\tau - 1$ refers to the subperiod preceding in case of a flow concept, or the beginning of τ(= the end of $\tau - 1$) in case of a stock concept.

It should be noted that an increasing number of subscripts of a basic symbol indicates a decreasing degree of aggregation, and vice versa.

A sub- or superscript below a Σ sign indicates the summation over the whole range of the pertinent script.

It may also be pointed out that in general we have tried to adhere to the following scheme: Uppercase letters refer to variables whose units are other than dollars; lowercase letters refer to variables expressed in dollars; Greek letters are used for denoting parameters. Since the border between exogenous variables and parameters is occasionally vague, the latter distinction cannot always be relied upon. Finally, it is important not to confuse basic symbols with subscripts; this danger could not be avoided since the limited number of letters requires the use occasionally of one and the same letter for a symbol as well as for a subscript.

Key to Symbols

- F Quantitative performance in units (hours, etc., depending on the basis of factory overhead costs) of producing departments.
- G Quantitative performance in units (hours, etc., depending on the basis of overhead costs) of service departments.
- I Finished goods inventory (including partly finished goods inventory in equivalent units).
- J Raw material inventory (in t, pounds, m^3, etc.).
- L Labor hours.
- M Raw material purchases (in t, pounds, m^3, etc.).
- N Raw material consumption (in t, pounds, m^3, etc.).
- P Production (in equivalent units).
- S Sales (in units).
- a Addition in capital budget (cost value of added fixed assets).
- b Bad debt reserve (addition during period).
- c Cost or expense item (not mutually exclusive with e, f, l, m, etc.).
- d Depreciation charge (not mutually exclusive with e, f, l, m, etc.).
- e Operating expenses (administrative and selling expenses).
- f^* Factory overhead expenses of producing departments *before prorating* service departments.
- f Factory overhead expenses of producing departments *after prorating* service departments.
- g Factory overhead expenses of service departments.
- h Cash holding.
- i Cost of finished goods inventory.
- j Cost of raw material inventory.
- k Fixed asset (average).
- l Labor cost.
- m Cost of raw material purchases.
- n Cost of raw material consumption.
- o Owners' equity increase through additional investment in cash.
- p Cost of production.
- q Collection of accounts receivable.
- r Accounts receivable (balance).
- s Sales revenues (net).
- t Income tax cash payments.
- u Repayment of debt capital.
- v Variable operating expenses.
- w Variable factory overhead cost of producing departments after prorating service departments.
- w^* Variable factory overhead cost of producing departments before prorating service departments.
- x Cash expenditures.

y Owners' equity decrease (dividends, etc.).
z Liquid funds to be procured during period.
α Coefficient (parameter) expressing the sales (in units) as a percentage of sales of the previous period.
β Coefficient expressing the sales (in units) of a subperiod as a percentage of the corresponding sales for the whole budgeting period.
γ Coefficient expressing the quantity of raw material required (= to be consumed in production process) in a subperiod as a percentage of the quantity of the raw material requirement for the budgeting period.
δ Coefficient expressing the purchases of raw material in a subperiod as a percentage of the corresponding concept for the budgeting period.
ϵ Fixed cost portion of operating expenses.
ζ Unit cost of finished goods inventory.
η Coefficient expressing the production performance during a subperiod as a percentage of the corresponding concept for the budgeting period.
θ Coefficient expressing the production activity in units of the basis on which factory overhead costs are calculated.
ι Fixed portion of factory overhead costs of service departments.
κ Standard rate of labor (in hours per equivalent product unit).
λ Wage rate (in dollars per labor hour).
μ Unit cost of raw material.
ν Coefficient prorating variable factory overhead costs of service departments to producing departments.
ξ^* Variable rate of factory overhead costs of producing department before prorating service departments.
ξ Variable rate of factory overhead costs of producing departments after prorating service departments.
π Unit cost of production.
ρ Raw material requirement (in material units) per product unit.
σ Sales price per unit of finished product (average).
τ Coefficient of capital (asset) addition distribution during budgeting period.
υ Depreciation rate.
ϕ^* Fixed portion of factory overhead cost of producing departments before prorating service departments.
ϕ Fixed portion of factory overhead cost of producing departments after prorating service departments.
χ Variable rate of factory overhead costs of service departments.
Ψ Variable overhead rate of operating departments (after prorating service departments).
ω Coefficient prorating fixed factory overhead costs of service departments to producing departments.
Γ Applied factory overhead rate.
Φ Function (or parameter) expressing accounts receivable solicitation in terms of sales or accounts receivable.
Ω Function (or parameter) expressing expenditures as a function of costs.

MODEL OF A GENERALIZED PERIODIC BUDGETING SYSTEM

Sales budget:

$$s = \sum_i s_i = \sum_i \sigma_i S_i = \sum_i \sum_\tau \sigma_i \beta_i^\tau S_i^\tau$$

$$s = \sum_i \sigma_i \alpha_i S_i^{t-1}$$

Production budget:

$$S_i = I_i^{t-1} + \sum_\tau P_i^\tau - I_i$$

$$P = \sum_i P_i = \sum_i \sum_\tau P_i^\tau$$

$$\pi_i = \frac{\sum_\tau \pi_i^\tau}{12}$$

$$p = \sum_i \sum_\tau \pi_i^\tau P_i = \sum_i \left(\pi_i^\tau \sum_\tau \eta_i^\tau P_i \right)$$

Raw material and purchasing budget:

$$M_j^\tau = J_j^{\tau-1} + \sum_i \delta_{ij}^\tau N_{ij} - J_j^\tau = \gamma_j^\tau M_j$$

$$m = \sum_j \mu_j \left(J_j^{t-1} + \sum_i \sum_\tau \delta_{ij}^\tau N_{ij} - J_j \right)$$

$$m = \sum_j \left(j_j^{t-1} + \sum_i n_{ij} - j_j \right)$$

Direct labor budget:

$$l^\tau = \sum_i \sum_j \sum_d \kappa_{ijd} \lambda_j \eta_{ijd}^\tau P_{ijd}$$

$$l = \sum_j \sum_d \lambda_j L_{jd}$$

Factory overhead cost budget, producing departments and service departments:

$$f = \sum_j \sum_d (\phi_{jd} + w_{jd})$$

$$= \sum_j \sum_d \sum_\tau \left(\frac{\phi_{jd}}{12} + w_{jd}^\tau \right)$$

$$f_d^\tau = \sum_j \frac{\phi_{jd}}{12} + \xi_d^\tau F_d^\tau$$

$$\Gamma_d = \frac{f_d}{F_d} = \xi_d + \frac{\sum_j \phi_{jd}}{F_d}$$

$$\zeta_d = \frac{\sum \zeta_d^{\tau}}{12} = \frac{w_d}{F_d}$$

$$f_d = \overset{*}{\phi_d} + \sum_h \omega_{dh}\iota_h + \overset{*}{w_d} + \sum_h \nu_{dh}\chi_h G_h$$

$$g_h = \iota_h + \chi_h G_h$$

Operating expense budget:

$$e_j^{\tau} = \frac{\epsilon_j}{12} + \psi_j \sum_i s_i^{\tau}$$

$$e_j = \epsilon_j + v_j$$

Capital additions budget and depreciation schedule:

$$a = \sum_j a_j = \sum_j \sum_{\tau} \tau_j a_j = \sum_j \sum_{\tau} a_j^{\tau}$$

$$d = \sum_j d_j = \sum_j k_j v_j = \sum_j \sum_{\tau} d_j^{\tau} = \sum_j k_j \frac{v_j}{12}$$

The expense items e, f, l, and m are mutually exclusive among themselves but are not mutually exclusive with the expense items b, c, and d.

Accounts receivable collection budget:

$$q = \sum_i q_i = \Phi_i^{t-1}(r_i^{t-1} - b_i^{t-1}) + \sum_{\tau} \Phi_i^{\tau} s_i^{\tau}$$

Cash budget:

$$x_j = {}_c c_j + {}_p c_j - {}_b c_j$$

$$x = \sum_j x_j = \sum_j \Omega_j c_j = \sum_j ({}_e c_j + {}_p c_j - {}_b c_j)$$

$$\begin{array}{l}
h^{t-1} + q^1 - u^1 + o^1 - x^1 - y^1 - t^1 + z^1 = h^1 \\
h^1 + q^2 - u^2 + o^2 - x^2 - y^2 - t^2 + z^2 = h^2 \\
\cdot \qquad \qquad \qquad \qquad \qquad \qquad \qquad \cdot \\
\cdot \qquad \qquad \qquad \qquad \qquad \qquad \qquad \cdot \\
\cdot \qquad \qquad \qquad \qquad \qquad \qquad \qquad \cdot \\
h^{11} + q^{12} - u^{12} + o^{12} - x^{12} - y^{12} - t^{12} + z^{12} = h^{12} = h
\end{array}$$

The symbol c_j ($j = 1, \cdots, r$) may represent any cost or expense item. That means it may stand for n_1 or l_3 or f_5 or g_6 or e_7, etc.

The prescripts b, p, and e of the symbol c indicate beginning balance, purchases, and ending balance, respectively (beginning and ending balances, of course, refer to deferred or accrued items in the broadest sense of the word).

In a similar way (i.e., by further use of nonmutually exclusive variables) a projected balance sheet and income statement may be constructed. Both statements can be developed from the previous equations by mere accounting identities without the use of further behavioral parameters (it is, however, possible to include parameters in the form of liquidity coefficients and other statement ratios if one insists on a certain statement structure—obviously, the best way to achieve this is to impose certain constraints on the model). Another aspect is the possibility of combining Stedry's limited substitution maximization model with the above aggregation system.

Within this framework, such a maximization problem would assume the following form if our interpretation of Stedry's model is correct:[15]

Maximize:

$$\sum_i \left[\Delta^{\tau}_{id} P^{\tau}_{id} - \sum_j \left(\mu_j \frac{N^{\tau}_{ijd}}{\rho^{\tau}_{ijd}} + \lambda_j \frac{L^{\tau}_{ijd}}{\kappa^{\tau}_{ijd}} \right) \right]$$

subject to the following constraints:

$$\sum_j (N^{\tau}_{ijd} + L^{\tau}_{ijd} - \rho^{\tau}_{ijd} \kappa^{\tau}_{ijd} P^{\tau}_{ijd}) = 0$$

$$\sum_j \rho^{\tau}_{ijd} P^{\tau}_{ijd} \leq N^{\tau}_{jd}{}^{\max}$$

$$\sum K^{\tau}_{ijd} P^{\tau}_{ijd} \leq L^{\tau}_{jd}{}^{\max}$$

$$*I^{\tau}_i{}^{\max} \geq *I^{\tau-1}_i + *P^{\tau}_i - S^{\tau}_i \geq *I^{\tau}_i{}^{\min}$$

---

[15] In comparing Stedry's model [see below], the reader will notice that the above maximization model has not only been translated into our symbolism but also had to be adjusted somewhat to make it conform to the structure of our aggregation model.

Maximize:

$$\sum_i^m \left(c_i y_i - \sum_{j \epsilon q_i} \sum_{k=1}^{nj} c_{ijk} x_{ijk} \right)$$

subject to:

$$\sum_{k-1}^{nj} x_{ijk} - y_i = 0 \qquad i \doteq 1, \cdots, m; j \in q_i$$

$$\sum_{i=1}^{m} b_{ijk} x_{ijk} \leqq b_{jk} \qquad k = 1, \cdots, n_j; j \in q_i$$

$$y_i \leqq U_i$$
$$-y_i \leqq -L_i$$

For the sake of comparison, we have stated here the original model *without*, however, listing the pertinent *key* of symbols. For the latter, see Stedry, *op. cit.*, p. 120. Note that in contrast to Stedry, we assume above that the limitations set by machine (and buildings) capacity are incorporated in the constraints set by $N_{jd}{}^{\tau\max}$ and $L_{jd}{}^{\tau\max}$, and hence do not need separate consideration.

At this point a new symbol and three superscripts have to be explained.
Δ_i^τ · · · the contribution per unit of the *i*th item to profit and costs (for subperiod τ); the superscript "max" refers to the *maximum* (capacity) of a certain material or labor factor (in a certain department) or of an inventory level permissible for a certain raw material; corresponding to the latter, the superscript "min" refers to the *minimum* inventory level. The *asterisks* in the last equation merely indicate that I and P refer to *completely* finished goods and are not (as previously; cf. key to symbols) determined on an equivalent unit basis.

The reader will have noticed that the concept Δ_i^τ (or in Stedry's notation, c_i) is a contribution margin, which, however, is not identical to the contribution margin of direct costing. By employing such a concept, Stedry circumvents the difficulty of incorporating some overhead costs in his model. This, of course, does not solve the overhead cost problem but only shifts it to another level (a level outside the maximization model). It should be added that Stedry offers concrete suggestions for computing his maximization model by means of a linear programming approach with "diadic" arrangement.[16]

In this connection, we ought to draw the reader's attention to another proposal made by Kenneth J. Arrow,[17] who also emphasizes departmental profit maximization. Arrow shows under which circumstances suboptimization can lead to overall optimization and presents concrete suggestions for using interdepartmental *shadow prices* for the attainment of this goal. He furthermore recommends, for the purpose of determining the profit maximum, step-by-step approximations—eventually by means of computing machines—but does not rely, as Stedry does, on linear programming methods. Arrow's paper pivots around the question whether and when decentralization within a firm is possible and thus illuminates the problem from an entirely different point of view. Some of the results of this study, however, seem to be relevant to our problem and will shortly be summarized.

Under perfect competition and absence of purely "internal goods" (those not available in the market) the optimum policy for the firm is simply to instruct each process manager independently to maximize profits, computed at market prices. "There may indeed be problems of control to insure that maximization does take place and it is clear that such problems present a challenge to the accounting procedures as well as incentive schemes."[18] If, however, internal goods that are not traded in the market are admitted, we can again have decentralization by instructing the manager to maximize a

---

[16] A. Charnes, W. W. Cooper, and M. H. Miller, "Dyadic Problems and Sub-Dual Methods" (mimeo), Carnegie Institute of Technology (cited from Stedry, *op. cit.*).

[17] Kenneth J. Arrow, "Optimization, Decentralization, and Internal Pricing in Business Firms," in *Contributions to Scientific Research in Management,* Proceedings of the Scientific Program following the dedication of the Western Data Processing Center, Graduate School of Business Administration, University of California, Los Angeles, 1959, pp. 9–18.

[18] *Ibid.*, p. 12.

shadow profit, that is, the profit computed by valuing the commodities at their market price and the internal good at its shadow price, which can be found through a process of successive approximations.

Let some central agency within the firm announce a tentative shadow price for the good which is used only internally. Then let the manager of each process maximize his shadow profit, as given by formula 8 [here not reprinted]. As a result, it will be found in general that the total amount demanded of good 3 [the internal good] within the firm is greater or less than the amount available. These demands and supplies are forwarded by the process managers to the central office. If the demand in total exceeds the supply, the shadow price is raised for the next period; otherwise it is lowered. This provides a new shadow price, on the basis of which the process managers again optimize. It can be shown, under certain conditions, that if this process is continued long enough, the operations of the firm will gradually converge to a position of maximum total profitability.[19]

Under imperfect competition, complete decentralization is not possible, since there has to be some single agency to supply the marginal revenues which are affected by the actions of the process managers. "It would not be correct to allow each process manager to maximize his profits taking account of the effect of his output on his own prices but not taking into consideration the effect of his output on the prices received by the other process manager."[20]

PRACTICAL APPLICATION AND CONCLUSION

At this stage the reader who is not familiar with the application of mathematical models for practical purposes and with computer simulation may ask: How can the budgeting model presented in this paper serve a particular purpose in actual practice? We will try to answer this question by indicating the various steps necessary for the implementation of such a simulation system.

1. The existing budgeting system will have to be examined and translated into mathematical terms, step by step, each subbudget for itself, as shown in the previous model. One must not forget that our model is only an illustration, and the idiosyncrasies of each individual budgeting system have to be reflected through appropriate choice of variables, parameters, and model structure. If desired, one might at this point consider certain changes that improve upon the structure of the previously available budgeting system. It also must be taken into consideration that in our presentation we received the benefit afforded by the application of *general* sub- and superscripts like $i(i = 1, \cdots, n)$, $(j = 1, \cdots, r)$, etc. For practical purposes, however, each sub- or superscript must be spelled out; this increases immensely the number of variables, parameters, and equations. Finally, it must be borne in mind that in our exposition we have selected only a few equations—namely, the more interesting and significant ones—out of a whole system of simul-

[19] *Ibid.*, p. 13.

[20] *Ibid.*, p. 15.

taneous equations. Such a system must be tested for determinacy (ordinarily, the number of independent equations must be equal to the number of endogenous variables).

2. The complete model now has to be translated into machine language, conveniently by way of an automatic coding system and the necessary flow diagrams (beware that not all coding systems are suitable for our model; e.g., the most frequently applied IBM FORTRAN language cannot be used without difficulties, since it permits only three dimensions, while our model uses four). In writing the computer program, attention also has to be paid to some of the items listed below.

3. Values must be assigned to the exogenous variables and to the parameters, based on the data, estimates, forecasts, and past experience of the enterprise. In this connection, it has to be decided which of the alternative business situations shall be computed; that means which exogenous variables (and perhaps even parameters, although in this case the distinction between exogenous variable and parameter might become vague) shall be varied and within which ranges that shall be done. This, of course, involves the decision which exogenous variables shall be varied with each other. That is to say, one has to decide how many *combinations* of "basic alternatives" shall be computed. Hence, in many cases a whole set of values will have to be assigned to a single exogenous variable.

4. After this preparatory work the computation in the electronic data processing system can be carried out, and the output should yield the budgeting data of the firm simulated under a large number of different conditions. These conditions may partly depend on the entrepreneurial policy or on external, and in many cases uncontrollable, conditions. The computer output can be arranged in such a way as to *print* a sales budget, a production budget, etc., and finally a cash budget, as well as projected position and income statements—each of them with all desired alternatives. The selection of that alternative which appears to be most satisfactory (with regard to the controllable exogenous variables) can be done by visual inspection and comparison of the various alternatives. In case of too large a number of alternatives (especially where one cannot rely on a limited number of key figures, as, for example, net profit, sales volume, asset and capital structure, liquidity ratio, etc., for selection of the most satisfactory alternative), it should be feasible to complement the program with satisficing criteria such that the computer selects automatically the most "satisfactory" choice or a more limited number of "best" alternatives, from which the top executives can make their own selection.

5. Finally, in case of internal or external changes of data during the business year a recomputation with the newly assigned values (of exogenous variables or parameters)—but the original computer program—can be carried out. In this way a revised budget can be calculated rapidly; furthermore, one can afford to compute revisions more frequently than is possible under present circumstances.

Using electronic computers, the calculation of even a large number of alternatives should not be very time-consuming, and the suggested method is by no means restricted to firms in possession of an EDP system. Computations outside the enterprise, at statistical service or consulting firms, should be within the range of feasible expenses and will facilitate the general application of the proposed approach. Obviously, the models presented here are designed for use in connection with a *digital* computer; however, the application of *analog* computers to budgetary and related managerial planning might offer decisive advantages (less expensive, handier, data more compact and concise, etc.) and deserves serious consideration. Since the output of analog computers can best be arranged in the form of a graph, it is conceivable to arrange this output in the form of a *multidimensional* break-even chart. Thus, with the help of a somewhat modified model and the necessary input data, the analog computer would be in a position to supply a set of diagrams containing whole families of cost, revenue, and profit curves, offering information of different alternatives for one and the same purpose as well as for different managerial goals. Proposals for improving and expanding the application of break-even charts as made by Dean,[21] Eiteman,[22] Barber,[23] and others may in this way approach a fuller realization. Dean's assertion that "break-even analysis has not measured up to its potential usefulness, but it can if it embodies these kinds of cost forecasting and thus becomes a versatile device for flexible comparison of conjectural income statements under a variety of projected conditions"[24] still holds.

So far, we have assumed that most of the data are being supplied by the individual departments without worrying about the way in which these data were created—that means we have gone only as far as textbook budgeting reaches. If, however, the budgeting activity on the departmental level is to be incorporated into the simulation approach, it will be necessary to develop a model, perhaps even a maximization model *à la* Stedry, for each department. Thus, many of our previous exogenous variables will have to be converted into endogenous variables, and a long array of new exogenous variables will emerge; needless to say, this increases considerably the number of simultaneous equations and complicates the program. If departmental optimization models are to be used, it may be advantageous to compute these departmental optima independently from, and prior to, the overall budget model. This *independent* treatment, however, is probably not feasible if an *overall* optimization by way of interdepartmental prices and shadow prices *à la* Arrow is

[21] Joel Dean, "Methods and Potentialities of Break-Even Analysis," *Australian Accountant*, October–November, 1951; reprinted in David Solomons (ed.), *Studies in Cost Accounting* (London, 1952), pp. 227–66.

[22] Wilford J. Eiteman, "Application of Break-Even Charts to Cash Situations," *Controller*, June, 1951; reprinted in W. E. Thomas (ed.), *Readings in Cost Accounting, Budgeting and Control* (2d ed.; Cincinnati, 1960), pp. 472–75.

[23] Raymond J. Barber, Jr., "When Does Part of a Business Break Even?" *NACA Bulletin*, May, 1951; reprinted in Thomas, *op. cit.*, pp. 463–71.

[24] Dean, *op. cit.*

intended. This second or extended stage of budgeting simulation will have to be experimented with at some length before detailed recommendations can be made. In the long run, this second stage will, however, become as important as is the first. Finally, it is hoped that in time the two extreme approaches of simulating the firm, the "flow model" on one side and the budgeting model on the other, will move toward each other. Then we may hope for the day when it is possible to fuse them to such a degree that an economic model of the firm emerges which corresponds to the needs and facilities of a particular enterprise without being unsound from the viewpoint of hypothesis formulation. This no doubt is a dream at present, but where would we stand today had our ancestors failed to indulge in their own dreams?

Act. of Com. Sim. Sim. Design (Naylor [ed.], 1969, p. 5) cont...

(4) <u>Analysis of Simulated Data</u>. Consists of following steps:

a) Collection and processing of simulated data.
b) computation of test statistics
c) intrepretation of results.

47

The authors describe a single-period linear programming model which maximizes an end-of-period balance sheet, subject to various specific constraints. The technique of constructing the model is elaborated upon in considerable detail. After an optimal solution is computed, the relevant management information implicit in this solution (and the related dual solution) is described and discussed.

*A LINEAR PROGRAMMING MODEL FOR BUDGETING AND FINANCIAL PLANNING**†

Yuji Ijiri, F. K. Levy, and R. C. Lyon

INTRODUCTION

This paper reports on an experiment in applying modern mathematical methods to management problems in budgeting and financial planning. In this experiment the techniques of linear programming and double-entry accounting are joined by means of suitable models and interpretations in order to see what might be gained in the way of a unified approach to total enterprise planning.

Two very general aspects of this study may be identified. Starting from an initial statement of the balance sheet accounts, the first aspect of this study was concerned with devising ways of planning (and identifying) the transaction flows that would in terms of some relevant objective (1) bring the corporation into the best possible end-of-the-period balance sheet and (2) make due allowance for other aspects of management policy, technological limitations, etc. The second aspect of this study was concerned with synthe-

* Reprinted from *Journal of Accounting Research*, Autumn, 1963, pp. 198–212.

† This paper was written as part of the contract "Planning and Control of Industrial Operations" with the Office of Naval Research and the Bureau of Ships, at the Graduate School of Industrial Administration, Carnegie Institute of Technology. Reproduction of this paper in whole or in part is permitted for any purpose of the United States government. Contract Nonr–760(01), project NR–047011. The authors are indebted to Professor W. W. Cooper, Carnegie Institute of Technology, who not only guided the research on this paper but also provided numerous suggestions that have been incorporated.

sizing information that could be utilized by management to evaluate all aspects of the problem. That is, it was desired to erect a model which could be used to supply information by means of which a company's management might readily determine the dollar consequences that could be expected to flow from altering the firm's policies or the environment in which it operated, and so on.

To accomplish both of these study objectives simultaneously, the so-called "direct" and "dual" aspects of a linear programming approach were utilized.[1] Briefly, the direct linear programming model was used to synthesize an optimum program, under given conditions (or constraints), in order to achieve a best end-of-the-period balance sheet as outlined under the first of the study aspects noted above. Then the dual linear programming model was utilized to provide information on how the initially stated conditions might be altered, as outlined above, for the second aspect of this study.

It would have been desirable, of course, to test or otherwise validate (and study) this kind of application in the context of an actual business firm. This was not done. Instead, an application was made in the setting of the business game operated by the Graduate School of Industrial Administration at Carnegie Tech. (Fortunately, this game is sufficiently complicated[2] so that it will bear the weight of the applications of modern operations research techniques like linear programming in more than trivial or unchallenging ways.) The application proceeded as follows. Acting as a hypothetical operations research group[3] within one of the functioning firms, various aspects of a model were synthesized and tested against data that were assembled for this purpose. In particular, electronic computer runs[4] were made and compared with actual operations for a representative period of months. Significant improvements were noted, but since this involved an ex post facto comparison, it cannot be considered a wholly valid test of the model under the conditions of the game, where large amounts of uncertainty, the need for coordinated action (as contrasted with coordinated plans), and like considerations must also be handled. For this reason, and also because it will permit us to simplify parts of the (direct) model, we do not propose to emphasize this aspect of the study. We shall try instead to emphasize the possible managerial uses of the so-called "dual evaluators" which emerge from the direct model after developing the direct model in sufficient detail to provide a basis for understanding (1) the actual operating problem that was studied and (2) the kinds of interrelations that obtain between any pair of direct and dual linear programming models.

[1] Cf., e.g., chap. i in Charnes and Cooper [2] for an explanation and a managerial interpretation of "direct" and "dual" linear programming models.

[2] This game is built around a detailed model of the packaged detergent industry. For further discussion and description, see, e.g., Cohen *et al.* [4] or Dill *et al.* [6].

[3] This was done actually as part of an assignment for the graduate course in operations research taught by Professor Cooper, and the present paper is based largely on the operations research report to the firm in question, prepared as part of that assignment.

[4] Carnegie Tech's Bendix G–20 computer was used for this purpose.

Synthesizing the Model

To synthesize the one-period model with which we are concerned, it is convenient to start with the balance sheet shown in Table 1 (p. 662). This is the actual beginning-of-the-period balance sheet for an operating firm. Note that certain accounts have been combined in order to achieve some desirable simplifications.

Note also the letter codes that appear alongside the account captions. By means of the "spread-sheet" conventions of double-entry accounting,[5] these letters will be paired in a way which will provide the debit-credit relations needed for accounting interpretations of the transactions. For instance, observe in Table 2 (p. 662) that the letter pair *CB* refers to the class of entries debit cash, *C*, and credit securities, *B* (= bonds). In each case, we employ the variable X to refer to the "amount" of the transaction. Thus, in Table 2, X_{CB} = \$9,703,000, the amount which is debited to cash and credited to securities. In every case the debit entry will be symbolized as the left member of a letter pair, and the corresponding credit entry will be symbolized by the letter appearing on the right.

Model Constraints

These debit-credit letter pairs for the transaction flows must be supplemented by symbols for the balance sheet (stock) amounts. To represent these figures, we shall use the symbol K with an appropriate subscript. For instance, K_C = \$7,260,000 refers to the opening cash balance, while K_B = \$12,000,000 refers to the opening balance of the securities account, and so on.

The balance sheet accounts and the transaction flows will of course be related by the usual accounting identities. In addition, we need to impose certain conditions (or constraints) which limit the transactions. As a case in point, for this one period model, we impose:

1. The firm's sale of securities cannot exceed the beginning balance in this account, viz.:

$$X_{CB} \leq K_B \tag{1}$$

where, in this case, K_B = \$12,000,000[6]

In addition to *inequality* constraints like constraint 1, we also wish to incorporate *equations* which we now illustrate by means of one part of the data for the game:

2. Interest earned is calculated by multiplying the end-of-the-period

---

[5] See, e.g., Charnes, Cooper, and Ijiri [3]. See also the references cited therein and especially Kohler [7].

[6] All constraints will represent dollar limits or their equivalents.

security balance by the appropriate interest rate; here the periodic rate is 0.229 percent. Hence:

$$X_{CE} = 0.00229(K_B + X_{BC} - X_{CB}) \tag{2}$$

K_B is the opening balance for securities, X_{BC} refers to securities purchased during the period, and X_{CB} refers to the cash debits realized by sales of securities during the period. Hence, $(K_B + X_{BC} - X_{CB})$ correctly states the ending balance when, as the Carnegie Tech game requires, all such transactions are effected only in cash. Applying the indicated interest rate of 0.229 percent, we obtain X_{CE}, the amount which is debited to cash and credited to the stockholder's account.[7]

In the model we use, direct reference to income account details will be avoided. This greatly simplifies the model and does so with no great loss, since supplementary analyses of the transactions, with the aid of the model (and its associated spread sheet), can always be undertaken to synthesize an income statement when desired. (See Table 4 [p. 663].)

The point to be emphasized is: Our model is one in which *all* constraints must be *simultaneously* satisfied. For example, the X_{CB} which appears in expression 1 is exactly the same as the one that appears in equation 2. It will perhaps serve to illustrate our intended meaning by rearranging terms in expressions 1 and 2 and positioning the constant, K_B, on the right to achieve the pair of expressions:

$$\begin{array}{lcl} 0.00229X_{CB} + X_{CE} - 0.00229X_{BC} & = & 0.00229K_B \\ X_{CB} & \leq & K_B \end{array} \tag{2.1}$$

In particular, note how the variable X_{CB} has been positioned in these expressions. This is intended to reflect the simultaneity aspect of the constraints for this model. If, in any solution, an amount is assigned to the variable X_{CB} in one of these expressions, then this same value must be assigned to this variable in the other expression. The admissible values for the variables must therefore satisfy *all* of the constraints simultaneously.

Bearing this in mind, we proceed to formulate the remaining constraints:

3. Since the firm's terms of sale are 30 days net, its maximum collection of receivables during the month is given by the beginning balance in the receivables account:

$$X_{CR} \leq K_R \tag{3}$$

4. The beginning-of-the-period cash balance limits the purchase of securities:

$$X_{BC} \leq K_C \tag{4}$$

5. The firm's per unit selling price during the period studied was 9.996^+; its per unit standard cost of production was $2.10. The following constraint

[7] In the Carnegie Tech game, all interest income is realized as immediate cash income, and the price of the bond is held constant throughout the game periods.

represents the "contribution"[8] on a unit sale in terms of the corresponding deduction from finished goods inventory:

$$X_{RB} = 3.76X_{RG} \tag{5}$$

6. Standard cost for a unit of finished goods ($2.10/unit) includes material cost (X_{GM} = $1/unit) and conversion cost (X_{GE} = $1.10/unit) which consists of direct labor cost and direct overhead:

$$X_{GE} = 1.1X_{GM} \tag{6}$$

7. Production capacity limits conversion during the period. Here, production capacity is expressed in the value of raw materials (at standard cost) that can be converted:

$$X_{GM} \leq 1{,}300{,}000 \tag{7}$$

8. Conversion is also limited to raw materials on hand at the beginning of the period:[9]

$$X_{GM} \leq K_M \tag{8}$$

9. Market conditions limit sales in the current period to 2 million units[10] ($4.2 million at standard cost):

$$X_{RG} \leq 4{,}200{,}000 \tag{9}$$

10. Sales during the period are further limited to the beginning balance of completed units:[11]

$$X_{RG} \leq K_G \tag{10}$$

11. Repayment of loans is limited by the outstanding loan balance at the beginning of the period:

$$X_{LC} \leq K_L \tag{11}$$

12. Because the firm is allowed 30 days for payment of materials purchased, the payment of accounts payable is limited to the sum of the beginning balance of accounts payable plus expenses of the current period:

$$X_{PC} \leq K_P + X_{EP} \tag{12}$$

13. Monthly depreciation charges are 0.833 percent of the net fixed assets owned at the beginning of the period:

$$X_{EF} = 0.00833K_F \tag{13}$$

---

[8] *Contribution* is the term used here to describe the difference between revenue and incremental, variable, or direct cost. Thus, each unit sold gives rise to a contribution of $7.896^+ ($9.996^+ − 2.10), which is 3.76 · $2.10.

[9] In this case, K_M = $1,499,000, so that the preceding constraint (7) is controlling. We have, however, represented both constraints for the sake of completeness in cases where K_M < $1,300,000.

[10] Obtained from the relevant market forecast, determined as an expected rate, a maximum, and a minimum. The maximum is entered here as an exact upper limit for subsequent study by reference to the relevant dual evaluators.

[11] Cf. n. 10. It should also be observed that this constraint is intended to reflect the lag on shipments from the plant to the relevant distribution centers.

14. Costs to be incurred during the current period include manufacturing cost (other than materials) and operating costs which consist of the following four items: (*a*) fixed operating expenses, \$2,675,000; (*b*) variable conversion cost, X_{GE}; (*c*) effective interest penalty for discounts not taken on accounts payable (3.09 percent per period); (*d*) interest (periodic rate, 0.291 percent) on loans payable at the end of the period:

$$(14)\ X_{EP} = 2{,}675{,}000 + X_{GE} + 0.0309(K_P + X_{EP} - X_{PC}) + 0.00291(K_L + X_{CL} - X_{LC})$$

15. Income tax is accrued at 52 percent of the net profit. In addition, the firm's policy is to declare a dividend equal to \$83,000 plus (minus) 5 percent of the excess (shortage) of what it considers a standard net profit after taxes, \$1.86 million:

$$X_{ED} = 0.52(X_{CE} + X_{RE} + X_{GE} - X_{EF} - X_{EP}) + 83{,}000 + 0.05[0.48(X_{CE} + X_{RE} + X_{GE} - X_{EF} - X_{EP}) - 1{,}860{,}000]$$

Simplifying:

$$(15)\ X_{ED} = 0.544X_{CE} + 0.544X_{RE} + 0.544X_{GE} - 0.544_{EF} - 0.544X_{EP} - 10{,}000$$

16. Company policy requires a minimum cash balance of \$4 million at the end of each period:

$$(16)\ K_C + X_{CB} + X_{CR} + X_{CL} + X_{CE} - X_{BC} - X_{PC} - X_{DC} - X_{LC} \geq 4{,}000{,}000$$

17. Because of an impending price rise in the next period—i.e., in the period following the one under study—the firm requires the ending balance of finished goods inventory to be at least as great as the minimum sales expected during the following period (expected sales of 1.7 million units at \$2.10 standard cost/unit, or \$3.75 million):[12]

$$(17)\qquad K_G + X_{GM} + X_{GE} - X_{RG} \geq 3{,}570{,}000$$

18. The firm also expects to produce 1.2 million units in the next period. Thus the ending balance of raw materials must be sufficient for this expected production (at \$1 raw material cost/unit the end-of-the-period raw materials balance must be \$1.2 million):[13]

$$(18)\qquad K_M + X_{MP} - X_{GM} \geq 1{,}200{,}000$$

19. All outstanding income taxes payable and dividends declared, including those accrued or declared during the period, have to be paid by the end of the current period:

$$(19)\qquad K_D + X_{ED} - X_{DC} = 0$$

In addition to these constraints, all transaction variables (X's) are required to be nonnegative. This is done to avoid any confusion between the debit and

[12] Note that this amount, too, is subject to treatment by means of the dual evaluators. For instance, such an analysis will show how much is being lost from current profit opportunities in order to provide for the future in this manner.

[13] See preceding footnote.

credit entries which would otherwise have to be given a reverse (credit-debit) interpretation for negative values of any X. Either way of proceeding can be elected, but it simplifies the exposition merely to arrange the model so that the nonnegativity condition can be enforced on all variables.

Statement of Objectives and Completion of the Model

As indicated, an explicit statement of the profit and loss accounts (in their usual sense) is eliminated in the model that we are synthesizing. Thus, in place of assuming that profit maximizing is controlling, we consider that this firm wishes to maximize its net addition to retained earnings.[14] This is given by:

Net additions to retained earnings

$$= X_{CE} + X_{RE} + X_{GE} - X_{EF} - X_{EP} - X_{ED}$$

Because the objective is maximization, we can refer to the preceding constraint details and set forth the full linear programming model as:

Maximize

$$X_{CE} + X_{RE} + X_{GE} - X_{EF} - X_{EP} - X_{ED}$$

subject to

$$\begin{array}{lll}
(1) & X_{CE} - 0.00229X_{BC} + 0.00229X_{CB} & = 0.00229K_B \\
(2) & X_{CB} & \leq K_B \\
(3) & K_{CR} & \leq K_R \\
(4) & X_{BC} & \leq K_C \\
(5) & X_{RE} - 3.76X_{RG} & = 0 \\
(6) & X_{GE} - 1.1X_{GM} & = 0 \\
(7) & X_{GM} & \leq 1{,}300{,}000 \\
(8) & X_{GM} & \leq K_M \\
(9) & X_{RG} & \leq 4{,}200{,}000 \\
(10) & X_{RG} & \leq K_G \\
(11) & X_{LC} & \leq K_L \\
(12) & X_{PC} - X_{EP} & \leq K_P \\
(13) & X_{EF} & = 0.00833K_F
\end{array}$$

$$(14)\ X_{EP} - X_{GE} - 0.0309X_{EP} + 0.0309X_{PC} - 0.00291X_{CL} + 0.00291X_{LC} = 2{,}675{,}000 + 0.0309K_P + 0.00291K_L$$

$$(15)\ X_{ED} - 0.544X_{CE} - 0.544X_{RE} - 0.544X_{GE} + 0.544X_{EF} + 0.544X_{EP} = 10{,}000$$

$$(16)\ X_{CB} + X_{CR} + X_{CL} + X_{CE} - X_{BC} - X_{PC} - X_{DC} - X_{LC} \geq 4{,}000{,}000 - K_C$$

$$\begin{array}{lll}
(17) & X_{GM} + X_{GE} - X_{RG} & \geq 3{,}570{,}000 - K_G \\
(18) & X_{MP} - X_{GM} & \geq 1{,}200{,}000 - K_M \\
(19) & X_{ED} - X_{DC} & = -K_D
\end{array}$$

$$X_{CB}, X_{CR}, X_{CL}, X_{CE}, X_{BC}, X_{RG}, X_{RE}, X_{GM}, X_{GE}, X_{MP}, X_{PC}, X_{DC}, X_{LC}, X_{EF}, X_{EP}, X_{ED} \geq 0$$

That is, we are to search for amounts X_{ij} which satisfy all constraints, including nonnegativity for all variables; and among the entire collection of such

[14] It is not proposed to enter into a statement of whether this is the proper objective or whether any *one* objective is ever proper for a business. If, for instance, break-even or other objectives are wanted, then recourse may be had to the devices discussed in Charnes, Cooper, and Ijiri [3]. Some caution may be needed in considering *multiple* objectives, since policy conditions (like "stable employment," etc.) can be reflected in the constraints. On the other hand, when multiple objectives are desired, recourse may be had to approaches like those given in chap. ix of Charnes and Cooper [2].

values, we are to single out one set that makes the net addition to retained earnings a maximum. The solution methods of linear programming—e.g., the simplex method[15]—are designed to produce exactly this result.

THE RESULTS

By substituting the figures in the beginning balance sheet (Table 1) for the K's in the above constraints, and by applying the simplex method, a solution to the above problem was readily achieved. We now summarize the results in

TABLE 1

BEGINNING BALANCE SHEET

C	Cash	$ 7,260,000	*P*	Accounts payable	$ 3,592,000
B	Securities	12,000,000	*D*	Dividends and taxes payable	2,922,000
R	Accounts receivable	6,999,000			
G	Finished goods	4,032,000	*L*	Loans payable	4,400,000
M	Raw materials	1,499,000	*E*	Stockholders' account	46,876,000
F	Fixed assets	26,000,000			
		$57,790,000			$57,790,000

the following series of tables. In Table 2, we list the transactions which achieve the maximum possible net addition to retained earnings.

Next, we utilize this information to obtain the following projections of the balance sheet and income statement (Tables 3 and 4).

Notice that we now have the main documents that are usually deemed to

TABLE 2

OPTIMUM PROJECTED TRANSACTIONS

CB	Sell securities	$ 9,703,000
CR	Collect accounts receivable	6,999,000
CL	New borrowing	....
CE	Collect interest on securities	6,000
BC	Buy securities	....
RG	Cost of sales at standard cost	3,192,000
RE	Gross profit on sales	12,002,000
GM	Material consumption (transfer from raw materials to finished goods inventory)	1,300,000
GE	Variable conversion costs	1,430,000
MP	Material purchased	1,001,000
PC	Payment of accounts payable	7,697,000
DC	Payment of dividends and taxes	7,871,000
LC	Refund of loans	4,400,000
EF	Depreciation	217,000
EP	Manufacturing and operating expenses	4,105,000
ED	Accruals of income taxes and dividends	4,949,000
	Net addition to retained earnings	4,167,000

[15] We used this method as one part of the available G–20 electronic computer code without attempting to apply or devise other, possibly more efficient methods. For further remarks on this topic, see Charnes, Cooper, and Ijiri [3].

TABLE 3

PROJECTED BALANCE SHEET
End of Period

C	Cash	$ 4,000,000	P	Accounts payable	$ 1,001,000
B	Securities	2,297,000	D	Dividends and Taxes Payable	....
R	Accounts receivable	15,194,000			
G	Finished goods	3,570,000	L	Loans payable	....
M	Raw materials	1,200,000	E	Stockholders' Account	51,043,000
F	Fixed assets	25,783,000			
		$52,044,000			$52,044,000

be pertinent for financial planning purposes. Additional documents—e.g., flow of funds statements, cash budgets, etc.—can also be generated if desired.[16] Instead of pursuing these, we intend to indicate how the results of this analysis can be used for planning and execution by various kinds of management. The details of Table 2 lend themselves to ready translation for the direction of operating managers, or other persons, who are not immediately concerned with the overall aspects of financial planning. For instance, the production manager may be directly instructed to plan to produce $2.73 million worth of finished goods during this period and further to allocate $1.3 million of this amount for the purchase of raw materials and to expend the rest ($1.43 million) on conversion costs. In turn, the purchasing department may be instructed to purchase $1,001,000 worth of raw materials, and so on.

Of course, the usual information for a coordinated assessment and review by top management is also available in the form of projected balance sheets, income statements, etc. In addition, the linear programming solution provides valuable by-product information in the form of the dual evaluators.[17]

TABLE 4

PROJECTED INCOME STATEMENT FOR THE PERIOD

Sales ($RG + RE$)		$15,194,000
Incremental cost (RG)		3,192,000
Contribution (RE)		$12,002,000
Manufacturing costs and operating expenses (EP)	$4,105,000	
Depreciation	217,000	
Manufacturing costs charged to finished goods (GE)	−1,430,000	
Unabsorbed manufacturing costs and operating expenses		2,892,000
Operating profit		$ 9,110,000
Interest income (CE)		6,000
Net income before tax		$ 9,116,000
Accruals of income taxes and dividends (ED)		4,949,000
Net addition to retained earnings		$ 4,167,000

16 See Charnes, Cooper, and Ijiri [3] for further discussion.

17 The G–20 code (like most linear programming codes) provides these data automatically, at the end of its run, as well as other (equally valuable) results which enable the user to test the program's sensitivity to errors in the data, etc. See, e.g., Charnes and Cooper [2], chap. xiii, for a discussion in the context of the so-called "revised simplex code" for IBM computers.

We propose, therefore, to elaborate on this topic in the next section and then show how this information can be assembled to form a new type of accounting document for use in integrated management planning.

An Accounting Statement for the Dual Evaluators as Opportunity Costs

A dual evaluator, at least in a managerial-accounting-economics context, indicates the change in net addition to retained earnings that can be secured if the constraint corresponding to the given evaluator were relaxed by $1. For

TABLE 5

ANALYSIS OF OPPORTUNITY COSTS*
$3.59 per Unit Increase in Production Capacity

(1)	Incremental sales resulting		$9.996000
	Less: Cost of incremental sales		2.100000
(2)	Contribution		$7.896000
(3)	Deduct: Income taxes and dividends (54.4%)		4.295424
(4)	Net retained from sales after taxes and dividends		$3.600576
(5)	Deduct: Opportunity cost of cash needed to finance expansion:		
	Cash required for raw materials†	$	
(5*a*)	Conversion to finished product	1.100000	
	Total	$1.100000	
(5*b*)	Add: Cash required for income taxes and dividends	4.295424	
(5*c*)	Total cash required	$5.395424	
(6)	Total of interest earnings forgone on securities sold ($5.395424 @ 0.00104533)		0.005640
(7)	Net retained realization per unit increase in production capacity		$3.594936

* This statement is based on optimal adjustments being effected in all pertinent transactions.
† All required raw material is available from inventory or hand.

example, the dual evaluator of constraint number 7 (production capacity) has a value of $3.594936. This means that if production capacity were increased so that exactly one additional dollar's worth of raw material can be processed, then retained earnings will be increased by $3.594936. This figure, which is obtained (automatically) as a so-called "evaluator," really summarizes a whole complex of interrelated opportunities. Hence, some further accounting aids to managerial interpretations and uses are indicated.

In order to show that the dual evaluators take into account every constraint of the model in *mutatis mutandis* fashion, the evaluator of production capacity will now be analyzed in more detail.[18] Let it be desired to alter the firm's raw material processing capacity by one unit. This activates a whole complex of transactions, which are set forth in Table 5.

Notice that the end result is the $3.59 figure which was predicted by the dual evaluator; also, notice that each of the indicated transactions are carried

[18] See Charnes and Cooper [2] for further elaboration and distinctions between *ceteris paribus* and *mutatis mutandis* approaches.

out optimally (relative to one another) in order to produce this optimal return from the indicated increase of one unit of capacity. The single figure of $3.59 summarizes all of these transactions, but it needs accounting elaboration if the purposes of managerial use and understanding are to be adequately served. The above statement is intended to supply this kind of service.

The data of Table 5 were drawn from the by-product results furnished automatically by the computer calculations after appropriate supplementation by economic-accounting considerations. We now elaborate on this as follows.

In constraint 1, we observe that the incremental capacity increase has resulted in a sale of goods. The needed raw material is presently on hand, since K_M = $1,499,000 (Table 1) is greater than X_{GM} = $1,300,000 (Table 2). Therefore an additional raw material unit is drawn from inventory. This unit is processed at $1.10 conversion of finished goods which, valued at standard, costs $2.10. The unit of finished goods can be sold at once, since the firm has unfulfilled demand in the present month of $1,008,000 of product (valued at standard cost—see constraint 9, remembering X_{RG} = $3,192,000).

Segments 2, 3, and 4 give the net profit realized from this sale as determined by constraints 5 and 15 of the model.

The transaction analysis is not yet complete, as the gross profit ($3.600576) is higher than the dual evaluator ($3.59436). The difference ($0.00564) can be accounted for by turning to the cash account and recalling that the program has pushed up against the $4 million stipulated minimum balance. Therefore the additional cash outlays needed for production must be obtained in one of three ways: (1) sell securities at the monthly interest rate 0.229 percent; (2) borrow from the bank at the monthly interest rate of 0.291 percent; (3) postpone payments on accounts payable at a monthly interest rate of 3.09 percent. The least costly of these three ways is obviously achieved in the sale of securities. The $0.00564 shown opposite segment 6 in Table 5 represents the opportunity cost incurred because of the interest income that must be forgone if securities are sold to obtain the needed cash. This is derived as follows: Segments 5*a* and 5*b* give the amount of cash needed to increase production by one unit. Segment 5*a* represents the conversion cost which is paid at the end of the period. Segment 5*b* represents dividends and taxes payable on the profit generated in segment 4, and cash must be obtained to pay these at the end of the period. The total cash requirement is therefore the sum of segments 5*a* and 5*b* or $5.395474,[19] which is the figure shown opposite segment 5*c*. Segment 6 multiplies the number of dollars needed by the opportunity cost per dollar to obtain the total opportunity cost of obtaining cash.

The opportunity cost per dollar is obtained via the following reasoning:

The firm forgoes interest income of $0.00229 for every dollar of securities sold. However, the loss is reduced to $0.00104424 by taking into account savings on taxes and dividends. Since the interest income would normally be

[19] Note that two other cash flows (accounts receivable and payments on raw material accounts) are affected by the capacity increase. However, they have no effect on the flow in the present period, as they are not received (or paid) until the following period.

collected in cash at the end of the period, the \$0.00104424 of income forgone reduces the end-of-period cash balance by \$0.00104424. This reduction in cash balance violates constraint 16 (minimum cash balance constraint); and to compensate for this reduction, the firm must sell an additional \$0.00104424 of securities and forgo ($0.00104424 \times 0.00104424$) dollars of net interest income, as well as ($0.00104424 \times 0.00104424$) reduction in the cash balance.

The total reduction of net profits after taxes and dividends resulting from this sale of securities needed to obtain an additional dollar of cash is given by the sum of the infinite series:

$$0.00104424 + (0.00104424)^2 + (0.00104424)^3 + \cdots$$

$$= \frac{0.00104424}{1 - 0.00104424} = 0.00104533$$

Therefore, 0.00104533 appears as the unit opportunity cost in segment 6.

Finally, in segment 7, we see that the net effect of relaxing the production capacity constraint by one unit is equal to the difference between net profit (after taxes and dividends) realized from the sale of goods and the opportunity cost of securing additional cash required. That is, \$3.600576 − \$0.005640 = \$3.594936. This figure is precisely equal to the dual evaluator associated with production capacity.

Notice in particular that any one dual evaluator provides the opportunity cost information that is relevant when *every* possible transaction is altered to a new optimum level in response to a change anywhere in the system. This is, in fact, the intended meaning of the term *mutatis mutandis* which has been accorded to this determination of opportunity costs in contrast to other approaches which assume that only a few variables are adjusted while all others are held constant.

Of course, we have singled out only a small portion of the total dual evaluator information printed out by a computer at the end of a run on a linear programming model. Evidently, further extensions can be made by considering collections of these evaluators simultaneously, and still other kinds of extensions can also be made. The main point here is that the *mutatis mutandis* approach will generally involve a complex series of transaction interactions. Technically speaking, there is no real trouble in assessing the dual evaluators. On the other hand, some forms of guidance and assistance undoubtedly have to be supplied if management is to make intelligent and understanding use of this information. One form of assistance has been suggested by the accounting statement which we have exhibited. Undoubtedly, other kinds of statements will also be devised, especially where more complex transaction interactions are considered. Some exercise of ingenuity and some period of experimentation will be required for this purpose.

CONCLUSION

We now try to point out some of the conclusions and further elaborations suggested by this study. First, we should observe that linear programming is not the only possible mathematical method of approach to accounting and financial planning.[20] It does, however, offer a highly flexible instrument and is associated with an extremely sharp and general (underlying) mathematical theory. Our analysis and interpretation of the dual evaluators should be taken as partially illustrative of the type of further extensions that are readily available from the linear programming model. Sensitivity analysis offers still another alternative course of immediate extensions which would show the effect of changes in the objective function or constraints (including additions of new variables and constraints) on the optimum solution of the model. As in the above, all sensitivity changes within any specific part of the model are evaluated in terms of their effect on the entire model. In general, this evaluation can be done without re-solving the entire problem.

Other applications of linear programming to accounting have shown the relationships between programming to goals and break-even budgeting.[21] This could be combined with our application to form a unified approach to planning when multiple (and sometimes conflicting) objectives exist among the various divisions of a firm. Such an approach might be in order, for example, to determine a system of transfer prices for guiding decentralized operations in a way that will produce the best *overall* results from each department's operations. These applications are available as a result of previous research in the theory and applications of linear programming. Additional research might produce further advantages if it were devoted to, say, investigating accounting models and applications as such. As Charnes *et al.*[22] have shown, the network features of accounting models offer promising avenues of exploitation. With suitably arranged objective functions, linear programming and simulation approaches can be joined together with further increases in the scope and power of each.

Finally, all of these topics are closely associated with the rapidly evolving developments and uses of electronic computers for business purposes. Further research in this direction is also warranted if the full value of these devices for managerial accounting applications is to be achieved.

BIBLIOGRAPHY

1. Bonini, C. P. *Simulation of Information and Decision Systems in the Firm.* Englewood Cliffs, N.J.: Prentice-Hall, Inc., 1963.
2. Charnes, A., and Cooper, W. W. *Management Models and Industrial Applications of Linear Programming.* New York: John Wiley & Sons, Inc., 1961.
3. Charnes, A.; Cooper, W. W.; and Ijiri, Yuji. "Breakeven Budgeting and Programming to Goals," *Journal of Accounting Research,* Spring, 1963.
4. Cohen, K. J., *et al.* "The Carnegie Tech Management Game," *Journal of Business,* October, 1960, pp. 303–21.

[20] For example, see Bonini [1] or Cyert, Davidson, and Thompson [5].

[21] Charnes, Cooper, and Ijiri [3].

[22] *Ibid.*

5. Cyert, R. M.; Davidson, J.; and Thompson, G. L. "Estimation of the Allowance for Doubtful Accounts by Markov Chains," *Management Science*, April, 1962, pp. 287–303.

6. Dill, W. R., *et al.* "Experiences With a Complex Management Game," *California Management Review*, Spring, 1961, pp. 39–51.

7. Kohler, E. L. *A Dictionary for Accountants*. Englewood Cliffs, N.J.: Prentice-Hall, Inc., 1952.

48

A matrix model is derived in a step-by-step fashion for determining the number of times that various classes of information are available to each of several uniquely defined business functions. A product of this exposure is the degree of redundancy evident in processing. While the author does not suggest an optimal data processing system, the advantages of the model of an existing system are carefully evaluated.

*A MATHEMATICAL MODEL FOR INTEGRATED BUSINESS SYSTEMS**

Irving J. Lieberman

THE BUSINESS FIRM is not merely "facts" modified by logic, engineering, and intuition forming communication networks among rational individuals with predictable reactions.

Nevertheless, it is true that intercommunication of facts is necessary for continuance and that the prosperity of the firm does depend to a significant degree on the efficiency, effectiveness, and application of facts toward operations thoughout the enterprise.

The form and manner of data transmittal must be prescribed and organized. It is to this portion of the problems of management that the considerations in this paper are directed.

To further designate the boundaries of the problems we are investigating, let us look at the total problem in the following manner.

At all times, we are concerned with an entity that defies thorough definition or description, but we hope to make it operate as "an integrated business system" that attempts to adjust optimally to its changing environment.

We might therefore divide up our conception of an integrated business system in some major areas. Those concerned with information we can designate as

1. Integrated data processing
2. Control of the system and its parts
3. Decision-making process
4. Management conclusions

Though none of these functions is independent of the others, it is our purpose at this time to focus our attention on the first, that is, the problem of providing

* Reprinted from *Management Science*, July, 1956, pp. 327–36.

efficient data processing for disseminating effective information through our integrated business system.

Recently, there have been numerous investigations of methods to integrate the data processing of an organization. Most of these have been instigated by the thought of the potentialities of electronic computer systems. In order to efficiently utilize electronics systems, techniques have been devised to translate into machine language the source data of various functions of an organization —e.g., accounting, production, sales, personnel, etc. This "common language" approach is fundamental to a truly integrated data processing system.

Data collection and processing are only a part of the business system. We ask, what are the information requirements of a modern enterprise? Management must know how well its carefully laid plans are faring. If something goes wrong, there must be some corrective action. Thus, reports must be timely as well as be able to pinpoint the source of any trouble. Few reporting systems serve their purpose well in the control and decisions situations.

The utilization of electronic processing equipment has helped to lighten the burden of preparing reports. Information can now be processed faster and the necessary data transmitted to management sooner. But we still have no answer to the basic question. Once the requirements are established, electronic processing gives us the means to satisfy them. We are on the way to getting our answer. There are reported cases where a processing technique has led to a change in the business system and where most of the gains made can be attributed to the system change. In fact, reversion to older processing techniques and further system changes sometimes result in even greater gains. These results highlight the need for continued work in analyzing the business system. Also, it points to the lack of a good working description of the system.

The business system can be thought of as a communication network. Information is disseminated from one point and used at another. Thus a worker originates information which is used by the foreman as well as assembled by the accounting department for reporting to various other points in the organization. The organization can thus be described in terms of the communication network or information flow.

Descriptions of such a communication (business) system are seen in the flow diagrams of the systems analyst. Those diagrams, which integrate the complete system of an enterprise, have proven to be cumbersome and incomprehensible. The analyst has therefore broken the diagrams into parts corresponding to the various functional parts of the organization. These are woven together by still another chart which leaves out the details of each of the parts and gives an overall view. The analyst has now built a model of an organization by parts in which it is difficult to look at the totality in detail.

What the systems man would like to devise is the optimum system which satisfies the information requirements of the enterprise. To obtain this, he must build a model of the business system which simultaneously

1. Presents the total system in an easily comprehensible form
2. Presents the details of the system

3. Has a method for manipulation
4. Shows effects of system changes

If the model could accomplish all of these, then the analyst would be able to answer the question, "What are the information requirements?" This model will enable the analyst to test data processing systems for the information being presented to management. He can test the effects of changes in the system on the information presented. This experimentation with the system combined with interviewing the persons affected by the changes in information flow will aid the analyst in determining the information requirements of management. Also, mathematical models for scheduling and management decision making point out some of the information needs for effective planning and control.

What I propose in this paper is a mathematical technique for investigating integrated business systems. This technique will be based on the mathematical notion of matrices.

Essentially, it will be assumed that the information requirements of the various business functions are known. The problem is to find an optimal data processing system for such requirements, given a series of "report levels."

The model presented here is by no means the complete model of a business system. It is the simplest one which will be considered, but it is useful. Now, let us consider only the formal reporting structure. By investigating this model, it will become apparent that a more sophisticated version, to be described at some later date, could meet the requirements for a model of an integrated business system. Here, we shall construct matrices which will describe the details of the data flow as well as the overall picture. Manipulating and examining the matrices will answer some of the questions which the systems analyst asks. The result of this manipulation will be other matrices which will indicate the availability of data as well as a measure of its usefulness and redundancy. Further developments in this technique will be indicated at the end.

Elements of the matrices will determine the relationship between information and the communication of information through source documents and reports to various parts of the organization. It is practical to consider the structure of the system from the viewpoint of function within the organization. We shall consider an existing (or proposed) data collecting and processing system. In this network, there will occur first the original or source data. This source information will be put on source forms from which, by various operations, report forms will be prepared. There will usually be a number of stages of reporting before the information is used in some function. You will notice that the lowest level in the reporting structure—the source of data—can be workers, a foreman, or even the president of the company. Therefore the reporting level cannot be compared to management levels. But in general, the number of reporting stages probably will be about the same as the number of management levels.

Before we can proceed to build the model, it is necessary to define the symbols and terms which will be used in constructing the matrices. These definitions are not rigid and are used only to convey the concepts of the model.

B, a business function, we define to be a set of managerial activities which are assigned to a group according to types of duties.

In this definition, we are trying to separate the various aspects of control or action taking in the organization. The functions are usually fairly well recognized within an organization; but if they are difficult to define, then for our purposes they may be grouped in some arbitrary manner. Examples of business functions are purchasing, accounting, production operations, inventory operations, budgeting, etc.

In this treatment, we shall consider that *C*, a *class of information*, consists of one or more pieces of information having all common qualities. A class may have any number of members.

What we are essentially trying to do is differentiate between the kind of information and the quantitative measure of that kind of information. For example, the straight-time hours, overtime hours, total hours, name, date, etc., are all different classes or kinds of information; and the number of overtime hours worked, etc., is the quantitative measure of that particular class of information. Thus, two different people work overtime hours, which belong to the same class of information which may have different quantitative measures.

We shall distinguish between two different *types of classes of information.*

First there is the *identification type of class of information* (i). These classes describe or identify a form or document. As examples of this type of information class, we have date, invoice number, purchase order number, name, address, description of material, etc., all tending to identify the document.

The number of hours worked, number of pieces ordered, number of people, etc., all are examples of the *quantitative type of class of information* (q). These are the classes of information which give a quantitative measure.

Information is entered on a document or form. The distinction between forms and documents is given by the following definitions for a *form* (F): Two documents are said to be of the same form if they have all of the same classes of information and no other classes. An example of two different documents are two timecards, one for one person and another for someone else, or one for you on one day and the other for some other day. In both cases, these timecards are the *same form.*

Another concept which we have mentioned is report and source forms. They are defined as follows:

Source data forms (S): Those forms upon which information is recorded for the first time and is not obtainable from any other form by using some operation or combination of operations.

Report forms (R): Those forms which arise from performing an operation or combination of operations on source data forms.

With these definitions and symbols in mind, we are now in a position to construct a matrix model. The first matrix constructed will display the classes of information which are used in each source data form.

What we want to know about the relationship of the information and the forms is whether a class of information is used or not used in a source form. The cell which is designated by the intersection of the column headed by the name or symbol for the form and the row headed by the name or symbol of the information will contain a one or a zero according to whether the information is used or not used in that particular form. Thus, if the source forms are listed in a row on top and all the classes of information in a column on the left-hand side of a matrix, the remainder may be filled in with ones and zeros as required.

TABLE 1

M_s—SOURCE DATA FORMS

Classes of Information		*Timecard* S_1	*Labor Realization* S_2
Identification (i):			
(Date)	i_1	1	1
(Department)	i_2	1	1
(Section)	i_3	1	1
(Name)	i_4	1	1
(Employee number)	i_5	1	1
(Shift)	i_6	1	1
(Job number)	i_7	0	1
(Machine number)	i_8	0	1
Quantitative (q):			
(Straight-time hours)	q_1	1	0
(Overtime hours)	q_2	1	0
(Rate of pay)	q_3	1	0
(Number of pieces made)	q_4	0	1
(Number of pieces bad)	q_5	0	1
....			
....			
....			

This first matrix we shall call M_s. If there are n classes of information and m forms, then there will be n rows and m columns. Let us fill in a typical matrix, (M_s)(information on source data forms). (See Table 1.)

In a similar manner the other matrices are constructed. M_1, the matrix of source data forms used in the first report level, is constructed as follows: We let R^1 stand for the first report level. R_1^1, R_2^1 etc., are different reports at this level. For example, R_1^1 might be the payroll report, R_2^1 the customer order summary, etc.; S_1, S_2, etc., refer as above to the source data forms.

$$(M_1) \qquad \begin{array}{c|cccc} & R_1^1 & R_1^2 & \cdots & R_p^1 \\ \hline S_1 & b_{11} & b_{12} & \cdots & b_{1p} \\ S_2 & b_{21} & b_{22} & \cdots & b_{2p} \\ \cdot & \cdot & & & \cdot \\ \cdot & \cdot & & & \cdot \\ \cdot & \cdot & & & \cdot \\ S_m & b_{m1} & \cdots & & b_{mp} \end{array}$$

Thus, in this matrix, b_{12}, for example, tells us whether S_1 is used in the second first-level report, R_2^1. Each of these b_{ij}'s are either zero or one. Matrix (M_2), the first-level reports used in the second level of reports, is constructed (here, R^2 means the second-report level):

$$
(M_2) \qquad \begin{array}{c|cccc}
 & R_1^2 & R_2^2 & \cdots & R_v^2 \\
\hline
R_1^1 & C_{11} & C_{12} & \cdots & C_{1v} \\
\cdot & \cdot & & & \cdot \\
\cdot & \cdot & & & \cdot \\
\cdot & \cdot & & & \cdot \\
R_p & C_{p1} & \cdots & & C_{pv}
\end{array}
$$

Thus, if $C_{11} = 1$, this means that the first-level report, R_1^1, is used in preparing the second-level report, R_1^2. As many matrices as are needed for the particular system under consideration are constructed in a similar manner.

After some finite number of steps, we come to the last matrix which is to be filled out. This represents which functions use each report. This last matrix is constructed as follows: We let $B_1, B_2, \ldots, B_w$ represent w business functions. Suppose there are just two report levels. Then (M_B), the final matrix, is

$$
(M_B) \qquad \begin{array}{c|cccc}
 & B_1 & B_2 & \cdots & B_w \\
\hline
R_1^2 & d_{11} & d_{12} & \cdots & d_{1w} \\
\cdot & \cdot & & & \cdot \\
\cdot & \cdot & & & \cdot \\
\cdot & \cdot & & & \cdot \\
R_v^2 & d_{v1} & \cdots & & d_{vw}
\end{array}
$$

We now scrutinize each matrix for certain criteria. If the sum of the elements of a row is greater than or equal to one, then this indicates the information or form has been used in preparing a number of other forms. The number gives us an index of how many times the same information is repeated (sum $= 0$, means it is useless). If the sum of the elements of a column is greater than or equal to one, then this indicates the amount of information in that form which heads the column (sum $= 0$, means no information is used in the form).

Now we manipulate the matrices, by the usual matrix multiplication technique, in a number of ways. We may, for example, find the R^1's available to the functions, B's, or the i's (identification information), and q's (quantitative information) available to the R^2's, etc. At each stage, we can analyze the result according to the criteria of repetition, redundancy, and amount of information. We can then get the basic data, i's and q's, used in the function (B).

Let us follow a theoretical example through this system. First, we construct the matrices:

(M_s)

	S_1	S_2	S_3	S_4	S_5	
i_1	1	0	0	1	1	⋯
i_2	1	1	1	0	1	⋯
i_3	1	0	0	1	1	⋯
i_4	0	0	0	1	1	⋯
q_1	1	0	0	0	1	⋯
q_2	0	0	1	0	1	⋯
q_3	0	1	0	1	0	⋯
	.	.	.	.	.	
	.	.	.	.	.	

(M_1)

	R_1^1	R_2^1	R_3^1	R_4^1	R_5^1	R_6^1
S_1	1	0	0	1	1	1
S_2	0	0	1	1	0	0
S_3	0	0	0	0	1	0
S_4	0	1	1	0	0	1
S_5	1	1	0	0	0	0

(M_2)

	R_1^2	R_2^2	R_3^2	R_4^2
R_1^1	1	0	1	1
R_2^1	1	1	0	0
R_3^1	0	0	0	1
R_4^1	1	0	0	0
R_5^1	0	1	0	0
R_6^1	1	0	0	1

(M_B)

	B_1	B_2	B_3	B_4	B_5	B_6
R_1^3	1	0	1	1	0	0
R_2^3	0	1	0	0	0	1
R_3^3	1	0	0	1	0	0
R_4^3	0	0	1	0	1	1
R_5^3	0	0	0	0	0	1

What can we find out at this point? Returning to M_s, let us sum the elements in each row and column. These numbers indicate the relative amount of information on each form and the number of times the same information is used on different forms.

1. S_5 contains nearly all the information.
2. S_2 contains very little information.
3. In nearly all the source forms, i_2 is repeated, and so on.

This can be done for each of the matrices.

(M_s)

	S_1	S_2	S_3	S_4	S_5	Sum
i_1	1	0	0	1	1 · · ·	3
i_2	1	1	1	0	1 · · ·	4
i_3	1	0	0	1	1 · · ·	3
i_4	0	0	0	1	1 · · ·	2
q_1	1	0	0	0	1 · · ·	2
q_2	0	0	1	0	1 · · ·	2
q_3	0	1	0	1	1 · · ·	3
	·	·	·	·	·	
	·	·	·	·	·	
	·	·	·	·	·	
Sum	4	2	2	4	7	

It is evident we can now try to eliminate some of the duplication of information. Let us multiply the matrices. If we multiply M_1 by M_s:

(M_s)

	S_1	S_2	S_3	S_4	S_5
i_1	1	0	0	1	1
i_2	1	1	1	0	1
i_3	1	0	0	1	1
i_4	0	0	0	1	1
q_1	1	0	0	0	1
q_2	0	0	1	0	1
q_3	0	1	0	1	0

$X(M_1)$

	R_1^1	R_2^1	R_3^1	R_4^1	R_5^1	R_6^1
S_1	1	0	0	1	1	1
S_2	0	0	1	1	0	0
S_3	0	0	0	0	1	0
S_4	0	1	1	0	0	1
S_5	1	1	0	0	0	0

we obtain:

	R_1^1	R_2^1	R_3^1	R_4^1	R_5^1	R_6^1
i_1	2	2	1	1	1	2
i_2	2	1	1	2	2	1
i_3	2	2	1	1	1	2
i_4	1	2	1	0	0	1
q_1	2	1	0	1	1	1
q_2	1	1	0	0	1	0
q_3	0	1	2	1	0	1

$X(M_2)$

	R_1^2	R_2^2	R_3^2	R_4^2
R_1^1	1	0	1	1
R_2^1	1	1	0	0
R_3^1	0	0	0	1
R_4^1	1	0	0	0
R_5^1	0	1	0	0
R_6^1	1	0	0	1

This means, for example, that in preparing the form R_1^1, i_1 was available twice (as shown by the element in the first row and first column). We now proceed further with this multiplication. By multiplying this result of the first multiplication by M_2, we obtain:

	R_1^2	R_2^2	R_3^2	R_4^2
i_1	7	3	2	5
i_2	6	3	2	4
i_3	7	3	2	5
i_4	4	2	1	3
q_1	5	2	2	3
q_2	2	2	1	1
q_3	3	1	0	3

$X(M_3)$

	R_1^3	R_2^2	R_3^3	R_4^3	R_5^3
R_1^2	1	1	0	0	1
R_2^2	1	0	0	1	0
R_3^2	1	1	0	0	1
R_4^2	0	1	1	1	1

=

	R_1^3	R_2^3	R_3^3	R_4^3	R_5^3
i_1	12	14	5	8	14
i_2	11	12	4	7	12
i_3	12	14	5	8	14
i_4	7	8	3	5	8
q_1	9	10	3	5	10
q_2	5	4	1	3	4
q_3	4	6	3	4	6

$X(M_B)$

	B_1	B_2	B_3	B_4	B_5	B_6
R_1^3	1	0	1	1	0	0
R_2^3	0	1	0	0	0	1
R_3^3	1	0	0	1	0	0
R_4^3	0	0	1	0	1	1
R_5^3	0	0	0	0	0	1

=

	B_1	B_2	B_3	B_4	B_5	B_6
i_1	17	14	20	17	8	36
i_2	15	12	18	15	7	31
i_3	17	14	20	17	8	36
i_4	10	8	12	10	5	21
q_1	12	10	14	12	5	25
q_2	6	4	8	6	3	11
q_3	7	6	8	7	4	16

The resultant matrix indicates the classes of information available to each of the business functions. The number of times this information is available to each function is indicated by the number at their intersection. This gives a measure of the *redundancy in the processing*.

Let us follow an example through the system. The first matrix shows that i_1 occurs in S_1, S_4, and S_5, which are used in preparing the R^1's. Multiplying these matrices results in i_1 being available to all of the R^1's and available to some of them from more than one source.

The next multiplication results in a matrix in which the information is available to the next level of reporting, R^2. This shows that i_1 is available to R_1^2 seven times. The number 7 is seen to come from the previous result plus the occurrence of R_1^1, R_2^1, R_4^1, and R_6^1 in preparing R_1^2. In a similar way, we look at the information available to the R^3's and the business functions.

It was not necessary to start with the information (i's, q's). We could have started from the opposite end and found the R^2's used in the B's, the R^1's available to the R^3's or the B's, etc.

Thus, we have a model that can be investigated and manipulated. If changes are made at any stage, the results of these changes on the rest of the system will immediately become apparent. When a desired result is known, i.e., the i's and q's available to the B's, then, by "inverting" the matrix, the previous matrix can be found. By progressively "inverting" each matrix, all the matrices become known.[1] In this way an optimum system can be devised for any information requirements of management. Notice also that the size of each succeeding matrix does not necessarily increase.

If we consider the reporting structure as only a part of the communications within the organization, we can see immediately that there is also an

[1] This is *not* the usual type of matrix inversion.

informal communication network existing. The formal reporting structure is always augmented by the informal, by people in various functions speaking to people in other functions. In many cases, this informal structure is more effective in controlling the operation than the reporting structure. Thus the informal communication network must be woven into our model.

There are several ways to construct the informal communication model; each depends on the amount of information which can be obtained about the structure. One technique is to consider the information being communicated between the various functions. Then we may construct the following matrices:

$$
(I_1)\quad
\begin{array}{c|cccc}
 & B_1 & B_2 & \cdots & B_n \\
\hline
i_1 & k_{11} & k_{12} & \cdots & k_{1n} \\
i_2 & \cdot & \cdot & & \cdot \\
\vdots & \vdots & \vdots & & \vdots \\
q_1 & \cdot & \cdot & & \cdot \\
\cdot & \cdot & \cdot & & \cdot \\
q_n & k_{m1} & k_{m2} & \cdots & k_{mn}
\end{array}
\qquad
(I_2)\quad
\begin{array}{c|cccc}
 & B_1 & B_2 & \cdots & B_n \\
\hline
B_1 & b_{11} & b_{12} & \cdots & b_{1n} \\
B_2 & \cdot & \cdot & & \cdot \\
\vdots & \vdots & \vdots & & \vdots \\
B_n & b_{n1} & b_{n2} & \cdots & b_{nn}
\end{array}
$$

The matrix resulting from multiplying $I_1 \times I_2$ then corresponds to the resultant matrix of the formal system. Therefore the total system—both formal and informal—may be constructed in an integrated model.

A modification to this model can be made with the introduction of a timing notation. This will give us a relationship of the periodicity of the information flow. Also, the time it takes to go from one stage to the next—the lag time—must be considered.

The model can be made to describe the real information flow and processing by the introduction of operation matrices. This gives us the facility to reduce the system to a minimal from the operating and economic point of view. These models will be described at some future date.

The value of these matrices does not lie in the fact that they show anything which could not be represented in other ways—e.g., by 300-foot rolls of paper or voluminous manuals. Rather, the value lies in the fact that the analyst has called upon mathematics for presentation of information in condensed and manipulable forms.

Not only does the model enable the analyst to picture the whole of a very complicated situation in a relatively simplified form, but it offers other advantages. For example, because the relationships are delineated and grouped so precisely, it becomes relatively easy to divide the systems study work among the members of an analysis group. Each can be given a different part of the study, with precise knowledge as to how his part fits into the whole picture.

Equally important, because the items are defined clearly and their flows established, it becomes much easier to provide the electronics engineers with the volume, quality, and routing specifications which are so hard to obtain for present data processing systems. It is in this direction that improvement in special electronic systems can most profitably be sought.

Another advantage is the experimentation which can be carried on with the model, to determine the effects of certain suggested system changes, without disturbing the actual system. This is a scientific advantage which it is almost impossible to obtain using present methods. In present systems the direct effects of a systems change can usually be foreseen, but the second- and third-order effects, together with overlaps and other difficulties, are almost impossible to determine in advance. Indeed, they frequently go unrecognized even after the system change is put into effect. Efficiency suffers, but the cause is not ascertained.

Comparison of information transferred by the informal system and that by the formal net will give a new picture of the communication process. It will be possible to decide the extent to which the informal net should be encouraged, the amount of data which should be repeated over the formal net for verification purposes, and so on.

There are many other advantages afforded by the use of this type of model. However, the last we shall mention here is the important opportunity which is offered the analyst to incorporate in his system the advances which are taking place in programming, scheduling, and feedback—both conceptually and in terms of electronic equipment.

IX

Performance Review

TABLEAU IX

Methodological Analysis

Methodology / *Article*	*Statistical Theory*	
	Sampling	*Regression and Correlation Analysis*
49. Sampling and the Auditor	X	
50. Some Basic Concepts of Statistical Sampling in Auditing	X	
51. Use of Sampling Procedures in Internal Auditing	X	

PERFORMANCE REVIEW

Performance review implies, among other things, that periodic audits be made of the financial records of business enterprises. Because of the plethora of data that must be examined, it is logical to assume that some statistical sampling techniques may be profitably employed. Nonetheless, special problems are posed in such a circumstance, especially when the client enterprise or the independent auditor does not fully accept or regard as valid the results of the sample, or when significant errors are found in the sample data. The articles in this section suggest several answers for the above situations. They indicate why statistical sampling should be used in many instances and discuss the general techniques of statistical sampling as they relate to the attest function.

49

The author laments that generally accepted sampling methods do not currently exist in the auditing field and suggests that reeducation for present practitioners is required. Estimation sampling, acceptance sampling, and discovery sampling are each defined. The questions of "what" and "how" to sample are also dealt with, as well as sample size and interpretation of results.

*SAMPLING AND THE AUDITOR**

Herbert Arkin

EARLY AUDITORS performed their examinations on a 100 percent basis. However, as business grew, this approach became obviously impossible due to the mass of entries confronting the auditor. The auditor then resorted to the technique which has become known as the "test." This technique involved examining part of the entries or records with the view of drawing a conclusion about all of them. Thus the audit test is a sampling operation. The sampling methods to be used became entirely a matter of decision by the individual auditor.

STANDARDS OF TEST LACKING

The independent commercial auditor, no matter what methods of sampling be used, could fall back on the fact that he certified that his audit was conducted in accordance with "generally accepted auditing standards." However, it is apparent that insofar as sampling methods are concerned, there are no standards. The method and size of the test has been left entirely to the judgment and whim of the individual auditor.

For instance, *Generally Accepted Auditing Standards*,[1] published by the American Institute of Certified Public Accountants, merely states that "the appropriate degree of testing will be that which may reasonably be relied upon to bring to light errors in about the same proportion as would exist in the whole of the record being tested" and that "the testing technique thus rests for its justification upon its reasonableness, which in turn involves a variety of circumstances. . . ." However, no inkling is given as to how this worthwhile

* Reprinted from *Federal Accountant*, December, 1961, pp. 137–46.

[1] American Institute of Certified Public Accountants, *Generally Accepted Auditing Standards: Their Significance and Scope* (New York, 1954), pp. 37 and 35.

objective is to be obtained. Nor does examination of current practices disclose any "standard" techniques universally used in the test method.

Yet the techniques of statistical sampling, an objective and scientific method, have been available and widely used in virtually every other field where sampling is required. The application of statistical sampling methods in accounting and auditing situations is relatively new, perhaps due to the reluctance of auditors and accountants to apply these methods due to the misconception that they must become statisticians in order to do so. Nothing could be further from the truth. However, it will be necessary for the auditor to learn these techniques and the principles underlying them.

REEDUCATION REQUIRED

This education of the auditor in a new field will require effort on his part, but such a requirement for reeducation is not new. At their inception the auditor had to educate himself in punched card techniques, which were then new to him; and more recently, education in the area of electronic data processing has become necessary. It is the fate of those working in any professional field to continuously reeducate themselves as new and better techniques become available. It is the auditor's responsibility to undertake such a reeducation, or he will find himself seriously outmoded with considerable jeopardy to his professional standing.

In recent years, there has been an astoundingly large growth in interest in the use of statistical sampling in the audit tests. This has been reflected in the literature of the field of auditing, where numerous articles and books on statistical sampling in auditing have appeared. Various accounting firms and governmental agencies have developed training programs for their personnel. Among these groups, the U.S. Army Audit Agency has taken a leading position with a training course which provided such education for hundreds of their auditors. The various accounting societies have all formed committees to investigate this area; and some, particularly the Federal Government Accountants Association, have sponsored courses for their members.

Fear has been expressed by some auditors that the use of statistical methods will make the audit test a mechanical operation with no room for the exercise of the auditor's judgment. Actually, in any test the auditor exercises his judgment primarily in determination of test objectives (what to sample) and the audit interpretation of the findings. Statistical techniques do not intrude on either of these situations but merely provide assurance that the data compiled from a test, and thus comprising the facts to which the audit judgment is applied, are actually the facts, with a known margin of error due to the fact that a sample was taken. In no way is the exercise of audit judgment limited.

The auditor requires a sampling procedure which is unbiased, objective, and defensible. The "judgment" sample usually used by the auditor becomes indefensible when the audit test fails and under any circumstance rests for its justification upon the judgment of the individual auditor. Yet, ability at judgment varies not only from auditor to auditor but even for the same auditor at various times. The statistical sample has its justification in the mathematical principles on which it rests and is defensible at all times, even in courts of law.

SAMPLING APPROACH

The form of the statistical sampling approach to be used in a given test will be dependent upon the objectives of that test. There are three approaches of value in auditing:

1. Estimation sampling
2. Acceptance sampling
3. Discovery (exploratory) sampling

Estimation sampling answers the question as to *how many* or *how much*. How many errors, evasions of regulations, etc., exist in a set of documents? This form of estimation sampling is termed *attributes* sampling. On the other hand, the interest may be in the estimation of the dollar value of these errors or of an inventory. This form of estimation sampling is referred to as *variables* sampling.

Acceptance sampling is a technique by means of which a field is accepted or rejected as being good or bad. This is accomplished by selecting a sample of a given size from a field of documents or entries of a specified size and examining the sample for errors. If the sample contains more than a specified number of errors, the field is rejected; if not, it is accepted.

While acceptance sampling was generally recommended as the most useful approach in early auditing literature on this subject, and to some extent it still is, present thinking indicates that, generally speaking, the auditor will find estimation sampling more useful.

The objective of discovery (or exploratory) sampling is different. Here the purpose is to give reasonable assurance to the auditor that if some type of event (errors, evasions, fraud, etc.) exists in the field with some minimum frequency, he will include at least one example of such an event in his sample. The method indicates how large a sample it is necessary to take to achieve this end.

Obviously, then, some decision must be reached as to the approach to be used; and this, in turn, stems from the test objectives. There is a need for specific statements of test objectives here which has proved quite beneficial apart from the needs of statistical sampling by requiring a reexamination of test purposes. Vague objectives cannot be used to develop statistical sampling plans.

WHAT AND HOW TO SAMPLE

The sampler in any field is confronted by four questions:

1. What to sample?
2. How to sample?

3. How much to sample?
4. What do the sample results mean?

While the determination of the test objective by the auditor generally defines what is to be sampled, there are considerations relating to the field and sampling unit as well.

It is to be noted at this point that, contrary to some beliefs, the use of statistical sampling techniques does not require the sampling of all items when the auditor's interest is in certain items only. If the auditor decides he is interested in only those vouchers in excess of $100, there is nothing in the statistical method requiring him to include other vouchers in his test. However, it must be remembered that the results of such a test may be projected to state the condition of these items only, and no conclusion can be drawn about types not given an opportunity for inclusion in the sample. It is to be emphasized that sample results can be projected to represent only the field from which they were drawn, and if the auditor chooses to rule out part of the original field, his results are projectable only to that portion sampled.

The advantages of statistical sampling, including the ability to make an advance determination of the required sample and the appraisal of sample reliability, arise from the application of the mathematical theory of probability. However, this is possible only if the sample is a true statistical sample. Such a sample is called a *probability* or random sample.

A probability or random sample must be obtained in a certain way so that there is an equal probability of inclusion of any sampling unit in the field or in some cases a subdivision of the field. This does not mean that a random sample can be obtained by haphazard choice. A probability sample can be obtained by two methods: (1) random number sampling and (2) systematic sampling.

Random number sampling makes use of random number tables such as those published by the Interstate Commerce Commission's Bureau of Transportation, Economics, and Statistics ("Table of 105,000 Random Decimal Digits") or that published by the RAND Corporation ("A Million Random Digits"). The choice of the sampling units to be included in the sample is determined by the numbers listed in such tables.

In *systematic sampling*, every *n*th sampling unit is included, *beginning with a random* start. While many consider this method to be simpler than random number sampling, it is less preferred because of the danger of a bias when the sampling units are arranged in some form of pattern.

HOW MUCH TO SAMPLE

In order to determine the appropriate sample size for an estimation sample, either attributes or variables (how many or how much), the auditor must arrive at certain decisions. He must decide how closely it is necessary to establish the projection. Is it necessary to know the actual rate of errors to within ± 0.1 percent, ± 1 percent, or 2 percent, etc.? This sampling tolerance is called the sample *reliability* or *precision*.

In addition, since there is a risk attached to any sampling operation, no matter how large the sample, he must establish the risk he is willing to run, remembering that the smaller the risk, the larger the resulting sample. This risk is generally expressed as the probability that the sample projection will actually be no further from the value obtainable by a 100 percent sample than the previously determined sample precision. This is called the *confidence level.* Confidence levels are, then, the expression of the probability that the auditor will be correct, when he projects the sample result to estimate the value obtainable from a complete examination, to within a certain amount of that value. Confidence levels of 90, 95, and 99 percent are quite widely used. The auditor will have to select the proper confidence level in terms of the objective he has in mind.

The sample size required to achieve the desired sample precision and confidence level can now be determined from appropriate tables. If the sampling is for attributes (rate of occurrence) and the auditor wishes to minimize his sample size, it will be necessary to estimate the maximum probable rate of occurrence in the field. While sampling sizes can be fixed without such a determination, they will be unnecessarily large. A section of such a table is reproduced as Table 1.

TABLE 1

SAMPLE SIZES FOR SAMPLING ATTRIBUTES FOR RANDOM SAMPLES ONLY
Expected Rate of Occurrence Not Over 5 Percent
Confidence Level 95 Percent

Number of Items in Field	*Sample Size for Reliability of:*				
	±1%	*±2%*	*±3%*	*±4%*	*±5%*
200			101	73	53
300			121	83	59
400			135	89	62
500		238	144	93	64
1,000		313	169	102	68
1,500		350	179	106	70
2,000	954	371	184	108	70
2,500	1,055	386	187	109	71
3,000	1,134	396	190	110	71
3,500	1,199	403	192	110	71
4,000	1,253	409	193	111	72
4,500	1,298	414	194	111	72
5,000	1,336	418	195	111	72
6,000	1,399	424	196	112	72
7,000	1,447	428	197	112	72
8,000	1,485	431	198	112	72
9,000	1,517	434	198	113	72
10,000	1,543	436	199	113	72
15,000	1,626	443	200	113	73
20,000	1,672	446	201	113	73
25,000	1,700	448	201	113	73
50,000	1,760	452	202	114	73
100,000	1,791	454	202	114	73

TABLE 2

SAMPLE RELIABILITY FOR RELATIVE FREQUENCIES FOR RANDOM SAMPLES ONLY
Rate of Occurrence in Sample 6 Percent
Confidence Level 95 Percent

	For Sample Size of:													
	50		*100*		*200*		*300*		*500*		*1,000*		*2,000*	
Field Size Is:	*Lower Limit*	*Upper Limit*	*Lower Limit*	*Upper Limit*	*Lower Limit*	*Upper Limit*	*Lower Limit*	*Upper Limit*	*Lower Limit*	*Upper Limit*	*Lower Limit*	*Upper Limit*	*Lower Limit*	*Upper Limit*
200	1.9%	15.2%	3.3%	10.7%										
300	1.7	15.7	2.9	11.4										
400	1.6	15.9	2.7	11.7	4.0%	9.0%								
500	1.5	16.0	2.6	11.9	3.8	9.3								
1,000	1.4	16.3	2.4	12.3	3.5	9.8	4.0%	8.7%	4.7%	7.7%				
1,500	1.3	16.3	2.4	12.4	3.4	9.9	3.9	8.9	4.5	8.0				
2,000	1.3	16.4	2.3	12.4	3.3	10.0	3.8	9.0	4.4	8.1	5.0%	7.2%		
2,500	1.3	16.5	2.3	12.5	3.3	10.0	3.8	9.1	4.3	8.2	4.9	7.3		
3,000	1.3	16.5	2.3	12.5	3.3	10.1	3.8	9.1	4.3	8.2	4.9	7.3		
3,500	1.3	16.5	2.3	12.5	3.3	10.1	3.7	9.1	4.3	8.3	4.8	7.4		
4,000	1.3	16.5	2.3	12.5	3.3	10.1	3.7	9.2	4.2	8.3	4.8	7.4	5.3%	6.8%
4,500	1.3	16.5	2.3	12.5	3.2	10.1	3.7	9.2	4.2	8.3	4.8	7.5	5.3	6.8
5,000	1.3	16.5	2.3	12.5	3.2	10.1	3.7	9.2	4.2	8.3	4.8	7.5	5.2	6.9
6,000	1.3	16.5	2.3	12.5	3.2	10.1	3.7	9.2	4.2	8.3	4.8	7.5	5.2	6.9
7,000	1.3	16.5	2.3	12.6	3.2	10.2	3.7	9.2	4.2	8.3	4.7	7.5	5.2	7.0
8,000	1.3	16.5	2.3	12.6	3.2	10.2	3.7	9.2	4.2	8.4	4.7	7.5	5.1	7.0
9,000	1.3	16.5	2.3	12.6	3.2	10.2	3.7	9.2	4.2	8.4	4.7	7.6	5.1	7.0
10,000	1.3	16.5	2.3	12.6	3.2	10.2	3.7	9.2	4.2	8.4	4.7	7.6	5.1	7.0
15,000	1.3	16.6	2.3	12.6	3.2	10.2	3.7	9.3	4.1	8.4	4.7	7.6	5.1	7.0
20,000	1.3	16.6	2.3	12.6	3.2	10.2	3.7	9.3	4.1	8.4	4.6	7.6	5.1	7.1
25,000	1.3	16.6	2.3	12.6	3.2	10.2	3.6	9.3	4.1	8.4	4.6	7.6	5.1	7.1
50,000	1.3	16.6	2.2	12.6	3.2	10.2	3.6	9.3	4.1	8.4	4.6	7.6	5.0	7.1
100,000	1.3	16.6	2.2	12.6	3.2	10.2	3.6	9.3	4.1	8.4	4.6	7.6	5.0	7.1

If the auditor should overestimate or underestimate this maximum rate of occurrence used to determine the sample size, he is protected by the later appraisal of the sample result which is necessary under all conditions. However, he may find that he has achieved a better or worse sample precision than he had desired.

Similar methods may be used to establish the sample size for variables. In this case the sample size determination is affected by the variability of the values in the field. A preliminary sample will provide that information. The details of the method are beyond the scope of this limited discussion.

WHAT THE SAMPLE RESULTS MEAN

After the sample is at hand, it is possible to reappraise the result for a final determination of the sample reliability actually achieved. This is done by reference to tables such as that shown in Table 2.

For instance, if a sample of 300 is drawn from a field of 10,000 for an attributes estimation sample and the rate of occurrence of 6 percent, the table indicates that 95 chances in 100 (or 95 percent confidence level) the sample came from a field containing not less than 3.7 percent nor more than 9.2 percent. Tables for variables estimation samples provide a similar ability to reappraise such sample data on the basis of the field sample.

Discovery sample tables such as that reproduced in Table 3 provide an

TABLE 3

PROBABILITIES OF INCLUDING AT LEAST ONE OCCURRENCE IN A SAMPLE
For Random Samples Only

	When Occurrence Rate is:						
	0.05%	*0.1%*	*0.5%*	*1%*	*2%*	*5%*	*10%*
When Sample Size Is:	*Probability of Finding at Least One Occurrence Is:*						
	Field Size Is 3,000:						
10	0.3%	1.0%	4.9%	9.6%	18.3%	40.2%	65.2%
100	5.0	9.7	39.9	64.0	87.2	99.5	100.0
200	9.8	18.7	64.6	87.5	98.5	100.0	100.0
400	19.3	34.9	88.4	98.7	100.0	100.0	100.0
600	28.4	48.8	96.5	99.9	100.0	100.0	100.0
800	37.2	60.6	99.4	100.0	100.0	100.0	100.0
1,000	45.6	70.4	99.8	100.0	100.0	100.0	100.0
	Field Size Is 10,000:						
100	4.9%	9.6%	39.5%	63.6%	86.9%		
200	9.6	18.3	63.6	86.9	98.3		
500	22.6	40.1	99.3	99.4	100.0		
1,000	41.0	65.1	99.5	100.0	100.0		
	Field Size Is 15,000:						
100	4.9%	9.6%	39.5%	63.5%	86.9%		
200	9.6	18.9	63.4	86.8	98.3		
500	22.4	39.9	92.2	99.4	100.0		
1,000	40.4	64.5	99.4	100.0	100.0		

ability to determine the sample size required to obtain any degree of assurance desired of including an instance of the type sought, if it occurs in the field at not less than some specified rate. A very complete set of such tables has been published by the Auditor General of the U.S. Air Force.

For instance, it can be seen from Table 3 that a sample of 200 from a field of 3,000 will provide an 87.5 percent assurance that *at least* one such event will be found in the sample if the rate of occurrence in the field is 1 percent.

In this brief discussion, it is not possible to examine the more sophisticated sampling techniques. While the auditor can operate without these techniques, knowledge of these methods can result in a very considerable reduction in the required sample size, with the attendant saving in audit costs.

In closing, it might be said that while the use of statistical sampling may require a greater effort on the part of the auditor, it is to be remembered that an unbiased, objective projection with a known sample reliability will result. There may be easier ways to sample, but it must be emphasized that *it is better not to sample at all than to sample incorrectly or inadequately.*

50

The general features of statistical sampling are examined, and the argument is made that this technique does not encroach upon the auditor's professional judgment. The author provides a simple explanation of mathematical probability, after which he discusses the hypergeometric, binomial, and Poisson distributions. An auditing application using the Poisson distribution is illustrated. The author also briefly comments upon confidence, precision, and sample size as they relate to this distribution.

*SOME BASIC CONCEPTS OF STATISTICAL SAMPLING IN AUDITING**

Kenneth W. Stringer

IN RECENT YEARS, accounting literature has included many interesting articles on statistical sampling. In the earlier stages of developments in this field, many of these articles reflected the conflicting views of opponents and advocates of sampling and some disagreement among the advocates concerning the relative merits of different sampling methods. More recent articles have related principally to case studies or proposals dealing with specific applications or to certain sampling tables and formulas.

UNDERSTANDING THE CONCEPTS

The writer believes that the progress of statistical sampling in auditing has reached the stage where many auditors who have given little attention to the subject may now be interested in developing an understanding of the basic concepts, and this article is intended for this purpose. An understanding of basic concepts is desirable as a general background for auditing applications of statistical sampling, although a study of the more complex concepts does not seem essential.

Some auditors who are not familiar with statistical sampling may regard it with complete skepticism, with unrealistic expectations, or with unwarranted apprehension. It is desirable that these extreme views be replaced by a realization that statistical sampling is not highly theoretical, on the one hand,

* Reprinted from *Journal of Accountancy*, November, 1961, pp. 63–69.

or a means of performing the impossible, on the other, but that it is simply a rational and understandable method for recognizing the probabilities associated with audit tests in a given situation. If this can be demonstrated through illustrations of some simple situations, auditors may accept more readily the application of the same concepts in other situations where the mathematical symbols or computations appear more complex.

AUDITOR'S JUDGMENT

Before considering basic concepts, it may be worthwhile to mention briefly one matter that often is of primary concern to auditors who are not familiar with statistical sampling techniques. This is the fear that use of these techniques would encroach on the auditor's judgment. This is a legitimate concern because auditors, quite properly, have the highest regard for the importance of professional judgment. Therefore, it appears desirable to emphasize that auditors who have studied statistical sampling thoroughly are in general agreement that these techniques would not supplant the auditor's judgment but would only serve as a useful tool in applying it. In fact, there are indications that the use of these techniques would bring certain aspects of judgment into sharper focus. While this conclusion is asserted without discussion at this point, it is believed that its validity will become apparent on further study of this subject.

FEATURES OF STATISTICAL SAMPLING

It seems appropriate to introduce the discussion of basic concepts by pointing out the principal common feature of statistical sampling and audit testing. Both of these techniques are designed for the purpose of forming conclusions concerning the whole of a group of data by examining only a part of it. It should be clearly understood that the application of either of these techniques presupposes a willingness to accept some degree of uncertainty. The justification for accepting some uncertainty, either in statistical work generally or in auditing, lies in the relationship between such factors as the cost of examining the data, the time required, the decisions to be made from the resulting conclusions, and the adverse consequences of erroneous decisions. Where these factors do not warrant the acceptance of some uncertainty, the only alternative is a complete examination or enumeration of the data. However, it is important to recognize that even complete examination may not give absolute assurance because various kinds of mistakes may be made in spite of complete coverage. For example, in examing all vouchers for a given period, an auditor may fail to recognize some that include errors. Obviously, the same kind of mistakes may be made in testing or sampling. Statisticians refer to mistakes of this kind as "nonsampling errors," and such errors are excluded from all of the discussion that follows.

The distinguishing feature of statistical sampling is that it provides a means for measuring mathematically the extent of the uncertainty that results from examining only a part of the data instead of all of it. The principal advantage offered by statistical sampling follows from this unique feature. By being able to measure the extent of uncertainty, the auditor may determine the sample sizes necessary to confine it to the limits that he considers acceptable in any particular situation. While this is the fundamental advantage offered by statistical sampling, this may manifest itself in different ways. It may result in more uniformity in the extent of audit tests in comparable situations; it may possibly, but not necessarily, reduce the extent of tests; and perhaps most important, it may result in an increase in the auditor's confidence in his tests and in his ability to demonstrate objectively to others the basis for such confidence.

Since the crux of statistical sampling is the measurement of uncertainty, it is important to understand some of the elementary aspects of the mathematics of probability, which is the basis for the measurement. In fact, statistical sampling is sometimes referred to as probability sampling. Although mathematical probability may be defined in various ways, it is satisfactory for auditing purposes to regard it *as the ratio of the number of possibilities for the occurrence of a particular event in a given set of mutually exclusive and equally likely events to the total number of possibilities for the occurrence of each of the events.*

MATHEMATICAL PROBABILITY

The concept expressed in this definition may appear complex but is easily comprehended in its simpler applications. It is often explained by reference to such familiar incidents as tossing coins, throwing dice, or drawing cards. For example, we recognize intuitively that the probability of drawing a spade on one draw from an ordinary deck of cards is one out of four, or ¼. Table 1, relating to this simple example, may be used to illustrate the definition given above.

TABLE 1

SAMPLE OF ONE

Possible Sample Results	*Number of Possible Sample "Combinations"*	*Probabilities*
One spade	13	0.25
One club	13	0.25
One diamond	13	0.25
One heart	13	0.25
	52	1.00
No spades	39	0.75
One spade	13	0.25
	52	1.00

The "particular event" in the definition is the event for which the probability is being considered. In this illustration, it could be the drawing of any one of the four suits, as shown in the top part of the first column; or if the drawing of a spade were the event of interest, the possible sample results could be stated as shown in the bottom part. Also, the drawing of a card of some particular value, with or without regard to its suit, could have been specified as the "particular event" but with results different from those shown in Table 1.

The "set of events" in the definition is the total number of possible distinct samples that could be drawn. In this example a sample of one card could produce any of the 52 cards in the deck, and these 52 distinct possibilities comprise the set of events. (The term *combinations* is discussed in connection with the next illustration, where its significance is more apparent.) The events in this set are "mutually exclusive" because each card is different from the others; they may or may not be "equally likely" depending on the way the sample of one card is selected. If it is selected so that any one card has the same chance of being drawn as any other, this requirement in the definition is satisfied. In cases where the selection is made in such a way that the chances for each individual item to be included in the sample are not equal but are determinable, techniques are available for making the adjustments necessary to satisfy this requirement. The need for using random numbers or other statistical selection techniques to comply with this requirement is one of the important basic concepts of statistical sampling. If the selection is made otherwise, the situation is outside the realm of mathematical probability, and none of the remaining discussion is relevant.

With this explanation of the terminology, the application of the remainder of the definition seems self-evident. In the foregoing example, there are 13 separate possibilities for drawing a card of any particular suit, and the related probabilities are simply the ratio of these possibilities to the total possibilities, with the latter being expressed as 100 percent or as one.

As the number of possibilities increases, the application of the definition of probability may become somewhat more difficult to visualize, but it should be reassuring to the auditor to understand that the basic simplicity of the concept remains the same. This may be illustrated by considering the effect of increasing the sample to include two cards, the second being drawn without replacing the first. Assuming that the particular event we are concerned with is the drawing of spades, the probabilities are as shown in Table 2.

In this case the only change in the possible sample results is that the possibility of drawing two spades has been added. However, the number of possible sample combinations has increased substantially, and it may be helpful to explore this in some detail. As in the previous illustration, the first card drawn may be any one of the 52. The second card may be any one of the remaining 51. Therefore, for each of the first 52 possibilities, there are 51 second possibilities. This produces a total of 2,652 possibilities, which is merely the product of multiplying 52 by 51. Each of these possibilities constitutes a

TABLE 2

SAMPLE OF TWO—WITHOUT REPLACEMENT

Possible Sample Results	*Number of Possible Sample "Combinations"*	*Probabilities*
No spades	741	0.55882
One spade	507	0.38236
Two spades	78	0.05882
	1,326	1.00000

separate way of drawing a pair of cards, and each is described technically as a "permutation." In computing permutations, each different sequence or order of the same items is counted separately. For example, the drawing of the ace of spades followed by the king would be one permutation, while the king followed by the ace would be another. When the sequence is disregarded, a particular grouping of items is known as a "combination." Thus the ace and king of spades would be only one combination, although it could be drawn in two ways. Since the sequence of items in a sample ordinarily is not important, probability computations of the type illustrated here are usually based on the possible sample combinations. In this illustration the combinations are computed by dividing the 2,652 permutations by 2.

The number of combinations that would include no spades will be considered next. To obtain such a sample, the first card drawn could be any one of the 39 cards of other suits, and the second could be any one of the remaining 38. Using these figures, the number of possibilities for a sample that would include no spades can be computed by the method just explained for computing the total of all the possibilities ($39 \times 38 \div 2 = 741$). The other possible sample combinations can be computed in a generally similar way.

The discussion of these computations is not intended to enable the reader to make similar ones for his own use; therefore, no formulas are given. Such detailed computations would not be necessary in auditing applications because the desired probabilities or satisfactory approximations can be obtained from available tables or simpler computations. On the contrary, the sole purpose here is to demonstrate that the probability computations underlying statistical sampling are a realistic method for giving the proper weight to all of the possible results that could be obtained from a sample of a given size from a given group of data.

One more illustration is given to show the tremendous increase in the possible combinations that results from even a small increase in sample size. For this purpose the sample size is increased to four, and the possibilities are shown in Table 3. The large number of possible combinations in this case, in spite of the small "population" (group of items from which the sample is drawn) and the small sample size, indicates quite clearly the futility of trying

TABLE 3

SAMPLE OF FOUR—WITHOUT REPLACEMENT

Possible Sample Results	*Number of Possible Sample "Combinations"*	*Probabilities*
No spades	82,251	0.30382
One spade	118,807	0.43885
Two spades	57,798	0.21349
Three spades	11,154	0.04120
Four spades	715	0.00264
	270,725	1.00000

to apply the concept of probability without resort to mathematical formulas or tables.

PROBABILITY DISTRIBUTIONS

The tabulations that have been presented are examples of the "hypergeometric distribution," which is one of several types of "probability distributions." Since some of these distributions are referred to frequently in sampling literature, a brief discussion of their applicability and relation to each other may be worthwhile.

The hypergeometric distribution is applicable to sampling from finite populations without replacement of the sample items, which corresponds to the usual practice in audit testing. However, for useful sizes of populations and samples, hypergeometric probabilities are burdensome to compute, and the most extensive tables that the author is aware of show only the probabilities of finding at least one error or other feature of interest if a given number is present in the population. This limits the usefulness of these tables in auditing situations where it may be desirable to know the probabilities applicable to samples that include one or more errors.

A second type of probability distribution is the "binomial," which applies to sampling from an infinite population or from a finite population with each of the sample items being replaced before the next is drawn. In these circumstances the proportion of the items of interest in the population does not change as each sample item is drawn. For example, if the sampling from a deck of cards is with replacement, the probability that any single card drawn will be a spade remains constant at 0.25, or $13/52$. Further, this probability is also 0.25, or $26/104$, if two decks are combined; and it does not change if more are added. This illustrates the concept—which sometimes is not clear on initial consideration—that the size of the population has no bearing on the sample size where the sampling is with replacement and the sample is concerned with the proportion of some feature of interest in the population.

If such sampling is without replacement, the size of the population has some effect on the probabilities and related sample sizes, but this effect is much less than proportional to the differences in population sizes. For example, if the sampling is without replacement, the successive probabilities that any single card drawn from one deck will be a spade (until the first spade is drawn) are $13/52$, $13/51$, $13/50$, etc.; if two decks are combined, such probabilities are $26/104$, $26/103$, $26/102$, etc. Because the effect of the population size may be so small, binomial probabilities are often a satisfactory approximation of hypergeometric probabilities. The available binomial tables give more complete distributions than the hypergeometric tables, but the range of sample sizes covered may not be adequate for some auditing purposes.

A third type of probability distribution is the "Poisson." This distribution is not strictly applicable to sampling either with replacement or without replacement, but it provides an approximation to the hypergeometric distribution that seems satisfactory for most auditing purposes where both the expected percentage of errors or other features of interest in the population and the percentage of the population included in the sample are less than 10 percent. The first of these conditions is likely to prevail in most auditing situations, but the second may not. In the latter event a satisfactory adjustment may be computed by a fairly simple formula. Poisson tables that give complete distributions for a wide range of situations are available in a form that is more compact than either of the other types of tables referred to above. For these reasons the Poisson distribution appears to be suitable for use in many auditing situations.

Table 4 shows a comparison of the three distributions discussed above. In this table the population and sample size and the proportion of the feature of interest are more relevant to auditing situations than those in the preceding illustrations, but the basic concept underlying the computations is the same. The hypergeometric probabilities were computed and the others were taken from published tables.[1] The individual probabilities are shown on the lines with the respective numbers of errors, and the cumulative probabilities are shown on the other lines. The individual probabilities are those of obtaining exactly the indicated number of errors in a sample; and the cumulative probabilities, as presented here, are those of obtaining less than the number of errors indicated on the following line.

If the sample in this illustration were exactly representative of the population, it would include three errors, which is the product of the sample size multiplied by the proportion of errors in the population. This product is sometimes referred to mathematically as the "expected" sample result and indicated by the symbol np (n being the number of items in the sample and p the proportion of the items of interest in the population). It may be observed from Table 4 that the cumulative Poisson probabilities for any number of

[1] H. G. Romig, *50–100 Binomial Tables* (New York: John Wiley & Sons, Inc., 1947); E. C. Molina, *Poisson's Exponential Binomial Limit* (Princeton: D. Van Nostrand Co., Inc., 1942).

TABLE 4

SAMPLE OF 100 ITEMS
FROM A POPULATION OF 1,000 ITEMS CONTAINING 30 ERRORS

Possible Sample Results —Number of Errors in Sample	*Probabilities— Individual and Cumulative*		
	Hypergeometric	*Binomial*	*Poisson*
0	0.04035	0.04755	0.04979
1	0.13897	0.14707	0.14936
	0.17932	0.19462	0.19915
2	0.22879	0.22515	0.22404
	0.40811	0.41977	0.42319
3	0.23971	0.22748	0.22404
	0.64782	0.64725	0.64723
4	0.17958	0.17060	0.16803
	0.82740	0.81785	0.81526
5	0.10245	0.10131	0.10082
	0.92985	0.91916	0.91608
6	0.04629	0.04961	0.05041
	0.97614	0.96877	0.96649
7	0.01701	0.02061	0.02160
	0.99315	0.98938	0.98809
8	0.00518	0.00741	0.00810
	0.99833	0.99679	0.99619
9	0.00132	0.00234	0.00270
	0.99965	0.99913	0.99889
10 or more	0.00035	0.00087	0.00111
	1.00000	1.00000	1.00000

errors less than the "expected" number is greater than the corresponding hypergeometric probabilities. This is a general characteristic of the Poisson distribution which assures conservative results in terms of audit protection when this distribution is used as illustrated in the next section. As mentioned earlier, satisfactory adjustment may be made when this feature is likely to result in excessive conservatism in computing sample sizes or in evaluating sample results for auditing purposes.

The "normal" distribution is another type that is referred to frequently in sampling literature and is useful in many sampling applications, including some in accounting and auditing. In common with the distributions discussed above, it provides a basis for computing or approximating the distribution of all possible sample results for the purpose of estimating probabilities associated with samples, but it employs a different mathematical technique. This technique is based on the "standard deviation" of the population items from the population average. In practice, both the population standard deviation and the average are usually estimated from the sample. The extent to which these estimates should be relied upon depends on (1) the sample size and (2) the degree of difference between the "normal" distribution and the actual distribution of the population (for example, in terms of the monetary value of items or of errors). Consequently, both of these factors should be considered carefully in auditing applications that make use of the normal distribution. Further discussion of normal distribution theory or application is beyond the scope of this paper.

ILLUSTRATIVE AUDITING APPLICATION

The preceding discussion and illustrations have dealt with probability distributions in situations where the proportion of errors or of other features of interest in the population was known. In auditing, as in other sampling applications, this proportion is not known, and the purpose of sampling is to obtain information concerning it. Consequently, the use of probability in sampling requires a transition from the known to the unknown. This transition may be made by substituting a hypothesis for the unknown proportion and testing the sample results against the hypothesis by reference to the related probabilities.

To illustrate the application of this technique to auditing, it may be assumed that an auditor wishes to sample a population of 10,000 disbursement vouchers for the purpose of deciding whether the degree of compliance with the prescribed internal control procedures is satisfactory. For this purpose the auditor must supply the criterion for a "satisfactory" degree of compliance, based on his judgment in the circumstances. Obviously, he would prefer to have absolute assurance that there were no deviations or procedural errors, but this would require examination of all of the vouchers. As mentioned earlier, a willingness to tolerate some degree of uncertainty is implicit in any form of testing, whether by statistical techniques or others.

Assume further that in the auditor's judgment a procedural error rate in excess of 0.03 would require further consideration and possibly additional audit work. This upper limit of 0.03 becomes the hypothesis to be tested, and it is one of the ways of expressing the statistical measurement known as the "precision limit." This is the first of two measurements which, taken together, express the degree of assurance that is attributable to a statistical sample. The second of these measurements is referred to as the "confidence level" (or "reliability") or, conversely, as the "sampling risk." The confidence level is also a matter to be determined in the light of the auditor's judgment.

The meaning of these terms may be shown more concretely by considering the above assumptions in relation to Table 5. This excerpt shows for selected values of np (the product of the number of sample items multiplied by the proportion of the errors or other feature of interest in the population) the probabilities of obtaining no errors in a sample and of obtaining one or more. As used in this illustration, the first probability expresses the "sampling risk," and the second expresses the "confidence level."

If the auditor wants a confidence level of at least 95 percent, the middle column can be used to determine the approximate minimum sample size.

TABLE 5

CONDENSED EXCERPT FROM POISSON DISTRIBUTION

Possible Number of Errors in Sample	Probabilities		
	$np = 2.3$	$np = 3.0$	$np = 4.6$
None	0.10026	0.04979	0.01005
One or more	0.89974	0.95021	0.98995
	1.00000	1.00000	1.00000

This column shows that an *np* equal to 3.0 is required. The desired precision limit of 0.03 in this illustration is *p;* therefore the sample size *n* becomes 100 ($n = np/p$; $3.0/0.03 = 100$).

If the sample of 100 includes no procedural errors, the upper precision limit with respect to such errors at the selected confidence level would be 0.03; if it includes one error, the limit would increase to approximately 0.048 (based on the lowest value of *np* for which the probability of two or more errors in a sample is at least 95 percent—which is not shown in the foregoing condensed excerpt); and each larger number of errors in the sample would require a correspondingly (but not proportionately) higher precision limit if the desired confidence level is to be maintained. The confidence attributable to such samples is derived from knowing that at least 95 percent of all possible combinations of vouchers that could have been selected in a sample of 100 would have included more than the respective number of errors if the error rate in the population were greater than the respective precision limits. If the precision limit indicated by the sample results is not satisfactory to the auditor, he has the problem of satisfying himself by extending the sample or by some other means.

The reader may observe that the Poisson probabilities and the sample size in this illustration concerning a population of 10,000 items are the same as in Table 4 concerning a sample from a population of 1,000. The limited effect of population size, and of sampling without replacement, on sample size was discussed in the section dealing with probability distributions (p. 697). As a further example of this limited effect, a comparison of the actual and approximated confidence levels for a sample population of 100 is presented in Table 6. This comparison also illustrates the earlier statement that the Poisson

TABLE 6

Size of Population	Confidence Level	
	Actual—Hypergeometric	Approximate—Poisson
1,000	0.960	0.950
10,000	0.953	0.950

approximations are conservative in terms of audit protection. This is so because the actual confidence level is greater than that shown by the Poisson approximations when the latter are used in the manner explained above.

CONFIDENCE, PRECISION, AND SAMPLE SIZE

It is apparent from the preceding discussion that there is a three-way relationship between confidence, precision, and sample size. This relationship is such that any one of these factors is a function of the other two, and the other two may be combined in various ways. This may be observed from Table 7

TABLE 7

ILLUSTRATIVE COMBINATIONS OF CONFIDENCE, PRECISION, AND SAMPLE SIZE, WHERE SAMPLE INCLUDES NO ERRORS—BASED ON POISSON DISTRIBUTION

Approximate Confidence Level	*Upper Precision Limit —Error Rate*	*Sample Size*
0.90	0.023	100
0.95	0.03	100
0.95	0.01	300
0.99	0.01	460

by comparing the first and second, second and third, and third and fourth lines, in which the sample size, confidence, and precision, respectively, are constant with the other two factors varying. Readers may find it helpful to trace the development of this table to the foregoing condensed excerpt from the Poisson distribution.

The terminology in this article is not used uniformly by all writers on sampling. Other terms that are sometimes used include *reliability*, *confidence coefficient*, *sampling error*, *confidence limits*, *confidence interval*, and *tolerance interval*. To avoid confusion in this area, it is necessary to determine the sense in which the terminology is applied by a particular writer. Fortunately, this usually is stated or is evident from the context.

Having considered some of the basic concepts and an illustration of a simple application of statistical sampling, the reader may be in a better position to evaluate the earlier remarks concerning its relation to the use of judgment in auditing. It should be evident from the foregoing discussion that in any application of statistical sampling the auditor's judgment would be the sole factor in determining the audit purpose of the sample, the related criteria as to what should be treated as an error, and the confidence level and precision limit deemed appropriate in the light of internal control, materiality, and other relevant factors. After these decisions were made, the sample size necessary to satisfy the auditor's requirements would be determined from probability tables or formulas. The use of statistical techniques for selecting a sample from a large group of items with no apparent unusual features would not conflict with the examination of any additional items that appear, on the basis of judgmental criteria, to warrant special attention. In examining the individual items in the sample, the auditor's judgment would be applied in deciding whether they were satisfactory or were to be treated as errors. The quantitative significance of the results shown by the sample would then be evaluated by reference to the applicable probabilities and to the requirements established by the auditor. If these requirements were not met, the auditor's course of action would be determined on the basis of his judgment in the circumstances.

While the purpose of this article has been to present basic concepts in a simplified manner, it would be unfortunate if this were achieved at the expense of oversimplification. Readers should be aware that the discussion has not dealt with some of the more difficult problems involved in auditing applications.

Some of the principal problems relate to the areas of judgment mentioned in the preceding section. The auditing illustration in this article dealt with precision limits in terms of numbers of errors rather than monetary amounts, but this may be an inadequate criterion for the purpose of many audit tests. Therefore the determination of precision limits in terms of monetary amounts of items or of errors is another important problem. A further group of problems relates primarily to sampling efficiency. These include the choice of a sample evaluation method, sample design, and selection technique that will provide the desired degree of assurance at the approximate minimum cost in typical auditing situations.

51

This discussion accents the application of statistical procedures to the auditing function, including specific consideration of problems posed by errors discovered in audit samples, possible corrective measures if the error rate proves to be higher than a prescribed limit, etc. The overall impact of sampling on internal auditing is emphasized; minimal attention is given to any specific experience.

USE OF SAMPLING PROCEDURES IN INTERNAL AUDITING*

K. F. Schumann

THE APPLICATION of statistical sampling techniques to auditing is still all but virgin territory. Some case studies are on record, but there is much research to be accomplished. This article adds the experience of Deere & Company. This experience already has a history. The quality control departments of the various factories have been delegated the responsibility, for a number of years, of verifying the inventory counts being made by the counting teams. The procedure of counting 15 tags of each lot of 100 inventory tags in a normal examination and allowing an average of from 1 percent to 3 percent variation in count (dependent upon factory) before requiring a recount of the remainder of the lot has come to be considered to be an efficient method for maintaining satisfactory quality in inventory counts.

Now, we are approaching the use of statistics in auditing on a broader basis. Means of applying to various auditing procedures certain statistical tools developed for us by the quality control department are actively under study. We have already realized the following advantages:

1. A means whereby we can establish standards and evaluate the quality of work is provided.
2. The extent of our audit verifications is determined on a more scientific basis; and in some cases, reduction in tests has been possible. The longer the period is which is being reviewed, the smaller proportionately are the tests in cases where sample sizes were previously designated on the basis of monthly, semiannual, or annual intervals. The corollary to this is that sounder reasons can be given to the

* Reprinted from *NAA Bulletin*, published by the National Association of Accountants, December, 1957, pp. 17–23.

independent public accountants for our reduction of tests, while they can still rely on our work.

3. In other cases the original application of quantitative statistical measurements indicates the possible need of an increase in the amount of audit testing. In such cases, our entire approach has been reexamined and weighed in the light of reasonable cost and acceptable risk.
4. In some cases, our tests have become still more of a random sample. The more random the sample, the greater the number of files examined, which in turn impresses employees still more as to the thoroughness of the examination. The psychological effects of such impressions are considerable.

These statistical tools now at our disposal will help us in the handling of our sampling problems in the auditing process, although they will not by themselves solve auditing problems, which are to ascertain the accuracy of the balance sheet and profit and loss statement, the extent of compliance with company policies, plans, and procedures, the effectiveness of internal controls and the prevention and detection of fraud.

APPROACH TO STATISTICAL PROCEDURES

The tools given us are the acceptance sampling tables for attributes based on the government publication Mil-Std 105*A* and are based on quality levels which will be accepted 95 percent of the time. It has seemed appropriate to us to concern ourselves only with single sampling at the outset. Single sampling is defined as a type of sampling in which a decision to accept or reject is reached after one sample from the inspection lot has been checked. A lot is a group from which a sample may be drawn. Sampling of each lot is based on an acceptable quality level. This level is the percent defective established by management which, if exceeded, will generally result in rejection of the inspected lot. When a lot is rejected, screening takes place to improve the lot quality to a desired quality level. The sampling tables are prepared for three levels of inspection. The lowest inspection level is the least rigid and requires the least inspection. The opposite holds true for the highest level. Each inspection level also has three degrees of inspections: reduced, normal, and tightened.

When establishing our quantitive measurements, we must first decide what a "lot" is to be. For example, in considering the application of the tables to a footing procedure, should we consider a unit within a lot to be a month, a page, a day, a footing group, or a line? In this, a page proves most practical and allows more random sampling than heretofore accomplished when an entire month was examined, as well as a reduction in work. Another problem arises in the verification of inventories. In counting complete machines, for example, should a unit be considered to be cultivators, tractors, and wagons as groups; or should they be defined more clearly, such as 400 or 800 series cultivators, or 40 or 50 series tractors, or should we be more specific by considering 411, 412, 811, and 812 cultivators as units and 40*C*, 40*S*, 40*T*, and

40*U* tractors as units? We prefer the last-named basis when verifying complete machines. Granted that this is a change from our previous philosophy, which considered units according to series. However, we now have tools by which we can make better determinations as to the quality of work.

Following our definition of a lot, we can determine the lot size and then establish the size of the sample to be taken, based upon the acceptable quality level established and the inspection level and degree of inspection being applied. This process is referred to as determining the sampling plan. First, however, since an acceptable quality level relates to the percent defective or the number of errors in the sample, we must determine what rates of error we can tolerate in our auditing approach to the subject under review, as well as what standards of accuracy are desirable of attainment by the clerical force.

PROBLEMS POSED BY ERRORS DISCOVERED IN THE SAMPLE EXAMINED

Bringing up the question of rate of error determination immediately poses another problem for when we speak of rates of error, we must then ascertain what is to be considered an error. This will vary for each testing procedure. For example, in the examination of vouchers, the list of descriptive errors or defectives reads as follows:

1. Invoice not authentic
2. Duplicate payment
3. Endorsement to check incorrect
4. Invoice not checked to purchase order or accepted at different price without authority
5. Invoice not checked to receiving report or not checked correctly
6. Arithmetical computations incorrect
7. Discount incorrectly computed or not taken
8. Payment not approved or check not properly signed
9. Invoice not stamped with date paid
10. Purchase order not attached to voucher
11. Credit not filed or taken when it should have been
12. Charged to wrong account, or allocated to wrong costing code or wrong product group
13. Company's invoice number not stamped on vendor's invoice when item was to be rebilled, as system provides

Some errors, such as the first three in the list, will be of the nature that, if found, they will require a detailed investigation. But if more emphasis is to be placed upon some types of defectives than others, should we not assign weights to the errors? It is true that we could possibly classify defectives into three groups: those indicating fraud, major errors, and minor errors. However, we believe that in the early stages of the application of statistical methods to auditing, it is adequate, as a general rule, to differentiate only between errors which give evidence of possible fraud and all others. Later, when it has been determined that the desired acceptable quality level is generally being met, it will probably be desirable to assign values to the varying types of defective items in an effort to upgrade quality still further.

Other problems present themselves. In a confirmation procedure, for example, should an error be measured by the amount of the transaction, by the amount of the account, or as a breakdown in internal control? Our audit objectives determine this. In other words, our main concern is correct statement of our accounts. Of secondary concern is the account involved and, lastly, the size of the account. The fact that violations of internal control principles are classified as defective items in the sample has its interesting and beneficial aspects. When an auditor's recommendations for changes in procedures for reasons of internal control have not been accepted, it seems reasonable to assume that with the application of scientific measurements and comparisons, more convincing material will be available.

Before leaving the subject of errors, it should be pointed out that it is important to recognize an error as items are reviewed. If we incorrectly classify an item, it may have an important bearing on our decisions as to the adequacy of the audit phase involved. Likewise, it is important that all phases of the examination be performed. For example, in the review of cash vouchers, it is important that we review each one for all error definitions.

It is equally important that we record and analyze the results. The recording process, when applying to statistical procedures, will not only include recording the number of errors and comparing it to the acceptable number but will also include such things as recording the page number of footings, recording the number of vouchers examined, and maintaining counters for recording postings checked. The auditor may in some instances find it desirable to expand the working papers to provide for checking off various items verified under each audit procedure.

INTERRELATIONSHIPS AND SELECTION OF SAMPLES

Earlier, selection of the inspection level and degree of inspection was mentioned. This will sometimes vary. For example, in performing inventory tests, it may be desirable to use a higher or lower inspection level and a different degree of inspection, dependent upon the amount of inventory adjustment. In our experience, it has seemed desirable to test the parts inventory at level 2 (reduced), with an acceptable quality level of 6 percent if the inventory adjustment is not more than one tenth of 1 percent of warehouse sales or one quarter of 1 percent of average warehouse inventories. If the adjustment is over these levels, it appears desirable to test on level 3 (reduced), with acceptable quality level of 10 percent. In this procedure, we find that because of the method of intracompany shipments (shipments of pallet loads between factories and branches being measured by weight), it is also practical to weigh the defectives and consider as defective only those variances of more than 1 percent of the number on hand plus the number sold since the last inventory. However, if we are verifying an inventory count of branch-house parts inventories, a defective is then described as 2 percent of the number on hand.

Still other relationships exist. Various tests of the accuracy of clerical work in annual inventory procedures are excellent for application of statistical sampling when the inventory adjustment is a shortage. While there is nothing to prevent the same approach when the inventory adjustment is an overage, a more pointed approach rather than a random sample is generally called for. This is because when we are looking for an overage, we are concerned with large values and find that a review of all parts items aggregating more than $500 will often locate some of the difference. When such an approach is used, the randomness of the work under surveillance is destroyed because a specific segment of the universe is reviewed. If, however, we were to select only a portion of the items aggregating more than $500 for testing, then we would still have the random selection qualifications but of a different universe. A similar situation would exist if we were to limit our test check of check vouchers to a universe of check vouchers over $50.

We might elaborate a bit on this subject of randomness by saying that the term *random* does not necessarily imply that a systematic procedure of checking, for example, every seventh or every twenty-first item cannot be applied. The requisite, if such a plan is adopted, is that the starting place be not predetermined for some particular reason and that the same day of the week or month is not regularly included in the sample. There are some cases in which it might be desirable to select the sample through the use of tables of random numbers.

MORE ON THE ACCEPTABLE QUALITY LEVEL

A few more words might be said about the acceptable quality level. In establishing this level, we must use a realistic approach and be fair in deciding how high a rate of error we are willing to accept. We might also set a level as to the low rate of error which we consider desirable. One must remember that when including all types of errors, i.e., those of serious proportions and those of minor nature, in the list of definitions for defectives, a higher acceptable quality level is necessarily called for than would otherwise be the case. In our own applications the error acceptance level has varied from 0.5 percent to 10 percent, depending upon the nature and importance of the item under examination. Another approach might be to establish separate quality levels for serious and minor errors. We are of the opinion, however, that it is more practical during the early stages of applying the principles of statistical sampling to refrain from practicing such refinements. It may well be that even after establishing the level with the most discriminating approach, the auditor may find that it is in need of adjustment upward or downward. Any adjustments in an upward direction should be made only after a painstaking review of the entire concept and of the objectives of the auditor's approach to the work.

PROCEDURE TO FOLLOW WHEN ERROR RATE IS HIGHER THAN LIMIT

What do we do if errors found in the sampling plan for a particular acceptible quality level are excessive? This will depend on the kind of errors, their dollar value, and the subject under review. When applying statistical sampling plans to manufacturing operations, rejection of lots and the screening of them is a requirement. However, in auditing, as long as the errors are not of the kind to indicate fraud, there will always be reason for considering suspension of further examination. If the item does not materially affect the financial statements or unit operations, or, although it may affect the financial statements, the dollar value of errors has been insignificant, we are of the opinion that it is generally adequate to consider the work subpar but to do no more sampling. Our problem then will be to determine what action can be taken to eliminate such errors in the future and to convince management of the necessity and practicality of our suggestions designed to rectify the trouble. There may be some isolated instances in which it will appear judicious to extend our examination or to recommend that the branch or factory recheck for a certain period the type of work which has been under inspection. Specific examples of this latter situation would be where there have been excessive errors in cash discount allowances or in the computation of invoices or credits.

In cases in which it appeared that an extension of our audit inspection was definitely needed, we would be required to examine the remainder of the lot according to strict interpretation of statistical formulas; but when lot sizes generally are based on the audit period, such an approach would be prohibitive in cost. We find that it is practical to convert one's thinking to the basis that the single sample size utilized is a portion of the total sample to be taken in a double sampling procedure. The work then would be extended to the limits called for in the double sampling procedure. The switching between a single and a double sampling plan appears practical from an administrational and operational standpoint. Statistically, it would require that the operating characteristic curves of the two plans be nearly enough alike to provide a similar degree of protection.

POSSIBLE FUTURE MODIFICATION OF SAMPLING PLANS

As we gain further experience with statistical sampling, we visualize further reduction in work and costs of auditing through the adoption of the double sampling plan. In the use of double sampling, we also consider it practical to convert the plan to a single sample plan if the first sample indicates that the acceptable quality level is not satisfactory. Likewise, if the acceptable quality level is not satisfactory when the sample has been converted to the single sampling concept, we would reconvert our approach to the double sampling plan. This approach resembles what is referred to as a multiple sampling; and indeed, it may be possible eventually to adopt this third plan of sampling. The decision to convert to such plans will be commensurate with the risks which will appear capable of being assumed after our foundation in this modern and scientific approach to auditing has been more firmly established.

Because statistical sampling as an approach to auditing is a new experience for us, it has appeared best, as indicated previously, to use the single sampling plan for a period of time with occasional conversions to double sampling tables until all components of the approach have been proven satisfactory and quality levels have been achieved or revised in either direction, as may be indicated. One of the principal results from the application of a statistical sampling plan to auditing is the valuable information it gives regarding the quality of work. The single sampling plan provides more precise information regarding quality than a double or multiple sampling plan because the first samples of the latter plans are smaller. The single sampling plan has in most cases provided a reduction in work from our previous quantitative measurements.

Statistical sampling plans are available tools for modernizing and making auditing and accounting work more scientific. The method of our application of statistical sampling plans to auditing procedures has been outlined here together with our interpretation of results. We find that statistical sampling is a desirable, practical, and economical method for performing certain audit work.